THE ROYAL AIRCRAFT FACTORY
FE2b/a
& Variants in RFC, RAF, RNAS & AFC Service

ROYAL AIR FORCE museum

in collaboration with

CROSS & COCKADE INTERNATIONAL

THE FIRST WORLD WAR AVIATION HISTORICAL SOCIETY • 2009

REGISTERED CHARITY NO 1117741

Title page: **They kept them flying – ground crew and FE2b.** *Below:* **The first Boulton & Paul built FE2b, 5201.**

First published in Great Britain in 2009 by
Cross & Cockade International

© **Cross & Cockade International 2009**

All original artwork and profiles remain
the copyright of the individual artists

ISBN: 978-0-9555734-1-5

Printed by Warwick Printing Company Limited

The CCI Monographs Series:
1: Nieuports in RNAS, RFC and RAF Service (2007)
2: The Royal Aircraft Factory FE2b/d and Variants (2009)
3: The Airco DH2 (in preparation)

Copies are available from the Society website **www.crossandcockade.com** or from
The Sales Manager, Cross & Cockade International, 6 Cowper Road, Southgate, London N14 5RP
sales.manager@crossandcockade.com

For subscription information contact
Membership Secretary: Roger Tisdale, 11 Francis Drive, Westward Ho! Bideford, EX39 1XE
membership.secretary@crossandcockade.com

Acknowledgements

The Society would like to thank the members and the many individuals and organisations
who have contributed with information or photographs from their collections, including
The Royal Air Force Museum (Andrew Cormack, Peter Dye, Andrew Renwick, Richard Simpson);
Boulton & Paul Association (Archivist: Les Whitehouse); Imperial War Museum, The National Archives, Royal Aero Club Trust,
CCI Archive, Lance Bronnenkant, Mick Davis, John Flannigan, Ross Gochenaur, Barry Gray, Paul Hare, Eric Harlin, Trevor Henshaw,
William Higgs, Colin Huston, Alex Imrie, Philip Jarrett, Eddy Lambrecht, Paul Leaman, Stuart Leslie, John McKenzie, Tony Mellor Ellis,
Mike O'Connor, Colin Owers, Chas Schaedel, Stewart Taylor, Greg van Wyngarden, Mike Varley, Harry Woodman, Peter Wright,
and is particularly grateful to all the WWI personnel without whose efforts these collections and this publication could not exist.

Colour profiles by Ronny Bar; line drawings by Mick Davis.
Project Editor/Designer, Colin Huston; Adobe InDesign™ Prepress, Barbara Huston.

Royal Aircraft Factory production lines.

FE2b A5478 'Gold Coast No 10', a typical night bomber, fully armed and ready for action.

Introduction

Those who flew the FE2 (Fee) always spoke with affection about the aircraft, but its subsequent reputation has been overshadowed by the heavy losses suffered in the spring of 1917 – when it was clearly outclassed by a new generation of German fighters.[1] Of the 275 aircraft lost by the Royal Flying Corps (RFC) during 'Bloody April' more than 70 were flown by day squadrons operating the FE2b or FE2d.

Even so, the popular image of a hapless, lumbering two-seater, out-fought by faster and more nimble German fighters, is largely misplaced and certainly ignores the Fee's outstanding performance in 1916, when (together with the DH2, and the equally underestimated BE2c) the RFC soundly defeated the German air arm during the Battle of the Somme, achieving air superiority – if not air supremacy – for several months.

Flown aggressively, and with a good air gunner, the Fee (and particularly the FE2d with its more powerful Rolls-Royce Eagle engine) was able to give a good account of itself in air combat – even as late as the summer of 1917. A number of German aces discovered just how dangerous the Fee could be – not least Manfred von Richthofen who was badly wounded on 6 July 1917 by return fire from 2Lt A.E. Woodbridge in an FE2d of 20 Sqn flown by Capt D.C. Cunnell.[2]

Another reason for the Fee's mixed reputation may be its less than glamorous appearance. To modern eyes, the pusher configuration looks particularly antiquated (somehow more incongruous than other aircraft of the period). The Fee never possessed the angular menace of its Royal Aircraft Factory stablemate the SE5a, the powerful sleekness of the Albatros D.III or the delicate elegance of the Nieuport 17.

A big, large-boned aircraft, it looked old before its time, yet performed outstandingly well in a wide variety of roles from day-fighting to bombing, from reconnaissance to anti-submarine operations and from training to air defence.

The Fee saw longer service on the Western Front than any other type – from all the air forces engaged. Given that the Fee's lineage could be traced to before the start of the war, this was an incredible achievement and testimony to its simple design, good flying characteristics and intrinsic strength – qualities that allowed a succession of variants and modifications to be introduced as the war progressed – all borne with quiet fortitude.

More than 1,900 Fees were produced and further substantial orders were in progress at the Armistice. Despite the large numbers that served on the Western Front, no complete example of the type survived beyond the 1920s. One of the last remaining Fees was scheduled to appear with an SE5a at the 1921 Hendon Air Pageant to illustrate 'the progress of aeroplane design', but suffered technical problems en-route.[3] A solitary specimen did linger on in civilian guise, as G-EAHC, but soon disappeared from sight.[4]

Just as the Fee faded away, so did the efforts of those who flew and sustained the aircraft. The historiography of the First Air War has, for perhaps understandable reasons, focussed largely on aerial fighting and in particular those units that operated single-seat scouts.

The Fee has never fitted this simple picture and yet the contribution of those who built, flew, fought, repaired, modified and maintained the aircraft deserves to be told. It is an important story embracing thousands of individuals at home and overseas. For many of them, however, we have neither photographs nor names, yet their achievements are none the less impressive. The scale of their contribution to the air war and, ultimately, to the creation of the Royal Air Force, deserves to be more widely known.

We have endeavoured, throughout this monograph, to highlight the individual stories of those involved with the Fee during its short operational life. Sadly, this effectively excludes the many thousands of ground crew working on the flying squadrons or in the depots and also largely ignores

non-commissioned aircrew. Unfortunately, they have left few records or personal reminiscences. For these unknown airmen, this history is offered as belated recognition.

The experience of 2Lt Thomas Archibald Mitford Stuart Lewis, an observer with 20 Squadron, provides a small insight into what it was like to fly the Fee. He has left us a personal account of his last flight, on Friday 27 July 1917.[5]

Detailed to fly an Offensive Patrol with seven other FE2d machines, he and 2Lt George Thomas William Burkett were tasked with 'clearing the air' of enemy aircraft. Taking off in the early evening from their home airfield at St-Marie-Capelle, they soon discovered that their engine was not running well, causing them to slip behind the rest of the formation. Once over the lines, and at a height of about 5000ft, they were attacked by two large groups of Albatros fighters. Lewis used both his forward and rear guns against them and claimed at least one destroyed.

With his controls badly damaged, Burkett turned the Fee for home and dived for the lines. Lewis fought off further attacks, claiming one machine out of control, but by now his pilot had been wounded in the shoulder while he had been struck in the leg by a phosphorous bullet. Unable to stand and fire over the top wing, Lewis could only operate the forward gun lying on his back, although Burkett swung the aircraft to give him a better field of fire. Fortified by some brandy from a hip flask, several more Albatros were fought off, including another out of control. On occasions, in the desperate struggle to avoid being shot down, the aircraft nearly turned over and Lewis only managed to stay in the cockpit by gripping the gun. Eventually, after just an hour in the air, Burkett landed the badly damaged Fee at Bailleul airfield where both occupants were rushed to the adjacent Casualty Clearing Station for immediate operations.

For their actions on that day, both Lewis and Burkett received the Military Cross.[6] You would have to read Lewis' account quite carefully to discover any hint that his leg had had to be amputated before he returned to England – effectively ending his flying career. His cheery tone and self-deprecating humour underline the innate modesty and bravery of a generation that rarely spoke about its achievements or the price paid in damaged bodies or lost comrades and friends.

The opportunity to recreate a Fee from substantial surviving components has been the dream of successive curators at the RAF Museum for more than 30 years. With the support of the Trustees of the RAF Museum and the efforts of numerous individuals and organisations, this ambition has now been fulfilled and the Fee will join the Lancaster, Halifax and Wellington on permanent display in the Bomber Command Hall of the Royal Air Force Museum.

To mark the occasion, members of Cross and Cockade International, The First World War Aviation Historical Society, and the staff of the RAF Museum, have worked together to produce this monograph detailing the history of the Fee and all its variants, from design to operational service. It is hoped that these combined efforts will bring back to life an important yet long-neglected aircraft and properly celebrate the achievements of all those associated with the Fee throughout the First World War.

Perhaps the last word should be left to the late Jack Bruce, noted aviation historian and Deputy Keeper at the RAF Museum, who had always hoped to see the Fee reborn: *It was a gallant, plodding, hard-working, but essentially obliging aeroplane, willing at least to try to do whatever was demanded of it. It was essentially a machine of war, and, like the good old soldier it was, it faded unobtrusively away.*[7]

Peter Dye
Director Collections Division
RAF Museum
June 2009

1   W.E. Johns recorded the great affection felt by all that flew the Fee and described how the low musical hum of their Beardmore engines was unmistakable 'as they pursued their murky way through the war-stricken skies'. Johns, *Popular Flying*, February 1933, p 637. Not everyone was always so charitable about the 'Fee'. One pilot 'objected to the feeling of being pushed and pushed around the wide-wide skies on the end of a shovel.' *Flight*, 5 September 1930, p 987.
2   Other aces wounded or killed in air combat with the 'Fee' include: Obltn Max Immelmann (15 victories) reportedly shot down on 18 June 1916 by Cpl J.H. Waller in FE2b 6346 of 25 Sqn flown by 2Lt G.R. McCubbin; Ltn Walter Göttsch (20 victories), wounded by FE2ds from 20 Sqn on 3 February 1917 (and again on 27 June 1917); and Ltn Karl Schäfer (30 victories) shot down on 5 June 1917 by Lt H.L. Satchell and Lt T.A.M.S. Lewis in FE2d A6469 of 20 Sqn.
3   *Flight*, 30 June 1921, p 435.
4   G-EAHC was first registered on 14 July 1919 and withdrawn from use on 7 August 1921.
5   TNA AIR1/733/185/4.
6   Lewis' citation reads 'For conspicuous gallantry and devotion to duty. Whilst acting as Observer his patrol engaged a superior force of enemy scouts. His Pilot was wounded, but they continued to fight, destroying one enemy machine. He was then severely wounded, but continued to work his gun lying on his back. By this means they were able to destroy a second enemy machine. Afterwards, when returning to our lines with their machine badly damaged, he and his Pilot drove off two machines which were pursuing them, having displayed the greatest gallantry and presence of mind.'
7   Bruce, 'The FE2 Series', *Flight*, 12 December 1952, p 724-728.

Many of the photographs and much of the operational detail appearing in this monograph have been drawn from the archives of the Royal Air Force Museum. The Department of Research and Information Services (DoRIS) holds a large collection of documents and photographs covering the entire history of the Royal Air Force, including the work of the Air Battalion, Royal Flying Corps and Royal Naval Air Service. Some 360000 separate items have been added to the Collections Database over the past 10 years: this includes over 400 individual logbooks from the First World War.

Researchers wishing to use this material should contact the department directly at: DoRIS, Royal Air Force Museum Hendon, London, NW9 5LL. Email research@rafmuseum.org. Telephone 020 8358 4873 The Museum is keen to expand its collection and welcomes donations of material covering all aspects of the Royal Air Force to be preserved for future generations and to support an ongoing programme of research, exhibitions and academic publications.

De Havilland's original FE1 fitted with a passenger seat. The removal of the forward elevator was an important step in the evolution of the design.

Geoffrey de Havilland left the Royal Aircraft Factory in January 1914 after developing the FE2. He moved to the Air Inspection Directorate, then joined the Aircraft Manufacturing Company (Airco) in July but was briefly called to active service before returning to Airco as a designer.

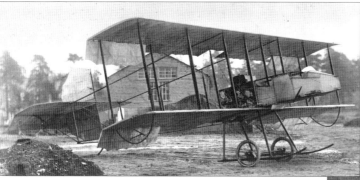

Below: FE2 tested as a floatplane on Fleet Pond.

Above: The original FE2 with lower tailplane removed and wing-tip skids added. The nacelle covering is all fabric.

Below right: The 1911 FE2 showing off its armament whilst on a visit to the Military Aeroplane Competition at Larkhill in August 1912. The gun is wrapped in cloth but whether for protection or disguise is unknown.

FE2 with 50hp Gnome rotary in January 1912.

Right: The uncovered nacelle of the second FE2 at the Royal Aircraft Factory in 1913, fitted with 70hp Renault engine, but awaiting a propeller .

Below: The machine gun, with its muzzle lashed down with a length of rope, is clearly of the the Maxim type as fitted during August 1912: possibly another view from the Military Trials.

The Development of the FE2 Series

The FE2b had its origins in the first successful aeroplane created by Geoffrey de Havilland, a forward elevator pusher of what was, for 1910, a fairly conventional layout. De Havilland financed the construction of the machine with a gift of £1000 from his grandfather and once he had completed his trials with it and, at the same time, taught himself to fly, he was at something of a loss as to what to do next as returning to his previous position as a draughtsman in the motor industry now had little appeal.

A fortuitous meeting with a friend, F.M. Green, who was then employed as 'Engineer Design' at Farnborough, led de Havilland to successfully seek employment there too, securing a position as designer and test pilot and, at the same time, selling them the aeroplane for £400. One condition of the purchase was that de Havilland should demonstrate the machine's ability to stay airborne for an hour. This he did, successfully, on 10 January 1911.

The organisation which de Havilland joined had started back in 1878, initially to build observation balloons for the army before diversifying into the construction of non-rigid airships and, following a similar advancement by the military, was now seeking to start work with aeroplanes. Known as H.M. Balloon Factory for most of its life, it was re-named H.M. Army Aircraft Factory in 1911 before becoming the Royal Aircraft Factory in April 1912.

Once at Farnborough the de Havilland built machine became the first aeroplane designated under the system devised by the Factory Superintendent, Mervyn O'Gorman and, as the first experimental aeroplane in class 'F' (so called because, like the design made famous by Henry Farman, it had a forward elevator) it became FE1.

Experiment and development of the design led to a larger tailplane which improved fore and aft stability. The addition of wing extensions increased lift, allowing a second seat for de Havilland to give air experience to many members of the Air Battalion whilst they were camping on Farnborough Common. These flights revealed some difficulty in turning with two people aboard which was simply overcome, before the end of May, by the provision of larger rudders. Adjustments to the rigging ensured that the forward elevator 'carried no weight', following which it was removed completely and, on 3 July, de Havilland flew the aircraft in this new configuration. The absence of the forward elevator meant that all links with the Farman design after which the type had been named were lost, but the unobstructed forward field of view so obviously lent itself to the fitting of a gun that henceforth the 'F' designation would stand for 'Fighting'.

On 15 August FE1 was taken up by Lt T.J. Ridge, the Factory's Assistant Superintendent, who had only recently learned to fly, and was damaged in a crash, although fortunately Ridge was unhurt. Its

Mervyn O'Gorman

development over, it was not repaired and never flew again.

The next day, 16 August 1911, saw de Havilland make the first trial of a new design, FE2, broadly similar in layout to its predecessor, but powered by a 50hp Gnome rotary and equipped with a simple fabric covered nacelle of rather unfinished appearance. At this stage the pilot occupied the front seat with the passenger, when carried, behind him where his weight was closer to the centre of gravity, thereby reducing trim problems.

At this time, despite its name, Army Aircraft Factory had no authority to construct new aeroplanes, it functions in connection with heavier-than-air flight being limited to the repair of the army's few existing machines, the manufacture of spares, the higher training of mechanics and what is today called research and development. The existence of the FE2 was therefore explained away as a rebuild of FE1, which it clearly was not, a subterfuge which the War Office, to whom the Factory was responsible, appeared happy to accept and which would be employed on many future occasions, but which has confused researchers ever since.

The new machine's first take-off was aborted when the engine failed due to a broken piston. Two days later, with the engine repaired, it took off without further incident at 16.30, de Havilland reporting that the Centre of Gravity was too far aft, making gliding difficult; not entirely surprising as the general arrangement drawings clearly show a large and impressive nose-mounted gun. 50lb of lead weights were added in the nose and another flight made the same evening, but FE2 was still tail heavy and modifications to the tailplane were immediately put in hand to adjust the balance.

Development was dogged by engine problems until the following year when a replacement Gnome, this time of 70hp, was fitted. Thus powered, FE2 was equipped with floats and test flown from nearby Fleet Pond by E. Copland Perry before being fitted with a Maxim type machine gun in a fork mounting which allowed the muzzle to rest on the forward rim of the cockpit when not in use. Mervyn O'Gorman's report on the trials of this gun,

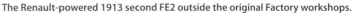

The Renault-powered 1913 second FE2 outside the original Factory workshops.

dated 26 July 1912 state that the trials had been delayed whilst the control runs were modified so as to move the pilot to the rear seat. Even then the range of elevation was unsatisfactory, the gunner needing to stand up to depress the muzzle beyond 30°, whilst an elevation of more than a mere 6° brought the breech down into the gunner's lap. However the gun was still mounted when it visited Larkhill on Salisbury Plain during the Military Aeroplane Competition held there in August 1912, where it was widely photographed by the Press attending the event, after which it seems to have passed into obscurity.

In the spring of 1913 Superintendent O'Gorman received a request to provide an armed aeroplane which, in those days, dictated a pusher design. The Factory therefore returned to the FE2 concept, creating a new design which was ostensibly a re-construction of the earlier machine. Powered by a 70hp air-cooled V8 Renault engine, it was a two seater with the crew housed in a neatly rounded nacelle. The general arrangement drawings to which it was built show a large gun mounted above the rim of the forward cockpit. Wings were copied from those of the BE2a, the strut positions modified to suit the new design and with the addition of mounting points for the tail booms. The tailplane was mounted on the upper tail booms, with a balanced rudder and, as was common at the time, no fin. Remarkably, in view of its raison d'être, no armament was ever fitted.

On 23 February 1914 FE2 spun and crashed near Wittering, the pilot Ronald Kemp suffering a badly broken leg whilst his passenger, E.T. Haynes, was killed outright.

Henry Phillip Folland
and his preliminary sketch and notes for the
FE2a Gun Carrier

The FE2a

Although FE2 was lost the concept of an armed aeroplane continued and by the middle of 1914 a new design, FE2a, began to emerge under the direction of Henry Folland, whose preliminary sketches bear the title 'FE2A Gun carrier' and so leave no doubt about its intended role.

FE2a was larger than the earlier designs, with a wide centre section extending outboard as far as the tail boom attachments, with BE2c wings employed as its outer panels, giving a three bay rigging arrangement and a span of close to 50 feet. The centre section struts splayed outwards slightly and the entire trailing edge of the upper centre section could be lowered as an air-brake by means of a wheel in the

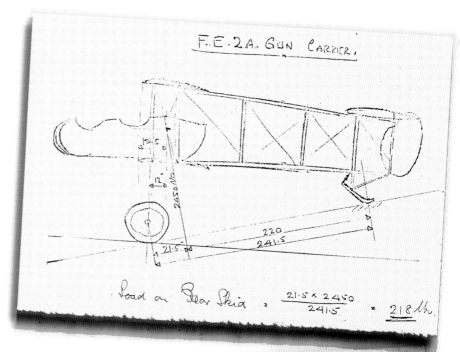

The 1913 second FE2, and its fatal crash at Wittering.

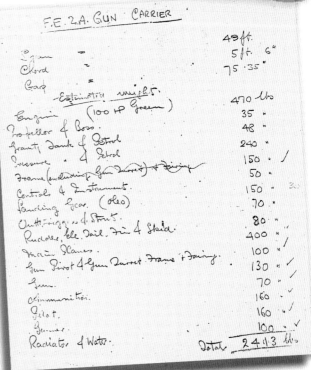

The first FE2a, 4227, with 100hp Green engine, seen on Farnborough Common with the whirling arm, used for testing propellers, in the background. This machine has the full undercarriage and a two blade propeller.

cockpit in order to shorten the landing run and so ensure that it could operate from the small airfields often found in France.

The nacelle was built around a framework largely constructed of metal tubing, with wooden formers supporting aluminium panels. The drawings show armour plate fitted to the nacelle floor but there is some doubt whether this was included in the completed machines. The pilot occupied the rear cockpit and the passenger the front giving him a clear field of fire throughout almost the entire forward hemisphere.

Although the drawings again show the fitting of a powerful looking 'pom-pom' gun the machine, when built, was actually armed with a Lewis gun on a simple swivel mount fixed to the cockpit floor. The undercarriage, with its sturdy oleo legs and buffer nose wheel had previously been tested on a BE2 and assisted in achieving smooth landings on poorly prepared surfaces, whilst the sprung tailskid, which Folland had calculated would carry a load of 218lb whilst on the ground, was copied directly from the BE2c.

As in the earlier FE2 the tailplane was mounted on the upper tail booms ahead of the steel tube framed, balanced rudder but, mindful of the cause of the crash of the previous model, this time fin area was provided both by the fabric covering of the kingpost bracing the tailplane, two ribs being added to keep the fabric in shape, and by the unusually broad chord of the rearmost vertical struts. The machine was powered by a six-cylinder, 100hp water-cooled Green engine, an example of which had recently won a prize in a competition

The third FE2a, 2864, with the 120hp Austro-Daimler engine which was used instead after the Green was found to be unsuitable.

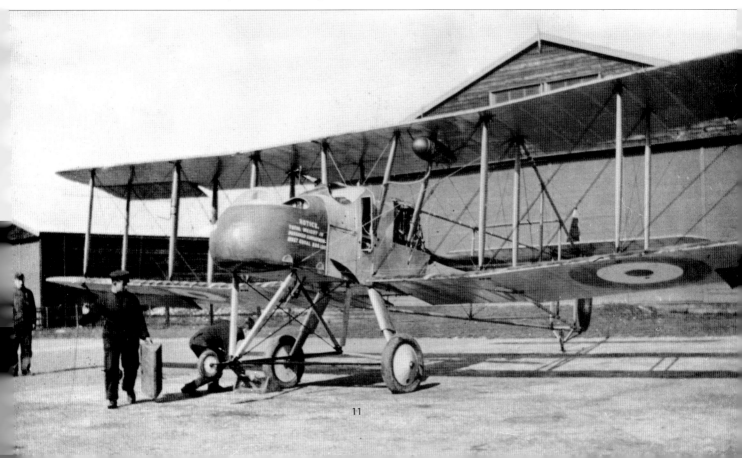

to find the best British aero engine. To reduce resistance, the radiator was fitted within the nacelle, between the pilot and the engine, air being admitted thereto via slim vertical scoops on each side of the nacelle. In this position it not only kept the engine cool but also helped keep the pilot's back warm.

All in all it was a very attractive and practical design and production of a batch of twelve was ordered 'off the drawing board', the Royal Aircraft Factory now seemingly released from any restriction regarding aircraft construction, a development which was regarded with some animosity by commercial aeroplane companies. The first FE2a to be completed was presented for inspection on 22 January 1915 and made its first flight four days later, with Frank Goodden at the controls.

The Green engine proved to be too heavy for its power output and plans were quickly made to substitute the 120hp Austro-Daimler, originally designed in 1910 by Ferdinand Porsche, which had been put into production, under licence, in March 1914 by Wm Beardmore Ltd, who had modified the design to include dual ignition and twin carburettors. The

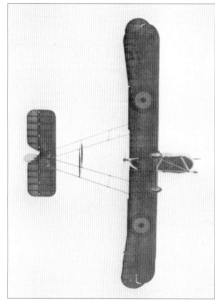

Three views of 2864, during tests with the balanced ailerons, which were not adopted.

engine change necessitated modification not only to the engine mountings but also to the fuel system, a circular section streamlined gravity tank being added under the centre section. The first machine thus modified was therefore the third production example, the second machine

being already too far advanced for the conversion to be easily carried out. The Beardmore powered machine, 2864, was test flown by Goodden on 16 March and showed such an improvement over the original that this engine was approved for the rest of the production run.

2864 was then fitted with inversely tapered ailerons, with balance areas presumably because it was thought that the increased control surface area would improve the rate of roll. The next two production examples were similarly fitted, after completion, their original ailerons being returned to stores as BE2c spares. No significant advantage was gained by the modification, the original ailerons being judged to be equally effective, and the three machines were re-converted upon arrival in France, whilst the remainder of the production run were completed as designed.

Meanwhile 2864, complete with balanced ailerons, was sent to the Central Flying School at Upavon on 30 March for evaluation, and was flown by three different instructors, in both bumpy weather and calm. The CFS report states that it was judged to be both easy to fly and to land, very stable fore and aft, and to a certain degree self banking. The cockpit was considered very comfortable, although the pilot's windscreen was criticised as ineffective, goggles being required at all times. The report was also critical of the clearance afforded to the propeller by the tail surface control wires, which it was thought might foul the propeller if allowed to get slack. The ground clearance was also thought to be inadequate since it was judged that the propeller might touch the ground if the oleo struts were at their maximum compression and both tyres were flat. These latter criticisms were ignored and 2864 went to join 6 Squadron in France.

Unfortunately delays in manufacture, seemingly of both engine and airframe, meant that deliveries of the FE2a were extended through the summer, the last of the twelve, 5648, not being completed until 5 October 1915.

FE2b

The 11th example FE2a, 5648, was completed with a simple wooden Vee undercarriage and without the centre section airbrake which, it had been found, was rarely if ever used in service. The incorporation of these modifications have led to this machine being regarded as the prototype FE2b, although by the time of its completion hundreds of this new model were already on order, the first of them, 5201, being completed on 2 October 1915, before the last FE2a. This was the first aeroplane built by Boulton & Paul of Norwich, a company previously famous for the manufacture of wooden buildings, including those for Captain Scott's ill-fated Antarctic expedition, and appears to have been tested extensively and photographed with evident pride, before finally being handed over. (*see p2/3*)

The FE2b differed from the FE2a only in the omission of the airbrake, which allowed some simplification of control cable runs, and in the substitution of a flat sided gravity tank, streamlined only in plan, a change which had no discernible effect on the machine's performance. The oleo undercarriage was retained and the cockpit floor was cut from plywood instead of the armour plate originally intended.

In addition to a batch of 50 ordered from the Royal Aircraft Factory, manufacture was

Another view of FE2a 2864, which was also used for comparison tests with the Voisin LA before being sent to France where it had an active service life of about four months.

undertaken by a number of contractors including Boulton & Paul; Ransomes, Sims & Jefferies; and G. & J. Weir.

When the FE2b first entered service a memo from the Assistant Director of Military Aeronautics at the War Office informed the RFC administration that the machine should be officially referred to as the 'Fighter Mark 1', the SE4 becoming 'Scout Mark 1' but there is little evidence that any notice was taken of the instruction. In signal jargon the FE2b became the 'Fetubi', and the big pushers were also occasionally referred to, in official circles, as 'battleplanes' but to the airmen who flew them, and serviced them, it was called simply, and not without affection, the 'Fee'.

However development did not stop once the type had entered production and when, early in 1916, the aerofoil section of the BE2c was changed from RAF6 to RAF14

a similar change was made in the wings of the FE2b which shared the design, the first machine so equipped being 6354. This gave a noticeable improvement in climb albeit with a small reduction in overall ceiling.

The normal finish applied was for the upper surfaces to be painted with the green/brown preservative PC10 and for the under surfaces to be left in natural linen, clear varnished. However, in March 1916 6361 arrived in France with its nacelle painted yellow, prompting Brig Gen Trenchard, Commander of the RFC in France to write to the Assistant Director of Military Aeronautics at the War Office requesting that in future all nacelles should be painted a 'dull service colour'.

Attempts to improve performance by the introduction of a simple wooden 'Vee' undercarriage met with some resistance from the RFC in France, where it was feared

FE2a 5648 with 'Vee' undercarriage. The location is again Farnborough Common and the machine in the background is an RE7, its Beardmore engine running uncowled. 5648 differed from other FE2as in lacking the airbrake on the upper centre-section trailing edge. The vertical rear end to the radiator cowling was common to all production FE2as.

An FE2b with its nacelle fabric removed. Bomb racks have been fitted beneath the lower centre section and a cranked No 10 Mark 1 gun mounting at the rear of the front cockpit. The undercarriage has ungone the Trafford Jones modification

that heavy landings might cause damage to the airframe which could not easily be repaired in the field. After deliberate heavy landings showed that the undercarriage itself broke, the axle bending, before the nacelle frame bent, resistance to the new innovation lessened and the 'Vee' undercarriage was grudgingly accepted. However Lt Trafford Jones (a Canadian pilot from Tortonto) of 20 Squadron devised a modification to the oleo undercarriage in which the nose wheel and its supporting struts were removed and the horizontal radius rods locating the axle were angled upwards to connect to the now vacant attachment points for the nose wheel legs. This gave a reduction in resistance almost equal to that obtained with the 'Vee' type whilst retaining the springing of the oleo type and, on 3 June 1916 the RFC requested that all future FE2b should be thus modified before being sent to France. Unfortunately Lt Trafford Jones did not live to see the widespread adoption of his modification as he was killed in action on 16 May 1916 whilst flying 6359, his observer being wounded.

The 'Vee' type undercarriage was re-introduced later in the war when the FE2b's role changed to bombing as it allowed the carriage of a 230lb bomb beneath the nacelle, which the oleo undercarriage, in either form, did not.

The petrol tank included in the original design held 24 gallons and gave a maximum endurance of 2½ hours. This

Lt Trafford Jones

proved inadequate in service if only because other machines could stay aloft for three hours or more and on 1 March 1916 Trenchard again wrote to the War Office, this time requesting that the FE2b should be provided with an enlarged tank, to hold an additional 8 gallons. The Royal Aircraft Factory's response was to redesign the tank, increasing its capacity by 16 gallons, and utilising the vacant space under the pilot's seat, thus not only providing the additional endurance needed but also anticipating the increase in consumption that would result from the fitting of a more powerful engine.

The tailplane incidence, designed to keep the machine flying level with two occupants appears to have caused concerns at 8 TDS,

Netheravon too for, during the summer of 1918, an air mechanic, employed as a draughtsman, was instructed to devise a tail trimmer for the FE2b. The result, which even its designer admitted was a 'rather Heath Robinson affair' comprised a vertical fast-screw attached to the apex of the triangle formed, in plan, by the upper tail booms and a nut fixed to the rear spar of the tailplane, with the tailplane being hinged at the front spar to the upper tail booms. At the bottom of the vertical screw was an ordinary bicycle chain wheel round which passed a yard of chain from the ends of which two cables were taken forward to the pilot's cockpit where another length of chain went around another chain wheel to which a crank was fitted. There is no record of this device being widely adopted.

Armament

The Fee was designed when aerial fighting was in its infancy, and when the synchronizing gear which would allow a gun to be fired forward, through the propeller arc of a tractor design had yet to be conceived. Thus the machine was a pusher and was designed to allow the widest possible field of fire forwards and to the sides so that, like a warship at sea, it could engage the enemy at whatever quarter it might appear, by manoeuvring the gun not the vehicle carrying it. Therefore the FE2a was equipped with a drum fed Lewis machine-gun on a simple swivel pillar mounting, allowing freedom

of movement in both elevation and traverse to cover as much of the forward hemisphere as was practicable. Firing to the rear was not considered: if the enemy were behind it was expected that the machine would turn to face its attacker. Only experience would show the deficiencies in this idea.

Early examples of the FE2b were fitted with the No 2 Mark 1 gun mount which comprised a horizontal bar to which the gun was attached between two inverted vees fixed to the nacelle, thus positioning the gun above the cockpit rim and allowing the muzzle to be depressed some way below the horizontal as well as allowing it to be elevated and traversed over a reasonable arc. It was obviously not entirely satisfactory as a Mark II version which allowed an improved range of movement was soon introduced.

This mounting was itself superseded in April 1916 by the No 4 Mark 1 mount which was a swivelling pillar not dissimilar to that originally provided in the FE2a, whilst the Mark III version which replaced it could be swung from side to side, rocking from a pivot just above its attachment to the cockpit floor, and affording a much enhanced field of fire downwards at each side of the nacelle.

Still the range of movement was insufficient to allow the Lewis gun to be aimed in every direction thought necessary until the introduction of the final refinement, the No 4 Mark IV or Clark Mounting, which incorporated a universal joint and so allowed the pillar to be swung in any direction. Spring clips were fixed at points around the cockpit rim to secure the mount in position as required. In addition it was common for posts to be fitted on either side of the nacelle, more or less in line with the pilot's windscreen to allow the more aggressive pilot to fire obliquely forwards or, by reversing the gun, the occupant of the forward cockpit could fire downwards to the rear to cover the area beneath the machine's tail.

Firing directly to the rear was another matter entirely as the area immediately behind the nacelle was covered by the propeller arc. The solution lay in the No 10 Mark 1 mounting, a telescopic, cranked, swivelling pillar which was in turn fixed to an Anderson arch, a metal hoop at the rear of the front cockpit, secured to the floor. In order to use a gun fixed to this mount, as the gunner was obliged to do for defence against attack from behind, it was necessary for him to stand up either on the ammunition locker, or even on the rim of the cockpit, if he wished to fire clear of the upper wing. This dangerous looking practice was accepted with the fortitude characteristic of that generation most of whom were volunteers, many choosing to fight as aerial gunners rather than endure the squalor of the trenches.

At first only one Lewis gun was fitted, it being necessary to move it from mount to mount as occasion demanded, but later a second gun was carried, ready on the rear mounting. Each gun was provided with a leather pouch in which spent cartridge cases collected to prevent their flying back in the slipstream and causing damage to either the engine or propeller. A total of ten 97-round drums of ammunition were normally carried, allowing around two minutes of continuous fire. At least one FE2b, 4873 was fitted with twin Lewis guns, yoked together so that they could be aimed as one, the installation being carried out by the Armament Experimental Station at Orfordness in the summer of 1917, but it is not known whether the machine saw service so armed.

For reconnaissance duties a camera was sometimes carried, usually mounted on the starboard side of the forward cockpit, the observer needing to lean overboard in order to change the plates.

A series of posed shots showing the how the gunner could, if both agile and courageous, fire in almost any direction.

The front cockpit of this Fee has been faired over to produce a single seater. The lower Lewis gun is fixed and connected to a container for spent cartridge cases within the nacelle.The upper gun, which can be swivelled, has the usual leather pouch.

FE2b 4282, with a camera mounted on the starboard side. 4282 was later converted to an FE2c.

Below: The first FE2c conversion, 6370 in a lineup at Farnborough in July 1916.

A few FE2bs, in service with training units, had their front cockpit modified to allow a Scarff ring to be fitted. However the cockpit sides remained fairly shallow and the occupant must have been obliged to squat down to use the gun.

FE2c

In October 1915, contemporary with the completion of both the last FE2a and the first FE2b, a new variant with reversed crew positions was proposed and, logically, designated FE2c. Placing the pilot in the front cockpit gave him a much improved view, especially when landing. Presumably it was considered that this improved view would eliminate the risk of a nose-over when landing and that the buffer nose wheel would not therefore be required as a wooden 'Vee' undercarriage was provided rather than the oleo type.

The nacelle of the FE2c was distinguished by a more streamlined nose contour than the FE2b with an elegant sweep to the cockpit rim, and the horizontal spacer bar between the cockpit was made curved in order to accommodate the back of the front seat.

The pilot was provided with a Lewis gun mounted in the nose of the machine, roughly level with his knees, its limited movement being aligned to a sighting bar in front of the windscreen. A tubular Anderson arch at the rear of the pilot's cockpit provided a mounting for the observer's gun, allowing a reasonable field of fire forwards and upwards, although his position close to the wings prevented his firing to the rear. The pilot must have found it rather unnerving to have a machine

An operational FE2c, with the gunner in the rear cockpit.

gun firing immediately above, and thus potentially at, the back of his head. 6370 and 6371 were both modified to become FE2cs, the latter being presented for AID inspection on 19 March with the second machine joining it the following day.

6371 was sent to France in April, possibly in mistake for an FE2b, and served with 22 and 25 Squadrons until 17 July when it was wrecked in exactly the kind of landing accident its reversed crew positions were designed to prevent. 6370 was retained at the Royal Aircraft Factory where it underwent further development, including being fitted with dual controls and an oleo

undercarriage, as well as being employed in testing bombsights, until it was written off in a crash on 9 May 1917.

The dual control concept, which blurred the distinction between the FE2b and c, obviously had some merit for pilot training and during the spring of 1916 drawings were prepared for a system which could be applied to either type. The two rudder bars were simply joined by cable, running internally, the rear rudder bar being lengthened for unexplained reasons. The two control columns were linked by a tube, close to their bases, to allow either to operate the elevators, the control horn

being outside the forward cockpit, but each stick had separate aileron cables which joined at triangular wiring plates a few few inches short of the pulleys fixed to the lower wing. The rear cockpit's control column was made detachable by means of a tapered plug and socket joint.

A number of such conversions were made and saw service with training units in England.

The FE2c design was revived in the spring of 1918 when a number of FE2bs were converted with new nacelles built by the Royal Aircraft Factory and were employed for ground attack.

D9124 was a single seat conversion carried out by 51 Squadron, with two fixed Lewis guns firing through the holes in the nacelle front. A5543, shown on p 57, is a different interpretation of the same principle, with the guns in a different position within the structure.

The prototype FE2d, 7995, 250hp Rolls-Royce Mk I. The exhausts run forward to discharge above the upper wing.

FE2d

Once in service it was soon found that the 'Fee', although able to put up a good fight once battle was joined, an ability well respected by its opponents, lacked sufficient speed to chase the enemy machines, especially the new Fokker scouts, and initiate combat. Trenchard, whose policy was one of constant aggression, did not like his fighters to have to wait to be attacked and promptly wrote to the War Office demanding that something be done to improve its performance.

An up-rated version of the Beardmore engine with modified cylinders, increasing the bore from 5 to 5½ inches and raising the power output to a nominal 160hp with only a 77lb increase in weight, was under development but was, initially, somewhat unreliable suffering both from overheating and from the early failure of the cylinder

holding down bolts. The nominal rating turned out to be somewhat conservative as, on the bench the up-rated engine gave 192hp at 1450 rev/min. Rather than simply wait and hope that this new engine would soon become available the Royal Aircraft Factory considered all available alternatives and, in January 1916 put forward a proposal for a new version, FE2d, which would be powered by the new V12 that was Rolls-Royce's first venture into aero engine production. Later named 'Eagle', the new engine had a swept volume of 20 litres and was initially rated at a conservative 250hp and had its first run in March 1915. Based on Mercedes practice it had an aluminium crankcase and steel cylinders with forged valve ports welded to the heads. Unusually, it had an epicyclical reduction gear, reducing propeller speed to around two-thirds of crank speed, so

allowing higher engine speeds.

Modifications to the airframe necessary to accommodate the more powerful engine included increasing the capacity of the main petrol tank from 24 to 36 gallons by the simple expedient of making it rectangular instead of cylindrical so that it could occupy the same space, although both strength and ease of manufacture were slightly compromised by the change. The rear of the nacelle was modified so that the radiator, which had previously been inside of the nacelle, where it had enjoyed a measure of protection, was fully exposed, and was secured in place by diagonal bracing rods fixed to the centre section struts. This new location, although more vulnerable, increased its efficiency both by improved thermodynamic circulation due to its top connection being higher above the engine, and by improved cooling since

FE2d A5 in German hands after the crew ferrying it to France became lost and made a bad landing on the wrong side of the lines.

it now enjoyed the full effect of the air flow over it.

The prototype, fitted with engine No. 1/250/31, was completed ready for AID inspection on 4 April 1916 and made its first flight on the 7th, piloted by Frank Goodden. As expected its performance was much improved compared with the 120hp FE2b; it climbed quicker, it ceiling had risen from 11000 to 17000 feet and, most importantly its speed was increased from 80 to 92 mile/hour which, although hardly spectacular, was enough to satisfy Trenchard's demands.

50 were ordered from the Royal Aircraft Factory and 300 from Boulton & Paul, who sub-contracted the nacelles to Richard Garrett & Sons of Leiston, later contracted to build complete aeroplanes.

On 7 May the prototype, now accepted by the RFC and given the serial 7995,

With demand for the Eagle engine forever outpacing supply some machines ordered as FE2d were completed as FE2b, fitted with the 160hp engine.

The prototype FE2d, 7995, as was commonplace at the Royal Aircraft Factory, had been fitted with exhausts which discharged above the upper wing, an arrangement which, in a tractor design, ensured that the exhaust fumes were kept clear of the crew's faces but which, in a pusher like the FE2d, served no useful purpose and a simpler arrangement was substituted for production examples.

Unfortunately the enemy quickly became all too familiar with the FE2d, almost before meeting it in combat as, on 1 July 1916 a crew ferrying an early production example, A5, over to France, a country which they had not previously visited, landed at an aerodrome on the

occasionally removed altogether.

The first 30 examples built by the Royal Aircraft Factory were fitted with the 250hp Eagle Mark 1 but this engine was thereafter reserved for the DH4, so A31 and later machines received the 275hp Mark III. Final examples were fitted with an even later model Eagle, rated at 284hp.

The gravity tank, initially mounted under the upper centre section, above the nacelle, was later moved and mounted above the upper surface although the reason for the change is not recorded. The FE2d was originally built with the full oleo undercarriage but on 15 August 1916 7995, then in service with 20 Squadron was given the Trafford Jones modification which proved sufficiently successful that on 24 September it was decided that all future FE2ds would receive the modified undercarriage.

FE2d 'A1' with Rolls-Royce engine, photographed in a checkerboard scheme at 1AD.

went to the CFS where it was reported as being heavy to manoeuvre, making it tiring to fly and tricky to land. With the type already in production this opinion was ignored; the machine could fly and fight, and at that stage of the war that was really all that mattered as the enemy had effective fighter aeroplanes and the RFC did not. Fortunately once the FE2d entered service it was soon realised that the CFS report was highly subjective and the majority of service pilots found the machine quite pleasant to fly. It had, in any event, only ever been considered as a 'stop-gap' and since the problems with the 160hp Beardmore had been more or less resolved and, installed in FE2b 6357 had made its first flight, piloted by B.C.Hucks on 11 May, the Director of Aeronautical Equipment informed Trenchard on 29 May that it was not proposed 'to perpetuate the FE2d' once existing contracts were fulfilled.

wrong side of the lines and made a present of both the aeroplane and its Rolls-Royce engine to the enemy.

The radiators fitted to the earliest examples differed slightly, some having an arched top and others being square, but they all had one thing in common, they were too big and over-cooled the engine. The provision of shutters, although attempted was ineffective partly because no thermometer was fitted, the pilot needing to rely on experience, or intuition to gauge the engine temperature, and partly because in combat he had more pressing matters to attend to. The eventual solution was simple; the smaller radiator design for use with the Beardmore engine was adopted instead but mounted in the fully exposed position which characterised the FE2d. Shutters were still provided but only as a means to accelerate engine warm-up but were never used in the air and were

The type remained on active service in France until late in 1917 with remaining examples then being re-assigned to other duties – making it a long-lived 'stop-gap'.

FE2 e-f-g-h

Whilst the 160hp Beardmore was still under development and with the Rolls-Royce Eagle engine perpetually in short supply attempts were made to fit various alternative engines to the FE2. The first to be tried was the Royal Aircraft Factory's own RAF5, a development of the air-cooled V12 RAF4a that powered such aeroplanes as the BE12 and RE8, but fitted with a cooling fan and a modified thrust bearing to render it suitable for pusher applications. Two examples of the new design, FE2e, were created by the conversion of 6360 which was completed early in February 1916 and 4256, built by Weir, which joined it in April. Each had a tall scoop behind the

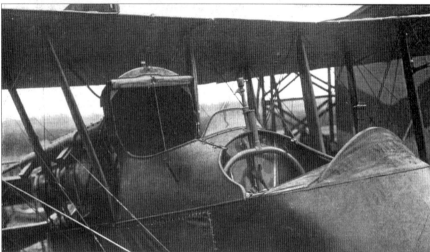

Two views of BHP engined FE2h A6545, the lower one showing the radiator blind, Anderson arch gun mounting and observer's folding windscreen.

rated at 120hp, could almost match.

The two FE2es were not sent to France and both took part in bombsight tests at Orfordness during the summer of 1916 and later in various other experiments, some designed to assess the effect of weather on aircraft performance. Although 4256 was still extant in March 1918 their eventual fate is unknown.

FE2f was to have been powered by the Royal Aircraft Factory RAF3, a water-cooled V12 designed to produce at least 200hp whilst the FE2g would have been fitted with the up-rated RAF5b but there is no evidence that either type progressed beyond the design stage.

Late in 1917 FE2d A6545 was modified, by Ransomes, Sims & Jefferies, to accept the BHP engine which had been developed from the Beardmore by further increasing both bore and stroke and by substituting Hispano-Suiza type closed end cylinder liners. It was nominally rated at 200hp, but the prototype had produced 236hp on the bench.

The new type was designated FE2h and evidently showed some promise as three more machines, A6501-6503, which although built, like A6545, by Boulton & Paul, were converted by Ransomes, Sims & Jefferies and re-numbered E3151-3153. The engines with which they were fitted were a further development of the Austro-Daimler/Beardmore/BHP design modified for production by Siddeley-Deasy and now named the 'Puma'. Siddeleys had again re-designed the cylinders which now had open ended liners and aluminium heads and promised 300hp, but once in service it was found that valves burned

pilot to direct cooling air onto the cylinders and the rear centre section struts were bound in asbestos cord to prevent their being burned by the exhaust manifold, which passed very close. As was usual with Royal Aircraft Factory engines they were fitted with four blade propellers.

Despite the reduction in weight from the omission of the radiator and its attendant plumbing, the performance of the FE2e was little better than that of the standard FE2b, hardly surprising given that the RAF5 only developed 140hp, a figure which a well tuned Beardmore, although nominally

FE2e 6360 at Farnborough. This machine was fitted with a 150hp RAF engine and used to test the RAF gyroscopic bombsight (*see p 68*) **in the summer of 1916. BE2c 4094 is just visible on the left.**

out and cylinder blocks failed, so it was reluctantly de-rated to 230hp which reduced its problems to an acceptable level, but destroyed any advantage it may have offered over previous engine designs. The performance of the FE2h was therefore little improved over the FE2b with the 160hp Beardmore, and use of the 'Puma' was largely confined to the DH9 which had been designed around it, although as a result of the reduction in power, its performance never came up to expectations.

The FE2h never saw active service but at least one was employed at the Isle of Grain in tests with the Davis 'recoilless' gun which fired a 2lb projectile.

Post-war usage.

Production ended fairly abruptly once the Armistice was signed, unfulfilled orders being cancelled, and the FE2b quickly disappeared from service use, being declared obsolete early in 1919, although 149 Squadron which formed part of the Army of Occupation held on to its Fees until it was disbanded on 1 August 1919. One example, D9108, served with the Instrument Design establishment at Biggin Hill in 1919 before being returned to Farnborough were it remained at least until November 1924 as a test vehicle for various experiments.

The 'Fee' was not popular as a vehicle for passenger flights both because of the comparative difficulty in entering and leaving the forward cockpit and the relative thirst of its powerful engine but one, D3832, entered the civil register as G-EAHC, and embarked upon a new career giving joyrides with the Bournemouth Aviation Company, its former serial number initially displayed on the sides of the nacelle to proclaim its military pedigree. At least one of the small number sold to the US Government performed a similar service in America, its nacelle bearing the legend 'The Flying Bathtub'. Another found a role as a camera platform in the motion picture industry.

In Australia A778, which had become CFS-14 after its arrival 'down under', now became G-AUCX and formed one of the swarm of aeroplanes that greeted the Vickers Vimy G-EAOU on its arrival after completing the first flight from England. It later embarked upon an attempt to fly around the country, selling rides, but was written off when engine failure on take-off caused it to crash on 7 February 1922.

A790, which had found its way to India where it had its radiator repositioned above the nacelle, as in the FE2d, to aid cooling in the subtropical climate, survived until 1920 when it was damaged in a landing accident and was scrapped.

A790 in India, undergoing maintenance, *above*; and *right*, after its landing accident.

Below: An FE2b being used for aerial camera work in the USA.

Bottom: D3832 on the UK civil register, with two passengers in the front cockpit.

TheFE2b/d in Training Units

The RFC training system, at the time that FE2as were operational with the BEF and the FE2b was entering service, was not properly developed. Reserve Aeroplane Squadrons (RAS) took ab-initio pilots and trained them to solo standard. The RAS were equipped with a miscellany of types that were, largely, obsolete. Graduates then passed to service squadrons, in the process of mobilisation, for advanced training and most were posted overseas with less than 40 hours noted in their logbooks. There was no specialist training in weaponry, photography and tactics, these skills had to be learnt 'on the job'.

The 1916-1917 planned expansion of the RFC was coupled with an overhaul of the training system. Reserve Squadrons (RS), as the RAS had been re-designated, were categorised into elementary and advanced units. All prospective pilots were given initial training at elementary RS, with civilian schools, such as those at Hendon, accommodating any surplus. Upon achieving solo status, trainees moved on to an advanced RS which then had type specialisation. Pilots gained experience of their intended operational machines, but there was still no systematic training in operational techniques.

Several advanced RAS/RS were devoted to the training of FE2b/d pilots by December 1916. 9 RS, at Norwich/Mousehold Heath had an intended establishment of nine Henri Farman F.20s and 9 FE2bs. Pupils were instructed in flying pushers on the former type before graduating to the operational machine. Those attending 19 RS, at Hounslow, may have had a better grounding as its establishment was nine

DH1s and nine FE2bs. The AMC type, unlike the rotary-engined HF F.20, had a static engine, the 80hp Renault, which would have been a better introduction to the 120hp Beardmore of the FE2b. 27 RS, at Gosport and formed from the initial 41 Sqn, also had FE2bs and DH1s before it was re-designated as an elementary RS and received Maurice Farmans, The FE2d had entered service by the end of 1916 and both 46 RS, at Bramham Moor/Tadcaster, and 59 RS, at Yatesbury, were designated to provided pilots for 20, 25 and 57 Sqns operating that variant with the BEF. To that end, each of those RS was given an establishment of six DH1s, for initial training, six FE2bs, for type introduction, and six of the more powerful FE2ds, for advanced training.

28 Squadron, at Gosport, also served in a training role, and was equipped with both FE2bs and FE2ds. It had, however, been intended to become operational with the BEF. The RFC Programme of Development, dated 8 November 1916 stated that the squadron would fly 250hp FE2ds in the fighter-reconnaissance role, receive its first three operational machines by 31 December and be fully equipped (presumably ready for posting to France) on 1 March 1917. That deployment did not take place, probably because higher authority recognised that the type was outdated operationally and

that Rolls-Royce engines would be better employed in the DH4. Concurrently, both 35 and 64 Sqns, at Thetford and Sedgeford respectively, each operated a flight of FE2bs as interim equipment and took pilots from elementary Reserve Squadrons for advanced training.

A move toward developing the training system further was made in January 1917, with the opening of dedicated (Auxiliary) Schools of Aerial Gunnery; 1 (Aux) SAG at Hythe and 2 (Aux) SAG at Turnberry. The former specialised in observer training and the Scottish-based unit was, mainly, intended for pilots of single-seat scouts but had FE2bs on charge to provide gunnery practice against both towed and ground/moored targets.

The Reserve Squadrons were re-titled during May 1917 to become, more appropriately, Training Squadrons. The FE2b and FE2d were, by that time, outclassed by the opposition on the Western Front and replacement by Bristol F2Bs and DH4s was beginning to take place. That should have seen the end of the FEs in training units but the FE2b received a new lease of life; one that continued until the end of hostilities.

The reason for this was a combination of the decision to re-equip the northern squadrons of the Home Defence Wing

46 TS, at Bramham Moor (Tadcaster) was responsible for training FE2d pilots. Most of its equipment was, however, FE2bs and this photograph, taken shortly before the unit moved to Catterick, for re-equipment with DH4s, may show one of the elusive dual control conversions. There appears to be a spade grip for a control column in the front cockpit and pitot leads running down both front centre-section struts.

with the type and the introduction of it into the squadrons of the BEF's newly formed night light-bombing force. Both types of squadron needed pilots who were trained in night flying and a further aspect of the RFC's training programme developed to meet that demand.

When 100 Squadron, the first of the night light-bombing units, was formed on 11 February 1917, the sole night training unit was 98 Depot Squadron at Rochford, created three days earlier by the re-designation of 11 RS. 98 DS had neither the extra manpower nor the FE2bs to serve 100 Sqn during its short mobilisation period. Instead, 100 Sqn was attached to 51 (HD) Sqn, the HD Wing's only FE2b unit, with headquarters at Hingham, and its crews worked up on the flight stations at Harling Road, Mattishall and Narborough. The brevity of 100 Squadron's mobilisation may have resulted in it receiving insufficient FE2bs, or crew trained to fly the type, because its initial equipment with the BEF included four BE2es.

The formation of a second bombing unit, 101 Squadron, stretched the training resources of the HD Group, as the HD Wing had been re-titled, to the limit. The availability of FE2bs from the Training Squadrons, due to the type's replacement in France, allowed the creation of further Depot Squadrons for specialist training of pilots for the northern HD squadrons and the night-light bombing force.

99 DS formed at Rochford on 1 June 1917 and moved to its intended base at East Retford twenty-two days later, where it joined 200 DS, which was already in residence. 99 DS was re-designated 199 DS on 27 June. A further Depot Squadron, 192 DS, formed for FE2b training; its nucleus moved from Gainsborough to East Retford, where it became operational, and then Marham, before finally settling down

2 (Auxiliary) SAG formed at Turnberry in January 1917 in order to give pilots, destined for BEF service, some training in gunnery and tactics. This atmospheric view shows one of the unit's FE2bs on landing approach, with RE7s parked outside the Bessonneau hangars.

4972 saw service with 19 RS at Hounslow, one of the units dedicated to the training of FE2b pilots. Among its pupils was 2Lt E. Mannock, who flew this machine on 12 and 13 January 1917. Mannock went on to greater things and 4972 survived until, at least, May 1918.

4279 saw training service with 192 NTS at Newmarket, with which unit it crashed, with fatal consequences, on 21 January 1918. It, too, may have been a dual control conversion. There are twin pitot heads and the position of the front cockpit's seated occupant suggests that he could have been holding a control column.

A800 had the unusual addition of a Scarff ring to the observer's cockpit. After service with the BEF, this machine was in use at Marske as a gunnery trainer.

Lt Robin Arthur Grosvenor transferred to the RFC from the 2nd Dragoons and was posted to 2 RS at Brooklands for initial flying instruction. He made his first flight on 16 August 1916, in MF Se.11 A910, and the earliest stages of his training, by a Lt Millman, concentrated on landing practice. He soloed after exactly eleven days six hours of dual instruction, making a 17 minute flight in A2175 at 06.23 on 27 August. He was awarded his 'ticket' on 7 September, after a further nine solo flights, all of which had been made at less than 2000 feet. His course at Brooklands finished on 11 September, on which day he took A2175 to 3000 feet on a flight to Staines Reservoir. With 16hr 19min flying time behind him, Grosvenor progressed to a higher Reserve Squadron.

19 RS at Hounslow had a responsibility for training FE2b pilots but Grosvenor's advanced training began on DH1s, whose 80hp Renault engines (the same as used on the MF Se.11 'Shorthorn') made them a good introductory type to the more powerful FE2b. General flying and landing practice came first and he embarrassed himself by crashing 4640 on 22 September and 4638 two days later. He was involved in a further crash on 18 October, but that time he was flying as a passenger to Lt Napier, attempting to deliver FE2d A1933 from Farnborough to Bramham Moor. After one successful forced landing at Peterbrough, they came down in thick fog near Wakefield and ran into an iron fence.

His return to Hounslow saw a resumption of landing practice and some camera obscura work before he was introduced to the FE2b on 26 October, flying as a passenger on a formation flight to Reading. Grosvenor soloed the following day, on 4887, and followed that with three further landing practice flights. By 1 November, he had progressed to shooting practice, on 7673, wireless training for a test the following day, formation flying, SA (split-arse) turns and camera gun practice. His training at Hounslow brought his flying time up to 31hr 58min.

He must have been earmarked for active service on FE2ds and was posted to 46 RS at Bramham Moor, where he first flew the Rolls-Royce engined variant on 13 November, with a 15 minute flight ending in a successful forced landing after engine failure. A landing practice flight, a formation flight and two practice reconnaissance flights, on the second of which he became lost and force-landed, brought an end to his training. With 34hr 58min flying time, he joined 57 Squadron for active service on 4 December 1916.

He flew and fought with the squadron until 8 May, when he joined 2 Aircraft Depot at Candas. After a month of what seem to have been familiarisation flights on tractor machines, mainly, a BE2e and a Martinsyde G.102, Grosvenor was posted to Home Establishment and duty as a ferry pilot at the Lympne AAP.

199 NTS trained night light bomber pilots and marked its FE2bs with a distinctive white lazy M on the front of their nacelles. A5717 is seen having come to grief in a ground collision with A5523 of 200 NTS at East Retford on 12 October 1917.

at Newmarket. 192 and 199 DS were the initial units supplying the FE2b night bombing units of the BEF, being joined later in the year by 200 DS, which gave up its HF F.20s and DH1as. The Depot Squadrons were re-designated, again more appropriately, as Night Training Squadrons on 21 December 1917, by which time 190 and 191 had been formed. These latter units were for basic training and graduates moved to East Retford or Newmarket for introduction to the FE2b.

The FE2b had superseded ageing BE2 variants in 33, 36, 38 and 76 (HD) Squadrons from July 1917, again the release of former Training Squadron machines allowed this to take place. 76 (HD) Sqn soon relinquished its FEs and reverted to being a BE2/BE12 unit for another year but the others were also brought into the training programme, providing pilots and observers for the Home Defence Group, which was expanded to become the Home Defence Brigade and then VI Brigade. The introduction of the FE2b to these units was made in the knowledge that the type's ceiling was well below that of the latest German airships, suggesting that the training function was paramount. HD pilot and observer trainees were teamed and given conjoint training exercises to speed up the programme. Those exercises

A821, devoid of any armament fittings, was a training machine that served with 9 TS at Norwich (Mousehold Heath) until crashed on 6 July 1917. It had the V-strut undercarriage.

A6433 was an FE2d and served with 28 Sqn at Gosport. The unit was intended to join the BEF with FE2ds for fighter-reconnaissance duties but, with the impending replacement of FEs by Bristol F2Bs and DH4s, remained in England and mobilised as a scout unit with Sopwith F1 Camels.

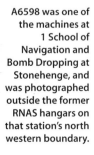

A6598 was one of the machines at 1 School of Navigation and Bomb Dropping at Stonehenge, and was photographed outside the former RNAS hangars on that station's north western boundary.

B1862 is shown at Yatesbury and this photograph has previously been captioned to state that it was a 66 TS machine. That unit, however, trained Corps-Reconnaissance pilots and it is more likely that the FE2b was on the strength of the co-located 59 TS, which was an FE2 unit. B1862 should have been an FE2d and, while built as an FE2b, retained the over-wing gravity tank position of the Rolls-Royce engined type.

included bombing (both by day and by night), aerial fighting practice, flying in searchlights and reconnaissance.

The northern night training programme reached its final development by mid 1918. All prospective FE trainees attended one of the elementary NTS which, by then, were 186 and 187 NTS, at East Retford and 190 NTS at Bury/Upwood. Here, they passed through Stage A of the programme and achieved 15 hours solo. The best of the graduates then moved to one of the northern HD squadrons for training through Stages B and C on the FE2b, which then qualified them as Northern Defence pilots. The more heavy handed moved

on to one of the FE2b equipped Night Training Squadrons for training through Stages B and C as Night Light Bombing pilots. Those squadrons were then 191 at Upwood, 192 at Newmarket and 199 and 200 NTS which had moved to Harpswell. Stage B was identical for all pilots but Stage C, for night light-bombing pilots, included 10 hours night flying, practice night landings using restricted lighting and a written examination on topics related to their intended operational tasks. A 100 mile night reconnaissance was part of the general syllabus but it was common for this to be made in daylight, with pilots wearing tinted goggles to simulate

conditions of darkness.

1917 RFC planning for the following year envisaged the introduction of the HP O/400 as a heavy night bomber. This coincided with a further revision to the main training programme. The existing practice of training via elementary and then advanced Training Squadrons was expensive in terms of time and resources. A solution, based on the French training model, was the creation of Training Depot Stations. Most of these were the equivalent of three training squadrons and occupied a single aerodrome. Trainees were taken all the way through the training syllabus and each TDS had a type function. Those for the HP O/400 were 8 and 12 TDS at Netheravon, 13 TDS at Ternhill, 58 TDS (initially 213 TDS) at Cranwell and 59 TDS at Scopwick. DH6s and, later, Avro 504s provided initial training and students then moved on to the FE2b for practice with larger machines before being introduced to the twin-engined Handley-Pages. The nominal establishment for such units was 30 Avros, 20 FEs and 10 HPs, although 58 TDS, being the equivalent of only two training squadrons, had, respectively, 20, 18 and 8 of these types.

The development of the, by then RAF, training programme introduced a further, final phase for pilots of heavy night and light day bombers. 1 School of Aerial Navigation and Bomb Dropping (the word Aerial was soon dropped from the title) had been formed at Stonehenge in January 1918, by the re-designation of 2 TDS, and incorporated RNAS Handley-Pages from Manston. It developed into a finishing school where future bomber pilots were taught the tactical skills implied by the unit's title. For prospective HP pilots, this

D9157 had seen operational service with 58 Sqn before returning to England and being issued to 8 TDS at Netheravon, in whose service it crashed on 22 October 1918. This angle shows the serial number presented on the rear side of the nacelle.

included night flying and, again, the FE2b was used as an interim trainer. The unit establishment was two Avros, two Sopwith Scouts and 48 DH4/9 for day work and six MF.Se.11, 40 FE2b and 10 HPs for night flying training. The 'Shorthorns', by then redundant in the earlier stages of training, were for practice in pusher flying before an introduction to night work on the FE and graduation to the heavies as the final stage, if that was to be their intending operational posting. Two further such schools were opened at home and that at Andover, 2 SNBD, was given the same establishment as that at Stonehenge.

The 1918 re-equipment of the Northern Home Defence squadrons with Avros, Bristol Fighters and Pups left a void in the training of observers for the night light bombing force and that was filled by the SNBD. Trainee observers were posted in and followed a similar training sequence to their pilot counterparts.

The scope and thoroughness of 1918 RAF training were in marked contrast to that of 1916 and the FE2b played an important part. 343 of the 563 FE2bs on RAF charge at the end of October 1918 were with home-based units. 69 were noted as being with RAF Areas, i.e. TDS, 38 with schools, i.e. SNBD, and 97 were with VI Brigade, the vast majority of those being with NTS.

There was no place for the FE2b in the post-war RAF. The rapid disbandment of the night light-bombing force, the reduction in the number of Handley-Page squadrons and the replacement of the final HD machines with Snipes negated the need for FE2b trainers and, by mid 1919, the type had all but disappeared from home service.

FE2b Night Light Bomber Pilot Training 1918

2Lt Joseph Helingoe had a disrupted training as a pilot but its final stages demonstrate how the Night Training and Home defence squadrons worked in conjunction to produce pilots for the night light bombing force that operated with the BEF.

His elementary training began at 7 RS, Netheravon, where he made his initial flight in MF Se.11 A7071 on 16 February 1916. He soloed after nine instructional flights that involved circuits and landings and 4 hour 25 minutes in the air. A further six solos and three flights with an instructor brought his total time to 12 hours 55 minutes and he moved on to 38 RS at Rendcombe, where his first flight, on Avro 504A 5919, was on 1 March. After 2 hours 20minutes flying with that unit, he had a brief attachment to 15 RS at Doncaster, where he made a single flight, practising turns in Avro 504A A558 with an instructor.

Helingoe must have been intended to become a Home Defence pilot because he then joined 36 (HD) Sqn at Seaton Carew and first flew there on 10 April; the flight to the Thornaby landing ground, with Lt Turnbull as pilot, was in BE2c 2738, the machine flown by 2Lt I.V.J. Pyott to destroy the Zeppelin L34 on 27 November 1916. Six more instructional flights brought a temporary conclusion to his flying career.

That career resumed on 4 February 1918, when Helingoe joined 199 NTS at East Retford. The reason for the hiatus was not recorded. His earlier attachment to 36 (HD) Sqn may have had a bearing on this posting and his earlier training may have negated any requirement for him to attend one of the elementary NTS.

His introduction to the FE2b was made on 12 February, a landing practice flight with Lt Chaplin on B461, and was followed by solo flights, practising turns and landings and two cross-country flights of more than two hours duration. Despite his unit's title, Helingoe made only one night flight during his posting and that was his final one, in A781 on 25 February, during which he made six landings.

He progressed, two days later, to 33 Sqn C Flight at Elsham for advanced training, after 23 hours 35 minutes flying time at East Retford. That training hitherto must have been on 120hp machines, because his first log entry with the new unit, noted that A5595 was his first flight on a 160hp FE2b. He took up his first passenger on 28 February, on a cross-country flight that was probably preparatory to the 60 mile night reconnaissance made on the following night. Bomb dropping practice by day was followed by that at night from 8 March and then night shooting practice at a lighted target. His final days at training with 33 Sqn were spent with A Flt at Scampton, practising night landings by both hurricane lamps and searchlights, a 100 mile night reconnaissance and a cross country flight, during which sixteen bombs were dropped, ten of which were classed as 'OKs'.

With a further 25 hours 40 minutes flying noted in his log and after a fortnight's leave, Helingoe was posted to 148 Sqn at Ford Junction (which he noted by its alternative name of Yapton), a unit that was working up for active service with the night light bombing force. His first flight from Ford Junction was on 5 April, a cross country exercise in B469 on 5 April, and other training flights followed (they totalled 21 hours 35 minutes) until the unit proceeded overseas fifteen days later.

The missing year in his log may be accounted for by his log entries at this point. He wrote 'Flying overseas again for the 3rd time', 'Total Solo Day 465 hrs', 'Total solo Night 212 hrs', 'Time in Air 690 hrs'.

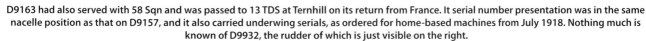

D9163 had also served with 58 Sqn and was passed to 13 TDS at Ternhill on its return from France. It serial number presentation was in the same nacelle position as that on D9157, and it also carried underwing serials, as ordered for home-based machines from July 1918. Nothing much is known of D9932, the rudder of which is just visible on the right.

Day Operations on the Western Front

FE2a 2864, seen here without the balanced ailerons fitted experimentally for a short period, as shown on p12. Lt L.A. Strange delivered this machine to 6 Squadron on 20 May 1915.

Although the FE2a had done well in the evaluation trials conducted by CFS in early 1915[1] – in comparison to the Voisin – full scale production was not feasible until increased quantities of the 120hp Beardmore could be made available. As a result, the 'Fee' did not appear in significant numbers on the Western Front until the beginning of 1916 – even though orders for 450 examples had been placed as early as the spring of 1915.

Meanwhile, the few FE2a machines that were produced, albeit with the 120hp Beardmore rather than the inferior 100hp Green, were immediately sent to France to gain operational experience. There has been subsequent criticism that this lengthy delay prolonged the 'Fokker Scourge' and that the RFC could have regained air superiority much sooner. However, this ignores the significant engineering and supply problems that had

Capt L.A. Strange

to be overcome before quantity production could commence.

Only 12 FE2a were built, serving largely with 6 Sqn (the exception being FE2a 5647 which was allocated to 16 Sqn). The new aircraft was well received, although its impact was muted by the slow rate of deliveries. Capt Louis Strange was one

of the first to fly the FE2a in combat and wrote in his logbook that: *The FE is a fine machine and would be ideal if it were only a little faster. As it is, the Hun always seems to see us in time and avoids us like the plague, so that we seldom catch him. It is, however, a splendid reconnaissance and photographic machine.*[2]

Unfortunately, there were never more than four to six machines with 6 Sqn at any one time. Meanwhile, the first production FE2b (5201) was handed to the RFC on 2 October 1915 and allocated to 16 Sqn just four weeks later. By the end of the year a total of seven aircraft were on the strength of the BEF – four FE2a with 6 Sqn and three FE2b with 16 Sqn.

The first complete FE2b squadron to reach the Western Front was 20 Sqn which arrived with its complement of 12 aircraft on 23 January 1916. As it transpired, 20 Sqn would become the longest serving

The first of the type to be built and the first to be lost, FE2a 4227, re-engined with a 120hp Austro-Daimler, was delivered to 6 Squadron from England on 14 May 1915 and was successful in combat until 5 September, when Capt W.C. Adamson and Lt E.C.R.G. Braddyll were shot down and killed by AA fire.

William Campbell Adamson

9.10.16, 8.20pm: Machine, FE **4862**:
Pilot Capt Callaghan: Time in mins, 100:
Duty, Night Bombing.

Crossed the line at LE SARS at 8.50pm at 4500ft. Velu at 9.0pm. No activity seen at Velu but could see conspicuous lights on the ground in a northern direction so went to see what they were.

There were three lights on the ground – two white ones and one red one. The two white ones were about 50 yards apart and the red one formed the apex of an isosceles triangle and was 200 yards distant from the white lights. The red light pointed into wind.

Green and white Very's lights were being fired into the air at long intervals. We had a good look at the place and could see hangars on the north western side of the flares.

The position of this aerodrome is (51B) V.4b.4e (centre of landing ground).

At 9.15pm from 5000ft dropped 3 Hales 20lb HE bombs. The first two burst about 200yds south of the hangars and the other one was about 100yds south of the hangars.

All lights were immediately put out and as we hovered over the aerodrome to drop our remaining bombs a machine was wheeled out of a hangar and took off into wind. We followed him and by keeping our nose down we kept him in sight. We were getting quite close to him (we were at 4000ft and he was about 1500ft below us) when he turned sharply and we turned to get on top of him.

He was drawing away from us so I opened fire on him and gave him a drum. He then went out of sight and we followed in his direction.

As we came over the aerodrome again we dropped our remaining three bombs – two burst on the aerodrome and the third one hit a hangar. No fire was caused.

We hovered round but could not see the hostile machine. No indications could be seen on the ground pointing out direction. Another aerodrome could be seen lit up in the direction of Marcoing. We did not go there as we had no bombs left.

At 9.35pm when over DOIGNIES the engine started missing and stopped. The pilot pushed her nose down and switched over to the gravity tank. The prop nearly stopped when the engine picked up. BEAUTIFUL SENSATION.

A repetition of this occurred over ALBERT later.

At 9.40pm when over BAPAUME saw lights on BAPAUME-ERVILLERS road just north of BAPAUME. Fired a drum at them. Re-crossed at LIGNY-THILLOY at 9.45pm and landed.

Observation was clear underneath but hazy in the distance.

10.10.16, 10.5pm: Machine, FE 4915:
Pilot Capt Callaghan: Time in mins, 185:
Duty, Night Bombing.

Crossed the lines at COURCELETTE at 10.40pm at 5000ft. Patrolled east of BAPAUME looking for aerodromes. At 11.5pm when over ACHIET LE GRAND saw a machine flying at about1000ft going north east. We tried to keep him in sight but he was considerably faster than us and we lost him.

At 11.10pm saw a number of AA shells bursting over HERMIES.

We could not find any aerodromes lit up, we decided to have a look for activity in CAMBRAI.

At 11.25pm when over HAVRINCOURT, two searchlights, one at K.26c.9.4 and the other at K.20b.4.2 (Sheet 57C) tried to pick us up. We were slightly archied but the shooting was not good. At 11.30pm a searchlight played from (57C) L.16a.2.1.

Reached CAMBRAI at 11.35pm. Height 6500ft. A searchlight played from (51A).5.26d.9.4. Heavily archied but not accurate.

Nothing doing in Cambrai station so went on to VALENCIENNES.

At 11.40pm a dozen or so faintly lit lorries were on IWUY-CAMBRAI road at T.15 going south. When we were above IWUY, the town of DENAIN

was well lit up but on our approach, all lights were extinguished.

At 11.50pm train on line at (51A) K7b.8.3 heading southwards but not moving.

Arrived VALENCIENNES at 11.55pm. Height 7000ft. The station on the north west corner was lit up. MONS which could be seen in the distance was well illuminated. We had a good look at the town and came down about 1000ft. A number of trains (about 4) could plainly be seen in the station.

At 12.10am dropped 6 Hales 20lb HE bombs all together. The bombs burst in the centre of the station at (51A) E.3c Central. A small fire broke out and burned merrily for 3 minutes. It then went out. By this time all lights in the neighbourhood had been extinguished. There was no searchlight or AA activity.

We returned to CAMBRAI passing over DENAIN at 12.20am. Stationary train on line at (51A) N.6c.9.7 heading south at 12.25am. Another stationary train heading towards CAMBRAI at (51A) K.23c.7.4. Could not see an aerodrome.

At 12.40am the two searchlights at K.26c.9.4 and K.20b.4.2 tried to pick us up so we dived from about 6500 – 5300ft and I fired two drums at them. The one at K.26c.9.4 was put out but my firing had no effect on the other one.

At 12.40am a red light was burning on the ground at (57C) 0.2c.1.6.

We re-crossed the line at LIGNY-THILLOY at 12.55am.

Observation was very clear.

No moving trains were seen.

On our return there was considerable bombardment of the German trenched east and north of COURCELETTE.

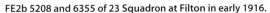

FE2b 5208 and 6355 of 23 Squadron at Filton in early 1916.

Lt Eynon George Arthur Bowen, RGA

A pre-war regular, Lt Eynon George Arthur Bowen had served in France with a Heavy Battery before transferring to the RFC as an observer in August 1915. He joined 6 Sqn, operating with the BE2c from Abeele, and flew with them until December when he was sent for pilot training at 9 Reserve Sqn Norwich. Having soloed on a Maurice Farman, and completed some 8 hours flying, Bowen was transferred to 35 Sqn at Thetford where he converted to the FE2. After a further 9 hours flying, he was posted on 19 May 1916 to 22 Sqn at Bertangles, itself recently arrived from England and equipped with the FE2b.

Although Bowen's period in training seems particularly short it was not unusual for the period. It should be remembered that he had already seen a year's service on the Western Front, including 5 months as an observer with 6 Sqn. Nevertheless, as the war progressed it was recognised that training programmes needed to be longer. By 1918, some pilots had over 100 hours flying experience before they joined an operational unit.

After an initial test flight, Bowen was soon flying operational patrols of 3 hours duration, covering the front from Bienvillers to the Somme. These long patrols, interspersed with the occasional photographic sortie, continued through May and June, operating at heights between 3000 and 8000 ft. The opening of the Battle of the Somme saw more formation patrols and greater anti-aircraft fire but no encounters with German aircraft. Emboldened by the lack of enemy air activity, Bowen strafed the German front line from low level on 15 July at the end of a routine patrol, an action that gained favourable comment from headquarters. The situation gradually changed as more enemy aircraft arrived on the Somme front. During photography of the German rear lines on 21 July, Bowen and his regular observer, Lt W.S. Mansell were attacked by a 'Roland' over Combles. They quickly turned the tables and shot it down. A further air combat occurred on

26 July involving several LVGs but this time with no outcome.

From now on, increasing numbers of enemy aircraft were encountered as the German Air Service attempted to wrest air superiority from the RFC. Nevertheless patrols and photography continued much as before during the remainder of July and into August, with the occasional inconclusive combat. Most missions were between 2 and 3 hrs duration and usually flown above 10000 ft, where the cold and lack of oxygen took their toll. Bowen's last flight, before some well-earned leave, was to photograph Le Sars on 25 August. It was on his return that he was shot down and killed, together with his observer Lt Robert Macallan Stalker. They were flying FE2b 4921 on another photographic sortie when they were attacked by enemy aircraft and reported as falling in flames. The victor was probably the German ace, Hpt Oswalde Boelcke leading the newly-formed Jasta 2 – created in direct response to the RFC's Somme success. Neither Bowen nor Stalker have a known grave and are commemorated on the Arras Memorial.

Bowen's squadron commander, Major Barry Martyn, wrote that he had been popular and valuable officer with an extensive knowledge of flying. His comrades "very much felt his loss". In his letters home, Bowen didn't disclose much detail about his war flying. He did comment that he liked the FE2, although he also thought it could have been faster. There is no indication that he felt outclassed by the enemy machines he met, indeed it was not until August that he encountered any in quantity. In July he was able to write that "we are right in the middle of the push and get plenty of work in consequence but we have got the Boches properly scared in the air down here, so we aren't much worried." By the beginning of August he was noting that German airmen were more active, although he was more concerned about the summer heat than air combat.

Fee unit employed on day operations – relinquishing the type only in September 1917. Further squadrons followed as production allowed: 25 Sqn in March 1916; and 18, 22 and 23 Sqns in April 1916 – significantly increasing the frontline strength of the RFC in anticipation of the Battle of the Somme.

Cecil Lewis has left us a typically evocative picture of 23 Sqn's departure from Gosport: *We stood on the tarmac watching them go. And still after twenty years, my heart swells at the memory of the sight. I can hear the strong engines and smell the tang of the burnt oil. I can see them as they came hurtling up, their goggled pilots and observers leaning down to wave a last farewell before they passed in a deafening flash of speed and smoke fifty feet overhead.*[3]

The FE2b and the DH2 pusher scout are popularly credited with the end of the 'Fokker Scourge' – the aerial dominance enjoyed by the Fokker single-seat monoplane. There is no doubt that the FE2b offered a much improved field of fire and good visibility as well as a reasonable turn of speed and a reliable engine. The most important development, however, was the operational transformation it brought about. The overwhelming technical superiority of the Fokker – although never present in large numbers – had forced the RFC to adopt a defensive strategy that saw the introduction of formation flying for all missions east of the German lines.

With the arrival of the FE2b a degree of parity emerged, such that individual pilots felt confident enough to take the fight to their adversaries. These changes did not happen overnight: German fighters continued to be dominant for the next few months but by May 1916 the tide was definitely turning. There were now five

25 Squadron lost FE2b 4909 *Baby Mine* in combat on 18 June 1916. 2Lt J.R.B. Savage fatally wounded, AM2 Robinson PoW.

A rare unposed photograph of a Flight from 22 Squadron preparing to depart for France.

fully-equipped FE2b squadrons in France; a total of over 60 machines. From this point onwards, the RFC never returned to a defensive strategy. The FE2b was the catalyst for this fundamental change in RFC's thinking about air warfare and the doctrine of the 'strategic air offensive'.

Typical of this period were 25 Sqn's experiences on 18 June 1916 when, in separate combat patrols, a total of 3 Fokker E.IIIs were claimed (including the leading ace Oblt Max Immelmann) for the loss of

FE2b 4849 joined 22 Squadron on 4 September 1916.

two of their own crews – Lt C.E. Rogers and Sgt H. Taylor in FE2b 6940 and 2/Lt J.R.B. Savage and AM Robinson in FE2b 4909.

The Fee soon proved to be a popular aircraft, both for its flying and for its fighting characteristics. Cecil Lewis described the FE2b as *a fine machine, slow, but very sturdy* and added that *with good battle tactics, a flight of these machines was very deadly, even to an enemy with far greater speed and manoeuvrability.*[4] Although the defensive arrangements looked quite ungainly, with up to three Lewis guns (and 1000 rounds of ammunition) mounted on a variety of pillars that sometimes required the observer to stand on the edge of the nacelle in order to fire rearwards over the top wing, they provided coverage against attack from almost all quarters. There was a blind spot immediately to the rear but the solidity of the engine provided a degree of protection for the pilot and observer. It is not clear when the idea of forming a defensive ring first emerged but

FE2d A18, which was lost with its crew on 20 July 1916.

Flt Sgt James Byford McCudden

James McCudden also flew the FE2, albeit briefly, during the Battle of the Somme. When he arrived on 20 Sqn at Clairmarais he had had no previous experience on the 'Fee'. His first flight was in FE2d A6 on 7 July 1916. During the month he served with the squadron, he was employed in hostile aircraft patrols, reconnaissance, bombing and photography. Flying as high as 12000ft, McCudden saw few German fighters, the majority being engaged further south. The most serious incident during his time came about because of the weather. An aircraft early patrol on 20 July was caught out by low mist and three machines out of five failed to return, including Capt G.N.Teale and Cpl J.W. Stringer who were killed in FE2d A18.

In leaving 20 Sqn, McCudden wrote that he was *sorry also to leave my cumbersome old F.E. for these aeroplanes had certainly earned for themselves the wholesome respect of the German pilots and with good cause too.*

FE2b A5481 'Gold Coast No 13', delivered to 18 Squadron BEF on 23 January 1917.

it soon became standard practice, allowing each aircraft in the formation to defend the other's tail, the observer of one machine firing his top gun and the observer of the next machine using his front gun so that any attacker had at least two guns firing at them – anticipating the 'Lufbery Circle' of 1917 and echoing the Bf.110's tactics employed during the Battle of Britain. As a result, Fee formations were able to fight their way home – even when confronted by large numbers of faster and more manoeuvrable German fighters.[5]

A good feel for the Fee's fighting record can be judged from the brief biographies and comprehensive individual aircraft histories accompanying this monograph. The latter lists over 500 combat claims. The most successful machine was FE2d A6430, 'AJMER', flown regularly by Capt F.J.H. Thayre and Capt F.R. Cubbon of 20 Sqn,

with at least 20 victories to its credit. The Fee was clearly no slouch in air combat, boasting at least 18 fighter/observer aces (15 of these serving, at one time or another, with 20 Sqn).[6]

Capt F.J.H. Thayre

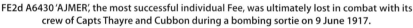

FE2d A6430 'AJMER', the most successful individual Fee, was ultimately lost in combat with its crew of Capts Thayre and Cubbon during a bombing sortie on 9 June 1917.

A considerable number of personal reminiscences and histories have been published over the years by those that flew the Fee.[7] All testify to the great strength of the airframe and its ability to endure strenuous manoeuvring and to return safely after absorbing damage that would have brought down most other aircraft. This point is underscored by the limited number of field modifications needed to keep the airframe airworthy or to incorporate urgent operational requirements. Between the end of 1916 and the summer of 1918, the Military Aeronautics Directorate had to authorise just six alterations to the FE2 compared to 73 for the RE8 and 130 for the AWFK8.

During the summer and autumn of 1916, the 120hp Beardmore was gradually replaced by the 160hp Beardmore. The new engine increased the FE2b's top speed by up to 10mph and the service ceiling from 9000 to 11000 feet, although this was still inferior to the Rolls-Royce powered FE2d which began to appear on the Western Front at much the same time – albeit never in large numbers. As much as these improvements were welcome, the squadrons discovered that (initially at least) reliability was significantly worse.

With more aircraft available, the opportunity was taken to increase squadron establishments from 12 to 18 aircraft. This process saw 20 Sqn give up the FE2b (the remaining machines were largely re-allocated to 22 and 25 Sqns) in favour of the FE2d. On the afternoon of 23 November, two flights from 25 Squadron found themselves fighting 20 German fighters, and a 30 mile an hour headwind, on their return from bombing Brebières village. The 12 FE2bs, led by Capts A.W. Tedder[8] and R. Chadwick, fought their way

Flt Sgt Thomas Mottershead, VC

In numerical terms, the heyday of Fee daylight operations came in January 1917 when a total of over 120 machines equipped seven of the 38 RFC squadrons serving on the Western Front – including the recently arrived 57 Sqn, equipped with the FE2d. This was also the month that saw a member of 20 Sqn become the only non-commissioned officer to win the Victoria Cross for valour in the air. Flt Sgt Thomas Mottershead had joined the RFC on the outbreak of war and was selected for flying training in May 1916. After brief service as an instructor, he joined 25 Sqn at Auchel on 6 July 1916. Mottershead soon proved to be a brave and energetic pilot, winning the Distinguished Conduct Medal on 22 September (flying FE2b 6998, with 2/Lt C. Street as observer), in an attack against

Lt W.E. Gower, Mottershead's observer in FE2d A39.

back across the lines, claiming several machines out of control and an Albatros D.I destroyed (2/Lt C.H.C. Woollven and Sgt G.R. Horrocks in FE2b 7024, east of Oppy). Three of 25 Squadron's pilots had to make force-landings – Sgt W.D. Matheson (damaged radiator), 2/Lt F.S. Moller (wounded in the back) and Lt A.P. Maurice (wounded in the arm).[9]

As early as August 1916 individual FE2bs were undertaking night bombing against German airfields and the transportation system, anticipating the role that they were to perform for the remainder of the war. The success of these early operations, and the limited interference from searchlights, anti-aircraft fire and enemy fighters, may well have influenced the later decision to employ the Fee exclusively on night bombing.

Ltn Walter Göttsch of Jasta 8, who is thought to have damaged Mottershead's FE2d.

the railway station at Somain; destroying an ammunition train and shooting down an attacking monoplane. Early in the New Year, after a period of home leave, he was posted to 20 Sqn, based at Clairmarais. On 7 January 1917, Mottershead and his observer, Lt W.E. Gower, were detailed for a hostile aircraft patrol over Ploegsteert Wood. Attacked by two Albatros scouts, and with their aircraft (FE2d A39) badly on fire, Mottershead somehow managed to return across the lines and make a safe landing – even though terribly burnt – saving the life of his observer. Sadly, Mottershead succumbed to his injuries on 12 January 1917.[10]

As the Fee declined in fighting abilities so its front line strength also began

On 6 April 1917 Lt T.F. Burrill/ Pte F. Smith, 57 Sqn, became PoWs. Brought down by Ltn H. Gontermann of Jasta 5 in FE2d A1959 'A4' near Cambrai.

A photo-reconnaissance observer records his escorting Flight leader.

to diminish. Within four months of Mottershead's action, there were fewer than 80 machines on the Western Front. The first unit to lose its aircraft was 23 Sqn which started to exchange its FE2bs for SPAD VIIs in February, completing the process by the end of March. The next to follow was 57 Sqn, which handed over all of its FE2ds after less than five months operations (the residual airframes largely going to 20 and 25 Sqns), replaced by the DH4. 11 Sqn converted to the Bristol Fighter in June, as did 22 Sqn during July and 25 Sqn to the DH4 a month later. When 18 Sqn finished its conversion to the DH4 at the end of August only 20 Sqn was left to soldier on with the FE2d. It would be wrong, however, to conclude that the Fee was now hopelessly outclassed. During the summer of 1917 the aircraft showed time and time again that handled aggressively, and with a well-trained crew, it was able to inflict losses on enemy fighters that, on paper at least, outperformed it in every respect.

The Fee's darkest phase was undoubtedly 'Bloody April'. In the effort to support the British Army's Arras offensive, which opened on Monday 9 April 1917, the RFC suffered extremely heavy losses in machines and personnel. Since their Somme failure, the German air service had reorganised and re-equipped. The RFC's forward strategy, involving hostile aircraft patrols at least six miles beyond the lines, coupled with an interdiction campaign against targets in the rear areas, invited substantial attrition in the face of German technical superiority. However, the scale of the wastage was unprecedented. Over 30% of frontline machines and nearly 20% of pilots were lost in combat. The six Fee

squadrons paid the highest price, seeing 70 aircraft destroyed from a frontline strength of just over 100 machines. Typical of this unequal struggle was the fate of a mixed formation of FE2bs and FE2ds from 25 Sqn returning from a bombing raid against Henin-Liétard in the early evening of Friday 13 April. A group of enemy fighters from Jastas 4 and 11, led by Manfred von Richthofen, quickly shot down 3 of the 6 machines (2/Lt A.H. Bates and Sgt W.A. Barnes in 4997, Sgt J. Dempsey and 2/Lt W.H. Green in A784 and Capt L.L. Richardson and 2/Lt D.C. Wollen in A6372) with the loss of their crews before the Nieuports of 40 Sqn could intervene.

The only compensating factor, in the face of such heavy losses, was that the fighter squadrons succeeded in largely protecting the RFC's army co-operation aircraft, allowing their crews to direct accurate and sustained artillery fire in support of the ground offensive.[11]

The Fee, even the more powerful FE2d, should by now have been replaced by higher performance aircraft but production delays with the DH4 and Bristol Fighter meant that it had to soldier on for a further five months. Although by now outclassed, the Fee was not entirely defenceless. On 6 July 1917, Manfred von Richthofen, the highest scoring ace of the First World War, was brought down by fire from 2/Lt A.E.

2Lt Albert Edward Woodbridge

Woodbridge in an FE2d of 20 Sqn flown by Capt D.C. Cunnell.

Later that month, in a carefully planned operation, a formation of 20 Sqn machines deliberately enticed a large group of German fighters into a pre-arranged trap over Polygon Wood. The supporting squadrons were slow to arrive and the eight FE2ds had to conduct a running fight against superior numbers for over 40 mins. More than 30 enemy fighters were eventually claimed destroyed – for the

loss of just one Fee (A6512) flown by 2/ Lts G.T.W. Burkett and T.A.M. Lewis, who had lagged behind the main formation because of engine problems.[12] In reality, German losses were significantly fewer than claimed, but the incident underscores the point that even in the twilight of its career as a day fighter the Fee was able to hold its own.

20 Sqn's last victories with the Fee were recorded on 17 August 1917, bringing their total to over 200 since February 1916 – a remarkable record.[13] It is equally remarkable that the Fee had by now been serving successfully on the Western Front for over two years and would do so (at night) for another 16 months. No other aircraft type employed during the First World War could boast a similar longevity or, arguably, excite the same level of affection from those that flew her. It is a hugely impressive story for a machine designed before the First World War even started.

ENDNOTES
1 TNA AIR1/209/3/246.
2 Strange, L.A. *Recollections of an Airman*, pages 117-119, John Hamilton Ltd, London, 1933.
3 Lewis, C.A. *Sagittarius Rising*, pages 25-29, Peter Davies, London, 1936.
4 Lewis, op cit, page 25.
5 Although less manoeuvrable and with a slower top speed, the FE2 had a smaller turning radius than both the Albatros D.II and D.III.
6 The squadron's combat record has been well described in two articles. Bailey & Franks, 'Combat Log No 20 Sqn RFC/RAF', pp 24-53, *Cross & Cockade USA*, Vol 26 No 1, Spring 1985. Bailey & Franks, 'Top Scorers', pp 32-45, *Cross & Cockade GB*, Vol 4 No 1, 1973.
7 Kleiser, 'Narrative of the Experiences of Arch Whitehouse' (22 Sqn), *Cross & Cockade USA*, pp 313-321, Vol 4 No 4 Winter 1963. Manning, 'Sgt Taylor–25 Sqn', pp 117-126, *Cross & Cockade USA*, Vol 8 No 2, Winter 1967. Cambray, 'We Stood to Fight' (20 Sqn), *Flight International*, pp 1072-1073, 26 December 1968 & pp 14-15, 2 January 1969. Harvey, J. *'Pi' In The Sky* (22 Sqn), Colin Huston, Leicester, 1971. Hopkins, 'Pusher Pilot' (22 Sqn), *Cross & Cockade GB*, pp 45-67, Vol 3 No 2, 1972. Price, 'No 23 Sqn Dec 15–Jul 16', pp 162-167, *Cross & Cockade USA*, Vol 16 No 2, Summer 1975. Wright, 'Sense of Duty' (18 Sqn), pp 94-98, Cross & Cockade International, Vol 27 No 2, 1996.
8 Later Marshal of the Royal Air Force Lord Tedder.
9 The 12 FE2bs were 7003, A5439, 7025, 7686, 4946, 4925, 7683, 7024, 4877, 7693, 7007, & 7672.
10 Their opponent is believed to have been Ltn Walter Göttsch of Jasta 8, who had further encounters with 20 Sqn bringing down seven of their number in total but at the price of being wounded twice.
11 Although the corps squadrons represented some 50% of the RFC's strength they only suffered 35% of the casualties during 'Bloody April'.
12 They still managed to make a safe landing at Bailleul. TNA AIR1/733/185/4
13 Franks & Bailey, 'The Record of 20 Squadron RFC/RAF', pages 32-44, *CCI Journal* Vol 4 No 1, 1973.

Maj 'Casey' Callaghan & 2Lt Burton Ankers

Cpl Burton Ankers joined the RFC on 28 January 1915, as an Airman 2nd class. At 21 he was slightly older than his contemporaries, possibly accounting for his rapid promotion to Cpl and selection for observer duties. By the end of the year he was serving with 'B' Flt, 18 Sqn, based at Treizennes, flying the Vickers FB5 'Gunbus'. The bulk of the squadron's work comprised patrols and photography with some artillery co-operation. During April the squadron started to re-equip with the FE2b. By this time, he had gained slightly under 70hrs operational flying – largely with Lt (later Capt) G. Wenden. Ankers' first flight in the new aircraft took place on 8 April when, together with Lt Maurice Le Blanc-Smith in FE2b 4903, he registered targets for 13 Siege Battery. After a period of leave, Ankers returned to operations on 12 July 1916 when he flew an artillery patrol with Capt Joseph 'Casey' Cruess-Callaghan in FE2b 6941. Over the next four months this pairing would fly over 60 sorties together.

The arrival of the FE2b saw a change in the squadron's tactics in the form of larger formations and the introduction of bombing raids against airfields and transportation targets – particularly railway stations. Ankers' log book for this period is full of detail recording German ground activity and the individual positions registered. It also regularly notes the absence of enemy aircraft and balloons. An exceptional event recorded on 28 August was his first night flight, with Capt Callaghan in FE2b 4933, when they bombed Sallaumines. A full month passed before their next bombing duty (9 October), when they flew twice. On their second sortie, flying FE2b 4933, the target was the railway at Cambrai, where Ankers scored a direct hit on a train in the station. They met strong searchlight activity and anti-aircraft fire but returned safely after an hour and a half in the air. For the remainder of the month the pair carried out a mixture of night bombing and day patrols, once again without interference from enemy aircraft.

Ankers received his commission at the beginning of November 1916, leaving 18 Sqn for Home Establishment and pilot training with nearly 200hrs operational flying on the Western Front to his credit. In recognition of their achievements Callaghan was awarded the Military Cross and Ankers the Distinguished Conduct Medal. Ankers returned to France in 1918, flying Sopwith Dolphins with 87 Sqn, under the command of his old pilot, Major Callaghan, who was shot down and killed on 2 July 1918. Ankers survived the war (although he was badly wounded on 8 August 1918 while with 23 Sqn) and remained with the RAF. He had risen to the rank of Wg Cdr when he was killed in a flying accident at Kutumba, India on 9 August 1939.

... a deafening flash of speed and smoke fifty feet overhead — FE2b 6940 'Punjab 32 Montgomery' takes to the air.

Night Bombing 1917 to 1918

One important component of this air weapon was a capability to fly at night. There were limits, imposed primarily by the weather – virtually all flying still needed reasonable weather to be truly effective. An operational capability at night meant attacks waged through the day could be continued through the hours of darkness. Some sought tactical destruction and disruption close behind the battle – typically the work of the FE2bs, though as will be seen later, some FE2bs made attacks to extraordinarily remote destinations. Deeper strategic strikes at the enemy's war potential remained the work of the big Handley Page bombers.

Night flying also enabled very useful reconnaissance of road and rail movements and troop concentrations. Being nocturnal they were laid on at exactly the best time to uncover these hopefully covert movements. Enemy airfields were also watched and

After ninety years of increasing research and examination of the first air war, night operations remain relatively forgotten – odd when night bombing has become a bedrock of modern air offensives. By late 1917 the ground war was unfolding with a vast, remorseless momentum and diversity – a diversity which in particular the air forces had to serve. Whilst the great ground offensives might swell and recede as the resources were alternately provided and swallowed up, by this time the air offensive never let up. It was a proven means of keeping significant pressure on the enemy whilst ground forces went through their inevitable cycles of regrouping. The air weapon was expected to account for itself not just from day to day, but from hour to hour. It had the challenge of many different roles, requiring adaptability and a great variety of skills from its personnel. Just as common purpose and comradeship bound the RFC together, there was also a great diversity of effort expected of them. Well planned, well managed, well resourced and well executed diversity is a very powerful asset in warfare. The British Forces had an air weapon eminently capable of all this as 1918 opened.

A852 of 100 Squadron ready for a night bombing raid. It has the sturdy V-strut undercarriage – most characteristic of night bombing FE2bs – and beneath the nose the flare chute. Technically designated 'RL Launching Tubes', for their derivation from the Royal Laboratories, Woolwich, these ignited RL Reconnaissance or Parachute Flares electronically when the flares were slid through them.

bombed. Thus night operations made the air weapon all the more comprehensive, numbing and demoralising to the enemy.

Of necessity, however, night fliers were fighting an unusual war, where things were just a little different. Their work would never attract the glamour which came to be attached to the fighter pilot – their challenges were quite different from those confronting their daytime fellows. In terms of war flying, per se, it was rarely anywhere near as perilous, and yet operating at night in WWI was indeed a dangerous and often deadly affair. The airman's foes became the reliability of the machine and the hazards of the lonely darkness. He needed self reliance and a constant reserve of flying skills. Compared with day operations, the success of night bombing depended almost entirely on the capabilities of individual crews. Each FE2b proceeded independently to the target and from the time it left the ground the pilot and observer were on their own. The job of navigating to the area of the target and then locating it precisely was totally in their hands.

Squadron armourers fitting the tail fuse of a 230lb RFC HE bomb mounted on a skeleton carrier. The night bombers' V-strut undercarriage made it possible to carry these heavy bombs. A clutch of 25lb Cooper bombs and a Michelin parachute flare are visible beneath the starboard wing as are the permanent special metal ribs, fitted to the main spars, which allowed a range of carriers to be fitted rapidly under the wings.

Reminiscences reveal that crews felt very isolated on these flights. A new pilot on his first few night raids often had no idea where he was from the moment he left the aerodrome until he was back over it again. A.R. Kingsford of 100 Squadron described the sensation in his autobiography *Night Raiders of the Air*.

… there was not a light to be seen anywhere, just blank, impenetrable darkness, broken only by the red glare of the exhaust and the glow of the dashboard.

Crews usually carried out two, three, or even four shorter raids through the night rather than long single journeys, though the distance to the target and weather conditions obviously controlled this. The FE2b could be adapted to provide up to five hours flying time by the fitting of a second fuel tank beneath the upper wing However, it was found that by deploying relatively briefly and often over the objective a machine was not only exposed to less focused AA fire but could deliver a greater number of bombs, causing an extended period of mayhem and destruction.

The Michelin Flare was more commonly used on operations as, by comparison, the RL Parachute Flare had poor illuminating power, frequently failed and entailed additional work for the observer. Also visible are the navigation lights (fitted on the upper surface of the lower wing) outboard of the outer struts, and the fixed Holts Flares (providing illumination during landings) on the under surface of the lower wings.

The nature of the FE2: 'Never Say Die' with its ground crew.

The effect of night bombing was as much on morale as in material damage; the more continuous it could be the more the enemy might be hampered. A single aeroplane overhead making mischief had much the same effect as many.

Longer flights were far more influenced by the vagaries of the weather. For the FE2b, some raids were to targets more than 70 miles away – a long night journey at an average speed of around 60mph. 100 Squadron ventured as deep as Trier [Trèves] on one occasion, to bomb barracks – a round trip of 180 miles. Cancellation or recall was therefore bound to follow any doubt about conditions. The practice of making multiple shorter raids had ramifications on night bombing casualties and accidents, as will be seen shortly, for the numbers of take-offs and landings were greatly multiplied.

Birth of a Night Bomber

Why did the FE2b find such an effective role in night work? The machine has been described as a plodding workhorse and looks an archetypal 'flying machine' – its pusher configuration ensuring it was an aircraft in a design cul-de-sac. A workhorse it may have been, and its performance certainly shared very little with the two-seaters which replaced it in daytime roles in 1917 and 1918. Yet the pilots who flew it at night almost universally wrote about it with deep affection and trust. Its engines gave cause for concern, and its low speed made already demanding operations still more protracted and lengthy, but otherwise it was clearly a sturdy and reliable aeroplane for night bombing and reconnaissance work. It was so fit that production, which had died to a trickle by late 1917, was raised to well over five hundred in the last seven months of the war to ensure supply.

The FE2b served as the short-range night bomber of choice with eight squadrons in France from Spring 1917 until the Armistice. These were, in order of their arrival in France, 100, 101 and 102 Squadrons in 1917, and 58, 83, 148, 38 and 149 Squadrons in 1918. It additionally served with I Flight, an intelligence gathering Special Flight. Its replacement only really began with the deployment of the Handley Page O/400 bomber in two of these units, 100 and 58 Squadrons, in the last months of the war. All the other units continued to fly FE2bs until the end of the fighting.

Of the units mentioned above, 100 Squadron was unique for not only being the first night bombing unit to reach France, in March 1917, but also because it spent most of its time on more southerly fronts, initially within 41st (Bombing) Wing and then with the Independent Force which grew out of this. With their emphasis on strategic and thus longer-range operations the IF's usual machine was the twin-engined Handley Page heavy bomber, and yet 100 Squadron operated their FE2bs until August 1918. Even as the Handley Pages were replacing the FE2bs in some units in late 1918, the actual numbers of the light bomber in France never dropped below 100 machines, from a peak of

A line-up of matt-black painted FE2bs: believed to be 102 Squadron at the point of their departure for France in September 1917.

around 130 in June 1918, equating to about 8% of RAF summer strength. The value and usefulness of the FE2b night bomber was always acknowledged.

Evolution

While the development of the Royal Aircraft Factory FE2b is covered elsewhere, it is worth briefly recalling the factors which led to the superseding of the fighter pusher type by the tractor configuration: the introduction of interrupter gear and the latter's greater efficiency of flight. Neither speed nor efficiency were first priorities for a night bomber, but robustness, relative reliability and good visibility were, and the FE2 types would excel in these areas.

It had already been used as a day bomber before the Somme, with bomb racks placed low down under the centre section, but problems of adapting its oleo undercarriage for this purpose meant that at the time its capacities in this regard were limited. 6 Sqn had tried it as a night flying aeroplane as early as late 1915, and found it excellently suited.

18 Sqn made the first serious attempt to use the type as a night bomber on the night of 10/11 November 1916, with surprisingly good results. As the potential usefulness of night bombing came to be appreciated, it was realised that the FE2b was in fact very suited. When 100 Sqn came to France on 24 March 1917 specifically in this role it therefore brought not only BE2es but FE2bs as well, and was soon fully equipped with the latter type. Back in England, some night flying home defence squadrons also adopted the machine, although its poor climb to altitude made it less effective for this work. By late 1917 several night training squadrons had been set up to ensure a steady supply of pilots familiar with the type. The FE2b had taken on a new lease of life.

Flying At Night

Under cover of darkness its lack of performance which had brought such dire consequences in its day work through 1917 was no longer so critical. But it also brought positive assets to the role. It could lift a reasonable load of bombs and carry them, albeit slowly, a long way into enemy territory. It also had an exceptionally good forward view, useful for bombing as much as for landing more safely at night. It was also tough, and could take a battering at landing – more likely in night operations. Additionally, whilst quite capable of giving its crew some tense and anxious moments, it was hardly ever known to suffer structural failure in the air.

The configurations which came to be used for night operations all retained the 160hp Beardmore engine – probably

The somewhat unreliable 160hp Beardmore, with Lang propeller.

its weak link. Fully loaded with bombs its cruising speed was between 60 and 70mph. It took just over seven minutes to reach 3000ft and around nineteen minutes to reach 6500ft, although on night operations it would rarely fly above 4000ft. It could carry a 230lb bomb or a pair of 112lb bombs. Otherwise, brackets of four 25lb bombs could be placed under each wing, and there were instances of twelve being carried. By war's end this comparatively light load of bombs was identified as a problem, in that much time, effort and skill was being expended to drop a few hundred pounds of explosive, but for the great majority of its service as a night bomber this was simply a fact of life. It was its bomb carrying requirements which led to the adoption of the V-strut undercarriage, a trademark of night

flying FE2bs, in place of the earlier and more complex oleo undercarriage with its oil-filled telescopic buffers. With the latter, 230lb bombs could not be fitted, so the V-strut became standard, with little or no loss to the aircraft's resilience in a hard night landing.

The quality of general strength and toughness, which the FE2b certainly possessed, was a key advantage of the type for night flying. An emergency landing at night was a particular peril. In daytime flying a forced landing was a matter of training, judgment and skill, but at night, as A.R. Kingsford described, it was down to little more than luck:

..you see nothing, your engine cuts and you have to get down as best you can, without killing yourself and knowing nothing of what lays beneath.

Bombing up at St-Omer, 18 July 1918. An FE2b of 149 Sqn is loaded with 112lb RL and 25lb Cooper bombs. A Michelin flare is visible mounted under the starboard wing.

Sergeant Eric Ewart Jones, 58 Squadron

Sgt Eric Ewart Jones, seen here standing before his FE2b, was a very rare night bird. The only Flight Sergeant to serve with his unit, he was perhaps the only one in the night bombing force. On 22 September 1918 he was finally promoted to Second Lieutenant, but by this time he had been flying FE2b/ds for most of the previous two years – as a ferry pilot, then as an instructor, and then bombing with them at night. His mastery on the type got him out of several deadly scrapes. Given his extraordinarily long acquaintance with FEs he may well have flown more hours on them than any other British pilot.

Jones trained at 17 RAS at Croydon from late December 1915 until moving on to Brooklands for further training the next May. In August 1916 he became a ferry pilot, specialising almost exclusively in piloting FE2bs and FE2ds, feeding fighter reconnaissance units in the Battle of the Somme. As its daytime use waned and night bomber deployment began, it was a good enough reason to give Jones' talents new life as a night bombing instructor. He attended the Aerial Gunnery School at Turnberry in July 1917 and then joined 192 Night Training Squadron at Newmarket in November 1917.

In mid May 1918 it was time for him to join the fighting forces in France. He flew out to 58 Squadron's summer base at Fauquembergues, and was almost immediately flying night bombing raids. With his usual observer 2Lt F.W. Roadhouse he quickly gained a reputation in the squadron as an expert flyer. On 2 September the pair were aloft on a moonless night returning from a raid when his prop burst and an emergency landing near the aerodrome was required. The rescue team, which had heard their aircraft in distress, found the pair standing beside their FE2b in a field of waist high corn, with not a scratch or a wire out of place except for the shattered propeller.

In late August 1918 58 Squadron began receiving Handley Page heavy bombers, and unlike most of the squadron's FE pilots who moved on, Jones quickly retrained whilst still bombing and was piloting raids on his O/400 within a couple of weeks. At the end of October Jones was accidentally injured in the thigh and was convalesced home. He joined 191 Night Training Squadron at Ramsey on 1 January 1919 where it was his sorry duty to ferry many of the last remaining night bombing FE2bs off to be broken up. His photograph of them in his album is affectionately captioned 'The Last Muster of Good Old FE's Before Being Broken Up'.

Pilots were encouraged to scour their locality in daylight to familiarise with shapes of features in the landscape, such as woods or lakes, which at night might momentarily orientate crews. Some attempted to use flares to assist in emergency landings, and there was even practice on airfields with landing aids dimmed. Out on operations, however, there was always tension associated with the prospect of an emergency arising. Targets were usually at least ten or twenty miles behind the lines, often reached over thirty miles of old battlefields where every yard on either side of the line might be pock-marked with shell holes. This made a crash almost inevitable in a forced landing, but the FE2b offered a high factor of safety for its crew. As both pilot and observer were both well forward of wings and engine and high above the ground when wheels touched, thanks to the high undercarriage, they were usually thrown clear on impact, often able to walk away.

The rule of thumb was to land with tail down. At least then if an obstruction was hit the undercarriage would likely be lost and the machine simply sit down on its wings. Observers were in the forward position in the nacelle, and some record how in an emergency landing they assumed a crouched position on their toes to ensure an effective catapulting. Only when they hit an obstruction like a building or a tree, or in a particularly steep crash, would circumstances then be reversed and the configuration of a pusher aircraft become a mortal liability, especially for the pilot,

2Lt A.I. Orr-Ewing and Capt E. Marshall of 101 Squadron crash-landed uninjured but became PoWs when their FE2b A856 was brought down during a night bombing raid on Ledeghem on 21 September 1917.

directly in front of the engine. Its mass would bring it forward, tearing at the fuel pipes and quite possibly resulting in fire.

Besides robustness, the other main asset of the FE2b at night was its excellent view forward and down to the sides. This was invaluable not only for landing the machine on very minimally lit and darkened air strips, but also for reconnaissance and for the sighting and dispatch of bombs over the target. The pilot's seat was well enclosed by the sides of the nacelle, which were cut down on each side to enable this good lateral vision downwards. In front of his face was a small hinged windshield of safety glass.

The observer, sitting in front was in contrast very exposed, as the sides of the nacelle fell away sharply, curving down to a blunt nose not much higher than a seated man's knees. Here he sat on an improvised seat (there was not one provided for him in the FE2b) which might be his wireless set or simply an old petrol tin. There was no harness or belt, and he made himself as comfortable as possible, his feet awkwardly placed around the pole mount of his

Capt H.J. Whittingham

machine gun. Only the aerodynamically shaped nose of the nacelle, deflecting some of the slipstream up and over his head, gave him any protection from the full force of the gale.

The observer's Lewis machine gun could

be lifted and re-mounted on a selection of brackets for re-directing and was fitted with a shell bag to collect spent cartridges and to ensure that none flew back into the propeller. Usually eight to ten drums of ammunition were carried, mostly stowed in the front cockpit.

Variations on the arrangements so far described were known but not common. In March 1918 58 Squadron carried out some interesting experiments with the Vickers 1.59in breech loading gun. This fired a 2lb shell, one at a time. Lt R.A. Varley, with his pilot Capt H.J. Whittingham, used it for the first time in their FE2b B489 on a raid to Menin on the night of 13 March, and then three nights later attacked a train and a lighted house with eight shells. It received spasmodic use over the next ten days, even through the move to their next aerodrome at the height of the March Offensive, but its use then quickly lapsed, its handling proving difficult and its rate of fire slow.

100 Squadron used two or three FE2bs adapted to carry a pom-pom gun in their nacelles. Several operations with it are described in *Rovers of the Night Sky*,

---

NIGHT BOMBING OBSERVER 1917
Based on the unpublished memoirs of, then, 2Lt J.A. Stedman, 100 Squadron

As far as our work was concerned, it was a bit scary. One's vitality is rather low at night and the sight of searchlights waiting for us did not improve matters. However, we had a lucky machine which suffered many bullet holes through the wings but none through the body of the machine. Correction. One night, when we were on our way home and I was half asleep, there was a ping on my gun and something hit me in the face. I got up to remonstrate with the pilot for throwing things at me. He replied that I should not be a bloody fool; he would not think about throwing things around in a pusher machine because the things might fly back through the propeller. When we got home I found a bullet hole in the floor, a scratch on my gun and no mark on my face. I may have been the only man to have been hit in the face by a bullet without having a mark to show for it.

My cockpit was quite bare, a plywood floor and nothing else. I used a 2 gallon petrol tin to sit on; laid flat for cruising, on one edge when I wanted a better view and on end when nearing the target, to get a better view still. To communicate with the pilot, I had to stand up and turn round and shout at him, while he leaned forward as far as he could. Some might call it primitive.

As time wore on, the Germans began to dislike us and we found more and more machine guns, more and more searchlights and anti-aircraft shells bursting from a thousand feet upwards. One memorable night, our target was in the middle of a town called Courtrai (our targets were always small things, such as ammunition dumps, but sometimes these were in the centre of a town).

We approached Courtrai from the north, at about 2000 feet, and saw a column of hate over the town; the tracer from any number of machine guns, plus searchlights plus shell bursts above. My pilot called me and we had a conference. He said, 'I don't like the look of this' and I said, 'Neither do I'. After some discussion,

we decided we would have to go in, so he throttled down and turned towards the target on a glide. At that moment, all the machine gun and shell fire stopped, the searchlights waved about for a bit and then concentrated in two clusters, one to the east and one to the west of the town. We guessed that the Hun was doing what our people did; that is to say, stop the noise and listen. Apparently they had heard two machines, one to the west and one to the east of

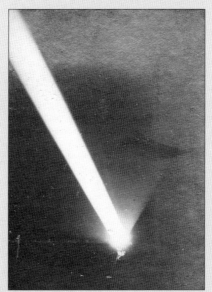

the town. The searchlights converged on them and the machine guns and anti-aircraft guns followed. We glided down through the middle, dropped our bombs and were away before anyone noticed.

Comparing notes when we got home, we found that two of our chaps had been very badly shot up over Courtrai. We felt very much like thanking them but decided not to.

Another exciting journey was when we had to bomb an aerodrome near the town of Valenciennes. This was about 35 miles over the line, about the furthest we had ever been. On arrival, we were about to make our run-in when the pilot saw what appeared to be kite balloons ahead and above us. Non-one ever likes flying under kite balloons because it would be fatal to tangle with their steel cables. He pointed them out to me and said would I like to have a shot at them. We climbed up to their level and then found out the were not balloons but anti-aircraft bursts – nice round puffs of smoke.

As we were preparing to resume our run-in on target, there was a loud bang; the engine started to make horrible noises and the whole machine was vibrating like mad. I got up to confer with the pilot, who asked if I would prefer to take a chance on landing there, with the certainty of being taken prisoner, if nothing worse, or to keep the engine running and try to get home. I think being taken prisoner was the thing, next to fire and fog, that we all disliked most and we both voted for home.

We were at about 1000 feet and 35 miles from the lines but that dear old engine, a 6 cylinder engine with one cylinder out of action, pulled us all the way back. I tried to keep my mind off the possibilities by working on my gun, which of course had jammed at the critical moment. At last we found ourselves over an aerodrome, fired off a Very light and someone kindly put some landing lights on for us, so we were home and safe. They bedded us down for the rest of the night and next day we made our way home and, of course, the machine was attended to in due course.

We considered our machine to be a lucky one. We were often shot up, but never with any serious results. On one occasion, we counted 23 shots that had hit vital parts, like flying wires, struts, spars and so on, with numerous holes through the fabric of the wings, but not one through the body of the machine.

58 Squadron Observer Lt R.A. Varley perched on B489, specially adapted to carry the Vickers 1.59in breech loading gun, as described in the text. On the nose is painted a cat and the name 'Black Eyed Queen'.

by W.J. Harvey, but as with the breech-loading gun mentioned above these adapted machines with special weapons soon departed owing to the complicated nature of their use. In June 1917 one 100 Squadron FE2b was forced down for an emergency landing when its pom-pom blew up on a raid to Cambrai!

In January and February 1918 100 Squadron also flew a handful of an exotic variation of the FE2b known as the FE2c, wherein the pilot and observer positions were reversed. Several anecdotes survive about flying this type and nearly all are surprisingly positive: a pilot in the front nacelle, which was more fully faired over, had greater room for his legs and feet, and it was reputed to handle better. Yet

The Pom-Pom gun. In the much modified nose of this 100 Squadron FE2b (named 'GABY') can be seen the muzzle of a Vickers automatic one-pounder gun. The slot permits a degree of elevation, and illuminated Hutton sights are fitted for night use.

the observer had correspondingly less room to sit and found use of the gun more restricted – how a machine gun operating immediately above one's head might have affected a pilot's concentration can only be guessed at. Despite high commendations from Commanding Officer down, the type soon disappeared from use.

It is worth noting here that FE2ds rarely if ever served with night flying units. The increased power and performance of this type was simply not an asset in this role, especially when its engine could find usefulness in a DH4 day bomber.

Many factors could affect bombing plans. Research was carried out on the effects and characteristics of different moonlight, as well as on other climatic or atmospheric variables affecting flying or navigation at night, particularly relating to finding or seeing the target. These are described in more detail later, but for example basing plans on clear visibility was erroneous – on most nights on which flying was possible the visibility was only moderate or poor.

Enemy aerodromes were particularly important, if difficult, targets. 100 Squadron spent much of its first six months in France targeting these, including Richthofen's fighter base at Douai, which the squadron attacked on its first night of operations on 5/6 April 1917. The raid obviously made an impression on the Red Baron as he described it in some detail in his autobiography *Der Rote Kampfflieger*. These targets were well defended, and there was often good warning of anything like a concentrated attack on an airfield target owing to the sophisticated liaison between the enemy air forces and its searchlight batteries. The German Air Force had no more intention than the RFC or RAF did of revealing their locations at night.

An attack was usually only possible if one chanced upon a field with its flares lit for one of its returning machines. Chances could be improved if a selection of known aerodromes in a particular area was made and a form of what came to be known in the next war as 'pathfinding' was carried out. A few wireless machines would be sent to the area first in order to relay back which aerodromes were the most lit up. Bombing machines would then take off and concentrate on these.

Another practice Kingsford described was on dark nights for the leader to carry phosphorous bombs in order to set fire to something and light the surroundings for the subsequent attackers.

Engine Problems

Whilst sturdy and structurally sound, the FE certainly came to suffer from engine unreliability. Under the demands of sustained and numerous operations the

83 Squadron preparing to leave for France in March 1918, from their base at Narborough in England. (*see also p166*).

old design was bound to be affected. Just as the night bombing units which had arrived in 1917 had been required to operate through some appallingly cold winter months, so as the weather warmed through the 1918 summer the problems of overheating increased dramatically and it became practically difficult to muster enough aeroplanes for basic operational requirements. The reduced lift in the hot evening air also meant that additional caution was needed at take-off, the heavily laden machines needing longer runs to become safely airborne. Abandoned flights or accidents attributable to engine failures or other technical mishaps rapidly increased. Virtually every anecdotal record left to us from 1918, concerning the FE2b in the night role, mentions this growing problem of reliability at some point. Lt H.N. Hampton of 58 Sqn typically recollected:

As the summer advanced the original FEs began to wear out. Engines required overhaul more frequently. The arrival of new mechanics led to less skilled maintenance. We began to have serious engine trouble in June and on the average, the squadron had three or four forced landings every week during July. I came back from one reconnaissance at the end of that month, after spending nearly two hours over the line, with three cylinders loose, three valves with no clearance and ignition incorrectly timed. During August our engines used to get so hot that we began to fly without any radiator cowling. Continuous night flying is a strain, but with unreliable engines it becomes a great strain ... we were a very compact and experienced unit, composed of pilots and observers who had learnt to do their work thoroughly with the least risk to themselves. For example, we found out that the safest height to fly was very low. Casualties became fewer, and by June our chief enemy was the Beardmore engine.

Looking at some statistics, there are 451 Casualty Returns in the National Archives at Kew dealing with night bombing FE2bs. An astonishing number of these, about a third, mention engine problems, although most of these relate to 'non-war flying'. Failed take-offs and landings are the next

most mentioned cause of problem: the FE2b being deployed in several sorties through the night no doubt exacerbated this statistic.

107 of the 451 do relate to 'enemy action'. Within these, there are 130 individuals who became casualties. The high number of 83 became prisoners and a bare 20 more were killed in action or died as a result of it. The causes of these night losses in action with the enemy are often hard to tie down – almost half don't give a reason for going missing. The vast majority of stated reasons mention AA and ground fire. Only four mention night combats. It was very difficult to see other machines in the air at night, and meetings were rare. Crews might occasionally be caught on reconnaissances, circling down around their flares, the light attracting attention. When they were, the best defence was to dive rather than fight it out. The FE2b was never renowned for its high speed or rate of climb, but it really could dive very effectively and safely. Many of those 'missing' doubtless conceal engine problems, as their machines gave out over the lines.

Total casualties to FE2b night flying units in France, therefore, amount to 20 killed in action, 83 taken prisoner, 27 wounded or injured from enemy action, 27 died from or killed in accidents, and 96 were injured in accidents.

Squadron Organisation

A night bombing squadron needed to operate its own unique regimen and timetable. Operations being heavily dependent on the weather their viability could alter at very short notice. In essence, however, they were a unit operating at night in a service essentially organised for daytime, and they needed to establish their own patterns of activity. Practice flying and testing of aircraft could be done by day, usually in the afternoons. Yet elements of the same ground crews were needed to see off and welcome crews home safely in the middle of the night. There would also be those not due to fly, who would want to have a normal night's sleep.

The ground crews, universally admired

and fêted by airmen in their memoirs for their devotion and effort, would have completed many tasks through the day. Riggers would have been checking for any bullet or shrapnel damage. Mechanics would be thoroughly overhauling engines, or filling tanks with benzine for testing, in which they were expected to participate by going aloft with the pilots. Some of the latter felt taking a fitter or rigger aloft on a test impressed on their men the importance of being careful and thorough in their work, for their own lives thus depended on it.

The Gun Room, under the control of the Armament Officer, would have been as busy as anywhere on the base. Here the all-important guns were stored, cleaned, repaired and tested. Records of jams and other problems were also kept, each gun with its own logbook. A faulty gun was worse than no gun, it was said.

The Equipment Officer would be almost as important as the Armament Officer. He was responsible for all the kit, the store, tents, huts, lorries, oil, petrol and furniture issued or loaned to a squadron. He was also known to possess certain 'arbitrary powers', which by the provision of a vehicle for a relaxing excursion to the

58 Squadron's summer 1918 aerodrome at Fauquembergues, from 2000 feet. The circular tents housed pairs of airmen, and the FE2b-shaped tents protected individual aircraft.

This is almost certainly a captured 100 Squadron FE2b, notable for displaying twin tanks, fitted to extend a machine's range. This conversion may have been more common than first thought, for at least six images are known of different 100 Squadron machines so adapted. The empty CFS 100lb carriers and undamaged appearance suggest it may have been a victim of engine failure while returning from one of the long-distance night raids.

coast, or the offer of help to assemble an evening's entertainment surely made the difference for countless young men finding themselves at war.

The vagaries of the weather made any major changes to the usual hours of meals unworkable. To move the evening meal to around midnight would have created difficulties on nights when flying was not possible. The only regular exception to this was the morning meal following a night of flying. Crews would return, and sleep through until perhaps 10.30, and then have breakfast. After testing of machines a mid-afternoon lunch would follow. If no flying was expected, then the evening meal would be at 18.00 or 19.00; but if operations were on, then dinner would be postponed, crews having it after returning from the first show, usually around 21.00 or 22.00. The key of course was flexibility.

On Operations

Descriptions of night operations on the FE2b which have come down to us describe an odd amalgam of danger and determination mixed with boredom and loneliness. As the time to depart approached, one would find a line of FE2bs across the aerodrome being bombed up and prepared. Finished all over in dull matt black, to ensure no shine should betray their forms to searchlights, and with cockades and other markings reduced to a bare minimum, they sought to slip through the night unnoticed.

Pilots and observers would be moving around, the latter carrying their machine guns to their aircraft. Bombing up would only occur just prior to departure. Engines would be started one by one, the roar increasing until it was deafening. Observers would be testing guns as crews

awaited the signal from the Commanding Officer to depart. For some units this meant the flashing of a green light from the roof of his office or else a Morse signal sent down from a senior officer, aloft to check conditions. The machines then taxied to the starting point for take-off. Lighting on the airfield varied greatly between squadrons and as the war progressed. The aim was of course to be seen as little as possible by the enemy, who, in the same way as was the aim of the Allies, might be waiting overhead at these moments to make his own attacks. A searchlight aimed down the take-off line, into wind, might be provided, with a row of paraffin flares down one side. Alternatively the facilities might be as minimal as single lights in a 'T' shape. In either circumstance there would be a red light at the far end of the field, showing the safe extent of the strip.

Take-offs were usually a minimum of five minutes apart, to allow for machines that needed to return or for other mishaps. Before squadrons became more organised, a scramble would take place upon the signal from the CO to get into first place, so a system of queuing was instituted, with each pilot allotted a letter. At his turn the pilot flashed his letter to the control pit to ask for permission to approach the flare path. The Flares Officer would flash the letter back on his Aldis lamp when he wanted the machine to come up to the strip, and the lighting would be switched on. Mechanics would finally swing it into place, facing down the flare path. A last adjustment of goggles and throttling up to full power would take the crew down the line and up into the dark. Having gained a sufficient height the pilot would make a single circuit of the airfield in case of a last

minute signal or recall, and then head east towards the night's objective.

Once aloft, flight organisation ceased, the success of the operation now resting solely in the determination and skill of the crew, acting independently until once again over the aerodrome. After having set off for these flights it became rather a race to reach the target first. The reason was that the first crews had the advantage of surprise and could often approach the destination fairly stealthily, by throttling down and gliding in on the target. Those that followed, or came on subsequent raids during the night, usually met ready and well prepared defences. It seems strange that there was not more attention paid to surprise. In general, it was a matter of routine to dispatch all machines as soon as it was dark, and the result was that the enemy was therefore often ready for them. On nights where weather meant a delayed start, maybe at 02.00 or 03.00, crews were often able to reach and bomb objectives unmolested.

The practice of grouping the departure of night machines on raids, which did not always result in the most effective outcome over the target, may have been a hangover from the received wisdom of day bombing operations which held that a concentrated attack delivered by several machines was the most effective practice – in terms of accuracy and impact. Night bombing attacks, in contrast, could aim for such a concerted attack but could never ensure it simply because crews were necessarily independent of one another. The effect of night bombing on morale was different as well: if attacks were delivered unpredictably through the night their impact was so much more telling.

Navigation at Night

Navigation at night was far from easy. Much time would have been spent before the raid in the Map Room – the centre of business life of a squadron – where not only orders for the night were received and assimilated, but also a compass course was carefully studied and worked out with bearings for the outwards and return trip. W.J. Harvey, in *Rovers of the Night Sky*, described its walls *'bristling with facts'*, be these photographs of aerodromes and towns, trench systems or battery positions.

Taking this navigational information into the air, however, only then saw the challenges really begin. The FE2b had about a dozen luminous instruments to fly by, but none dealt with drift. In poor conditions the pilot would be grimly watching his air speed through the pitot tube and keeping a close eye on his compass. To maintain the machine on an even keel was his entire aim, especially in bad weather or nil visibility: corrections had the bad habit of resulting in not knowing where one was flying, inverted even. If the speed increased dramatically it was the only way of knowing one had probably begun to dive. The night flying machines were set up to be stable, generally rigged to climb slightly with hands off and to fly level with throttle half closed. In a black and sightless dive at night the procedure therefore was to centralize your controls, hands off stick, rudder dead straight, and let the machine get herself out. One could do little more with any margin of safety. The pilot would also be watching the oil pressure valve to ensure the engine was not over-revving – a common problem with the Beardmore engine – and found

to be often mitigated by tipping the blades with brass to correct the weight. A purring 1200rpm was the aim.

A safe height to cross the lines would be between 3-4000 feet. The observer would navigate his pilot to the target by compass and map reading. He would have many navigational aids on the ground – not only on his own side of the lines but also in German territory as well, and he would utilize all of them. These included repeating beacons each with its own particular signal, navigational search-lights and, on the German side in addition, 'flaming onions' or aerial navigational lights: glowing phosphorous balls chained together and launched from the ground. The latter had the additional benefit of penetrating cloud canopy so that on bad nights they were a vital help to crews. All of these were at established locations, which the crews knew well.

In fact the lighthouses were absolutely pivotal to night operations – whether offering aids to navigation or to ensure night fliers took routes which avoided their own side's defensive screens of searchlights and anti-aircraft batteries. Exact bearings from particular lights back to their own aerodrome would all be known. Locations and identifying codes were regularly changed to maintain secrecy. It was the job of the officer in charge of the Squadron Map Room, usually a senior observer, to ensure all the latest meteorological reports and intelligence relating to these aids was available. Information might include other temporary landmarks, such as a big fire.

Lastly, at all times the observer would be looking for clues in the landscape. Whether for navigational reasons or for the purposes

Signalling lighthouses were essential tools for all airmen operating at night. Set to pulse a particular Morse number or letter, they could be readily identified from the air and were used for navigation.

of reconnaissance, crews needed to be skilled at interpreting these: the shadows and shapes on moonlit roads, the positions of rivers and lakes which were both very apparent at night, woods of a particular shape or else railway lines, which were easy to see on moonlit nights.

In the summer of 1918 there was a trial in France of a special night flying map. Only prominent objects like woods, rivers, main roads and railways were shown, along with just the larger towns. Information about details not usually seen from the air at night was omitted. This might have seemed like a good idea, to simplify map reading, but it proved a

This curiously relaxed scene, evidently well inside German territory, shows another captured FE2b, fitted with twin tanks and navigation lights. It is known from photos that in the summer 1918, which this appears to be, there were still 100 Squadron FE2bs operating with twin tanks, although the more distant operations were rarely undertaken by then.

failure. It was based on what could be seen on a bright moonlit night with good visibility, whereas such conditions were the exception. On most nights, navigation consisted of picking one's way along from point to point with no more than moderate visibility, often interpreting only brief glimpses of ground. The more information and detail one had on a map the better – especially on really bad nights.

Flying to the target would almost certainly take them on routes over towns defended by searchlights and anti-aircraft firing up shells and 'flaming onions', as well as general ground fire. Usually only a single light would search, and then having found a machine all the others in the area would uncover. Advanced searchlights near the lines would pick up an aircraft and then hand it on to the next, always extinguishing before coming in range of the aeroplane's own guns or bombs, whilst the crew themselves would be doing all they could to escape the beams.

Once caught in searchlights violent maneuvering was about the only option, side-slipping and 'split-arsing' down out of the beams, the observer firing into the light as best he could. A couple of dives followed by a simple climbing turn was often enough for a moderately experienced pilot to elude them. There were also methods to confuse the enemy below about one's altitude and position by combining various manoeuvres to change position quickly, whilst simultaneously altering engine speed and sound to further mislead them about what the machine was doing. More than once, Kingsford employed the ruse of firing parachute flares, in order to draw off the attentions of searchlights onto the brightly descending flare.

The chances of reaching the target were dependent on many factors, the skill and experience of the crew being paramount, because success or failure was almost totally in their own hands. The weather was a big factor in deciding whether less experienced crews would make it through to the objective; on the other hand, engine problems on the FE2b could hit young and old hands alike.

Once over the target, the observer began bomb aiming. Bomb sights were relatively primitive, but effective enough at the low speeds and altitudes being flown. Much guesswork came into it as well. It was commonly accepted that the key to effective bomb dropping at night was to come in low. The same applied to night reconnaissance, where the ground features became notably clearer below 1000ft. Ground mist usually necessitated this in any event. Whilst the chances of accurate bombing improved the lower one came, one was also more exposed to fire. Observers, with no control over these affairs, no doubt suffered at these times.

Some bombing took place from as low as 200 feet, but the best results were usually achieved from around 700 to 1000 feet. The better the defences around the objective, the higher the initial approach would be, so as to have a longer glide with the engine silent. At the chosen moment, away would go the first bombs and then around and away, the observer loosing off his Lewis at the target or searchlights, the pilot banking and side-slipping to escape the lights and dodge the AA fire. Another turn over the target, and more bombs away, and then to head west at speed, into the safety of the darkness. A further tactic was to fly down even lower before opening up again, making one's escape from as low as fifty feet. This made it much harder to be picked up by searchlights and enemy fire and made use of diving

to reach higher speeds to get beyond the danger area before restarting the engine, which naturally exposed one's position.

Both men would be trying to assess the night's work before leaving the target, the observer making notes of what could be seen. From now on, all efforts would be bent on nursing engine and machine back to the aerodrome, usually on a simple reverse heading, unless adjustments were called for to miss the night's trouble spots. It was always a matter of honour to re-cross the lines having fired off all ammunition, although some crews held one drum in reserve in case they met an enemy aircraft. This was not common, as we have seen.

One of the most difficult parts of an operation remained to be accomplished: to land safely down the flare path at one's airfield. Relatively elaborate landing procedures had been developed to minimize the risk of being bombed, involving severe restrictions on lighting and landing aids. It can never have been an easy task.

Dummy Aerodromes

By late in the war pilots would often have just a dim T-shape of Aldis lamps to guide them in, with a searchlight only being used on very dark nights. Anything more elaborate really required the use of a dummy aerodrome. The purpose of these was not only to provide a decoy, as the name might suggest. They were also a vital tool for crews by which they returned safely to their airfields. By early 1918 danger of attack to returning night flying crews began to be a serious problem. At this time, the recognized L-shaped flare path was still used on aerodromes and machines all flew with navigation lights on west of the line so as to avoid being shot by their own AA. On the other hand, on clear nights it enabled the enemy to see aeroplanes approaching the Lines or for enemy machines to follow one back to an aerodrome.

In late March it became apparent that this was happening and major changes in night flying organization were instituted. Navigation lights were eventually abandoned, although this meant now attracting friendly AA. Aerodromes were still lit, however, and being visible for upwards of twenty miles they provided easy targets for German bombers. Airfields had to be more hidden, and so dummy airfields were used.

Returning from an operation, reverse headings were not taken to bring crews back to their main field, which was now kept in maximum darkness, but instead to their dummy aerodrome. It was then through signals passed between the personnel

A5662 of 102 Squadron well protected from the elements. The twin tanks are just visible. This aircraft was damaged in raids on enemy aerodromes on 27 October 1917 when it was hit by ground fire, and the pilot Capt I.A.J. Duff was wounded.

and the crews above that clearance came to head on to the main landing strip. In this way, not only did the dummy strip withstand the brunt of the enemy bombing, but it enabled the machines to proceed back to base and land only when it was completely safe to do so.

The dummy aerodrome was positioned and constructed to look as much like the real landing strip as possible. Its surface did not matter, but its position was very important. It had a proper L-shaped flare path, correctly placed and aligned for the wind. Within reason, and to an extent which would not create suspicion, as much light as possible was in evidence. Along one side of the dummy site, low wooden frames were built with wire stretched across them about two feet off the ground. By covering these with old Bessoneau canvas they simulated aircraft hangars. Hurricane lamps were placed beneath. The officer in charge would also fire off various coloured rockets and Very lights through the night. In this way, the light and activity not only sought to deceive enemy night bombers but enabled returning pilots to locate it.

As a pilot recrossed the lines on his return journey and picked up the lighthouse nearest his dummy aerodrome, he would set off on his established compass course towards it, gradually losing height and finally approaching it at about 500 feet. The observer would signal down his code letter, using the identification light under the nacelle of his FE2b. As many as eight aircraft might be circling here, following each others' tail lights, awaiting permission to land at the real aerodrome beyond.

If no hostile aircraft were in the vicinity, the control officer at the dummy aerodrome would signal back permission by repeating the code letter with a white light. If enemy were about a warning red light was used. In this event the pilot either

An FE2b of 58 Sqn sets out at dusk.

waited longer for circumstances to ease, or if urgently needing to land, set off for his airfield knowing he could expect little or no landing aids to help him down. If a steady red beam was directed back at the returning pilot it meant permission to land was definitely refused.

With permission gained he would fly directly home with all lights switched off to ensure he approached it in darkness. He would circle at 100 feet to locate any landing aids, shut off and glide in over the strip and touch down. The crew usually landed with only red danger lights to mark obstacles and probably a T of two red lights at the near end of the strip with a third at the far end. As soon as the machine pulled up, it was turned towards the hangars and guided in by green torch light.

Regarding dummy aerodromes there were many precautions taken to fool German reconnaissance. Though the dummy aerodrome sounds complicated, it was actually erected and dismantled every night and every morning, taking six men about fifteen minutes to do so, withdrawing the lights and stowing canvas away in dug

outs. It was essential to keep the location a secret, and that is why all signs were always removed a good half hour before dawn. There would often be bomb craters across it, however, after a night's activities, and these were harder to hide from the enemy photographic reconnaissances of the morning.

A solution was found through the School of Camouflage at Boulogne. Coloured chalk impressions of the colour of the main and dummy aerodromes were made from the air and large painted canvas sheets of camouflage including ground patterns and plain ground colours were prepared. Hundreds of dummy bomb craters were also painted.

Just before dawn, a team would be sent out and any holes which could not be filled in quickly were overlaid with plain painted canvas strung on wires. From the air, no bomb holes remained visible and it looked again like an ordinary cultivated piece of land. Meanwhile, at the main aerodrome, another team would be busy placing dummy craters at various points around the sheds and flare path, taking care to orient their shaded sections properly for the morning sun. Mock-ups of damaged aircraft were also utilized. This work took about half an hour, and in this way when German reconnaissance came over the secret was apparently comprehensively kept. No evidence suggests that the Germans discovered these methods, though in all likelihood they probably operated similar arrangements.

What is certain is that dummy aerodromes were sufficiently realistic to cause aircraft from both sides to land on them in error at various times and to be bombed in anger. Throughout the Summer and Autumn of 1918 they became a useful and integral part of the organization of night flying squadrons in France.

100 Squadron lost 7714 'Zanzibar VII' on a night bombing raid to Douai aerodrome on 6 April 1917, when it was forced down intact by Ltn W. Frankl from Jasta 4. 2Lt A.R.M. Richards/ AM2 E.W. Barnes became PoWs. 7714 is seen here having been carefully dismantled for removal by rail.

In my 'kip' at 11.30am: time for correspondence.
Sgt Eric Jones of 58 Squadron relaxing. His fleece-lined flying coat lies on his bunk, with boots, goggles and helmet all to hand.

Billets

To return once more to the strange life and routine by which the night flyer often conducted his war, there were also some unusual billeting arrangements for these airmen. A more surprising one, in the case of 58 Squadron, was being billeted in cottages in the neighbouring village. A crew might take over a ground floor front room, for instance. The Madame of the house would keep the place clean and make their beds and even provide them with their breakfast – bed and breakfast – the other meals being taken in the Mess. There was little else to attract them to their abode except to sleep, which the nature of their operations made very unpredictable.

The mess at the flying field might consist of a snug hutment, equipped with deck chairs and card tables. A gramophone and a large pile of records stood in the corner, and in the middle was a wood burning stove. Meals were often taken in an annex to this main hut and in general it appears there was no shortage of good food and drink. In summer many squadrons operated from canvas bell tents and hangars. It was often blisteringly hot in the afternoons, and in their free time the men would sit in deck chairs in the shade and consume mineral drinks. Others might walk to a local river and swim. Having the day relatively free even enabled visits to the coast. Action and the demands of war would come as evening fell, but in common with all air crews in war the hours spent not flying were a precious time to unwind.

Developing the Science of Night Bombing

At higher levels within Headquarters RAF there was a good deal of investigation and reflection on what could be learnt from the unfolding air war, not least of all considering night bombing.

For some months IXth (HQ) Brigade, within which 54th Wing operated, had been working under the orders of the French. When the Brigade returned from the French Area on 21 June, policy regarding the bombing of the enemy's rail network was re-assessed and some new directives initiated. These looked at both day and night bombing, and had the effect of introducing a more strategic element, as well as providing an opportunity to broadly review and articulate what methods and practices were most useful and productive.

The aim was to find the most effective means of disruption of the enemy rail network. The most telling targets, such as bridges, viaducts, water tanks etc. were in their turn small and difficult to hit. Destruction of track at railway stations was important but the enemy usually had a number of lines it could use and as repair gangs were quickly mobilized, disruption was not comprehensive. However, a straight stretch of line between stations was an easier target. If it was an important line and could be damaged, for instance in a cutting, dislocation was certain.

As regards night bombing, the enemy's particular use of his rail network just before sundown and just after dawn meant that the usual daylight attacks needed to be continued and maintained at intervals through darkness. Whilst continuous bombing was not generally practical it should still be regular and sustained, and to be most effective should be on carefully selected targets of greatest importance: few in number but comprehensively attacked. So long as conditions would permit, this would preferably mean maintaining attacks for a continuous period of at least six to seven nights. With these ground rules established, work then centred on where these concentrations should be, and eventually enabled the general classifying of targets in terms of their size and type.

So many other factors could, however, impinge on any bombing plans, and these too had to be quantified, explained, and ordered where possible. In the case of night flying, this was done by bringing together received opinion about its every aspect, through an on-going series of conferences and discussions, which started that month. These included detailed examinations of the effects and characteristics of different moonlight, as well as other climatic or atmospheric variables known to affect one's ability to fly or navigate at night, and in particular, relating to how one found or saw the target. This led to establishing optimal heights for attacking particular objectives, and for perhaps the first time established the importance of choosing targets of a kind and size that were visible and locatable in night conditions. Until this time, most targets were set on the basis of clear visibility, when in fact on most nights when flying was possible, visibility was only moderate or poor. The choice of target also involved assessing how well it was defended, and if the weapon of surprise could be useful, or the timing of raids increase their impact. The final determining characteristic of a target was the effort required to get to it, namely how far away it was and if it was difficult to find.

Thus this valuable research gradually gathered knowledge that without doubt

There is no better proof of the topsy-turvy world of the night bombing airman than this 'Pyjama Parade' in June 1918. Here a comradely group of flyers stands blinking in the late morning light, recently awoken from their slumbers, no doubt, as that *other* war surges on around them. These 58 Squadron pilots are 2Lt C.M. MacBlain, 2Lt K.Y. Gliddon, Capt W.A. 'Bill' Leslie, Sgt E.E. Jones, Capt C.C. 'King' Cole, 'Tich', 2Lt R.K. Fletcher, Lt A.H. Padley, and Lt S.G.E. Inman-Knox.

A5478 'Gold Coast No 10' of 100 Sqn, fully loaded with eight 25lb Cooper bombs underwing plus a 230lb heavy bomb.

led to greater operational success and survival of crews. Targets came to be better chosen and the men in the machines could fly more effectively. Mistakes were still made: crews still felt they were often sent to ill-conceived and dangerous targets, given the brightness of the moon for instance; or else asked to find difficult objectives on dark or stormy nights, when the only option was to come down low to vulnerable and exposed heights. Another complaint was that Headquarters was too slow in introducing the policy of giving crews alternative targets, which in certain conditions would have led to more effective operations overall. However, there is no doubt there was an effort made from mid 1918 onwards to understand and improve the methods of both day and night bombing.

Such lessons took most of 1918 to learn, but the very great power of bombing was no longer in doubt by the last months of the war. Trenchard wrote an illuminating dispatch on 1 January 1919 summarizing what he and the Independent Force had learned, and what would have developed that year. This is cited in *The Annals of 100 Squadron*, assembled by Maj C.G. Burge, and in it Trenchard described the relationship between day and night bombers – how each would be significantly less effective without the other. There were always numerically about twice as many day bombing aircraft as their night counterparts on the Western Front.

Though the day bombers suffered higher casualties, without their efforts the night bombers' role would be quite marginal, for the enemy could simply make his preparations by day and then retreat to safety at night. If the majority of bombing had been done at night, then the enemy would not have been forced to concentrate his men and material into defensive measures. Night bombing might also be 'safer,' but the potential for mistakes and misapprehensions were greater – meaning there were difficulties in not only locating the target but also practical problems in assessing the real damage caused. Trenchard had also realized that to successfully attack Germany itself it was essential to attack their aerodromes heavily, precisely to prevent them attacking Allied airfields, as well as to destroy their own attacking potential. In 1919 *... at least half of my force would be attacking the enemy's aerodromes, whilst the other half carried out attacks on long-distance targets in Germany.*

Special Night Reconnaissance

Mention has been made of that other nocturnal activity: the night reconnaissance. It is easy to overlook this, but it remains a fact that this work was ever-present within the FE2b night bombing squadrons. From the middle of June 1918, special reconnaissances took on a very great importance, and the scope and extent of areas required to be observed increased significantly. Night reconnaissances were thought to be a very special and vital class of work, to be carried out virtually 'at all costs'. They were commonly very dangerous and demanding. Crews could find them either over-long and monotonous, as they usually lasted three to four hours, or else very perilous because of the conditions under which they had to be flown.

For a while, in some night bombing units such as 58 Squadron, bombing practically took on a secondary role. Numbers of machines so employed increased to six and later eight, and these operations were expected to be carried out on any night on which flying was at all possible, two or three crews being out at the same time.

When reconnaissance operations had been re-commenced in May, they had largely concentrated on the area of Arras, Cambrai and Bapaume, some 40 miles to the south-east. However in June, attention was switched to the Lille-Tournai and the Valenciennes-Douai areas, which were very long flights for the FE2b, especially if winds were westerly. Once or twice reconnaissances were sent as far as Le Cateau and Wassigny, well beyond Cambrai, which meant flights of over 180 miles, on the very limits of what was possible. For instance, on the night of 31 May, Lts Jeffrey and Booth, in FE2b A5636, set off at 21.55 to carry out a surveillance of the railway lines from Arras-Douai-Somain-Anzin-LeQuesnoy-Solesmes-LeCateau-Wassigny-Busigny-Cambrai-Denain, and then back to their summer airfield at Fauquembergues. Later the same night Capt Whittingham and Lt Varley flew A5647 some 150 miles to reconnoitre the railway from La Bassée-Lille-Orchies-St.Amand-Anzin-Somain-Douai-Arras. These distances were not uncommon.

To complement their reconnaissance role at this time squadrons' FE2bs were fitted with small wireless sets, by which information could be sent back in Morse. After crossing the lines a considerable length of copper wire would be unwound, trailing below and behind the machine, and a wireless operator back at the airfield would take any messages sent. Observers were responsible for the sets and were encouraged to transmit as often as they liked, apparently in an effort to confuse the enemy in some way. The messages would then be passed to the Squadron Intelligence Officer, who in turn would forward them to Wing Headquarters. Crews used Michelin flares to help in reconnaissance as well as to light the target and to assess any damage caused.

B1877 'St Andrews No 1' with 100 Squadron in July 1918, visibly well equipped with bomb/flare release levers for both pilot and observer. With C9802, on the right, it was eventually transferred to the USAS in September 1918.

Dropped from about 4000 feet, from here on a good night the ground was visible. By gliding down and keeping above and to one side the maximum amount of detail could be seen.

An additional feature of reconnaissances late in the war was that they always carried a sizeable bomb load, to drop on searchlights, ammunition dumps, or railway lines as they went. They were encouraged to shoot up these targets wherever possible. Reconnaissances were not a success at first, inexperience leading to problems, but once made reliable they became most valuable.

The reconnaissance would be more affected by moonlight and atmospheric conditions than bombing. Beyond the level of experience of the airmen involved, which was again of prime importance, three main factors contributed to effectiveness. Self evidently, the more moonlight there was, the greater the likely usefulness of a night reconnaissance. Then the visibility of particular features on the ground played a part: a wider, straighter road or length of rail track made for easier observation.

If enemy forces were using side roads or moving through woods or changing terrain then what could be made out was greatly reduced. The final factor was the altitude at which the work was able to be done.

These three factors were all connected. For example, if the light from the moon was dim then unless the observer was particularly experienced the only options were to come lower or to use flares. Even then, something like the shadow of trees on a road could look much like troops on the move. On a bright moonlight night most movement on main roads could be detected from about 3000 feet, and the type of movement made out from between 2000 to 1500 feet. Rail movements were also easy to discern from these altitudes, by the smoke from the stacks and the glow of the fire box.

A half moon night made a great difference. Even at 1500 feet the outline of objects on the ground became vague and observations were unlikely to be really valuable unless machines descended to 1000 feet. Parachute flares were particularly useful on these nights. Yet

from many points of view a half moon night brought considerable advantages to the observer: it left sufficient darkness for their own concealment, permitting the crew to operate at lower levels than on brighter nights, with a larger factor of safety from attack. In addition, on a half moon night the enemy was also found to be generally more careless about his own concealment, leading to more sightings. Moderate visibility, such as encountered on half moon nights, however, was also found to yield only moderately accurate reports. The use of flares was less likely in these conditions and information gathering was indeed challenging, crews relying more on their eyes. It is worth recalling, however, that the enemy did not make the task of reconnaissance easy for the FE2b crews. The German forces made huge efforts to conceal their activities. They used minor roads, there were no lights used at night in any of their areas going back at least fifteen miles behind the trenches, and German transport remained entirely unlit on nights it was likely the British would be out observing. There was conjecture that the 'flaming onion' battery signals were in fact warnings to troops near the lines to conceal their movement, just as much as they were navigational aids for the flyers.

At natural light levels less than this, namely at quarter moon or starlit nights, it was essential to employ flares on any reconnaissance. Paradoxically, a quarter moon night was probably the best for bombing, for crews could descend when near to their targets and approach at relatively low altitudes from where they could bomb more accurately, whilst they themselves remained much more concealed from the enemy defences. On really dark nights the fundamental problem became the actual navigation to the target owing to the lack of visible ground features. Major

A6562 of 102 Sqn, in night bombing paint scheme, with navigation lights and underwing flares.

roads or large woods of which the crew might have a knowledge were very useful, but the network of navigational lights on the ground, described elsewhere, were the most invaluable aids to steering a course, be it to the target, or for getting home. Poor weather, even such as clouds, made both bombing and reconnaissance on darker nights almost impossible, for even with the use of flares the task of finding the target itself was extremely challenging.

Reconnaissance came to be generally disliked by crews, chiefly owing to its monotony. On occasions crews could also be sent up when conditions were dangerous. The most unpopular piece of work was always the last sortie of the night because this meant staying up and starting one's job when everyone else had finished and gone to bed. It also meant as often as not returning in daylight, when an FE2b would be an easy target for any enemy fighter.

Possibly one of the more unusual experiments which one finds mentioned in reports in the last weeks of the war were the attempts to take night photographs with the aid of flares. There is very little of substance in the records about this, but experiments were carried out, and they were doubtless in connection with this reconnaissance work.

'I' Flight

Also of a more unusual nature were the espionage operations carried out in particular by 'I' Flight, a Special Duty Flight involved in intelligence gathering. 'I' Flight operated with various night flying units through 1918, but for most of the summer made their secretive, dangerous flights from within 58 Squadron at Fauquembergues. The work consisted of special missions often up to 50 miles over the lines, far into eastern France, to drop messenger pigeons to contacts there or even to land in order to drop or pick up agents. These operations not only called for tremendous nerve from a special sort

A5564 of 100 Squadron. One of the very few FE2bs to serve with RNAS night bombing units, this machine joined 100 Squadron from 16 (Naval) Squadron on 5 March 1918, and served until it hit a rut on take-off for a night bombing raid and crashed on 31 May 1918.

of pilot, but for pin-point accuracy in navigation as well, the crew having to find a particular wood or building in remote, hostile, and completely unknown territory. The fate of a crew if caught many miles behind the lines, in a machine clearly adapted for special operations was rarely in question, for spies were believed to be commonly shot. Cockpits were equipped with an assortment of strange gadgets, pistols, pigeon holders and elaborate transmitting equipment. It would be all too obvious what they were doing there.

Conclusion

The FE2b night bombers played a unique part in the first air conflict. Their nocturnal role meant all those who flew and looked after them in France confronted a unique set of challenges, which is why emphasis has been laid on the service experience of flying the FE2b rather than a purely operational appraisal. And now, for the first time in 90 years, it is possible to stand beside a night flying FE2b, constructed and recently installed at the Royal Air

Force Museum at Hendon, in London.

The FE2b as a wider aircraft type has a meritorious place in the history of the Royal Flying Corps and the early Royal Air Force because it served in such substantial numbers through a period of events of the highest order. It was one of the first aircraft designed to have a fighter capability. It helped grasp air superiority throughout the Somme in 1916, and then fought on through the attrition and suffering of Bloody April 1917. By this time, however, it was already being comprehensively redeployed in its new role as a night bomber – a role it generally performed admirably for eighteen months until the end of the war. The FE2b was a successful night bomber.

The arrival of the FE2b in operational night-black matt finish as a new display at the Royal Air Force Museum is therefore very fitting. It recalls and remembers those young men who went to work as the moon rose. As the motto of the Royal Air Force has it: *Per Ardua ad Astra*: Through Adversity to the Stars.

FE2b D9967 of 101 Squadron, post-Armistice, before 2Lts K.L. Graham/ J.H. Pringle were injured when they side-slipped it into a hangar on 18 February 1919.

References relating to night bombing with the RAF FE2b

GENERAL

AIR1/15/312/196 — Notes on Night Reconnaissances and Bombing, July 1918.

AIR1/27/15/1/131 — Instructional Notes for Night Flying Observers. Complied by Lt A.H. Clegg, RAF

AIR1/512/16/3/68 — Formation of Night Flying Squadrons RFC for Duty with BE Force. Squadron Nos. 100, 101, 102, 148 and 149.

AIR1/725/97/5 — Army Squadron Night Bombing – Ground Arrangements, Flares etc

AIR1/1916/204/230/10 — Night Flying in France During the Last Year of the War. A lecture delivered by WgCdr R.G.D. Small to officers of the Fighting Area.

38 SQUADRON

AIR1/173/15/165/1 — History of 38 Squadron 1916 – 1919

AIR1/691/21/20/38 — History of 38 Squadron – Air Historical Branch

AIR1/1919/204/236/1 — Operation Orders 65th Wing (38 Sqn) Oct – Nov 18

AIR1/1919/204/236/2 — 38 Squadron Record Book, June 18 – Jan 19

AIR1/1919/204/236/3 — 38 Squadron Bomb Dropping Reports, June – Oct 18

AIR1/1920/204/236/5 — 38 Sqn Fortnightly Casualty Returns, Oct 18 – Jan 19

AIR1/1920/204/236/6 — 38 Sqn Personnel Flying Times, June 18 – Jan 19

AIR1/1920/204/236/8 — 38 Squadron Reconnaissance and Bomb Raid Reports, Nov 1918

AIR1/1920/204/236/12 — 38 Squadron Field Returns, Jun 18 – Feb 19

AIR1/1920/204/236/15 — 38 Squadron Daily States, Oct 18 – Jan 19

Cole, C and Cheesman, EF. *The Air Defence of Britain 1914-1918*. London: Putnam, 1984.

Walford, L.O.T., *No.38 Squadron 1916 – 1963*. Malta, 1964.

58 SQUADRON

AIR1/11/15/1/9 — 54 Wing Return of Bombs Dropped March 22-31st 1918; 58 and 83 Squadrons – Return of Small Arms Ammunition Fired.

AIR1/173/15/178/1 — Brief History of 58 Squadron. Maj D. Gilley DFC

AIR1/174/15/178/2 — 58 Squadron Record Book

AIR1/720/42/7/1 — Night Flying. Lt G.R. Thornley

AIR1/955/204/5/1032 — Bomb Dropping Reports: May – June 1918, 58 Squadron and others.

AIR1/1166/204/5/2578 — Move of 58 Squadron to Egypt, Dec 18 – May 19.

AIR1/1225/204/5/2634 — Combat Reports: 58 Squadron, Aug – Sept 1918

AIR1/1914/204/230/4 — Combat Reports: 58 and 151 Squadrons, Sept-Oct 1918.

AIR1/2390/228/11/132 — Staff College Reports: War Recollections of 2Lt A.P. Ledger

AIR1/2392/228/11/184 — Staff College Reports: Service Experiences of 2Lt H.N. Hampton

IWM 80/26/1 — War Recollections of 2Lt D.R. Goudie

Bowyer, C. *Handley Page Bombers of The First World War.* Bourne End, Bucks: Aston Publications, 1992.

Henshaw, T. 'The War At Night – Bombing with the RAF FE2b in 1918'. *Cross and Cockade International*, Vol. 30, No. 4, 1999.

Robertson, F.A.deV., Colson, C.N., Cook, W.A. *Squadrons of the Royal Air Force and Other Units.* London: Flight Publishing Co. Ltd, 1935.

83 SQUADRON

AIR1/11, 176, 694, 956, 1770-71*

AIR1/11/15/1/9 — 54 Wing Return of Bombs Dropped March 22-31st 1918; 58 and 83 Squadrons – Return of Small Arms Ammunition Fired.

AIR1/176/15/190/1 — History of 83 Squadron, 1917 – 1918

AIR1/694/21/20/83 — History of 83 Squadron, 1917 – 1931, Air Historical Branch

AIR1/956/204/5/1032 — Bomb Dropping Reports: May – June 1918, 83 Squadron and others

AIR1/1770/204/145/1 — 83 Squadron, Emergency measures in event of invasion, May – Dec 1917

AIR1/1770/204/145/3 — 83 Squadron, Instructions for Flying Overseas, 1917

AIR1/1770/204/145/4 — 83 Squadron, Mobilisation Instructions, Sept – Nov 17

AIR1/1770/204/145/9 — 83 Squadron, Officers Recommendations, Feb 17 – Jan 18

AIR1/1770/204/145/11 — 83 Squadron, Reconnaissance and Bomb Raid Reports, Mar – Nov 1918

AIR1/1771/204/145/12 — 83 Squadron, Flying Times Book, Mar – Nov 1918

AIR1/1771/204/145/13 — 83 Squadron, Flying Times Book, Oct 18 – Jan 19

AIR1/1771/204/145/14 — 83 Squadron, Record Book, Mar 18 – Jan 19

AIR1/1771/204/145/15 — 83 Squadron, Programme of Development, Mar 17 – Jan 18.

AIR1/2389/228/11/103 — Staff College Reports: Service Experiences of Lt AO Lewis Roberts DFC.

Low, R.G. & Harper, F.E. *83 Squadron RAF 1917-1969.* Compaid Graphics, 1997.

100 SQUADRON

AIR1/176/15/199/1 — History of 100 Squadron, 1917 - 1918

AIR1/512/16/3/68 — Formation of Night Flying Squadrons RFC for Duty with BE Force. Squadron Nos. 100, 101, 102, 148 and 149.

AIR1/694/21/20/100 — History of 100 Squadron, 1917 – 1930, Air Historical Branch

AIR1/863/204/5/490 — Resumés of Operations of 100 Squadron, Apr – Sept 17

AIR1/1731/204/129/1 — 100 Squadron Record Book, Aug 1917.

AIR1/1734/204/134/1 — 83rd Wing RAF: History Data, also 97, 100, 115, 215 and 216 Squadrons, July – Dec 1918

Bowyer, C. *Handley Page Bombers of The First World War.* Bourne End, Bucks.: Aston Publications, 1992

Burge, C.G. *The Annals of 100 Squadron.* London: Bivouac Books, Reprint 1975.

Kingsford, A.R. *Night Raiders of the Air.* London: The Aviation Book Club, 1939.

Morris, A. *First of Many. The Story of Independent Force, RAF.* London: Jarrolds Publishers, 1968.

Rennles, K. *Independent Force: The War Diary of the Daylight Bomber Squadrons of the Independent Air Force, 6 June to 11 November 1918.* London: Grub Street, 2003.

Skelton, M.L. 'The Long Plod Home: Lt Roy Shillinglaw recalls 100 Squadron'. *Cross & Cockade International*, Vol. 10, No. 3, 1979.

Skelton, M.L. 'Lt J.H.L. Gower of 100 Squadron RAF: His Shows'. *Cross & Cockade International*, Vol. 14, No. 1, 1983

101 SQUADRON

AIR1/176/15/200/1 — History of 101 Squadron, 1917 - 1919

AIR1/512/16/3/68 — Formation of Night Flying Squadrons RFC for Duty with BE Force. Squadron Nos. 100, 101, 102, 148 and 149.

AIR1/694/21/20/101 — History of 101 Squadron, 1917 – 1938, Air Historical Branch

AIR1/886/204/5/642 — Bombing Reports and Operation Orders 101 Squadron, Sep – Dec 1917

AIR1/956/204/5/1032 — Bomb Dropping Reports, May – June 1918, 101 Squadron and others.

AIR1/1732/204/130/4 — 101 Squadron Record Book, Aug 17 – Feb 18.

AIR1/1732/204/130/5 — 101 Squadron Orders and Instructions on Various Subjects, Apr 16 – July 18.

AIR1/1732/204/130/6 — 101 Squadron Operation Reports, Sept 17 – Apr 18.

AIR1/1733/204/130/7 — 101 Squadron Operation Orders and Reports, May – Nov 1918.

AIR1/1733/204/130/8 — 101 Squadron History Data, Jul 17 – Jan 19.

AIR1/1733/204/130/9 — 101 Squadron Operation Orders, Nov 17 – June 18.

AIR1/1733/204/130/10 — 101 Squadron Operation Orders, June - Oct 1918.

AIR1/1733/204/130/11 — 101 Squadron Operation Orders, Oct – Nov 1918.

AIR1/1733/204/130/12 — 101 Squadron Officers Record of Flying, 1917 – 1918.

AIR1/1733/204/130/13 — 101 Squadron Officers Record of Flying, 1918.

AIR1/1733/204/130/14 — 101 Squadron, Code Names Allotted to RAF Units, Nov 1918.

AIR1/1733/204/130/15 — 101 Squadron, Establishment: Reductions in 5 and 9 Brigades, Feb 1919.

AIR1/2387/228/11/53 — Staff College Reports: Service Experiences of Lt L.G.S. Payne.

Montgomery, D.H. *Down The Flare Path.* London: John Hamilton, 1937.

Whetton, D. 'From Dusk till Dawn. Recollections of Claude Wallis, late Lt Observer 101 Squadron RFC'. *Cross & Cockade International*, Vol. 7, No. 2, 1976.

102 SQUADRON

AIR1/176/15/201/1 — History of 102 Squadron, with Extracts from Squadron Record Books, Operations Reports, etc., 1917 – 1918

AIR1/512/16/3/68 — Formation of Night Flying Squadrons RFC for Duty with BE Force. Squadron Nos. 100, 101, 102, 148 and 149.

AIR1/694/21/20/102 — History of 102 Squadron, 1917 – 1938, Air Historical Branch

AIR1/956/204/5/1032 — Bomb Dropping Reports: May – June 1918, 102 Squadron and others.

AIR1/1942/204/247/1 — 102 Squadron, Recommendations for Honours and Awards, Jan – Dec 1918

AIR1/1942/204/247/2 — 102 Squadron, Orders for Moves and Nominal Rolls of NCOs and Men, Sept – Oct 1917

AIR1/1942/204/247/3 — 102 Squadron, Notes on Night Fighting in France, Aug 1917

AIR1/1942/204/247/4 — 102 Squadron, Resumé of Operations, Sept 17 – Jan 18

AIR1/1942/204/247/5 — 102 Squadron, Record of Personnel Operations, Sept 17 – Aug 18

AIR1/1942/204/247/7 — 102 Squadron, Record Book, Oct 17 – May 18

AIR1/1943/204/247/6 — 102 Squadron, Record Book, Aug – Nov 1918

AIR1/1944/204/247/8 — 102 Squadron, Record Book, Jun 18 – Jan 19

AIR1/1944/204/247/9 — 102 Squadron, Bomb Raid and Reconnaissance Reports, Feb – Nov 1918

AIR1/1944/204/247/10 — 102 Squadron, Recommendations for Promotion, Oct 17 – Jan 19

AIR1/1945/204/247/19 — 102 Squadron, Operation Orders: Wings and Brigade, Sep 1917 – Nov 1919

AIR1/1945/204/247/22 — 102 Squadron, Technical Correspondence, Oct 17 – Feb 19

AIR1/1945/204/247/23 — 102 Squadron, Bomb Raid and Reconnaissance Reports, Aug 1918

Levyns, J.E.P. *The Disciplines of War. Memories of the War of 1914-18.* New York: Vantage Press, 1984.

148 SQUADRON

AIR1/176/15/207/1 — History of 148 Squadron, 1918

AIR1/512/16/3/68 — Formation of Night Flying Squadrons RFC for Duty with BE Force. Squadron Nos. 100, 101, 102, 148 and 149.

AIR1/956/204/5/1032 — Bomb Dropping Reports: May – June 1918, 148 Squadron and others.

149 SQUADRON

AIR1/176/15/208/1 — History of 149 Squadron, 1918

AIR1/512/16/3/68 — Formation of Night Flying Squadrons RFC for Duty with BE Force. Squadron Nos. 100, 101, 102, 148 and 149.

AIR1/956/204/5/1032 — Bomb Dropping Reports: May – June 1918, 149 Squadron and others.

Johnston, J. & Carter, N. *Strong by Night: History & Memories of No 149 (East India) Squadron RAF, 1918/19 - 1937/56.* Tonbridge, Kent: Air Britain.

Every picture tells a story ... This photograph is associated with the name Patey, so may possibly show Capt A.L. Chick and Lt W.O. Patey of 102 Sqn with a souvenir of their escape after A5587 was damaged by ground fire during a raid on 22 May 1918. The levers and 'freestyle' cable runs resemble those on B1877 of 100 Sqn (*see p50*).

The FE2b In Home Defence

The Home Defence aerodromes that operated FE2b and FE2d were spartan sites, chosen for their strategic locations. Hylton was typical, as photographed in April 1918. It had a coupled pair of HD pattern sheds and FE2bs can be seen inside. The Bessonneau hangar was used to shelter MT and was replaced with purpose-built MT sheds by the autumn of that year.

The threat posed by the German airship force led to the formation of RFC Home Defence squadrons from February 1916, after wrangling over responsibilities had been ironed out with the RNAS. The BE2c became the standard RFC machine for such operations and acquitted itself well during the autumn of that year, with four airships destroyed in action by 39 and 36 (Home Defence) Squadrons, a fifth as a partial consequence of a 39 (HD) Squadron BE2c's interception and a sixth destroyed by an RNAS BE2c from Yarmouth.

Those successful BE2c encounters were by machines flown as single seaters but the latest generation of German airships were designed to operate above the type's ceiling. The FE2b was seen as a possible replacement but, at the time, all available examples of the type were needed to support the RFC's operations in France.

The FE2b's first involvement in Home Defence had already taken place but it was purely a coincidental one. In addition to its airship raids, the German Navy operated 'hit and run' attacks on Channel ports, using seaplanes of See Flieger Abteilung 1, based at Zeebrugge. Such a raid, by seven machines and the largest to date, took place on 19 March 1916, shortly after 6364 had taken off from Lympne on its delivery

flight to St-Omer. The FE was crewed by 2Lt R. Collis and Flt Sgt A.C. Emery and they noted one of the German machines making for Deal. Collis, an experienced pre-war NCO pilot, did not give immediate chase but positioned his machine to intercept the enemy on its return. The seaplane, a Hansa Brandenburg, was piloted by Ltn Friedrich Christiansen, destined to become Germany's leading naval airman, with the Zeebrugge CO, Oberleutnant-zur-See von Tschirschky as his observer.

Collis positioned the FE behind the seaplane as it flew homeward, allowing Emery to discharge a drum of Lewis gun ammunition. His fire damaged the enemy's radiator, forcing the seaplane to make an

emergency landing in the Channel. The British crew had lost sight of their quarry and continued on their delivery flight. A temporary repair was made by von Tschirschky and Christiansen was able to ease the machine back to base. The FE2b passed through 1 AD at St-Omer to 23 Sqn, with which unit it lasted little over a month, before crashing on a practice flight.

FE2bs began to be issued to the Home Defence Wing during late September 1916. Only limited numbers were available, sufficient to equip 51 HDS, with its HQ then at Thetford and its flights dispersed to Mattishall, Harling Road and Marham. The unit's B Flight at Harling Road received the first examples; these were probably 7004 and 7005, and the latter did not last long, crashing during a forced landing while on patrol against the airship raid on the night of 1/2 October. Conversely, 7004 had a long career with the squadron, still being on charge more than a year later.

All three 51 HDS flights had re-equipped with the type by November and flew ineffective patrols against the last airship raid of the year. The successes of the HD Wing and the lull in airship raids over the winter of 1916-1917 brought a false sense of security to War Office thinking. This was combined with the decision to form FE2b-equipped night light bombing squadrons for service in France. 100 Squadron was the first such unit and formed at Hingham, the new HQ for 51 HDS, with its personnel attached to the HD unit's flights. Trained night pilots were in short supply and some 51 HDS personnel were drafted into the new squadron. The extent to which this then affected its ability to operate is demonstrated by the fact that by 7 March 1917, 51 HDS may have been over-equipped, with 20 FE2bs on charge, but undermanned; there were only eight pilots available.

51 HDS had sacrificed four of its FE2bs to allow 100 Squadron's formation and was, at the time experimenting with a new weapon. Several of its machines had been

The accidental pioneers: 2Lt R. Collis, *above*, and FE2b 6364.

converted to a single-seat configuration, with a Vickers 1.59in quick-firing gun (a pom-pom) fixed in a forward-firing position in a modified nacelle front. Photographs show that there were variations in the style of that nacelle modification. [*see pp 64/5 and 91*] Two of these modified machines found their way to 100 Squadron.

The situation in 51 HDS had improved by the time of the first German airship raid of 1917, when six Zeppelins made an abortive attack on London. The squadron was able to dispatch twelve machines, but none made contact with the enemy. All the FEs returned safely to their bases.

Daylight aeroplane raids on London had begun during May and the oncoming shorter summer nights should have seen a halt to airship raids. Against all expectations, an airship raid was mounted on the night of 16/17 June and an FE2b was involved in the destruction of one of the participating Zeppelins, L48.

B401 had been issued to the Armament Experimental Station at Orfordness. The station, along with several Training Squadrons, had been given a temporary HD commitment as a result of the Gotha raids. Zeppelin L42 crossed the Kent coast and bombed targets in that area but L48, suffering from mechanical problems, made landfall almost directly above Orfordness. Lt F.D. Holder and Sgt S. Ashby took off in B401 shortly before 02.00, following a BE2c into the air. The airship's engine problems ruled out an attack on London and so its commander, Kapitänleutnant F.G. Eichler, bombed Harwich, by which time the BE2c, piloted by Lt E.W. Clarke, had given up the chase. Holder had coaxed the FE2b up to 14000 feet, still well below the airship's altitude. Both

51 (HD) Sqn was the first Home Defence squadron to equip with the FE2b and the last to operate the type. 4871, a 120hp FE2b with tricycle undercarriage, was re-allotted for HD duty on 25 April 1917, after having been earmarked for 100 Sqn, and went to 51 (HD) Sqn B Flt at Marham. It crashed during a practice flight on 26 August, killing 2Lts P.G. Shellington and H.W.H. Marshall. It is fitted for night flying, with wing-tip navigation lights and underwing brackets for Holt's flares.

FE2b Night Fighter Pilot 1918: Lt E.T. Carpenter

Lt Edgar Theodore Carpenter began his pilot training with 5 RS at Castle Bromwich during November 1916. He progressed to 11 RS at Rochford later that month; then the sole Reserve Squadron dedicated to training pilots for night flying. He was then posted, in January 1917, to 37 HDS, also at Rochford and served with that unit until May and two of his flights were with Lt W.A. Bishop, who was soon to receive a reputation as a high-scoring fighter pilot with 60 Sqn.

After a brief attachment to 51 RS at Wye, then Waddington, Carpenter joined 100 Sqn, in which his night training was put to use. His, log at the time, recorded 76hr 43min flying time of which 6hr 10min were night flying. He served with that pioneering night-bomber squadron until mid December, bringing his total flying time up to 189hr 13min, 78hr 29min of this being at night. He had dropped 5ton 8cwt 16lb of bombs on the enemy, which he claimed was then the record for a 100 Sqn pilot.

Carpenter was posted to Home Establishment and, after the customary leave, joined 36 Sqn C Flt at Seaton Carew, making his first flight there on 11 January 1918. He assumed temporary command of B Flt, at Ashington, fifteen days later before taking over A Flt on 4 February. This interchange of aircrew between the night light bombing squadrons and HD units was commonplace.

His logbook only recorded eleven flights during that month, none of more than an hour and only two at night, one of which was of a mere ten minutes duration. March 1918 saw airship raid alerts on two successive nights, those of the 12th and 13th, and Carpenter was airborne for both, with Lt T.V. Preedy, in his usual mount, A6474. He landed at Ashington during the first and recorded having a drink with Capt J.A. Boret, before returning to Hylton. A6474 was coaxed up to 12300ft on the second, the night that L42 attacked Hartlepool, and patrolled the area between Newcastle and Blyth, before landing in mist after 75min. Both these sorties were recorded merely as night flights, with no mention of the airship menace.

The majority of Carpenter's recorded flights were for routine purposes; frequent engine tests, co-operation with searchlights, instructional sessions, inspection of landing grounds, gun firing practice and occasional height tests.

On 4 April, he recorded that A6474 had been 'streamlined' (if such was possible with a FE2b) and 'converted to single seater'. He made a height test in it the following day and recorded reaching 17700ft during the 1hr 40min flight, loaded with two Lewis guns and three double drums of ammunition.

Carpenter tested a concession to pilot comfort on 16 April; recording 'Electric Clothing Test, OK' against a 30 minute flight in A6474 but on the following day noted that the equipment was 'dud after ½ an hour'.

He made 18 flights during the first fortnight in May, only three of them on a FE2d. The remainder were on a pair of Bristol F2Bs. 36 Sqn was scheduled to be re-equipped with 22 of those machines by June and there appears to have been a spurt of intensive familiarisation flights. Delivery of the new machines was slow and Carpenter returned to the FE2. Instructional flights continued and he made reference, on 7 June, to B5555 having dual control when he used it for landing practice with a Lt Turner. There were occasional flights in F2Bs but the planned re-equipment was amended, with each of the unit's flights intended to receive four F2Bs and four Pups. A6474 remained as his usual mount but it had been restored to two-seat configuration by mid June. Carpenter recorded a flight with AM1 Hutchinson on 7 August, when he put that machine through 'spins, stalls, dives at 140mph'.

Despite the fact that he was instructing pupils, Carpenter had no training in that skill until 22 August, when he spent five days with the North East Area Flying Instructors School at Redcar to learn the recommended techniques.

His return to Hylton marked the virtual end to his time as a pilot of the FE2. He and Lt Macdonald took D9773 as far as Doncaster on 30 August and continued on to Bury (Upwood) the following day. Presumably, the machine was handed over to one of the NTS at that station. Carpenter tested Pup B1805 there on 3 September before flying it northward, via Seaton Carew, to B Flt at Ashington.

Flights from then on, until his posting out of 36 Sqn in January 1919 were, all except one, in Pups and Brisfits. The exception was on 29 September. FE2b A5738 was still on unit charge, probably the last of its breed, and Carpenter flew it on an inspection of the landing grounds at Rennington, Acklington and Snipe House.

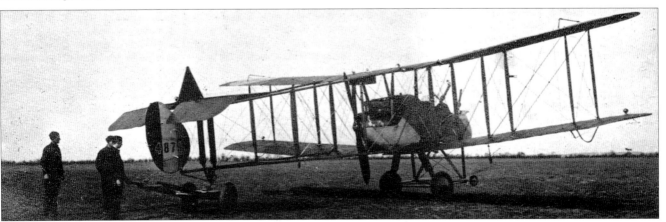

This atmospheric scene looking out of a Bessonneau hangar at Marham. 4871 is seen again, at right, with night-flying equipment but a colour scheme that was unsuitable for its role. The machine to the left was 7682, [*see p64*] an FE2b converted to mount a Vickers 1lb QF gun. Unlike 4871, it had the 160hp engine and a sloping nacelle front that may have been armoured.

pilot and observer fired, optimistically, at the Zeppelin and kept following. The airship then began to descend, possibly as a result of its mechanical problems and the FE2b was able to move in closer. Ashby had fired more than four drums of ball and incendiary ammunition when the Zeppelin caught fire. The FE2b crew was not alone in the interception. A DH2, flown by Captain R.H.M.S. Saundby, had also taken off from Orfordness and fired on the airship, as had a BE12 of 37 HDS from Goldhanger, piloted by Lt L.P. Watkins. The airship fell to earth near Theberton with three of its crew surviving. It was difficult to reconcile the reports of the British participants and the decision was taken to award the credit for the Zeppelin's destruction to Watkins; a move that was probably political in rewarding a member of the permanent HD organisation. All three pilots, however, were awarded the MC and Ashby the MM; probably a fairer reflection on their contributions. A FE2b from Orfordness also flew against the Gotha raids of 4 and 7 July, with little chance of climbing to the enemy's altitude of 14000 feet in time or of matching the enemy for speed.

The withdrawal of FE2bs from the day fighting squadrons in France led to greater numbers of the type being made available for Home Defence. The decision was taken to equip the northern squadrons of the Home Defence Group, as the HD Wing had been re-designated, with the type from July. 33, 36 and 38 HDS were duly equipped and some were initially issued to 76 HDS, but soon withdrawn, probably because its area of operations was less strategically important – this also being the likely reason why 77 HDS, covering lowland Scotland, and 38 HDS, covering the South Midlands, remained equipped for the time being with BE variants. By the summer of 1917, the disposition of the FE2b equipped HD squadrons was:

33 HDS	HQ	The Lawns, Gainsborough
	A Flt	Scampton (Brattleby)
	B Flt	Kirton Lindsey (Manton)
	C Flt	Elsham
36 HDS	HQ	Monaise, Fernwood Road, Jesmond, Newcastle
	A Flt	Seaton Carew (became C Flt 12.8.1917)
	B Flt	Hylton (became A Flt 12.8.1917)
	C Flt	Ashington (became B Flt 12.8.1917)
51 HDS	HQ	The Old Grammar School, Hingham
	A Flt	Harling Road then Tydd St Mary from 14.9.1917
	B Flt	Marham
	C Flt	Mattishall

The FE2s given over to Home Defence work

This typical early FE2d A12 had the Beardmore type radiator. It was issued to 20 Sqn and served with the BEF until being flown back to England on 22 November 1916. Issued for training, it saw use by 46 Sqn at Bramham Moor, before being re-allotted for HD duty. It was with 33 (HD) Sqn C Flt at Elsham and crashed near its aerodrome during an anti-airship patrol on 24 September, killing 2Lt C. Pinnock and and Lt A. Menzies.

received little in the way of modification. Brackets for electrically ignited Holt's flares were mounted under the lower wingtips, at the attachment point for the outer forward strut, and navigation lights mounted above those wing-tips. Signalling lights were fitted for both air-to-air and air-to-ground communication and instrument markings were radiumised. Surprisingly few HD FE2s were given the colouring or toned down markings associated with their nocturnal duties.

The Home Defence Group had been expanded to Brigade status during August and assumed responsibility for the training of night flying pilots of the night light bombing force. The existing Depot Squadrons were, at the time, incapable of meeting that demand and so training, which had been removed from HD squadrons in 1916, was re-introduced. There was much interchange of personnel between HD Brigade units and the night light bombing force. Both newly-qualified and experienced HD pilots were posted to units in France and night bombing pilots were posted to HD units on return to Home Establishment. The HD squadrons also trained observers for night bombing work and a syllabus was written for conjoint pilot/observer training. Training flights were not without hazard and, as the serial listing shows, a substantial number of FE2bs were wrecked in night-flying accidents – engine failure a primary cause.

A few FE2ds were also issued to HD units from August 1917 but Rolls-Royce engines were needed for higher priorities and so many of the airframes carrying FE2d serial numbers were, in fact FE2bs with 160hp Beardmores substituted.

There were to be no further attempts to attack London with airships, the capital becoming the target for further daylight and then night aeroplane raids. It was different for the Midlands and Northern England, with Zeppelin attacks continuing until the summer of 1918 and FE2s of the northern HD squadrons hopelessly

Cpl Clarke Chapman with 90cm searchlight.

Mascots were often carried for luck on nacelles, like the doll on this early FE2b of 51 (HD) Sqn in a Bessonneau at Marham. The observer's Lewis gun was mounted on a No.4 Mk IV Clark mounting while the pilot's was on a cranked pillar attached to an Anderson arch. Neither gun had an illuminated sight, despite the unit's nocturnal activities.

outclassed attempting to reach an enemy that often flew at 20000 feet.

A fleet of eight airships set out to attack the Midlands on the night of 21/22 August, although it would seem that only one bombed. 33 HDS was still re-equipping but sent up eight FEs, two of which were definitely FE2ds, but none was able to get anywhere near a high-flying enemy.

The two FE2ds of 33 HDS, B1882 and B1883, were transferred to 78 HDS at Sutton's Farm by the following month; possibly their (slightly) better performance seen as making them suitable for intercepting Gothas which were, by then, raiding London by night from heights below 10000 feet. Both made fruitless patrols against the raid of 24/25 September.

That same night saw an airship attack against the Midlands and Yorkshire and all three FE2b units of the HD Brigade had machines in the air; 33 HDS launched seven FE sorties, 36 HDS two and 51 HDS eight. None met with any success and 36 HDS lost A6461, which was assumed to have been lost at sea with 2Lt H.J. Thornton and 2Lt C.A. Moore posted missing. 38 HDS had begun re-equipment with the type and sent up one, which abandoned its patrol due to engine trouble. The squadron was fully re-equipped by the following month, when its component units were distributed as follows:

38 HDS	HQ	Scalford Road, Melton Mowbray
	A Flt	Stamford
	B Flt	Buckminster
	C Flt	Leadenham

Attempts to reduce the deficit in the FE2's ceiling had involved some being flown without an observer and a development was the conversion of a number of machines to single-seat configuration. This usually involved the simple expedient of fairing over the observer's cockpit with fabric and mounting a fixed, forward-firing Lewis gun alongside the pilot's cockpit, usually to starboard, and another on a moveable mounting. There is evidence of a more elaborate conversion to a 51

Listening for the Zeppelins. Lt Loughlin waits with a searchlight crew at their switchboard.

A number of FE2bs on Home Defence duty were converted to single-seaters. This usually entailed the fitting of a canvas fairing over the front cockpit, using the rail for the observer's folding windscreen as a support. Pilots' logbooks often refer to such modification as streamlining. B419 was so modified and was initially issued to 76 (HD) Sqn, but soon moved on to 38 (HD) Sqn. It went to France with the squadron when it became a night-light-bombing unit and survived until October 1918, when it was damaged in a crash landing and passed to 4 ASD at Guines.

HDS FE2b at Tydd St Mary, comprising a faired plywood nose enclosing a pair of internally mounted, fixed Lewis guns. Such streamlining and the lack of an observer's weight had some effect on performance but the ceiling was still only 16000-17000 feet, more than half a mile below that at which airships then tended to operate.

The next raid on the Midlands occurred on the night of 19/20 October and an FE pilot came close to a successful interception. Eleven airships took off but five were lost, to the weather and not the Home Defence organisation. Although there was early warning of the raid and numerous machines airborne to intercept only two pilots were able to fire on the enemy. One of these was Lt G.H. Harrison of 38 HDS C Flight in FE2b B422, which had been converted to single seat configuration. Harrison attacked an airship near Leicester and his machine was hit, harmlessly, by return fire. His gun then jammed and he was forced to abandon the chase. Harrison's was one of eight sorties launched by his squadron; 33 HDS launched fifteen and 51 HDS six. The unreliability of Beardmore engines meant that six of these sorties had to be abandoned. 33 HDS lost A5656 with 2Lt H.P. Solomon killed and 2Lt H. Preston

Single seat FE2b night fighters were usually armed with a pair of Lewis guns on Anderson mountings. The starboard one was fixed, the other on a moveable mount. A5724 was so armed and had Neame illuminated sights on the guns, with batteries strapped to the barrel casings. Unusually for the period, the guns had the single 47-round drums. Spent cartridge cases could damage the propellers of pusher machines and so collection bags were fitted to the guns.

shaken when the machine crashed on take-off from the small landing ground that served the squadron HQ at Gainsborough.

The words Home Defence were dropped from unit titles in November 1917. The squadrons still maintained the training commitment and pilots were also expected to perform other duties apart from that and their primary one. They had to be competent in signalling and bomb dropping; the HD units would support the Army in the event of invasion. The FE2bs of the Hylton flight of 36 Sqn and the Elsham flight of 33 Sqn were equipped with wireless transmitters and their crew trained in range-finding to assist local coastal batteries.

Training accidents continued but not all calamities were due to the unreliability of engines. A5698, became victim to 'friendly fire' when, on the night of 3/4 January 1918, 2Lt E.F. Wilson of 38 Squadron accidentally passed into the London area defences during such a training exercise.

2Lt Herbert Philip Solomon

Wilson fired an incorrect recognition flare and was promptly fired on by AA. The FE was hit but Wilson, luckily, walked away from the ensuing forced landing.

Although intended for the Midlands, the first airship attack of 1918, on the night of 12/13 March, only penetrated as far as east Yorkshire, with weather conditions hampering both intruders and defenders. 33 Squadron put up a pair of FE2bs, which were landed due to the weather after twenty minutes. It was better further north and 36 Sqn launched three sorties as a precaution, but these were unnecessary.

That raid was followed by another the next night, against which 36 Sqn sent out eight FEs. Strong winds forced two of the airships to return home but the third, L42, waited off the Northumberland coast until after dark and then attacked Hartlepool from the north. Most of the FEs were already airborne and 2Lts E.C. Morris and R.D. Linford, from Seaton Carew in A6422, picked out the airship and fired, ineffectively, from extreme range. Although they followed the Zeppelin out to sea,

7675: another 51 (HD) Sqn FE2b armed with a Vickers 1lb QF gun. The weapon and sighting rod are shown in the elevated position. It had the 120hp Beardmore and tricycle undercarriage. It appears to have had a navigation light on the upper starboard mainplane tip and a telescopic mounting for a Lewis gun on the port fuselage side, ahead of the pilot's cockpit.

they were unable to climb high enough to make a purposeful attack. The night's disappointment was compounded by the wreck of A5683, which crashed landing at Seaton and the death of Sgt Arthur Joyce, from Hylton. Joyce had taken off shortly before the airship attacked, in A5740, and crashed below Pontop Pike. That hill is well to the west of the coast and Joyce may have become disorientated and lost. A memorial still stands on the outskirts of Annfield Plain to mark the crash site.

The shortcomings of the FE2b in the Home Defence role had not gone unrecognised and some hope was pinned in the FE2h as its replacement. This had a basic FE2b airframe with a 230hp BHP engine, which should have improved deficiencies in speed and climb. Tests took place during March and results were disappointing enough to cause its rejection.

The penultimate airship raid on Britain was on the night of 12/13 April with 38 and 51 Sqns providing all but two of the sixteen machines sent out to intercept it. Once again, the FEs could not climb to the height of the attackers, with Lt F. St C. Sergeant of 51 Sqn, in A5753, coming closest and firing from extreme distance at Zeppelin L62 which he had followed from Norfolk to Northamptonshire. It was probably this same airship that was sighted and attacked near Birmingham, again at long range and without effect, by Lt C.H. Noble-Campbell in A5707 from 38 Sqn and based at Buckminster. The January mishap of Wilson may have been repeated on this night because Noble-Campbell then crashed in circumstances that were never explained. His own account stated that he had been hit on the head but by what was unknown. The press reports of the time stated that he had been brought down by fire from the airship, but no guns were fired from L62. 38 Sqn also lost A5578, from Stamford, that night, with Lt W.A. Brown surviving its crash near Radford

aerodrome, near Coventry.

38 Squadron left the Home Defence organisation on 31 May 1918. It had been mobilised as a night light bombing squadron and departed for Cappelle on that date. It did, however, leave behind a Depot Detachment of FE2bs to maintain the defence of the South Midlands. The Depot HQ was at Buckminster, but the

other two of the squadron's flight stations were still used.

The inadequacy of the FE2b for Home Defence and the disappointment of the FE2h led RAF authorities to look toward urgent replacement. It was decided to re-equip 33 and 36 Sqns with the Bristol F2B, which was already in service with 39 and 141 Sqns. That process began in June

4890 served with 19 RS before being fitted with night flying equipment and issued to 51 (HD) Sqn at Marham. It flew against the airship raid of 23 March 1917 and was still on charge two months later. Lt Alexander was the culprit behind this mishap, on an unrecorded date.

A5729, also with 51 (HD) Sqn. Issued from 8 AAP on 12 October 1917, two days after its 'Gold Coast No.9' designation, it was converted to a single seater with a canvas fairing over the observer's cockpit, and given two Lewis guns. The fixed gun had a chute that fed spent cartridge cases to an internal collection bag, the moveable gun had the bag attached. Lt T.H. Gladstone flew A5729 against the airship raid of 12 April 1918.

Sgt Arthur Joyce pictured standing in the cockpit of A5657 which he wrecked by a crash landing on 20 February 1918. Shown picketed down after its crash, that FE2b appears to have had flare brackets under the forward cross member of its tail boom and, like several other 36 Sqn machines, had a pair of RFC wings painted on the nose of its nacelle.

Sergeant Arthur John Joyce

NCO pilots were never numerous in the RFC and RAF but they faced the same dangers as their officer counterparts. There were more fatalities to aircrew in the UK and Ireland than in France. The majority of these were on training units but a posting to an operational squadron on Home Defence duties was not without dangers.

36 Squadron suffered ten fatalities during the Great War, one of these being Sergeant (9932) Arthur John Joyce, from Clapham, London.

The photograph at the top of the page shows the result of a landing accident at Hylton where Joyce served with the squadron's A Flight. Joyce is shown standing in the pilot's cockpit of FE2b A5657, after wiping off its undercarriage on 20 February 1918. The FE2b was unarmed but it carried wing-tip navigation lights. Like several other of the squadron's machines, a small pair of RFC wings was painted on the front of the nacelle. Joyce was dead three weeks later.

The picture in this panel shows FE2b A5740.

Joyce took off in this machine at 21.15 on 13 March 1918, one of two sorties made by A Flight in response to that night's raid on Hartlepool by Zeppelin L42. Joyce flew it solo, suggesting that it may, by that date, have been converted to single seat configuration. Alternatively, ballast may have been secured in the observer's cockpit.

The aeroplane crashed on the southern slopes of Pontop Pike, shortly before 23.00, killing its pilot. The crash site was some eight miles west of Durham and well away from Joyce's patrol line. It would appear that he may have become disorientated. His body was returned to his family for burial at Wandsworth.

A memorial to him was erected at the crash site, now on the outskirts of Annfield Plain, and is shown at left. The memorial was re-dedicated in 1959, by AVM G.R. Bromet, after the addition of a flanking wall to commemorate local airmen who perished during WWII.

1918 but was slow. 51 Sqn was destined to continue operating the FE2b.

When the final airship raid by five Zeppelins was mounted on 5/6 August, FE2bs were still among the Home Defence machines sent up to intercept. The early destruction of L70 by a 4 Group crew from Yarmouth and damage to L65, combined with poor navigation by the remaining three airships meant that the raid came to nothing. Fighters were airborne, however. 33 Sqn put up three FE2bs, as well as three of its new Bristol Fighters. The 38 Sqn detachments at Leadenham and Buckminster put up an FE2b each, while 51 Sqn sent out two from each of its flight stations. None made any contact. This was the last operation by FE2bs on Home Defence duty.

38 Squadron's detachments were absorbed into the new 90 HD Sqn, formed at Buckminster on 14 August. Initially they flew the inherited FE2bs. The squadron re-equipped with the Avro 504K (NF) during the following month.

36 Sqn relinquished all of its FEs by the end of August, when it suffered its last casualty on the type. Lt A. Wald MC, who had been decorated for his night bombing work on 100 Sqn FE2bs, had taken off from Ashington on a night flying exercise in C9793 and crashed in a spin near the aerodrome. Each of the squadron's flights was given an establishment of four Bristol F2Bs and four Sopwith Pups.

33 Sqn never fully re-equipped with the Bristol F2B and, under a revised plan also received the Avro 504K. Its FE2bs were also gone by September 1918.

That left 51 Sqn, which soldiered on with the type until the last month of the war. Initially intended to receive Sopwith Camels as replacement equipment, it received Snipes instead and the FE2b had ended its days as a fighter. There can have been no other WWI machine that performed such a front-line duty for so long.

This FE2d saw successful action with 20 Sqn in France before being flown back to England on 9 September 1917. It was with 36 Sqn at Hylton by 24 February 1918 and was flown on an anti Zeppelin patrol on 10 March by Sgt Mann and Cpl Douglas. Two days later, Lt Downing was responsible for the distress shown in this photograph. Although a later Fe2d, with a Beardmore type radiator, A6429 had the style of pilot's 'bathtub' associated with the first production batch. The only visible concession to its night-flying activities was a flare chute that projected though the floor of the observer's cockpit.

Lt Thomas Hugh Gladstone

Some Home Defence pilots had prior type experience with FE2b fighting/reconnaissance squadrons in France. One such was T.H. Gladstone who completed his training at 19 Reserve Sqn, Hounslow in October 1916 with nearly 30 hours solo to his credit and was posted to 22 Sqn at Bertangles. After three familiarisation flights, he did his first line patrol, with Lt Brassington as his observer, on 10 November 1916 in FE2b 5207. For the next few weeks he carried out a mixture of defensive patrols and photography. No enemy aircraft were encountered but strong winds, low cloud, mist and engine problems provided their own challenges. His first experience of air combat came on 20 December when on photographic escort duties. The fighters involved were driven off but from now on more and more enemy aircraft were encountered. Gladstone recorded the loss of Aspinall and Miller (the latter shot in the knee) on 2 February 1917, and two days later was himself forced to land near Trones Wood with two bullets in the petrol tank of FE2b A5456.

The early months of 1917 had seen a significant increase in photographic activity – both leading and escorting. In the weeks leading up to the Arras offensive, the squadron's efforts

returned to offensive patrols, interspaced with reconnaissance and bombing. It was during a reconnaissance of St Quentin on 6 April that Gladstone recorded one enemy fighter crashed and one forced to land by the escorting Sopwith Pups of 54 Sqn. Notwithstanding Bloody April's subsequent reputation, the remainder of the month proved very quiet. A succession of patrols, bombing and photographic missions were carried out without opposition, although

anti-aircraft fire caused damage to his aircraft on several occasions. The lull did not last for long. A photographic patrol on 6 May was attacked by five enemy fighters and, although all were driven off, the squadron was not so lucky on 19 May. On this occasion, 2/Lts Goodban and Ward were shot down in flames in FE2b A5457.

For the next few weeks offensive patrols continued but operational difficulties faced by the squadron were reflected in the need to provide an escort of 12 Sopwiths for two FE2bs conducting a reconnaissance on 15 June. There must have been some relief, therefore, with the arrival of the first Bristol Fighters during July which would replace the FE2b by the end of the month. Gladstone did not remain to see this process completed. After more than six months on the Western Front, he returned to Home Establishment, joining 51 Home Defence Sqn at Marham – although still flying the FE2b. He stayed with 51 Sqn for over a year, returning to France with 38 Sqn in November 1918 – once again flying the FE2b but this time in the night bombing role. His last recorded flight in an FE2b was on 11 January 1919, making Gladstone one of the longest serving 'Fee' pilots on the Western Front – with more than two years continuous operations and over 300 hours on type.

FE2d B1883 had a lengthy HD career. It was first issued to 33 (HD) Sqn by August 1917 but transferred to 78 (HD) Sqn at Sutton's Farm during the following month, for use on anti-Gotha patrol. 78 Sqn re-equipped with Sopwith two-seaters and B1883 was issued to 36 Sqn B Flt at Ashington by January 1918 and flew against two airship raids. It went to 36 Sqn's A Flt at Hylton by the end of March and was still there three months later.

Experimental Work with the FE2b

Given that one of the functions officially assigned to the Royal Aircraft Factory was the study of aerodynamics it was almost inevitable that the FE2, like any of only a handful of aeroplanes available at Farnborough at any given time, should be employed in various tests and experiments that were not immediately concerned with the development of the airframe itself but with aeronautical research pure and simple.

For example it was common practice at 'The Factory' for stress calculations to be verified by practical experiment, thereby maintaining the accuracy of future calculations of a similar nature and ensuring that design factors of safety were being achieved. Whilst some loads, such as the tension in a wire, could be simply measured with specially designed instruments, others could only be tested by applying an ever-increasing load until the component failed. In the most spectacular of all such tests the entire aeroplane was inverted and its wings loaded with a measured quantity of sand or lead shot until they finally collapsed. Such a fate befell FE2d A40 which, after a brief period of service in France, was returned to the Royal Aircraft Factory in October 1916, and its engine removed before it was tested to destruction so its design calculations could be verified, and the factors of safety employed thereby proved.

Floats and Flotation

One early Royal Aircraft Factory experiment began on 3 April 1912 when FE2 was briefly modified to become a floatplane, as described on p9/10. This experiment seems to have served no immediate purpose beyond that of simply demonstrating that it was possible for an aeroplane to operate from water, as was being proved contemporaneously by other people, and in other countries. The point clearly made, the trials were discontinued and FE2 returned to a wheeled undercarriage.

The idea of fitting floats to an FE2 was resurrected early in 1917 when work began on the design of a seaplane version of the FE2d for service on coastal patrols and other roles involving flying over water. However in April the idea was dropped in favour of the Royal Aircraft Factory's only flying boat design, CE1 which, in turn, proved inferior to the American Curtiss flying boat designs and was therefore not put into production.

The assignment of the FE2b to anti-submarine patrols over the North Sea early in 1918 brought about a renewal of interest in its aquatic abilities, with a view to ensuring that it would remain afloat if forced to ditch into the sea, so that the crew could be rescued, and the machine recovered. Experiments were carried out with A6536 at the former RNAS base at the Isle of Grain to develop emergency flotation gear which comprised large cylindrical air bags fitted under the lower wing roots, next to the nacelle, and small floats added to the wing tips.

A trial ditching took place on 30 May 1918 and, although the aeroplane remained afloat satisfactorily a fair volume of water was swept into the forward cockpit as it entered the water. The machine was therefore further modified by the provision of a wooden twin skid undercarriage of rather old fashioned appearance to which was attached a hydrovane designed to keep the nose up when ditching and prevent the cockpits from being swamped. A further ditching trial on 29 June, with the hydrovane in place, was entirely successful but by this time the employment

FE2b A6536 as it appeared on arrival at Grain. It was fitted with carriers for 112lb bombs and the over-painting of its rudder striping suggests prior use by an HD squadron.

A6536 fitted with flotation bags and wing-tip floats. A sturdy-looking hydrovane undercarriage has replaced the Trafford Jones design seen on the left.

Opposite: **FE2b with flotation bags inflated.**
Below: **A successful ditching.**
Right: **Recovering the aircraft after ditching, with the flotation bags still inflated.**

Braking parachute experiments in progress, February 1915. The screens along the factory fence were not permanent.

of the FE2b on anti-submarine patrols was already being discontinued in favour of more suitable machines and the emergency flotation gear never passed beyond the experimental stage. This may perhaps have been partly because events had proven that it was not necessary; two 'Fees' had been forced to ditch whilst patrolling over the North Sea and whilst neither had been equipped with flotation gear both crews had been recovered although, admittedly, the aircraft had been lost.

Braking Experiments

The landing run of the FE2a, although short by the standards of later years was somewhat longer than that of other, lighter, contemporary types and appears therefore to have been a cause for concern at the Royal Aircraft Factory, especially with regard to the comparatively small size of some of the fields in France. Efforts

were made to reduce the landing run by the introduction of the mechanism whereby the trailing edge of the upper centre section could be wound down, by a wheel in the pilot's cockpit, to increase drag and so act as a brake on landing. This device proved unpopular with pilots who were busy enough when landing and it saw little, if any, use in service. As recorded elsewhere it was deleted on the FE2b and later variants as an unnecessary complication.

However the Royal Aircraft Factory was not discouraged from its efforts to reduce the landing run and in a remarkably innovative experiment, initially conducted on 9 February 1915, fitted an FE2a with a small parachute attached to a length of cable which could be released on landing to provide a braking force. The report of the trials has not been located but the device was obviously not adopted for

wide-scale use, and the braking parachute was forgotten, only to be re-invented some decades later.

Experimental Armaments

In August 1916 a trial was conducted in which an FE2b, 6377, was finally fitted with a weapon very similar to that included in the original design concept, namely the 37mm Vickers quick firing gun which had first seen service in the Boer War where it had acquired the nick-name the 'Pom-Pom' gun from the noise it made when fired. A belt of forty 1lb shells was provided. The gun was positioned off-centre to starboard with the gunner to port to retain the balance, and to place him beside rather than behind the breech of the gun.

Trials were conducted at Orfordness as a result of which a number of other machines were similarly equipped and saw limited operational service with 100 Squadron, attacking road and rail transport. Most appear to have been converted to single seaters, again with the gun offset to starboard and with their shortened nacelles subjected to a variety of modifications, almost all equally ugly.

August 1916 also saw the trial of another heavy weapon, the 0.45in calibre Vickers-Maxim machine gun and at least two Fees equipped with this weapon entered service but the 'pom-pom' was the more effective weapon for the ground attack role and the heavy machine guns were soon replaced.

In another experimental installation the whole forward cockpit was replaced with an armoured structure with two machine guns and an Aldis sight built into the front surface. Although the guns had some movement in both traverse and elevation the whole of the plate into which they

The RAF drawings of the conversion of the FE2b to carry a Vickers 1lb QF gun envisaged a simple rounded nacelle nose. *Left:* This 160hp FE2b, possibly 6337, had a more substantial fairing, with high cockpit sides. The gun was a lightened version of the Army's weapon, with a shortened barrel, and a sighting rod attached to the gun, which could be elevated. The ammunition box was fitted over the breech mechanism. *Right:* A similar conversion, with slightly lower cockpit sides and rather longer nose. There is an access door to the spent shell-case box, fitted on the right-hand side of the gun. The RAF proposals were for a machine in which the gun could be depressed as well as elevated. It also showed three small searchlights, fitted in the position of the single one shown here, that were linked to the gun and moved with it, presumably to illuminate targets.

were fitted was hinged so that the guns could be fired downwards at a steep angle, facilitating ground attack.

In March 1918 a 58 Squadron FE2b, B489, was experimentally fitted with a 1.59in calibre Vickers-made weapon which weighed only 46lb but fired a 2lb shell. Although popularly called the 'Crayford Rocket Gun' it was in reality a conventional artillery piece. Its light weight was obtained by eliminating all frills and leaving it completely manual in operation, even to the ejection of spent cartridge cases. This made it very slow to load and fire but its fire power was too

impressive to ignore and B489, with the gun still mounted, saw limited service with 58 Squadron.

Another attempt to provide aerial artillery saw at least one of the Puma engined FE2hs built by Ransomes, Sims & Jefferies being stationed at the Isle of Grain and experimentally equipped with the so-called 'recoilless' gun invented by Commander Cleland Davis of the US Navy. This formidable looking weapon comprised a long barrel, the smallest being 40mm calibre, from which was fired an explosive shell nominally weighing 2lb, whilst, simultaneously, a counterweight of shot

7682, also a 160hp machine, was one of the Vickers QF conversions issued to 51 (HD) Sqn and its nose modifications left the weapon more exposed. The lower projection of the nose fairing was added to several of the FE2bs that were so armed and led to the conversion being nicknamed NCR (National Cash Register, as its shape resembled shop tills of the time).

Above: 7679 had the 120hp Beardmore and, although it too had the lower nose projection, featured a rounded front to the main body of the nacelle. This FE2b was initially issued to 51 (HD) Sqn but later saw service with 100 Sqn.

Top right: Another 120hp machine with a nose modification very similar to that of 7682.

Below: Details of the hinged twin gun installation shown on the opposite page.

Above: The 'Crayford Rocket Gun'.
Below: The modification to the nacelle frame needed to secure the gun.

and grease was ejected to the rear, the two reactions effectively cancelling each other out, eliminating recoil, and so placing no strain on the mounting or airframe. Each barrel had to be loaded separately and then re-joined for firing, which made it effectively a 'one shot' weapon and it was, obviously, essential to take note of where both ends were pointing which, in an FE2 type, meant that the muzzle had to be depressed well below the horizontal if the rearward discharge was not going to damage some part of the machine, the upper wing being particularly at risk, as was the pilot! The trials, although quite extensive, were discontinued without the

The 'Fees' used to carry out night bombing raids had special equipment, including navigation lights and landing flares to facilitate the performance of these duties but these are described in the chapter dealing with such operations.

A small number of FE2bs were converted, in service, into single seaters, partly in the hope that the reduction in weight would bring about an increase in performance and partly because a gunner was not really necessary for their projected role as night fighters as part of the effort to combat the Zeppelin menace.

The front cockpit was faired over to reduce resistance and the tail-plane incidence adjusted to compensate for the changed position of the centre of gravity.

Left: **One of three FE2h conversions made by Ransomes, Sims & Jefferies, seen at Grain, where they were fitted with Davis recoilless guns that should, technically, have been described as recoilless rifles (the barrels were rifled). The 97in long weapon may have been intended for Marine Operations. The angle at which it had to be fired without the rearward discharge damaging the machine is clear. Glazed panels were inserted in the modified noses and the nacelles extended rearward, possibly as compensation for the added weight of the weapons.** (*see also p91*)

Below: **There were several attempts to fit FE2bs with searchlights for anti-airship operations. This carried a substantial light, whose power was generated by the nose propeller.**

weapon being adopted for service use.

In early October 1916 the Royal Aircraft Factory's instrument department devised a searchlight system designed to allow the FE2b to carry out ground attacks at night and so 4928, built by Weir, was fitted with a searchlight mounted above the nose wheel of its oleo undercarriage, power being provided by a generator mounted in the nose of the nacelle. The light, which was out of reach of the crew, was fixed and so always pointed in the direction of flight, which proved a handicap in practice, especially with target acquisition. By March 1917 a more powerful lamp, a French made Sautter-Harlé, was installed in a swivel mount at the front of the forward cockpit of another Weir built FE2b, A781. This had a propeller driven generator mounted below the nacelle, almost in the same position of the lamp in the previous experiment, although this machine had a Vee undercarriage. Twin Lewis guns were mounted along with the lamp, one on each side of it, the whole assembly being aimed together. Clearly it failed to impress as, once the tests were completed, the equipment was removed and A781 returned to service as a standard FE2b.

A more warlike searchlight installation was made by the RAF to A781 during March 1917. The French Sautter-Harlé light was yoked to a pair of Lewis guns and had an external, propeller-driven generator. Lt W.S. Farren (later head of the RAE) is shown above, demonstrating the installation.

A single movable Lewis gun was provided for the pilot, its mount supported by an Anderson arch at the rear of the front cockpit, while an additional fixed, forward-firing Lewis gun was provided with an internal catchment area for spent cartridge cases instead of the usual leather pouch. .

At Tydd St Mary, in the Lincolnshire fens, 51 Squadron carried out a more ambitious conversion of A5543, D9121 and D9124, moving the pilot's cockpit forward to a mid point and installing twin Lewis guns firing through holes in the re-contoured nose.

Bombsights

The two RAF5 powered FE2es, 4256 and 6360, were retained by the Royal Aircraft Factory at Farnborough as test vehicles in which capacity they were employed on experiments into the development of gyroscopic bomb sights.

The earliest attempts at aerial bombing had quickly demonstrated that aiming any kind of projectile from a moving aeroplane is far from being a simple matter and that an acceptable level of accuracy is unobtainable, regardless of practice, without mechanical aid. When a bomb is released from an aeroplane flying at altitude, although it immediately begins to drop vertically due to the influence of the earth's gravity, it retains its forward motion, due to inertia, until slowed by air resistance and therefore its path to earth initially follows a parabolic curve. The path of this curve is fairly easy to calculate provided that the aeroplane's height and speed are precisely known, this calculation being the function of a bombsight. But the instrument's accuracy is adversely affected by any variation from the straight

This elaborate Home Defence conversion of FE2b A5543 was made by 51 (HD) Squadron. The repositioning of the pilot's seat meant that the controls were moved to the position they occupied in the FE2c. Twin internal Lewis guns were fitted; their position would have facilitated magazine changing by the pilot. The alterations to the upper nacelle included a cowling that completely enclosed the 160hp Beardmore. A similar conversion, D9124, is shown on p 17.

The CFS Mk 4b bombsight, invented by 2/Lt (later Lt-Col) R.B. Bourdillon while employed with the CFS experimental flight based at Upavon in late 1914/early 1915. The sight proved effective, simple to use and reliable. Over 2000 were manufactured for the RFC (at £4 each) and, although production ceased in 1917, it continued to be used until the Armistice. The sight employed both fixed and moving sighting wires allowing, with the use of a stopwatch, bombs to be dropped with relative accuracy (an average error of 30 yards from 6000 ft was claimed for a moderately skilled pilot). Bourdillon subsequently received a substantial inventions award.

This bombsight was widely used from 1916 onwards for medium altitude bombing. Invariably fitted on the starboard side of the nacelle, the actual position varied on whether the observer or pilot was acting as bomb aimer [see p122]. The sight was attached by screwing the two end-flanges to wooden backing strips which in turn were secured by wires to the fuselage structure, and adjusted so that it was level when the aircraft was in its flying position. Its use at night seems to have been limited and it became the custom for squadrons to drop their bombs at low level – on the hand signals of the observer - as the target disappeared under the nose of the aircraft.

Above and right: **CFS Mk 4 bombsights mounted on the starboard side of the nacelle.**

Below: **An experimental gyroscopic bombsight installed, offset to port, in the nacelle of 6360. The wires on the cockpit floor run from the generator underneath.**

and level at the moment of release and it is this variation that the gyroscopic bombsight was designed to reduce. Research, development and testing of bombsights continued throughout the war, and beyond, with A5540 being involved in bombsight testing at Orfordness in August 1917 and D9108 following suit with the Instrument Experimental Unit at Biggin Hill in the summer of 1918 before moving to Farnborough to continue its career as a test vehicle, remaining in service until 1924.

Front view of gyroscopic bombsight trial installation showing generator.

Two views (starboard and port) of a combination underwing rack for a single 112lb and two 25lb bombs, plus outboard, the carrier for a Michelin flare with its distinctive notched clip for locking the fusing vane.

Bombs and Bomb Gear

Throughout the FE2b's service life there were numerous experimental bomb carrier fitments, both under the wings and suspended beneath the nacelle.

In the bombing role, to which the 'Fee' was re-assigned once out-classed as a fighter, mounting rails were fitted beneath the underside of each lower wing centre section for the attachment of carriers for different bombs or flares, frequently four 20lb Cooper bombs.

In night bombing configuration, one 230lb bomb could be carried in a cradle mounted beneath the nacelle, provided a modified 'Vee' undercarriage was fitted, with a small cutout in the back of the axle fairing to ensure that the nose of the bomb dropped past it without making contact. Alternatively up to three 120lb bombs could be carried under the nacelle, on a special mounting.

A rack of 20lb Hales bombs, and the standard 20lb bomb rack, *below*.

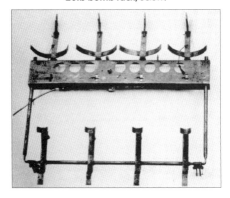

Below: **FE2b of 83 Squadron in October 1918 with two Cooper bomb racks fitted in tandem beneath the centre-section .**

Fusing and arming a 112lb bomb, mounted on a centre-line bomb rack.

An empty Twin 112b rack fitted beneath the centre-section – looking forward. There is an empty generator clip on the port undercarriage leg. The rear notch in the axle fairing, to avoid fouling a 230lb bomb when carried beneath the centre section, can be clearly seen.

A 230lb RFC bomb (containing 140lbs of Amatol) fitted to a skeleton carrier suspended under the centre-section of a 9 Wing FE2b in October 1917. Although the arrangement of cables and struts looks haphazard and fragile, it proved reliable and effective. Also visible is the 'notch' cut in the axle fairing, to provide adequate clearance on release; the fixed metal frames under the starboard wing for the bomb carriers, and (towards the wing-tip) a Holts Flare.

Below: The **FE2b** squadrons experimented throughout the war with a variety of field modifications to increase carrying load and reduce the time taken for role changes (different targets required different combinations of HE and incendiary bombs). Here a combination of Cooper and 112lb RL racks under each wing allowed a total load of 548lbs to be carried – in addition to a single Michelin Flare.

Initially bombs were released by either pilot or observer by toggles attached to the outside of the nacelle, (*see also the lower photo of 7691 on p 144*) but lever systems were developed later, and an example, probably from 102 Squadron, appears on the machine shown on p 53.

Michelin flares for illuminating bombing targets were often mounted singly, directly onto the underwing carrier rails, but the photo below shows a standard 20lb bomb rack with an extension that could hold four of these flares, which, as the bottom picture indicates, were over 30in long.

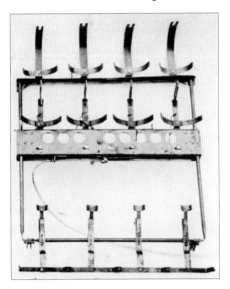

Navigation lights were fitted to the top of the lower wingtips, centre section and tail.

Holt's patent magnesium landing light. Electrically operated, they gave a single-use, one-minute burn time, and were mounted on rods below the wing tips, and on some machines, below the tail booms. The detail of D9108, left, shows a later version on a relatively short 'stalk', with a fairly large tri-lobe 'light shade' which would give protection to the wing fabric and and also reduce glare for the pilot. A Holt's flare on a longer stalk mounting can be seen just above the fin of the 230lb bomb opposite, top. Other types of installation are noted in photo captions throughout.

The flares could be ignited separately via a double switch in the cockpit. Instructions issued in 1916 state 'In use, the flare on the opposite side to that on which the pilot usually looks out on landing, should be lighted'. Thus they did offer two attempts at landing at night.

Some night bombers, like A852 (p 36) had a chute installed in the floor of the observer's cockpit for dropping RL parachute flares, but more machines had the rack-mounted Michelin flares, as seen below, with a simple attachment loop.

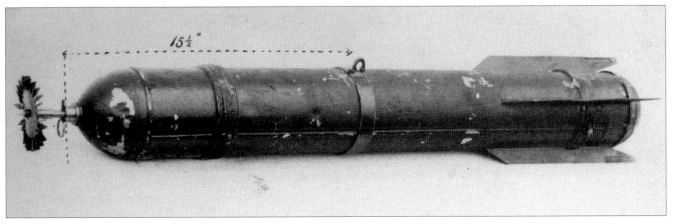

Wireless

During June 1916 production FE2b 4914 was fitted with an improved spark gap type wireless transmitter developed by Dr R. Widdington of the Royal Aircraft Factory's Instrument department and retained at Farnborough for trials which appear to have been of the wireless equipment rather than the installation, with the Fee's roomy front cockpit providing a convenient test bed for the equipment. The transmitter was installed to the left of the cockpit, with the morse key mounted on the right, convenient to the operator's hand and with the drum from which the aerial was wound out close to the key.

Whatever the result of the tests the equipment was removed, and 4914 sent to France by the beginning of July.

On active service wireless transmitters were usually carried only by aeroplanes engaged on artillery observation duties, to report fall of shot back to the battery concerned and so correct aim. FE2b crews were not normally assigned to such duties and were rarely equipped with wireless.

Wireless development continued throughout the war, first at Farnborough, and at Brooklands then, from early 1917, at the Wireless Experimental Establishment at Biggin Hill in Kent a location, later famous, chosen as being an elevated, level site, free from obstruction and interference. Here FE2bs A5773 and D9116 both served as test vehicles.

Photography

Normally cameras were employed to photograph the ground immediately below the aircraft, with overlapping images to ensure full coverage, but occasionally a camera was mounted to take oblique photographs the better to highlight fortifications. In the Fee, such cameras, when fitted, were installed behind the gunner's feet, inside the nacelle, with the lens pointing through a clear panel in the nacelle side.

Top left: The cockpits of a night bomber FE2b, identified by the curved elevator horns necessary to give clearance when the V-strut undercarriage was fitted. The Spartan observer's cockpit has a folded canvas windscreen and a Lewis gun carried on a No.4 Mk.IV mounting, clipped to the forward nacelle rail. Further clips are fitted at the sides of the rail. A camera is installed on the left , and there is a wireless unit with aerial reel handle and morse key on the right. The pilot released the bombs, using the lever on the outside of his cockpit.

Left: The wooden brass-bound Thornton-Pickard type-C aerial camera was a development of the RFC's first aerial camera, the Thornton-Pickard type-A of 1915. In 1916 the type-C was the camera most often found mounted on FE2b/ds. It was superseded in 1917 by the type L, a lighter metal-bodied camera. The type-C was semi-automatic, the photographic plates being gravity fed by a slide motion, operated by the handle on the left, from the upper magazine and transferred after exposure to the lower receiving magazine, on the right.

Top: **Cpl A.L. Hitchin is shown here demonstrating an extented plate-changing lever on a Thornton Pickard type-C camera at East Retford. The camera here is set up for operation by the pilot, and the shutter release cable also extends back to his cockpit. This FE2b had an additional stay cable between its forward centre section struts.**

Right: **The camera on this early Weir-built FE2b was operated manually by the observer and carried on an outsized wooden framework. It is fitted with lenses of two different focal lengths, long and wide angle, mounted side by side. The machine had been modified, with air-scoops for the radiator attached to the sides of the pilot's 'bathtub' replacing the standard door arrangement.**

Below: **'Special 24in whole-plate camera' installation for oblique photography. This FE2b may have been 6982, one of two machines to bear the presentation inscription 'Newfoundland 4'. 6982 was allocated for photographic experiments in July 1916 and was with 11 Sqn by that September. The nose markings are reminiscent of those used by that unit.**

Above: **B401, still with its factory-fitted bomb rack under the nacelle and brackets for Holt's flares, is shown with the balloon fender tested by Lt Roderic Hill at Orfordness.**

Right: **The nacelle cockade suggests that this FE2b, also built as a night bomber, was *not* B401 with an alternative design of balloon fender. The location was Farnborough, with the sheds on Jersey Brow visible in the background of this photograph.**

Balloon Fenders

On the night of 24 January 1918 FE2b A852 of 100 Squadron ran into the cable of a balloon whilst returning from a night bombing raid on Trier railway station and, although the crew survived the resulting crash the aeroplane was totally wrecked. This was not the first such incident, 6971 having suffered a similar fate on 16 September 1916, its crew being killed, but none the less it sparked off an investigation into ways in which a further recurrence might be avoided. As a result modifications were made to FE2b B401, which had already had a long and distinguished career both on active service where it participated in the destruction of the Zeppelin L48, and as a test vehicle both at Farnborough and Orfordness. The modifications, carried out at the Experimental Station at Orfordness, comprised a spar fixed to the underside of its nacelle, projecting forward like the bowsprit of a sailing ship, from the front of

Opposite: **A dual camera with different focal length lenses for oblique photography was fitted in this 11 Sqn machine, 4993, making the observer's cockpit very cramped. The pilot appears to have a fixed Lewis gun, attached to the upper longeron of the nacelle by a stay-rod, but documentation exists which suggests that it may in fact have been a sighting device, adapted from a stripped-down Lewis.**

which a wire ran back past each wing tip, where additional struts had been fixed to receive it, and hold it clear of the machine. The idea was that should the aeroplane then strike a balloon cable it would be fended off by the wire with which it would then remain in contact, sliding along until it was deflected clear of the wing tip.

A brave test pilot, Roderic Hill, then deliberately flew into the cable of a balloon which had been deployed specifically for that purpose to test the effectiveness of the device. The shock of the impact was greater than had been anticipated and slewed the aeroplane around causing it to fall into a spin, from which Hill was fortunately able to recover, and on landing it was discovered that the wing tips had been damaged.

The test was rightly judged to have been a failure, the angle of the wire, from nose to wing tip being insufficiently acute to

achieve the desired effect and, as it was not practicable to fit a spar of sufficient length for the necessary angle, the trials were discontinued. B401 was repaired and, the apparatus removed, it continued to serve as a test vehicle for various armament experiments until the summer of 1918, though nothing so spectacular was ever asked of it again.

... but one unofficial experiment!

75

Marine Operations and the FE2b

It is sometimes difficult, at this distance in time, to realise the industrial importance of North East England to the war effort. Coal from the Durham and Northumberland coalfields was shipped to the south-east for factories and homes. That same fuel formed a basis of the iron and steel industry of the region which, in turn, led to the growth of its engineering, armament and shipbuilding industries. Sunderland, at the time, was launching a higher tonnage of ships than any other town or city in the world and the Armstrong Whitworth shipbuilding and armaments concern, based in and around Newcastle, was a world leader. Such industrial importance made the region a prime target for German attack which had initially been from surface vessel bombardment and then from airships.

Both of these threats had diminished by the time 36 (HD) Squadron began, in June 1917, to receive FE2bs as replacements for its, virtually, obsolescent BE2es and BE12s. That re-equipment took place shortly after Germany had introduced a policy of unrestricted submarine warfare.

The North East war channel was an obvious target, with large numbers of vessels, mainly merchantmen, plying its waters on a daily basis. The sole RNAS operational presence was the seaplane depot and repair base at South Shields, which operated a war flight that comprised a handful of Short 184s and Sopwith Babys. The radius of its patrols was extended with the opening of a sub-station in the Tees estuary but a suggested plan to open a flying boat base on Holy Island was not realised. A detachment

of HP O/100s operated temporarily from Redcar for a month from October 1917, met with some success and demonstrated the greater efficiency of land based machines for Marine Operations. The Handley-Pages were withdrawn for use in France and, although further such detachments were proposed, were not replaced. There was the future prospect of the Blackburn Kangaroo entering service but, by January 1918, the prototype, B9970, was still with the Experimental Station at Martlesham Heath. Disposition lists for naval aeroplanes and seaplanes, for that month, show B9970 on the books of RNAS Redcar. There is no evidence of it actually serving there but it would have been an ideal choice of station to assess its potential in the Marine Operations role.

The Martlesham trials had highlighted

FE2b A5542 was with 36 HDS C Flt by 24 September 1917 when 2Lt R.J. Paull and 2Lt G.H. Box flew it on a Home Defence sortie. It was still with the Seaton Carew flight during the following spring and took part in three attacks on enemy submarines, being force-landed on the last of those, on 19 June. It is shown here during a visit to Catterick.

A pair of Ashington-based FE2bs are shown with visiting F1 Camel B6261 that belonged to 73 TS.

several shortcomings in the Kangaroo's design and it would be four months before production machines were ready. An interim measure was needed and a War Office meeting, in January, produced the agreement that two flights of 36 Squadron would be placed at the disposal of the Admiralty, for Marine Operations duties, from March. The time delay is likely to have been necessary to allow for the provision of munitions and the supply and fitting of bomb carriers to the aircraft.

1917 had been an operationally inactive year for the unit, with some standing patrols flown but a large proportion of its efforts devoted to the training of night flying crews. The squadron's A Flight, at Hylton, was already tasked with the further role of co-operation with coastal defence batteries and so B Flight at Ashington and C Flight at Seaton Carew were designated to take on the new role.

A history of 36 Squadron was compiled after the Armistice and it claimed that the unit's FE2bs had been responsible for the sinking of six enemy submarines. Official assessments of the attacks, carried out at the time, concluded that two resulted in

possible slight damage while the others were unclassified, i.e. no damage caused.

A5542, crewed by Lts MacDonald and McMillan, had the distinction of making the squadron's first attack on a U-boat, on 26 April. They had sighted the vessel, at 12.14 when two miles south east of Seaham, in the process of sinking a merchantman. The FE2b descended to drop a single bomb, and its explosion was followed by a small quantity of oil rising to the surface. The attack was judged to have had no damaging effect.

8 May saw Seaton Carew based machines make two further attacks. Lt Ainscon in A5542 dropped a bomb on a submarine which he found 15 miles east of Redcar at 19.05. Patches of oil again rose to the surface, as also happened when Lt E.J. Penny and Lt Bell had earlier, at 13.20 in A6586, also dropped a single bomb on a U-boat that was four miles east of Seaham. Penny, in his unpublished memoirs, claimed that the vessel was destroyed.

The aeroplane attack had been followed up by depth charges from a drifter but no official claim was made. It is likely that pilots were under the impression that rising

oil, and air, indicated serious damage.

U-boat construction comprised a cylindrical pressure hull encased in a keeled outer shell, with air and oil tanks sandwiched between the two. A single ruptured tank, or connecting pipe, could release quantities of oil or air but did not mean serious damage had been done.

The Ashington based flight finally made contact with the enemy that day. Lt Taylor was patrolling in A5684, one of B Flight's single-seater conversions, and attacked a submarine, at 13.35, that was 13 miles south east of Seaham. His single bomb was dropped to no effect.

The 160hp Beardmore engine of the FE2b was never noted for its reliability and there was the real possibility of pilots having to make forced landings at sea when engaged on Marine Operations duty. Such a possibility became a reality on 25 May, when A5561 came down in the water, five miles north of the Tyne, after engine failure. Its crew were picked up almost immediately but the machine could not be taken in tow and sank.

Efforts were already being made to alleviate the dangers of ditching.

Five FE2bs of 36 Squadron's B Flight lined up at Ashington during early 1918.
The station's machines and those at Seaton Carew were detailed for Marine Operations.

A6536 had been delivered to the Grain experimental station by 25 May, probably from 36 Squadron, and was fitted with floatation gear, which was successfully tested five days later.

Both FE2b attacks deemed to have caused damage to enemy submarines were made on 31 May. Lts Riley and de Escolet, from Ashington, were patrolling the north Northumberland coast, in A5738, where they found and attacked an enemy submarine five miles off Beadnell. Two bombs were dropped, one seeming to explode on the edge of the vessel's conning tower. Possible slight damage was the official classification, as it was for the earlier attack by A6535 from Seaton Carew.

That FE2b was piloted by Lt Beal, who, at 09.18, dropped two 100lb bombs on a submarine found five miles east of Seaham. Oil and bubbles had again risen to the surface and the destroyer HMS *Locust* was on hand to follow up the attack with depth charges, but it was later revealed that the submarine, UC49, was only damaged. The repeated references to Seaham are a reflection of that port's importance to the shipping of coal. Its artificial harbour, built by the Londonderry family, was a major outlet for shipments, via colliers, for coal from the East Durham coalfield to South-East England.

The final attack on a U-boat by a 36 Squadron FE2b was made at 06.40 on 19 June. Lt Toyne of C Flight from Seaton Carew, with AM Taplin as observer, was on convoy patrol in A5542 when he identified an enemy submarine off the coast a mile to the south of Seaham. Two bombs were dropped and, with only bubbles of air and a small patch of oil left on the surface, no claim was allowed.

A5542 did not make it back to base. The Beardmore engine gave trouble on the short southward journey and Toyne was obliged to land. He was probably making for the Easington landing ground when the FE2b came down at Littlethorpe, on the lower ground a half-mile to the east of that prepared site. Toyne and Taplin's effort was the sixth and last by 36 Squadron and it seems likely that the squadron historian mistook all attacks for destructions.

Patrolling continued, as replacement units built up to operational readiness. The final event of note in 36 Squadron's, and the FE2b's, brief flirtation with coastal patrol occurred on 7 June, when A6589 came down in the sea. Its crew, Capt Stanley and Lt Lock were rescued and, although taken in tow, the FE2b sank.

Meanwhile, at Grain, A6536 was continuing in experiments to alleviate the dangers of ditching. A hydrovane was then fitted and tested successfully on

A5684 was with 36 HDS B Flt Ashington as single-seat conversion by 14 October 1917, when it was flown by Lt J.H. Matthews. It too was still operational in 1918 and was involved in an unsuccessful attack on a U-boat on 6 May.

29 June. The FE2b was then dispatched, early in July, to 36 Squadron but crashed en-route and returned to Grain for repair. The experimental station's efforts were, by then, too late. 495 Flt had formed at Seaton Carew, initially within 252 Squadron, with Blackburn Kangaroos and had built up to its intended establishment of eight machines. 252 Squadron had also formed four DH6 Flights at Tynemouth, Redcar and Seaton Carew, with 256 Squadron doing likewise at Ashington, New Haggerston and Seahouses. The FE2bs were withdrawn from Marine Operations, the timing of this coinciding with their replacement by more suitable machines, Bristol Fighters and Sopwith Pups, for Home Defences duty. Although a few examples lingered on until August, the FE2b had all but ended its year plus of service in the North-East.

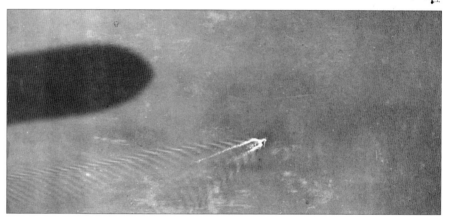

Above: **Tracking a U-boat periscope.** *Below*: **Depth charge exploding in the North Sea.**

The FE2b in Australia

*I*nformation pointing to the probability of an enemy seaplane carrier with one or more seaplanes operating the South Gippsland coast was given me at 7p.m. on 19th April and at midnight of the same date I received orders to proceed by air and establish a station either at Toura or Alberton.

... wrote Capt F.H. McNamara, VC, CBE as he commenced his Report as the O.C. Air Reconnaissance, South Gippsland. McNamara had won his VC in the Middle East flying with No 1 Squadron, AFC. He was sent home and was on the Aviation Instructional staff at Point Cook, Victoria. He selected the sole FE2b biplane of the Central Flying School (CFS) as the aircraft for the task.[1]

In fact, the FE2b was the only aircraft in Australia at the time that could be called a warplane. It came to Australia via the gift of £2,250 for the purchase of a 'Battleplane' by Alfred M. Simpson, Young House, Parkside, South Australia. Simpson offered to provide £2,250 for the purchase of a 100hp Gnome powered Gun Biplane that would be accepted by the Australian military authorities. Lt Col E.H. Reynolds recommended that the machine be sent to the CFS as the School did not have a modern fighting aeroplane. Simpson was advised that as the complete equipping of No.1 Squadron, AFC was being provided by the Home Government, the military authorities preferred that his gift be brought to Australia to provide for the training of future pilots in a modern fighting aeroplane.

On 25 May 1916, the War Office wrote to the Australian High Commissioner that a

... 120H.P. Beardmore-Engined Gun Aeroplane (Type FE2B) together with Gun and proportionate spare parts for the Machine Engine, and Gun, can be supplied by this Department for the Military Forces in Australia on payment of the following rates:-

FE2b Aeroplane	*£1,160*
120 H.P. Beardmore Aero Engine	*970*
Aeroplane mix spare parts	*710*
Engine	*160*
Lewis Gun complete with spare Parts	*175*
	£3,1752

The extra funding for the aircraft was to be met by the government and Victorian Order No 1073 was raised to cover the purchase of the machine and signed on 5 July 1916.

On 24 August 1916, External Affairs wrote to Defence that as to Victorian Order 1073, they regretted that urgent requirements prohibited the issuing of the FE machine until 15 September.[3]

'Portions of this machine' arrived at the CFS 'during the months of November and December 1916,' and 'the remaining parts arrived about two months later.'[4] The FE2b was recorded as having arrived and had been erected at the CFS, Point Cook, although the engine, gun and bombs were not yet to hand.[5] This machine was A778, the first FE2b of a batch of 100 built by G. & J. Weir of Cathcart. On 27 July it was officially recorded by the CO of the CFS as having just flown.[6]

It was flown by McNamara for the first time on 12 July 1917, after which Major Eric Harrison suggested that Mr Simpson be asked to come to the CFS to see the machine flying. Unfortunately, however, Mr Simpson died on 28 September. His son suggested that the inscription to be painted on the machine be 'Presented by Alfred Muller Simpson, Parkside, SA, 1916'.[7] This was painted in 6in high white lettering on the front of the nacelle. A778 was given the CFS serial CFS-14 which was carried in addition to its British serial.

The cruise of the German raider SMS

FE2b A778/CFS-14 at Yarram with the Presentation inscription on the nacelle.

CFS-14 nearing completion: the gun mounting has not yet been fitted.

WOLF was largely unknown during the war, but strange lights and activities were regularly reported and increased once war was declared. It was thought that there was the possibility that one to four German raiders may have been operating in Australian waters and the Navy and Army were asked to search for these ships, hence McNamara's orders. Lt R.F. Galloway, another instructor at the CFS, was also ordered to take an aircraft to Twofold Bay, NSW, to carry out searches from that area.

McNamara wrote that he left Laverton in the FE2b, accompanied by WO S.J. Hendy as gunner for the Lewis Gun in the front cockpit, at 15.00 on 20 April 1918. The rest of the 11-man ground party, together with naval wireless ratings, left Melbourne by train that morning. McNamara did not reach Toura until dusk due to strong easterly winds over Mornington. As he considered the landing grounds poor, he flew onto Alberton and landed there at 18.37. As the grounds here also proved unsuitable he moved to Yarram the next day where they were much better, and because petrol was available from a local garage.

The field selected for the landing ground proved to have a four foot fence and a deep drain running parallel to the fence across the whole field. This drain had an 18in bank and was hidden by weeds. On the 23rd

... when landing on return from reconnaissance the under carriage struck this bank and I crashed. The crash was not a very serious one, but owing to the fact that no spare landing chassis was available, steel tubing had to be obtained from Melbourne and a new one made up at Yarram. On 30.4.18 the machine was again serviceable and patrols were resumed.

Problems with the engine began to manifest themselves. A crack in the crankcase *which had been there for some months* appeared to be becoming worse. Then one of the bolts holding down No.6 cylinder broke. *This necessitated practically the dismantling of the engine to get the bolt.* A new bolt was made up and on the afternoon of 10 May, the machine was test flown. After only 15 minutes the radiator developed a leak. A new radiator was fitted and he left for Laverton on 11th. This radiator developed a leak and he was forced to land at Powlett River. He resumed the journey at 14.25 on 12th. Rain storms were met the whole journey back. *It took 3 hours 35 minutes to cover this distance (72 miles) and it was dark while I was halfway across the bay.*

For the period from 21 April to 10 May 1918, eight reconnaissance patrols and three movement flights were made. During its time at Yarram the aircraft was subject to considerable exposure from rain and dew and McNamara recommended that several portable RAF hangars be obtained for *future movements of a detachment.*[8]

Albert Newberry was about seven when McNamara arrived at Yarram. The aeroplane was the first he had seen and of course created much interest in the area. One day when the family was sitting at their midday meal there was a knock at the door and to his delight it was some men in uniform. The observer in the plane had observed something strange in the backyard and they had been sent to investigate. *The strange object was a rotary clothes line. Rotary clothes lines were rare in those days. Dad had this one specially made; and to the men in the air, it was a mysterious looking affair.* After Albert's mother demonstrated the line, the men

Ground crew including Naval personnel recovering CFS-14 after the landing accident which destroyed the undercarriage.

left the family to resume their meal.[9] This amusing incident spotlights the paranoia that the war had caused with people seeing mysterious lights, ships, and spies.

The Commonwealth Government was desirous of constructing aircraft in Australia to overcome the problems with supply from the UK. An Aeroplane Construction Committee was set up in 1918 to examine the feasibility of the proposal. A Mr Harry Wilson, a well known consulting Engineer, was engaged to ascertain the capabilities of various engineering firms as to whether they could manufacture aircraft components. *Drawings and components of the FE2b, the machine selected as a guide only* were supplied to the firms and their responses recorded for the Committee.[10]

On 24 July the Committee wrote to the CGS asking for the use of *certain metal components of the FE2B (Fighter) on charge to the* CFS. It was understood from the Commanding Officer of the CFS that the some of the required parts were not carried as spares and would be required to be removed from the machine and *thus prevent its re-assembling, but the Fighter is not a flying instructional machine, and this will not entail any handicap to the work of the school.*[11]

This was the whole problem with the use of the FE2b in Australia. The CFS only taught pupils elementary flying to eliminate those who had no aptitude for flying. Then the pupils would go to the UK to finish their training. There were few pilots at the CFS who had the experience to fly the FE2b.

The machine was reassembled for the display of aircraft held at the Exhibition Building in Melbourne between 19 June and 2 July 1920. This exhibition included AAC aircraft and the AFC and German aircraft returned from Europe. Only two of the German aircraft survived until today, the Albatros D.Va and Pfalz D.XII now in the Australia War Memorial's collection.

After the war the FE and other aircraft were surplus to the New Australian Air Corps requirements. Avro 504K trainers and Sopwith Pups had been obtained from the UK and the Imperial Gift of aircraft was in the offing. Much of this equipment was put up for sale. There were a number of offers to purchase the FE2b. Capt R.D. McKenzie offered £500 on 27 May 1920, and an offer of £650 was made for the aircraft, Beardmore engine and spares on 29 October.

CFS Routine Orders No.84 of 12 November 1920 states that the FE2b fitted with 120hp Beardmore engine WD1242, MN172, had been sold and struck off the strength of the CFS.[12] A 120hp Beardmore had been received at the CFS on 17 November 1916, together with an 80hp

Capt McNamara VC running up CFS-14 at Yarram to search for the suspected German raider.

Wolseley Renault, *forwarded as gifts by the War Office for instructional purposes.*[13] This engine may have been installed after the reconnaissance flights from Yarram given the description of the engine problems in McNamara's report. The purchaser of the FE2b was not recorded, however Aviation Ltd of Glenroy, Victoria, purchased an aircraft and spares around November 1920. The firm purchased an FE2 aileron from the Department on 22 November 1920.[14]

Aircraft for 15 January 1921 reported that amongst the aircraft entered for the Aerial Derby that was flown on Boxing Day at Epsom racecourse, Victoria, were an FE2b entered by Mrs Yule and F.H. Huxley, and another FE2b entered by Aviation Ltd and flown by Capt H.A. Rigby. Rigby won the Derby in a 120hp FE2b. Thus by this time there were at least two FE2 biplanes in Australia.[15]

A778/CFS-14 stripped down for the Aeroplane Construction Committee.

The 120hp FE2b, which must have been ex-CFS-14 never made the civil register. In his long running article *Civil Aircraft in Australia 1919-21*, the editor of *Aircraft* lists an FE2b amongst the 45 casualties that never made the transition from the 1918-1920 period to the new Civil Aviation Branch period of Australian aviation. What the fate of the aircraft was, is not recorded.

Huxley took the FE2b to Tasmania on 4 January 1921. The machine was damaged in a gale on the 26th with the result that one wing, the tailplane and the centre section were affected. Huxley obtained the spares from Aviation Ltd in Melbourne.

On 26 March, he had another mishap that rendered him unconscious for a day. The biplane nose-dived into the ground throwing all three occupants out of the machine. Damage was repaired by the 22 April when he flew the aircraft over Hobart. Aviation Ltd had not received the spares from the Defence Department as it had not paid the amount of the contract, so it seems probable that parts of CFS-14 were used to repair Huxley's machine, given the short time it took to return it to the air.[16]

Huxley made a flight from Stanley in Tasmania to Melbourne in his FE2b. The newspaper announcement of this successful flight also recorded that he had sold the FE2b to Ray Parer who announced he would use it to fly around Australia.[17]

On 2 August 1921, R.J.P. Parer of Crystal Café, Bourke St, Melbourne, received a Certificate of Airworthiness No 28 for FE2b G-AUCX. The letter notes that *...I am directed to draw your attention to the total allowable load... will not permit of the **extra** twenty gallons of petrol being carried at the same time as a Pilot and two passengers.*[18]

G-AUCX was fitted with a 160hp Beardmore.[19] Ray Parer operated Geelong Air Services.

Parer operated close to the limits of

A778 as CFS-14 at Yarram during the search for the German sea raider.

financial collapse for most of his career and the FE2b was no exception. Rupert U. Hoddinott recalls:

... Ray Parer had just arrived and was giving joy rides with his FE plane. I noticed that his engine was giving off clouds of black smoke when he took off and mentioned to him that his engine needed adjustment. I came back that afternoon and seeing that the engine sounded normal, I asked the mechanic what fault had been found. 'Oh', said the mechanic, 'we found that she wasn't pulling too well at Ouyen so we reamed out the jet, but just now we found two splits in the induction pipe had caused the trouble. We bound them up with insulating tape and she is good again.'

Shortly before, Parer had been hurt when swinging the prop of the FE and had tied it up to a fence for a few weeks while he recovered. The gaping seams of the nacelle were evidence of this, but since the induction pipe had been bound up the plane appeared to operate well and safely.[20]

Parer had a crash at Boulder on 7 February 1922 and wrote off G-AUCX.

After to and fro correspondence with the Department, Parer wrote that preparatory to leaving Boulder for Southern Cross, he ran up the engine, and when warm and on leaving the ground the engine

... failed as we were lifting over the end of the racecourse. It sounded like a carburettor was starving.

Realizing a crash was inevitable I avoided a locality of houses and took the force of the crash on my right wing against a telegraph pole.

The machine first hit the wires and fortunately slid along them about 30 feet

when they broke owing to the increasing weight of the machine caused by the slackened speed. The pole was hit and broken.

My cousin and self sustained bruises and abrasions and nerve shock.[21]

On 17 February 1922, the department wrote to Parer at the Government Hospital, Boulder, asking for the return of the Certificate of Registration for G-AUCX owing to the machine *having been wrecked*, so ending the story of the FE2b in Australia.[22]

Note AA = Australian National Archives at either Canberra, ACT or Melbourne, Victoria.

1 For details of McNamara's wartime achievements and his post-war problems see Chris Coulthard-Clark's *McNamara, VC: A Hero's Dilemma*, Air Power Studies Centre, ACT, 1997.

2 AA Melb CRS MP367 File 524/10/25.

3 AA ACT CRS A2023/1 File A38/3/401 *Shipment of 100 h.p. Gnome Gun Biplane.*

4 Report *Central Flying School – Laverton, Financial Year 1916-17.* AA MP 367/1 File 600/4/15.

5 PM to Premier of SA, 21 March 17. AA ACT CRS A2/1 File 17/3712, Aeroplanes, Gifts of.

6 Defence Minister to PM, 27 July 17. AA ACT CRS A2/1 File A38/3/694.

7 AA Melb CRS MP367. File 524/10/25. Letter of 17 October 17.

8 AAA B187 Defence Secret and Confidential Correspondence Files Multiple Number Series 1906-1935. File 2021/1/168/ *Report on Air Reconnaissance, South Gippsland.* 7.06.18.

9 Letter to Fred Morton from AH Newberry, 18 September 79. Copy in J Hopton's archives.

10 AA ACT CRS A2180 File 1821/1/6. Construction of Aircraft in Australia 1918: Aeroplane Construction *Committee – Correspondence & General File.* Copy letter dated 03 July 18.

11 AA ACT CRS A2180 File 1821/1/6. Construction of Aircraft in Australia 1918: Aeroplane Construction Committee – Correspondence & General File. Letter: Aeroplane Construction Committee to CGS, 24 July 18.

12 Copy in RAAF Museum, Point Cook, Victoria.

13 Report *Central Flying School – Laverton, Financial Year 1916-17.* AA MP 367/1 File 600/4/15.

14 Air Board Agenda No.45, 24 March 21.

15 A photograph showing two FE2b biplanes amongst a line-up at Glenroy aerodrome in November 1920, appears on P.34 of Parnell, N. and Boughton, T. *Flypast: A Record of Aviation in Australia*, AGPS, Canberra, 1988.

16 The matter was not settled until 17 January 1923, with the Liquidator of Aviation Ltd.

17 'From Tasmania to Melbourne', *Sydney Morning Herald*, 22 July 1921.

18 AA CRS A705 File 35/6/273. Secretary, Air Council to PJP Parer. 02 August 21.

19 *Aircraft*, 20 September 1921.

20 Hoddinott, RY: *Years that have flown*, autobiographical manuscript. Copy in AWM MSS0791. Hoddinott served in the Royal Australian Engineers pre-war and trained as a gunner in the RFC in 1917. Worked post-war in the Department of Civil Aviation and its predecessors. Served in WWII as CO Works & Building Branch RAAF in Port Moresby.

21 AA A705 Dept of Air Correspondence files, multiple number (Melbourne) series. 1922-1960. File 38/1/133. The Dept were apparently acting due to adverse newspaper comments by Capt Larkin.

22 Air Council to RJP Parer, 17 Feb 22. AA CRS A705 File 35/10/42.

G-AUCX, the second FE2b in Australia, seen at Tarcoola in South Australia during a fund-raising flight. Ray Parer is standing in the pilot's cockpit, and passenger Hazel Abernethy (later Higgs) is in the front with Mark Parer, Ray's cousin.

Airframe Development, FE2a – FE2h

A crew with excess baggage prepare to leave Farnborough for France in FE2d A2 in June 1916. This early production aircraft has the Beardmore radiator but retains the original tricycle undercarriage and three spigots for mounting a Lewis gun around the rim of the observer's cockpit. A2 went on to serve with 20 Squadron but was wrecked on 2 July 1916.

The Royal Aircraft Factory's two most enduring designs, the BE2 and the FE2 series, changed little over the course of the war. Once the basic geometry had been established, any changes introduced in sub-variants were in design detail.

With the FEs, the mainplane and tailplane sizes and shapes, the span of the centre section, the tail-boom arrangement, the rudder and the nacelle wooden box girder were basically identical in each variant.

FE2a No.1

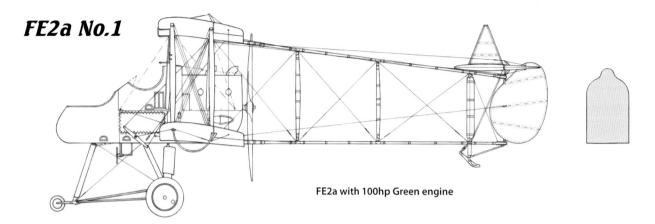

FE2a with 100hp Green engine

The first FE2a, with the 100hp Green engine, had a shallower pilot's cockpit than those that followed and had a small radiator, mounted on the upper longerons of the nacelle. The aluminium decking that enclosed the radiator was contoured at its top, to provide the basis of a pilot's headrest, and had small, high-mounted doors that could open to allow airflow to the radiator itself. The engine was intended to be fully cowled but the top section of the cowling (which appeared on Factory drawings of the type) is absent in all known photographs. Its intended shape is indicated on the drawing.

Fuel supply was provided by an internal tank, L-shaped in side view, to follow the contours of the forward part of the crankcase. The fuel pump must have been internal.

The centre-section airbrake, which appeared on all but one of the FE2as, was actuated by cables connected to a hand-wheel, located on the starboard side of the pilot's cockpit and exited the nacelle adjacent to the elevator control horns. The duplicated rudder cables ran, via pulleys at the pilot's seat, to exit the fuselage just ahead of the line of the wing leading edges and thence to further pulleys on the rear lower tailbooms before continuing aft on the outside of the tail-boom assembly. Aileron cables were led, via pulleys, to the hollow interior of the elevator rocker shaft and exited the ends of that shaft to pulleys under the lower mainplanes and thence to the control horns on the lower mainplanes. Cables connected the lower and upper ailerons, which were of single action. The upper aileron control horns were attached to elasticated cord that was secured to the front spar. Control horns on the ends of the elevator shaft secured cables that led first to pulleys inboard on the underside of the centre-section rear spar, then to other pulleys at the outboard lower edges of that spar and on, again outside the tail-boom assembly, to the elevator control horns.

The port and starboard tail boom structures were cross-braced in the second and third bays with lateral struts, top and bottom, at the rear of those bays. There was no cross-bracing in the first bay, because of the propeller, and the only lateral bracing was a cable that connected the tops of the struts at the rear of that bay. The lack of a lower cable was due to the need for working space when removing/installing the engine. The complete tail-boom structure was braced to the wing cellule by drift wires that ran from the top booms, at the rear of their first bay, to the top of the rear upper mainplane spars at the connection points for

the inner struts. Factory drawings show that anti-splinter rings were intended only at points flanking the strut attachments but a further pair was fitted, equally spaced, in each bay. The tail skid, mounted on the rear lower cross strut of the booms, was non-steerable.

Drift wires braced the nacelle to the wing cellules. Duplicated cables led from the front undercarriage strut pick-up points on the lower longerons to the tops of the rear outer centre-section struts. Another set ran from the upper longerons, at the rear of the observer's cockpit, to the base of the outer rear centre-section struts. Others were intended, as shown on RAF drawings, but apparently not fitted. Their locations are indicated on the drawing above by broken lines.

In addition to the typical bracing between the struts of the mainplanes and centre section, there was a supplementary flying wire that ran from the lower front inboard mainplane strut to the front spar of the upper mainplane, at a point approximately central between the inner and outer struts. The lower mainplanes were fitted with semi-circular cane skids, mounted at the line of the outer struts.

The outer faces of the airbrake followed the angle of taper set by the tail-booms and the surface itself was of slightly less chord than that from the mainplane rear spar to the trailing edge. The lower centre section had a straight trailing edge and was of the same chord as the upper one (with airbrake). The reduced chord was a consequence of the need for propeller clearance.

Armament was intended to be a Lewis gun, carried on a swivelling, cranked pillar that was bolted to the centre of the floor in the observer's cockpit.

Access to the cockpits was provided by a braced footstep hung from the port lower longeron and reinforced footholes cut in the fabric of the nacelle's port side.

The tricycle oleo undercarriage gave a total length of 32ft 3in. That length has been previously quoted for the subsequent sub-variants but it should be noted that it only applied if the tricycle undercarriage was fitted.

The introduction of the 120hp Austro-Daimler necessitated the use of a larger radiator and this led to a revision of its cowling shape and section. The cowling was not extended to cover the engine and terminated with a vertical rear edge.

The engine itself, which was later developed into the 120hp Beardmore, can be distinguished from the latter, which had its

Later FE2a

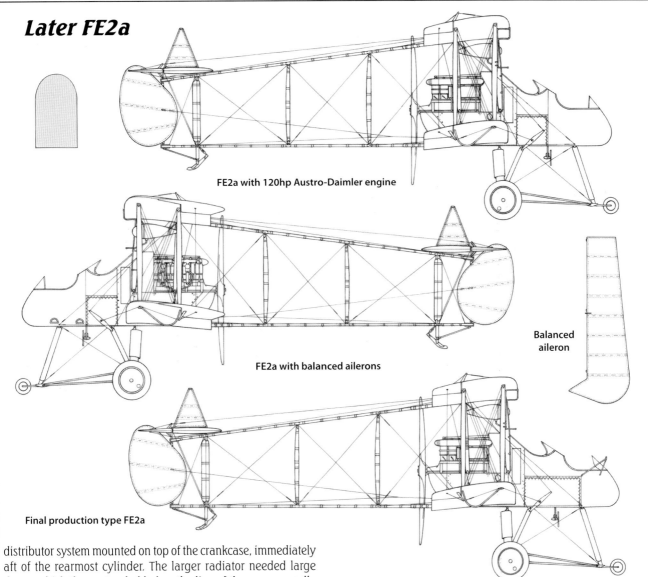

FE2a with 120hp Austro-Daimler engine

FE2a with balanced ailerons

Balanced aileron

Final production type FE2a

distributor system mounted on top of the crankcase, immediately aft of the rearmost cylinder. The larger radiator needed large doors, which then extended below the line of the upper nacelle longerons. The introduction of those doors meant that the aluminium panelling of nacelle sides and radiator cowling was extended forward to a point ahead of the wing leading edges.

The thirstier 120hp engine was longer than the Green and necessitated a revision to the fuel system. A cylindrical main tank was carried on the floor of the nacelle, under the engine and a tear-drop shaped gravity tank, of circular cross section, was carried under the centre-section, to port of the centre line. A cuboid oil tank was mounted to starboard of the cylinders.

Although the nacelle framework was unchanged, the length of the nacelle was extended by lengthening the curved aluminium bowl which formed its rear end. That lengthening was also due to the greater size of the Austro-Daimler. There were differing styles of nose fairing, that on earlier machines extending further aft, affecting the extent to which the nacelle sides were fabric covered. A propeller-driven fuel pump, for the main tank, was mounted under the nacelle.

The elevator control run was re-designed. The cables from the rocker shaft control horns led through apertures in the centre-section to pulleys that were carried inboard on the upper surface of the rear centre-section spar and then directly to the elevator control horns, passing perilously close to the airscrew arc.

Perhaps in an effort to increase purchase, the airbrake cables were re-routed, running rearward through the nacelle and exiting below the rear centre-section strut.

The rudder cable run was also changed, with the internal pulleys moved to the rear of the pilot's seat. The cables then exited the fuselage at points on line with, and just above, the leading edges of the lower centre section.

The number of anti-splinter rings on the tailbooms, was increased. The position of the pitot head was changed to the inner front starboard mainplane strut on most of the later machines, the gravity tank fuel line taking up the run down the front port centre-section strut.

There was also a revision of the nacelle to wing cellule drift wires. That from the lower longeron was retained but the upper one was dispensed with. Instead, a second drift wire was led from the front undercarriage strut pick-up point to the underside of the lower centre-section spar below the outer strut. The shape of the wingtip skids was changed to an asymmetrical one.

Windscreens were designed and fitted; the observer's being of differing shape between early and late production machines. The Lewis gun mounting changed to the No.2 Mk.1 rail type mounting, which gave the observer greater room for manoeuvre in his cockpit but reduced the gun's field of fire. Its operation must have been hampered by the windscreen.

The airbrake was dispensed with on the 11th FE2a and the new, one-piece centre-section was of the same chord as the lower one. That machine was also fitted with an experimental V undercarriage.

Balanced, inversely-tapered ailerons were tested on three FE2as and found to have no significant improvement on control. Their fitting increased the span from 47ft 9in to 50ft 1in.

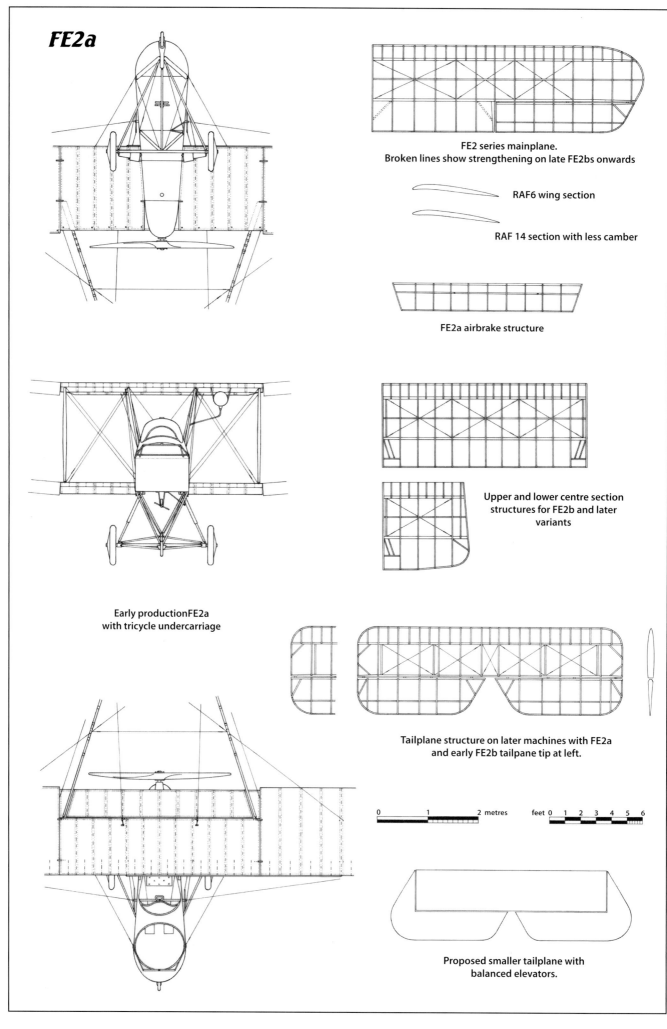

FE2a

FE2 series mainplane.
Broken lines show strengthening on late FE2bs onwards

RAF6 wing section

RAF 14 section with less camber

FE2a airbrake structure

Upper and lower centre section
structures for FE2b and later
variants

Early productionFE2a
with tricycle undercarriage

Tailplane structure on later machines with FE2a
and early FE2b tailpane tip at left.

0   1   2 metres   feet 0 1 2 3 4 5 6

Proposed smaller tailplane with
balanced elevators.

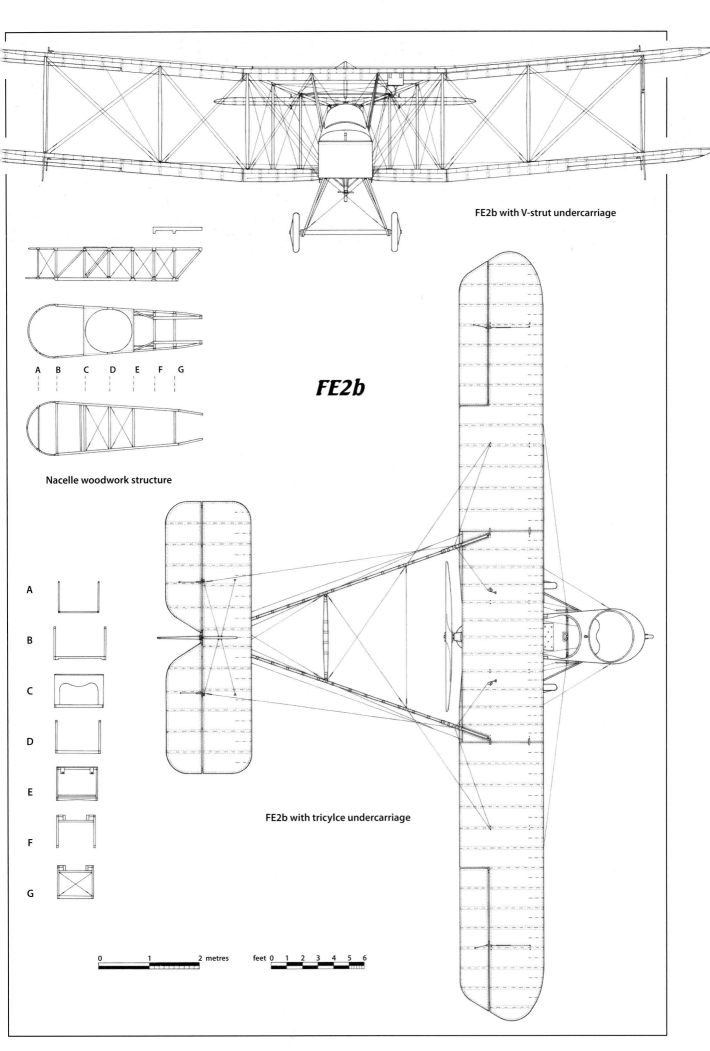

FE2b with V-strut undercarriage

Nacelle woodwork structure

A B C D E F G

FE2b

A

B

C

D

E

F

G

FE2b with tricylce undercarriage

0   1   2 metres

feet 0   1   2   3   4   5   6

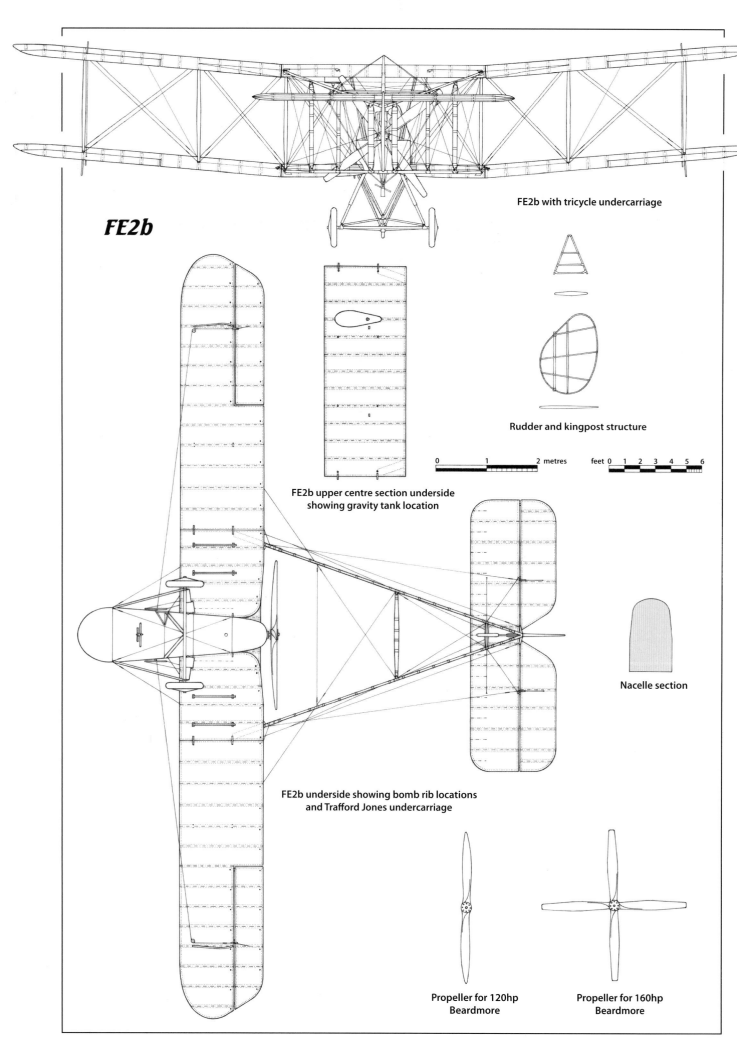

FE2b

FE2b with tricycle undercarriage

Rudder and kingpost structure

0   1   2 metres   feet 0 1 2 3 4 5 6

FE2b upper centre section underside
showing gravity tank location

Nacelle section

FE2b underside showing bomb rib locations
and Trafford Jones undercarriage

Propeller for 120hp
Beardmore

Propeller for 160hp
Beardmore

FE2b

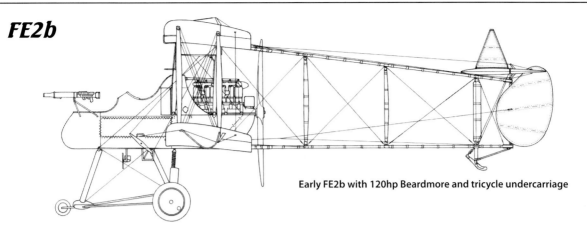

Early FE2b with 120hp Beardmore and tricycle undercarriage

Although the FE2b was essentially an FE2a with a Beardmore engine replacing the Austro-Daimler, there were subtle design changes from the outset of production and others made in light of operational experience.

The FE2b incorporated the one-piece upper centre-section used on FE2a No.11 but the trailing edges of the lower centre-section stub wings were radically altered. Outboard, the chord was that of the mainplanes for two rib spaces but then tapered to reduce the chord before being rounded to meet the sides of the nacelle. This was probably to give clearance for mechanics working on the engine, and access to the front end of the engine was catered for by the fitting of aluminium tread-plates on the lower centre-section next to the nacelle.

The radiator was still mounted mainly above the longerons and inside the cowling immediately behind the pilot. The cooling doors were totally above the longerons and, in their closed position, faired the plywood pilot's 'bathtub' to the shape of the rear cowling. A forward extension of the cowling top, forward of the radiator, served the same purpose. The rear edge of the radiator cowling swept downward in a graceful curve to the upper longerons at the rear centre section strut pick-up points.

The streamlined gravity tank of the FE2a was replaced by a slab sided one that was mounted, in the same offset position, directly to the wing lower surface.

The unsatisfactory elevator control run of the later FE2as was replaced. The pulleys above the upper rear centre section spar were re-angled to take the cables to further pulleys that were mounted on top of the front 'knuckles' of the top tail booms and thence to the elevator control horns. The tension this placed on the tail boom pulleys was countered by the addition of drift wires, from their mountings to the top of the rear upper mainplane spar, at a point above the inner strut mounting.

The rudder cable routing was, initially, the same as that for later FE2as but the aileron control run was modified. The cables led directly from the control column to the pulley under the lower mainplane, exiting the fuselage through an aperture in the fabric covering. The rudder cable pulleys were moved from the tailbooms to positions on the inboard tops of the rear lower mainplane spars (this may have also been the case with later FE2as, but there is no photographic evidence available). Rudder cables were duplicated and bound together aft of the wing-mounted pulley.

A steerable tailskid was fitted. Its cables were spliced into the rudder cables at a point just behind the wing trailing edge and connected to control horns on the top of the tailskid's pivot. The position of the splice was further forward on later machines.

The position of the footstep was moved rearward and the footholes of the FE2a were dispensed with. On later machines, a footplate was added on the upper port longeron, immediately below the pilot's cockpit.

There were two early changes to the airframe. Initial machines, including the first Weir-built batch, had elevators that were identical to those of the FE2a. These were replaced by components that incorporated an extra rib at their outer ends. Operational experience suggested that endurance was insufficient and so an extra fuel tank was installed. The new, rectangular tank replaced the pilot's seat bearers and the seat then bolted on to the new tank. This meant that the rudder control run had to be altered. The pulleys in the nacelle were repositioned ahead of the new tank and then exited the nacelle sides in a position similar to that which had been used on FE2a No.1.

1916 saw a change in the wing section, with the less cambered RAF 14 section replacing RAF 6. This coincided with a change to dual action ailerons. Pulleys replaced the attachment points for the elasticated cord return springs on the upper mainplane front spars and a balance cable, fed through guides along the spars, connected the upper aileron control horns.

The tricycle undercarriage was initially fitted and benefited from the addition of a fairing around the strut joints at the nose-wheel. The Trafford Jones undercarriage was introduced

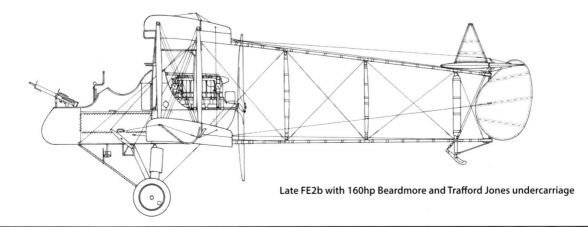

Late FE2b with 160hp Beardmore and Trafford Jones undercarriage

and reduced the overall length to 31ft 9in. There is no known photograph of the initial modification but that made with official approval incorporated a pair of stay cables that attached to the underside of the nacelle at a point on line with the wing rear spars.

The introduction of the 160hp Beardmore brought the use of a four bladed propeller; hitherto a two blade unit had been used on all FE2as and FE2bs.

The No.1 Mk.II gun mounting was initially fitted to FE2bs

The new undercarriage incorporated a pair of spreader tubes, around which a fairing was built. It was found that the 230lb weapon could strike that fairing as it was dropped, and so a small notch was created in the fairing's trailing edge to prevent this from happening. The V-strut undercarriage would have fouled the elevator control horns, so those components were given a curved shape that provided the necessary clearance.

In addition to the 230lb RL bomb, the other heavy ordnance carried was the 100lb and 112lb RL bombs. The relative sizes

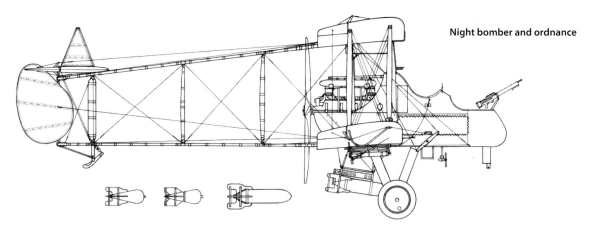

Night bomber and ordnance

but its limited field of fire resulted in the adoption of various alternatives. An Anderson Arch (a curved steel tube) was mounted inside the rear of the observer's cockpit and mounted a telescopic, swan-necked pillar for a Lewis gun, the No.10 Mk.1 mounting, enabling the observer to fire rearward, over the upper wings. The standard forward gun mounting became the No.4 Mk.I, which was a fixed pillar, attached to the steel tubing of the nacelle nose. That was replaced by the No.4 Mk.III mounting, a rocking pillar that could be slid laterally along a horizontal tube, welded to the upper steel tubing of the nacelle. The final solution was the No.4 Mk.IV mounting. This pillar mounting was carried on a universal joint that fixed to the cockpit floor. Spring clips were arranged around the rim of the cockpit to steady the pillar for firing and to stow it when not in use.

The introduction of the FE2b into night bombing brought further modifications. Greater range was provided by the adoption of a rectangular sectioned main tank to replace the original cylindrical one and provide an extra 10 gallons of petrol. Some night bombing FE2bs were given even greater range by the fitting of a second gravity tank, located centrally under the centre-section. The main external difference was the use of the V-strut undercarriage. This was introduced to permit the carrying of a 230lb bomb under the nacelle. The complicated bomb carrier for that ordnance could not be fitted with the Trafford Jones undercarriage, whose rear stay cables were in the way.

and shapes of these weapons are shown on the accompanying drawing.

The introduction of parachute flares, as an aid to night reconnaissance, required the addition of a flare chute that projected downward below the observer's cockpit. Navigation lights were fitted to the tips of the lower mainplanes and brackets for Holt's flares, used to aid landing, were carried below those surfaces, usually under the attachment point for the rear inboard mainplane strut, where the glare would not blind the pilot. Some units, notably 102 Sqn, fitted a 'light-shade' to the brackets, to further reduce glare.

The earliest FE2bs had been fitted with the same styles of windscreens as used on the FE2a but that was abandoned and most were flown either without any screen or with an Avro-type screen for the pilot. A concession to observer comfort came with the introduction of a folding canvas windscreen attached to the steel tubing of the nacelle nose.

FE2bs on HD duty were also fitted to carry navigation lights and Holt's flares and also mounted signalling lights, one below the nacelle and one on the upper centre section. Flare brackets were occasionally mounted on the lower tailbooms, either on the booms themselves or on the first horizontal cross-member. Although there were elaborate single-seat conversions on HD duty, most such conversions simply involved placing a detachable canvas fairing over the observer's cockpit.

The most elaborate FE2b conversions were those machines

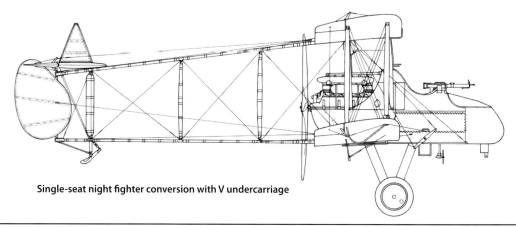

Single-seat night fighter conversion with V undercarriage

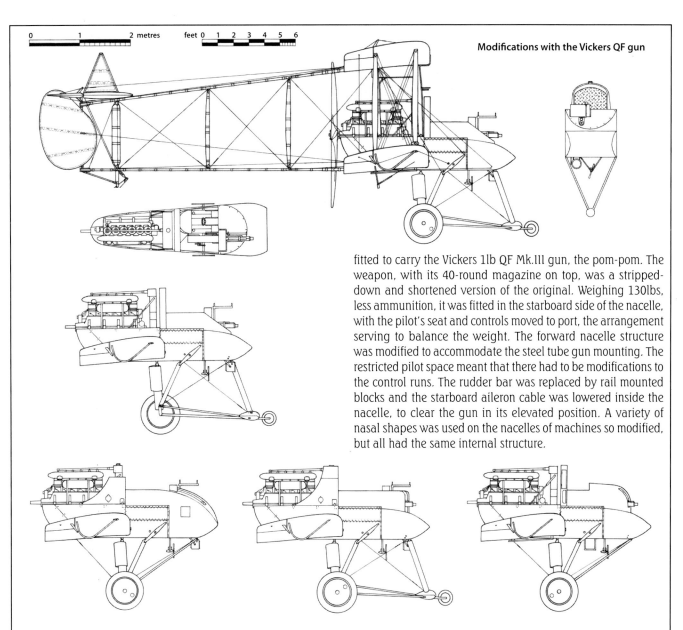

fitted to carry the Vickers 1lb QF Mk.III gun, the pom-pom. The weapon, with its 40-round magazine on top, was a stripped-down and shortened version of the original. Weighing 130lbs, less ammunition, it was fitted in the starboard side of the nacelle, with the pilot's seat and controls moved to port, the arrangement serving to balance the weight. The forward nacelle structure was modified to accommodate the steel tube gun mounting. The restricted pilot space meant that there had to be modifications to the control runs. The rudder bar was replaced by rail mounted blocks and the starboard aileron cable was lowered inside the nacelle, to clear the gun in its elevated position. A variety of nasal shapes was used on the nacelles of machines so modified, but all had the same internal structure.

The original FE2c conversion may have been made from an FE2a, but there is no evidence, either documentary or photographic, of this. The earliest known conversions were made from early, single main tank FE2bs with single action ailerons and 120hp engines, with only the nacelle front being altered. The transposition of seating, with the pilot's legroom being a prime consideration, meant that the pilot's seat was placed in line with the second vertical wooden spacer of the nacelle. The corresponding top spacer, an integral part of the plywood cockpit divider in the FE2b, would have interfered with this and so a rearward curving steel tube spacer was substituted. The elevator shaft was moved forward accordingly and, from its control horns, the cables followed the same pulley routing as used in the FE2b. The rudder bar was in the extreme nose and its cables were carried rearward in the nacelle to pulleys that were also in the FE2b position. The aileron cables, however, exited the fuselage through apertures adjacent to the elevator horns. The revised plywood nosing was slightly longer than that of the FE2b, bringing the length to 32ft, without the tricycle undercarriage. The communal cockpit had formed plywood

FE2c

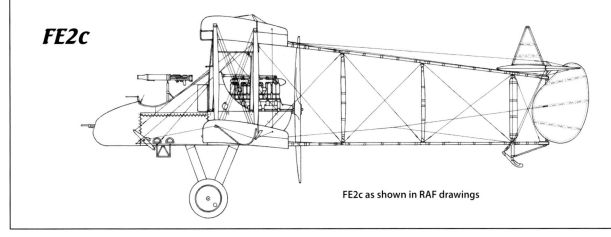

FE2c as shown in RAF drawings

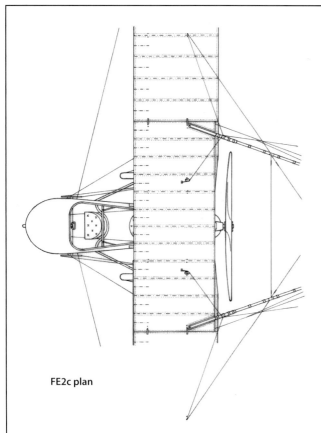

FE2c plan

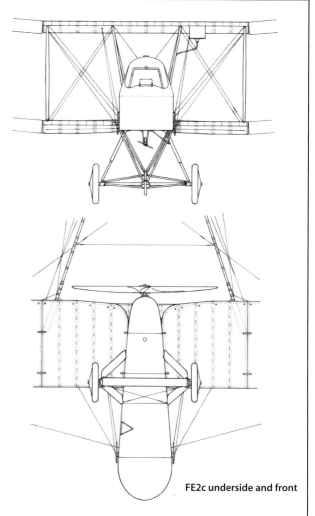

FE2c underside and front

sides that faired into the existing FE2b metal panelling around the radiator. The footstep was moved forward and reinforced foot-holes were provided in the fabric of the nacelle, one for each of the aircrew.

RAF drawing A7220, dated 10 November 1915, shows that a V-strut undercarriage was intended, one identical to that fitted to FE2a No.11. More significant was the armament arrangement, which seems to show that the Factory wanted to enhance the FE's fighting qualities. The observer, perched on a bench seat in front of the radiator, still had a Lewis gun, mounted on an angled, steel tube arch above the position of the pilot's head. A second Lewis gun was intended for pilot use and was to be mounted in the nacelle nose. The mounting arrangement was the same remote one as had been designed for the FE8, which had flown the previous month. The weapon was mounted on a linkage, connected to a sighting bar, which allowed limited movement. There is no photographic or documentary evidence of the nose armament having been fitted.

Later FE2cs had the 160hp Beardmore, dual main tanks and the revised rudder cable routing that dictated. The mounting for the observer's gun was an Anderson arch and V-strut undercarriages were fitted.

Dual Control Conversions

Despite repeated and tantalising logbook references to dual control FE2bs in use from 1917 onward, photographic and documentary evidence is scanty. The original DC conversion may have been made to FE2c 6370 at Farnborough. Drawings exist for such a conversion, dated 6 April 1916. The pilot's seat was raised slightly and a second rudder bar fitted under it. A second rocker shaft was fitted across the observer's cockpit with the aileron column pivoting on it. A detachable control column, with tapering end, fitted into the aileron column. A linkage rod passed under the pilot's seat to connect the two control columns. Aileron cables led from each control column, through apertures in the nacelle fabric, to meet at joining plates near the wing-mounted aileron pulleys, from which single cables led to the control horns. 6370 was photographed in this guise and had an instrument board fitted to the redundant gun arch.

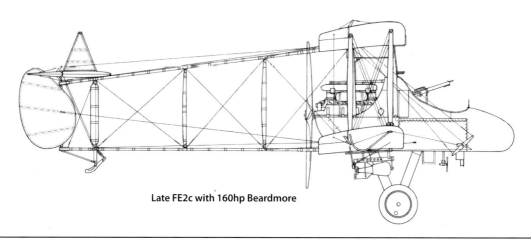

Late FE2c with 160hp Beardmore

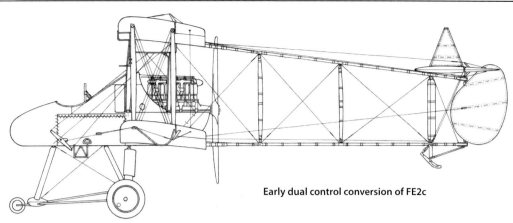

Early dual control conversion of FE2c

Drawing A16653, dated 2 June 1916, shows alterations to the gunner's cockpit floor of the FE2b for dual control. A 2in hole was cut near the floor nose to accept the rudder bar pivot and traverse ash battens (9in x 1.75in x 0.5in high) fixed ahead of and behind this as reinforcement. Further apertures were made to accommodate foot-pans that gave easier access to the rudder bar for the pilot's feet. A 3in circular hole was cut for the control column, flanked by a pair of rectangular holes, centred 15.25in from the centre line, which must have been for the elevator rocker shaft bearers.

The only other evidence for dual control is photographic. Control column spade grips can be discerned in front cockpits in some shots. The presence of twin pitot heads on some machines is an obvious clue – that the front cockpit of a DC conversion would have carried some basic instrumentation, an ASI being a necessary one. The exit points for the aileron cables from the front cockpit, in a similar arrangement to that made on FE2c 6370, can be identified and, on at least one machine of 192 NTS, shown in the panel p.40, there is evidence of an external elevator shaft link rod under the nacelle.

FE2d

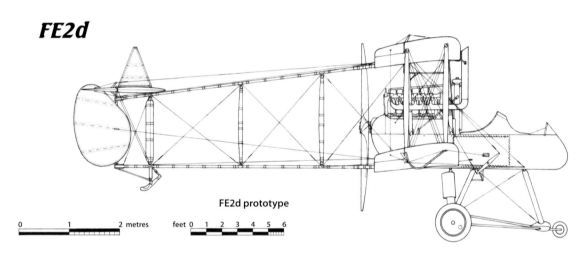

FE2d prototype

0   1   2 metres   feet 0 1 2 3 4 5 6

The 250/275hp Rolls-Royce engine was longer and heavier than the Beardmores of the FE2b. It was also designed for tubular engine bearers and so these had to be mounted above the existing wooden ones, raising the thrust line. The greater engine length meant that the radiator was moved further forward, to the line of the wing leading edge. The pilot's cockpit had then to be moved forward and consequently the position of the controls did likewise. That repositioning was allowed by the use of a single, flat bulkhead between the cockpits that doubled as an instrument board. The position of the new engine altered the centre of gravity and so the nose of the observer's cockpit was lengthened. With or without the tricycle undercarriage, the length was 32ft 3in.

The new nose brought the ply covering as far aft as the rear of the observer's cockpit and so the laced fabric sides, behind this, were proportionally shorter. The aluminium rear sides of the nacelle incorporated louvres to assist crankcase cooling.

A large rectangular radiator was initially fitted and the gravity tank repositioned to the centre of the centre-section underside. Aileron control was of the single action type on the first machines.

There were two distinct styles of pilot cockpit. The first was a very low cut one, which allowed maximum airflow to reach the radiator. It was created, on the prototype, by cutting down the sides of the original higher-sided component. The engine crankcase and most of the reduction gear were cowled but those aluminium panels were sometimes removed in service. The prototype had forward exhaust extensions to its engine manifolds and these were brought forward of the wing leading edge and turned through 90° to rise above the upper centre section. That unnecessary arrangement was abandoned on all production machines, on which the exhaust pipes were turned outward.

The original radiator was found to be too efficient and was replaced by a standard FE2b component that was mounted wholly above the line of the upper longerons. Early FE2ds could be seen with either style of radiator. A revised pilot's cockpit, on later Boulton-Paul machines, had very high sides that faired into the sides of the radiator. That high cockpit was sometimes cut down in service, often on the starboard, to allow a fixed Lewis gun on a Dixon-Spain mounting for pilot use.

The gravity tank was repositioned on later FE2ds and was carried just to starboard of centre, above the centre section. This coincided with the introduction of dual action ailerons and the front of the tank had a guide for the balance cable. The new tank had its sight gauge on its front face, invisible to the pilot but,

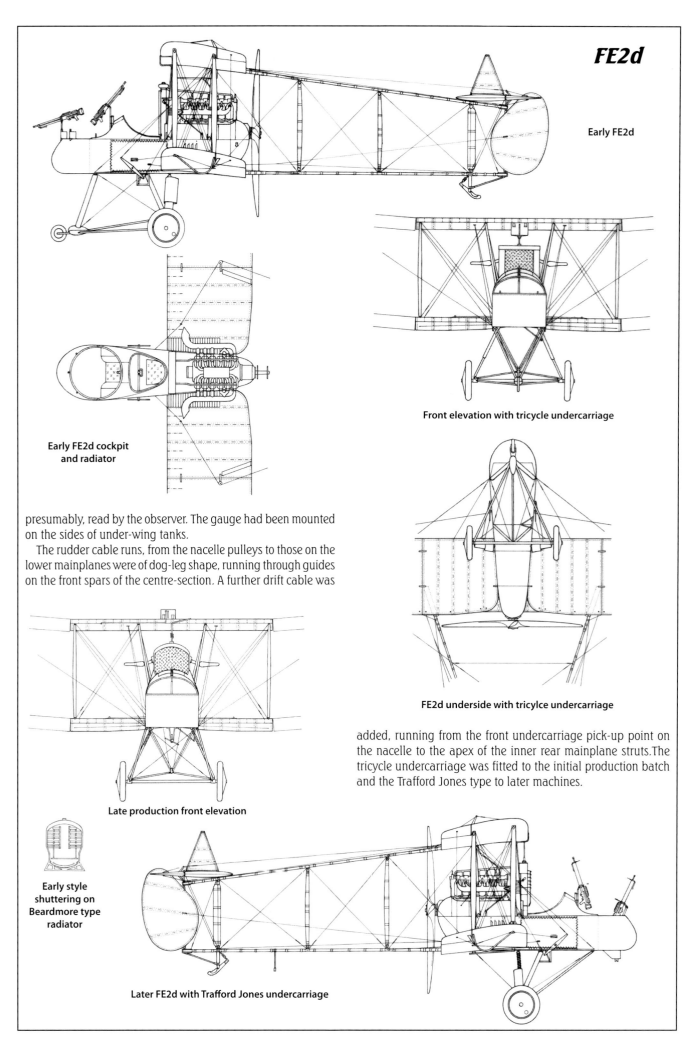

FE2d

Early FE2d

Early FE2d cockpit and radiator

Front elevation with tricycle undercarriage

FE2d underside with tricylce undercarriage

presumably, read by the observer. The gauge had been mounted on the sides of under-wing tanks.

The rudder cable runs, from the nacelle pulleys to those on the lower mainplanes were of dog-leg shape, running through guides on the front spars of the centre-section. A further drift cable was added, running from the front undercarriage pick-up point on the nacelle to the apex of the inner rear mainplane struts. The tricycle undercarriage was fitted to the initial production batch and the Trafford Jones type to later machines.

Late production front elevation

Early style shuttering on Beardmore type radiator

Later FE2d with Trafford Jones undercarriage

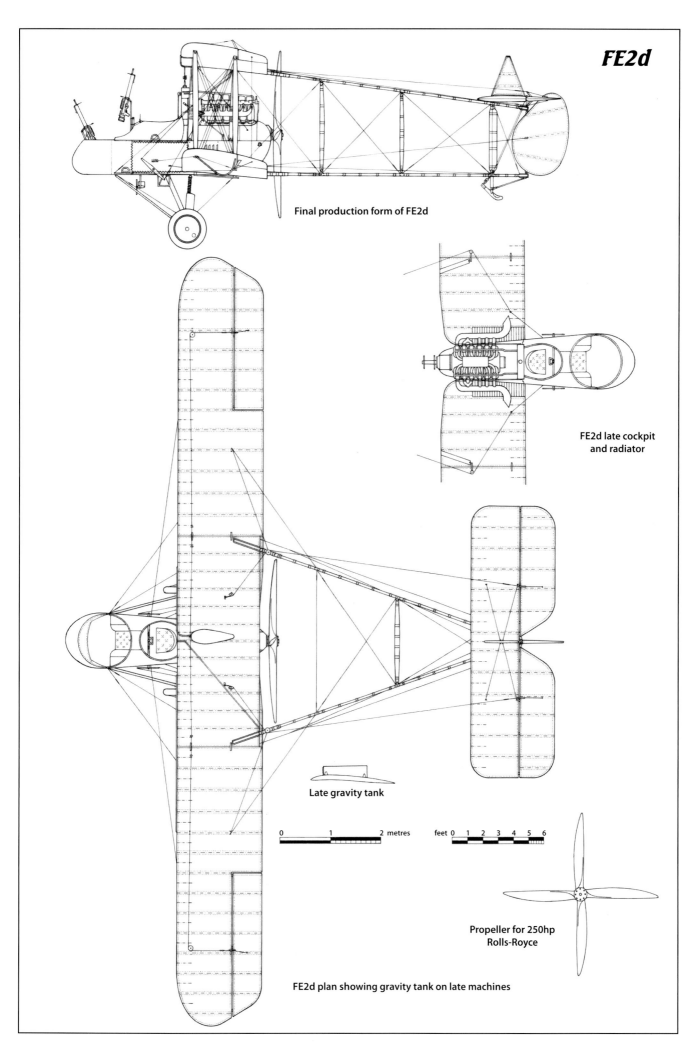

FE2d

Final production form of FE2d

FE2d late cockpit
and radiator

Late gravity tank

0   1   2 metres

feet 0   1   2   3   4   5   6

Propeller for 250hp
Rolls-Royce

FE2d plan showing gravity tank on late machines

FE2e

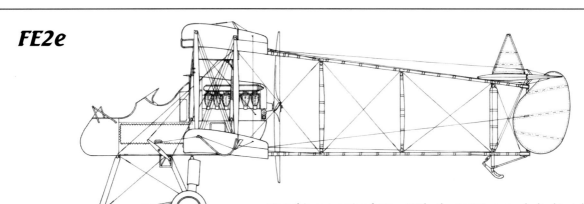

On this conversion from a FE2b, the RAF 5 engine bolted to tubular bearers which, again, raised the thrust line. The crankcase was cowled and a characteristic RAF engine air-scoop placed between and above the cylinder blocks. The sides of the pilot's cockpit were modified to blend in with the air-scoop and the crankcase cowling and incorporated a cooling louvre.

FE2h

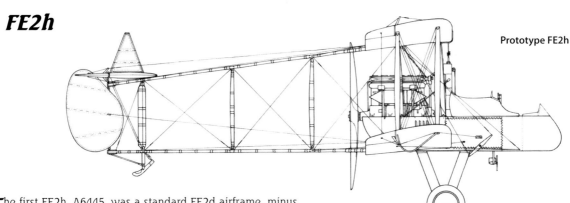

Prototype FE2h

The first FE2h, A6445, was a standard FE2d airframe, minus its tubular engine bearers and with a 200hp BHP engine replacing the Rolls-Royce and bolting onto the existing wooden bearers. A two-bladed propeller was fitted. This variant required a larger oil tank, which had conical ends.

The three further conversions differed significantly from the original. The 230hp Puma was essentially similar to the BHP but the rear of the nacelle was lengthened by the addition of an extra bay. That brought the engine, and therefore the radiator, further aft and a new radiator shroud was fitted, one which tapered forward and downward to meet the existing high sided FE2d pilot's cockpit. The shroud incorporated doors, as on the FE2b, which allowed cooling air to be deflected through the radiator. The lower nose of the observer's cockpit was modified to incorporate a flat, glazed observation panel.

The lengthened nacelle was probably an attempt to maintain the centre of gravity when the intended weapon, the 6lb Davis gun, was fitted in the front cockpit.

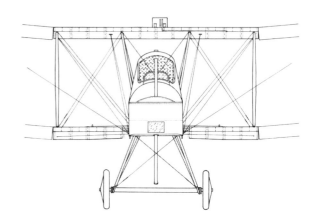

FE2h front view showing sighting panel for Davis gun

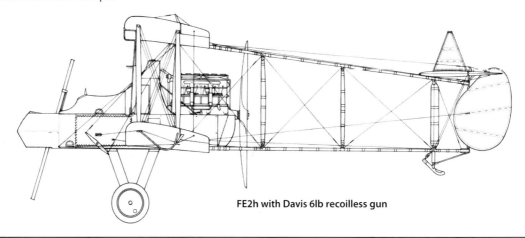

FE2h with Davis 6lb recoilless gun

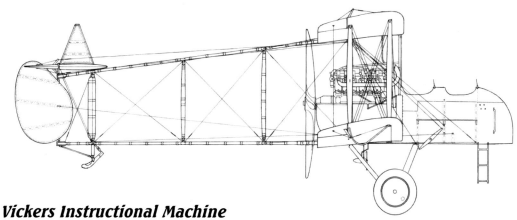

Vickers Instructional Machine

The ultimate development of the FE2 series was made in 1920. Although technically outside the scope of this book, its details are included for the sake of completeness. Vickers had received a contract to supply Vimy Commercials to the Chinese Government plus the necessary training (both personnel and equipment).

The Shorts Tucano and BAe Hawk have a common cockpit layout that facilitates conversion to the fast jet. The idea is not novel. Vickers, in need of a machine to train Chinese Vimy pilots, came up with the idea of fitting Vimy controls and cockpit equipment to FE2b airframes. 35 machines, named VIM (Vickers Instructional Machine) were built, probably converted from airframes that had been placed in storage at the war's end. The mainplanes, tailbooms and tail surfaces were unmodified FE2b components but the nacelle, engine, upper centre section and its struts, undercarriage and cooling system were revised.

The nacelle was a slab-sided one, dispensing with the dished aluminium end piece. Its rear sides were raised to the level of the bearers for its Rolls-Royce Eagle VIII engine. That 360hp unit served a double purpose. It provided the extra power needed for the added equipment but also allowed the use of similar controls to the Vimy (which also had that engine). The engine's cooling system incorporated a pair of flank radiators whose leading edges were in line with the wing leading edge. The radiator pipes formed an inverted V shape, which was connected to the engine via a further pipe, and were braced to the front spar of the upper centre section.

The forward nacelle was deeper than that of the FE2b, probably necessary to accommodate the aileron control wheels, which were Vimy components. A ladder and handrail were fixed at the starboard nose and a ledge ran at mid fuselage depth to allow access to the rear cockpit.

The oleo undercarriage was replaced by a V-strut unit, with wheels of larger diameter. The undercarriage unit was, however, shorter than that of the FE2b and reduced the machine's overall height to 12ft 4in.

The upper centre section was supported by struts made from tubing. The forward pair used the same fuselage attachment points as the FE2b but the rear pair attached to the lower longeron of the nacelle. A notch was made in the trailing edge of the upper centre section, probably to facilitate engine change. An over-head FE2d-type gravity tank was fitted. Although the mainplanes were standard FE2b components, they incorporated extra flying wires that ran from the base of their forward inboard struts to a mid bay position on the bottom of the front spar.

The positioning of the flank radiators precluded the use of FE2b control runs. The aileron actuating cables were led through the nacelle, to exit at points under the front lower centre section spars and led, via an extra pulley, to the existing pulleys ahead of the aileron actuating horn. A standard aileron cable balance cable completed the run. Dual control was provided with the elevator control shaft in the rear cockpit having FE2b-type control horns. The internal linkage between the two cockpits was probably similar to that used on FE2b and FE2c dual control conversions. The elevator cables ran to pulleys mounted under the lower spar of the upper mainplanes in corresponding positions to the rudder control pulleys on the FE2b. Those pulleys for the rudder cables were retained but the cables exited the nacelle at the front of the rear cockpit.

Photographs and Profiles

Various alternative exhausts were tried, from the six individual straight stubs *above* to the more substantial manifold arrangement *left and below*, which would carry the exhaust clear of the propeller arc. (*see also p 102*)

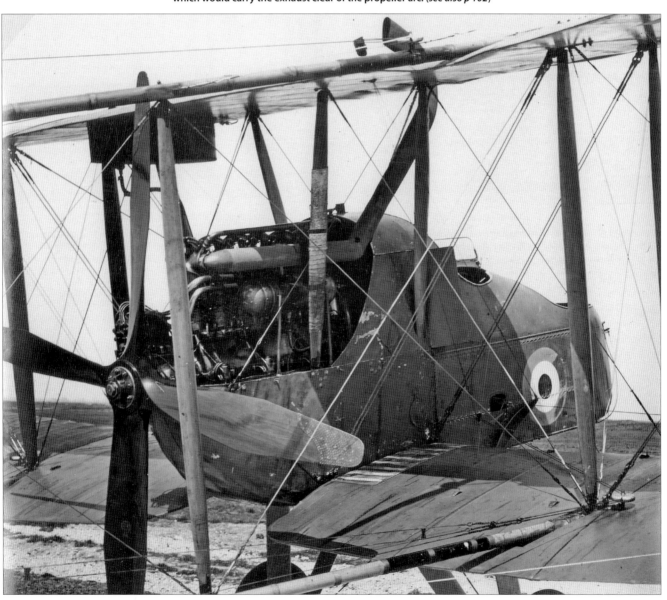

Interesting nacelle nose markings; *left*, a stylised 'A' on an unidentified single seat conversion, and *right*, a swastika (at this time simply an ancient good luck symbol) decorates the front of this night bomber.

Above: Running up an FE2d with a substantial searchlight that must have added considerable drag.

Below: An FE2b of 192 Night Training Squadron at Newmarket in 1917 about to depart on a practice operation to the bombing ground at nearby Lakenheath. Armourers can be seen finishing fusing the 20lb Hales HE bombs fitted to carriers under each wing. The Hales (containing 4.5 lbs of Amatol) had been developed for the RNAS but was widely employed by the RFC until replaced by the 25lb Cooper during 1917.

A Fee in the early days of the RAF, the date suggested by the transitional mixture of uniforms. Two pilots, a Lieutentant RAF and a Flight Sub-Lt (ex-)RNAS share the front cockpit. The officer, also a pilot, leaning his elbow on the wing is a Lieutenant RAF, wearing a 1918 RAF cap and a Highland regimental pattern cutaway tunic with Sam Browne belt. The rest of the group are ground crew, representative of the various trades whose skills were needed to keep the Fees flying throughout the war.

Often forgotten is the sheer size of the FE2 types, demonstrated here by the group of riggers and mechanics straining to service one, somewhat precariously, in a hangar. Oliver Stewart, who flew FE2bs with 22 Squadron, wrote in *The Clouds Remember*: 'A cow, a blunderbuss, a domestic pet, a kitchen range with wings on, a threshing machine, ... a brute ..., yet among the aeroplanes of the War period, indubitably one of the great world's workers. That was the FE2b, a forerunner of the FE2d and creator of the essentially big FE qualities'. Nearly thirteen feet high, half as wide again as an SE5, and in all 'quite contemptuous of streamlining', to quote Stewart again. The FE was a big aeroplane.

A surprising outfit for flying a Fee, even in summer.

No shorts for this aviator at Risalpur, India, with A790 behind.
This FE2b had exhaust stubs, rather than the usual,
single exhaust manifold. [see also p 99]

All aircraft movements between England and the Aircraft Depots and
Squadrons in France were recorded on these pink cards at 1 AD.

Unreliability of both rotary and in-line engines at this time made life
jackets essential for ferry pilots when crossing the Channel.

The pilot's cockpit of an FE2d, showing the single, flat bulkhead, incorporating a glazed panel that separated this from the observer's cockpit. The bulkhead doubled as an instrument board. The standard compass was mounted, centrally on a shelf, with the magneto switches below. The characteristic spade grip of the control column is clearly visible. The cluster of instruments on the port side included an altimeter, an ASI and an air pressure gauge, as well as a watch. Interestingly, the key instruments have lighting, unusual for a FE2d in BEF service and suggesting that the machine was in home use, either for Home Defence or experimental work.

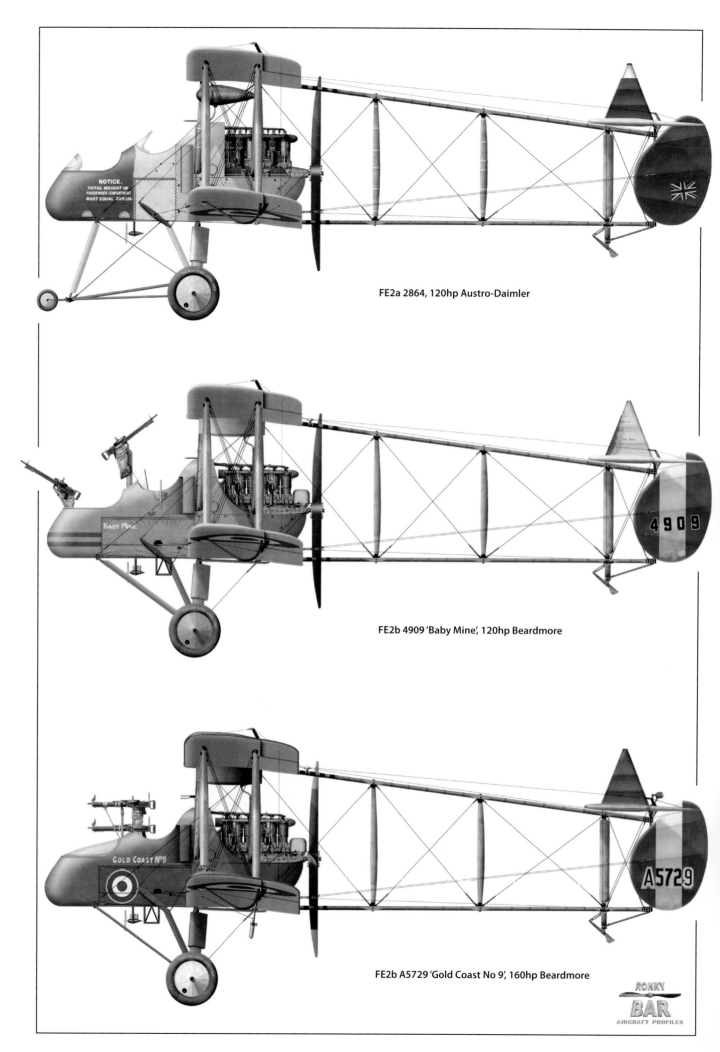

FE2a 2864, 120hp Austro-Daimler

NOTICE.
TOTAL WEIGHT IN
PASSENGER COMPARTMENT
MUST EQUAL 225 LBS.

FE2b 4909 'Baby Mine', 120hp Beardmore

BABY MINE.

4909

FE2b A5729 'Gold Coast No 9', 160hp Beardmore

GOLD COAST Nº9

A5729

RONKY
BAR
AIRCRAFT PROFILES

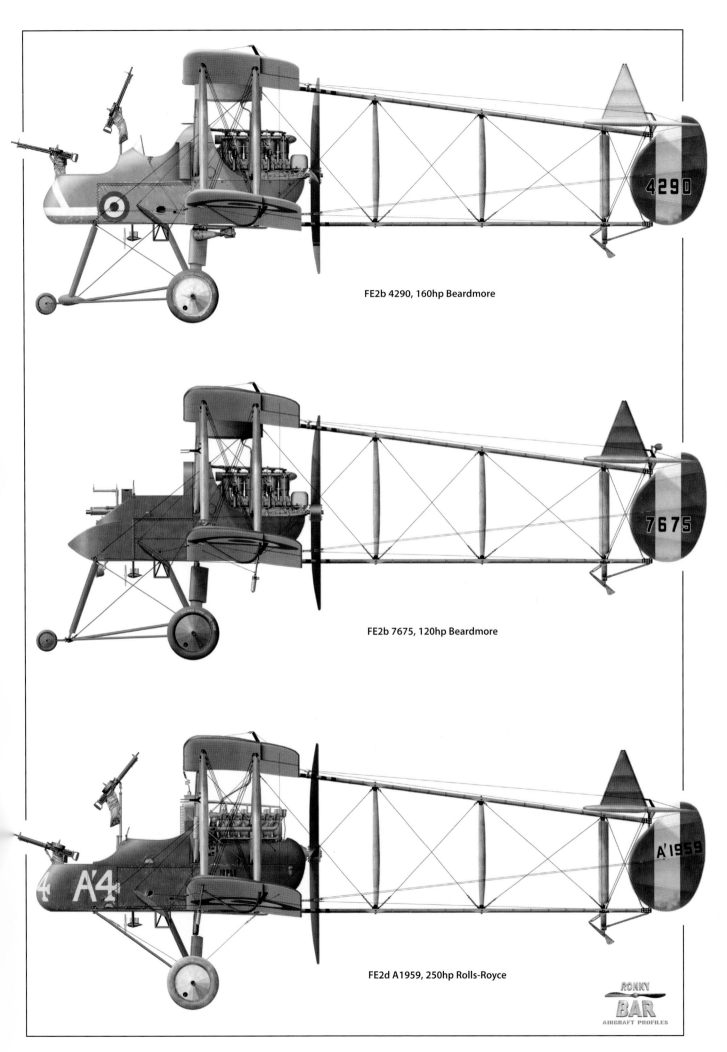

FE2b 4290, 160hp Beardmore

FE2b 7675, 120hp Beardmore

FE2d A1959, 250hp Rolls-Royce

RONKY
BAR
AIRCRAFT PROFILES

The first FE2s to be employed in France were all delivered via No 1 Aircraft Depot at St-Omer which continued to support the type for the remainder of the war, albeit based at Marquise from March 1918. In this evocative photograph taken on a late Autumn day, towards the end of 1916, a number of FE2bs stand awaiting deployment to squadrons. In the foreground is A5448 which would serve only briefly with 18 Sqn, crashing and then being salvaged for spares within two weeks. A5450 beyond also went to 18 Sqn and lasted until Boxing Day when it suffered damage in the air from a British shell. At this time more than one in six RFC aircraft in France were FE2b/ds.

These FE2bs, occupying what was the town's pre-war race course, are parked on the southern edge of the depot, adjacent to the St-Omer/Longuenesse road. Bldg 17 (left, distance) was the Tinsmiths' Shop. The airfield remains largely unchanged to this day, although the area on the far side of the road is now occupied by a prison. *Inset*: The British Air Services Memorial, erected in 2004 through the efforts of Cross & Cockade International, stands about 50 metres behind the camera position.

1 Aircraft Depot Saint-Omer

2 Aircraft Depot Candas

Aircraft lined up outside the repair sheds at 2AD Candas during early 1917 before an inspection visit by General Haig. Types visible include an FE2b (second from right). Candas supplied many of the FE2 squadrons on the Western Front, including 11, 18, 22, 57, 58, 83, 100, 101, 102 and 148 Sqns.

Col Vere Bettington, whose signature appears on the 'Incoming' card on p 102, seated front row centre, in this later group of officers after he had taken charge of 2 ASD. The Chaplain (*see opposite and below*) is seated front left.

Vertical view of 2ASD (Bahot) in the summer of 1918, after the depot had been relocated from Candas during the German Spring Offensive. It was at Bahot that the famous scene (*opposite*) of the 2 ASD Chaplain preaching from the nacelle of an FE2b was photographed.

The depots erected, fitted out and issued all the FE2b and FE2d aircraft employed on the Western Front. They also repaired, modified and reconstructed airframes and engines received from the squadrons in the field. On occasion, there could be more than a dozen FE2 machines in work or stored (sometimes just the nacelles). It was also the depots that struck off wrecked aircraft and reduced them to spares for use within the depot or for despatch to the issue sections and field squadrons. It was not unusual to find individual airframes retained for experiments and development purposes. For example, on 28 February 1917, 14 FE2b aircraft (160hp Beardmore) were available serviceable at Candas with a further 4 machines in repair and 1 retained for photographic experiments (5229). There were also 5 FE2b machines (120hp Beardmore) on charge of which only one was serviceable (7704). On the same day, two wrecked machines were received (FE2b 4970 from 23 Squadron and FE2d A1940 from 57 Squadron).

The delivery of serviceable aircraft between Home Establishment and the depots, and between the depots in theatre, was largely the task of dedicated ferry pilots while deliveries to the squadrons fell to individual squadron pilots. Aircraft that were time-expired, but still of utility, were either returned to Home Establishment in cases or flown back direct via Lympne.

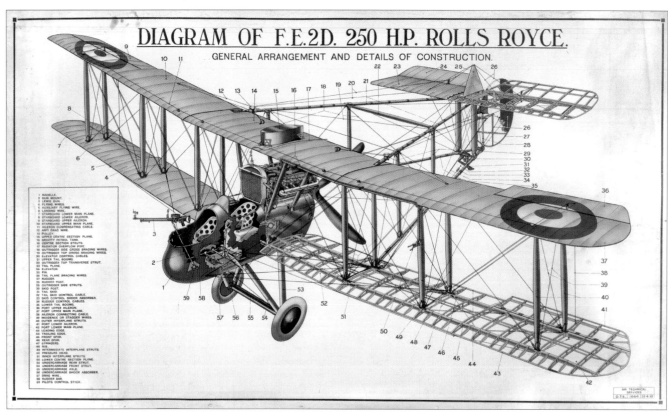

A contemporary training diagram of the FE2d.

FE2b crashed by Lt Price, 199 Squadron, Retford, 14 Ocober 1917. Accidental damage reveals internal detail.

TYPES and SERIALS
1915-1919

'NO WATER IN RADIATOR'. *This beautifully clear photo, presumably taken during the winter of 1916-17, shows all the salient features of a mid-production FE2d. While retaining the cut down pilot's cockpit, tricycle undercarriage and under-wing gravity tank of the original production machines, a Beardmore radiator was fitted, mounted on a cradle that rested on the upper longerons. The variety of duties imposed on FE2d crews is reflected by the machine's equipment. The observer's Lewis gun is shown on a No.4 Mk.IV mounting, clipped to the starboard side of the nacelle nose tubing, with an extended telescopic mounting for rear defence. Battens, for attaching a camera, were fixed to the starboard side of the nose and there were under-wing bomb carriers fitted to ribs under the lower centre section.*

Abbreviations used in the Serials Listing

@	at least	HD	Home Defence	SOC	struck off charge *see Note below*
AA	anti-aircraft fire	HDS	Home Defence Sqn	Sqn	Squadron
AAP	Aircraft Acceptance Park	IIA	injured in accident	Sqn Cdr	Squadron Commander
AAP	Army Aircraft Park	IIFA	injured in flying accident	TDS	Training Depot Station
AD	Aircraft Depot	KIA	killed in action	TS	Training Squadron
AES	Aeroplane Experimental Station	KIFA	killed in flying accident	wdd	wounded
AFS	Aerial Fighting School	LIA	lost in action	w/e	week ending
AGP	Anti Gotha Patrol	Lt	Lieutenant	wef	with effect from
AID	Air Inspection Directorate	2Lt	Second Lieutenant	WEE	Wireless Experimental Establishment
AIS	Air Issues Section	NARD	Northern Aircraft Repair Depot	WIA	wounded in action
ALG	Advance Landing Ground	NLG	Night Landing Ground		
AM1	Aircraft Mechanic, 1st Class	NTS	Night Training Squadron		
AM2	Aircraft Mechanic, 2nd Class	NWR	not worth reconstruction		
AP	Aircraft Park	OOC	out of control		
ARS	Aeroplane Repair Section	OP	offensive patrol		
ASD	Aeroplane Supply Depot	POW	prisoner of war		
AWM	Australian War Memorial	RAE	Royal Aircraft Establishment		
AZP	Anti Zeppelin Patrol	RAF	Royal Aircraft Factory		
BEF	British Expeditionary Force	RAS	Reserve Air Squadron		
Capt	Captain	RFC	Royal Flying Corps		
CFS	Central Flying School	RNAS	Royal Naval Air Service		
dd	delivered	RP	Repair Park		
DBR	damaged beyond repair	RS	Reserve Squadron		
DS	Depot Squadron	SAG	School of Aerial Gunnery		
EA	enemy aircraft	SAD	Southern Aircraft Depot		
ff	first flown	SARD	Southern Aircraft Repair Depot		
Flt	Flight	SD Flt	Special Duties Flight		
FSL	Flight Sub Lieutenant	SMA	School of Military Aeronautics		
GI	ground instruction	SN&BD	School of Navigation/Bomb Dropping		

Note

The expression 'struck off charge' has been used to indicate only a machine's transfer out of an RFC/RAF unit and not its final writing off. Instead, the naval expression 'deleted' has been used throughout to indicate that a machine was of no further use to the services.

In the listing below:

1 Units given in **bold characters** *are those confirmed by documentary, logbook or photographic evidence.*

2 *Units given in* normal characters *have appeared in published works but cannot be verified.*

3 *102 Sqn acted as a Demobilisation Squadron in January 1919, receiving large numbers of FEs from other units which were reduced to cadre status.*

Service Units Operating FE2s

6 SQUADRON RFC
Joined the BEF as a general purpose squadron 7.10.14 and, in 2 Wing, received FE2as at Abeele from 5.15, as part of mixed equipment. Some FE2bs received from 12.15 but given up 2.16. FE2as withdrawn 3.1916 and unit became a Corps Squadron with BE2cs.

Commanding Officers
Capt A.G. Board, 28.9.14–23.11.14.
Maj C.G. Hoare, 24.3.15–6.11.15.
Maj F.L.J. Cogan, 7.11.15–15.7.16.

11 SQUADRON RFC
Joined the BEF as a fighting squadron 25.7.15 and, in 13 (Army) Wing, received FE2bs at Savy from 6.16, initially as part of mixed equipment. To Izel-le-Hameau 31.8.1916, fully equipped with FE2bs. Began to receive Bristol F2Bs 5.17 and fully re-equipped with that type by 6.17.

Commanding Officers
Maj T.O'B. Hubbard, 10.11.15–17.10.16. Maj K.P. Atkinson, 17.10.16–30.3.17.
Maj C.T. McClean MC, from 30.3.17.

Unit Markings
A white triangle on the nacelle nose with bars extending from its base. Large white flight letter marked on inboard area of upper port mainplane, with flight number in equivalent position to starboard.

12 SQUADRON RFC
Joined the BEF as a general purpose squadron 6.9.15 and, in 3 Wing, received a few FE2bs at Vert Galant 2.16, as part of mixed equipment during that month only.

Commanding Officers
Maj J.C. Halahan, 1.16–10.16.

15 SQUADRON RFC
Joined the BEF as a corps squadron 23.12.15 and, in 2 Wing, received a few FE2bs at Droglandt 2.16, for escort duty during that month only.

Commanding Officers
Maj H.leM. Brock DSO, 7.11.1915–19.12.1916.

16 SQUADRON RFC
Formed in the BEF as a general purpose squadron 11.2.15 and, in 1 Wing, received FE2as and some FE2bs at Merville from 6.15, initially as part of mixed equipment. Moved to La Gorgue 12.12.15 and FE2as given up 1.16, FE2bs 2.16.

Commanding Officers
Maj F.V. Holt, 8.2.15–23.7.15..
Maj H.C.T. Dowding, 23.7.15–1.16.
Maj D.W. Powell, 1.16–5.8.16.

18 SQUADRON RFC
Joined the BEF as a fighting squadron 18.11.15 and, in 1 (Corps) Wing, received full complement of FE2bs at Bruay from 4.16. To Treizennes and 10 (Army) Wing 22.7.16, returning to Bruay and 1 (Corps) Wing 2.8.16 then to Laviéville and 14 (Army) Wing 6.9.16, St-Leger-les-Authie 10.12.16, Bertangles in 22 Wing 27.1.17 and Baizieux in 13 (Army) Wing 25.5.17. Began to re-equip with DH4s 6.17 and all FE2bs withdrawn that month.

Commanding Officers
Maj G.I. Carmichael, 11.5.15–19.12.16.
Maj R.S. Maxwell MC, 19.12.16–30.3.17.
Maj G.R.M. Reid DSO MC*, 30.3.17–24.11.17.

Unit Markings
The squadron is variously reported to have marked coloured (red?) diamonds and/or triangles on the nacelle noses of it FE2bs.

20 SQUADRON RFC
Mobilised as a fighting squadron with FE2bs at Filton in 4 Wing and joined the BEF at St-Omer as a fighting squadron 16.1.16 moving to Clairmarais and in 2 Wing 23.1.16. Transferred to 10 Wing 2.16. Re-equipped with FE2ds from 6.16. Moved to Boisdinghem 19.1.17 and then Ste-Marie-Capelle 15.4.17, still in 10 (now Army) Wing. Began re-equipment with Bristol F2Bs 8.17 and all FE2ds withdrawn by 9.17.

Commanding Officers
Capt C.W. Wilson MC, 1.9.15–21.3.16.
Maj G.J. Malcolm, 21.3.16–10.7.16.
Maj W.H.C. Mansfield DSO, 10.7.16–15.10.17.

22 SQUADRON RFC
Mobilised as a fighting squadron with FE2bs at Gosport in 6 Wing and joined the BEF at St-Omer as a fighting squadron 1.4.16 moving to Vert Galant and in 14 (Army) Wing 1.4.16. Moved to Bertangles 16.4.16 then to Chipilly 27.4.17, Flez 1.5.17, Warloy 3.7.17, still in 14 (Army) Wing. Began

re-equipment with Bristol F2Bs 7.17, moving to Izel-le-Hameau in 13 Wing 5.7.17 and all FE2bs withdrawn by 8.17.

Commanding Officers
Maj RB Martyn, 10.15–2.17.
Maj LW Learmont DSO MC, 2.17–3.18.

Unit Markings
Flight letter/number combination painted in white below observer's cockpit on either side of nacelle. Black disc under each lower mainplane contained flight letter/number in white.

23 SQUADRON RFC
Mobilised as a fighting squadron with FE2bs at Gosport in 6 Wing and joined the BEF at St-Omer as a fighting squadron 15.3.16 moving to Fienvillers 16.3.16 then Le Hameau in 13 Wing 18.3.16. To Fienvillers and 15 (Corps) Wing 1.9.16 then Vert Galant and 22 (Army) Wing 5.9.16. Re-equipped with SPAD S.VIIs from 3.17. Moved to Baizieux, still in 22 (Army) Wing 5.3.17 and all FE2bs withdrawn by 4.17.

Commanding Officers
Capt L.A. Strange, 21.9.15–21.1.16
Maj R.E.T. Hogg, 22.1.16–24.4.16
Maj A. Ross-Hume, 4.16–1.17
Maj J.B.T. Leighton MC, 1.17–5.17

Unit Markings
Flight letter painted in white on front of nacelle, with flight number marked in white on both sides of the nacelle, below the observer's cockpit.

25 SQUADRON RFC
Mobilised as a fighting/reconnaissance squadron with FE2bs at Thetford in 7 Wing and joined the BEF at St-Omer as a fighting squadron 20.2.16 moving to Lozingham and in 10 (Army) Wing 1.4.16. Re-equipped with FE2ds from 3.17. Began re-equipment with DH4s 6.17 and all FE2ds withdrawn by 8.17.

Commanding Officers
Maj F.V. Holt, 25.9.15–14.3.16.
Maj T.W.C. Carthew 14.3.16.
Maj R.G. Cherry, 15.3.16–5.17.
Maj the Hon. O.M. Guest from 3.6.17.

Unit Markings
Flight marking of dark, usually black, horizontal

bars around the nose of the nacelle–1 bar for A Flt, 2 for B Flt and 3 for C Flt.

28 SQUADRON RFC
Serving as a training unit in 17 Wing at Gosport, received FE2bs and FE2ds as part of mixed equipment from 4.16. Scheduled for service with BEF as fighting-reconnaissance unit with 250-hp FE2ds from 1.3.17, but FEs given up on move to Yatesbury 23.7.17 for mobilisation as a scout squadron.
Commanding Officers
Maj . Shekleton, 28.2.17–25.5.17.
Capt R.D. Oxland, 7.6.17–28.6.17.
Capt P.C. Campbell, 28.6.17–12.7.17.
Maj H.F. Glanville from 12.7.17.

31 SQUADRON RFC
Operating as a general purpose squadron on the NE Frontier of India, with HQ at Risalpur and numerous detachments, received one FE2b 7.17 and flew it until 1920.
Commanding Officers
Maj S. Hutcheson, 5.17–1.12.18.
Maj E.L. Millar, 1.12.18–10.8.19.
Sqn Ldr D.H.M. Carberry MC DFC, 8.19–1.20.

33 SQUADRON RFC/RAF
Operating as 33 (Home Defence) Squadron in Lincolnshire under Home Defence Group, with HQ at Gainborough and A Flt at Brattleby (Scampton), B Flt at Kirton Lindsey and C Flt at Elsham re-equipped with FE2bs and some FE2ds from 6.17. Under Northern HD Wing from 1.9.17 and 48 Wing from 29.10.17. Function dropped from unit title 1.11.17. HQ to Kirton Lindsey 12.6.18. Partially re-equipped with Bristol F2Bs from 6.18 and all FE2bs/FE2ds withdrawn when fully re-equipped with Avro 504K (NF) from 8.18.
Commanding Officers
Maj C.G. Burge from 21.11.16.
Capt G.M. Turnbull, 5.6.18–@ 1.19.

35 SQUADRON RFC
Serving as a training unit in 7 Wing at Thetford, received some FE2bs as part of mixed equipment from 2.16. To Narborough, still in 7 Wing and mobilised as a corps squadron from 10.16, when FE2bs were withdrawn.
Commanding Officers
Maj B. Vernon Harcourt, 13.3.16–22.2.17.

36 SQUADRON RFC/RAF
Operating as 36 (Home Defence) Squadron in NE England under Home Defence Group, with HQ at Jesmond (Newcastle) and A Flt at Seaton Carew, B Flt at Hylton and C Flt at Ashington re-equipped with FE2bs and some FE2ds from 6.17. Flights re-titled 12.8.17 with A Flt at Hylton, B Flt at Ashington and C Flt at Seaton Carew. Under Northern HD Wing from 1.9.17 and 46 Wing from 29.10.17. Function dropped from unit title 1.11.17. HQ to Hylton 12.6.18. Partially re-equipped with Bristol F2Bs from 4.18. HQ to Hylton 1.7.18 (re-named Usworth 15.7.18) and all FE2bs/FE2ds withdrawn when fully re-equipped with Bristol F2Bs and Sopwith Pups from 9.18.
Commanding Officers
Maj J.H.S. Tyssen MC from 22.1.17.
Maj S.W. Price MC from 1.1.18.
Maj W.J. Tempest DSO MC, 26.7.18–16.1.19.
Unit Markings
Small RFC wings painted on front of nacelle nose on several FE2bs.

38 SQUADRON RFC/RAF
Operating as 38 (Home Defence) Squadron in the South Midlands under Home Defence Group, with HQ at Melton Mowbray, A Flt at Stamford (Wittering), B Flt at Leadenham and C Flt at Buckminster re-equipped with FE2bs from 8.17. Under Midland HD Wing from 1.10.17 and 47 Wing from 29.10.17. Function dropped from unit title 1.11.17. HQ to Buckminster 25.5.18. Mobilised as a night light bombing squadron and joined the BEF in 82 Wing at Cappelle 31.5.18. Moved to Beauregard 24.8.18, St-Pol 29.9.18, Harlebeke 26.10.18 and Serny 16.12.18, all still in 82 Wing.

FE2bs handed to 102 (Demobilisation) Sqn 1.19 and unit reduced to cadre.
Commanding Officers
Capt Pretyman from 7.17.
Maj C.C. Wigram, 18.7.17–21.10.18.
Maj R.D. Oxland, 21.10.18–17.1.19.
Capt G.T. Wix from 17.2.19.

38 SQUADRON DEPOT DETACHMENT RAF
Detachment remained with 47 Wing, operating from Stamford, Leadenham and Buckminster when squadron joined the BEF 31.5.18. Disbanded into 90 Sqn 14.8.18
Commanding Officers
Capt Burdett, 31.5.18–14.8.18.

39 SQUADRON RFC
Operating as 39 (Home Defence) Squadron in London area under Home Defence Wing, with HQ at Woodford Green and A Flt at North Weald Bassett, B Flt at Sutton's Farm and C Flt at Hainault Farm received at least one FE2b 1916.
Commanding Officers
Maj T.R.C. Higgins, 1.5.1916–13.6.1916.
Maj W.C.H. Mansfield, 13.6.1916–12.7.1916.
Capt (later Maj) A.H. Morton MC, 26.7.1916–20.3.1917.

42 SQUADRON RFC
At Filton, in 4 Wing, received at least one FE2b whilst training during the early summer 1916 and prior to mobilisation as a corps squadron.
Commanding Officers
Maj J.K. Kinnear, 4.16–11.16.

45 SQUADRON RFC
Training at Sedgeford in 7 Wing, received at least one FE2b during early summer 1916, prior to mobilisation as a fighting & reconnaissance unit.
Commanding Officers
Maj W.R. Read MC, 24.4.16–24.4.17.

51 SQUADRON RFC/RAF
Operating as 51 (Home Defence) Squadron in East Anglia under Home Defence Wing, with HQ at Hingham and A Flt at Harling Road, B Flt at Mattishall and C Flt at Marham began to re-equip with FE2bs from 9.16. Fully re-equipped by 2.17, then under Home Defence Group. HQ to Marham 7.8.17. Under South Midland HD Wing from 1.9.17. A Flt to Tydd-St-Mary 14.9.17. Under 47 Wing from 29.10.17. Function dropped from unit title 1.11.17. Flights re-organised 2.18 with A Flt at Mattishall, B Flt at Tydd-St-Mary and C Flt at Marham. Re-equipped with Sopwith Snipes from 10.18 and all FE2bs withdrawn by 11.18.
Commanding Officers
Maj H. Wyllie, 18.7.16 to 11.9.1917.
Maj F.C. Baker, 11.9.17–18.3.18.
Maj H. Wyllie, 23.3.18–16.6.18.
Capt H.L.H. Owen, 21.8.18–13.6.19.

57 SQUADRON RFC
Mobilised as a fighting squadron with FE2ds at Bramham Moor (Tadcaster) in 8 Wing and joined the BEF at St André-aux-Bois in 9 (HQ) Wing 16.12.16, moving to Fienvillers 22.1.17. Re-equipped with DH4s from 5.17 and all FE2ds withdrawn by 6.17.
Commanding Officers
Maj L.A. Pattinson from 5.17–4.11.17.
Unit Markings
White flight letter/number combination, separated by an apostrophe, on either side of the nacelle nose.

58 SQUADRON RFC/RAF
Operated as a training unit and mobilised at Cramlington in 19 Wing as a night light bombing squadron, moving to Dover (St Margaret's) in 6 Wing for re-equipment with FE2bs 12.17. Joined the BEF at St-Omer 10.1.18 and moved to Treizennes in 9 (HQ) Wing 13.1.18. Moved Clairmarais in 11 Wing 1.2.18. Moved to Auchel 25.3.18, Fauquembergues 23.4.18 then Alquines 31.8.18, all in 54 (Night) Wing. Began re-equipment with HP O/400 8.18 and all FE2bs withdrawn by 10.18.

The Special Duties Flt/I Flt was attached to the squadron from 23.6.18–31.8.18.
Commanding Officers
Maj E.D. Horsfall, 8.6.16–5.1.18.
Maj J.H.S. Tyssen MC, 5.1.18–25.6.18.
Maj D. Gilley DFC from 25.6.18.

64 SQUADRON RFC
Serving as a training unit in 7 Wing at Sedgeford, received some FE2bs in B Flt as part of mixed equipment from 4.16. Mobilised as a scout squadron from 6.17 and FE2bs withdrawn.
Commanding Officers
Maj B.E. Smithies from 8.16–12.16.

76 SQUADRON RFC
Operating as 76 (Home Defence) Squadron in NE England under Home Defence Group, with HQ at Ripon and A Flt at Copmanthorpe, B Flt at Helperby and C Flt at Catterick partially re-equipped with FE2bs from 6.17 but these were withdrawn 8.17.
Commanding Officers
Maj EM Murray DSO MC 10.10.16 to 31.1.1918.

78 SQUADRON RFC
Operating as 78 (Home Defence) Squadron for London under Eastern Home Defence Wing at Sutton's Farm, received 2 FE2ds ex 33 (HD) Sqn 9.17 as part of mixed equipment. FE2ds withdrawn 10.17.
Commanding Officers
Maj C.R. Rowden MC, 8.7.17–20.4.18 (KIFA).

83 SQUADRON RFC/RAF
Operated as a training unit, mobilised at Narborough in 7 Wing as a night light bombing squadron with FE2bs 12.17. Joined the BEF at St-Omer 6.3.18 and moved to Auchel in 54 (Night) Wing 7.3.18. Moved to Franqueville 2.5.18, Lahoussoye 9.10.18, Estrées-en-Chaussée 26.10.18, all still in 54 (Night) Wing. To Serny 13.12.18 in 82 Wing 13.12.18. FE2bs handed to 102 (Demobilisation) Sqn by 2.19 and unit reduced to cadre.
Commanding Officers
Maj V.A. Albrecht, 16.5.17–1.3.18.
Maj E.L.M.L. Gower, 1.3.18–28.7.18.
Maj S.W. Price, 27.8.18–14.1.19.
Capt C.W. Stonehouse from 14.1.19.

90 SQUADRON RAF
Re-formed as a Home Defence squadron with FE2bs in 47 Wing from 38 Sqn Depot Detachment 14.8.18, with HQ at Buckminster and A Flt at Leadenham, B Flt at Buckminster and C Flt at Stamford (Wittering). FE2bs withdrawn when re-equipped with Avro 504K (NF) 9.18.
Commanding Officers
Capt Burdett, 14.8.18–23.8.18.
Maj W.B. Hargreave, 23.8.18–24.10.18.
Capt Burdett, 24.10.18–@ 1.19.

97 SQUADRON RFC/RAF
Mobilising in 4 Wing at Netheravon, used several FE2bs 3.18–5.18.
Commanding Officers
Maj V.A. Albrecht MC, 4.4.18–4.3.19.

100 SQUADRON RFC/RAF
Formed at 51 HDS HQ Hingham 23.2.17 as the first night light bombing squadron and worked up on that unit's aerodromes. To Farnborough 2.17 and joined the BEF in 13 (Army) Wing at St-André-aux-Bois 27.3.17 with some BE2es in addition to the main FE2b equipment. Moved to Izel-le-Hameau 1.4.17 then Treizennes and 19 (Army) Wing 10.5.17. BE2es withdrawn by 8.17. Came under 9 (HQ) Wing 9.17. To Ochey and 41 Wing 11.10.17, moving to Villeseneux 1.4.18 and returning to Ochey 9.5.18 and on to Xaffévillers 10.8.18. FE2bs withdrawn and replaced by HP O/400s 8.18.
Commanding Officers
Maj M.G. Christie DSO MC, 23.3.17–11.12.17.
Maj W.J. Tempest DSO MC, 11.12.17–13.3.18.
Maj C.G. Burge, 13.3.18–3.19.

101 SQUADRON RFC/RAF
Formed at South Farnborough 12.7.17 with personnel only. Joined the BEF under 9 (HQ) Wing

at St-André-aux-Bois 25.7.17, receiving FE2bs on arrival and moved to Clairmarais South 31.8.17. Special Duties Flt attached to the unit from 4.9.17 until 14.2.18. To Auchel 2.2.18, Catigny 16.2.18, still under 9 (HQ) Wing, but with 54 (Night) Wing 3.18. To Fienvillers 24.3.18, Haute Visée 25.3.18 and Famechon 7.4.18, all in 22 (Army) Wing. Moved to La Houssoye, Proyart East then Hancourt 25.10.18, all in 54 (Night) Wing. Joined 89 (Army) Wing at Catillon, 12.11.18 then moved to Stree 29.11.18 and Morville 13.12.18, both in 15 (Corps) Wing and transferred to 82 (Corps) Wing then 91 (Army) Wing 1.19. To Laneffe 12.3.19 and FE2bs withdrawn. Cadre moved to Filton 16.3.19.

Commanding Officers
Maj the Hon L.J.E. Twisleton-Wykeham-Fiennes, 19.7.17–31.10.17.
Maj W.B. Hargrave 31.10.17–27.7.18.
Maj E.L.M. Leveson Gower 27.7.18–17.8.18.
Capt A.R. Brook 17.8.18–23.8.18.
Maj J. Sowrey 23.8.18–11.1.19.
Capt C.W.D. Bell, 11.1.19–13.1.19.
Maj S.W. Price MC, 13.1.19–28.1.19.
Maj W.J. Tempest DSO MC, 28.1.19–15.3.19.

102 SQUADRON RFC/RAF
Formed at 51 HDS HQ Hingham 9.8.17 and joined the BEF in 13 (Army) Wing at St-André-aux-Bois, already with FE2bs, 24.9.17. Moved to Izel-le-Hameau 28.9.17, Treizennes and 9 (HQ) Wing 3.10.17 then returned to Izel-le-Hameau 5.3.18, temporarily in 54 (Night) Wing then in 13 (Army) Wing. Moved to Surcamps 10.4.18 then Famechon 19.9.18, Hurtebise Farm 19.10.18 and La Targette 23.10.18, all still in 13 (Army) Wing. To Bevillers 27.10.18 and transferred to 90 (Army) Wing then to Serny in 82 Wing 14.12.18. Acted as Demobilisation Squadron for 38 and 83 Sqns. FE2bs withdrawn by 23.3.19 when cadre moved to Lympne for disbandment on 1.7.19.
Special Duties Flt attached to the squadron from 14.2.18 until 3.5.18.

Commanding Officers
Maj H. Wyllie, 11.9.17–20.3.18.
Maj F.C. Baker, 20.3.18–15.2.19.
Capt M.L. Taylor from 15.2.19.

115 SQUADRON RAF
Mobilising in 4 Wing at Netheravon, used several FE2bs 3.18 until 6.18.

118 SQUADRON RAF
Training in 4 Wing at Netheravon, used several FE2bs 4.18 until 6.18.

131 SQUADRON RAF
Training at 29 Wing Shawbury, used several FE2bs 4.18 until 8.18.

148 SQUADRON RFC/RAF
Working up and mobilised at Ford Junction in 21 Wing as a night light bombing squadron with FE2bs 3.18. Joined the BEF at Auchel 25.4.18 in 54 (Night) Wing and moved to Sains-lès-Pernes in 10 (Army) Wing 3.5.18. To Camblain-l'Abbé 22.10.18 then Erre 31.10.18. To Serny in 82 Wing 9.12.18 and all FE2bs withdrawn by 2.19.
I Flt was attached to the squadron from 31.8.18 until 1.19.

Commanding Officers
Maj I.T. Lloyd, 10.2.18–1.19.

149 SQUADRON RFC/RAF
Working up and mobilised at Ford Junction in 21 Wing as a night light bombing squadron with FE2bs 3.18. Joined the BEF at Marquise 2.6.18 and moved to Quilen 4.6.18 then Alquines 16.6.18 in 11 (Army) Wing, with one flight detached to operated from Abeele then Clairmarais North. To Clairmarais North 16.9.18 then Ste-Marguerite 25.10.18, still in 11 (Army) Wing. To Fort Cognelée in 54 (Night) Wing 26.11.18 then Bickendorf with Army of Occupation 24.12.18. To Tallaght 26.3.19 reduced to cadre and FE2bs withdrawn before disbandment 1.8.19.

Commanding Officers
Maj BP Greenwood, 3.3.18–2.19.

216 SQUADRON RAF
see 16 SQN RNAS

SPECIAL DUTIES FLIGHT RFC/RAF
Formed in the BEF at Vert Galant in 9 (HQ) Wing 4.17 for the dropping of agents and carrier pigeons. Operated several FE2bs as part of mixed equipment from 1917. To Liettres 31.5.1917 and Clairmarais South, attached to 101 Sqn and still under 9 (HQ) Wing, 4.9.17. To Auchel attached to 102 Sqn 14.2.18 and under 54 (Night) Wing from 4.3.18. To Sains-lès-Pernes 3.5.18 then Fauquembergues 23.6.18, still in 54 (Night) Wing and attached to 58 Sqn. Re-titled I Flight 9.7.18.
Commanding Officers
Capt JW Woodhouse DSO MC Apr–Sept? 17

I FLIGHT RAF
Formed in the BEF and 54 (Night) Wing 9.7.18 ex Special Duties Flight at Fauquembergues and attached to 58 Sqn. To Sains-les-Pernes and attachment to 148 Sqn in 10 (Army) Wing 31.8.18, moving with that squadron to Camblain-l'Abbé 22.10.18 and Erre 31.10.18. To Serny, in 82 Wing, 9.12.18 and disbanded 1.19.
Commanding Officers
Capt PWB Lawrence by 8.18–@ 11.18.

16 SQUADRON RNAS
Formed ex A Sqn RNAS in 41 Wing RFC at Ochey 8.1.18 and received several FE2bs which operated alongside the main HP O/100 equipment. Became 216 Sqn RAF 1.4.18. FE2bs withdrawn by 5.18.
Commanding Officers
Sqn Comm KS Savory DSO 8.1.18.
Sqn Comm/Maj HA Buss DSC 19.1.18–1.9.18.

9 RESERVE/TRAINING SQUADRON RFC
Operating as 9 RS in 7 Wing at Norwich (Mousehold Heath) from 6.1916 and designated as a Higher Reserve Squadron with establishment 23.12.16 set at 9 HF + 9 FE2b. Re-designated as 9 TS 31.5.17. FE2bs withdrawn by 8.17 and replaced with DH4s.

19 RESERVE/TRAINING SQUADRON RFC
Operating as 19 RS in 6 Wing at Hounslow and designated as a Higher Reserve Squadron with establishment 23.12.16 set at 9 DH1 + 9 FE2b. Re-designated as 19 TS 31.5.17. FE2bs withdrawn by 8.17 and replaced with DH4s.

25 RESERVE SQUADRON RFC
Operating in 7 Wing at Thetford, with at least one FE2b by 5.17.

27 RESERVE SQUADRON RFC
Formed in 6 Wing at Gosport 22.5.16 by re-designating 41 Sqn and operated some FE2bs. To 17 Wing, still at Gosport, 9.8.16. Designated as an Elementary Reserve Squadron with establishment 23.12.16 set at 18 MF and FE2bs withdrawn by 1.17.

28 TRAINING SQUADRON RFC
Operating in 25 Wing at Castle Bromwich, reported as having at least one FE2b on charge 7.17–possibly a clerical error relating to 28 Sqn.

46 RESERVE/TRAINING SQUADRON RFC
Formed in 8 Wing at Doncaster 23.10.16, moving to Bramham Moor (Tadcaster) 17.12.16. Designated as a Higher Reserve Squadron with establishment 23.12.16 set at 6DH1 + 6 FE2b + 6 FE2d. Re-designated as 46 TS 31.5.17. To Catterick, still in 8 Wing, 23.7.17 with FE2bs and FE2ds withdrawn by 8.17 and replaced with DH4s.

59 RESERVE/TRAINING SQUADRON RFC
Formed at Gosport in 17 Wing 1.2.17, with nucleus from 28 Sqn. Had been designated to form as as a Higher Reserve Squadron with establishment 23.12.16 set at 6 DH1 + 6 FE2b + 6 FE2d. To Yatesbury and 21 Wing 30.4.17. Re-designated as 59 TS 31.5.17. FE2bs withdrawn by 8.17 and replaced with RE8s.

187 NIGHT TRAINING SQUADRON RAF
Operating as a preliminary NTS at East Retford

in 48 Wing, operated several FE2bs during mid 1918. Fully re-equipped with Avro 504K by 11.19.31.5.19.
Commanding Officers
Maj T.R. Irons, 2.6.1918–@ 1.1919.

192 DEPOT SQUADRON RFC
see 192 Night Training Squadron

191 NIGHT TRAINING SQUADRON RFC/RAF
Formed as 191 Depot Squadron at Marham in 47 Wing 6.11.17, with nucleus from 51 Squadron. Re-designated 191 NTS 21.12.17 and fully equipped with FE2bs. To Bury (Upwood) 1.7.18, still in 47 Wing. Disbanded 26.6.19.
Commanding Officers
Capt A.T. Harris from 6.11.17.
Maj A.T. Harris from 1.1.18.
Capt J.G. Griffiths from 10.6.18.
Maj J.G. Griffiths, 1.7.18–@ 1.19.

192 DEPOT SQUADRON RFC
see 192 Night Training Squadron

192 NIGHT TRAINING SQUADRON RFC/RAF
Formed as 192 Depot Squadron at Gainsborough 5.9.17, with nucleus from 33 (HD) Squadron. To East Retford 24.9.17 in 48 Wing. To Marham, in 47 Wing 10.10.17 and fully equipped with FE2bs. To Newmarket 14.11.17, still in 47 Wing. Re-designated 192 Night Training Squadron 21.12.17. Disbanded 31.5.19.
Commanding Officers
Maj J. Sowrey, 24.10.17–22.8.18.
Maj M.L. Taylor, 22.8.18–3.9.18.
Maj W.H. Tolhurst, 3.9.18–@ 1.19.

198 DEPOT SQUADRON RFC/RAF
Formed as 98 Depot Sqn at Rochford 8.2.17, by re-designating 11 RS. Re-designated 198 DS 27.6.17 and operated several FE2bs, discarding them before being re-designated 198 NTS on 26.12.17.
Commanding Officers
Maj B.F. Moore, 30.10.16(11 RS)–22.11.17.
Capt C.O. Usborne, 30.11.17–2.2.18.

99 DEPOT SQUADRON RFC
see 199 Night Training Squadron

199 DEPOT SQUADRON RFC
see 199 Night Training Squadron

199 NIGHT TRAINING SQUADRON RFC/RAF
Formed as 99 Depot Squadron at Rochford 1.6.17. To East Retford and North Midland Home Defence Wing 23.6.17 with FE2bs as part of mixed equipment. Fully equipped with FE2bs by 11.17. Re-designated 199 Depot Squadron 27.6.17. Re-designated 199 Night Training Squadron 21.12.17. Under 48 Wing from 1.2.18. To Harpswell 26.6.1918. Disbanded 1.5.19.
Commanding Officers
Maj J.T. Lloyd, 1.6.17–10.2.18.
Maj J.O.C. Orton, 11.2.18–@ 1.19.
Unit Markings
White 'lazy M' marking around the nacelle nose on FE2bs.

200 DEPOT SQUADRON RFC
see 200 Night Training Squadron

200 NIGHT TRAINING SQUADRON RFC/RAF
Formed as 200 Depot Squadron at East Retford, in the North Midland Home Defence Wing, 17.6.17 with FE2bs as part of mixed equipment. Fully equipped with FE2bs by 11.17. Re-designated 200 Night Training Squadron 21.12.1917. Under 48 Wing from 1.2.18. To Harpswell 10.11.1918 and disbanded 13.6.1919.
Commanding Officers
Maj C.H.R. Johnston, 17.6.17–26.2.18.
Maj W.E. Collison, 27.2.18–@ 1.19.
Unit Markings
White vertical bar on each side of the nacelle nose on FE2bs.

8 TRAINING DEPOT STATION RAF
Formed in 4 Wing at Netheravon 1.4.18 to train

HP pilots. Establishment set to include 18 FE2b, as intermediate training machines. Re-designated 8 TS 15.5.19, by which time FE2bs had been withdrawn.
Commanding Officers
Maj Mc Ewan by 6.18–@ 1.19.

12 TRAINING DEPOT STATION RAF
Formed in 4 Wing at Netheravon 1.4.18 to train HP pilots. Establishment set to include 18 FE2b, as intermediate training machines. Disbanded 15.5.19, by which time FE2bs had been withdrawn.

13 TRAINING DEPOT STATION RAF
Formed in 29 Wing at Ternhill 1.4.18 to train HP pilots. Establishment set to include 18 FE2b, as intermediate training machines. Re-designated 13 TS 14.3.19, by which time FE2bs had been withdrawn.

15 TRAINING DEPOT STATION RAF
Formed in 27 Wing at Hucknall 1.4.18 to train DH pilots but had at least 2 FE2bs on strength.

58 TRAINING DEPOT STATION RAF
Formed in 59 Wing at Cranwell 1.4.18, by re-designating 213 TDS, to train HP pilots. Establishment set to include 10 FE2b, as intermediate training machines. Re-designated 59 TS 14.3.19, by which time FE2bs had been withdrawn.

59 TRAINING DEPOT STATION RAF
Formed in 26 Wing at Portholme Meadow 1.4.18, by re-designating 211 TDS, to train HP pilots. Establishment set to include 18 FE2b, as intermediate training machines. To Scopwith and 59 Wing 15.10.18. Disbanded 13.3.19.

1 SCHOOL OF NAVIGATION & BOMB DROPPING
Formed in 33 Wing at Stonehenge 5.1.18, by re-designating 2 TDS, to instruct day and night bombing crews in tactics. Establishment set to include 40 FE2b, as intermediate training machines. Disbanded into the School of Air Pilotage, Andover, 23.9.19, by when FE2bs had been withdrawn.
Unit Markings
Stylised bomb marking under lower mainplanes.

2 SCHOOL OF NAVIGATION & BOMB DROPPING
Formed in 36 Wing at Andover 23.6.18 to instruct day and night bombing crews in tactics. Establishment set to include 40 FE2b, as intermediate training machines. Disbanded into the School of Air Pilotage, at Andover, 23.9.19, by when FE2bs had been withdrawn.

1 (AUXILIARY) SCHOOL OF AERIAL GUNNERY
Formed at Hythe 1.1.1917 by re-designating existing School of Aerial Gunnery, with detachment at Lympne–2.1917 and operating several FE2bs and FE2ds. Re-designated 1 (Observers) School of Aerial Gunnery 9.3.1918 when amalgamated with 3 (Auxiliary) School of Aerial Gunnery, by which time FE2s had been withdrawn.

2 (AUXILIARY) SCHOOL OF AERIAL GUNNERY
Formed at Turnberry 1.17 to instruct pilots in tactics and gunnery. Establishment set to include FE2b, for firing at ground, moored and towed targets. Disbanded into 1 School of Aerial Fighting & Gunnery, at Turnberry 10.5.18, by when FE2bs had been withdrawn.
Commanding Officers
Maj L.W.B. Rees VC.
Unit Markings
Large white station numbers painted either side of the nacelle nose.

4 (AUXILIARY) SCHOOL OF AERIAL GUNNERY
Formed at Marske 1.11.17 to instruct pilots in tactics and gunnery. Establishment set to include some FE2b, for firing at ground, moored and towed targets. Disbanded into 2 School of Aerial Fighting & Gunnery, at Marske 6.5.18, by which time FE2bs had been withdrawn.

TESTING SQUADRON RFC
Formed at Upavon, within CFS, to evaluate new designs/developments, including FE2s. To Martlesham Heath 16.1.17. Re-designated Aeroplane Experimental Station 16.10.17.

AEROPLANE EXPERIMENTAL STATION
Formed at Martlesham Heath 16.10.17 by re-designating the Testing Squadron and evaluated several FE2s. Continued post war and re-designated A&AEE 23.3.24.

ARMAMENT EXPERIMENTAL SQUADRON RFC
Formed at Orfordness 20.5.16 by re-designating 37 Sqn and evaluated guns, bombs and sighting arrangements using several FE2s. Re-designated Experimental Armament Station 13.10.17.

ARMAMENT EXPERIMENTAL STATION
Formed at Orfordness 13.10.17 from the existing Experimental Armament Squadron and evaluated guns, bombs and sighting arrangements using several FE2s. Continued post war absorbed into Aeroplane ES Martlesham Heath 16.3.20.

WIRELESS EXPERIMENTAL ESTABLISHMENT
Formed ex Wireless Testing Park at Biggin Hill 14.12.17 and operated several FE2bs as part of mixed equipment. In SE Area and Experimental Group from 1.4.18. Re-designated Instrument Design Establishment 1.11.19.

INSTRUMENT DESIGN ESTABLISHMENT RAF
Formed at Biggin Hill 1.11.19 and continued to operate several FE2bs as part of mixed equipment until 5.24.

1 AIRCRAFT PARK RFC
Formed at St-Omer from existing un-numbered Aircraft Park 17.3.15, responsible for the preparation, supply and repair of machines for squadrons on the northern part of the front and the primary receipt point for aeroplanes flown to and from England.

1 AIRCRAFT DEPOT
Formed at St-Omer 13.12.15 by re-designating 1 Aircraft Park and responsible for the supply, repair and reconstruction of machines on the northern part of the British Front. Moved to Guines 18.5.18, Petite Synthe 31.10.18 with advanced detachment at Croix, later Cognelée. To Arques, post war, then Dormagen by 15.7.19. Disbanded 5.11.19.
Commanding Officers
Lt Col S.A. Hebden by 8.18–@ 11.18.

2 AIRCRAFT DEPOT
Formed at Candas 13.12.15 by re-designating 2 Aircraft Park and responsible for the supply, repair and reconstruction of machines on the southern part of the British Front. Moved to Rang-du-Fliers 3.18, Grofliers by 6.18 and Vron by 11.18, with advanced detachment at Cambrai. Disbanded 19.
Commanding Officers
Lt Col A. Christie DSO by 8.18.
Lt Col W.H. Lang by 11.18.

3 AIRCRAFT DEPOT
Formed at Courban 3.18 and responsible for the supply, repair and reconstruction of machines of Dunkerque Command. Transferred to Independent Force 6.6.18. Disbanded 5.11.19.
Commanding Officers
Lt Col W Wright DSO by 8.18.

1 AEROPLANE SUPPLY DEPOT
Formed within 1 AD at St-Omer 11.17 for the distribution of machines to active squadrons. Moved to Marquise 10.4.18 and Merheim 18.7.19. Disbanded 19.
Commanding Officers
Lt Col B.F. Moore by 8.18.

2 AEROPLANE SUPPLY DEPOT
Formed within 2 AD at Fienvillers 11.17 for the distribution of machines to active squadrons, with Repair Park at Verton. Moved to Hesdin by 5.18 and Berck-sur-Mer by 7.18. Disbanded 19.
Commanding Officers
Lt Col V. Bettington by 8.18.

3 AEROPLANE SUPPLY DEPOT
Formed within 3 AD at Courban 3.18. Transferred to Independent force 6.6.18. Disbanded 19.

4 AEROPLANE SUPPLY DEPOT
Established in 5 Group at Guines 3.18. Disbanded 12.18.
Commanding Officers
Lt Col E.W. Stedman by 8.18.

1 AIR ISSUES SECTION
Formed within 1 AD at Serny 11.17, responsible for the final preparation of machines for issue to squadrons. Moved to Rely by 3.18. Disbanded 19.
Commanding Officers
Capt E. Digby-Johnson by 11.18.

2 AIR ISSUES SECTION
Formed within 2 AD at St-André-aux-Bois 25.3.18., responsible for the final preparation of machines for issue to squadrons. Moved to Fienvillers 7.10.18 and Cambrai 10.11.18. Disbanded 19.
Commanding Officers
Capt A. Denison MC by 11.18.

RECEPTION PARK
Formed within 1 ASD at Marquise for the receipt of machines from England. Disbanded 1919.
Commanding Officers
Maj E. Ainslie MBE by 11.18.

3 AIRCRAFT ACCEPTANCE PARK
Formed at Norwich (Mousehold Heath) in Eastern Area Command 1917, replacing existing AID section and responsible for the storage, testing, preparation and issue of FE2s from Boulton Paul, Ransomes Sims & Jefferies and Garretts. Re-designated 3 (Norwich) AAP 12.10.17. In 3 Area/Midland Area under 15 Group then Technical Group from 1.4.18. Disbanded 1919.

4 AIRCRAFT ACCEPTANCE PARK
Formed at Lincoln (West Common) in Northern Area Command 1917, replacing existing AID section and responsible for the storage, testing, preparation and issue of FE2s from Boulton Paul and Garretts. Re-designated 4 (Lincoln) AAP 12.10.17. In 3 Area/Midland Area under 15 Group then Technical Group from 1.4.18. Disbanded 1919.

6 (GLASGOW) AIRCRAFT ACCEPTANCE PARK
Formed at Renfrew (Glasgow) in Scottish Area Command 10.3.18 and responsible for the storage, testing, preparation and issue of FE2s from the Weir Group. In 5 Area/NW Area under 23 Group then Technical Group from 1.4.18. Disbanded 1919.

7 (KENLEY) AIRCRAFT ACCEPTANCE PARK
Formed at Kenley Common in Eastern Area Command 1917 and responsible for the storage, testing, preparation and issue of some FE2bs from 1918. In 1 Area/SE Area under 6 Group then Technical Group from 4.18. Disbanded 1919.

8 AIRCRAFT ACCEPTANCE PARK
Formed at Lympne 1917 in Eastern Area Command as the primary departure/destination point for machines issued to/returning from BEF units. Re-designated 8 (Lympne) AAP 12.10.17. In 1 Area/SE Area under 6 Group then Technical Group from 4.18. Disbanded 1920 (or 21?).

NORTHERN AIRCRAFT REPAIR DEPOT
Also referred to as Northern Aircraft Depot in Northern Area Command, functioning at Coal Aston from 28.4.17, for the repair and reconstruction of airframes, including FE2bs. Re-designated 2 (Northern) ARD 12.10.17.

SOUTHERN AIRCRAFT REPAIR DEPOT
Also referred to as Southern Aircraft Depot, formed at Farnborough in Aldershot Command by 1917, for the repair and reconstruction of airframes but also responsible for the testing of new machines, including many FE2s, for the Aeronautical Inspection Department. Re-designated 1 (Southern) ARD 12.10.17.

WESTERN AIRCRAFT REPAIR DEPOT
Also referred to as Western Aircraft Depot, functioning at Yate in Western Area Command from 31.5.17, for the repair and reconstruction of airframes, including FE2bs Re-designated 3 (Western) ARD 12.10.17.

2 (NORTHERN) AIRCRAFT REPAIR DEPOT
Formed ex NARD at Coal Aston 12.10.17 and used for storage of FE2bs, under NE Area, late 1918.

6 STORES DEPOT
Formed at Ascot by 1918, under 1 Area/SE Area and 6 Group and responsible for the storage of airframes, including FE2bs.

ARMAMENT SCHOOL
Formed at Hillingdon House, Uxbridge 1917, to give ground instruction in weaponry. Had FE2bs as GI airframes. Disbanded 1919.

2 SCHOOL OF MILITARY AERONAUTICS
Formed at Christchurch College, Oxford 27.10.16 by re-designating 2 School of Instruction. Operated some FE2bs as GI airframes. Word 'Military' dropped from title 1.4.18. Disbanded 24.1.19.

4 SCHOOL OF MILITARY AERONAUTICS
Formed at Toronto 1.7.1917. Had one FE2b on charge. Word 'Military' dropped from title 1.4.18. Disbanded 3.19.

AERONAUTICAL INSPECTION DEPARTMENT
Formed at Farnborough (1913?) to accept and test aeroplanes, including many FE2bs, prior to issuing for service units, with testing performed by SAD/SARD personnel. Sub-units attached to centres of aeroplane manufacture from 1916, becoming Aircraft Acceptance Parks 1917, after which the acceptance/testing system was wholly decentralised.

EXPERIMENTAL CONSTRUCTIVE & ARMAMENT DEPOT RNAS/RAF
Formed at Grain 12.17 as Experimental Constructive Depot and Experimental Armament Depot which merged 1918. Some FE2bs operated in ditching trials 1918.

CENTRAL FLYING SCHOOL (Australia) RFC/AFC
Formed at Point Cook, Victoria, in 1913 and received one FE2b 1917.

Presentation Aircraft

Complete list of presentation names allocated to Fees, as not all the names are given in the full serials list that follows.
Names could be carried on from one machine to another, but not necessarily of the same type, after loss.

4269 FE2b Jack Cannuck [Canada]	6344 FE2b Zanzibar No.3	6981 FE2b Malaya No.17 'The Alma Baker No.3'
4295 FE2a Gibraltar	6346 FE2b Black Watch No.2	
4898 FE2b Government of Johore No.14	6347 FE2b 'South Australia'	6982 FE2b Newfoundland No.4
4965 FE2b South Australia	6348 FE2b Malaya No.9 'Balas'	6986 FE2b Montreal No.4
4969 FE2b Shanghai No.3 'Shanghai Exhibition'	6350 FE2b Baroda No.13	6987 FE2b British Guiana
	6351 FE2b Baroda No.14	6988 FE2b Malaya No.8 'The Manessa Meyer'
4970 FE2b Punjab No.4 'Jind'	6352 FE2b Baroda No.15	
4971 FE2b Johore No.6	6357 FE2b Shanghai Britons No.3	6989 FE2b Newfoundland No.3
4974 FE2b Punjab No.10 'Kalabagh'	6356 FE2b donor unknown	6992 FE2b Shanghai Race Club No.2
4994 FE2b HH the Sultan of Kedah No.2	6359 FE2b Baroda No.17	6993 FE2b Baroda No.14
4996 FE2b Montreal No.3	6361 FE2b Montreal No.3	6994 FE2b Montreal No.3
4997 FE2b Baroda No.17	6363 FE2b Junagadh No.1	6996 FE2b Punjab No.5 'Nabha'
4998 FE2b Ceylon No.3 'A Nightjar from Ceylon'	6364 FE2b Junagadh No.2	6997 FE2b Punjab No.28 'Shalpur'
	6365 FE2b Mauritius No.2	6998 FE2b Trinidad Chamber of Commerce
5201 FE2b Bombay No.1	6366 FE2b Jamaica No.1	6999 FE2b Junagadh No.2
5202 FE2b Newfoundland No.4	6368 FE2b Junagadh No.3	7000 FE2b H. Teesdale Smith Adelaide
5203 FE2b River Plate	6369 FE2b Ceylon No.2 'A Devil Bird From Ceylon'	7002 FE2b Gold Coast No.2
5204 FE2b Montreal No.4		7003 FE2b Baroda No.18
5211 FE2b Bombay No.3	6928 FE2b Malaya No.12 'Perak Federated States Civil Service' [unconfirmed]	7004 FE2b Zanzibar No.4
5220 FE2b Bombay No.2		7005 FE2b Punjab No.4 'Jind'
5222 FE2b Punjab No.2 'Bahawalpur'		7006 FE2b Shanghai No.3 'Shanghai-Exhibition'
5224 FE2b Punjab No.4 'Jind'	6929 FE2b Malaya No.13 'The Alma Baker No.2' [unconfirmed]	
5225 FE2b Punjab No.5 'Nabha'		7007 FE2b Nova Scotia
5226 FE2b Punjab No.6 'Nabha'	6930 FE2b Malaya No.14 'The Garland Hope' [unconfirmed]	7008 FE2b Baroda No.13
5227 FE2b Punjab No.7 'Faridkot'		7009 FE2b Baroda No.15
5228 FE2b Punjab No.8 'Faridkot'	6931 FE2b Malaya No.15 'The Knoo Cheow Teong Gan Ngoh Bee' No.1 [unconfirmed]	7014 FE2b Maori
5229 FE2b Punjab No.9 'Kalsia'		7015 FE2b Gold Coast No.4
5230 FE2b Punjab No.10 'Kalabagh'		7017 FE2b Gold Coast No.8
5231 FE2b Malaya No.9 'Balas'	6932 FE2b Malaya No .16 'The Menang' [unconfirmed]	7018 FE2b Punjab No.32 'Montgomery'
5232 FE2b British Guiana		7019 FE2b Punjab No.3 'Jind'
5233 FE2b Trinidad	6933 FE2b Malaya No.17 'The Alma Baker No.3'	7020 FE2b Punjab No.34 'Jhelum'
5234 FE2b 'South Australia'		7021 FE2b Punjab No.33 'Ludhiana'
5235 FE2b Dominica	6934 FE2b Punjab No.26 ' Jullundar'	7022 FE2b Ceylon No.2 'A Devil Bird from Ceylon'
5236 FE2b Newfoundland No.1	6935 FE2b Punjab No.27 'Lyallpur'	
5238 FE2b The Akyab, Burma	6937 FE2b Punjab No.29 'Rawlpindi'	7023 FE2b Australia No.1 South Australia No.1 'The Sidney Kidman'
5239 FE2b Gold Coast No.1	6939 FE2b Punjab No.31 'Multan'	
5240 FE2b Gold Coast No.2	6940 FE2b Punjab No.32 'Montgomery'	7024 FE2b Gibraltar
5241 FE2b Gold Coast No.3	6943 FE2b Malaya No.11 'The Joffna' [unconfirmed]	7025 FE2b Government of Johore No.1
5242 FE2b Gold Coast No.4		7026 FE2b Government of Johore No.2
5243 FE2b Gold Coast No.5	6944 FE2b Newfoundland No.4	7027 FE2b Government of Johore No.3
5244 FE2b Gold Coast No.6	6945 FE2b Rajpipla	7666 FE2b Government of Jahore No.4
5245 FE2b Gold Coast No.7	6946 FE2b Zanzibar No.2	7669 FE2b Government of Johore No.5
5246 FE2b Gold Coast No.8	6947 FE2b Baroda No.6	7670 FE2b Government of Johore No.6
5247 FE2b Montreal No.1	6948 FE2b Ceylon No.4 'Flying Fox'	7671 FE2b Government of Johore No.7
5249 FE2b Ceylon No.3 'A Nightjar from Ceylon'	6949 FE2b Jungadh No.2	7672 FE2b Government of Johore No.8
	6950 FE2b Newfoundland No.2	7677 FE2b Government of Johore No.9
5250 FE2b Colony of Mauritius No.3	6951 FE2b HH the Sultan of Kedah No.1	7678 FE2b Government of Johore No.10
5642 FE2a Montreal No.1	6952 FE2b City of Adelaide, Presented by Mrs Harry Bickford	7680 FE2b Government of Johore No.11
5645 FE2a Montreal No.2		7681 FE2b Government of Johore No.12
5646 FE2a Nova Scotia	6953 FE2b Zanzibar No.1	7683 FE2b Government of Johore No.13
5647 FE2a Bombay No.2	6955 FE2b Punjab No.5 'Nabha'	7684 FE2b Government of Johore No.14
5648 FE2a Newfoundland No.3	6956 FE2b Malaya No.9 'Balas'	7685 FE2b Subjects of All Races in Siam
6329 FE2b Newfoundland No.2	6957 FE2b Gold Coast No.5	7686 FE2b Australia No.2 N.S.W. No.1 'The White Belltrees'
6330 FE2b Manitoba	6058 FE2b Sind	
6331 FE2b Ceylon No.2 'A Devil Bird from Ceylon'	6961 FE2b Jamaica No.2	7687 FE2b Australia No.3 N.S.W. No.2 'The White Edenglassie'
	6962 FE2b Gold Coast No.3	
6332 FE2b Malaya No.8 'The Manessa Meyer'	6963 FE2b Punjab No.7 'Faridkot'	7689 FE2b Australia No.4 N.S.W. No.3 'The Mrs P Kirby & Son'
	6968 FE2b Zanzibar No.3	
6333 FE2b Jamaica No.1	6969 FE2b Malaya No.18 'Singapore No.1'	7691 FE2b Australia No.5 N.S.W. No.4 'The F.J.White Sumarez & Baldblair'
6334 FE2b Montreal No.3	6970 FE2b Malaya No.19 'Singapore No.2'	
6335 FE2b Trinidad Chamber of Commerce	6971 FE2b Malaya No.20.'The Straits Times'	7692 FE2b Dominica
6336 FE2b British Guiana	6972 FE2b Malaya No.21 'The Tan Jiak Kim'	7693 FE2b Punjab No.6 'Nabha'
6338 FE2b Ceylon No.3 'A Nightjar from Ceylon'	6973 FE2b Malaya No.22 'The Sime Darby'	7694 FE2b Gold Coast No.7
	6974 FE2b Malaya No.23 'The Malacca'	7695 FE2b Baroda No.16
6339 FE2b Nova Scotia	6975 FE2b Malaya No.24 'The Penang No.1'	7696 FE2b Baroda No.19
6341 FE2b Zanzibar No.1	6978 FE2b Baroda No.19	7697 FE2b Punjab No.5 'Nabha'
6342 FE2b Zanzibar No.4	6979 FE2b Punjab No.1 'Bahawalpur No.1'	7698 FE2b Zanzibar No.2
6343 FE2b Zanzibar No.2	6980 FE2b Punjab No.6 Nabha	7699 FE2b Malaya No.21 'The Tan Jiak Kim'

7700 FE2b	Malaya No.29 'The Negri Sembilan'	
7701 FE2b	HH Sultan of Kedah No.2	
7702 FE2b	Malaya No.9 'Balas'	
7703 FE2b	Punjab No.9 'Kalsia'	
7704 FE2b	Gold Coast No.2	
7705 FE2b	Montreal No.4	
7706 FE2b	Toungoo District of Burma	
7707 FE2b	H. Teasdale Smith of Adelaide	
7708 FE2b	Jamaica No.1	
7709 FE2b	The Akyab, Burma	
7710 FE2b	Presented by the Residents of Aden	
7711 FE2b	Auckland	
7712 FE2b	Zanzibar No.5	
7713 FE2b	Zanzibar No.4	
7714 FE2b	Zanzibar No.7	
7715 FE2b	Zanzibar No.8	
A9 FE2d	Residents in the Punjab	
A778 FE2b	Alfred Muller Simpson, Parkside, S.A.	
A784 FE2b	Black Watch No.2	
A785 FE2b	Newfoundland No.1	
A789 FE2b	Punjab No.28 'Shahpur'	
A800 FE2b	Zanzibar No.5	
A801 FE2b	Australia No.7, N.S.W. No.6 'The White Edenglasssie'	
A802 FE2b	Malaya No.11 'The Joffna'	
A804 FE2b	Australia No.9, N.S.W. No.8 'The F.J. White Sumarez & Baldblair'	
A5438 FE2b	Zanzibar No.9	
A5439 FE2b	Zanzibar No.10	
A5440 FE2b	Zanzibar No.11	
A5441 FE2b	Zanzibar No.12	
A5442 FE2b	Malaya No.26 'The Malacca Chinese No.2'	
A5443 FE2b	Malaya No.27 'The Women of Malaya'	
A5444 FE2b	Malaya No.28 'Singapore No.3'	
A5445 FE2b	Malaya No.20 'The Straits Times'	
A5446 FE2b	Malaya No.11 'The Joffna'	
A5447 FE2b	Australia No.6, N.S.W. No.5 'The White Belltrees'	
A5448 FE2b	Australia No.7, N.S.W. No.6 'The White Edenglassie'	
A5449 FE2b	Australia No.8, N.S.W. No.7 'The Mrs P Kirby & Son'	
A5450 FE2b	Australia No.9, N.S.W. No.8 'The F.J. White Sumarez & Baldblair'	
A5451 FE2b	Punjab No.29 'Rawlpindi'	
A5452 FE2b	Baroda No.17	
A5453 FE2b	Montreal No.3	
A5454 FE2b	Junagadh No.2	
A5455 FE2b	Gold Coast No.5	
A5456 FE2b	Punjab No.32 'Montgomery'	
A5457 FE2b	Punjab No.3 'Jind'	
A5458 FE2b	River Plate	
A5459 FE2b	Baroda No.14	
A5460 FE2b	Manitoba	
A5461 FE2b	Montreal No.2	
A5462 FE2b	Punjab No.30 'Mainwale'	
A5463 FE2b	Malaya No.22 'The Sime Darby'	
A5464 FE2b	Sind	
A5465 FE2b	Punjab No.26 'Jullundar'	
A5466 FE2b	Baroda No.13	
A5467 FE2b	Newfoundland No.3	
A5468 FE2b	Malaya No.8 'The Manessa Meyer'	
A5469 FE2b	Ceylon	
A5470 FE2b	Zanzibar No.3	
A5471 FE2b	Shanghai Race Club No.2	
A5472 FE2b	Gold Coast No.1	
A5473 FE2b	HH Maharajah of Bikanir No.5	
A5474 FE2b	HH Maharajah of Bikanir No.6	
A5475 FE2b	HH Maharajah of Bikanir No.7	
A5476 FE2b	HH Maharajah of Bikanir No.8	
A5477 FE2b	Gold Coast No.9	
A5478 FE2b	Gold Coast No.10	
A5479 FE2b	Gold Coast No.11	
A5480 FE2b	Gold Coast No.12	
A5481 FE2b	Gold Coast No.13	
A5482 FE2b	Gold Coast No.14	
A5483 FE2b	Gold Coast No.15	
A5484 FE2b	Gold Coast No.16	
A5485 FE2b	Bombay No.1	
A5486 FE2b	City of Adelaide, Presented by Mrs Harry Bickford	
A5487 FE2b	British Subjects in Siam No.2	
A5518 FE2b	Mauritius No.15	
A5537 FE2b	Zanzibar No.1	
A5594 FE2b	Johore No.4	
A5601 FE2b	Gold Coast No.10	
A5629 FE2b	Malaya No.11 'The Joffna'	
A5630 FE2b	Punjab No.5 'Nabha'	
A5648 FE2b	Baroda No.14	
A5661 FE2b	Montreal No.2	
A5692 FE2b	Punjab No.1 'Bahawalpur'	
A5709 FE2b	Junagadh No.3	
A5729 FE2b	Gold Coast No.9	
A5731 FE2b	HH the Sultan of Kedah No.1	
A5732 FE2b	Malaya No.30 'The Ashworth Hope'	
A5733 FE2b	Waringford Burma	
A5735 FE2b	Mauritius No.13	
A5740 FE2b	Zanzibar No.3	
A5760 FE2b	Johore No.4	
A5761 FE2b	Mauritius No.15	
A5764 FE2b	HH the Sultan of Kedah No.2	
A6351 FE2d	Newfoundland No.2	
A6352 FE2d	Malaya No.29 'The Negri Sembilan'	
A6353 FE2d	Johore No.2	
A6355 FE2d	Gold Coast No.6	
A6356 FE2d	Ceylon No.4 'Flying Fox'	
A6357 FE2d	Punjab No.27 'Lyallpur'	
A6355 FE2d	Bombay No.2	
A6359 FE2d	Overseas Club Empire Day 1916 No.4	
A6360 FE2d	Australia No.10, N.S.W. No.9 'The Tweed'	
A6361 FE2d	Australia No.11, N.S.W. No.10 'Duplicate Tweed No.9'	
A6364 FE2d	Mauritius No.3	
A6384 FE2d	Newfoundland No.2	
A6385 FE2d	Punjab No.27 'Lyallpur'	
A6386 FE2d	Overseas Club Empire Day 1916 No.4	
A6387 FE2d	Punjab No.44 'Lahore No.4'	
A6388 FE2d	Punjab No.45 'Jhelum River'	
A6389 FE2d	Punjab No.46 'Chenab'	
A6390 FE2d	Punjab No.47 'Ravi'	
A6391 FE2d	Punjab No.48 'Beas'	
A6392 FE2d	Punjab No.49 'Sutley'	
A6393 FE2d	Punjab No.50 'Manjha'	
A6394 FE2d	Punjab No.51 'Malwa'	
A6395 FE2d	Udaipur No.1	
A6427 FE2d	Udaipur No.2	
A6428 FE2d	Johdpur	
A6429 FE2d	Bundi No.1	
A6430 FE2d	Ajmer	
A6431 FE2d	Kotah No.1	
A6432 FE2d	Kotah No.2	
A6433 FE2d	Rajputana No.1	
A6434 FE2d	Waringford Burma	
A6435 FE2d	People of Mauritius No.2	
A6442 FE2d	Toungoo District of Burma	
A6443 FE2d	Punjab No.29 'Rawlpindi'	
A6444 FE2d	Johore No.7	
A6445 FE2d	HH the Sultan of Kedah No.1	
A6446 FE2d	Malaya No.17 'The Alma Baker No.3'	
A6447 FE2d	Colony of Mauritius No.1	
A6448 FE2d	Mauritius No.2	
A6455 FE2d	Mauritius No.3	
A6456 FE2d	Mauritius No.4	
A6457 FE2d	Australia No.9 N.S.W. No 8 'The F.J. White Sumarez & Baldblair'	
A6480 FE2d	Mauritius No.5	
A6485 FE2d	Mauritius No.6	
A6498 FE2d	Mauritius No.7	
A6499 FE2d	Mauritius No.8	
A6500 FE2d	Mauritius No.9	
A6510 FE2d	Baroda No.13	
A6511 FE2d	Mauritius No.10	
A6512 FE2d	Mauritius No.11	
A6513 FE2d	Mauritius No.12	
A6516 FE2d	Mauritius No.13	
A6522 FE2d	Mauritius No.14	
A6527 FE2d	Mauritius No.15	
A6528 FE2d	Australia No.12 N.S.W. No.11 'The Macintyre Kayuga Estate'	
A6547 FE2d	Australia No.13 N.S.W. No.12 'The Macintyre Kayuga Estate'	
A6548 FE2d	Malaya No.30 'The Ashworth Hope'	
A6555 FE2d	Malaya No.31 'The Kuala Kangsar'	
A6581 FE2d	Malaya No.6 [unconfirmed]	
A8950 FE2b	Leeds [Imperial Air Fleet Gift to India]	
B439 FE2b	Malaya No.17 'The Alma Baker No.3'	
B440 FE2b	Gold Coast No.14	
B441 FE2b	Mauritius No.4	
B442 FE2b	Malaya No.28 'Singapore No.2'	
B443 FE2b	Johore No.7	
B453 FE2b	Junagadh No.2	
B454 FE2b	Shanghai No.3 'Shanghai Exhibition'	
B455 FE2b	Rajpipla	
B456 FE2b	Malaya No.8 'The Manessa Meyer'	
B457 FE2b	Zanzibar No.5	
B483 FE2b	Mauritius No.15	
B485 FE2b	Punjab No.29 'Rawlpindi'	
B1863 FE2d	Malaya No.32 'The A.N. Kenion'	
B1865 FE2d	Falkland	
B1873 FE2d	Punjab No.5 'Nabha'	
B1874 FE2d	Junagadh No.2	
B1877 FE2b	St Andrews No.1	
B1880 FE2d	Punjab No.29 'Rawlpindi'	
B1888 FE2d	British Residents in the Netherlands East Indies No.1	
B1889 FE2d	Bundi No.1	
B1896 FE2d	Orissa States No.1	
B1897 FE2d	Australia No.14, N.S.W. No.13.'The Tweed Armidale'	
B1900 FE2d	British Residents in the Netherlands East Indies No.1	
C9786 FE2b	Malaya No.11 'The Joffna'	
C9789 FE2b	Malaya No.17 'The Alma Baker No.3'	
C9790 FE2b	Gold Coast No.10	
C9791 FE2b	Shanghai No.3 'Shanghai Exhibition'	
C9828 FE 2b	Mauritius No.4	
C9829 FE2b	Malaya No.19 'Singapore No.2'	
C9833 FE2b	Punjab No.27 ' Lyallpur'	
C9834 FE2b	Shanghai No.3 'Shanghai Exhibition'	
D3824 FE2b	Punjab No.16	
D3829 FE2b	Kaffraria (Residents of South Africa)	
D3830 FE2b	Punjab No.36	
D9917 FE2b	Montreal	
D9964 FE2b	Gold Coast Aborigines No.2	
D9991 FE2b	API, Presented by the Paramount Chief & Basuto Nation	
D9993 FE2b	Australia No.6	
D9998 FE2b	Australia No.1, South Australia No.1	
D9999 FE2b	Australia No.16	
E7037 FE2b	Hawkes Bay New Zealand	
E7042 FE2b	Baroda No.6	
E7043 FE2b	Johannesburg No.2	
E7044 FE2b	British Residents in the Netherlands East Indies No.2	
E7046 FE2b	Malaya No.4 'The Wi-Cheng Kim'	
E7052 FE2b	Central Argentine Railway Aeroplane	
E7056 FE2b	Malaya No.16 'The Menang'	
E7064 FE2b	South Africa	
E7068 FE2b	Baroda No.13	
E7074 FE2b	Madras No.1	
E7078 FE2b	Mauritius No.1	
E7080 FE2b	Punjab No.6 'Nabha'	
E7081 FE2b	Faridkot No.3	
E7082 FE2b	Leeds [Imperial Air Fleet Gift to India]	
E7085 FE2b	Toungoo District of Burma	
E7086 FE2b	Punjab No.5 'Nabha'	
E7087 FE2b	Malaya No.24 'The Penang No.1'	
E7088 FE2b	Malaya No.17 'The Alma Baker No.3'	
E7089 FE2b	Zanzibar No.10	
E7090 FE2b	Punjab No.11 'Kalabagh'	
E7092 FE2b	Britons Overseas No.11	
E7093 FE2b	'Masupha No.1' The Paramount Chief & Basuto Nation	
E7094 FE2b	'Makhabanejara' The Paramount Chief & the Basuto Nation	
E7095 FE2b	A.D.P. Non Mihi Sed Patriae	
E7096 FE2b	Junagadh No.3	
E7097 FE2b	Britons Overseas No.10	
E7100 FE2b	Huddersfield	
E7101 FE2b	North China Aeroplane	
E7102 FE2b	Rio de Janeiro Britons No.3	
E7103 FE2b	Britons in Nicaragua	
E7104 FE2b	Citizens Town & District of Thana	
E7105 FE2b	'Lepoqo' The Paramount Chief & Basuto NationLepoqo	
E7106 FE2b	Australia No.21, N.S.W. No.19	
E7107 FE2b	Imperial Order of Daughters of the British Empire (USA)	

2864: 1 RAF FE2a (120hp Austro-Daimler) built by the Royal Aircraft Factory, Farnborough under War Office authority.

2864 Third machine ff 16.3.15 (Capt FW Goodden). **CFS** dd 20.3.15 for comparative tests with Voisin LA. Allotted to BEF. **1 AP**. **6 Sqn** dd ex 1 AP 20.5.15 (Lt L Strange). **1 AP** ex 6 Sqn 22.5.15. **6 Sqn** re-issued ex 1 AP 29.6.15, in combats on recce 25.7.15 (2Lt MK Cooper-King/2Lt EW Leggatt engaged an EA near Linselles), on recce 28.7.15 (Capt LA Strange/Lt ECRG Braddyll OK after hit by fire from an Aviatik near Ypres), on recce 1.8.15 (2Lt MK Cooper-King/2Lt EW Leggatt engaged an EA over Polygon Wood), on recce 2.8.15 (Capt LG Hawker/2Lt HJ Payn sent an EA down near Houthem and drove off two others), on patrol 12.9.15 (2Lt MK Cooper-King/Lt MW Thomas engaged an Aviatik near Westroosebeke) and 21.9.15 on art obs then recce (Lt JL Kinnear/Lt RC? Morgan engaged an twin engined EA near Hooge and then sent an EA down smoking near Polygon Wood). Deleted 22.9.15.

4227 – 4228: 2 RAF FE2a (120hp Austro-Daimler) built by the Royal Aircraft Factory, Farnborough under War Office authority.

4227 First machine, completed 22.1.15 with 100hp Green and flown 26.1.15 (Capt FW Goodden). Converted to 120hp Austro-Daimler and ready by 17.4.15. **6 Sqn** dd ex England 14.5.15, in combat 20.6.15 (Lt JL Kinnear/Lt GA Parker engaged an EA near Roulers), 2.8.16 (Capt LG Hawker/Lt A? Payze forced an EA C-type to land near Wulverghem) and 11.8.15 (Capt LG Hawker/Lt N Clifton forced down an EA C-type near Houthem and a Fokker near Lille) then LIA 5.9.15 (Capt WC Adamson/Lt ECRG Braddyll KIA – shot down by AA).

4228 Second machine, fitted with 100hp Green but converted to 120hp Austro-Daimler and ready by 3.5.15. **6 Sqn** dd ex England 14.5.15, damaged 16.5.15, repaired and in combats 3.6.16 (Capt LA Strange/Lt GA Parker engaged an EA near Houthulst Wood), 6.6.16 (Capt LA Strange/Lt GA Parker drove off an EA near Polygon Wood), 16.6.16 (Capt LA Strange/Lt GA Parker sent an LVG

The ungainly appearance of the extended oleo undercarriage is very clear as Capt Frank Goodden brings the first FE2a, 4227, 100hp Green engine, in to land on 26 January 1915.

down over Polygon Wood). **1 AP** ex 6 Sqn 17.6.15.

4253: 1 RAF FE2a (120hp Austro-Daimler) built by the Royal Aircraft Factory, Farnborough under War Office authority.

4253 Fourth machine. **6 Sqn** Abeele dd ex Administrative Wing 19.5.15, in combat 31.7.15 (Lt WHC Mansfield/Lt ECRG Braddyll engaged an Albatros near Tournai). **1 AD** ex 6 Sqn 2.10.15 and deleted 19.10.15.

4256 – 4292: 37 RAF FE2b (120hp Beardmore) built by G & J Weir Ltd, Cathcart under Contract 94/A/210.

4256 RAF fitted with 150hp RAF 5 engine 27.4.16 and tested with RAF gyroscopic bomb-sight 9.16 and still at RAF 4.17. Armament ES . Still on RFC charge 3.18.

4257 RAF Farnborough 16.2.16.

4258 **22 Sqn** dd ex Glasgow 26.2.16. **18 Sqn** dd ex 1 AP 19.5.16, damaged landing 10.7.16 and damaged in combat with 7 EA near Gommecourt 9.11.16 (Capt GH Norman WIA/2Lt CP Murchie OK). **1 AD** ex 18 Sqn 4.12.16 and flown to England 20.12.16. Allotted to Training Brigade 22.12.16.

4259 **28 Sqn** dd 9.3.16. **22 Sqn** dd ex 28 Sqn 2.4.16. At Dover 15.4.16. **18 Sqn** by 17.6.16.

4260 **35 Sqn** A Flt dd 15.3.16 and deleted 4.8.16.

4261 **35 Sqn** B Flt dd 15.3.16. Burnt out 14.4.16

4262 **RAF** with RAF 5, allotted to BEF but re-allotted to **Reserve Aircraft Park** 22.5.16. **RAF** 16.6.16.

4263

4264 **35 Sqn** dd ex Farnborough 11.5.16, visited Northolt 6.16 (Lt Russell). **9 RS** dd ex 35 Sqn 5.7.16.

4265 **19 RS** dd 12.6.16. **1 AD** tested 5.7.17. Deleted 7.17.

4266 Thetford (35 Sqn?) by 23.5.16. **42 Sqn** dd ex Castle Bromwich 8.6.16; SOC and deleted 14.7.16.

4267 Allotted to BEF 20.5.16. **20 Sqn** dd ex 1 AD 31.5.16. **22 Sqn** by 16.6.16 ('new machine from 20 Sqn') and vict 21.7.16 (2Lt EGA Bowen/2Lt WS Mansell sent a Roland D-type OOC near Leuze Wood at 10.00) then wrecked and deleted after overturned in landing crash near Grovetown railhead after combat 7.9.16 (2Lt FD Holder/Lt E Ambler OK.) 120hp Beardmore. Flying time 184hr 48min. **2 AD** ex 22 Sqn 9.9.16 and deleted 12.9.16, serviceable parts to store.

4268 **27 RS** by 9.16.

4269 Presentation a/c *Jack Cannuck*. **RAF** allotted to BEF 20.5.16 (120hp Beardmore). **25 Sqn** dd ex 1 AD St-Omer 22.5.16, wrecked in crash 18.6.16 (Lt Read/Lt JA Mann OK). 1 AD, deleted 18.6.16, NWR, Flying time 24hr 13min.

4270 Fitted with 140hp RAF 4a (1012/WD3642). **10 RS** 6.16. **19 RS** dd 8.8.16, deleted 9.11.16.

4271 **23 Sqn** damaged taking off on photo sortie (hit road) 10.7.16. **2 AD** under re-build 1.9.16, 1.10.16, 31.12.16 and 28.2.17. **100 Sqn** dd ex 2 AD 7.4.17. Flown to England ex

FE2b 4270 experimentally fitted with a 140hp RAF 4a engine, in front of 1915 pattern flight sheds, probably at 19RS Hounslow.

1 AD 17.6.17 (120hp Beardmore).

4272 Allotted to BEF 20.5.16. **RAF** 24.5.16 (120hp Beardmore 538/WD6918). **18 Sqn** dd ex 1 AD 31.5.16. **25 Sqn** damaged when binoculars hit propeller 21.6.16 (Lt GR McCubbin/Cpl J Waller OK) and vict 15.7.16 (2Lt K Mathewson/AM1 JM Booth destroyed a Fokker E.III near La Bassée at 05.00) then LIA in combat with EA near Lens 3.8.16 (Lt K Mathewson/Sapper EM des Brisay KIA shot down in flames by a Fokker E-type. Flying time 85hr 27min).

4273 **RAF** 7.6.16. Crashed at Gosport.

4274 **10 RS**, allotted 21.6.16 (engine WD1353).

4275 **RAF** 9.6.16. **23 Sqn** by 28.6.16. **28 Sqn** by 17.7.16.

4276 **RAF** 9.6.16. **35 Sqn** dd ex Gosport 16.6.16. **64 Sqn** dd ex 35 Sqn 15.8.16. But 18 Sqn wrecked in crash 8.8.16 (2Lt HMB Law KIFA).

4277 **9 RS** and wrecked in crash from stall 30.9.16 (Sgt WM Jackson KIFA).

4278 Farnborough 27.6.16 allotted to BEF (120hp Beardmore). **10 RS** re-allotted to EF. **2 AD** 12.7.16. **11 Sqn** damaged landing on delivery flight ex 2 AD 15.7.16. **22 Sqn** and LIA on photo sortie 1.8.16 (Capt WA Summers/Flt Sgt LC Clarkson KIA – hit by AA SW of Bapaume. Flying time 12hr 6min).

4279 **SAD** allotted to BEF 9.6.16. **23 Sqn** dd ex 2 AD 10.11.16. **1 AD**, wrecked, ex 2 AD 4.12.16 (120hp Beardmore) and to England for reconstruction. **64 Sqn** by 3.17 until @ 4.5.17. **76 HDS** by 6.17 until @ 7.17. **192 NTS** and wrecked in crash after control lost on slow down-wind turn on bombing practice 21.1.18 (Lt HP Freeman/2Lt CE Rooke KIFA, 120hp Beardmore 229/WD1297M).

4280 Allotted to BEF 13.6.16. **25 Sqn** dd ex 1 AD 29.4.16. **Pilots Pool 1 AD** as practice machine and wrecked 1.9.16. To England in packing case ex 1 AD 28.9.16 (120hp Beardmore, flying time 74hr 13min). **SARD** tested 29.3.17. **19 RS** crashed 23.4.17 (crew injured).

4281 Allotted to BEF 9.6.16. **25 Sqn** dd ex 1 AD 18.7.16 and wrecked landing short 28.8.16. **1 AD** ex 25 Sqn 1.9.16 and deleted 1.9.16 (120hp Beardmore, NWR, flying time 73hr 47min).

4282 Converted to FE2c and tested at **SARD** 11.7.17 (pressure dud).

4283 At Renfrew 17.6.16, allotted to BEF. **25 Sqn** dd ex 1 AD 24.6.16 and victs 26.6.16 (2Lt LL Richardson/AM2 LS Court forced a Fokker E-type to land near Annoeullin) and 2.7.16 (2Lt LL Richardson/Lt M Vaughan Lewes forced an Albatros C-type to land near Habourdin) then crashed at Bailleul after fuel fault 18.7.16 (2Lt LL Richardson IIFA/Lt M Vaughan-Lewes fatally IIFA). **1 AD** and deleted 20.7.16 (NWR, flying time 34hr 50min).

4284 At Renfrew 24.6.16, allotted to BEF. **SAD** 20.9.16, re-allotted to Training Brigade. **19 RS** dd ex SAD 22.9.16. Crashed at Tonbridge en-route for EF.

4285 Allotted to BEF 19.6.16. **22 Sqn** and LIA on recce 25.8.16 (Lt RD Walker/2Lt C Smith POW after engine failed, 120hp Beardmore 475).

4286 At Renfrew 29.6.16, allotted to BEF. **22 Sqn** and vict but damaged in combat near Guedecourt 30.7.16 (Lt GHA Hawkins/2Lt CPF Lowson OK – sent an EA D type OOC near Guedecourt at 12.40) damaged in combat near Guedecourt 30.7.16 (Lt GHA Hawkins/2Lt CPF Lowson OK – tank hit and landed at 4 Sqn) and again damaged in combat 8.8.16 and force landed at 4 Sqn aerodrome (Lt GHA Hawkins WIA/2Lt CM Clement OK).

4287 Allotted to BEF 24.6.16. **22 Sqn** dd ex 2 AD Candas 16.7.16 and damaged in accidental

4285 'Rolls Rabbit' in German hands after capture on 25 August 1916.

fire 25.12.16. **2 AD** ex 22 Sqn 28.12.16 and deleted 29.12.16.

4288 At Renfrew 30.6.16, allotted to BEF. **25 Sqn** dd ex 1 AD 28.7.16. **22 Sqn** and damaged in combat 8.8.16 (2Lt CPF Lowson OK/2Lt LWB Parsons WIA – landed at 4 Sqn) and hit in propeller during combat 3.9.16 (2Lt CM Clement/Cpl JK Campbell OK – propeller hit, force-landed at Baizieux). **2 AD** ex 25 Sqn 4.9.16 and deleted 12.9.16 (120hp Beardmore, NWR, flying time 84hr 6min, serviceable parts to store).

4289 Allotted to BEF 29.6.16 (120hp Beardmore. **25 Sqn** dd ex 1 AD 24.6.16. **2 AD** tested 15.8.16. **22 Sqn** and damaged in combat with 2 EA over Combles 25.8.16 (Capt JHS Tyssen/Lt SH Clarke OK – fuel tank hit). **18 Sqn** by 27.10.16. **1 AD** ex 18 Sqn 5.12.16. To England 20.12.16 and allotted to Training Brigade 22.12.16.

4290 At Renfrew 13.7.16, allotted to BEF. **2 AD** dd ex 1 AD 28.7.16. **11 Sqn** and LIA on 18.15 OP 2.9.16 (2Lt E Burton/2Lt FW Griffiths POW. 160hp Beardmore No.26. Flying time 16hr 35min).

4291 At Renfrew 3.7.16, allotted to BEF (120hp Beardmore). **1 AD** and deleted 14.7.16 (NWR, flying time 2hr 30min).

4292 At Renfrew 7.7.16, allotted to BEF (160hp Beardmore). **25 Sqn** dd ex 1 AD 6.8.16 and LIA near Oppy on bombing raid 10.10.16 (2Lt M Hayne KIA/Lt AHM Copeland POW wdd – brought down by EA. 160hp Beardmore. Flying time 76hr 25min).

4295: 1 RAF FE2a (120hp Austro-Daimler) built by the Royal Aircraft Factory, Farnborough under War Office authority.

4295 Presentation a/c *Gibraltar* wef 22.6.15. **RAF** 23.6.15 - 31.7.15, tested with 120hp Beardmore 135. Flown to France for 16 Sqn 2.7.15. **6 Sqn** dd ex 1 AP 6.7.15. **1 AP** for re-build ex 6 Sqn 13.8.15. **6 Sqn** ex 1 AP 27.9.15 and wrecked and dismantled 3.12.15 (flying time 36hr 25min). **1 AD** ex 6 Sqn and deleted 15.12.15.

4838 – 5000: 163 RAF FE2b (120hp Beardmore or RAF 5 specified, but Beardmore 120 & 160hp installed) built by G & J Weir Ltd, Cathcart under continuing Contract 94/A/210.

4838 Allotted to BEF (160hp Beardmore) 16.7.16. **2 AD** dd ex 1 AD 11.7.16. **11 Sqn** by 31.8.16 and force-landed on photo sortie 14.9.16 after map case hit propeller. **2 AD** ex 11 Sqn 16.9.16. Wrecked at 2 AD 27.9.16 and to England in packing case ex 2 AD 30.9.16 (120hp Beardmore). **19 RS** by 4.9.16.

4839 At Renfrew, allotted to BEF (160hp Beardmore) 13.7.16. **25 Sqn** by 1.5.16. **1 AD** ex 25 Sqn. **25 Sqn** ex 1 AD ARS 29.7.16 and vict 9.8.16 (2Lt NWW Webb/Lt CS Workman forced an Albatros C-type to land near Beaumont) then damaged in successful combat near Tourmignies 27.9.16 (2Lt VW Harrison/Sgt LS Court OK – had destroyed a LVG C type near Tourmignies but brought down by Ltn A Dissenbach/Obltn Schilling FAb 22) and further victs 17.3.17 (Capt LL

4290 of 11 Squadron, shot down by FAb22 on 2 September 1916.

119

Curious German soldiers gather round the smouldering remains of 4844, lost on 17 September 1916.

Richardson/2Lt DC Woollen destroyed an Albatros D.II in flames near Beaumont at 11.30), 26.4.17 (Lt C Dunlop/2Lt JB Weir sent an Albatros down in flames near Izel-les-Equerchin at 17.20) and 1.5.17 (2Lt RG Malcolm/Cpl L Emsden destroyed an Albatros D.II in flames near Bois Bernard at 18.00).

4840 Allotted to BEF (160hp Beardmore) 21.7.16. **25 Sqn** dd ex 1 AD 8.8.16 and wrecked in crash on bombing sortie 16.8.16 (2Lt AS Butler KIFA/AM1 ER Brotherton IIFA).

4841 At Renfrew, allotted to BEF (160hp Beardmore) 13.7.16. **25 Sqn** dd ex 1 AD 16.8.16 and victs 15.9.16 (2Lt NWW Webb/Lt CS Workman destroyed a Fokker E-type near Fresnoy) and 20.10.16 (Sgt GJ Mackie/Sgt GR Horrocks destroyed a Fokker E.III near Bauvin at 09.10)then wrecked in crash 10.11.16 (Lt ESP Hynes/Lt CH Birdmead KIFA – propeller disintegrated and destroyed tail booms). Wreckage to **1 AD** 11.11.16 and deleted 14.11.16.

4842 Allotted to BEF (120hp Beardmore) 21.7.16. **18 Sqn** by 8.16 and damaged in combat on photo escort near Flers 16.9.16 (Capt FC Baker/2Lt AV Sherwell OK). **1 AD** ex 18 Sqn 22.1.17 and flown to England 1.2.17.

4843 Allotted to BEF (160hp Beardmore) 15.7.16. **1 AD** and deleted 2.8.16 (160hp Beardmore, NWR, flying time 2hr 15min).

4844 Allotted to BEF (160hp Beardmore) 7.8.16. **11 Sqn** and vict 15.9.16 (2Lt TPL Molloy/Sgt GJ Morton destroyed an EA D type near Bapaume at 09.45) then LIA in combat on bombing escort near Marcoing 17.9.16 (2Lt TPL Molloy POW/Sgt GJ Morton POW wdd – shot down by Ltn W Frankl, Jasta 4. 160hp Beardmore. Flying time 64hr).

4845 Allotted to BEF (160hp Beardmore) 21.7.16. **1 AD** dd ex Farnborough 16.8.16. **25 Sqn** dd ex 1 AD 19.8.16. **2 AD** ex 25 Sqn 12.9.16. **18 Sqn** dd ex 2 AD 13.9.16 (120hp Beardmore) and damaged hitting mound on landing 21.11.16. **1 AD** ex 18 Sqn 5.1.17. Flown to England 23.1.17 (flying time 125hr 45min). Allotted to Training Brigade 27.1.17.

4846 RAF 10.1.17. **Armament ES**. Flown Orfordness to Hendon 28.5.18. **RAE** 29.5.18 for tests with adjustable tailplane.

4847 Allotted to BEF (120hp Beardmore) 9.8.16. **25 Sqn** dd ex 1 AD 2.8.16 and victs 16.10.16 (2Lt JLN Bennett-Boggs/2Lt AE Godfrey sent a Roland D-type OOC near Douai), 9.2.17 (Lt C Dunlop/2Lt JB Weir destroyed a Halberstadt D type in flames near Provin/La Bassée at 11.15) and 6.4.17 (2Lt B King/Cpl L Emsden destroyed a Halberstadt D type near Vimy at 10.45) then damaged in crash 16.3.17 (pilot OK/Sgt CWB Buchanan KIFA) and wrecked in crash near Vimy 26.4.17 (2Lt B King/Cpl L Emsden OK – 160hp engine, 226hr 37min flying time).

4848 Allotted to BEF (120hp Beardmore) 10.8.16. **1 AD** ex England 31.10.16. **2 AD** ex 1 AD 3.11.16 (Sgt T Mottershead) **18 Sqn** dd ex 2 AD 14.11.16 and LIA in combat near Warlencourt 20.11.16 (2Lt GS Hall POW fatally wdd/2Lt G Doughty KIA – engine 295/WD1357 – shot down by Ltn M Fr v Richthofen, Jasta 2).

4849 Allotted to BEF (120hp Beardmore) 15.8.16. **22 Sqn** dd ex 2 AD 4.9.16 and vict 20.10.16 (2Lt GH Hackwill/AM1 Edwards sent an Albatros D.I OOC near Grevillers at 09.30). **2 AD** ex 22 Sqn 6.11.16 with 120hp engine 6.11.16, serviceable 31.12.16 and deleted 20.2.17 (NWR, 104 flying hours).

4850 Allotted to BEF (160hp Beardmore) 15.8.16 and 21.8.16. **11 Sqn** dd ex 1 AD 17.9.16 and vict 11.3.17 (Lt NH Read/2Lt LN Smith destroyed an Albatros D.II near Monchy le Preux at 12.30) then LIA 27.4.17 (2Lt JA Cairns/AM1 EG Perry POW – engine 979/WD7589 – probably shot down by Ltn L v Richthofen, Jasta 11).

4851 Allotted to BEF 29.7.16. **2 AD**, serviceable, 1.9.16. **23 Sqn** dd ex 2 AD 3.9.16 and LIA in combat during OP 11.9.16 (2Lt GJ Firbank/2Lt LGH Vernon KIA (120hp Beardmore, flying time 12hr 19min).

4852 Allotted to BEF (120hp Beardmore) 8.8.16 and 1.9.16. **23 Sqn** dd ex 2 AD 1.9.16 and LIA on recce near Marcoing 17.9.16 (Sgt B Irwin/2Lt FG Thiery KIA – probably shot down by Hptm M Zander, Jasta 1, a/c had 120hp Beardmore and 28hr 7min flying time).

4853 Allotted to BEF (120hp Beardmore) 3.8.16. **25 Sqn** dd ex 1 AD 31.8.16. **2 AD** ex 25 Sqn 12.9.16. **18 Sqn** dd ex 2 AD 13.9.16 and LIA

on photo sortie near Le Transloy in combat with EA 23.9.16 (2Lt JL Tibbetts POW wdd/Lt WG Warn KIA. 120hp Beardmore, flying time 26hr 15min). BUT 2 AD wrecked ex 18 Sqn 8.11.16.

4854 Allotted to BEF (120hp Beardmore) 7.8.16. **18 Sqn** dd ex 1 AD 4.9.16 and damaged in combat near Flers 16.9.16 (2Lt F Hall/2Lt HS Royffe OK – fuel tank hit). **2 AD** ex 18 Sqn 19.9.16. To England, wrecked, in packing case ex 2 AD 30.9.16 (120hp Beardmore). **19 TS** Hounslow by 22.6.17.

4855 Allotted to BEF (120hp Beardmore) 9.8.16. **2 AD** ex 1 AD 1.9.16. **22 Sqn** dd ex 2 AD 6.9.16, fitted with 160hp Beardmore, and victs 16.10.16 (2Lt CS Duffus/Cpl F Johnson sent an EA D-type OOC near Guedecourt at 14.40) and 4.12.16 (2Lt AT Loyd/2Lt LC Welford sent an EA Type 'K' OOC near Beaulencourt at 10.10), 11.2.17 (2Lt PW Chambers/2Lt F O'Sullivan destroyed an Albatros D.II near Grevillers at 12.30) and 2.4.17 (Capt CR Cox/2Lt LC Welford destroyed a Halberstadt D type near Gouzeaucourt at 08.50 – shared with 24 Sqn).). **2 AD** ex 22 Sqn 5.7.17 and deleted 17.7.17 (recorded as A4855). **SARD** tested 2.8.17 (OK – recorded as A4855).

4856 Allotted to BEF (120hp Beardmore) 10.8.16 and 1.9.16. **2 AD** ex 1 AD 1.9.16. **18 Sqn** dd ex 2 AD 7.9.16 and LIA when wrecked hitting shell hole in forced-landing following combat near Morval 10.10.16 (2Lt CG Shaumer/AM1 L Hardinge OK, 120hp Beardmore, SOC with 41hr 55min flying time). **2 AD** ex 18 Sqn 14.10.16 and deleted 19.10.16 with serviceable parts to store.

4857 Allotted to BEF (120hp Beardmore) 11.8.16 and re-allotted 4.9.16. **2 AD** ex 1 AD 12.9.16. **23 Sqn** dd ex 2 AD 17.9.16 and damaged in combat near Bertincourt 24.9.16 (2Lt JC Griffiths OK/2Lt RS Osmaston KIA – engine shot up). **2 AD** ex 23 Sqn 28.9.16 (120hp Beardmore) and to England in packing case 27.10.16. **SARD** tested 19.3.17 and re-allotted to BEF 14.3.17. **25 Sqn** dd ex 1 AD 28.3.17. **1 AD ARS** ex 25 Sqn 31.3.17. **11 Sqn** dd ex 2 AD 12.4.17. **100 Sqn** wrecked in crash near Richebourg at 00.55 after hit by AA when night bombing 4.7.17 (Capt VE Schweitzer/Lt JS Godard OK – engine 820/WD6980). **2 AD** ex 100 Sqn 5.7.17 and deleted 6.7.17.

4858 At Weir allotted to Hounslow 2.9.16. Hounslow dd 7.9.16. **19 RS**. Recorded on 11 Sqn by 2Lt GN Anderson 31.8.16 – mistaken for 4838?

4859 Allotted to BEF (120hp Beardmore) 12.8.16. **25 Sqn** dd ex 1 AD 17.9.16 (Sgt Mottershead). **2 AD** ex 25 Sqn 1.10.16. **23**

4852, typically misidentified on this German postcard as a Vickers.

Sqn dd ex 2 AD 1.10.16. **2 AD** ex 23 Sqn 16.11.16. **1 AD** ex 2 AD 27.11.16 and flown to England 4.12.16 (120hp Beardmore, 74hr flying time, allotted to Training Brigade). **9 RS/TS** by 15.4.17 and crashed after engine failure flying downwind 17.7.17 (crew injured, engine 339/WD1403).

4860 Allotted to BEF (120hp Beardmore) 15.8.16. **22 Sqn** dd ex 1 AD 12.9.16 and victs 24.9.16 (Lt GW Robarts/2Lt JS Williams destroyed an EA D type near Epehy at 16.30, shared another OOC with 4924, 4935, 6372 and 6374 at 16.35 and destroyed an EA Type 'E' near St Pierre Vaast at 17.30) then crashed landing after losing wheel on patrol 25.9.16. **2 AD** ex 22 Sqn 27.9.16 (NWR, 120hp Beardmore, flying time 34hr 34min). Retaken on charge 29.9.16. To England in packing case ex 2 AD 3.10.16.

4861 Sold to Russian Government. Imperial Russian Air Fleet.

4862 Allotted to BEF (120hp Beardmore) 15.8.16. **2 AD** ex 1 AD 15.9.16. **18 Sqn** dd ex 2 AD 17.9.16. **1 AD** with 120hp engine ex 18 Sqn 22.1.17 and flown to England 25.1.17 (flying time 101hr 45min).

4863 At Renfrew allotted to BEF (120hp Beardmore) 31.8.16. **2 AD** ex 1 AD 15.9.16. **18 Sqn** dd ex 2 AD 16.9.16 and damaged in combat with 4 EA 16.9.16 (Sgt T Jones/Lt A Nesbitt OK) and with 5 EA 1.10.16 (2Lt FC Biette WIA/2Lt WA Mackay OK) then damaged in forced-landing on photo sortie 22.10.16. **2 AD** ex 18 Sqn 25.10.16 and to England in packing case 10.11.16.

4864 Sold to Russian Government. Imperial Russian Air Fleet.

4865 Allotted to BEF (120hp Beardmore) 30.8.16. **1 AD** ex England 20.9.16. **2 AD** ex 1 AD 16.10.16. **18 Sqn** dd ex 2 AD 25.10.16 (Capt JC Callaghan/Cpl B Ankers). **1 AD** ex 18 Sqn 27.11.16 and flown to England ex **1 AD** 4.12.16 (120hp Beardmore, flying time 38hr).

4866 Allotted to BEF (120hp Beardmore) 30.8.16. **1 AD** dd ex Farnborough 17.9.16. **25 Sqn** dd ex 1 AD 19.9.16. **2 AD** ex 25 Sqn 3.10.16. **23 Sqn** dd ex 2 AD 9.10.16 and LIA near Velu on recce 17.10.16 (2Lt JK Parker POW wdd/2Lt J Cooper-Wilson KIA, a/c had 120hp Beardmore and 29hr 30min flying time).

4867 Allotted to BEF (120hp Beardmore) 30.8.16. **SAD** allotted to BEF 20.9.16. **11 Sqn** dd ex 1 AD 21.9.16 and LIA near Douai on photo sortie 20.10.16 (2Lt NR de Pomeroy KIA/2Lt W Black POW wdd – probably shot down by Ltn E Bohme, Jasta 2, a/c had 160hp Beardmore and 24hr 56min flying time).

4868 Sold to Russian Government. Imperial Russian Air Fleet.

4869 Sold to Russian Government. Imperial Russian Air Fleet.

4870 At Glasgow allotted to BEF (120hp Beardmore) 8.9.16, re-allotted to Training Brigade 20.9.16. UK based training machine 5.1.17 (Lt GC Heseltine – 27 RS Gosport?). **59 TS** (120hp Beardmore). 51 HDS.

4871 Allotted to HD Wing but re-allotted to BEF 19.3.17 for 100 Sqn (120hp Beardmore) 30.8.16. Re-allotted to HD Wing 25.4.17. **51 HDS** B Flt and wrecked in crash after side-slipped on turn during practice flight 26.8.17 (2Lt PG Shellington/2Lt HWH Marshall KIFA – 120hp Beardmore 258/WD1324).

4872 **19 RS** by 2.17.

4873 **19 RS** by 23.10.16. **Armament ES** by 7.17, fitted with twin Lewis armament.

4874 **19 RS** dd ex Renfrew 25.9.16 (engine 508/WD2481) and on charge until @ 2.11.16.

4875 At Renfrew, allotted to Training Brigade 20.9.16. **28 Sqn** by 19.4.16. UK based training machine 20.1.17 (Lt GC Heseltine) – 27 RS Gosport? Crashed at Gosport.

4876 **51 HDS** A Flt Mattishall by 23.5.17 (2Lt EAW

FE2b 4858, 19RS: a good warm coat was as necessary for flying as the tall stepladder was for maintenance.

A good view of the No 2 Mk I gun mounting on 4870 while with A Flt, 59RS at Yatesbury. 1AM T.F. York in the front cockpit. Probably a dual control machine, with an exit hole for aileron cable in the side of the observer's cockpit and twin tubes from the pitot head. Unusually, its fuel pump is mounted on the front port centre section strut.

Kent/AM Brooker AZP).

4877 At Renfrew, allotted to BEF (160hp Beardmore) 25.9.16. **1 AD** ex England 11.10.16. **25 Sqn** dd ex 1 AD 14.10.16 and victs 22.10.16 (2Lt DS Johnston/2Lt WG Meggitt destroyed an EA scout near Lille at 16.20) and 17.11.16 (Sgt JHR Green/Cpl AG Bower shared the destruction of an EA near Vitry at 13.00 with 6990, 7022, 7024 and 7025). **1 AD** ARS ex 25 Sqn 2.4.17. **25 Sqn** ex 1 AD 7.4.17 and LIA in combat near Lieven 14.4.17 (160hp engine, 2Lt WE Davies/Lt NW Morrison KIA – a/c shot down in flames, probably by Ltn K Schäffer, Jasta 11 – engine 865/WD7475).

4878

4873 with experimental paired Lewis gun armament in 1917.

Maj L.W. Learmount, DSO MC with 4883. Here the machine has no camera and the bombsight is on the side of the observer's cockpit. The marking 'B1' appears in the discs on the lower underwing surfaces. The white flight identity on a black disc was continued when 22 Sqn re-equipped with the Bristol F2B.

Winter warriors: Capt H.R. Hawkins (left) and his observer of 22 Sqn return from a photo reconnaissance mission in FE2b 4883 in the cold and snowy conditions of 1916/17. There is a bombsight fitted to the side of the pilot's cockpit.

4879 SAD allotted to BEF 25.9.16 and 4.10.16. **1 AD** dd ex Farnborough 7.10.16. **18 Sqn** dd ex 1 AD 9.10.16. **2 AD** wrecked ex 18 Sqn 8.2.17, 160hp engine, and deleted 20.2.17 (NWR, 81hr 25min flying time).

4880 At Renfrew allotted to BEF (120hp Beardmore) 4.10.16. Allotment cancelled 7.12.16.

4881 SAD allotted to BEF (160hp Beardmore) 7.10.16. **RAF** 21.10.16. **1 AD** ex England 31.10.16. **2 AD** ex 1 AD 4.11.16. **22 Sqn** dd ex 2 AD 4.11.16, damaged after enine failed on take-off for patrol 26.2.17 and damaged in forced-landing on practice flight 14.3.17. **2 AD** ex 22 Sqn 18.3.17, SOC BEF charge 30.3.17 (160hp engine, NWR, 60hr 4min flying time) and to England in packing case 30.3.17.

4882 Allotted to HD Wing, re-allotted to BEF for 100 Sqn 19.3.17. **100 Sqn**, wrecked in crash during practice flight 3.3.17 (Capt J Sowery/AM2 CB Crickmore OK), Flying time 21hr 35min. **2 AD** ex 100 Sqn 9.4.17 and deleted that day.

4883 En-route Glasgow-SAD, allotted to BEF 5.10.16 (160hp Beardmore). **1 AD** ex England 2.11.16. **2 AD** ex 1 AD 4.11.16. **22 Sqn** dd ex 1 AD 4.11.16 as a/c *B-1* (named *Kookaburra*) and victs 4.12.16 (Capt CS Duffus/2Lt GO McEntee sent an Albatros D.I OOC near Barastre at 10.15 but a/c suffered damage) and 8.4.17 (2Lt CAM Furlonger/2Lt CW

Lane shared the destruction of an Albatros D.II near Regny with 4891, 7681, A796, A5454 and A5461) then LIA in combat near Brancourt 26.4.17 (Capt HR Hawkins/2Lt GO McEntee POW – probably shot down by OffSt Sturm, Jasta 5– 160hp engine 777/WD7137, flying time 103hr 58min).

4884 At Renfrew allotted to Training Brigade, re-allotted to BEF (160hp Beardmore) 5.10.16. **1 AD** dd ex Farnborough 9.11.16. **18 Sqn** dd ex 1 AD 23.11.16 and LIA in combat with 2 EA 20.12.16 (2Lt R Smith/2Lt H Fiske KIA – a/c shot down in flames).

4885 At Renfrew allotted to BEF (160hp Beardmore) 4.10.16, re-allocated as 120hp Beardmore 20.10.16 and allotment cancelled 7.12.16. **51 HDS** B Flt by 23.3.17 (Lt VE Schweitzer/Cpl Cruselle 2 AZPs) until @ 11.1.18.

4886 En-route Glasgow-SAD, allotted to BEF 7.10.16 (160hp Beardmore). **1 AD** ex England 4.11.16. **2 AD** ex 1 AD 8.11.16. **23 Sqn** dd ex 2 AD 16.11.16 and damaged during gun practice 7.2.17 (Lewis drum hit propeller). **2 AD** wrecked ex 23 Sqn with 160hp engine 13.2.17 and deleted (NWR, 53hr 47min flying time).

4887 **19 RS** dd 11.10.16 until @ 31.10.16.

4888 **9 RS** crashed after hit hedge on landing 5.1.17 (crew injured). **12 RS** 3.17. **64 Sqn** and wrecked and burnt after cross-wind take-off crash 6.5.17 (Lt RR Harkus injured). **38 HDS** by 8.17.

4889 **9 RS** crashed in bad landing 17.12.16 (crew injured).

4890 **19 RS** by 21.10.16 until @ 26.2.17. **51 HDS** C Flt by 23.3.17 (2Lt CO Bean/Sgt Bastable AZP) until @ 5.17.

4891 **22 Sqn** and vict 8.4.17 (Lt HG Spearpoint/Lt JK Campbell shared the destruction of an Albatros D.II near Regny at 07.00 with 4883, 7681, A796, A5454 and A5461). **199 DS** by 10.17. **200 NTS** by 12.17 until @ 2.8.18.

4892 At Renfrew allotted to BEF (160hp Beardmore) 28.10.16, re-allocated to Training Brigade (120hp Beardmore) 2.11.16. Flown St Albans (London Colney ?) to Hendon 4.12.16 (Lt DC Cloete). Northolt 5.12.16. UK based training machine 5.1.17 (Lt GC Heseltine) – 27 RS Gosport? **199 DS/NTS** by 11.17 (Lt Campbell) and with dual control by 31.12.17.

4893 **64 Sqn** by 3.17 until @ 4.5.17.

4894 **46 RS** by 4.17 until @ 5.17.

4895 **RAF** 6.12.16 allotted to Training Brigade, re-allotted to BEF (160hp Beardmore 856/WD7466) 8.12.16. **1 AD** ex England

20.12.16. **18 Sqn** dd ex 1 AD 24.12.16 and and damaged by AA on photo sortie 4.3.17 – landed safely at aerodrome (Lt CG Shaumer/2Lt RC Doughty OK). **2 AD** and deleted 17.3.17 (160hp engine, NWR, 23hr 55min flying time).

4896 Allotted to BEF 28.10.16 (160hp Beardmore). **RAF** 23.11.16. Folkestone ex Farnborough 28.11.16. **1 AD** ex England 9.12.16. **2 AD** ex 1 AD 5.1.17. **18 Sqn** dd ex 2 AD 12.1.17 and crashed and SOC BEF charge following landing after damaged on escort mission 17.3.17 (Lt C Parkinson OK/2Lt PS Taylor IIA – 160hp engine, 44hr 57min flying time). **2 AD** ex 18 Sqn 19.3.17 and to England in packing case 30.3.17.

4897 **AID** allotted to BEF (160hp Beardmore 666/WD7026) 15.11.16. **RAF** 21.11.16. **1 AD** dd ex Farnborough 4.12.16. **23 Sqn** dd ex 1 AD 11.12.16 and damaged on photo escort 3.4.17 (Sgt JA Cunliffe OK/AM2 J Mackie WIA). **2 AD** wrecked ex 23 Sqn 7.4.17, SOC BEF charge 10.4.17 (160hp engine, NWR, flying time 42hr 18min) and to England in packing case 10.4.17.

4898 Presentation a/c *Johore No 14* wef 29.12.16. **RAF** 8.12.16. Allotted to BEF 13.12.16. **2 AD** ex 1 AD 3.2.17, serviceable, 28.2.17. **18 Sqn** ex 2 AD 12.3.17 and vict 24.3.17 (2Lt EL Zink/AM2 J Walker sent a Halberstadt D-type OOC near Haplincourt/Reincourt at 11.59), damaged on photo escort 3.4.17 (AM2 J Mackie WIA), vict 12.4.17 (2Lt EWA Hunt/2Lt KA Fearnside-Speed sent an Albatros D.III OOC near Cagnicourt at 10.40) then LIA in combat 29.4.17 (Sgt G Stead/Cpl A Beebee KIA – engine 866/WD7476 – probably shot down by Ltn M Fr v Richthofen, Jasta 11 – 160hp engine 866/WD7476, flying time 43hr 50min).

4899 **RAF** 23.11.16. **AID** allotted to BEF 30.11.16. Gosport allotted to BEF, re-allotted for training 5.12.16. UK based training machine 6.1.17 (Lt GC Heseltine) – 27 RS Gosport? Crashed 18.1.17 (Lt RCB Riley injured/Cdr SS Riley KIFA).

4900 **RAF** 29.12.16. **AID** allotted to BEF 5.1.17. **2 AD** ex 1 AD 13.3.17. **22 Sqn** dd ex 2 AD 16.3.17 and deleted after wrecked in forced landing and shelling after combat 17.3.17 (2Lt FR Hudson/AM2 W Richman WIA, possibly by Ltn H Gontermann, Jasta 5. Engine 160hp 887/WD7497, flying time 6hr 35min).

4901 **22 Sqn** dd ex Glasgow 22.2.16, to BEF with unit and wrecked taking off on night flight 27.4.17; engine failed, hit hangar, overturned. **2 AD** ex 22 Sqn 7.5.16 and deleted 8.5.16 (NWR, flying time 22hr 15min).

4902 **28 Sqn** dd ex Glasgow 11.3.16. Still at Gosport 21.4.16.

4903 **18 Sqn** dd ex 1 AD 1.4.16 until and crashed in steep take off on practice flight 19.7.16 (2Lt HMB Law injured).

4904 **28 Sqn** dd ex Newhaven 26.3.16 until @ 7.5.16. Still at Gosport 17.6.16 (Capt Pemberton). 25 Sqn.

4905 **35 Sqn** dd ex Farnborough 30.4.16 until 15.5.16. **18 Sqn** by 16.6.16. **1 AD** and deleted 20.7.16 (NWR, 138hr 55min flying time).

4906 **35 Sqn** dd ex Farnborough 20.5.16. **51 HDS** Marham, photographed wrecked.

4907 **RAF** 22.5.16. **18 Sqn** Bruay dd ex 1 AD 27.5.16 and fitted with WT. **25 Sqn** damaged on artillery registration sortie over Bois de Biez 23.6.16, landing at 2 Sqn aerodrome (Lt HB Davey OK/Lt SRP Walter WIA), damaged landing from bombing sortie 20.7.16 and damaged on take-off for instructional flight 17.8.16.

4908 **RAF** 22.5.16. **RAP** allotted to BEF (120hp Beardmore) 20.5.16. **SAD** allotted to BEF

4899 after a fatal training crash in the severe winter of 1916/17. The wings, tail and struts are fringed with little icicles.

FE2b 4909 'Baby Mine' of 25 Sqn, claimed by Ltn Mulzer, but possibly, as stated on this postcard, the last victory of Hptm Immelmann who was killed in this combat. (See also p30)

21.5.16. **18 Sqn** Bruay dd ex 1 AD 27.5.16. **25 Sqn** dd ex 18 Sqn 3.6.16. **1 AD** ARS ex 25 Sqn 24.6.16 and flown to England 7.7.16 (flying time 40hr). **19 RS** by 7.16. Deleted 7.16.

4909 **AID** allotted to BEF (120hp Beardmore) 20.5.16. **RAF** 24.5.16. **25 Sqn** dd ex 1 AD 29.5.16 (Capt CT McClean/2Lt JC Barraclough) and named *Baby Mine*. LIA near Wingles 18.6.16 (2Lt JRB Savage fatally WIA/AM2 Robinson POW wdd – shot down in combat with 2 EA, possibly by Ltn M Ritt v Mulzer, KEK Nord. Flying time 25hr 30min).

4910 **SAD** allotted to BEF (160hp Beardmore) 22.7.16, re-allotted to Training Brigade 23.9.16. **9 RS/TS** by 7.2.17 and crashed and overturned following steep landing 27.6.17 (crew injured).

4911 **AID** allotted to BEF (120hp Beardmore) 20.5.16. **RAF** 25.5.16. **22 Sqn** dd ex 1 AD 29.5.16. **2 AD** Candas dd ex 1 AD 24.7.16. and deleted 5.8.16 (NWR, 77hr 59min flying time).

4912 **35 Sqn** dd ex Farnborough 17.6.16. Boulton & Paul Norwich dd ex 35 Sqn 5.7.16. **28 Sqn** and wrecked in crash from low stall on south coast 18.3.17 (2Lt WS Morrison KIFA/2Lt JJE Gray KIFA).

4913 **27 RS** by 9.16. Force-landed at Farnborough 15.1.17 (Lt GC Heseltine).

4914 At Renfrew allotted to BEF 5.6.16. **RAF** 11.6.16 fitted with RAF wireless set (120hp Beardmore). **25 Sqn** dd ex 1 AD St-Omer 4.7.16, unserviceable by 6.8.16. **1 AD** and flown to Paris 8.8.16 (39hr 25min flying time). **1 AD** and deleted 5.2.17 (NWR, 120hp engine, 120hr flying time).

4915 At Farnborough allotted to BEF 27.6.16 (120hp Beardmore). **18 Sqn** dd ex 1 AD 24.9.16, in landing collision with 7671 22.10.16 and vict 9.11.16 (Capt AW Tedder/2Lt EL Chadwick sent an Albatros D.II OOC near Douai at 09.00) then LIA in combat with EA near Ginchy 27.11.16 (Lt FA George WIA/AM1 O Watts KIA – a/c

shot down in flames, probably by Ltn W Voss, Jasta 2). **2 AD** ex 18 Sqn 30.11.16 and deleted that day (120hp Beardmore, NWR, flying time 40hr 12min, serviceable parts to store). BUT **11 Sqn** dd ex 2 AD 30.11.16.

4916

4917 Allotted to BEF (120hp Beardmore) 13.6.16. **18 Sqn** by 20.7.16 and damaged beyond repair in combat and by AA on photo sortie 5.8.16 (Capt FC Baker OK/2Lt EV Maclean WIA). 1 AD and deleted 9.8.16 (NWR, flying time 31hr 35min).

4918 At Renfrew allotted to BEF (120hp Beardmore) 17.6.16. **23 Sqn** and in combat 3.9.16 (Lt CJW Crichton/AM2 H Brothers OK) then LIA when crashed in shell-hole following combat near Achiet-le-Grand 10.10.16 (Capt RN Adams KIA/2Lt GJ Ogg OK. Abandoned and deleted with 120hp Beardmore. Flying time 227hr 34min).

4919 At Renfrew allotted to BEF (120hp Beardmore) 17.6.16. **23 Sqn** by 2.9.16. **2 AD** ex 23 Sqn 9.11.16. **1 AD** ex 2 AD 22.11.16. Flown to England ex **1 AD** 4.12.16 (120hp Beardmore, flying time 153hr). En-route to Hounslow for Training Brigade 9.12.16.

4920 Flown Farnborough to Norwich 7.7.16 and 27.7.16 (2Lt Livingstone).

4921 At Renfrew allotted to BEF (120hp Beardmore) 6.7.16. **2 AD** tested OK 24.7.16. **22 Sqn** and LIA near Le Sars on photo sortie 8.9.16 (Lt EGA Bowen/2Lt RM Stalker KIA – shot down in flames by Hptm O Boelcke, Jasta 2. 120hp Beardmore, flying time 54hr 24min).

4922 Allotted to BEF (160hp Beardmore) 12.7.16. **25 Sqn** dd ex 1 AD 23.7.16 and brought down by AA near Haubourdin 5.8.16 (2Lt WH Rilett/AM1 LS Court OK – a/c shelled to destruction. Flying time 30hr 42min).

4923 **9 RS/TS** by 14.2.17, force landed after carburettor came adrift 27.2.1917 (Lt AD

Pryor) and damaged in down-wind landing 17.7.17 (both crew injured, engine 412/ WD2384).

4924 At Renfrew allotted to BEF (120hp Beardmore) 13.7.16 and 14.8.16. **2 AD**, serviceable, 1.9.16. **22 Sqn** dd ex 2 AD 9.9.16 and vict 24.9.16 (2Lt A Cropper/Sgt F Johnson shared sending a Halberstadt OOC near Epehy at 16.35 with 4860, 4935, 6372 and 6374). **18 Sqn**. **1 AD** ex 18 Sqn 20.12.16. Flown to England 24.12.16. **SAD** by 4.1.17, allotted to Training Brigade. **46 RS** by 27.3.17.

4925 Allotted to BEF (160hp Beardmore) 28.7.16. **25 Sqn** dd ex 1 AD 10.8.16 and vict 23.1.17 (Lt B Mews/2Lt AV Blenkiron destroyed a Halberstadt D.II near Lens at 11.30) then wrecked 10.4.17. **1 AD** ex 25 Sqn with 160hp engine 12.4.17 and deleted (NWR, flying time 205hr 40min).

4926 At Renfrew allotted to BEF (160hp Beardmore) 13.7.16. **2 AD** Candas dd ex 1 AD 23.7.16. **11 Sqn** by 20.8.16 and damaged in forced landing after successful combat 28.8.16 (2Lt HH Turk/Lt DH Scott OK after destroying a Roland C type near Ligny/Tilloy at 18.40 – rudder had been shot away). **2 (Aux) SAG** and wrecked in crash near Maidens 26.6.17 (2Lt CA Cooper fatally IIFA/ AM2 II Towlson KIFA after machine stalled on a turn).

4927 **SAD** with RAF5 engine. **19 RS** dd ex SAD 15.9.16. **RAF**, tested with Kymograph 27.11.16 and fitted with RAF 5 engine by 4.17.

4928 At Renfrew allotted to BEF 13.7.16. Allocation changed to HD Wing 22.8.16. **RAF**, fitted with Whiddington searchlight on undercarriage and dynamo by 10.10.16.

4929 At Renfrew allotted to BEF (160hp Beardmore) 13.7.16. **25 Sqn** dd ex 1 AD 29.7.16. **1 AD** ex 25 Sqn 25.9.16 (old

4903 of 18 Squadron, with No 2 Mk I gun mounting and camera.

FE2b 4928 was used in searchlight experiments (see p66). Is the light-coloured nose preparation or restoration?

machine, would not climb). **18 Sqn** dd ex 1 AD 14.10.16 and vict 20.10.16 (2Lt FL Barnard/2Lt FS Rankin destroyed an Albatros D.II near Le Sars at 09.35) then wrecked after successful combat with 6 EA on photo escort near Bapaume 22.10.16 (2Lt FL Barnard WIA/Lt FS Rankin KIA– had sent one Albatros D.II OOC near Bapaume at 14.30. 120hp Beardmore. Deleted with 13hr 55min flying time).

4930 RAF5 engine. **19 RS** dd ex SAD 15.9.16 and wrecked hitting tree during forced landed after engine failed 4.1.17 (Sgt G Finevan OK/ Sgt SC Appleton injured).

4931 At Renfrew allotted to BEF (120hp Beardmore) 12.8.16. **SAD** dd ex Glasgow. BEF allotment cancelled, not repairable, to be written off.

4932 At Renfrew allotted to BEF (160hp Beardmore) 26.7.16. **25 Sqn** dd ex 1 AD 29.7.16 and crashed in fog 1.8.16. **1 AD** and deleted 3.8.16 (160hp Beardmore, NWR, flying time 14hr 25min).

4933 Allotted to BEF (120hp Beardmore) 21.7.16. **18 Sqn** by 8.16 and LIA near Le Transloy 26.10.16 (2Lt PF Heppel/2Lt HBO Mitchell POW wdd – possibly by Obltn Berr Jasta 5. 120hp Beardmore, flying time 85hr 20min).

4934 At Renfrew allotted to BEF 19.8.16. **22 Sqn** dd ex 1 AD 28.8.16 and LIA near Puisieux 20.9.16 (2Lt RN Carter/2Lt WJ Gray POW. 120hp Beardmore No 283, flying time 35hr 10min).

4935 Allotted to BEF (160hp Beardmore) 31.7.16. **1 AD** dd ex Farnborough 14.9.16. **22 Sqn** by 22.9.16 and vict 24.9.16 (2Lt JFA Day/Major RB Martyn shared sending a Halberstadt OOC near Epehy at 16.35hr with 4860,

4924, 6372 and 6374). **2 AD** ex 22 Sqn 6.11.16, engine adjustments 31.12.16 and serviceable 28.2.17. **23 Sqn** dd ex 2 AD 13.3.17 and damaged in landing crash on practice flight 3.4.17. **2 AD** wrecked ex 23 Sqn 7.4.17, SOC BEF charge 10.4.17 (160hp engine, NWR, flying time 115hr 18min) and to England in packing case 10.4.17.

4936 Allotted to BEF (120hp Beardmore) 9.8.16. **2 AD** ex 1 AD 12.9.16. **2 AD** ex 2 AD 18.9.16 until @ 3.10.16. Flown to England ex 1 AD 26.11.16 (120hp Beardmore, flying time 50hr 10min). **SAD** allotted to SAG Hythe 28.11.16. **SARD** allotted to EF (160hp Beardmore) 4.5.17. **1 AD** St-Omer, tested 5.6.17. **2 AD** ex 1 AD 10.8.17. **100 Sqn** dd ex 2 AD 22.8.17 and damaged in crash taking off on night bombing sortie 3.9.17 (2Lt FW? Wells/Prob Lt RC Pitman OK – engine failed).

4937 Allotted to BEF (120hp Beardmore) 7.8.16 and 1.9.16. **2 AD**, serviceable, 1.9.16. **18 Sqn** dd ex 2 AD 7.9.16 and LIA near Ginchy on photo sortie 22.9.16 (2Lt F Hall fatally WIA/Lt BF Randall OK – a/c landed by observer then shelled to destruction. 120hp Beardmore, flying time 27hr 15min)

4938 Allotted to BEF (120hp Beardmore) 9.8.16. **2 AD** ex 1 AD 7.9.16. **22 Sqn** dd ex 2 AD Candas 8.9.16 and LIA in successful combat with EA near Hardecourt 22.9.16 (2Lt HJ Finer IIA/Cpl A Winterbottom KIA after sending an EA OOC near Sailly-Saillisel at 09.45 – shot down, crashed, overturned and deleted. 120hp Beardmore, flying time 19hr 47min).

4939 Allotted to BEF (120hp Beardmore) 10.8.16 and 4.9.16. **2 AD** ex 1 AD 7.9.16. **18 Sqn** dd

ex 2 AD 9.9.16 and wrecked hitting ridge in forced landing after engine overheated on patrol 16.10.16. **2 AD** ex 18 Sqn 19.10.16 and to England in packing case 10.11.16.

4940 Sold to Russian government. Imperial Russian Air Fleet.

4941 Allotted to BEF (120hp Beardmore) 12.8.16. **1 AD** dd ex Farnborough 7.9.16. **2 AD** ex 1 AD 11.9.16. **23 Sqn** dd ex 2 AD 12.9.16. **1 AD** ex 23 Sqn 5.1.17 and flown to England by 7.1.17 (120hp engine, 135hr 5min flying time). At Hythe, allotted to Training Brigade, 9.1.17. **192 NTS** crashed 4.7.18 (pilot slightly injured).

4942 Allotted to BEF (120hp Beardmore) 15.8.16. **18 Sqn** dd ex 2 AD 14.9.16. **1 AD** ex 18 Sqn 4.12.16. Flown to England ex **1 AD** 11.12.16 (120hp Beardmore, flying time 90hr).

4943 Sold to Russian government. Imperial Russian Air Fleet.

4944 Allotted to BEF (120hp Beardmore) 30.8.16. **2 AD** ex 1 AD 14.9.16. **11 Sqn** dd ex 2 AD 20.9.16. **2 AD** ex 11 Sqn 27.9.16. **22 Sqn** dd ex 2 AD 27.9.16. **18 Sqn** Bertangles. **1 AD** ex 18 Sqn with 120hp engine 16.1.17 and flown to England 23.1.17 (flying time 97hr 25min).

4945 Allotted to BEF (120hp Beardmore) 30.8.16. **22 Sqn** dd ex 1 AD 23.9.16. **1 AD** ex 22 Sqn 11.12.16. Force landed at Calais en-route to England 16.12.16 and deleted but retaken on charge 22.12.16. To England in packing case by 9.1.17 (120hp engine, flying time 90hr 40min).

4946 Allotted to BEF (160hp Beardmore) 6.7.16. **25 Sqn** dd ex 1 AD 27.9.16 (Sgt Mottershead) and vict 24.1.17 (2Lt JL Leith/2Lt AG Severs destroyed an Albatros D.II near Lieven at 15.00) then crashed 5.2.17: engine cut and hit road when landing. **1 AD** ARS ex 25 Sqn with 160hp engine 7.2.17 and deleted 10.2.17 (NWR).

4947 Sold to Russian government. Imperial Russian Air Fleet.

4948 Sold to Russian government. Imperial Russian Air Fleet.

4949 At Renfrew allotted to BEF (160hp Beardmore) 16.9.16. **11 Sqn** dd ex 1 AD 27.9.16. Damaged in forced landing near Calais en-route from England to 1 **AD** 22.12.16. **11 Sqn** and damaged by ground fire on photo sortie 24.3.17 (crew OK). **1 AD** with 160hp engine ex 11 Sqn 28.3.17, SOC BEF charge 9.4.17 (NWR, flying time 112hr 9min) and to England in packing case 9.4.17.

4950 **64 Sqn** by 26.2.17 until @ 4.17. **42 TS** (19 RS?). BUT 12 RS Thetford by 3.17.

4951 **SAD** allotted to BEF (120hp Beardmore) 29.9.16. **1 AD** ex England 31.10.16. **2 AD** ex 1 AD 2.11.16 (Sgt T Mottershead). **18 Sqn** dd ex 2 AD 6.11.16. **1 AD** ex 18 Sqn 28.12.16. Flown to England by 15.1.17 (120hp engine, flying time 30hr 25min). **SARD** tested 21.2.17. **100 Sqn** by 7.4.17 (poor frame etc). **2 AD** ex 100 Sqn 20.4.17, with 120hp engine, allotted to HD Wing 25.4.17 but re-allotted to BEF and deleted 27.4.17 (NWR, flying time 50hr 40min.)

4952 At Renfrew allotted to BEF (160hp Beardmore) 25.9.16, re-allotted (120hp Beardmore) 20.10.16. **1 AD** ex England 31.10.16. **2 AD** ex 1 AD 2.11.16. **18 Sqn** dd ex 2 AD 4.11.16 and damaged in combat with EA near Bouzincourt 17.11.16 (Lt CH Windrum OK/Lt AV Sherwell WIA). **1 AD** ex 18 Sqn 27.12.16. 120hp engine. Flown to England by 4.1.17 (flying time 29hr 0min).

4953 At Renfrew allotted to BEF (120hp Beardmore) 25.9.16. **1 AD** ex England 11.10.16. **18 Sqn** dd ex 1 AD 14.10.16 and overturned in landing crash after patrol 5.11.16. **2 AD** ex 18 Sqn 8.11.16. **9 RS** Norwich by 2.17.

The crew of 4934 became lost in cloud and were forced to land and be captured, presenting the enemy with an untouched FE2b, as can be seen in this photo.

4954 **SAD** allotted to BEF 7.10.16. **RAF** 24.10.16 (160hp Beardmore 749/WD7109). **1 AD** ex England 2.11.16. **2 AD** ex 1 AD 9.11.16. **11 Sqn** dd ex 2 AD 10.11.16 and vict 15.3.17 (2Lt HC Calvey/AM2 HV Gosney sent an Albatros D.III OOC near Arras at 17.50) then LIA after becoming lost in storm and hit by AA 1.4.17 (Cpl A Wilson/AM2 F Hadlow POW. 160hp engine 836/WD7196, flying time 75hr 8min).

4955 At Renfrew allotted to BEF (120hp Beardmore) 29.9.16. **SAD** dd 9.10.16 ex Newcastle, via Hendon, 8.10.16. **1 AD** ex England 11.10.16. **23 Sqn** dd ex 1 AD 14.10.16 and damaged in take-off crash after propeller burst 27.12.16. **2 AD** ex 23 Sqn with 120hp engine 9.1.17 and to England in packing case 24.1.17 (flying time 46hr 47min). **2 (Aux) SAG**, flown by Capt JTB McCudden.

4956 At Renfrew allotted to BEF (120hp Beardmore) 29.9.16. **1 AD** ex England 18.10.16. **18 Sqn** dd ex 1 AD 21.10.16. **2 AD** ex 18 Sqn 1.2.17 and deleted 5.2.17 (NWR,

Above: 4939, with standard Trafford Jones undercarriage.

Below: Lt J.A. Hollis contemplates the damage to 4944.

4960 At Renfrew allotted to BEF (120hp Beardmore) 7.10.16. **1 AD** ex England 2.11.16. **2 AD** ex 1 AD 6.11.16 and serviceable 31.12.16 and 28.2.17. **23 Sqn** ex 2 AD 11.3.17 and wrecked in forced landing near Martinsart after combat 24.3.17 (Lt WF Fletcher/2Lt HS Elliot OK – engine 762/WD7122). **2 AD** Candas ex 23 Sqn 27.3.17, SOC BEF charge 30.3.17 (160hp engine, NWR, flying time 18hr 5min) and to England in packing case 30.3.17.

4961 **19 RS** dd 2.11.16.

4962

4963 **64 Sqn** by 28.2.17 until @ 5.17 (Lt C Campbell).

4964 **19 RS** dd 25.10.16.

4965 Presentation a/c *South Australia* wef 29.12.16. **AID** allotted to BEF 30.11.16. **RAF** (160hp Beardmore 877/WD7487) 15.12.16. **23 Sqn** dd ex 1 AD 7.1.17 and damaged in forced landing after combat on photo escort 4.3.17 (2Lt WE Jones OK/2Lt WA Golding

120hp engine, flying time 71hr 35min).

4957 At Renfrew allotted to BEF (160hp Beardmore) 4.10.16. **1 AD** ex England 13.10.16. **18 Sqn** dd ex 1 AD 21.10.16 (Capt JC Callaghan/Cpl B Ankers). **2 AD** ex 1 AD 14.11.16. **23 Sqn** and damaged in combat 6.3.17 (Sgt EP Critchley OK/AM2 G Brown WIA – engine 160hp 924/WD7534). **2 AD** ex 23 Sqn 11.3.17 and deleted 14.3.17 (NWR, flying time 53hr 59min).

4958 Allotted to Training Brigade 5.10.16. **28 Sqn** by 18.5.17 until @ 22.5.17.

4959 At Renfrew allotted to BEF (160hp Beardmore) 7.10.16, changed to 120hp Beardmore allotted to BEF 20.10.16. Allotment cancelled 24.11.16, machine crashed en-route to SAD and deleted.

One German finds the newspaper of more interest than the captured 4954, lost on 1 April 1917, while waiting for it to be towed away by horsepower. This machine also has Trafford Jones undercarriage, but with streamlined fairings on the forward struts.

At Hounslow, FE2b 4957 of 23 Sqn, in which observer 2AM G. Brown was wounded in combat on 6 March 1917.

FE2b 4962: carefully photographed, but its service history is completely elusive.

WIA – engine 877/WD7487). **2 AD** ex 23 Sqn 10.3.17. Deleted 7.5.17 (21hr flying time).

4966 At Renfrew allotted to BEF (160hp Beardmore) 28.10.16, re-allotted to Training Brigade (120hp Beardmore) 2.11.16. **19 RS** by 25.10.16 until @ 4.11.16.

4967 **RAF** 28.11.16. **AID** allotted to BEF (160hp Beardmore) 30.11.16. **18 Sqn** dd ex 1 AD 22.1.17. **2 AD** ex 18 Sqn 24.2.17. **18 Sqn** dd ex 2 AD 13.3.17 and LIA in combat with EA near Bapaume 5.4.17 (Lt HAR Boustead fatally WIA/2Lt G Mackintosh KIA, 160hp Beardmore 981/WD7591). **2 AD** wrecked ex 18 Sqn 11.4.17, with 160hp engine, SOC BEF charge 20.4.17 (NWR, flying time 26hr 43min) and to England in packing case ex 2 AD 20.4.17.

The bodies of the crew still lie beside the wreck of 4968, lost on an early night bombing raid by 18 Sqn on 1 May 1917.

4968 Allotted to HD Wing 13.11.16. **RAF** 28.11.16. **AID** allotted to BEF (160hp Beardmore 866/WD7376) 30.11.16. HD Wing allotment confirmed 2.12.16, changed to BEF 8.12.16. **2 AD** ex 1 AD 5.1.17. **18 Sqn** dd ex 2 AD 12.1.17 and LIA night-bombing 1.5.17 (2Lt EWA Hunt/2Lt GB Miller KIA – engine 726/WD7086).

4969 Presentation a/c *Shanghai No 3, Shanghai Exhibition*. **RAF** 10.12.16. **AID** allotted to BEF (160hp Beardmore 864/WD7474) 13.12.16. **1 AD** ex England 20.12.16. **18 Sqn** dd ex 1 AD 28.12.16 and victs 5.4.17 (2Lt VH Huston/2Lt GN Blennerhasset sent 2 Albatros D.II OOC near Inchy at 12.00) then damaged in crash 16.4.17 (Lt CG Shaumer/2Lt GB Miller OK). **2 AD** wrecked ex 18 Sqn 21.4.17 and under

overhaul 30.4.17. **2 AD** ex 1 AD 16.8.17. **102 Sqn** and LIA night bombing 9.10.17 (Lt DG Powell/Lt RF Hill POW).

4970 Presentation a/c *Punjab No 4, Jind* wef 29.12.16. **RAF** 10.12.16. **AID** allotted to BEF (160hp Beardmore) 13.12.16. **1 AD** ex England 20.12.16. **2 AD** ex 1 AD 26.12.16. **23 Sqn** dd ex 2 AD 29.12.16, damaged in crash 24.1.17 (Sgt L Booth KIFA), vict 7.2.17 (Sgt JA Cunliffe/AM2 AG Walker destroyed an Albatros D.III near Combles then damaged in forced landing near aerodrome after engine failed on recce 25.2.17 (Sgt J Cunliffe/2Lt R Law OK). **2 AD** ex 23 Sqn 28.2.17 and deleted 2.3.17 (NWR, flying time 39hr 33min).

4971 Presentation a/c *Johore No 6* wef 29.12.16. **AID** allotted to BEF (160hp Beardmore) 13.12.16. **RAF** 14.12.16. **22 Sqn** dd ex 1 AD 20.1.17 and wrecked in crash after combat near Eaucourt l'Abbaye 6.2.17 (Lt WN McDonald WIA/2Lt EDG Galley OK. 160hp engine, flying time 5hr 15min).

4972 Hendon ex Farnborough 12.1.17. **19 RS** by 12.12.16 until @ 13.1.17 (2Lt E Mannock). **76 HDS** by 8.17. **38 HDS** B Flt by 2.9.17. **192 NTS** dd ex Buckminster 22.5.18.

4973 4 Sqn wrecked. 2 AD ex 4 Sqn 29.5.16 too early?? – mistaken entry for BE2c 4073!). **9 RS** Norwich by 24.2.17.

4974 Presentation a/c *Punjab No 10, Kalabagh*. **AID** allotted to BEF (160hp Beardmore) 13.12.16. **RAF** Farnborough 18.12.16. At Lympne 5.1.17, BEF allotment cancelled. Issued to Capt FCV Laws for special duties (photography) in France. Deleted 4.17.

4975 **AID** allotted to BEF (120hp Beardmore) 23.12.16. **RAF** 3.1.17. Re-allotted to Training Brigade 11.1.17. **19 RS** by 18.2.17 and burnt in crash after engine failure 24.5.17 (crew injured).

4976 **36 HDS** A Flt damaged in take-off crash at Redcar 27.12.16 (Lt Townend/a mechanic OK). **2 AD** by 24.10.17. **100 Sqn** dd ex 2 AD 25.10.17.

4977 **AID** allotted to BEF (160hp Beardmore) 13.12.16. **RAF** 18.12.16. **23 Sqn** dd ex 1 AD 7.1.17 and damaged in landing crash in fog 16.1.17. **2 AD** ex 23 Sqn 20.1.17 with 160hp engine and to England in packing case 24.1.17 (flying time 4hr 22min). **SARD** allotted to BEF 4.5.17 and tested 9.5.17. **22 Sqn** by 23.6.17. **2 AD** ex 1 AD 10.7.17. **101 Sqn**. **100 Sqn** dd ex 101 Sqn 3.10.17 and damaged in landing crash near Jainllon 3.10.17. **2 AD** ex 100 Sqn 21.1.18. **2 ASD** deleted 12.2.18 (NWR, flying time 110hr).

4978 Allotted to HD Wing but re-allotted to BEF for 100 Sqn 19.3.17 (120hp Beardmore). **100 Sqn.** by 6.17. Flown to England 16.6.17.

4979 At Renfrew allotted to BEF 25.9.16. **AID** allotted to BEF (160hp Beardmore) 23.12.16. **RAF** 29.12.16. **11 Sqn** dd ex 1 AD 1.2.17 and damaged in in forced landing after successful combat near Grevillers 17.3.17 (Lt AC Woodman OK/2Lt RC Cox WIA after sending an Albatros D.II OOC near Grevillers at 10.00hr. 160hp 868/WD7478. Flying time 34hr 52min). SOC 11 Sqn 22.3.17. **2 AD** ex 11 Sqn 24.3.17 and deleted that day.

4980 **19 RS** by 2.17. **51 HDS** C Flt by 8.8.17. **51 HDS** B Flt by 20.9.17 until @ 22.9.17, photographed on nose In accIdent and also overturned in another and re-allotted to BEF 10.10.17. At Lympne allotted to BEF (160hp Beardmore) 13.10.17. **1 AD** dd ex England 14.10.17 (recorded as A4980, 160hp Beardmore 932/WD7542). **2 AD** ex 1 AD 18.10.17 (recorded as A4980, 160hp Beardmore 932/WD7542). **100 Sqn** and damaged in enemy bombing of aerodrome 6.12.17. **2 AD** ex 100 Sqn 6.12.17. **2 ASD** (recorded as A4980) and deleted 12.1.18 (NWR, flying time 86hr).

4981 Assembled by Barclay Curle. **51 HDS**. C Flt.

4982 Hendon dd ex Renfrew 25.1.17 (Lt Hay). Lympne AAP 28.1.17. **199 DS/NTS** by 30.11.17 until @ 6.18.

4983 **SAD** allotted to BEF (160hp Beardmore) 15.1.17. **RAF** 17.1.17. **2 AD** ex 1 AD 3.2.17. **22 Sqn** dd ex 2 AD 5.2.17, victs 8.4.17 (2Lt CAM Furlonger/Lt CW Lane shared the destruction of an Albatros D.III near Regny at 07.00 with 4891, 7681, A796, A5454 and A5461) and 13.4.17 (2Lt JV Aspinall/2Lt MK Parlee destroyed an Albatros D.III near Itancourt at 18.30) and damaged in forced landing after engine cut during patrol 19.4.17. **2 AD** wrecked ex 22 Sqn 25.4.17 and for England in packing case (160hp Beardmore), 30.4.17.

4984 **RAF** 11.1.17. **SAD** allotted to BEF (160hp Beardmore) 15.1.17. **2 AD** ex 1 AD 28.1.17. **18 Sqn** dd ex 2 AD 6.2.17 and victs 11.3.17 (Lt HAR Boustead/2Lt JR Smith destroyed an Albatros D.II near Velu-Bapaume at 11.45 and sent another OOC at 12.00) LIA near Dury in combat with Jasta 12 on photo escort 12.4.17 (Lt OD Maxsted POW/ Lt A Todd MC POW wdd. 160hp engine 960/ WD7570). Deleted 13.4.17.

4985 **51 HDS** by 3.17. **28 Sqn** by 8.5.17 until @ 6.17.

4986 **RAF** 14.1.17. **AID** allotted to BEF (160hp Beardmore) 16.1.17. **2 AD** ex 1 AD 28.1.17. **22 Sqn** dd ex 2 AD 9.2.17 and damaged in combat near Hesbecourt 24.3.17 (Capt WE Salter OK/2Lt EDG Galley WIA. Engine 160hp 957/WD7567, flying time 39hr 14min). **2 AD** ex 22 Sqn 28.3.17 and to England in packing case 30.3.17. **SARD** tested 8.5.17.

4987 **RAF** 12.1.17. **AID** allotted to BEF (160hp Beardmore 910/WD7520) 16.1.17 but allotment cancelled and under repair 26.1.17. **SARD** tested 23.3.17. **2 AD** by 3.17.

4988 **46 RS** by 4.17 until @ 5.17.

4989 Allotted HD Wing. Cramlington 19.3.17. Re-allotted to BEF for 100 Sqn 19.3.17. **100 Sqn** and damaged by AA night bombing 7.5.17 (2Lt HEK Eccles WIA).

4990 **AID** allotted to BEF (160hp Beardmore) 16.1.17. **RAF** 19.1.17. **1 AD** dd ex Farnborough 23.1.17 (had left 22.1.17, delayed by weather). **18 Sqn** dd ex 1 AD 24.1.17 and damaged in combat near Thiepval 17.3.17 (Lt VH Huston/Lt EA Foord OK – force landed in trench lines. Engine 920/WD7530). **2 AD** ex 18 Sqn 21.3.17, with 160hp engine, SOC BEF charge 7.4.17 (NWR, flying time) 49hr 45min and to England in packing case 7.4.17.

4991 **AID** allotted to BEF (160hp Beardmore) 16.1.17. **RAF** 20.1.17. **2 AD** ex 1 AD 11.2.17, serviceable, 28.2.17. **22 Sqn** and vict 5.4.17 (2Lt GM Hopkins/2Lt GO McEntee shared sending an Albatros D.III OOC near Honnecourt at 13.45 with 7697) then LIA on photo sortie 9.5.17 after combat with 3 EA near Lesdain (2Lt CAM Furlonger/2Lt CW Lane POW – engine 777/WD7137 – possibly shot down by Ltn W Voss, Jasta 2).

Possibly 4988, with V undercarriage. The large white station number suggests service with 2 (Aux) SAG at Turnberry.

FE2b 4974 with a new-looking presentation inscription. The wind-driven generator is clearly visible.

4992 **200 NTS** and wrecked in crash from spinning nose-dive following stall on turn 1.10.18 (2Lt CB Millington KIFA).

4993 **RAF** 28.12.16. **1 AD** dd ex Farnborough 6.1.17 (had left 3.1.17). **2 AD** ex 1 AD 13.3.17. **11 Sqn** dd ex 2 AD 17.3.17. **20 Sqn** and damaged in forced landing in cornfield after engine failed during OP 23.7.17.

4994 Presentation a/c *Kedah No 2*. **RAF** 9.2.17. **2 AD** ex 1 AD 16.3.17. **23 Sqn** dd ex 2 AD 26.3.17 and wrecked in crash after hitting wires during practice flight 1.4.17. **2 AD**

5.4.17 and deleted 11.4.17 (160hp engine, NWR, flying time 7hr 26min).

4995 **RAF** 6.2.17. **AID** allotted to BEF (160hp Beardmore) 8.2.17. **2 AD** ex 1 AD 1.3.17. **18 Sqn** ex 2 AD 12.3.17 and LIA near Epinoy in combat with Jasta 12 on photo escort 12.4.17 (Lt OT Walton/AM2 JC Walker KIA– 160hp engine 950/WD7560). Deleted 13.4.17.

4996 Presentation a/c *Montreal No 3* wef 1.17. **RAF** 19.2.17. **AID** allotted to BEF (160hp Beardmore) 17.2.17. **2 AD** ex 1 AD 13.3.17.

FE2b 4980 gave a year of service in home defence and as a night bomber that was not without incidents.

Something in the distance claims the attention of the German soldiers around 4984, captured on 12 April 1917, but it was evidently removed and dismantled later (left).

11 Sqn dd ex 2 AD 17.3.17**. 2 AD** wrecked ex 11 Sqn 20.4.17, with 160hp engine, and deleted 27.4.17 (NWR, flying time 23hr 50min).

4997 Presentation a/c *Baroda No 17*. **AID** allotted to BEF (160hp Beardmore) 17.2.17. **RAF** 19.2.17. **25 Sqn** dd ex 1 AD 21.3.17 and LIA bombing Hénin-Liétard 13.4.17 (2Lt AH Bates/Sgt WA Barnes KIA – engine 917/ WD7527 – brought down by Ltn M Fr v Richthofen, Jasta 11).

4998 Presentation a/c *Ceylon No 3, A Nightjar from Ceylon*. **AID** allotted to BEF (160hp Beardmore) 24.2.17. **2 AD** ex 1 AD 15.3.17. **18 Sqn** dd ex 2 AD 18.3.17 and victs 13.5.17 (2Lt VH Huston/Lt EA Foord destroyed a Halberstadt D-type near Cambrai at 17.15)

and 27.5.17 (2Lt VH Huston/Lt EA Foord shared the destruction of an Albatros D.V near Havrincourt at 07.45 with Sopwith Pup N6465) then crashed near Ferfay on night bombing sortie 8.8.17 (2Lt DE Marshall/2Lt A McMurray KIA). **2 AD** ex 18 Sqn 12.8.17 and deleted 13.8.17.

4999 **AID** allotted to BEF (120hp Beardmore) 24.2.17. **RAF** 1.3.17. **2 AD** ex 1 AD 15.3.17. **23 Sqn** dd ex 2 AD 26.3.17. **2 AD** ex 23 Sqn 7.4.17. **100 Sqn** dd ex 2 AD 13.4.17 and wrecked in crash during night bombing sortie 18.4.17 (crew OK. 120hp engine flying time 3hr). **2 AD** wrecked ex 100 Sqn 23.4.17 and deleted that day.

5000 At Lympne allotted to BEF (160hp Beardmore) 27.2.17. **2 AD** ex 1 AD 3.4.17. **11 Sqn** dd ex 2 AD 4.4.17 and wrecked in crash 6.4.17 (2Lt DS Kennedy/AM2 JF Carr OK). **2 AD** wrecked ex 11 Sqn 11.4.17, with 160hp engine 1014/WD7624, SOC BEF charge 20.4.17 (NWR, flying time 5hr 8min) and to England in packing case ex 2 AD 20.4.17.

5201 – 5250: 50 RAF FE2b (120hp Beardmore) built by Boulton & Paul Ltd, Norwich under Contract 94/A/136.

5201 Presentation a/c *Bombay No 1*. **AID** ex

Norwich 2.10.15. **RAF** 9.10.15. **1 AP** dd ex England 20.10.15 by Mr Stutt (engine 277/ WD1341). **16 Sqn** allotted and dd 30.10.15 to replace MF 5027, in combat 28.11.15 (2Lt AR Tillie/2Lt FR Hardine drove off an Aviatik and Lt GH Eastwood/Lt LN Gould drove off an Albatros). **1 AD** ex 16 Sqn 29.1.16. **12 Sqn** dd 1.2.16. **1 AD** ex 12 Sqn 24.2.16. **25 Sqn** dd ex 1 AD 1.3.16 and victs 16.5.16 (2Lt HB Davey/Cpl L van Schaik destroyed a Fokker E-type near Lille) and 17.6.16 (2Lt JRB Savage/AM2 Robinson shared a Fokker E-type OOC near Don with 6337 and 6938). Unserviceable 16.8.16. Flown to England 2.9.16. To Ransomes, Sims & Jefferies as pattern machine.

5202 Presentation a/c *Newfoundland No 4*. **AID** 15.11.15. **RAF** 16.11.15. **1 AD** dd 19.11.15 by Lt Dunn (engine 296/WD1360). **16 Sqn** dd ex 1 AD 20.11.15 and in combat 14.12.15 (Capt GH Eastwood/Lt Veitch engaged 7 EA near Douai), 19.12.15 (Capt GH Eastwood/2Lt LAK Butt engaged an Albatros near Erquinghem). **1 AD** ex 16 Sqn 24.1.16. **20 Sqn** dd ex 1 AD 25.1.16 and crashed in forced landing 16.4.16 (Capt EP Graves/Lt HLC Aked OK. Flying time 60hr 8min). **1 AD** ex 20 Sqn 18.4.16 and deleted

18 Squadron identified their Flights with different coloured diamond-shaped nose markings, as seen in this and the other views of 4984 above.

FE2b 5203 'River Plate' before and after.

25.4.16.

5203 Presentation a/c *River Plate*. **AID** dd 26.11.15. **22 Sqn** 30.1.16. **28 Sqn** crashed and deleted 12.10.16.

5204 Presentation a/c *Montreal No 4* wef 7.12.15. **RAF** 8.12.15. **1 AD** dd ex England 22.12.15 (engine 359). **6 Sqn** dd ex 1 AD 25.12.15. **20 Sqn** ex 6 Sqn 25.1.16 and wrecked when hangar blew down in gale 14.2.16.

5205 **20 Sqn** dd 21.12.15 (120hp Beardmore 201/ WD1271).

5206 **20 Sqn** dd 8.1.16 (120hp Beardmore 205/ WD1275) and to BEF with unit and LIA near Zandvoorde on recce escort 21.5.16 (Capt CEH James/Lt HLC Aked POW – combat with 2 EA; captured intact, probably brought down by Ltn Frankl. Flying time 87hr 5min).

5207 **22 Sqn** dd ex AID Norwich 8.3.16 and to BEF at with the unit and vict 29.7.16 (Lt AM

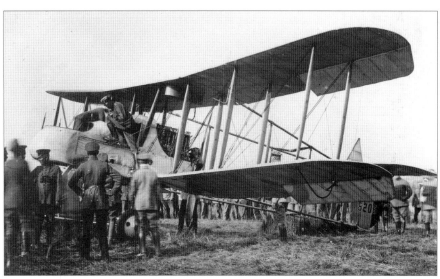

FE2b 5206 was seen by other members of its patrol force-landing near Zandvoorde on 21 May 1916. Curious German troops gather to inspect a fully intact FE2b.

Thomas/Flt Sgt J Stronach sent a Fokker E type OOC near Bapaume at 19.45) but shot through tank in continued combat and force-landed near La Houssoye with engine overheating (crew OK). **1 AD** ex 22 Sqn 18.12.16. Flown to England ex 1 AD 20.12.16. Allotted to Training Brigade 22.12.16.

5208 **23 Sqn** dd ex AID Farnborough 11.1.16, to BEF with unit. **2 AD** ex 23 Sqn 17.11.16. **1**

FE2b 5216 went to France with 22 Sqn in April 1916 and made the unit's first operational sortie from Bertangles on the 21st of the month. It accumulated over 230 flying hours.

Engine Fitter Cpl Frank Brook by the rudder of 5222.

AD ex 2 AD 23.11.16 and flown to England 4.12.16 (120hp Beardmore, flying time 347hr). Allotted to Training Brigade en-route to Hounslow 4.12.16. **19 RS** by 18.2.17.

5209 **25 Sqn** dd ex 1 AD 16.1.16 and victs 29.4.16 (2Lt Lord Doune/2Lt RU Walker destroyed a Fokker E-type near La Bassée at 11.05) and 16.5.16 (Lt HB Davey/Lt JA Mann shot down an Albatros near Lille at 09.45) then LIA near Hulluch 22.6.16 (2Lt JLP Armstrong POW fatally WIA/Sgt G Topliffe POW – by Ltn M Ritt v Mulzer, KEK Nord. Flying time 119hr 47min).

5210 **25 Sqn** and damaged in combat over Estaires 23.4.16 (Lt WE Collison OK/AM2 GF Atwell KIA – by Ltn M Ritt v Mulzer, KEK Nord). **1 AD** ex 25 Sqn 25.4.16 and deleted that day (NWR, flying time 60hr 30min).

5211 Presentation a/c *Bombay No 3*. **25 Sqn** dd ex 1 AD 23.1.16, and crashed 8.4.16. **1 AD** ARS wrecked ex 25 Sqn 9.4.16 (Flying time 70hr 5min) and deleted 22.4.16.

5212 **25 Sqn** dd ex 1 AD 26.1.16 damaged in combat near Radighem 2.4.16 (Capt W Milne/Lt Gilbert OK) and damaged on photo sortie 4.5.16 (2Lt H Dixon/Lt ER Davis OK – radiator shot up) and wrecked after combat near Mazingarbe 27.6.16 (Lt RCB Riley WIA/Lt EH Bird fatally WIA – probably by Ltn M Mülzer KEK Nord). 1 AD ex 25 Sqn and deleted 2.7.16 (NWR, flying time 143hr 21min).

5213 **23 Sqn** dd ex AID Norwich 9.2.16, to BEF with unit, damaged in combat and hit by AA on recce 1.7.16 (Capt H Wyllie OK/Lt AN Solly WIA) and vict 2.8.16 (Lt JC Griffiths/Lt AN Solly sent an EA scout OOC near Douai). **2 AD** ex 23 Sqn 9.11.16. **1 AD** ex 2 AD 16.11.16 and flown to England 22.11.16 (120hp Beardmore, flying time 379hr 38min). Allotted to SAG Hythe 23.11.16.

5214 **22 Sqn** dd ex AID Norwich 9.2.16, to BEF with unit and vict 21.7.16 (2Lt GH Hackwill/2Lt LWB Parsons destroyed a Roland C.II near Beaulencourt at 20.00) and on unit charge until @ 2.9.16. **2 AD** ex 18 Sqn 14.11.16 (unfit for active service). **1 AD** ex 2 AD 16.11.16 and flown to England 17.11.16 (120hp Beardmore, flying time 299hr 45min). **46 RS/TS** by 4.17 until @ 10.17.

5215 **23 Sqn** dd ex AID Norwich 22.2.16, to BEF with unit and damaged in combat 29.3.16 and vict 31.5.16 (Capt H Wyllie/Lt AN Solly shared sending an EA OOC near Marquion with 5235, 5249, 6354 and Martinsyde G.100 7280). **2 AD** ex 23 Sqn and deleted 20.7.16 (NWR, flying time 198hr 15min).

5216 **22 Sqn** dd ex AID Norwich 12.2.16, to BEF with unit, making its first war flight and damaged in landing crash on test flight 6.8.16. **2 AD** and deleted 8.8.16 (NWR, flying time 231hr 46min).

5217 **22 Sqn** dd ex AID Norwich 23.2.16 and deleted 8.3.16.

5218 **22 Sqn** dd ex AID Norwich 22.2.16, to BEF with unit and wrecked in landing crash on practice flight 29.4.16 (crew OK, 44hr 53min flying time, 120hp Beardmore 254/WD1320). **2 AD** ex 22 Sqn 4.5.16 and deleted 5.5.16 (NWR, flying time 44hr 53min).

5219 **20 Sqn** dd ex 1 AD 26.3.16 and crashed in side slip taking off on flight 21.4.16 to collect wounded pilot of 6332 (33hr 19min flying time). **1 AD** ex 20 Sqn 25.4.16 and deleted that day.

5220 Presentation a/c *Bombay No 2*. **18 Sqn** dd ex 1 AD 3.4.16 fitted with WT, damaged in crash 30.6.16 (2Lt FC Biette/2Lt HA Pearson OK) and damaged by ground fire on contact patrol 15.9.16 (2Lt FC Biette/2Lt PJ Smyth OK). **2 AD** ex 18 Sqn 19.9.16 and deleted 20.9.16 (NWR, 120hp Beardmore, flying time 198hr 25min, nacelle to England). **SMA** Reading as GI airframe.

5221 **35 Sqn** A Flt dd ex Norwich 9.3.16 (2Lt M Bell-Irving) and SOC 27.3.16.

5222 Presentation a/c *Punjab No 2, Bahawalpur*. **35 Sqn** dd ex Norwich 3.3.16 (2Lt M Bell-Irving). **Boulton & Paul** ex 35 Sqn 10.6.16. **27 RS** by 9.16. **28 Sqn**. Deleted 9.12.16.

5223 **22 Sqn** dd ex AID Norwich 9.3.16, to BEF with unit and damaged in landing crash 9.8.16 – had damaged undercarriage on take off. **2 AD** and deleted 12.8.16 (NWR).

5224 Presentation a/c *Punjab No 4, Jind*. **22 Sqn** dd ex AID Norwich 9.3.16 and to BEF with unit. **2 AD** ex 22 Sqn 5.4.16, deletion requested 6.4.16 and deleted 8.4.16 (Flying time 13hr 45min – the first FE2b handled by 2 AD).

5225 Presentation a/c *Punjab No 5, Nabha*. **22 Sqn** dd ex AID Norwich 9.3.16 and to BEF with unit and wrecked 11.5.16 and struck off unit charge 12.5.16. **2 AD** ex 22 Sqn 13.5.16 and deleted 14.5.16 (Flying time 50hr 25min).

5226 Presentation a/c *Punjab No 6, Nabha*. **22 Sqn** dd ex AID Norwich 9.3.16 to BEF with unit, damaged in forced landing on photo sortie 31.7.16 and wrecked in forced-landing 27.8.16. **2 AD** and deleted 1.9.16 (NWR, flying time 192hr 41min, repairing planes).

5227 Presentation a/c *Punjab No 7, Faridkot*. **18 Sqn** dd ex 1 AD 1.4.16 and damaged in landing crash 21.5.16 – hit fuel store. **1 AD** ex 18 Sqn 24.5.18 and deleted 27.5.16 (NWR, flying time 46hr 20min).

5228 Presentation a/c *Punjab No 8, Faridkot*. **35 Sqn** dd ex Norwich 20.3.16 (2Lt M Bell-Irving). **SAD** ex 35 Sqn 25.3.16 (Lt AK Tylee/2Lt TM O'Beirne). **51 HDS** C Flt fitted with Vickers 1lb QF gun. **100 Sqn**, still fitted with pom-pom and shelled to destruction after forced landing on night raid 4.6.17 (2Lt Chaplin OK – pom-pom had blown up). Deleted 6.17.

5229 Presentation a/c *Punjab No 9, Kalsia*. **35 Sqn** dd ex Norwich 23.3.16 (Lt AK Tylee). **9 RS** ex 35 Sqn 5.7.16. **SARD** and reported as deleted 23.8.16 but at SARD allotted to BEF 18.12.16. **2 AD** ex 1 AD 3.2.17 and for photographic experiments 28.2.17. **22 Sqn** dd ex 2 AD 20.4.17 and reported as 'old machine' 17.5.17. Flown to England 23.5.17 (160hp Beardmore 757/WD7117).

5230 Presentation a/c *Punjab No 10, Kalabagh*. **23 Sqn** dd ex 1 AD 29.3.16 and damaged in forced landing during patrol 30.9.16. **2 AD** ex 23 Sqn 4.10.16 (120hp Beardmore) and to England in packing case 27.10.16.

5231 Presentation a/c *Malaya No.9, Balas* wef 27.11.15. Deleted 30.4.16.

5232 **18 Sqn** dd ex 1 AD 6.4.16 fitted with WT and damaged by AA on photo sortie 26.4.16 (2Lt JC Callaghan OK/2Lt J Mitchell KIA – had destroyed a Fokker E-type). **1 AD** ex 18 Sqn and deleted 3.5.16 (NWR, flying time 21hr 50min).

5233 Presentation a/c *Trinidad*. **18 Sqn** dd ex 1 AD 21.4.16 and LIA when force-landed in no-mans-land 16.7.16 (2Lt HW Butterworth

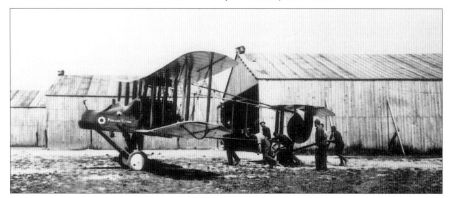

Identified as FE2b 5224 by its presentation inscription 'Punjab 4 Jind', this 22 Squadron aircraft was the first FE2b handled by 2 Aircraft Depot in France..

KIA/Capt JHF McEwan POW. Flying time 99hr 10min – reported in Aeroplane Casualties as 5253).

5234 Presentation a/c *South Australia*. **18 Sqn** dd ex 1 AD 6.4.16 fitted with WT, suffered engine fire 29.4.16 and crashed in forced-landing 16.10.16 (2Lt CG Shaumer/Lt BD Randall OK. 120hp Beardmore and SOC 18.10.16 with flying time 230hr 20min). 2 AD ex 18 Sqn 19.10.16 and deleted 20.10.16.

5235 Presentation a/c *Dominica*. **23 Sqn** dd ex 1 AD 21.4.16, damaged in combat with vict near Cambrai 31.5.16 (2Lt EF Allen OK/Lt LC Powell KIA after sharing sending an EA OOC near Marquion with 5215, 5249, 6354 and Martinsyde G.100 7280). Damaged in combat on recce 1.7.16 (Lt KL Gospill/Cpl AJ Cathie OK) also on bombing sortie 19.7.16 (2Lt ER Manning/2Lt CVJ Borton WIA) then LIA 31.8.16 (2Lt FG McIntosh/2Lt JDA Macfie POW wdd, engine Daimler 6903).

5236 Presentation a/c *Newfoundland No 1*. **28 Sqn** dd ex Norwich 11.4.16. Deleted 17.6.16.

5237 **28 Sqn** dd ex Norwich 10.4.16.

5238 Presentation a/c *'Akyab Burma'*. **25 Sqn** dd ex 1 AD fitted with WT, 18.4.16, damaged in successful combat 17.5.16 (Capt W Milne WIA/2Lt ER Davis OK after sending an EA C type OOC near La Bassée/Loos at 06.30) and victs 2.7.16 (2Lt HB Davey/Cpl W Paull destroyed a Fokker E-type near Lille), 19.7.16 (2Lt HB Davey & Capt HC Morley shared the destruction of a Fokker E.III near Provin with 5245) and 20.7.16 (2Lt HB Davey/Capt HC Morley shared the destruction of 2 Fokker E-types near Lens at 18.30 with 6932) then LIA in combat with Fokker E-types 6.9.16 (2Lt JL Robertson/Lt EC Kemp KIA – a/c went down in flames, pilot jumped. 120hp Beardmore, flying time 240hr 8min).

5239 Presentation a/c *Gold Coast No 1*. **18 Sqn** dd ex 1 AD 23.4.16 and LIA near Albert 19.10.16 (2Lt RL Dingley/Lt WHN Whitehead POW. a/c 120hp Beardmore, flying time 276hr).

5240 Presentation a/c *Gold Coast No 2*. **18 Sqn** dd ex 1 AD 23.4.16 fitted with WT and crashed landing on practice flight 7.7.16 (Lt G Haynes/2Lt GW Arkle OK). **1 AD** ex 18 Sqn and deleted 10.7.16 (NWR, 107hr 15min flying time).

5241 Presentation a/c *Gold Coast No 3*. **1 AD** ex England 18.4.16. **18 Sqn** dd ex 1 AD 21.4.16 fitted with WT and undercarriage wrecked in forced landing 16.5.16 (Capt GH Norman/2Lt ET Pruen OK, deleted. Flying time 36hr).

5242 Presentation a/c *Gold Coast No 4*. **22 Sqn** dd ex 1 AD 23.4.16 and LIA on photo sortie 31.7.16 (2Lt FD Holder/Pte Welford injured after forced landing following combat – a/c burnt). 2 AD and deleted 4.8.16 (NWR, flying time 188hr 24min).

5243 Presentation a/c *Gold Coast No 5*. **18 Sqn** dd ex 1 AD 22.4.16, crashed 29.4.16 (2Lt R Chidlaw-Roberts/2Lt GW Arkle OK) then undershot landing and hit road 6.5.16. **1 AD** ex 18 Sqn 8.5.16 and deleted 12.5.16 (NWR, flying time 17hr 30min).

5244 Presentation a/c *Gold Coast No 6*. **2 AD** (NWR 8.4.16, flying time 13hr 45min). **18 Sqn** dd ex 1 AD 23.4.16. **1 AD** ex 18 Sqn for examination and repair 10.5.16. Flown to England ex 1 AD 16.5.16.

5245 Presentation a/c *Gold Coast No 7*. **20 Sqn** dd ex 1 AD 23.4.16. **25 Sqn** dd ex 1 AD 19.6.16 and vict 19.7.16 (2Lt NWW Webb/2Lt JA Mann destroyed a Fokker E-type near Provin at 06.45 with 5238) then crashed landing on test flight 25.8.16.

5246 Presentation a/c *Gold Coast No 8*. **18 Sqn** dd ex 1 AD 3.5.16 fitted with WT until @ 10.6.16. **1 AD** and deleted 3.8.16 (NWR, flying time 110hr). 11 RS ?

5247 Presentation a/c *Montreal No 1*. **20 Sqn** dd ex 1 AD 1.5.16. **23 Sqn** by 10.16. **2 AD** ex 23 Sqn 9.11.16. **1 AD** ex 2 AD 16.11.16 and flown to England ex 1 AD 21.11.16 (120hp Beardmore, flying time 311hr 7min). Allotted for training 22.11.16. Allotted to BEF 7.4.17. **25 Sqn** dd ex 1 AD 19.4.17 and victs 24.4.17 (2Lt A Roulstone/2Lt EG Green destroyed an Albatros D-type near Fosse de Drocourt at 17.50) and 26.4.17 (Sgt JHR Green/2Lt HE Freeman-Smith sent an Albatros D.III OOC near Drocourt at 17.20) then damaged on practice flight 30.4.17. Deleted 6.5.17.

5248 **20 Sqn** dd ex 1 AD 29.4.16 and vict 15.5.16 (Lt AD Pearce/AM1 G Hodder sent a Fokker E.III OOC near Poelcapelle at 11.15) then wrecked landing in gale on practice flight 19.5.16. **1 AD** ex 20 Sqn 21.5.16 and deleted 27.5.16 with flying time 29hr 24min).

5249 Presentation a/c *Ceylon No 3, A Nightjar*

from Ceylon. **23 Sqn** dd ex 1 AD 3.5.16 and damaged in combat with vict near Cambrai 31.5.16 (2Lt AT Watson/2Lt CL Blake OK after sharing sending a EA OOC near Marquion with 5215, 5235, 6354 and Martinsyde G.100 7280) and again damaged in combat 8.6.16. **2 AD** ex 23 Sqn 10.11.16. **1 AD** ex 2 AD 16.11.16 and flown to England ex 1 AD 21.11.16 (120hp Beardmore, flying time 311hr 49min). Allotted for training 22.11.16. Deleted 15.12.16.

5250 Presentation a/c *Mauritius No 3*. **22 Sqn** dd ex 1 AD 1.5.16, damaged in combat 6.8.16 (Capt JG Swart OK/2Lt WS Mansell WIA), vict 17.8.16 (Capt JG Swart/2Lt LCL Cook destroyed an EA C type in flames near Pozières at 10.20, shared with 6931 – this a/c?) and LIA in combat near Bancourt 3.11.16 (Capt AJM Pemberton KIA/2Lt LCL Cook POW wdd).

5642 – 5648: 7 RAF FE2a (120hp Austro-Daimler) built by the Royal Aircraft Factory, Farnborough under War Office authority.

5642 Presentation a/c *Montreal No 1* wef 10.15. allotted to BEF 28.5.15. **1 AP** dd 4.9.15 (engine 279). **6 Sqn** dd 6.9.15, damaged by AA near Langemarck 19.10.15. **1 AP** ex 6 Sqn 7.11.15 (engine 294). **6 Sqn** returned 21.11.15 (with engine 195/WD1265) and forced to land after combat with Fokker near Poperinghe 30.11.15 (Lt EHP Cave/Lt EW Stubbs OK). **20 Sqn** ex 6 Sqn 25.1.16 and reported as unfit for service 7.3.16. **1 AD** ex 20 Sqn 10.3.16 and dismantled (flying time 65hr 57min).

5643 **AID** allotted to BEF 2.9.1915. **1 AP** dd ex England 14.9.15 (engine 282/WD1346). **6 Sqn** dd ex 1 AP 14.9.15 and in combat 26.10.15 (Lt JL Kinnear/2Lt JEP Howey engaged an EA near Boesinghe), 5.12.15 (Lt

Running up the engine of FE2b 5236, which saw training duties with 28 Sqn in 1916 at Gosport.

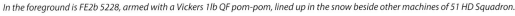

In the foreground is FE2b 5228, armed with a Vickers 1lb QF pom-pom, lined up in the snow beside other machines of 51 HD Squadron.

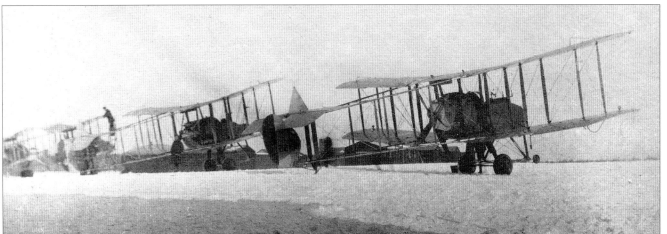

After combat, and a hit from AA fire which killed the pilot, the wounded observer of this 6 Sqn FE2a, 5644, 2Lt J.E.P. Howey, crawled onto the lap of his dead pilot and crash landed the aircraft over the lines. Below: The same machine offers a rare view of an FE2a in operational finish with an unusually large nacelle cockade.

EHP Cave/Lt O Nixon engaged an EA over Polygon Wood) and 17.1.16 (2Lt Raymond-Barker/2Lt Young engaged an LVG near Ypres). **20 Sqn** ex 6 Sqn 25.1.16 and wrecked on flight to 15 Sqn 4.2.16, had force-landed and hit tree taking off from Droglandt (2Lt CEH James/2Lt AH Dickinson injured).

5644 1 AP ex England 18.9.1915. **6 Sqn** dd ex 1 AP 23.9.15 (engine 291), in combat 4.11.15 (2Lt CH Kelway-Bamber/Lt HJ Payn sent a Fokker down near Zillebeke) and 5.11.15

(Capt JL Kinnear/2Lt JEP Howey engaged an EA near Merkem) then LIA 11.11.15 (2Lt CH Kelway-Bamber KIA/Lt JEP Howey POW – after combat with 2 EA).

5645 Presentation a/c *Montreal No 2* wef 11.15. Allotted to BEF 18.9.1915. **1 AP** dd ex England 23.9.15 (engine 278). **6 Sqn** dd ex 1 AP 1.10.15, damaged in combat near Bixschoote 19.12.15 (2Lt GEH Fincham/2Lt G Price OK) and wrecked when hit truck on take-off for patrol 2.1.16.

5646 Presentation a/c *Nova Scotia* wef 29.9.15. Allotted to BEF 23.9.1915. **1 AP** dd ex England 30.9.15 (engine 272/WD1336). **6 Sqn** dd ex 1 AP 2.10.15 and wrecked taking off on recce 5.12.15 – undercarriage wiped off and crashed. Deleted 6.12.15.

5647 10th machine. Presentation a/c *Bombay No 2*. **1 AP** dd 20.10.15 by Capt H de Havilland (engine 185/WD1253). **16 Sqn** dd ex 1 AP 26.10.15 by Lt Eastwood), unserviceable by 15.11.15 and reported dismantled awaiting rebuild 18.12.15. **1 AD** ex 16 Sqn 8.2.16. **20 Sqn** collected ex 1 AD 13.2.16 and damaged in forced-landing on delivery flight – no water, engine seized. **1 AD** and deleted 14.2.16 (NWR).

5648 11th machine. Presentation a/c *Newfoundland No 3* wef 25.10.15 (engine 288/WD1352). Fitted with V-strut undercarriage. Allotted to BEF 25.10.1915. **1 AP** dd 3.11.15 by Capt BC Hucks. **6 Sqn** dd ex 1 AP 7.11.15 and crashed 21.11.15 . **1 AD** ex 6 Sqn 22.11.15 and deleted – NWR.

6328 – 6377: 50 RAF FE2b (120hp Beardmore) built by the Royal Aircraft Factory, Farnborough under War Office authority.

6328 RAF 3.12.15; engine 363, airscrew T5638. **15 Sqn** by 2.16. **20 Sqn** and damaged in forced landing after combat near Ypres 18.3.16 (Lt RH Anderson/Capt EW Forbes OK). **1 AD** ex 20 Sqn and deleted 24.3.16 (NWR, 31hr 46min flying time).

6329 Presentation a/c *Newfoundland No 2* wef 18.11.15. **RAF** 10.12.15; engine 364, airscrew P3882. **20 Sqn** fitted with WT. **1 AD** ex 20 Sqn 23.4.16 for overhaul and rebuilding but deleted 3.5.16 (NWR, flying time 46hr 57min).

6330 Presentation a/c *Manitoba*. **RAF** 14.12.15; engine 218, airscrew 5798. **1 AD** dd ex England 26.12.15. **16 Sqn** dd ex 1 AD 28.12.15. **1 AD** ex 16 Sqn 27.1.16. **12 Sqn** dd ex 1 AD 1.2.16. **1 AD** ex 12 Sqn 24.2.16. **25 Sqn** dd ex 1 AD 25.2.16 and victs 16.5.16 (2Lt GRM Reid/Lt JA Mann destroyed an Aviatik C-type near Souchez), 19.5.16 (2Lt GRM Reid/Lt JA Mann destroyed a Fokker E-type near Mericourt at 16.00) and 21.5.16 (2Lt GRM Reid/Lt JA Mann destroyed an EA C-type near Lens at 18.15), crashed at Bruay 5.8.16 (Sgt Lane). **1 AD** ex 25 Sqn. **18 Sqn** damaged during practice landing on cornfield 5.8.16 and damaged by ground fire on photo sortie near Suzanne 19.9.16 (2Lt SF Heard/2Lt GT Richardson OK). **2**

FE2a 5647 'Bombay No 2' which saw action with 16 and 20 Sqns in France through the winter of 1915/16.

AD ex 18 Sqn 24.9.16 and deleted 24.9.16 (NWR, 120hp Beardmore, flying time 282hr 52min).

6331 Presentation a/c *Ceylon No 2* wef 22.12.15. **RAF** 15.12.15; engine 365, airscrew 5930. **1 AD** dd ex England 26.12.15. **6 Sqn** dd ex 1 AD 28.12.15. **15 Sqn** by 1.2.16. **20 Sqn** ex 6 Sqn 25.1.16 and vict 13.2.16 (2Lt PG Scott/2Lt FS Miller sent a Rumpler C type OOC near Mouscron at 15.40) then wrecked when hangar blown down in gale, before 14.2.16.

6332 Presentation a/c *Malaya No 8*. **RAF** 21.12.15; engine 3249, airscrew 5875. **20 Sqn** by 30.12.15, to BEF with unit and in combat near Roulers 14.3.16 (Lt NG McNaughton/2Lt C Chancellor OK) and 18.3.16 near Menin (Lt NG McNaughton AM1 Talbot) then damaged in combat 21.4.16 (2Lt NG McNaughton WIA/AM1 S Catton OK) and vict 24.4.16 (Capt EP Graves/2Lt C Chancellor destroyed an EA C type near Passchendaele at 08.45) then burnt after forced landing following combat near Poperinghe 29.4.16 (2Lt RD Sampson WIA/AM1 S Cotton KIA. Flying time 90hr 32min). **1 AD** ex 20 Sqn, deleted 30.4.16 (flying time 90hr 37min).

6333 Presentation a/c *Jamaica No 1*. **RAF** 19.12.15; engine 215, airscrew 5785. **20 Sqn** by 30.12.15, to BEF with unit and wrecked when hangar blown down in gale, before 14.2.16. 11 Sqn.

6334 Presentation a/c *Montreal No 3*. **RAF** 22.12.15; engine 221, airscrew 5892. **25 Sqn** dd ex 1 AD 5.1.16 and damaged by AA 22.6.16 (2Lt LC Angstrom WIA/2Lt HC Hadwick OK) and wrecked when shot down in combat near Cambrai 26.6.16 (2Lt R Sherwell OK/AM2 H Chadwick KIA). **1 AD** ex 25 Sqn and deleted 2.7.16 (NWR, flying time 217hr 20min).

6335 Presentation a/c *Trinidad Chamber of Commerce* wef 31.12.15. **RAF** 23.12.15; engine 216, airscrew 5824. **25 Sqn** dd ex 1 AD 5.1.16 and shot up and damaged in crash landing 31.3.16 (2Lt Collinson/AM2 Gevers OK). **1 AD** ARS ex 25 Sqn 1.4.16 and deleted (NWR).

6336 Presentation a/c *British Guiana* wef 5.1.16. **RAF** Farnborough; engine 234, airscrew 5823. 12 Sqn. **20 Sqn** and vict 13.2.16 (2Lt JT Kirton/Lt HF Billinge sent down a twin-engined EA near Mouscron at 16.15) then wrecked in forced landing on patrol 23.4.16 (flying time 72hr 26min). **1 AD** ex 20 Sqn 26.4.16 for deletion (flying time 72hr 25min).

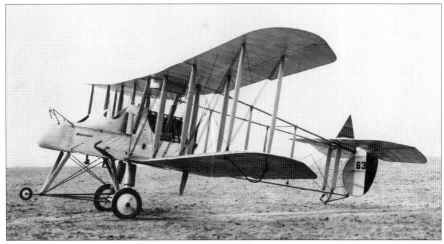

FE2b 6330 saw long service in France, flying with 16, 12, 25 and 18 Squadrons.

6337 **RAF** 28.12.15; engine 234, airscrew 5823. **CFS** Experimental Flt 6.1.16 – 5.16 (120hp Beardmore No.370) for Trials Report CFS 225. At CFS allotted to BEF 19.5.16 (120hp Beardmore). **18 Sqn** dd ex 1 AD 27.5.16. **25 Sqn** dd ex 18 Sqn 3.6.16 and vict 17.6.16 (2Lt LL Richardson/Lt MV Lewes shared sending a Fokker E-type OOC near Don with 5201 and 6938) then wrecked in crash on take off for bombing sortie 19.7.16. **1 AD** ex 25 Sqn and deleted 23.7.16 (NWR, flying time 111hr 20min).

6338 Presentation a/c *Ceylon No 3* wef 3.1.16. **RAF** 29.12.15; engine 260, airscrew 5879. **1 AD** dd ex England 8.1.16. **6 Sqn** dd ex 1 AD 15.1.16. **20 Sqn** ex 6 Sqn 24.1.16 and LIA on recce near Lille 29.2.16 (2Lt LA Newbold/2Lt HF Champion POW – shot down by EA C Type of Flt Abtl 3).

6339 Presentation a/c *Nova Scotia*. **RAF** 2.2.16; engine 387, airscrew 5925 – fitted with old section planes (RAF6). **20 Sqn** dd ex 1 AD 1.3.16 and in combat near Tournai 9.3.16 (Capt JR Howett OK/Sgt T May WIA) and

Face to face: an inscription on the nacelle records the capture of 6338, and the Eindekker in the upper photograph emphasises the point. Downed on 29 February 1916, this FE2b was the first loss in action for 20 Squadron. It has an unusual 'goal-post' type gun mounting between the cockpits.

Instead of having the Presentation name on both sides, this machine, and some others, are known to have carried a secondary name on the starboard side. FE2b 9341 was both 'Zanzibar No 1' and 'The Scotch Express'. The Presentation name transferred to FE2b 6953 when 9341 was lost.

'Recovery of an enemy aircraft'. FE2b 6341 of 25 Sqn after capture on 1 December 1915. Its pilot, Capt D. Grinell Milne, escaped in 1918 to become an ace with 56 Sqn. He wrote 'Wind in the Wires' about his experiences.

damaged in combat near Roulers 14.3.16 (Capt JR Howett OK/Lt HF Billinge WIA). **25 Sqn** and LIA bombing La Bassée 3.7.16 (2Lt R Sherwell/2Lt JCM Stewart KIA – shot down by AA. Flying time 122hr 53 min).

6340   RAF 30.12.15; engine 239, airscrew 5886. **1 AD** dd ex England 10.1.16. **12 Sqn** dd ex 1

AD 8.2.16. **1 AD** ex 12 Sqn 22.2.16. **20 Sqn** dd ex 1 AD 24.2.16 and vict 9.3.16 (2Lt PG Scott/2Lt GA Exley destroyed a Rumpler C type near Lille at 11.30). **23 Sqn** by 2.9.16 and crashed landing from OP 14.9.16 (Capt G Taylor-Loban/AM1 J Howcroft injured. 120hp Beardmore, flying time 254hr 6min).

2 AD ex 23 Sqn 17.9.16 and deleted 20.9.16 with serviceable parts to store.

6341   Presentation a/c *Presented by the Government of Zanzibar No 1, 'The Scotch Express'.* RAF 6.1.16; engine 391, airscrew 5935. **25 Sqn** dd ex 1 AD 18.1.16, to BEF with unit and vict 27.4.16 (2Lt RS Maxwell/2Lt SA Sharpe forced an Aviatik to land near Herlies) then LIA near Fournes on recce escort 16.5.16 (Capt D Grinell-Milne/Cpl D McMaster POW – shot down by 4 EA, a/c captured intact, flying time) 117hr 19min.

6342   Presentation a/c *Zanzibar No 4* wef 15.1.16. RAF 8.1.16; engine 389, airscrew 5926. **25 Sqn** dd ex 1 AD 18.1.16 and damaged in combat over Gheluwe with Fokker E.III 31.3.16 (Lt Norris OK/Capt H Seagrave WIA) then damaged taking off from forced-landing 17.7.16. **1 AD** and deleted 20.7.16 (NWR, flying time 223hr 40min).

6343   Presentation a/c *Zanzibar No 2.* RAF 7.1.16; engine 390, airscrew 5923. **25 Sqn**, damaged 2.1.16 (Capt C MacLean/2Lt JC Barraclough), to BEF with unit but damaged when overturned during forced landing in snow at Thérouanne after chasing EA 22.2.16 (Capt CT McClean OK/2Lt JC Barraclough injured). Deleted 24.2.16.

6344   Presentation a/c *Zanzibar No 3* wef 15.1.16. RAF 10.1.16; engine 406, airscrew 5915. **25 Sqn** dd ex 1 AD 20.1.16 and damaged by AA over La Bassée on photo sortie 16.4.16 (Lt CJ Hart/Cpl JH Waller OK) and damaged in crash taking off after forced landing 27.5.16. **1 AD** ARS ex 25 Sqn 29.5.16 and deleted ((NWR, flying time 149hr 47min. 38 Sqn?)

6345   RAF 10.1.16; engine 230, airscrew 5941. **23 Sqn** dd 18.1.16, fitted with experimental exhaust pipes 20.1.16, to BEF with unit and damaged by AA near Ayette on photo sortie 30.4.16 (Lt SHB Harris WIA/Lt AN Solly OK). and LIA on recce escort near Cambrai 31.5.16 (2Lt A Cairne-Duff/Cpl G Maxwell POW wdd – brought down by EA).

6346   Presentation a/c *Black Watch No 2.* RAF 12.1.16; engine 263, airscrew 5881. **25 Sqn** dd 18.1.16, to BEF with unit and damaged in forced landing 29.2.16. **20 Sqn** dd ex 1 AD 28.4.16. **25 Sqn** dd ex 20 Sqn 11.6.16 and vict 18.6.16 (2Lt GR McCubbin/Cpl JH Waller destroyed a Fokker E.III near Annay at 18.05) then damaged in combat near Beuvray 26.6.16 (2Lt GR McCubbin WIA/Cpl JH Waller OK). **18 Sqn** and *(named Elsa II)* LIA night bombing 15.10.16 (2Lt AR Crisp/AM1 L Hardinge POW. 120hp Beardmore, flying

time 163hr 45min).

6347 Presentation a/c *South Australia* wef 19.1.16. **RAF** 14.1.16; engine 251, airscrew 5880. **25 Sqn** dd ex 1 AD 24.1.16 and damaged in crash 5.5.16 (Lt JRB Savage/AM2 Walder OK, flying time 102hr 4min). **1 AD** ARS ex 25 Sqn for overhaul and repairs 6.5.16.

6348 Presentation a/c *Malaya No 9*. **RAF** 15.1.16; engine 252, airscrew 5929. **23 Sqn** dd ex AID 23.1.16, to BEF with unit and LIA near Biache 26.6.16 (Lt HB Russell POW wdd/Lt JR Dennistoun POW fatally wdd – shot down by 3 EA. Flying time 142hr 3min).

6349 **RAF** 18.1.16; engine 394, airscrew 5932. **23 Sqn** dd ex AID 25.1.16, to BEF with unit, being fitted with Strange gun mounting 24.3.16 and wrecked after losing fuel on test flight 22.5.16 (AM1 pilot blamed – 'poor flying'). **2 AD** ex 23 Sqn 27.5.16 and deleted 31.5.16 (Flying time 80hr 43min).

6350 Presentation a/c *Baroda No 13*. **RAF** 18.1.16; engine 250, airscrew 5920. **28 Sqn** dd ex AID 27.1.16. **23 Sqn** dd ex 28 Sqn 5.2.16, to BEF with unit and wrecked in crosswind crash landing at Wagnonlieu after combat 25.6.16 (2Lt KL Gospill IIA/Sgt HN Johnson WIA). 2 AD ex 23 Sqn and deleted 30.6.16 (NWR, flying time 141hr 6min).

6351 Presentation a/c *Baroda No 14*. **RAF** 19.1.16; engine 403, airscrew 5977. **28 Sqn. 23 Sqn** dd ex 28 Sqn 5.2.16, to BEF with unit and vict 20.5.16 (2Lt DC Cloete/Cpl P Havens destroyed an Aviatik near Adnifer Wood) then LIA near Peronne on recce 20.7.16 (2Lt DSC Macaskie/2Lt CI Sandys-Thomas POW wdd. Flying time 212hr 33min).

6352 Presentation a/c *Baroda No 15*. **RAF** 21.1.16; engine 407, airscrew 5993. **23 Sqn** dd ex AID 7.2.16, to BEF with unit and LIA near Queant in combat on recce escort 29.3.16 (2Lt FG Pinder POW wdd/2Lt EA Halford POW – a/c captured intact and displayed in Germany, probably shot down by Ltn M Immelmann FlAb 62. Flying time 23hr 3min).

6353 **RAF** 22.1.16; engine 408, airscrew 5885. **23 Sqn** dd ex AID Farnborough 9.2.16 to BEF with unit and LIA on Arras racecourse 16.3.16 on flight to France (Lt SHB Harris/2Lt EB Harvey OK – a/c hit by ground fire, force-landed on racecourse and shelled to destruction). Deleted 18.3.16 (engine and aeroplane logbooks destroyed with machine).

6354 **RAF** 25.1.16; engine 401, airscrew 5995 – fitted with new type planes (RAF14). **23 Sqn** dd ex AID 12.2.16 to BEF with unit and damaged in successful combat 20.5.16 (Capt RN Adams/AM1 DAR Chapman destroyed an Aviatik near Adnifer Wood) and vict 31.5.16 (2Lt DC Cloete/2Lt CE Pither shared sending an EA OOC near Marquion with 5215, 5235, 5249 and Martinsyde G.100 7280) then wrecked in crash in storm at St Pol after engine failed 4.7.16 (Sgt DAR Chapman injured/2Lt CE Pither OK). **2 AD** ex 23 Sqn and deleted 9.7.16 (NWR, flying time 164hr 24min).

6355 **RAF** 26.1.16; engine 214, airscrew 5922 – new section planes fitted (RAF14). **23 Sqn** dd ex AID Farnborough 5.2.16. **18 Sqn** dd ex 1 AD 14.4.16 and damaged in bad landing from test flight 23.5.16. **1 AD** ex 18 Sqn 25.5.16 and deleted 27.5.16 (NWR, flying time 43hr 30min.)

6356 **RAF** 28.1.16; engine 219, airscrew T5638 – new section planes fitted (RAF14). **12 Sqn** dd 15.2.16. **1 AD** ex 12 Sqn 24.2.16. **20 Sqn** dd ex 1 AD 1.3.16 and LIA near Ligny on recce escort 9.3.16 (Lt LR Heywood/2Lt DB Gayford POW. Flying time 7hr 50min).

6357 Presentation a/c *Shanghai Britons No 3*. **RAF** 1.2.16; engine 235, airscrew 5939 – section 14 planes fitted and fitted with 160hp Beardmore by 21.2.16 and tested 11.5.16

FE2b 6346 'Black Watch No 2' with 25 Sqn in summer 1916. The serial is painted high on the rudder.

After repair and transfer to 18 Sqn, 6346, now named 'Elsa II' and fitted with a klaxon for communication with ground troops, is seen in German hands after capture on 15 October 1916 on a night bombing raid.

Below: This photograph taken in a German hangar shows that when the machine was repaired and repainted the serial was placed on a lower segment of the rudder.

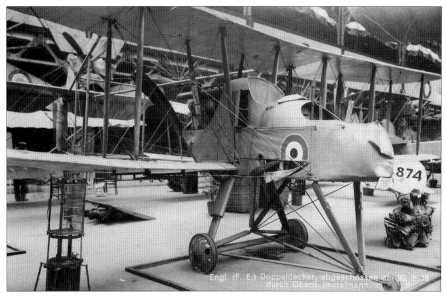

6352 on display in a German war exhibition, credited as shot down by Oblt Immelmann on 29 March 1916. It was 23 Squadron's first loss in action.

(Capt BC Hucks). **11 Sqn**, allotted 2.6.16, on charge by 26.6.16 and LIA near Bapaume on photo sortie 2.7.16 (2Lt JW Toone/2Lt EB Harvey POW, 160hp engine, flying time 55hr 25min).

6358   **RAF** 3.2.16; engine 246, airscrew 5884 – section 14 planes fitted. **20 Sqn** dd ex 1 AD 19.2.16 and wrecked landing from test flight 31.3.16. **1 AD** ex 20 Sqn 3.4.16 and deleted 22.4.16.

6359   Presentation a/c *Baroda No 17*. **RAF** 5.2.16; engine 419, airscrew 5887. **20 Sqn** dd ex 1 AD 19.2.16, in combat near Roulers 14.3.16 (2Lt JR Morton/Cpl May OK) and undercarriage modified by Lt E Trafford Jones by 12.5.16 then LIA 16.5.16 (Lt E Trafford Jones KIA/Capt EW Forbes WIA – wrecked in crash landing, by observer, in British lines after combat. Flying time 98hr 28min) and deleted 23.5.16.

6360   **RAF** 4.2.16 fitted with 150hp RAF No.SD1001 and airscrew 5981 and used in tests of RAF gyroscopic bomb-sight summer 16 and in tests to determine the effects of weather on performance.

6361   Presentation a/c *Montreal No 2*. **RAF** 6.12.15; engine 421, airscrew 5919 – old section planes fitted (RAF6). Subject of BEF complaint 3.16 – received from England with nacelle painted bright yellow. **20 Sqn** dd ex 1 AD 10.3.16 and damaged in combat near Ypres 21.4.16, forced landing on Ypres race course and wrecked by shellfire (Capt

CEH James/2Lt GA Exley OK, a/c had 34hr 15min flying time).

6362   **RAF** 10.2.16; engine 377, airscrew 5944 – old section planes fitted (RAF6). **28 Sqn** dd ex AID 5.3.16 and wrecked in crash from nose-dive following side-slip 11.3.16 (Capt GCN Nicholson/AM2 JH Martin KIFA). Deleted 23.3.16. BUT 19 RS by 1.17.

6363   Presentation a/c *Junagadh No 1*. **RAF** 11.2.16; engine 414, airscrew 5978 – old section planes fitted (RAF6). **28 Sqn** dd ex Farnborough 14.3.16. **19 RS** ex 28 Sqn 8.4.16 and crashed from side-slip after engine failed 24.5.17 (2Lt SGE Inman-Knox injured/AM3 Wardale injured). Deleted 4.6.17. BUT 9 RS Norwich 2.3.17 (Lt AD Pryor).

6364   Presentation a/c *Junagadh No 2*. **RAF** 15.2.16; engine 422, airscrew 5971. **AID** 15.2.16. **1 AD** dd ex Lympne 19.3.16 with combat en-route (2Lt R Collis/Flt Sgt AC Emery attacked and damaged a Brandenburg seaplane). **23 Sqn** dd ex 1 AD 25.3.16, in combat over Queant 29.3.16 (Lt SHB Harris/Lt LC Powell OK) and crashed landing near aerodrome on night practice flight 26.4.16. **2 AD** ex 23 Sqn and 3 AAP and deleted 2.5.16 (NWR, flying time 19hr 36min).

6365   Presentation a/c *Mauritius No 2*. **RAF** 15.2.16; engine 423, airscrew 5830. **20 Sqn** dd ex 1 AD 25.3.16 and damaged when hit hedge landing from practice flight 4.4.16. **22 Sqn** and LIA near Clery-Longueval on photo sortie 1.7.16 (Lt JH Firstbrook POW wdd/

Propaganda postcard of FE2b 6356, a 20 Sqn machine lost on 9 March 1916.

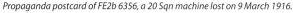

Lt R Burgess fatally WIA. Flying time 119hr 29min).

6366   Presentation a/c *Jamaica No 1*. **RAF** 17.2.16; engine 424, airscrew 5973 – old section planes fitted (RAF6). **25 Sqn** dd ex 1 AD 28.3.16 and damaged in successful combat 22.6.16 (Capt CT Maclean/2Lt JC Barraclough OK after destroying a Roland C type near Lens at 08.00). **1 AD** ex 25 Sqn 1.8.16. **22 Sqn** by 2.9.16 and LIA near Contalmaison 9.9.16 (Lt H Strathy-Mackay/Lt AJ Bowerman KIA – went down in flames. 120hp Beardmore, flying time 160hr 15min).

6367   **RAF** 19.2.16; engine 425, airscrew T5638/5888 – old section planes fitted (RAF6). **28 Sqn** dd ex Farnborough 31.3.16 and wrecked in crash from stall at 300ft 8.2.17 (crew injured).

6368   Presentation a/c *Junagadh No 3*. **RAF** 23.2.16; engine 235, airscrew 5995. **22 Sqn** dd ex AID Norwich 17.3.16 and to BEF with the unit and vict 25.8.16 (Lt H Strathy-Mackie/2Lt AJ Bowerman destroyed an EA C type near Flers at 12.55). **1 AD** ex 22 Sqn 11.12.16 and flown to England 16.12.16. **64 Sqn**.

6369   Presentation a/c *A Devil Bird from Ceylon*. **RAF** 29.2.16; engine 220, airscrew 5638. **20 Sqn** dd ex 1 AD 3.4.16. **25 Sqn** dd ex 20 Sqn 8.6.16 but unserviceable and to AD. **23 Sqn** and in combat over Vaulx 1.7.16 (2Lt GJ Firbank/Flt Sgt Adams OK). and wrecked in landing from bombing sortie 10.7.16. **2 AD** ex 23 Sqn and deleted 20.7.16 (NWR, flying time 120hr 22min).

6370   **RAF** as FE2c 20.3.16; engine 454, airscrew 5937. Retained at **RAF** for experimental work, inspected 19.4.16 for removal of V type undercarriage and fitting of oleo landing gear; crashed 9.5.17.

6371   **RAF** as FE2c 19.3.16; engine 464, airscrew 5993. **1 AD** dd 22(?).4.16. **22 Sqn** dd ex 1 AD 21.4.16 and crashed landing from practice flight 22.5.16. **25 Sqn** dd ex 1 AD St-Omer 19.6.16 and wrecked in landing crash 17.7.16 (flying time 105hr 47min). **1 AD** and deleted 20.7.16 (engine 464/WD2436, NWR, 105hr 47min flying time).

6372   **RAF** 30.3.16; engine 469, airscrew 5975 tested with V-strut undercarriage 7.4.16. **1 AD** dd ex England 14.4.16. **22 Sqn** dd ex 1 AD 23.4.16 and vict 24.9.16 (Capt JHS Tyssen/2Lt SH Clarke shared sending a Halberstadt OOC near Epehy at 16.35 with 4860, 4924, 4935 and 6374). **1 AD** ex 22 Sqn 18.12.16. Flown to England 24.12.16.

6373   **RAF** 29.3.16; engine 473, airscrew 5998. **20 Sqn** dd ex 1 AD 23.4.16. Reported as 15 Sqn 31.8.16 (???). **18 Sqn** and damaged in combat near Lille 1.9.16 (2Lt GK Macdonald WIA/Lt FS Rankin OK). **1 AD** ex 18 Sqn 4.9.16 and deleted 6.9.16 (120hp Beardmore, NWR, flying time 171hr 45min).

6374   **RAF** 12.4.16; engine 302, airscrew 600. **20 Sqn** dd ex 1 AD 19.5.16. **25 Sqn** dd ex 20 Sqn 2.6.16 and damaged by AA on photo sortie 16.7.16 (Lt HL Chadwick OK/Pte WH Truesdale WIA). **1 AD** ex 25 Sqn 1.8.16. **22 Sqn** by 2.9.16 and vict 24.9.16 (2Lt WE Knowlden/2Lt BWA Ordish shared sending a Halberstadt OOC near Epehy at 16.35 with 4860, 4924, 4935 and 6372) then LIA in combat near Bancourt 3.11.16 (2Lt WE Knowlden POW wdd/2Lt BWA Ordish POW).

6375   **RAF** 28.4.16; engine 229, airscrew 5876. **22 Sqn** dd ex 1 AD 16.5.16 and damaged in combat and shelled after forced landing 8.7.16 (Capt WA Summers/2Lt RM Chaworth-Musters OK. Flying time 63hr 14min). Converted to FE2d. **1 AD** dd ex 8 AAP 15.8.17.

6376   **RAF** 18.4.16; engine 293, airscrew 5939. **25 Sqn** dd ex 1 AD 7.5.16 and wrecked on

FE2b 6934 of 23 Sqn, lost on 3 September 1916 to Ltn G. Leffers of Ja1, who was flying a captured Nieuport Scout at the time.

landing 16.5.16 – hit shed. **1 AD** ex 25 Sqn 23.5.16 and deleted that day (NWR, flying time 10hr 40min).

6377 **RAF** 11.5.16; engine 330, airscrew 5827 fitted with Vickers pom-pom by 22.5.16.

6928 – 7027: 100 RAF FE2b (120hp Beardmore) built by Boulton & Paul Ltd, Norwich under Contract 87/A/265 dated 29.12.15.

6928 Presentation a/c *Malaya No 12* presented by the Federal Malay States Civil Service. **AID** by 3.12.15. **15 Sqn** by 1.2.16. **22 Sqn** dd ex 1 AD 12.5.16, in combat 25.6.16 (2Lt H Strathy-

Mackay/2Lt C Walsh engaged 2 Fokker E.IIIs near Acheux and then chased to lines by 21 EA) and LIA on photo sortie 1.7.16 (Capt GW Webb KIA/Lt WO Tudor-Hart POW wdd, a/c had 73hr 30min flying time).

6929 Presentation a/c *Malaya No 13*. **SAD** allotted to the BEF (160hp Beardmore) 16.1.16. **20 Sqn** dd ex 1 AD 6.5.16, fitted with WT. **22 Sqn** damaged in forced landing 18.8.16 (hit trench after engine failure). **2 AD** ex 1 AD 23.3.17. **22 Sqn** dd ex 2 AD 3.4.17 and LIA in collision with 24 Sqn DH2 7909 near Le Verguier 23.4.17 (Lt EA Barltrop/2Lt FO

Sullivan KIA. 160hp engine, flying time 216hr 10min).

6930 Presentation a/c *Malaya No 14*. **22 Sqn** Bertangles dd ex 1 AD 7.5.16, wrecked landing 20.5.16 and damaged in combat during photo sortie near Le Sars 3.9.16 (Capt GR Howard/2Lt JH Chester-Walsh OK. 120hp Beardmore, flying time 165hr 54min). **2 AD** ex 22 Sqn 6.9.16 and deleted 7.9.16.

6931 Presentation a/c *Malaya No 15*. **15 Sqn** by 1.2.16 (120hp Beardmore). **22 Sqn** dd ex 1 AD 7.5.16 and victs 17.8.16 (2Lt CS Duffus/ Cpl A Winterbottom shared the capture of an EA C-type near Pozières at 10.20hr with 5250) and 23.8.16 (2Lt CS Duffus/Cpl A Winterbottom sent a Fokker E-type OOC near Bapaume at 13.10) then damaged in combat near Ligny 30.9.16 (2Lt CS Duffus/ Cpl F Johnson OK – Lewis gun drum had hit propeller). **2 AD** ex 22 Sqn 4.10.16 (120hp Beardmore) and to England in packing case 27.10.16.

6932 Presentation a/c *Malaya No 16*. **25 Sqn** dd ex 1 AD St-Omer 7.5.16 and damaged by AA near Arras 26.5.16 (Capt BM Hay/2Lt JCM Stewart OK) and victs 20.7.16 (2Lt LL Richardson WIA/AM2 LS Court OK - shared destruction of 2 Fokker E-types near Lens with 5238 at 18.30) then crashed landing from test flight 18.8.16.

6933 Presentation a/c *Malaya No 17, the Alma Baker*. **18 Sqn** Bruay dd ex 1 AD 10.5.16 and

6937, 'Punjab 29 Rawalpindi', seen below after its capture on 22 September 1916, also carried the extra name of 'Dolores la Vivandière' [The Canteen-keeper] on both sides. The 18 Sqn nacelle marking is faintly visible.

A fine study of FE2b 6944 of 11 Squadron with the observer's folding windscreen raised.

Looking brand new in the sunshine, FE2b 6950 during its service with 11 Squadron, with 6949 behind.

FE2b 6949 of 11 Squadron, its crew shot down and burnt on 9 July 1916.

wrecked in crash on practice flight 11.6.16 (2Lt GK MacDonald/2Lt Evans OK – machine overturned landing in cornfield). 1 AD and deleted 17.6.16 (NWR, flying time 50hr 5min).

6934 Presentation a/c *Punjab No 26*. **23 Sqn** as a/c 6 and LIA near Bapaume on OP 3.9.16 (2Lt FDH Sams POW/Cpl W Summers POW wdd after combat with 5 EA. 120hp Beardmore, flying time 132hr 21min).

6935 Presentation a/c *Punjab No 27*. Allotment to BEF cancelled 21.5.16, aircraft wrecked. **25 Sqn**. Deleted 30.10.16.

6936 **22 Sqn** dd ex 1 AD 16.5.16 (120hp Beardmore). **2 AD** and deleted 9.7.16 (NWR, flying time 91hr 43min). BUT **22 Sqn** and LIA after hit by AA 9.2.17 (crew OK).

6937 Presentation a/c *Punjab No 29*. **18 Sqn** dd ex 1 AD 16.5.16, force landed at Chateau de la Haie 19.8.16 after propeller damaged by AA (Capt JC Callaghan/Cpl B Ankers OK) and LIA in combat with 2 EA near Ervillers 22.9.16 (Sgt T Jones POW fatally WIA/2Lt FAA Hewson POW wdd. 120hp Beardmore No.748, flying time 166hr 5min).

6938 **25 Sqn** dd ex 1 AD 17.5.16, damaged by AA near Bethune on photo sortie 4.6.16 (Lt Lord Doune OK/2Lt RE Walker WIA) and

victs 17.6.16 (2Lt HB Davey/2Lt JB Hinchcliff shared a Fokker E-type OOC near Don with 5201), 18.6.16 (2Lt JLP Armstrong/Sgt LC Chapman destroyed a Fokker E.III near Lens at 16.15) and 26.6.16 (Capt WA Grattan-Bellow/Lt WE Harper destroyed a Fokker E.III near Haisnes at 08.20). **22 Sqn** by 4.8.16 and damaged in forced landing after engine failed during patrol 21.9.16. **2 AD** ex 22 Sqn 24.9.16 and deleted 26.9.16 (NWR, 120hp Beardmore, 1 flying time 86hr 57min, serviceable parts to store).

6939 Presentation a/c *Punjab No 31, Multan*. Allotment to BEF cancelled, aircraft wrecked. Deleted 4.17.

6940 Presentation a/c *Punjab No 32*. **20 Sqn** dd ex 1 AD 22.5.16 (120hp Beardmore). **25 Sqn** dd ex 20 Sqn 15.6.16 and LIA near Arras 18.6.16 (Lt CE Rogers KIA/Sgt H Taylor POW wdd – shot down by EA, possibly Obltn M Immelmann FAb 62. Flying time 46hr 48min).

6941 **18 Sqn** dd ex 1 AD 16.5.16 and crashed in steep turn taking off on practice flight 8.8.16 (2Lt HMB Law KIFA). **1 AD** and deleted 11.8.16 (NWR, flying time 81hr).

6942 **18 Sqn** dd ex 1 AD 16.5.16 and crashed returning from night bombing Avion (Lt GK Macdonald OK – had lost flares and misjudged approach). **1 AD** and deleted 11.8.16 (NWR, flying time 87hr)

6943 Presentation a/c *Malaya No 11*. **SARD** allotted to BEF 30.3.16 (160hp Beardmore). **11 Sqn** by 1.9.16. **2 AD** damaged ex 11 Sqn 24.9.16 and deleted 26.9.16 (NWR, 160hp Beardmore, flying time 137hr 43min, nacelle to England). BUT **11 Sqn** and damaged in crash after stalled on landing approach after patrol 12.5.17.

6944 Presentation a/c *Newfoundland No 4*. **11 Sqn** and wrecked in crash after engine failure on night flight 18.6.16 (2Lt JB Anderson – machine struck railway signal. 160hp Beardmore, flying time 17hr 40min).

6945 Presentation a/c *Rajpipla*. **11 Sqn** (160hp Beardmore) dd 1.6.16, converted to V type landing gear on squadron 14.6.16 and damaged in combat 3.7.16 (Capt Rough/Capt ACW Field OK – landed at 4 Sqn). **2 AD** under reconstruction 1.9.16, being tuned up 1.10.16. **18 Sqn** dd ex 2 AD 16.10.16. **1 AD** ex 18 Sqn 7.12.16 and reported as special wireless machine, unserviceable, 14.1.17 and flown to England 15.3.17 (120hp engine, flying time 90hr 5min). **SARD** 22.3.17 with allotment to BEF cancelled, with DAE2a Repair Section.

6946 Presentation a/c *Zanzibar No 2*. **RAF** Farnborough 30.5.16. **11 Sqn** Savy by 20.6.16 and damaged landing 1.7.16 – struck wing, crew OK. **2 AD** and deleted 13.8.16 (160hp Beardmore, NWR).

6947 Presentation a/c *Baroda No 6*. **11 Sqn** by 4.8.16 (160hp Beardmore) and vict 9.9.16 (2Lt TPL Molloy/Sgt J Allen sent a LVG C type OOC near Monchy-au-Bois at 1800) then LIA near Frise 15.9.16 (2Lt FE Hollingworth/2Lt HMW Wells KIA. Flying time 85hr 20min).

6948 Presentation a/c *Ceylon No 4* wef 29.9.15. Allotment to BEF cancelled 1.6.16, aircraft wrecked.

6949 Presentation a/c *Jungadh No 2*. **11 Sqn** dd 1.6.16 (engine 613), converted on squadron to V landing gear 16.6.16 and LIA 9.7.16 (Lt HTL Spencer/2Lt WA Wedgwood KIA. 160hp Beardmore 423/WD6979, flying time 49hr 14min).

6950 Presentation a/c *Newfoundland No 2*. **11 Sqn** by 6.16 and damaged when propeller burst on patrol 9.7.16. **2 AD** under reconstruction 1.9.16, with engine being fitted 1.10.16. **22 Sqn** dd ex 2 AD 23.10.16 and wrecked in crash after controls damaged in combat near Pozières 17.11.16 (2Lt MR Helliwell/Pte FD Cox WIA. 160hp Beardmore, flying time 61hr 33min). **SMA** Reading by 2.18.

6951 Presentation a/c *Kedah No 1*. **11 Sqn** and

FE2b 6952 of 11 Sqn, also lost on 9 July 1916. A German soldier holds an ammunition drum from the wreck.

FE2b 6953 at Mousehold Heath before deployment to France.

damaged on recce 19.9.16 (Sgt AP Coupal/ Sgt Parke OK – landed safely on own aerodrome). **2 AD** damaged ex 11 Sqn 24.9.16 and deleted 29.9.16 (NWR, 160hp Beardmore, flying time 88hr 47min, nacelle to England).

6952 Presentation a/c *City of Adelaide*. To BEF 6.16 (160hp Beardmore). **11 Sqn** dd ex 2 AD 3.7.16 and LIA on patrol 9.7.16 (2Lt DH Macintyre POW wdd/2Lt J Floyd fatally WIA. 160hp Beardmore, flying time 16hr 17min).

6953 Presentation a/c *Zanzibar No 1*. To BEF 6.16 (160hp Beardmore). **11 Sqn** by 24.6.16 and damaged when propeller burst on patrol 7.7.16. **2 AD** under reconstruction 1.9.16 and 1.10.16. **22 Sqn** dd ex 2 AD 19.11.16 and LIA in combat with 18 EA on photo sortie near Gouzeaucourt 2.4.17 (2Lt PA Russell/Lt H Loveland KIA – a/c shot down in flames, probably by OffSt E Nathanael, Jasta 5. 160hp engine 914/WD7524, flying time 139hr 27min).

6954 To BEF 6.16 (160hp Beardmore 691/ WD7051). **11 Sqn** dd ex 2 AD 3.7.16 and damaged in landing crash after patrol 6.7.16. **2 AD**, under reconstruction 1.9.16 and 1.10.16, engine adjustments 31.12.17 and serviceable, 28.2.17. **18 Sqn** ex 2 AD 4.3.17 and undercarriage damaged on landing from practice flight 15.5.17. **1 SNBD** by 9.18.

6955 Presentation a/c *Punjab No 5* wef 1.6.16. Deleted 9.16.

6956 Presentation a/c *Malaya No 9* wef 1.6.16. **9 RS** by 6.17. **SMA** Oxford by 9.16.

6957 Presentation a/c *Gold Coast No 5* wef 1.6.16. **45 Sqn** by 6.16 until @ 7.16. **64 Sqn** and crashed landing 20.9.16 (2Lt WG Spence injured).

6958 Presentation a/c *Sind*. **35 Sqn** dd 11.6.16. **64 Sqn** dd ex 35 Sqn 18.8.16. Gosport (27 RS ?) by 14.2.17.

6959 **35 Sqn** dd 11.6.16. **9 RS** dd ex 35 Sqn 22.7.16.

6960 **35 Sqn** dd 16.6.16. **64 Sqn** dd ex 35 Sqn 18.8.16 until @ 28.9.16.

6961 Presentation a/c *Jamaica No 2*. **35 Sqn** dd 16.6.16. **64 Sqn** dd ex 35 Sqn 18.8.16 until @ 23.9.16. **9 RS** by 26.4.17. Deleted 6.17.

6962 Presentation a/c *Gold Coast No 3* wef 16.6.16. **35 Sqn** dd 25.6.16. **64 Sqn** dd ex 35 Sqn 18.8.16 until @ 24.9.16. Deleted 28.5.17.

6963 Presentation a/c *Punjab No 7*. At Norwich allotted to BEF 15.6.16 (120hp Beardmore). **22 Sqn** by 15.7.16 and damaged on photo sortie 31.7.16 (2Lt WRC daCosta OK/2Lt CG Riley WIA – hit by AA near Basieux)

and damaged in combat with 5 EA near Le Transloy 22.10.16 (2Lt A Cropper fatally WIA/Capt RH Rushby OK). **1 AD** ex 22 Sqn 11.12.16. Flown to England 16.12.16. **9 RS** by 2.17 until @ 3.17.

6964 At Norwich allotted to BEF 15.6.16 (120hp Beardmore). **23 Sqn** damaged in landing crash after photo sortie 15.7.16 and victs 2.8.16 (2Lt KL Gospill/2Lt RS Osmaston sent a Fokker E.II OOC near Vitry-en-Artois, shared with 6970) and 24.9.16 (2Lt KL Gospill/2Lt FWA Vickers sent a Roland C-type OOC near Bertincourt). **2 AD** ex 23 Sqn 15.11.16. **1 AD** ex 2 AD 17.11.16. Flown to England ex 1 AD 21.11.16 (120hp Beardmore, flying time 257hr 42min). **SAD** allotted for training 22.11.16. **46 RS** by 13.3.17.

6965 At Norwich allotted to BEF 15.6.16 and 26.7.16 (160hp Beardmore). **11 Sqn** and victs 16.8.16 (2Lt JB Quested/2Lt WJ Wyatt sent a Roland C.II OOC near Fampoux at 08.35), 2.9.16 (2Lt JB Quested/2Lt WJ Wyatt sent 2 Roland C.II OOC near Bapaume at 19.30) and 15.9.16 (2Lt JB Quested/Cpl G Monk destroyed an EA scout near Bapaume at 09.15) then LIA near Queant on photo sortie 17.10.16 (2Lt CL Roberts POW/2Lt JL Pulleyn KIA. 160hp Beardmore, flying time 170hr 35min).

6966 At Norwich allotted to BEF 15.6.16 (120hp Beardmore). **22 Sqn** damaged in combat 21.7.16 (Lt RD Walker/Cpl Capper WIA). **2 AD** and deleted 27.7.16 (NWR, flying time 50hr 17min).

6967 At Norwich allotted to BEF 15.6.16 (120hp Beardmore). **25 Sqn** dd ex 1 AD St-Omer 27.6.16 and wrecked on bombing sortie 10.10.16. **1 AD** ARS ex 25 Sqn 14.10.16 with 160hp Beardmore and deleted 15.10.16 (NWR, flying time 143hr 48min).

6968 Presentation a/c *Zanzibar No 3*. At Norwich allotted to BEF 15.6.16 (120hp Beardmore). **18 Sqn** damaged landing from practice flight 2.8.16 (2Lt CG Shaumer/AM1 L Hardinge) and damaged in combat with 9 EA on patrol near Bapaume 30.9.16 (2Lt C Parkinson/Lt FS Rankin OK). **2 AD** wrecked ex 18 Sqn 4.10.16 and deleted 5.10.16 (NWR, flying time 130hr 50min). BUT **22 Sqn** dd ex 1 AD 11.12.16.

6969 Presentation a/c *Malaya No 18, Singapore No 1* wef 23.5.16. At Norwich allotted to BEF 15.6.16 (120hp Beardmore). **23 Sqn** and in combat over Vaulx 1.7.16 (2Lt AT Watson/2Lt CL Blake OK). **2 AD** ex 23 Sqn 16.11.16. **1 AD** ex 2 AD 4.12.16 and flown to England 6.12.16 (120hp Beardmore, flying

time 184hr). Gosport ex 1 AD allotted for training 6.12.16 and still there (27 RS ?) by 5.1.17. Deleted 11.5.17.

6970 Presentation a/c *Malaya No 19, Singapore No 2* wef 23.5.16. At Norwich allotted to BEF 15.6.16 (120hp Beardmore). **1 AD** ex England 30.6.16. **23 Sqn** by 15.7.16 until @ 9.16 with vict 2.8.16 (Capt AT Watson/2Lt CL Blake sent a Fokker E.III OOC near Vitry-en-Artois, shared with 6964). **25 Sqn**. **1 AD** 5.1.17 and flown to England 23.1.17 (flying time 216hr 39min). **SAD** allotted to HD Wing 31.1.17. **51 HDS** B Flt Mattishall by 23.3.17 (Capt IAJ Duff AZP). **51 HDS** B Flt Marham by 28.9.17. 51 HDS C Flt Marham by 2.18 until @ 30.5.18.

6971 Presentation a/c *Malaya No 20, The Strait Times*. At Norwich allotted to BEF 15.6.16 (120hp Beardmore). **18 Sqn** by 25.7.16 and wrecked in crash 16.9.16 (2Lt TL Haywood IIFA/2Lt PJ Smyth KIFA – hit cable of balloon of 6 KBS. 120hp Beardmore, flying time 118hr 55min). **2 AD** ex 18 Sqn 19.9.16 and deleted 20.9.16.

6972 Presentation a/c *Malaya No 21*. At Norwich allotted to BEF 15.6.16 (120hp Beardmore). **22 Sqn** and damaged in combat on photo sortie 28.7.16 (Capt WA Summers/ 2LT RM Chaworth-Musters OK). **2 AD** and deleted 4.8.16 (NWR, flying time 29hr 4min).

6973 Presentation a/c *Malaya No 22, The Sime Darby* wef 23.5.16. At Norwich allotted to BEF 15.6.16 and 4.7.16 (160hp Beardmore). **11 Sqn** by 1.9.16 and LIA in combat with EA near Bapaume on bombing escort 30.9.16 (Lt EC Lansdale POW fatally wdd/Sgt A Clarkson KIA – shot down in flames by Ltn M Fr v Richthofen, Jasta 2. 160hp Beardmore, flying time 160hr 10min).

6974 Presentation a/c *Malaya No 23*. At Norwich allotted to BEF 15.6.16 (120hp Beardmore). **AID** dd ex Norwich 29.6.16 (with 7617 and 7668) and allotted to BEF 6.7.16. **23 Sqn** damaged in combat 28.7.16 (AM2 F Collinson WIA). **1 AD** ex 23 Sqn 5.1.17 and flown to England 7.1.17. At Hythe 9.1.17 allotted to Training Brigade. Deleted 28.2.17.

6975 Presentation a/c *Malaya No 24*. At Norwich allotted to BEF 15.7.16 (120hp Beardmore). **23 Sqn** by 15.7.17. **2 AD** ex 23 Sqn 15.11.16. **1 AD** ex 2 AD 4.12.16. Folkestone dd ex 1 AD 16.12.16. **SAD** dd ex Folkestone 19.12.16. **2 (Aux) SAG** and wrecked in crash near Turnberry lighthouse 1.5.17 (2Lt J Stevenson/Sgt CWH Bowers KIFA – stalled on turn at 300ft).

FE2b 6975, 'Malaya No 24, The Penang No 1', with abbreviated presentation inscription.

6976 At Norwich allotted to BEF 26.6.16 (120hp Beardmore). **23 Sqn** in combat with 6 EA near Bapaume on photo sortie 3.9.16 (2Lt EG Wheldon/AM1 Bayes OK) and damaged in combat near Achiet-le-Grand on recce 23.11.16 (2Lt EG Wheldon WIA/2Lt AW Phillips OK). **1 AD** 5.1.17 and to England in packing case for reconstruction 18.1.17 (120hp engine, 225hr 24min flying time).

6977 At Norwich allotted to BEF 26.6.16 (120hp Beardmore). **23 Sqn** by 2.9.16. **1 AD** ex 23 Sqn 7.1.17 and recorded as serviceable school machine 14.1.17. Flown to England, with 120hp engine, ex 1 AD 26.1.17 (239hr 29min flying time). Allotted to Training Brigade 27.1.17. **19 RS** by 28.2.17 until @ 4.3.17.

6978 Presentation a/c *Baroda No 19* wef 3.7.16. At Norwich allotted to BEF 26.6.16 (120hp Beardmore). **1 AD** ex England 1.7.16. **25 Sqn** dd ex 1 AD 18.7.16 and wrecked in crash in fog after successful combat 8.8.16 (2Lt HL Chadwick/Lt WE Harper OK after destroying a Roland near Pont-à-Vendin at 06.45). **1 AD** and deleted 11.8.16 (NWR, 45hr flying time).

6979 Presentation a/c *Punjab No 1* wef 3.7.16. At Norwich allotted to BEF 27.6.16 and 6.7.16

FE2b 6993 of 25 Sqn, forced down to be captured on a bombing operation on 22 September 1916.

(120hp Beardmore). **CFS** (160hp Beardmore) by 7.17, allotted to BEF but re-allotted to CFS Testing Flt 7.10.16. BUT deleted 20.9.17.

6980 Presentation a/c *Punjab No 6*. At Norwich allotted to BEF 27.6.16 (120hp Beardmore). **22 Sqn** and LIA after hit by ground fire 15.7.16 (2Lt RH Sievwright OK/ Lt JL Reid fatally WIA – a/c shelled after crash. flying time 31hr 27min).

6981 Presentation a/c *Malaya No 17*. At Norwich allotted to BEF 27.6.16 and 6.7.16 (160hp Beardmore). **2 AD** under reconstruction 1.9.16. **11 Sqn** dd ex 2 AD 23.11.16 and vict 27.12.16 (2Lt AC Woodman/2Lt W Hallitt destroyed an Albatros D.II near Warcourt at 11.15) then wrecked in crash after hit by AA 29.1.17 (Capt BL Dowling/Lt CF Lodge OK. flying time 30hr 32min). **2 AD** ex 11 Sqn with 160hp engine 756/WD7116 31.1.17 and deleted 2.2.17.

6982 Presentation a/c *Newfoundland No 4*. At Norwich allotted to BEF 27.6.16 and 6.7.16 (160hp Beardmore). Earmarked for experimental photo work 6.7.16. **11 Sqn** by 1.9.16. **2 AD** ex 11 Sqn with 160hp engine 24.12.16, engine fitted 31.12.16 and deleted 12.2.17 (NWR, 195hr 33min flying time).

6983 At Norwich allotted to BEF 27.6.16 and 6.7.16 (160hp Beardmore). **11 Sqn**, vict 22.8.16 (2Lt LBF Morris/Lt L Rees sent a Roland C.II OOC near Bapaume at 17.45, shared 6994) and 17.9.16 (Sgt Thompson & Sgt A Clarkson sent an EA D type OOC near Cambrai at 10.45) then reported as old machine 14.3.17 (186). **2 AD** ex 11 Sqn 17.3.17. **1 AD** ex 2 AD 23.3.17. Flown to England ex 1 AD 24.3.17.

6984 At Norwich allotted to BEF 27.6.16 and 6.7.16 (160hp Beardmore). **11 Sqn** and damaged landing from practice flight 1.8.16. **2 AD** and deleted 4.8.16 (160hp Beardmore, NWR, flying time 22hr 9min).

6985 At Norwich allotted to BEF 27.6.16 (120hp Beardmore). Hendon dd ex Norwich 13.7.16. Re-allotted to BEF 19.7.16 (160hp Beardmore). **11 Sqn** by 1.9.16 and vict 15.9.16 (2Lt WP Bowman/Sgt Walker destroyed and EA D type near Bapaume at 09.30) then LIA in combat with Jasta 2 near Delville Wood on recce 19.9.16 (Lt WP Bowman OK/Cpl G Munk WIA – a/c landed and was shelled to destruction. 160hp Beardmore, flying time 82hr 59min).

6986 Presentation a/c *Montreal No 4*. At Norwich allotted to BEF 27.6.16 and 13.7.16 (160hp Beardmore). **11 Sqn** by 17.7.16 (recorded as 6896 and described as 'new FE' by 2Lt GN Anderson 18.7.16) and damaged in crash on return from forced landing 13.8.16 (2Lt Malloy/Cpl Walker).

6987 Presentation a/c *British Guiana*. At Norwich allotted to BEF 27.6.16 and 13.7.16 (160hp Beardmore). **11 Sqn** by 17.7.16. **2 AD** ex 11 Sqn 12.9.16. **11 Sqn** dd ex 2 AD 24.9.16. **2 AD** ex 11 Sqn 14.11.16 and to England in packing case 8.12.16 (126hr flying time). **SARD** allotted to BEF 7.4.17. **18 Sqn** and victs 23.4.17 (2Lt HA Trayles/Cpl A Beebee sent an Albatros D.II OOC near Baralle at 17.30), 24.4.17 (Sgt T Whiteman/2Lt KA Fearnside-Speed destroyed an Albatros D.III in flames near Baralle at 08.15 – 2 other EA collided in this combat), 30.4.17 (2Lt MM Kaizer/Sgt F Russell destroyed an Albatros D.III around Baralle/Bourlon at 09.30 and sent 2 more OOC) and 1.5.17 (2Lt GA Critchley/AM2 WG Jones sent an Albatros D.V OOC near Epinoy at 10.30). **2 AD** deleted 11.7.17.

6988 Presentation a/c *Malaya No 8*. At Norwich allotted to BEF 13.7.16 (160hp Beardmore). **11 Sqn** by 1.9.16 and damaged in forced landing after successful combat near Pommier on bombing escort to Irles 9.9.16 (2Lt WHC Buntine WIA/Sgt GJ Morton OK in destroying a LVG C type near Achiet-le-

Petit at 16.30). **2 AD** ex 11 Sqn 11.9.16 and deleted 12.9.16 (160hp Beardmore, NWR, flying time 84hr 17min, serviceable parts to store).

6989 Presentation a/c *Newfoundland No 3*. At Norwich allotted to BEF 13.7.16 (160hp Beardmore). **11 Sqn** by 3.8.16, damaged in forced-landing on photo sortie 7.9.16 (Sgt Thompson/Flt Sgt Frudge.) **2 AD** ex 11 Sqn 10.9.16 and deleted 12.9.16 (160hp Beardmore, (NWR, flying time 84hr 57min, serviceable parts to store).

6990 At Norwich allotted to BEF 13.7.16 (160hp Beardmore). **25 Sqn** dd ex 1 AD St-Omer 29.7.16 damaged by AA on bomb raid near La Bassée 1.8.16 (Capt CH Dixon OK/2Lt JB Hinchcliff WIA) and victs 20.10.16 (Sgt JHR Green/Cpl WP Gilbert destroyed an EA scout near Lille at 15.15) and 17.11.16 (2Lt DS Johnson/2Lt I Heald shared the destruction of an EA near Vitry with 4877, 7022, 7024 and 7025) then damaged by AA on photo sortie 4.12.16 (Sgt JHR Green OK/Cpl AG Bower WIA) and vict 11.3.17 (Lt HE Davis/AM2 HG Taylor sent a Halberstadt D type OOC near Vimy at 11.15). **2 AD** with 160hp engine and deleted 27.4.17 (NWR, flying time 238hr 2min).

6991 At Norwich allotted to BEF 13.7.16 (160hp Beardmore). **25 Sqn** dd ex 1 AD St-Omer 1.8.16 and vict 8.8.16 (2Lt CHC Woollven/Lt C Nelson sent a Roland C.II OOC near Don at 06.40) and 20.10.16 (2Lt ESP Hynes & Sapper JR Smith sent an EA D type OOC near Provin at 08.50) then destroyed by fire on aerodrome 10.2.17 with flying time 204hr 34min, 160hp engine). **1 AD** ARS ex 25 Sqn 2.3.17.

6992 Presentation a/c *Shanghai Race Club No 2*. At Norwich allotted to BEF 13.7.16 (160hp Beardmore). **11 Sqn** by 1.9.16 and vict 15.9.16 (2Lt RP Harvey/2Lt AJ Cathie destroyed an EA D type over Le Sars Wood at 09.15 – given as 6922) then damaged in combat with Jasta 2 near Queant 19.9.16 (2Lt AJ Cathie WIA) then LIA in combat with EA near Bapaume on OP 10.10.16 (Sgt E Haxton/Cpl BGF Jeffs KIA – shot down in flames. Flying time 81hr 37min).

6993 Presentation a/c *Baroda No 14*. At Norwich allotted to BEF 13.7.16 (160hp Beardmore). **25 Sqn** dd ex 1 AD St-Omer 6.8.16 and victs 7.9.16 (2Lt AT Loyd/2Lt CS Workman shared sending a Fokker E-type OOC near Pont-à-Vendin at 17.50 with 6997 and 7003) and 9.9.16 (2Lt NWW Webb/Cpl LS Court destroyed an EA C-type near Pont-à-Vendin at 16.00) then LIA near Douai on bombing sortie 22.9.16 (2Lt KF Hunt/Cpl LO Law KIA – shot down by AA. Flying time 80hr, engine No.681).

6994 Presentation a/c *Montreal No 3*. At Norwich allotted to BEF 13.7.16 (160hp Beardmore). **11 Sqn** and victs 22.8.16 (Capt SW Price/Lt F Libby sent 3 Roland C.II OOC near Bapaume at 19.10, 1 shared 6983), 25.8.16 (Capt SW Price/Lt F Libby sent an Aviatik C-type OOC near Bapaume at 13.00) and 14.9.16 (Capt SW Price/Lt F Libby sent an EA C-type OOC near Bapaume at 09.30) then LIA in combat near Marcoing on bombing escort 17.9.16 (2Lt H Thompson fatally WIA/Sgt JE Glover KIA – possibly shot down by Ltn L Reimann, Jasta 2. 160hp Beardmore No.662, flying time 70hr 7min).

6995 At Norwich allotted to BEF 13.7.16 (160hp Beardmore). **25 Sqn** dd ex 1 AD 1.8.16 and wrecked in crash during forced landing in fog 8.8.16. **1 AD** and deleted 11.8.16 (NWR, 160hp Beardmore, flying time 17hr).

6996 Presentation a/c *Punjab No 5*. At Norwich allotted to BEF 13.7.16 (160hp Beardmore). Hendon dd ex Norwich 27.7.16. **25 Sqn** dd ex 1 AD 4.8.16 and LIA on patrol 9.8.16 (Capt

FE2b 6994 was one of three 11 Sqn FE2bs lost on 17 September 1916 when they met Jasta 2 pilots led by Boelcke for the first time. Richthofen scored his first victory in this combat (FE2b 7018).

CJ Hart/Lt JA Mann KIA – a/c burnt out. 160hp Beardmore, flying time 12hr 45min).

6997 Presentation a/c *Punjab No 28*. At Norwich allotted to BEF 13.7.16 (160hp Beardmore). **25 Sqn** dd ex 1 AD 8.8.16 and vict 7.9.16 (Capt CH Dixon/AM2 JH Booth shared sending a Fokker E-type OOC near Pont-à-Vendin at 17.50 with 6993 and 7003). **11 Sqn** and LIA in combat near Rouvroy 24.1.17 (Capt O Greig/Lt JE MacLennan POW – shot down by Ltn M Fr v Richthofen, Jasta 11. 160hp engine, flying time 155hr 3min).

6998 Presentation a/c *Trinidad Chamber of Commerce*. At Norwich allotted to BEF 13.7.16 (160hp Beardmore). **25 Sqn** dd ex 1 AD 1.8.16 and vict 22.9.16 (Sgt T Mottershead & 2Lt C Street destroyed a Fokker E.III near Brebières at 08.30) then damaged on bombing sortie 16.10.16 with Lewis drum hitting propeller. **1 AD** ex 25 Sqn 20.10.16. **2 AD** ex 1 AD 1.3.17. **18 Sqn** ex 2 AD 12.3.17 and damaged in forced landing on ALG after combat near Barelle 30.4.17 (Sgt T Whiteman WIA/AM2 JH Wynn fatally WIA – possibly brought down by Ltn H Klein, Jasta 4. 160hp engine, flying time 129hr 15min).

6999 Presentation a/c *Junagadh No 2*. At Norwich allotted to BEF 13.7.16 (160hp Beardmore). **1 AD** dd ex Farnborough 24.8.16. **11 Sqn** dd ex 2 AD 31.8.16 and LIA on recce near Marcoing 16.9.16 (2Lt AL Pinkerton/Lt JW Sanders POW – possibly shot down by Ltn O Hohme, Jasta 2. 160hp Beardmore and

flying time 22hr 35min).

7000 Presentation a/c *Presented by Mr H Teesdale-Smith, Adelaide*. At Norwich allotted to BEF 15.7.16 (160hp Beardmore). To BEF and damaged in crash on delivery 16.8.16 (both crew injured). Deleted 18.6.16.

7001 At Norwich allotted to BEF 15.7.16. **SAD** allotted to 16 Wing for HD 5.8.16. **RAF** fitted with 0.45in Maxim gun 24.8.16. Thetford dd ex Hendon 5.9.16 (Lt Gay).

7002 Presentation a/c *Gold Coast No 2*. At Norwich allotted to BEF 15.7.16 (160hp Beardmore). **25 Sqn** dd ex 1 AD St-Omer 17.8.16 and LIA crashed in trenches near Armentières after hit by AA 24.8.16 (Lt MT Baines/Lt WE Harper WIA – landed in lines and a/c shelled to destruction).

7003 Presentation a/c *Baroda No 18*. At Norwich allotted to BEF 15.7.16 (160hp Beardmore). **25 Sqn** dd ex 1 AD St-Omer 11.8.16 vict 7.9.16 (2Lt NWW Webb/Cpl H Brown shared sending a Fokker E-type OOC near Pont-à-Vendin at 17.50 with 6993 and 6997), damaged by ground fire near Somain on bombing mission 16.11.16 (2Lt H Sellers OK/2Lt WW Fitzgerald WIA) and victs 13.4.17 (Sgt WJ Burkenshaw/Sgt JH Brown shared the destruction of an Albatros D.III near Sallaumines at 19.30 with A782), 14.4.17 (Sgt WJ Burkenshaw/Sgt JH Brown shared the destruction of an Albatros D.III near Hénin-Liétard with A6383) and 1.5.17 (Capt CHC Woollven/Sgt JH Brown destroyed an Albatros D.III near Fresnoy at 18.00). **18 Sqn**

Too direct a delivery: FE2b 7000 crashed on arrival in France – and was deleted two days later.

FE2b 7009 lost half its fabric to an engine fire at Gosport. The pilot Major Hill was unhurt: the machine was not repaired.

and victs 23.5.17 (2Lt DE Marshall/2Lt GN Blennerhassett destroyed an Albatros D.III near Eswars at 13.25 and sent another OOC) then for deletion as old machine 30.7.17 with 284 flying-hours.

7004 Presentation a/c *Zanzibar No 4*. At Norwich allotted to HD Wing 3.8.16. **39 HDS**. **51 HDS** B Flt by 1.10.16 (Capt WE Collison AZP) and on further AZPs 28.11.16 (Capt WE Collison) and 24.3.17 (Capt P le G Gribble/Flt Sgt Johnson). **51 HDS** B Flt and on AZPs 24.9.17 (Capt RC Savery) and 19.10.17 (2Lt A Critchley) and still on charge 23.3.18.

7005 Presentation a/c *Punjab No 4*. At Norwich allotted to HD Wing 3.8.16. **51 HDS** B Flt and wrecked in forced-landing on AZP 1.10.16 (Lt Holmes OK – landed in wood by wing-tip flares). Deleted 9.10.16.

7006 Presentation a/c *Shanghai Exhibition* wef 15.8.16. At Norwich allotted to HD Wing 3.8.16. **25 Sqn**. Deleted 25.9.16.

7007 Presentation a/c *Nova Scotia* wef 15.8.16. At Norwich allotted to BEF 3.8.16 (160hp Beardmore). **AID** dd ex Norwich 17.8.16 (Capt Pixton). **25 Sqn** dd ex 1 AD 25.8.16 and vict 22.10.16 (Sgt WD Matheson/2Lt WG Meggitt destroyed an EA scout near Seclin at 09.00) and 24.1.17 (2Lt WD Matheson & 2Lt EG Green sent an Albatros D.II OOC near Rouvroy at 10.40). **1 AD** ex 25 Sqn 3.4.17. **25 Sqn** ex 1 AD ARS 10.4.17 and wrecked in crash on test flight 28.4.17 (Sgt J Burtenshaw/Lt P Smith, of 12 Sqn, KIFA. 160hp engine, flying time 231hr 30min).

7008 Presentation a/c *Baroda No 13*. At Norwich allotted to BEF 3.8.16 (160hp Beardmore). Dover dd ex Farnborough 20.8.16. **1 AD** dd ex Dover 21.8.16. **11 Sqn** dd ex 2 AD 24.8.16, converted to V type landing gear 29.8.16 and wrecked in crash after combat with Roland on OP 2.9.16 (2Lt GN Anderson WIA/2Lt GM Allen KIA. 160hp Beardmore, flying time 11hr 35min). Salved. **51 HDS** B Flt by 17.1.18.

7009 Presentation a/c *Baroda No 15*. At Norwich allotted to BEF 12.8.16 (160hp Beardmore) and re-allotted 7.9.16 (120hp Beardmore). **2 AD** ex 1 AD 11.9.16. **23 Sqn** dd ex 2 AD 15.9.16. **2 AD** ex 23 Sqn 19.11.16. **1 AD** ex 2 AD 23.11.16. Flown to England ex 1 AD 4.12.16 (120hp Beardmore, flying time 95hr). En-route to Gosport, allotted for training 4.12.16. Gosport (27 RS ?) by 7.1.17. Caught fire 30.3.17 (crew OK). Deleted 10.4.17.

7010 At Norwich allotted to BEF 12.8.16 (160hp Beardmore) and re-allotted 7.9.16 (120hp Beardmore). **2 AD** ex 1 AD 14.9.16. **18 Sqn** dd ex 2 AD 21.9.16 and LIA in combat near Englebelmer 3.11.16. (Sgt CG Baldwin/2Lt GA Bentham KIA – probably shot down by Ltn M Fr v Richthofen, Jasta 2).

7011 At Norwich allotted to BEF 12.8.16 (160hp Beardmore) and re-allotted 4.9.16 (120hp Beardmore). **1 AD** ex Farnborough 1.9.16. **25 Sqn** dd ex 1 AD 7.9.16 and wrecked 16.9.16 in aerodrome crash during night flying practice. **1 AD** ARS ex 25 Sqn 18.9.16 and deleted 19.9.16 (NWR, 120hp Beardmore, flying time 11hr 42min). **1 AD** 1.10.16 (presume retaken on charge). **23 Sqn** ex 1 AD 22.10.16. **2 AD** ex 23 Sqn 16.11.16. **1 AD** ex 2 AD 22.11.16, with 120hp engine 15.1.17 as 'old machine for home' but deleted 5.2.17 (NWR, flying time 37hr).

7012 At Norwich allotted to BEF 12.8.16 (160hp Beardmore) and re-allotted 7.9.16 (120hp Beardmore). **2 AD** ex 1 AD 12.9.16. **22 Sqn** dd ex 2 AD 21.9.16 and vict 21.10.16 (2Lt JV Aspinall/2Lt WM Taylor destroyed a Fokker E-type near Biefvillers at 14.05). **1 AD** ex 22 Sqn 14.12.16. Flown to England ex 1 AD 20.12.16. En-route from BEF allotted to Training Brigade 22.12.16. **1 AD** deleted 3.2.17.

7013 At Norwich allotted to BEF 12.8.16, re-allotted to Orfordness 19.8.16. Photo shows crashed.

7014 Presentation a/c *Maori*. At Norwich allotted to BEF 12.8.16. **2 AD**, serviceable, 1.9.16. **11 Sqn** dd ex 2 AD 3.9.16, converted to V type landing gear 3.9.16 and vict 30.9.16 (2Lt CL Roberts/Lt Collins destroyed an Albatros D.II in flames near Lagnicourt at 10.40). **2 AD** ex 11 Sqn 14.11.16 and to England in packing case 30.12.16. Deleted 4.17.

7015 Presentation a/c *Gold Coast No 4*. At Norwich allotted to BEF 12.8.16 (160hp Beardmore). **25 Sqn** dd ex 1 AD 1.9.16 and wrecked landing on night-flying practice 16.9.16. **1 AD** ARS ex 25 Sqn 20.9.16. To England in packing case ex 1 AD for reconstruction 28.9.16 (160hp Beardmore, flying time 16hr 30min). **SARD** allotted to BEF 30.3.17. **18 Sqn** and damaged in landing crash after formation practice 20.4.17 and SOC unit charge 21.4.17 (160hp engine, flying time 20hr 15min). **2 AD** wrecked ex 18 Sqn 25.4.17 and for England in packing case, 30.4.17.

7016 At Norwich allotted to BEF 12.8.16. **1 AD** dd ex Farnborough 28.8.16. **2 AD**, serviceable, 1.9.16. **11 Sqn** dd ex 2 AD Candas 6.9.16 and victs 9.9.16 (2Lt EL Foote/2Lt GK Welsford destroyed 2 EA near Irles at 16.30), 15.9.16 (2Lt EL Foote/2Lt GK Welsford destroyed an EA D-type near Ligny at 09.30), 23.9.16 (2Lt JB Graham/Lt FD Lutyens destroyed an EA D type near Quéant at 12.15) and 20.12.16 (2Lt JB Quested/Lt FD Lutyens sent an Albatros D.I OOC near Monchy-le-Preux at 14.20). **100 Sqn** by 5.7.17 and damaged in forced landing crash in fog near St Venant during night bombing sortie 25.9.17 (Lt HTO Winsor and Lt JW Price both injured).

7017 Presentation a/c *Gold Coast No 8*. At Norwich allotted to BEF 12.8.16 (160hp Beardmore). **SAD** re-allotted to BEF (120hp Beadrmore) 10.10.16 and 20.10.16. Crashed en-route to BEF and allocation cancelled 7.12.16. To England in packing case ex 2 AD 30.12.16. Deleted 21.5.17.

7018 Presentation a/c *Punjab No 32, Montgomery*. At Norwich allotted to BEF 12.8.16 (160hp Beardmore). **2 AD** ex 1 AD 6.9.16. **11 Sqn** dd ex 2 AD 9.9.16 and LIA near Marcoing on bombing escort 17.9.17 (2Lt LBF Morris POW fatally WIA/Lt T Rees KIA – shot down by Ltn M Fr v Richthofen, Jasta 2. 160hp Beardmore No.701, flying time 25hr 45min).

7019 Presentation a/c *Punjab No 3, Jind*. At Norwich allotted to BEF 12.8.16 (160hp Beardmore). **11 Sqn** dd ex 2 AD 11.9.16 and vict 14.9.16 (2Lt LBF Morris/Lt T Rees sent an EA C type OOC near Bapaume at 09.30) then LIA near Marcoing on bombing escort 17.9.16 (Capt DB Gray/Lt LB Helder POW – shot down by Hptm O Boelcke, Jasta 2. 160hp Beardmore, flying time 13hr 33min).

7020 Presentation a/c Punjab *No 34, Jhellum*. At Norwich allotted to BEF 14.8.16 (160hp Beardmore). **2 AD** ex 1 AD 7.9.16. **11 Sqn** dd ex 2 AD 15.9.16, damaged in combat with EA on OP 26.9.16 (2Lt LR Wren/LCpl Young OK). **2 AD** ex 11 Sqn 28.9.16 and to England in packing case 27.10.16. **SARD** allotted to BEF 30.3.17. **11 Sqn** and wrecked on recce 22.4.17 (Lt WF Fletcher/Lt W Franklin WIA – possibly by Ltn M Fr v Richthofen, Jasta 11. 160hp engine, flying time 32hr 50min). **2 AD**, wrecked ex 11 Sqn, 29.4.17.

7021 Presentation a/c *Punjab No 33 Ludhiana*. At Norwich allotted to BEF 14.8.16 (160hp Beardmore). **AID** dd ex Hendon 5.9.16. **11 Sqn** dd ex 1 AD 23.9.16 and listed as old machine 17.3.17. **2 AD** ex 11 Sqn 21.3.17. **1 AD** ex 2 AD 23.3.17. Flown to England ex

FE2b 7013 ended its days in a ditch, probably somewhere near Orfordness in late 1916.

1 AD 24.3.17. Allotted to Training Brigade 27.3.17. **SARD** tested twice 6.8.17 (very nose heavy, then OK). **51 HDS** B Flt by 24.9.17 (Lt TH Gladstone AZP) and crashed 3.12.17 after undercarriage damaged on take-off (Lt TH Gladstone/Lt Cock OK). **51 HDS** C Flt by 28.5.18 and on charge until @ 23.7.18. On RAF charge 11.18.

7022 Presentation a/c *Ceylon No 2* wef 23.9.16. At Norwich allotted to BEF 14.8.16 (160hp Beardmore). **25 Sqn** dd ex 1 AD 12.9.16 and vict 17.11.16 (Capt R Chadwick/Lt WG Meggitt shared the destruction of an EA near Vitry at 13.00 with 4877, 6990, 7024 and 7025) then LIA in combat near Thelus 4.12.16 (2Lt DS Johnson/Lt I Heald KIA – probably by Ltn O Splitgerber, Jasta 12. 160hp Beardmore, flying time 86hr).

7023 Presentation a/c *South Australia No 1*. At Norwich allotted to BEF 14.8.16 (160hp Beardmore). **11 Sqn** dd ex 1 AD 21.9.16 (160hp engine), damaged in combat 9.11.16 (Lt W Baillie OK/Lt GE Godden WIA) and wrecked in forced-landing during OP 4.2.17 (2Lt AP Coupal IIA/2Lt HL Villers KIA. Flying time 91hr 41min). Deleted 6.2.17.

7024 Presentation a/c *Gibraltar*. At Norwich allotted to BEF 14.8.16 (160hp Beardmore). **25 Sqn** dd ex 1 AD 12.9.16 and victs 16.11.16 (2Lt CHC Woollven/2Lt CH Marchant destroyed an Albatros D.I in flames near Somain), 17.11.16 (Lt C Dunlop/2Lt H Scandrett shared the destruction of an EA near Vitry at 13.00 with 4877, 6990, 7022 and 7025) and 23.11.16 (2Lt CHC Woollven/Sgt GR Horrocks destroyed an Albatros D.I near Oppy at 15.45) and 16.3.17 (Sgt GJ Mackie/Sgt JH Brown destroyed an Albatros D.II near Neuvireuil at 15.10) then crashed after test flight 28.4.17 (2Lt HF Walker injured).

7025 Presentation a/c *Johore No 1*. At Norwich allotted to BEF 30.8.16 (160hp Beardmore). **1 AD** dd ex Farnborough 15.9.16. **25 Sqn** dd ex 1 AD 16.10.16 and victs 17.11.16 (2Lt HL Chadwick/2Lt CJ Butler shared the destruction of an EA near Vitry at 13.00 with 4877, 6990, 7022 and 7024) and 4.3.17 (2Lt RNL Munro/Sgt G Goodburn shared the destruction of an LVG C-type near Courrières at 11.15 with 7693, A780 and A5439), damaged in combat near Oppy on OP 17.3.17 (Lt IW Parnell WIA/AM2 HG Taylor OK) then wrecked in forced landing following successful combat over Grosville 6.4.17 (2Lt DP Walter WIA/2Lt C Brown OK – had sent an Albatros D-type OOC near Arras at 08.55). **1 AD** ARS ex 25 Sqn 8.4.17 with 160hp engine 8.4.17. Deleted 10.4.17 (NWR, flying time 148hr 34min).

7026 Presentation a/c *Johore No 2*. Allotted to BEF 2.9.16 (160hp Beardmore), and re-allotted to Training Brigade 9.9.16. Allotted to BEF 27.9.16. **1 AD** ex England 18.10.16. **22 Sqn** dd ex 1 AD 20.10.16 and LIA in combat with 3 EA near Bancourt on recce 3.11.16 (Capt Lord AT Lucas KIA/Lt A Anderson POW wdd – probably down by Ltn M Muller, Jasta 2).

7027 Presentation a/c *Johore No 3*. At Norwich allotted to BEF 2.9.16 (160hp Beardmore). **11 Sqn** dd ex 1 AD 1.10.16, fitted with V type landing gear and victs 17.10.16 (Capt SW Price/Lt F Libby sent an Albatros D.I OOC near Mory at 11.15) and 20.10.16 (Capt SW Price/Lt F Libby shared sending an Albatros D.I OOC down in flames near Douxcette at 11.30) then damaged by AA near Gommecourt 22.10.16 (Capt CN Lowe/AM2 RE Tollerfield OK). **2 AD** ex 11 Sqn 25.10.16, under re-build 31.12.16 and 28.2.17 (160hp Beardmore). **100 Sqn** dd ex 2 AD 4.4.17 (120hp Beardmore) and overturned on landing from night bombing sortie 12.4.17. **2 AD**, for England in packing case (120hp Beardmore), 30.4.17. Deleted 9.5.17.

FE2b 7027 saw service with 11 Squadron in 1916, where this photo was probably taken, and then flew with 100 Squadron as a night bomber in 1917.

7666 – 7715: 50 RAF FE2b (120hp Beardmore) built by Boulton & Paul Ltd, Norwich under continuing Contract 87/A/265.

7666 Presentation a/c *Johore No 4*. At Norwich allotted to BEF (160hp Beardmore) 31.8.16. **2 AD** ex 1 AD 16.9.16. **11 Sqn** dd ex 2 AD 16.9.16 victs 21.10.16 (2Lt HH Turk/2Lt J Allen destroyed an LVG C type near Bois de Longest at 14.10 and sent an Albatros D.II down in flames near Achiet-le-Grand at 15.15) then damaged in forced landing after successful combat 27.12.16 (Capt JB Quested OK/2Lt HJH Dicksee WIA – had sent down a 'Nieuport' with, probably, Ltn G Leffers, Jasta 1, but then forced down by OffSt W Cymera, Jasta 1 near Warcourt at 11.15) and reported as old machine 14.3.17 (92hr). **2 AD** ex 11 Sqn 17.3.17. **1 AD** ex 2 AD 23.3.17. Flown to England ex 1 AD 24.3.17. 7666 reported as BE2 with 36 HDS C Flt Seaton Carew 8.17. **19 TS** Hounslow by 25.6.17 until @ 27.6.17. Wrecked in crash in UK – marked as *B-4* and force-landed in a wooded garden – possibly 19 TS.

7667 **9 RS** by 8.2.17.

7668 At Norwich 31.5.16. **AID** dd ex Norwich 29.6.16. **9 RS** by 8.2.17. **25 RS** and wrecked in crash from spinning nose-dive 19.5.17 (2Lt CL Beaumont/Capt JF St J Annersley KIFA).

7669 Presentation a/c *Johore No 5*. At Norwich allotted to BEF (160hp Beardmore) 31.8.16. **11 Sqn** dd ex 1 AD 27.9.16 and damaged in successful combat near Tillnoy 22.10.16 (2Lt JB Graham/Lt FD Lutyens sent an EA OOC near Tilloy at 16.20 but were forced to land). **2 AD** ex 11 Sqn 26.10.16 under reconstruction 31.12.16 and awaiting 120hp engine 28.2.17. HQ Wing ex 2 AD 23.3.17. **100 Sqn** and LIA night bombing 8.4.17 (Lt L Butler/AM2 R Robb POW – probably shot down by Ltn H Klein, Jasta 4. 120hp engine 227/WD1295, flying time 38hr 57min).

7670 Presentation a/c *Johore No 6*. At Norwich allotted to BEF (160hp Beardmore) 31.8.16. **1 AD** ex England 8.10.16. **2 AD** ex 1 AD 9.10.16. **11 Sqn** dd ex 2 AD 12.10.16 and LIA near Quéant on photo sortie 17.10.16 (Lt WP Bowman/2Lt G Clayton KIA – probably shot down by Obltn S Kirmaier, Jasta 2. 160hp Beardmore, flying time 10hr 38min).

7671 Presentation a/c *Johore No 7*. At Norwich allotted to BEF (120hp Beardmore) 31.8.16. **18 Sqn** dd ex 1 AD St-Omer 27.9.16 and damaged hitting 4915 when landing from photo escort 22.10.16. **2 AD** ex 18 Sqn 26.10.16 and to England in packing case 10.11.16.

7672 Presentation a/c *Johore No 8*. At Norwich allotted to BEF (160hp Beardmore) 31.8.16. **AID** dd ex Norwich 23.9.16. **1 AD** dd ex England 26.9.16. **25 Sqn** dd ex 1 AD 27.9.16 and victs 23.11.16 (Sgt JHR Green/Cpl AG Bower sent an Albatros D.II OOC near Oppy at 15.45) and 1.5.17 (2Lt RG Malcolm/Cpl L Emsden destroyed an Albatros D.III near Izel at 06.20 and captured another near Lens 06.45 but machine hit and observer WIA). **11 Sqn** and damaged by AA and forced to land 24.5.17 (Lt SNS Kennedy/Cpl C Beauchamp WIA).

7673 **19 RS** dd 12.10.16 and wrecked in crash into hangar during mis-judged landing 13.4.17 (both crew injured).

7674 Allotted for HD but re-allotted to BEF 22.9.16 (160hp Beardmore). **11 Sqn** dd ex 1 AD 25.9.16 and LIA near Arras on photo sortie 20.10.16 (Lt RP Harvey WIA/2Lt GK Welsford KIA – probably shot down by Hptm O Boelcke, Jasta 2. 160hp Beardmore, flying time 29hr 3min). **2 AD** ex 11 Sqn 23.10.16 and deleted 24.10.16 with serviceable parts to store.

7675 **51 HDS** B Flt, fitted with Vickers 1lb QF (120hp Beardmore).

7676 **51 HDS** C Flt by 23.3.17 (Capt Barnes AZP),

FE2b 7669 also served with 11 and then 100 Sqn. Unusually for a night bomber, it was claimed in combat on 8 April 1917, returning late from a raid, rather than falling victim to commoner night hazards.

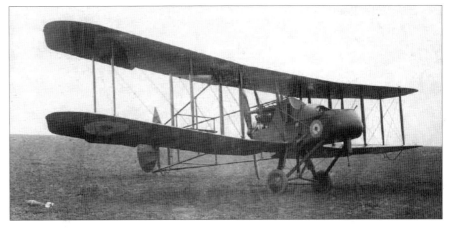

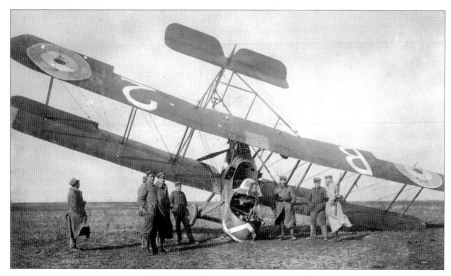

FE2b 7691 of 11 Sqn, Ltn K. Wolff's fifth victory on 31 March 1917.
The toggle-type bomb release is secured outside the pilot's cockpit.

re-allotted to BEF 4.4.17 but cancelled 5.4.17 and wrecked in crash on practice flight after spinning nose dive 22.8.17 (Lt GD Buckenridge KIFA – 120hp Beardmore 209/WD1279).

7677 Presentation a/c *Johore No 9*. At Norwich allotted to BEF (160hp Beardmore) 20.9.16. **1 AD** dd ex Farnborough 24.9.16. **11 Sqn** dd ex 1 AD 26.9.16 and vict 17.10.16 (2Lt HH Turk/2Lt J Allen sent an Albatros D.II OOC near Mory at 11.00) then wrecked in crash after combat 22.11.16 (2Lt F Crisp/2Lt JAV Boddy OK – shot down by Ltn E Konig, Jasta 2). **2 AD** ex 11 Sqn 25.11.16, deleted that day with 160hp Beardmore, flying time 45hr.

7678 Presentation a/c *Johore No 10*. At Norwich allotted to BEF (160hp Beardmore) 20.9.16. **11 Sqn** dd ex 1 AD St-Omer 24.9.16 and victs 30.9.16 (2Lt RP Harvey/2Lt W Black destroyed an Albatros C type in flames near Tilloy at 10.40) and 10.10.16 (2Lt RP Harvey/ Lt F Libby sent an EA scout OOC near Bapaume at 16.00) then crashed and burnt on landing from night bombing 9.5.17. Deleted 17.5.17.

7679 **51 HDS** A Flt by 23.3.17 (Capt LC Angstrom AZP). In France allotted to HD Wing but re-allotted to BEF 9.6.17. **100 Sqn** fitted with Vickers pom-pom gun and damaged when undercarriage collapsed on landing

from night bombing 26.2.18. **2 ASD** ex 100 Sqn 26.2.18. Still on BEF charge 30.6.18.

7680 Presentation a/c *Johore No 11*. For Training Brigade 13.9.16, re-allotted to BEF (160hp Beardmore) 20.9.16. Re-allotted for HD 25.9.16. **51 HDS** C Flt and wrecked in forced landing on Tibbenham NLG after engine failure on AZP 28.11.16 (Lt WR Gayner OK).

7681 Presentation a/c *Johore No 12*. For Training Brigade 13.9.16, re-allotted to BEF (160hp Beardmore) 20.9.16. **1 AD** ex England 1.10.16. **2 AD** ex 1 AD 3.10.16. **22 Sqn** dd ex 2 AD 9.10.16 and victs 28.1.17 (2Lt JV Aspinall/2Lt JMR Miller destroyed an Albatros D.I near Villers-au-Flos at 10.45) and 8.4.17 (Lt JV Aspinall & 2Lt MK Parlee shared the destruction of an Albatros D.II near Regny at 07.00 with 4883, 4891, 7681, A5454 and A5461) then LIA in combat on photo sortie 23.4.17 (2Lt JA Rossi/2Lt PH West WIA – a/c fell in flames. 160hp engine 959/WD7569, flying time 184hr 29min).

7682 **51 HDS** B Flt by 28.11.16 (Lt LC Angstom AZP). Fitted with Vickers QF 1lb pom-pom. On 51 Sqn charge allotted to HD Wing but re-allotted to BEF 4.4.17 but allotment cancelled 5.4.17. Re-allotted to BEF 13.4.17. **100 Sqn** and damaged in landing crash after night bombing sortie 27.7.17 – overshot aerodrome and crashed into a field.

7683 Presentation a/c *Johore No 13*. For Training Brigade, re-allotted to BEF (160hp Beardmore) 20.9.16. **25 Sqn** dd ex 1 AD 1.10.16 and damaged in combat 23.11.16 (2Lt FS Moller WIA/Sgt C Butler OK) then victs 17.3.17 (Capt JL Leith/AM2 L Emsden sent an Albatros D.III OOC near Arras at 17.25), 9.4.17 (Lt TN Southorn/2Lt HE Freeman-Smith sent an Albatros D-type OOC near Lievin at 19.05) and 14.4.17 (2Lt B King/Cpl HG Taylor sent a Halberstadt OOC near Lens. **1 AD** ex 25 Sqn 24.4.17. **2 AD** ex 1 AD 25.4.17 and reported wrecked (120hp Beardmore), 30.4.17. Deleted 12.5.17.

7684 Presentation a/c *Johore No 14*. At Norwich allotted to BEF (160hp Beardmore) 16.9.16. **1 AD** ex England 19.10.16. **11 Sqn** dd ex 1 AD 20.10.16 and LIA in low combat with EA near Gommecourt on OP 22.10.16 (2Lt ALM Shepherd POW fatally wdd/AM1 NL Brain KIA, a/c had 160hp Beardmore and 12hr 40min flying time).

7685 Presentation a/c *Subjects of all races in Siam*. At Norwich allotted to BEF (160hp Beardmore) 16.9.16. **1 AD** ex England 5.10.16. **2 AD** ex 1 AD 7.10.16. **22 Sqn** dd ex 2 AD 9.10.16, damaged in crash at Arvillers 5.1.17 and wrecked in combat near Combles 11.3.17 with controls shot away (2Lt LW Beal OK/AM2 AG Davin WIA – probably by Ltn W Voss, Jasta 2). 160hp engine 802/WD7162, flying time 56hr 9min SOC 22 Sqn 12.3.17. **2 AD** ex 22 Sqn 15.3.17.

7686 Presentation a/c *Australia No 2, NSW No 1, The White Belltrees* wef 4.10.16. At Norwich allotted to BEF (160hp Beardmore) 16.9.16. **25 Sqn** dd ex 1 AD 1.10.16 and victs 15.2.17 (Capt LL Richardson/2Lt WG Meggitt sent an EA C-type OOC near Avion at 16.30), 17.3.17 (2Lt EVA Bell/2Lt EG Green sent an Albatros D.III OOC near Oppy at 11.30) and 6.4.17 (2Lt A Roulstone/2Lt EG Green destroyed an EA in flames near Givenchy at 10.30) then damaged in crash 8.4.17. **1 AD** ex 25 Sqn 11.4.17 with 160hp engine and deleted 19.4.17 (NWR, flying time 170hr 37min). BUT. **11 Sqn** and overturned and wrecked in crash on patrol 17.5.17 (Lt LA Fuller KIFA/ Cpl C Beauchamp OK). Reported as 51 HDS 1917.

7687 Presentation a/c *Australia No 3, NSW No 2* wef 4.10.16. At Norwich allotted to BEF (160hp Beardmore) 20.9.16. **1 AD** dd ex Farnborough 23.10.16. **11 Sqn** dd ex 1 AD 25.10.16 and LIA 17.5.17 (2Lt LA Fuller KIA/ Cpl C Beauchamp WIA – a/c unsalvageable). BUT **2 AD** deleted for spares 2.6.17.

7688 Converted to FE2d and tested at Norwich 1.17. **9 RS** by 30.1.17 until @ 2.17.

7689 Presentation a/c *Australia No 4, NSW No 3, the Mrs P Kirby & Son*. At Norwich allotted to BEF (160hp Beardmore) 27.9.16. **1 AD** ex England 15.10.16. **2 AD** ex 1 AD 16.10.16. **18 Sqn** dd ex 2 AD 17.10.16. **1 AD** ex 18 Sqn 22.1.17 with 120hp engine and flown to England 23.1.17 (Flying time 33hr 45min). **SAD** allotted to HD Wing 1.2.17. **51 HDS** A Flt by 23.3.17 (Lt OE Ridewood/Cpl Dye AZP).

7690

7691 Presentation a/c *Australia No 5, NSW No 4, The FJ White Sumarez and Baldblair* wef 4.10.16. At Norwich allotted to BEF (160hp Beardmore) 27.9.16. **2 AD** ex 1 AD 31.10.16. **11 Sqn** dd ex 2 AD 4.11.16 and vict 27.12.16 (2Lt JB Graham/Pte HH Dyer sent an Albatros D.II OOC near Monchy le Preux at 11.15) then LIA after combat near Vitry-en-Artois on recce 31.3.17 (Lt LAT Strange POW/2Lt WGT Clifton POW fatally wdd – probably shot down by Ltn K Wolff, Jasta 11. 160hp engine 918/WD7528, flying time 100hr 27min).

7692 Presentation a/c *Dominica*. At Norwich

allotted to BEF (120hp Beardmore) 27.9.16. **1 AD** ex England in packing case 6.11.16. **18 Sqn** dd ex 1 AD 20.12.16 and damaged in forced landing near aerodrome on night flying practice 1.2.17. **2 AD** ex 18 Sqn with 160hp engine 6.2.17 and deleted 7.2.17 (NWR, flying time 28hr 10min).

7693 Presentation a/c *Punjab No 6*. At Norwich allotted to BEF (160hp Beardmore) 27.9.16. **1 AD** ex England 18.10.16. **25 Sqn** dd ex 1 AD 20.10.16 and victs 22.10.16 (2Lt JL Leith/ Sgt LS Court destroyed an EA scout near Seclin at 09.04), 9.11.16 (2Lt JL Leith/2Lt EL Chadwick sent a Fokker D-type OOC near Hénin-Liétard), 29.1.17 (2Lt JL Leith/2Lt DC Woollen destroyed an Albatros D.II near Harnes at 10.50) and 4.3.17 (2Lt RG Malcolm/ Cpl L Emsden shared the destruction of an LVG C-type near Courrières at 11.15 with 7025, A780 and A5439) then damaged in forced landing after successful combat near Cambrai-l'Abbé 16.3.17 (2Lt RNL Munro WIA/Sgt CHN Nunn OK after sending an Albatros D.II OOC near Neuvireuil at 15.10) and further vict 17.3.17 (Capt JL Leith/AM2 L Emsden sent an Albatros D.II OOC near Arras) then wrecked 18.3.17. **1 AD** ARS ex 25 Sqn 20.3.17 with 160hp engine 792/ WD7152 and deleted 20.3.17 (NWR, flying time 108hr 25min).

7694 Presentation a/c *Gold Coast No 7*. At Norwich allotted to BEF (160hp Beardmore) 27.9.16. **1 AD** ex England 16.10.16. **2 AD** ex 1 AD 17.10.16. **11 Sqn** dd ex 2 AD 18.10.16 and victs 22.11.16 (Capt HB Davey/Lt AL Harrow-Bunn captured an LVG C-type near Arras at 14.00), 4.3.17 (2Lt JB Graham/2Lt JAV Boddy captured an Albatros D.II near Tilloy at 16.10) and 11.3.17 (Lt ET Curling & Lt HW Guy sent an Albatros D.II OOC near Monchy le Preux at 12.15) then) damaged in combat near Fricourt 17.3.17 (Lt NH Read/2Lt L Nevile-Smith OK) and vict 24.3.17 (Lt ET Curling/ Lt HW Guy destroyed an Albatros D.III near Monchy le Preux at 12.15). **2 AD** ex 11 Sqn 27.3.17, SOC BEF charge 30.3.17 (160hp engine, NWR, 90hr 10min flying time) and to England in packing case 30.3.17.

7695 Presentation a/c *Baroda No 16*. At Norwich allotted to BEF (160hp Beardmore) 12.10.16. **1 AD** ex England 22.10.16. **11 Sqn** dd ex 1 AD 23.10.16 vict 9.11.16 (2Lt JL Leith & Sgt LS Court sent a Fokker D type OOC near Hénin-Liétard at 08.30) then and LIA in combat on

FE2b 7698 of 11 Sqn may have been another victim of Ltn K Wolff on 27 April 1917, but the crew managed to land in Allied lines.

FE2b 7702 of 11 Sqn was shot up and damaged on 14 April 1917, the observer being killed.

recce near Warlencourt on recce 17.3.17 (2Lt RW Cross and Lt CF Lodge POW – probably by Ltn W Voss, Jasta 2. 160hp engine 679/ WD7039, 7 flying time 5hr 39min).

7696 Presentation a/c *Baroda No 19*. At Norwich allotted to BEF (160hp Beardmore) 12.10.16. **1 AD** ex England 17.10.16. **2 AD** ex 1 AD 20.10.16. **11 Sqn** dd ex 2 AD 20.10.16. **2 AD** wrecked ex 11 Sqn 8.4.17 and for England in packing case 30.4.17. Deleted 11.5.17.

7697 Presentation a/c *Punjab No 5* wef 4.10.16. At Norwich allotted to BEF (160hp Beardmore) 12.10.16. **1 AD** ex England 2.11.16. **2 AD** ex 1 AD 4.11.16. **22 Sqn** dd ex 2 AD 5.11.16 and victs 11.12.16 (Capt CS Duffus/2Lt GO McEntee destroyed an EA C-type in flames

near Bapaume at 11.00, shared with DH2s 7930 and A305 of 24 Sqn) and 4.2.17 (Capt HR Hawkins/Sgt F Johnson destroyed an Albatros D.II near Haplincourt at 13.45) and 5.4.17 (2Lt FFHE Kolligs & 2Lt JO Stewart shared sending an Albatros D.III OOC near Honnecourt at 13.45 with 4991). **2 AD** ex 22 Sqn 27.7.17 (2Lt TH Gladstone). **1 AD** ex 2 AD 28.7.17. **2 AD** ex 1 AD 9.8.17. **18 Sqn** ex 2 AD 12.8.17. **2 AD** ex 1 AD 16.8.17. **101 Sqn** dd ex 2 AD 19.8.17 and listed as old and damaged 5.9.17 (258hr). Flown to England 11.9.17. Deleted 11.10.17.

7698 Presentation a/c *Zanzibar No 2* wef 4.10.16. At Norwich allotted to BEF (160hp Beardmore) 12.10.16. Allotment cancelled and under

FE2b 7705 of 25 Squadron was lost near Bapaume on 2 February 1917 and clearly drew a crowd from the town.

FE2b 7714 was 100 Sqn's first loss in action, bombing Douai airfield on the night of 5/6 April before being shot down by Ltn W. Frankl of Jasta 4. In the lower picture it is being drained of fuel or oil at the salvage dump, apparently still on the rail truck on which it is shown on p47.

repair 7.12.16. **SAD** allotted to BEF 18.1.17 (160hp Beardmore 727/WD7087). **11 Sqn** and overturned in forced landing in trenches following combat 27.4.17 (2Lt P Robinson WIA/AM2 H Tilley IIA – possibly brought down by Ltn K Wolff, Jasta 11).

7699 Presentation a/c *Malaya No 21, The Tan Jiak Kim* wef 4.10.16. At Norwich allotted to BEF (160hp Beardmore) 12.10.16. **1 AD** ex England 4.11.16. **2 AD** ex 1 AD 4.11.16. **23 Sqn** dd ex 2 AD 10.11.16 and in forced landing after radiator shot up 6.3.17 during successful combat with Halberstadt D.II (Capt CE Bryant/2Lt HS Elliot OK – EA sent OOC). **2 AD** ex 23 Sqn 11.3.17 and deleted 14.3.17 (NWR, flying time 77hr

FE2b 7715 of 11 Sqn was probably shot down by Lothar von Richthofen of Jasta 11 on 28 March 1917.

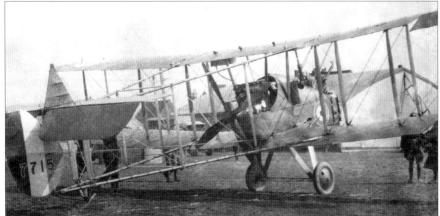

53min).

7700 Presentation a/c *Malaya No 29, The Negri Sembilan*. At Norwich allotted to BEF (160hp Beardmore) 12.10.16. **1 AD** ex England 20.10.16. **11 Sqn** dd ex 1 AD 21.10.16 used in message pick-up experiments and wrecked in crash when message pick-up wires snared propeller 3.11.16 (Lt HH Turk KIFA/Lt J Allen fatally IIFA). **2 AD** ex 11 Sqn 5.11.16 and deleted 6.11.16 with serviceable parts to store.

7701 Presentation a/c *Kedah No 2*. At Norwich allotted to BEF (160hp Beardmore) 12.10.16. **1 AD** dd ex Farnborough 21.10.16. **11 Sqn** dd ex 1 AD St-Omer 23.10.16 and wrecked after combat over Bapaume on bombing

escort 9.11.16 (2Lt JD Cowie WIA/Cpl CGS Ward KIA).

7702 Presentation a/c *Malaya No 9* wef 20.11.16. At Norwich allotted to BEF (160hp Beardmore) 12.10.16. **1 AD** ex England 20.10.16. **2 AD** ex 1 AD 21.10.16 under reconstruction 31.12.17 and engine fitted 28.2.17. **11 Sqn** dd ex 2 AD 3.4.17 and damaged in combat on photo-recce 14.4.17 (2Lt AW Gardner OK/Cpl W Hodgson KIA). **2 AD** wrecked ex 11 Sqn 17.4.17 and for England in packing case (160hp Beardmore), 30.4.17.

7703 Presentation a/c *Punjab No 9* wef 20.10.16. At Norwich allotted to BEF (160hp Beardmore) 12.10.16. **1 AD** ex England 21.10.16. **2 AD** ex 1 AD 22.10.16. **22 Sqn** dd ex 2 AD 23.10.16 and vict 4.12.16 (2Lt CM Clement/2Lt JK Campbell sent an Albatros D.I OOC near Baraste at 10.10 then damaged 10.5.17 (Major LW Learmount WIA) and wrecked in bad landing on gunnery practice 18.5.17 (2Lt JM Woods OK/ AM1 J McRobert injured).

7704 Presentation a/c *Gold Coast No 2*. At Norwich allotted to BEF (160hp Beardmore) 12.10.16. **SAD** departed for 1 AD St-Omer but force-landed at Marden 26.10.16 (2Lt H Slinsby) and returned to Farnborough 3.11.16. **1 AD** ex England in packing case 6.11.16. **2 AD** ex 1 AD 9.11.16. **23 Sqn** dd ex 2 AD 10.11.16. **2 AD** ex 23 Sqn 8.2.17 in exchange for SPAD S.VII, serviceable 28.2.17 (120hp Beardmore) and crashed on delivery flight to 101 Sqn 1.3.17 (Lt WF Lees OK). Deleted 5.3.17. **2 AD** with 160hp engine and deleted 5.3.17 (NWR, flying time 29hr 50min).

7705 Presentation a/c *Montreal No 4* wef 20.10.16. At Norwich allotted to BEF (160hp Beardmore) 12.10.16. **AID** dd ex Norwich 25.10.16, via Chingford 24.10.16. **1 AD** ex England 26.10.16. **22 Sqn** dd ex 1 AD, via 2 AD with 160hp engine 28.10.16. **23 Sqn** dd ex 2 AD 16.11.16 and LIA in combat near Bapaume on recce escort 2.2.17 (2Lt RT Whitney POW/Lt TG Holley POW wdd – shot down by Vzfw P Bona, Jasta 1. Engine 708/WD7068, flying time 35hr 10min).

7706 Presentation a/c *Toungoo District of Burma* wef 20.10.16. At Norwich allotted to BEF (160hp Beardmore) 12.10.16. **1 AD** ex England 26.10.16. **22 Sqn** dd ex 1 AD 2.11.16 and vict 22.11.16 (2Lt NH Tolhurst/Sgt F Johnson sent an Albatros D.I OOC near Bancourt at 13.30) then wrecked in landing crash and burnt out 15.1.17 after engine caught fire on gunnery practice. **2 AD** wrecked ex 22 Sqn 18.1.17 and deleted 18.1.17.

7707 Presentation a/c *Presented by H Teesdale-Smith of Adelaide* wef 20.10.16. At Norwich allotted to BEF (160hp Beardmore) 12.10.16. **1 AD** ex England 31.10.16. **2 AD** ex 1 AD 4.11.16. **22 Sqn** dd ex 2 AD 4.11.16 and wrecked in forced landing near Montauban after combat 4.3.17 (2Lt EA Mearnes/Lt H Loveland OK). **2 AD** ex 22 Sqn with 160hp engine 722/WD7082 15.3.17 and deleted 17.3.17 (NWR, flying time 73hr 57min).

7708 Presentation a/c *Jamaica No 1*. At Norwich allotted to BEF (160hp Beardmore) 12.10.16. **1 AD** ex England in packing case 6.11.16. **2 AD** ex 1 AD 10.11.16. **11 Sqn** dd ex 2 AD 12.11.16 and vict 27.12.16 (2Lt Taylor/Lt JAV Boddy sent an Albatros D.II OOC near Monchy le Preux at 11.15) then wrecked hitting lorry on take off for night flying practice 11.3.17 and SOC unit charge 12.3.17 (flying time 49hr 6min). **2 AD** ex 11 Sqn 18.3.17 and to England in packing case 9.4.17.

7709 Presentation a/c *The Akyab*. At Norwich allotted to BEF (160hp Beardmore) 12.10.16. Crashed en-route to BEF and allotment cancelled 24.11.16 **SARD** under repair, allotted to BEF 5.3.17 and tested 16.3.17.

11 Sqn and destroyed by fire in forced landing on recce 28.3.17 (2Lt Langwill/2Lt WGT Clifton OK. Flying time 11hr 8min). 2 AD wrecked ex 11 Sqn 31.3.17 and deleted 1.4.17.

7710 Presentation a/c *Residents of Aden*. At Norwich allotted to BEF (160hp Beardmore) 12.10.16. At **SAD** allotted to BEF but allotment cancelled 24.11.16 – aircraft crashed. Deleted 30.11.16.

7711 Presentation a/c *Auckland*. At Norwich allotted to BEF (160hp Beardmore) 12.10.16. **1 AD** ex England 2.11.16. **2 AD** ex 1 AD 4.11.16. **22 Sqn** dd ex 2 AD 7.11.16 with 160hp engine and wrecked in crash after hit by ground fire near Bapaume on photo escort 2.2.17 (2Lt JV Aspinall OK/2Lt JMR Miller WIA. Flying time 47hr 32min). **2 AD** ex 22 Sqn 5.2.17 and deleted 6.2.17.

7712 Presentation a/c *Zanzibar No 5*. At Norwich allotted to BEF (160hp Beardmore) 12.10.16. **1 AD** dd ex Farnborough 13.11.16. **2 AD** ex 1 AD 14.11.16. **23 Sqn** dd ex 2 AD 15.11.16 and damaged in combat with 5 EA 24.12.16 (2Lt WB Kellogg /2Lt TB Jones WIA). **2 AD** ex 23 Sqn 28.12.16 and deleted that day.

7713 Presentation a/c *Zanzibar No 4*. At Norwich allotted to BEF (160hp Beardmore) 20.10.16. **AID** dd ex Norwich 6.11.16. **1 AD** dd ex Farnborough 8.11.16. **2 AD** ex 1 AD 9.11.16. **23 Sqn** dd ex 2 AD 9.11.16 and LIA near Bapaume on photo escort 11.3.17 (2Lt CAR Shum/2Lt FC Coops POW – probably by Ltn H Gontermann, Jasta 5). Deleted on unit 12.3.17 (160hp engine 604/WD6964, flying time 83hr 30min).

7714 Presentation a/c *Zanzibar No 7*. At Norwich allotted to BEF (160hp Beardmore) 20.10.16. **1 AD** ex England in packing case 6.11.16. **100 Sqn** and LIA night bombing Douai aerodrome 6.4.17 (2Lt ARM Richards POW wdd/AM2 EW Barnes POW – shot down at night by Ltn W Frankl, Jasta 4).

7715 Presentation a/c *Zanzibar No 8*. At Norwich allotted to BEF (160hp Beardmore) 20.10.16, allotment cancelled and under repair at SAD 7.12.16. **25 Sqn** dd ex 1 AD St-Omer 21.3.17 and LIA in combat near Vimy 28.3.17 (2Lt NL Knight POW wdd/2Lt AG Severs KIA – probably shot down by Ltn L Fr v Richthofen, Jasta 11. 160hp engine 676/WD7036, flying time 19hr 20min).

7995: 1 RAF FE2d prototype (250hp Rolls-Royce) built by the Royal Aircraft Factory, Farnborough.

7995 First flown 7.4.16 (Capt FW Goodden). Given serial number by 20.4.16. **CFS** (engine 1/250/31 WD) and tested 7.5.16, producing Report No 41. 11th Wing dd ex 1 AD 27.6.16. **20 Sqn**, undercarriage modified by 2.9.16 and request for replacement 11.11.16. **1 AD** ex 20 Sqn 11.11.16. Flown to England ex 1 AD 21.11.16 (flying time 93hr 32min). Allotted to Training Brigade 27.11.16.

A1 – A40: 40 RAF FE2d (250hp Rolls-Royce Mk.I in first 30 and Mk.III in remainder) built by the Royal Aircraft Factory, Farnborough under War Office authority, Extract 147.

A1 **RAF** 12.5.16, engine 1/250/7, airscrew 10625. Allotted to BEF 1.6.16. **1 AD** dd 1.6.16 (Lt RR Archer). **20 Sqn** (engine 1/250/7 WD6149) propeller damaged when hit petrol tin flare 17.6.16 (Capt RS Maxwell/AM1 DA Stewart OK). 1 AD and deleted 24.6.16 ((NWR, flying time 16hr 42min).

A2 **RAF** 12.5.16, engine 17, airscrew 10626. Allotted to BEF by 17.6.16. **20 Sqn** and wrecked 2.7.16 (flying time 17hr 18min).

A3 **RAF** 24.5.16, engine 1/250/65, airscrew 11566/T28015. Allotted to BEF by 17.6.16. **20 Sqn** and victs 1.7.16 (Lt HE Hartney/AM2 A Stanley destroyed a Fokker E.II in

The 250hp Rolls-Royce engine of FE2d A1, with oil streaks on the cowling. The sight-glass gauge on the underwing fuel tank can be seen from this angle. The checkerboard markings on the forward nacelle are very unusual. (See also p19)

flames near Lille/Tourcoing at 05.30 and another in the same locality at 05.55) then severely damaged by AA near Wervicq 8.8.16 with controls shot up and force landed at Clairmarais (2Lt BL Dowling ASC/2Lt WG Pender OK – Pender 5 Sqn), 1 AD St-Omer under test 15.1.17. **20 Sqn** dd ex 1 AD 29.1.17, reported wrecked and deleted 4.2.17 (flying time 154hr 47min). **1 AD**, retaken on RFC charge 12.2.17. **20 Sqn** and victs 6.4.17 (2Lt EJ Smart/2Lt HN Hampson destroyed an Albatros D.III near Roulers at 10.15 and sent two more OOC at 10.20) then damaged in combat 25.5.17 (2Lt RG Dalziel WIA/Lt WH Chester OK – by Ltn Traeger, J.8. Engine 4/250/27 WD1214) then further victs 28.7.17 (Lt HL Satchell/Lt AN Jenks sent an Albatros D.V OOC near Tourcoing at 18.30) and 16.8.17 (2Lt RM Makepeace/Lt MW Waddington sent an Albatros D.V OOC near Zonnebeke at 09.05). **1 AD** and flown to England 18.10.17 (250hp RR 4/250/15/10065).

A4 **RAF** 20.5.16, engine 1/250/21, airscrew 10621. Allotted to BEF 30.5.16. **20 Sqn** and vict 6.9.16 (2Lt C Gordon-Davis/Cpl S Birch sent a Fokker D.II OOC near Passchendaele

at 12.45) then damaged in forced landing after engine failed on patrol 3.2.17 (Lt R Gordon-Davis/Cpl S Birch OK). **1 AD** by 10.2.17. **25 Sqn** and crashed after hitting wires on return from forced landing 7.5.17 (2Lt D Leishman IIFA/Pte J Billon fatally IIFA).

A5 **RAF** 23.5.16, engine 1/250/89, airscrew 10619. Allotted to BEF 30.5.16. Captured on delivery flight Farnborough – St-Omer 1.6.16 (2Lt SCT Littlewood/Lt D Lyall-Grant POW – lost and landed and turned on nose on Haubourdin aerodrome).

A6 **RAF** 26.5.16, engine 1/250/83, airscrew 10623. Allotted to BEF 5.6.16. **20 Sqn** flown by Flt Sgt JTB McCudden from 9.7.16, tested after overhaul 7.8.16 (Flt Sgt JTB McCudden/Cpl Farmer then Flt Sgt JTB McCudden/Cpl Hughes) and damaged by ground fire near Lille after successful combat on recce 20.10.16 (2Lt GG Callender WIA/2Lt HW Soulby OK – after sending an Albatros D.II OOC S of Lille at 09.15) and vict 21.10.16 (2Lt GG Callendar/2Lt WH Soulby sent an Albatros D.II OOC near Lille at 09.15 near Comines at 12.00). **1 AD** ex 20 Sqn 23.10.16 and deleted with flying time 140hr 21min. To

FE2d A2 at Farnborough. Probably the first FE2d to be fitted with the Beardmore type radiator.

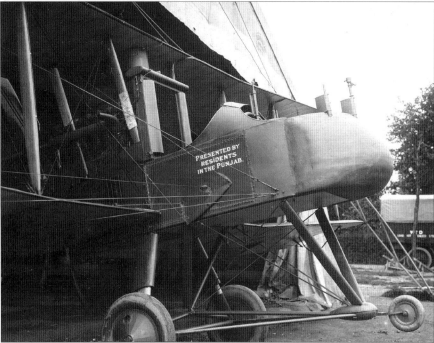

FE2d A9 of 20 Sqn with its original single-line presentation inscription, and then re-lettered following repairs to landing accident damage. The upper photograph shows the rudder stripes marked at an oblique angle to the thrust line. The RAF consistently inserted an apostrophe between the prefix letter and the rest of the serial.

England in packing case for reconstruction 17.12.16.

A7   RAF 29.5.16, engine 1/250/25, airscrew 10630. Allotted to BEF 12.6.16. **20 Sqn** by 10.7.16 (Flt Sgt JTB McCudden), force landed after engine failed on patrol 25.9.16 and damaged when over-turned taxiing on soft ground 2.1.17. **1 AD** and to England in packing case 18.1.17 (flying time 173hr 6min). En-route to SAD 26.1.17.

A8   RAF 28.5.16, engine 1/250/87, airscrew 10629. Allotted to BEF 12.6.16. **20 Sqn** damaged by AA over Lille and force landed near Fleurbaix 8.9.16 (2Lt DH Dabbs WIA/AM1 F Dearing OK – shelled after landing) and damaged in successful combat over Ypres 26.9.16 with forced landing near

Vlamertinghe (2Lt AF Livingstone WIA/AM1 F Dearing KIA – had destroyed an Albatros D.II near Ypres at 07.30) and vict 21.10.16 (2Lt ED Spicer/Sgt S Birch destroyed a Fokker D.II in flames near Comines at 12.00), request for replacement 11.11.16 and damaged in crash 6.1.17 and deleted on unit 7.1.17. **1 AD** 15.1.17, wrecked, unserviceable and for shipment to England in packing case (flying time 139hr 28min). To England in packing case 18.1.17. En-route to SAD Farnborough 26.1.17.

A9   Presentation a/c *Presented by Residents in the Punjab*. **RAF** 31.5.16, engine 1/250/49, airscrew 9597/T28010. Allotted to BEF 12.6.16. **20 Sqn** and crashed after tyre burst on take-off 10.8.16. **AD** ex 20 Sqn. **20 Sqn**

FE2d A19 of 20 Squadron met 20 enemy aircraft after crossing the lines on 29 April 1917, and was forced down by Jasta 18 machines. The crew survived this crash.

ex 1 AD 21.9.16 and damaged by ground fire on photo sortie 20.10.16, force landing near La Clyte (Lt HE Hartney/2Lt WT Jordan OK). **1 AD** ex 20 Sqn 23.10.16 and deleted with 99hr 19 min flying time. To England in packing case for reconstruction 17.12.16.

A10   RAF 5.6.16, engine 1/250/75, airscrew 10632/T28010. Allotted to BEF 16.6.16. Allotted to BEF by 17.6.16. **20 Sqn** and damaged taking off from forced landing during photo practice 8.7.16 (crew injured, pilot 2Lt E Birch). **1 AD** ex 20 Sqn and deleted 10.7.16 (NWR, 2 flying time 4hr 15min).

A11   RAF 5.6.16, engine 1/250/63, airscrew 10637/T28010. Allotted to BEF 12.6.16. **20 Sqn**, vict 1.7.16 (2Lt GPS Reid/Capt G Dixon-Spain destroyed a Fokker E-type near Wervicq at 05.10) and wrecked in forced landing crash in mist near Dieppe 20.7.16 (2Lt DS Davies/Cpl W Moore injured. Flying time 42hr 18min).

A12   RAF 7.6.16, engine 1/250/85, airscrew 10634/T28010. Allotted to BEF 12.6.16. **20 Sqn** by 2.9.16, request for replacement 11.11.16. **1 AD** ex 20 Sqn 14.11.16. Flown to England ex 1 AD 22.11.16 (flying time 161hr 50min). Allotted for training 23.11.16. **46 RS** by 28.3.17 until @ 5.17. Re-allotted for HD 27.7.17. **33 HDS** C Flt and crashed into trees near Elsham on AZP 24.9.17 (2Lt C Pinnock IIFA/Lt JA Menzies KIA, engine 4/250/31/WD10081).

A13   RAF 20.6.16, engine 1/250/43, airscrew 10638/T28010. Allotted to BEF 24.6.16. 11 Wing dd ex 1 AD St-Omer 27.6.16. **20 Sqn** and victs 21.7.16 (Capt RS Maxwell/2Lt HJ Hamilton sent an Albatros C type OOC near Lille at 09.45), 1.8.16 (Lt DH Dabbs/AM1 DA Stewart destroyed a Fokker E.III near Moorslede at 16.00) and 21.7.16 Capt RS Maxwell/2Lt HJ Hamilton sent a Rumpler C-type OOC near Lille) then wrecked in forced landing near Buysscheure 19.9.16 (crew injured, pilot Capt AG Deuchar. Flying time 130hr 34min). **1 AD** ex 20 Sqn and deleted 22.9.16. BUT **20 Sqn** dd 27.1.17.

A14   RAF 20.6.16, engine 1/250/27, airscrew 10642/T28010. Allotted to BEF 24.6.16. **20 Sqn** by 2.9.16 and wrecked in forced landing after fuel problems on patrol 7.9.16, had 96hr 8min flying time. **1 AD** ex 20 Sqn 10.9.16 and deleted 11.9.16.

A15   RAF 23.6.16, engine 1/250/59, airscrew 10631/T28010. Allotted to BEF 24.6.16. **20 Sqn** by 28.7.16 (Flt Sgt JTB McCudden) and wrecked after hitting telegraph wires in forced landing after successful combat 14.2.17 (2Lt FJ Taylor IIA/2Lt FM Myers KIA – after sending an Albatros D.II down in flames near Passchendaele at 17.00 – probably shot down by Ltn P Strähle, Jasta 18). Reported wrecked 15.2.17 (flying time 206hr 52min). **1 AD** and deleted 19.2.17.

A16   RAF 23.6.16, engine 1/250/45, airscrew 11568. Allotted to BEF 24.6.16. **20 Sqn** and wrecked in forced landing in mist near Fleurs Chateau 20.7.16 (Capt R Blatherwick/AM2 A Stanley injured. Flying time 23hr 56min).

A17   RAF 26.6.16, engine 1/250/53, airscrew 10635/T28010. Allotted to BEF 24.6.16. **20 Sqn** and in forced landing after engine failed on patrol 7.8.16.

A18   RAF 28.6.16, engine 1/250/29, airscrew 13084. Allotted to BEF 24.6.16. **20 Sqn** and wrecked in crash near Roellecourt on patrol 20.7.16 (Capt GN Teale/Cpl JW Stringer KIFA. Flying time 12hr 28min).

A19   RAF 29.6.16, engine 1/250/23, airscrew 10641/T28010. Allotted to BEF 24.6.16. **20 Sqn** and victs 3.8.16 (2Lt GPS Reid/Capt G Dixon-Spain sent an Aviatik C-type OOC near Hollebeke at 09.30), 31.8.16 (2Lt GPS Reid/2Lt LH Scott sent a Fokker D.II OOC

near Langemarck at 10.25), 5.9.16 (2Lt GPS Reid/2Lt HM Golding sent a Fokker E-type OOC near Passchendaele at 12.45), 31.8.16 (Capt GRM Reid/Lt LH Scott sent a Fokker D.II OOC near Langemarck) and 24.9.16 (Lt AD Pearce/2Lt WF Findlay shared the destruction of a Fokker D.II near Rumbeke at 12.10), request for replacement 11.11.16, damaged on test 22.1.17 when dog ran into propeller and LIA in combat with 20 EA on bombing sortie 29.4.17 (Sgt S Attwater/2Lt JE Davies POW – possibly shot down by Ltn E Weissner, Jasta 18. Flying time 190hr 26min, engine 1/275/81/WD13909).

A20 **RAF** 30.6.16, engine 1/250/41, airscrew 13080. Allotted to BEF 24.6.16. **20 Sqn** and burnt out in crash after sideslip on delivery flight 9.7.16 (Major CJ Malcolm/Lt GE Chancellor KIFA. Flying time 3hr 20min).

A21 **RAF** 11.7.16, engine 1/250/61, airscrew 13085/T28012. **20 Sqn** and damaged hitting hedge in forced landing after engine seized on escort 21.8.16. **1 AD** and deleted 25.8.16 (NWR) but re-taken on charge at 1 AD 11.9.16. **57 Sqn** dd ex 1 AD 5.1.17 and LIA after combat with 6 EA on OP 6.4.17 (2Lt DC Birch/Lt JK Bousfield POW – probably shot down by Hptm P v Osterroth, Jasta 12. Flying time 69hr 1min, engine 3/250/75/WD10069).

A22 **RAF** 12.7.16, engine 1/250/55, airscrew 13098/T28012. **20 Sqn** and victs 29.7.16 (Capt GRM Reid/Lt LH Scott destroyed a Rumpler C-type near Zandvoorde at 12.15) and 31.7.16 (Capt GRM Reid/Lt LH Scott destroyed an LVG C-type near Ypres at 11.35). **1 AD**, wrecked for reconstruction, ex 20 Sqn 8.9.16. **57 Sqn** dd ex 1 AD 4.1.17 and LIA in combat near Marquion 6.4.17 (Lt RTB Schreiber/2Lt M Lewis POW. Flying time 120hr 27min, engine 4/250/97/WD10096).

A23 **RAF** 17.7.16, engine 1/250/77, airscrew 13081/T2802. **20 Sqn** and vict 3.8.16 (Capt RS Maxwell/AM1 DA Stewart destroyed a Roland C.II near Gheluwe at 10.10) then reported as old and damaged 29.8.16. **1 AD** ex 20 Sqn for reconstruction 8.9.16. **20 Sqn** ex 1 AD 7.2.17 and LIA on bombing sortie 12.5.17 (2Lt H Kirby/Sgt TE Wait POW – engine 4/250/95/WD12092).

A24 **RAF** 18.7.16, engine 1/250/99, airscrew 13089/T28012. Allotted to BEF 24.6.16. **20 Sqn** by 28.7.16, flown 6.8.16 by JB McCudden, reported as old 5.9.16 but victs 23.9.16 (Lt S Alder/AM1 H Alexander destroyed a Fokker E type near Roulers at 17.25) and 24.9.16 (Lt S Alder/2Lt RW White

FE2d A23 of 20 Sqn, lost on a bombing raid on 12 May 1917. The removal of outer wing panels and upper cockpit fairing gives a clear view of the radiator shutters and telescopic gun pillar.

destroyed a Rumpler C type near Courtrai at 11.50 and a Fokker D.II near Rumbeke at 12.10 plus shared the destruction of a Fokker D.II near Rumbeke at 12.10 with A19 and A39) then crashed when engine failed on take off for patrol 30.9.16 (flying time 79hr 48min). **1 AD** ex 20 Sqn 1.10.16 and deleted 3.10.16.

A25 **RAF** 20.7.16, engine 33, airscrew 13093/T28012. Allotted to BEF 29.7.16. **RAF**, re-allotted for experimental purposes 3.8.16. Reconstructed 8.17 – engine 1/250/33, airscrew 14542/T28020.

A26 **RAF** 24.7.16, engine 97, airscrew 10653/T28010. Allotted to BEF 29.7.16. **20 Sqn** by 2.9.16 and victs 27.9.16 (2Lt JK Stead/Lt L Jefferson sent a LVG C type OOC near Zuydschoote at 11.30 shared with A29) and 28.9.16 (2Lt JK Stead/Lt L Jefferson sent an AGO C type OOC near Neuve Chapelle at 14.57) then wrecked taking off from forced landing made during patrol 4.11.16 (crew OK). **1 AD** ex 20 Sqn 7.11.16.

A27 **RAF** 29.7.16, engine 1/250/5, airscrew 10653/T28010 (recorded with same airscrew as A26). Allotted to BEF 3.8.16. **1 AD** dd 3.8.16. **20 Sqn** dd ex 1 AD 2.9.16 and reported as old with poor longerons 5.9.16. **1 AD** ex 20 Sqn 7.9.16 for repair. Fitted with 250hp R-R Mk.IV. **20 Sqn** re-issued ex 1

AD 30.12.16 and LIA on photo sortie Lille/Messines 17.3.17 (Lt W Anderson MC/Lt DB Woolley POW – shot down by Fwbl Hippert, FlA 227. Captured intact with 93hr 13min flying time, engine 4/250/141/WD12107).

A28 **RAF** 1.8.16, engine 1/250/7, airscrew 10652/T28010. Allotted to BEF 3.8.16. **20 Sqn** by 2.9.17 and vict 25.1.17 (2Lt RB Wainwright/2Lt JT Gibbon brought down a Halberstadt – location? time? this a/c?) then LIA in combat near Moorslede on photo-recce 1.2.17 (2Lt ED Spicer/Capt CM Carbert KIA – probably shot down by OffSt W Göttsch, Jasta 28. Engine 3/250/11 WD8150, flying time 139hr 28min).

A29 **RAF** 3.8.16, engine 1/250/17, airscrew 10651/T28010. Allotted to BEF 3.8.16. **20 Sqn** and victs 17.9.16 (Capt RS Maxwell/AM2 A Stanley destroyed an Albatros D type near Wervicq at 10.45), 27.9.16 (Lt HE Hartney/2Lt RS Dixon sent an LVG C type OOC near Zuydschoote at 11.30, shared with A26) 16.11.16 (Capt RS Maxwell/2Lt WT Gilson sent two Albatros D.II OOC near Abeele) and 26.1.17 (Lt RB Wainwright/Lt HM Golding sent an Albatros D.II OOC near Westroosebeke at 15.50) and 7.4.17 (2Lt SN Pike/AM2 AH Sayers sent an Albatros D.III OOC near Tourcoing at 18.30) then LIA near Sanctuary Wood on bombing sortie

Ltn W. Voss probably accounted for this FE2d, A32 of 25 Squadron, on 28 May 1917.

29.4.17 (2Lt EO Perry/AM2 TE Allum WIA – in combat with 7 EA but brought down by ground fire and shelled. Flying time 191hr 43min, engine 3/250/1/WD5506).

A30 **RAF** .8.16, engine 1/250/41, airscrew 10643/T28010. Allotted to BEF 3.8.16. **20 Sqn** dd ex 1 AD 31.8.16 with victs 3.9.16 (2Lt DH Dabbs/2Lt A Dewar destroyed a Fokker E.III near Roulers at 13.30), 20.10.16 (2Lt HE Hartney/2Lt WT Jourdan sent an EA D-type OOC near Lille), damaged in combat 1.2.17 (Capt JK Stead fatally WIA/2Lt WT Jourdan WIA) then wrecked taking off from forced landing made during bombing sortie 25.3.17. **1 AD** and deleted 17.4.17 (NWR, flying time 108hr 57min).

A31 **RAF** 16.8.16, engine 3/250/1, airscrew 10654/T28015. Allotted to BEF 3.8.16. **20 Sqn** dd ex 1 AD 8.9.16 and vict 26.1.17 (Lt JK Stead/2Lt WT Gilson sent an Albatros D.II OOC near Westroosebeke at 15.50) then LIA in combat with 6 EA near Moorslede 6.2.17 (Lt TCH Lucas/2Lt JT Gibbon KIA – probably by Ltn Traeger, Jasta 8. Engine 4/250/107 WD12096, flying time 115hr 44min).

A32 **RAF** 17.8.16, engine 51, airscrew 13082. Allotted to BEF 3.8.16. **20 Sqn** and victs 27.12.16 (2Lt J Blackwood/2Lt FH Bronskill destroyed a Halberstadt D.II near Roulers at 11.50) and 25.1.17 (Lt TCH Lucas/2Lt WT Gilson destroyed a Halberstadt D.II near Menin at 15.10) then damaged in heavy landing after recce 31.1.17 – pilot's goggles had frosted over – reported wrecked 1.2.17 (flying time 127hr 55min.) **2 AD** ex 1 AD 21.3.17. **25 Sqn** dd ex 2 AD 25.3.17 and vict 25.5.17 (2Lt EH Stevens/Lt V Smith sent an Albatros D.III OOC over Gloster Wood at 13.15) then LIA near Douai on recce 28.5.17 (2Lt EH Stevens POW fatally wdd/ LCpl C Sturruck POW wdd – probably shot down by Ltn W Voss, Jasta 5). Engine R22/275/WD13961

A33 **RAF** 18.8.16, engine 3/250/15, airscrew 13807/T28015. Allotted to BEF 3.8.16. **20 Sqn** dd ex 1 AD 8.9.16 and victs 15.11.16 (Lt RB Wainwright/Sgt S Birch sent a Halberstadt C type OOC near Ypres at 14.15 – Sgt Birch WIA that day, this a/c?), 27.12.16 (2Lt RB Wainwright/2Lt HR Wilkinson destroyed a Halberstadt D.II near Zonnebeke and another near Poelcapelle at c.11.55) crashed landing from recce escort 8.2.17 (crew injured). **1 AD** for deletion 14.2.17 (NWR, flying time 88hr 44min).

A34 **RAF** 22.8.16, engine 3/250/37, airscrew 10656/T28015. Allotted to BEF 3.8.16. **20 Sqn** dd 22.10.16 and LIA in combat with EA near Menin on recce 25.1.17 (2Lt S Alder/Lt RW White POW wdd – probably by Obltn Grieffenhagen J.18 but possibly by AA). Deleted as missing 26.1.17 (Engine 4/250/65 WD10093, flying time 44hr 43min).

A35 **RAF** 23.8.16, engine 3/250/9, airscrew 10657/T28015. Allotted to BEF 3.8.16. **1 AD** by c.1.10.16. **20 Sqn** dd 22.10.16 and wrecked in crash landing at Ste Marie Cappel after combat near Westroosebeke 26.1.17 (Sgt CJ Cox/2Lt LG Fauvel IIA). **1 AD** 29.1.17 (flying time 43hr 12min) and deleted 1.2.17.

A36 **RAF** 26.8.16, engine 3/250/31, airscrew 13524/T28020. Allotted to BEF 3.8.16. **1 AD** by c.1.10.16. **20 Sqn** dd ex 1 AD 6.11.16 and burnt out following forced landing near Berthen after hit at 100ft by ground fire 27.12.16 (2Lt DC Cunnell OK/Capt CM Carbert IIA). **1 AD** ex 20 Sqn 29.12.16 and deleted 1.1.17.

A37 **RAF** 25.8.16, engine 3/250/53, airscrew 10655/T28012. Allotted to BEF 31.8.16. **1 AD** dd ex Farnborough 9.16. **20 Sqn** dd ex 1 AD 30.9.16 and wrecked in forced landing after combat with 5 EA near Abeele 16.11.16 (2Lt JW Francis/Lt FRC Cobbold OK – probably brought down by UntOff WA Seitz J.8). **1 AD** ex 20 Sqn 20.11.16, had 28hr 43min flying time and deleted that day.

A38 **RAF** 28.8.16, engine 3/250/55, airscrew 13529/T28020. Allotted to BEF 2.9.16. **1 AD** dd ex Farnborough 1.10.16 (had left 30.9.16 but force-landed at Marden). **20 Sqn** dd 14.11.17 and LIA in combat with 6 EA near Moorslede on photo sortie 16.30 6.2.17 (2Lt ME Woods POW/Lt EB Maule KIA – probably shot down by Obltn Fr v Esebeck J.8). Engine 4/250/9 WD12110, flying time 36hr 7min .

A39 **RAF** 30.8.16, engine 3/250/45, airscrew 13521/T28020. Allotted to BEF 2.9.16. **1 AD** dd ex Farnborough 11.9.16 (had left 9.9.16 but delayed by fog at Pluckley and Folkestone). **20 Sqn** dd ex 1 AD 12.9.16 and victs 22.9.16 (Capt GRM Reid/2Lt LH Scott sent a Fokker D type OOC near Tournai at 09.25), 24.9.16 (Capt GRM Reid/Lt LH Scott shared the destruction of a Fokker D.II near Rumbeke with A19 and A24 at 12.10), 16.10.16 (Capt GRM Reid/Lt LH Scott sent an LVG C-type OOC near Wadizeele at 09.05) and 21.10.16 (Capt GRM Reid/Lt LH Scott destroyed an LVG C-type near Comines) and 9.11.16 (2Lt HG White/AM2 R Pope sent an Albatros D.II OOC near Habourdin at 11.00) then wrecked when crashed 3 miles N of Bapaume after combat at 9000ft with 2 EA 7.1.17 (Sgt T Mottershead fatally WIA/Lt WE Gower IIA – tank hit, down in flames, had possibly sent one of the EA OOC over Ploegsteert Wood at 12.00, Mottershead awarded VC for this action – probably shot up by Vzfw Göttsch, J.8). Engine 3/250/39 WD8152, flying time 81hr 50min. **1 AD** ex 20 Sqn 8.1.17 and deleted 11.1.17.

A40 Allotted to BEF 2.9.16. Re-allotted to **RAF** 7.10.16 and tested (engine-less) to destruction 6.11.16.

A778 – A877: 100 RAF FE2b (120hp Beardmore) built by G & J Weir Ltd, Cathcart under Contract 94/A/210 dated 9.6.16, with V-strut undercarraiage specified.

A778 Presentation a/c *Presented by Alfred Muller Simpson, Parkville, Adelaide.* Shipped to Australia as free gift 15.11.16. Used to search for the German commerce raider *Wolf*. **CFS** Point Cook. Exhibited by AWM in Melbourne 19.6.20 – 3.7.20.

A779 **RAF** 28.12.16. **SAD** allotted to BEF 15.1.17 (160hp Beardmore 888/WD7498). **2 AD** ex 1 AD 28.1.17, serviceable, 28.2.17. **11 Sqn** dd ex 2 AD 18.3.17. BUT **18 Sqn** ex 2 AD 11.3.17 and vict 30.4.17 (2Lt IC Barclay/AM2 LB Adcock sent an Albatros D.III OOC near Baralle at 09.30) then damaged by ground fire on trench strafe 19.8.17 (Lt JF Bryom/Lt EA Foord OK). **2 AD** ex 18 Sqn 23.8.17 and deleted 28.8.17.

A780 **RAF** 29.12.16. **SAD** allotted to BEF 5.1.17 **25 Sqn** dd ex 1 AD 6.2.17 and vict 4.3.17 (2Lt WD Matheson/Sgt WA Barnes shared the destruction of an LVG C-type near Courrières at 11.15 with 7025, 7693 and A5439) then wrecked in forced landing near Bray after combat 16.3.17 (2Lt WD Matheson/Sgt G Goodman WIA – possibly by Ltn K Kuppers, J.6. 160hp Beardmore 886/WD7496). **1 AD** ARS ex 25 Sqn 20.3.17 with 160hp engine and deleted 20.3.17 (NWR, flying time 33hr 35min).

A781 **RAF** 21.12.16 and fitted with twin Lewis guns and Sautter-Harlé searchlight 3.17. **SARD** tested 8.7.17 (pressure dud, 2nd magneto cutting) and 10.7.17 (twice – 2nd test OK). **199 DS/NTS** by 11.17 and damaged in crash at Hemswell 15.6.18. **187 NTS** by 7.18.

FE2b A781 with its experimental installation of twin Lewis guns coupled to a searchlight, also seen on p 67. Four smaller lights under each lower wing are also visible in this view – plenty of work for the large generator propeller.

A782 RAF 29.12.16. **SAD** allotted to BEF 15.1.17. **25 Sqn** dd ex 1 AD 26.1.17 and damaged in successful combat with 12 EA near Hénin-Liétard 29.1.17 (2Lt AW Shirtcliffe OK/2Lt AV Blenkiron WIA – sent 1 Halberstadt down OOC) and further victs 1.3.17 (Capt JL Leith/Lt GMA Hobart-Hampden sent an Albatros D.II OOC near Mericourt at 15.00), 17.3.17 (2Lt RG Malcolm/Lt CW Wilson destroyed an Albatros D.II near Oppy at 11.30) and 13.4.17 (Capt JL Leith/Lt GMA Hobart-Hampden destroyed an Albatros D.III near Sallaumines at 19.30) then crashed on Arras racecourse after combat with 4 EA 1.5.17 (2Lt B King OK/Sgt HG Taylor WIA).

A783 **2 AD** ex 1 AD 11.2.17, for radiator repair, 28.2.17 (160hp Beardmore). HQ Wing ex 2 AD 23.3.17. **100 Sqn** and wrecked in crash after hitting bushes on take-off for practice flight 8.4.17 (Cpl A Waite IIFA. 120hp engine, flying time 12hr 25min). **2 AD** wrecked ex 100 Sqn 13.4.17 and deleted 27.4.17.

A784 Presentation a/c *Black Watch No 2* wef 29.12.16. **AID** 30.11.16. **RAF** 17.12.16 (160hp Beardmore 880/WD7490). 1 AD ex England 24.12.16. **25 Sqn** dd ex 1 AD 2.1.17 and vict 29.1.17 (2Lt AW Shirtcliffe/Lt AV Blenkiron destroyed an Albatros D.II in flames near Harnes at 10.50) then LIA bombing Hénin-Liétard-Lietard 13.4.17 (Sgt J Dempsey POW/2Lt WH Green POW wdd – possibly by Vzfw S Festner, Jasta 11. 160hp engine 919./WD7929).

A785 Presentation a/c *Newfoundland No 1*. **RAF** 9.12.16. **SAD** allotted to BEF 14.12.16. **1 AD** dd ex Farnborough 24.12.16 (had departed 20.12.16 – engine trouble). **18 Sqn** dd ex 1 AD 5.1.17 and destroyed by shellfire after brought down in combat on photo escort 11.3.17 (2Lt JE Lewis IIA/Lt R Mayberry WIA – possibly brought down by Ltn Krefft, J.11 or by Ltn Schulte, J.12). 160hp engine. **2 AD** ex 18 Sqn 16.3.17 and deleted 18.3.17 (flying time 38hr 15min, engine 823/WD7183).

A786 **25 Sqn** by 4.3.17.

A787 **51 HDS** A Flt by 23.3.17 (Lt WR Gayner/Sgt Wigglesworth AZP) until @ 5.17

A788 Newcastle ex Ayr 30.10.17 for 199 DS. **199 DS** dd 30.10.17 (Capt GK Palmer).

A789 Presentation a/c *Punjab No 28 'Shahpur'*. **AID** allotted to BEF 16.1.1917 (160hp Beardmore 909/WD7519). **2 AD** ex 1 AD 29.1.17. **18 Sqn** dd ex 2 AD 8.2.17 and crashed in forced landing at Lavieville aerodrome after combat on photo sortie 4.3.17 (Lt H Lambourne/Pte J Collison WIA. Engine 909/WD7519). SOC 18 Sqn 7.3.17 (flying time 29hr 43min). **2 AD** ex 18 Sqn 10.3.17 and to England in packing case 12.4.17.

A790 Shipped to India. **31 Sqn**, first flown at Risalpur 18.7.17. Crashed 1920.

A791 **RAF** 24.1.17 (160hp Beardmore 934/WD9544). **AID** Farnborough allotted to BEF 16.1.1917. **2 AD** ex 1 AD 3.2.17. **23 Sqn** dd ex 2 AD 13.3.1917. **2 AD** ex 23 Sqn 4.3.17. **100 Sqn** dd ex 2 AD 7.4.17 (120hp Beardmore) until 6.17. Flown to England 16.6.17.

A792 **199 NTS** and wrecked in crash after entering spinning nose dive following stall on turn 24.12.17 (2Lt HS Sinclair KIFA, engine WD2348).

A793 **AID** allotted to BEF 16.1.17. **RAF** 26.1.17. **ES Orfordness** fitted with 1.59in gun. **2 AD** ex 1 AD 13.3.17. **11 Sqn** dd ex 2 AD 21.3.17. **100 Sqn**. **A Sqn** RNAS dd ex 100 Sqn 16.11.17. **16N Sqn** dd 8.1.18 and wrecked in enemy bombing of aerodrome 21.1.18 (flying time 188hr).

A794 **SARD** tested 19.6.17 (rev indicator dud).

A795 **RAF** 5.2.17. **AID** allotted to BEF 8.2.17. **11 Sqn** and vict 1.5.17 (2Lt WR Exley/Capt JA Le Royer destroyed an Albatros D.III near Biache at 09.30).

A796 **RAF** 7.2.17. **AID** allotted to BEF 8.2.17. **2** AD ex 1 AD 14.2.17, serviceable, 28.2.17. **22 Sqn** ex 2 AD 15.3.17 and vict 8.4.17 (Lt JFA Day/2Lt WM Taylor shared the destruction of an Albatros D.II near Regny at 07.00 with 4883, 4891, 7681, A5454 and A5461). **2 AD** ex 22 Sqn 20.7.17. **1 AD** ex 2 AD 28.7.17. **100 Sqn** dd ex 2 AD 4.8.17 and damaged by ground fire night bombing 24.9.17 (Lt FW Wells/Lt RC Pitman OK). Flown to England 27.9.17.

A797 **RAF** 7.2.17. **AID** allotted to BEF 8.2.17. **2 AD**, ex 1 AD 16.2.17 and serviceable, 28.2.17. **23 Sqn** ex 2 AD 11.3.17. **2 AD** ex 23 Sqn (160hp Beardmore) 8.4.17. **25 Sqn** dd ex 2 AD 13.4.17 (160hp Beardmore) and vict 22.4.17 (Sgt R Mann/Cpl L Emsden sent an Albatros D-type OOC near Noyell Godault) then wrecked in crash 25.4.17. **1 AD** ARS ex 25 Sqn 26.4.17. **22 Sqn** by 12.7.17. **2 AD** ex 22 Sqn 27.7.17.

A798 **AID** allotted to BEF 24.2.17. Allotment cancelled 6.3.17 – wrecked in Channel and deleted.

A799 160hp Beardmore. **AID** allotted to BEF 8.2.17. **SARD** tested 13.2.17. **RAF** 19.2.17. **11 Sqn** and vict 24.3.17 (2Lt RC Savery/AM2 RE Tollerfield sent an Albatros D.III OOC near Croiselles at 09.45), damaged in combat near Douai on recce 25.3.17 (2Lt Morrison/AM Tooley OK). **2 AD** wrecked ex 11 Sqn 29.3.17, with 160hp engine, SOC BEF charge 30.3.17 (NWR, flying time 15hr 43min) and to England in packing case 30.3.17.

A800 Presentation a/c *Zanzibar No 5*. **AID** allotted to BEF 8.2.17. **RAF** 19.2.17. **2 AD** ex 1 AD 13.3.17. **22 Sqn** dd ex 2 AD 18.3.17 and damaged on photo recce 10.5.17 (AM2 AG Whitehouse WIA). **2 AD** ex 22 Sqn 20.7.17. **101 Sqn** dd ex 2 AD 28.7.17. **1 AD** ex 101 Sqn 22.10.17. Fitted with Scarff ring at **4 (Aux) SAG** Marske.

A801 Presentation a/c *Australia No 7, NSW No 6* wef 21.5.17. **AID** allotted to BEF 24.2.17. **1 AD** dd ex Farnborough 28.2.17. **2 AD** ex 1 AD 16.3.17. **18 Sqn** dd ex 2 AD 18.3.17 and vict 1.5.17 (Lt C Parkinson/Lt JV Anglin sent an Albatros D.III OOC near Epinoy at 10.30). **101 Sqn** dd ex 2 AD 27.7.17 and LIA night bombing aerodromes 25.10.17 (2Lt JAM Fleming/2Lt ECS Ringer POW).

A802 Presentation a/c *Malaya No 11* wef 21.5.17. **AID** allotted to BEF 17.2.17. **RAF** 19.2.17. **25 Sqn** dd ex 1 AD 18.3.17 and wrecked in forced landing after engine failure on patrol 25.3.17. **1 AD** ex 25 Sqn 29.3.17. **100 Sqn** and burnt out in crash landing in fog near Poperinghe on night bombing sortie 25.11.17 (2Lt LA Bushe/Lt WV Hyde).

A803 Lympne 27.2.17 allotted to BEF. **11 Sqn** and LIA on recce Vaulx-Morchies 24.3.17 (Lt JR Middleton POW fatally wdd/AM2 HV Gosney KIA. Flying time 1hr 10min, 160hp Beardmore 845/WD7455).

A804 Presentation a/c *Australia No 9*. **AID** allotted to BEF 24.2.17. **RAF** 2.3.17. **2 AD** ex 1 AD 23.3.17. **11 Sqn** dd ex 2 AD 30.3.17 and crashed 10.4.17. **2 AD** wrecked ex 11 Sqn 13.4.17 and for England in packing case (160hp Beardmore, 30.4.17. Deleted 8.5.17.

A805 **AID** allotted to BEF 24.2.17. **2 AD** ex 1 Ad 25.3.17. **23 Sqn** dd ex 2 AD 2.4.17 and LIA in combat near Pronville 5.4.17 (Lt L Elsley KIA/2Lt F Higginbottom fatally WIA – probably shot down by Ltn Schlenker, J.3. 160hp engine, flying time 8hr 54min).

A806 **AID** allotted to BEF 1.3.17. **RAF** 6.3.17. **11 Sqn**. **2 AD** ex 11 Sqn, with 160hp engine, for deletion 10.4.17 (NWR, flying time 18hr) but to England in packing case 10.4.17. **1 AD** tested 20.8.17.

A807 **AID** allotted to BEF 1.3.17. **RAF** 6.3.17. **SARD** tested 8.3.17. **2 AD** ex 1 AD 23.3.17. **22 Sqn** dd ex 2 AD 23.3.17. **2 AD** ex 22 Sqn 3.7.17 and deleted 11.7.17.

A808 **AID** allotted to BEF 1.3.17. **RAF** 9.3.17. **11 Sqn** Izel-le-Hameau and LIA after direct hit by AA on recce 3.2.17 (Lt ETC Brandon/2Lt G Masters KIA. 160hp engine 984/WD7594, flying time 13hr 52min).

A809

A810 **RAF** 16.3.17. **AID** allotted to BEF 21.3.17. **2 AD** ex 1 AD 23.3.17. **11 Sqn** dd ex 2 AD 11.4.17 and wrecked in landing with combat damage on photo sortie 22.4.17 (Capt ER Manning OK/Cpl RE Tollerfield WIA). **2 AD** wrecked ex 11 Sqn 26.4.17, with 160hp engine, and deleted 27.4.17 (NWR, flying time 20hr 6min).

A811 **AID** allotted to BEF 13.3.17. **RAF** 20.3.17. **2 AD** ex 1 AD 23.3.17. **11 Sqn** dd ex 2 AD 31.3.17 and LIA on recce near Arras 6.4.17 (Sgt FH Evans POW/AM2 E Wood KIA – probably by Ltn W Frankl, J.4. 160hp engine 1005/WD7615, flying time 13hr 35min).

A812

A813 **AID** allotted to BEF 13.3.17. **RAF** 21.3.17. **SARD** tested 21.3.17. **25 Sqn** dd ex 1 AD 30.3.17 and vict 5.4.17 (Sgt J Dempsey/Sgt CHN Nunn sent an Albatros D.III OOC near

A790 with 31 Sqn at Risalpur, India, in a hangar with the engine removed.

A826, one of many victims of the dangerous 'spiral dive'.

Vimy Ridge at 12.00) then LIA on bombing raid on Mont St Eloi 8.4.17 (2Lt EVA Bell/2Lt AHK McCallum POW).

A814 Lympne, allotted to BEF 27.2.17 (160hp Beardmore). **2 AD** ex 1 AD 5.6.17. **22 Sqn** dd ex 2 AD 6.6.17 and damaged in crash after engine failed on take-off for test flight 14.6.17. **2 AD** ex 22 Sqn 17.6.17 and deleted.

A815 FE2c. En-route Ascot-Lympne 27.2.17, allotted to BEF. **25 Sqn** dd ex 1 AD 8.4.17 and vict 1.5.17 (2Lt B King/Lt G Hobart-Hampden sent an Albatros D.III OOC near Quiery la Motte at 07.20) then LIA near Rouvroy 1.5.17 (Lt GS French POW wdd/Lt GP Harding POW – shot down in flames at 18.55 S of Bois Bernard, probably by Ltn K Wolff, Jasta 11. Engine 160hp Beardmore 772/WD7132).

A816 En-route Ascot-Lympne 27.2.17, allotted to BEF. **11 Sqn** and damaged in crash after engine failed on take-off for test flight 28.5.17. **2 AD** and deleted for spares 23.6.17.

A817 **2 (Aux) SAG** and wrecked in crash at Dalquhat Farm after stalled on turn after take-off 19.6.17 (2Lt WHC Buntine/Sgt SC Appleton KIFA – a/c burnt out).

A830 and A834, both destroyed in accidents in the UK. Damage to the wing leading edges of A834 suggests some sort of collision.

A818 En-route Ascot-Lympne 27.2.17, allotted to BEF. **2 AD** ex 1 AD 3.4.17. **22 Sqn** dd ex 2 AD 5.4.17. **2 AD** ex 22 Sqn 9.4.17, with 160hp engine, SOC BEF charge 16.4.17 (NWR, flying time 3hr) and to England in packing case ex 2 AD 16.4.17.

A819 **AID** allotted to BEF 26.3.17. **RAF** 29.3.17. **SARD** tested 4.4.17. **11 Sqn** and LIA when wrecked in forced landing in lines after combat on OP 13.4.17 (Lt ET Curling WIA/2Lt J Rothwell OK – engine 1038/WD7648). **2 AD** and deleted 23.4.17.

A820 **AID** allotted to BEF 26.3.17. **RAF** 29.3.17. **11 Sqn** Izel-le-Hameau and LIA after combat 22.4.17 (Lt CA Parker OK/2Lt JEB Hasketh fatally WIA – a/c on fire and destroyed by shellfire. 160hp engine, flying time 32hr 58min).

A821 **9 TS** crashed after hitting hedge on take-off 6.7.17 (crew injured).

A822 Lympne, allotted to BEF 13.4.17 with 120hp Beardmore by 24.4.17. **2 AD** ex 1 AD 8.8.17. **18 Sqn** dd ex 2 AD 10.8.17. **2 AD** ex 1 AD 17.8.17. **100 Sqn** and LIA night bombing Gontrode airship shed after hit by AA near Thielt 30.9.17 (2Lt JF Bushe/2Lt LA Colbert POW – burnt a/c before capture).

A823 **AID** allotted to BEF 13.3.17. **SARD** tested 24.3.17. **2 AD** ex 1 AD 3.4.17. **18 Sqn** dd ex 2 AD 7.4.17 and vict 12.4.17 (2Lt EL Zink/Pte NG Jones sent an Albatros D.III OOC near Cagnicourt at 10.40) then damaged in successful combat 23.4.17 (2Lt EL Zink WIA/2Lt GB Bate OK after sending an Albatros D.III OOC near Baralle at 17.30). **2 AD** ex 18 Sqn 1.7.17. **101 Sqn** and wrecked in forced landing near Steenvoorde on night bombing sortie (2Lt DM Montgomery/2Lt DJ Stewart OK).

A824

A825 **RAF** 21.3.17. **AID** allotted to BEF 24.3.17. **2 AD** ex 1 AD 3.4.17. **22 Sqn** and LIA in combat near Brancourt on bombing sortie 26.4.17 (2Lt GM Hopkins/2Lt JDM Stewart POW – possibly shot down by Ltn Nebel, Jasta 5. 160hp engine, flying time 36hr 24min).

A826 Transferred to RNAS. **EAD** dd by rail 29.3.17 damaged by 3.6.17 and crashed in spiral dive 13.7.17 (TFSL RB Morrison fatally IIFA).

A827 **AID** allotted to BEF 26.3.17. **11 Sqn. 2 AD** wrecked ex 11 Sqn, with 160hp engine, 17.4.17 and deleted 18.4.17 (NWR, flying time 17hr 1min).

A828 Lympne, allotted to BEF 28.2.17 (160hp Beardmore). **22 Sqn** and wrecked in crash following slow take-off for test flight 21.5.17.

A829 **AID** allotted to BEF 1.3.17. **RAF** 21.3.17. **2 AD** wrecked ex 11 Sqn, with 160hp engine, SOC BEF charge 20.4.17 (NWR, flying time 26hr 28min) and to England in packing case ex 2 AD 20.4.17.

A830 **2 (Aux) SAG** dd ex Renfrew 2.3.17 (Major LA Strange, recorded as A803) and crashed from stall on low turn 14.4.17 (crew injured – recorded as A530).

A831 **AID** allotted to BEF 1.3.17. **RAF** 11.3.17. **11 Sqn** and wrecked then shelled in forced landing after combat on OP 13.4.17 (160hp engine, Sgt JA Cunliffe/AM2 WJ Batten WIA – possibly brought down by Ltn M Fr v Richthofen or Ltn K Schaeffer, Jasta 11. Engine 985/WD7595).

A832 **AID** allotted to BEF 7.3.17. **RAF** 14.3.17. **SARD** tested 15.3.17. **11 Sqn. 2 AD** wrecked ex 11 Sqn 8.4.17, with 160hp engine, for deletion 10.4.17 (NWR, flying time 17hr 7min) but to England in packing case 10.4.17.

A833 **9 RS** by 24.4.17 and wrecked in crash, hitting tree on landing 28.4.17 (crew injured).

A834 Photo shows wrecked in crash in UK.

A835 En-route Ascot-Lympne 27.2.17, allotted to BEF. **11 Sqn. 2 AD** ex 11 Sqn 14.6.17. **2 AD** ex 1 AD 17.8.17. **102 Sqn** and crashed landing

FE2b A857, lost on 5 June 1917 to ace Ltn W. Voss of Jasta 5. This was 22 Squadron's last FE2b lost in action before re-equipping with Bristol Fighters.

from engine test after oleo-undercarriage broke during flight. **1 AD** ex 102 Sqn 18.10.17.

A836

A837 En-route Ascot-Lympne 27.2.17, allotted to BEF. **25 Sqn** and LIA in combat near Willerval on escort 25.4.17 (2Lt CV Darnell/AM2 G Pawley KIA – in flames, probably shot down by Ltn K Schaefer, Jasta 11. 160hp engine 1043/WD7653, flying time 28hr 56min).

A838 **RAF** 6.7.17 with engine 760 and fitted with searchlight 8.17. **33 HDS** HQ Flt by 21.8.17 (2Lt GC Peters AZP). **51 HDS** by 30.9.17 wrecked landing too steeply 13.10.17 (2Lt L Rawnsley/2Lt D Deakin, 160hp Beardmore 696/WD7056). 38 HDS.

A839 At Lympne 16.4.17 allotted to BEF with 160hp Beardmore, re-allotted as 120hp machine 24.4.17. Flown to England ex 1 AD 7.6.17. (160hp Beardmore) **2 AD** ex 1 AD 5.8.17 and deleted 9.8.17.

A840 At Lympne 17.4.17 allotted to BEF with 160hp Beardmore, re-allotted as 120hp machine 24.4.17. **20 Sqn** dd ex 1 AD 6.6.17 and on charge until @ 22.7.17. **2 AD** ex 1 AD 5.8.17. **18 Sqn** dd ex 2 AD 9.8.17. **100 Sqn** and wrecked in take-off on move to Ochey 16 (6?).10.17 (2Lt WH Jones/Cpl AA Taylor OK). **1 AD** ex 100 Sqn 8.10.17 (160hp Beardmore 1112/WD6882) and deleted 10.10.17.

A841 At Lympne 19.4.17 allotted to BEF with 120hp Beardmore. **100 Sqn** and LIA when hit by AA night bombing Lille 29.5.17 (Lt EA Worrall WIA – force landed in flames near Steenwerck. Engine 492/WD2465).

A842 At Lympne 24.4.17 allotted to BEF. **25 Sqn** and wrecked in crash near Fiefs on return from bombing sortie 3.5.17 (Lt B King and Trumpeter JG Lawrence KIA).

A843 At Lympne 24.4.17 allotted to BEF. **22 Sqn. 2 AD** ex 22 Sqn 8.7.17. **101 Sqn** dd ex 2 AD 12.7.17. **1 AD** dd ex Lympne 21.10.17. BUT **101 Sqn** damaged in forced landing in dunes at Gravelines on night bombing sortie (Lt SA Hustwitt/Lt A Wardill OK). **1 AD** ex 101 Sqn 21.10.17.

A844 **SARD** allotted to BEF with 160hp Beardmore 25.4.17. **11 Sqn. 2 AD** ex 11 Sqn 9.6.17. **18 Sqn** ex 2 AD 14.7.17. **1 AD** tested 25.8.17. **2 AD** ex 1 AD 25.8.17. **100 Sqn** and wrecked in crash after take-off on practice flight 5.4.18 (2Lt LE Collins/2Lt N Ford KIFA.) Flying time 139hr 5min).

A845 **SARD** allotted to BEF with 160hp Beardmore 25.4.17 and tested 1.6.17. **100 Sqn** and wrecked hitting house after engine failed on night bombing sortie 5.7.17 (2Lt CR

Richardson/2Lt RJ Housden injured). **2 AD** ex 100 Sqn 8.7.17 and deleted 9.7.17.

A846 At Lympne 30.4.17 allotted to BEF with 160hp Beardmore. **20 Sqn** by 13.6.17 and crashed from stall on landing from practice flight 25.7.17.

A847 **SARD** allotted to BEF with 160hp Beardmore 18.4.17. **2 AD** ex 1 AD 23.4.17. **22 Sqn** dd ex 2 AD 24.4.17 and damaged when hit another machine when taxiing out for photo sortie 3.5.17. **101 Sqn** dd ex 2 AD 27.7.17.

A848 **SARD** allotted to BEF with 160hp Beardmore 18.4.17 and tested 21.4.17. **2 AD** ex 1 AD 24.4.17. **22 Sqn** dd ex 2 AD 24.4.17. **2 AD** ex 22 Sqn 27.7.17 and deleted 6.8.17.

A849 **SARD** allotted to BEF with 160hp Beardmore 25.4.17 and tested twice 12.5.17 (dud engine). **18 Sqn. 2 AD** ex 18 Sqn 1.7.17. **101 Sqn** dd ex 2 AD 6.7.17 and recorded as old machine 25.9.17 (flying time 85hr 51min). **1 AD** ex 101 Sqn, wrecked and un-serviceable, 30.9.17 (160hp Beardmore 1258/WD20167) and deleted 3.10.17.

A850 **SARD** allotted to BEF with 160hp Beardmore 25.4.17 and tested 11.5.17. **2 AD** ex 1 AD 3.6.17. **18 Sqn** dd ex 2 AD 4.6.17 and force landed after propeller burst on patrol 26.6.17. **2 AD** ex 18 Sqn 27.6.17 and deleted 28.6.17.

A851 **AID** allotted to BEF 12.4.17 (160hp Beardmore). **2 AD** ex 1 AD 21.4.17. **18 Sqn** dd ex 2 AD 21.4.17 and vict 30.4.17 (2Lt GA Critchley/2Lt OJ Partington sent an Albatros D.III OOC near Baralle at 09.30) then crashed in forced landing after engine failed on patrol 12.7.17. **2 AD** ex 18 Sqn 15.7.17 and deleted 16.7.17.

A852 **AID** allotted to BEF 12.4.17 (160hp Beardmore). **SARD** tested 20.4.17. **100 Sqn** and LIA night bombing Trier barracks and railway station 24.1.18 on the longest raid attempted by an FE2b unit (Lt LG Taylor/Lt FE LeFevre MC POW – hit by AA and hit balloon cable, flying time 182hr).

A853 **AID** allotted to BEF 12.4.17 (160hp Beardmore). **SARD** tested 26.4.17 and 27.4.17. **1 AD** dd ex Farnborough 27.4.17. **100 Sqn** and wrecked in crash after stall on landing from gunnery practice 12.6.17 (2Lt J Harper IIFA/Lt WE Lockhart KIFA).

A854 **AID** allotted to BEF 12.4.17. **RAF** 17.4.17 (160hp Beardmore 896/WD7506). **2 AD** ex 1 AD 22.4.17. **11 Sqn** dd ex 2 AD 24.4.17. **2 AD** ex 11 Sqn 14.6.17 and deleted 16.7.17.

A855 **AID** allotted to BEF 18.4.17. **RAF** 18.4.17 (160hp Beardmore 1074/WD7684). **2 AD** ex 1 AD 24.4.17. **22 Sqn** dd ex 2 AD 24.4.17 and vict 3.5.17 (2Lt EAH Ward/2Lt GG Bell

sent an Albatros D.III OOC at 13.30). **1 AD** tested 9.7.17 and 10.7.17. **101 Sqn** listed as old machine 29.9.17 (139hr). **1 AD** ex 101 Sqn 30.9.17 (160hp Beardmore 923/WD7533) and tested 1.10.17. Flown to England 2.10.17. **51 HDS** B Flt dd ex 8 AAP via Detling 18.10.17 (Lt TH Gladstone/Lt Hockey).

A856 Allotted to BEF 30.4.17. **2 AD** ex 1 AD 29.4.17. **22 Sqn** dd ex 2 AD 30.4.17 (160hp Beardmore) until @ 20.5.17. **1 AD** tested 9.7.17 (160hp Beardmore). **2 AD** ex 1 AD 10.7.17. **101 Sqn** dd ex 2 AD 15.7.17 and LIA night bombing Ledeghem 21.9.17 (2Lt AI Orr-Ewing/Capt E Marshall POW. Engine 855/WD7185).

A857 **RAF** 26.4.17 (160hp Beardmore 766/WD7126). Allotted to BEF 30.4.1917. **1 AD** dd ex Farnborough 29.4.17. **2 AD** ex 1 AD 29.4.17. **22 Sqn** as a/c *B-1* dd ex 2 AD 30.4.17 (160hp Beardmore) and LIA in combat with 6 EA on recce near Lesdain 5.6.17 (Capt FP Don/2Lt H Harris POW wdd – possibly shot down by Ltn W Voss, Jasta 5. Engine 1972/WD7682).

A858 **AID** allotted to BEF 24.7.17. **AAP** Lympne dd ex SARD 29.7.17. **2 AD** ex 1 AD 8.8.17. **18 Sqn** dd ex 2 AD 10.8.17. **100 Sqn** damaged crashing into soft ground on route for Ochey 11.10.17. **2 AD** dd ex 100 Sqn 11.10.17.

A859 **28 Sqn. 17 Wing ARS** Beaulieu ex 28 Sqn 18.7.17.

A860 **AID** allotted to BEF 1.5.17. **SARD** tested 1.5.17. **1 AD** dd ex 2.5.17. **2 AD** ex 1 AD 20.8.17. **102 Sqn** dd ex 2 AD 2.10.17. **1 AD** ex 102 Sqn 9.10.17 (160hp Beardmore 643/WD7003). Flown to England 24.10.17. **33 HDS** C Flt by 6.2.18. **38 Sqn** by 11.6.18, force-landed on night bombing sortie 18.6.18 and crashed in fog on night bombing sortie 15.10.18 (crew OK, engine 178, Capt FG Haney had made 66 successive flights in this machine 27.6.18 to 25.8.18 and a further 18 successive flights 1.10.18 to 16.10.18). **4 ASD** ex 38 Sqn 18.10.18. Flown to England 24.10.18.

A861 **AID** allotted to BEF 9.5.17. **SARD** tested 10.5.17. **22 Sqn** by 6.17 and wrecked in spin from 400ft after engine failed on take-off for recce 14.7.17 (2Lt GW Foreman/2Lt AA Creasey KIFA). **2 AD** ex 22 Sqn 15.7.17 and deleted 16.7.17.

A862 **199 NTS** by 15.1.18 until @ 4.18.

A863 Allotted to BEF 9.5.17. **1 AD** dd ex Farnborough 7.5.17. **18 Sqn** and shelled after forced landing following combat near Agny on patrol 14.7.17 (2Lt W Birch/2Lt D Logan WIA – possibly by Ltn J Schmidt, J.3). **2**

FE2b A862. Prior to its 199 NTS service, it may have been at Turnberry, where station machines were marked with large white numerals. Similar markings appear on FE2b 4988, p127.

AD ex 18 Sqn 17.7.17 and deleted 18.7.17.

A864 AID allotted to BEF 9.5.1917 (160hp Beardmore). **100 Sqn** by 13.8.17, converted to single-seater by 29.11.17 (recorded by Lt ET Carpenter) and wrecked and burnt out in forced landing after engine over-heated and seized on night bombing sortie 17.5.18. (flying time 162hr 50min) **2 ASD** ex 6 AP 18.6.18 and deleted that day (recorded as 160hr 6min flying time).

A865 AID allotted to BEF 5.6.1917 (160hp Beardmore). **100 Sqn**, reported wrecked 21.1.18 (flying time 133hr) but damaged in crash near Lixières after engine failed on night bombing sortie 31.1.18 (Capt WG Albu/Cpl R Lindsay OK) and wrecked 26.2.18 when bomb exploded while being loaded – 5 killed).

A866 AID allotted to BEF 5.6.1917 (160hp Beardmore). Lympne AAP by 23.6.17. **1 AD** tested 5.7.17 and 20.7.17. **2 AD** ex 1 AD 22.7.17. **101 Sqn** dd ex 2 AD 28.7.17 and force-landed 28.9.17. **100 Sqn** dd ex 101 Sqn 3.10.17 wrecked in forced landing near Verdun on night bombing sortie 24.10.17 (2Lt HC Chambers/Lt ER Howard injured).

A867 AID allotted to BEF 5.6.1917 (160hp Beardmore). **100 Sqn** by 4.7.17 and burnt out after catching fire on take-off 23.1.18 (Capt WG Albu OK, flying time 117hr).

A868

A869 33 HDS C Flt by 21.8.17 (Capt G Mackrell AZP).

A870

A871 199 DS by 20.8.17.

A872 19 TS Hounslow by 18.6.17.

A873 Yatesbury 1917, burnt (59 TS?).

A874 36 HDS B Flt by 30.8.17 (Lt JH Matthews) until @ 10.9.17.

A875 76 HDS by 7.17.

A876 Halton Camp as GI machine.

A877

A1932 – A1966: 35 RAF FE2d (250hp Rolls-Royce Mks.I, II or III or 275hp Rolls-Royce Eagle III) built by the Royal Aircraft factory, Farnborough under Contract 87/A/530 and War Office authority dated 12.7.16.

A1932 Allotted to BEF 11.9.16. **RAF** 22.9.16; engine 4/250/37, airscrew 13520/T28020. **SAD** allotted to BEF 5.10.16. **46 RS** by 30.3.17.

A1933 Allotted to BEF 11.9.16. **RAF** 22.9.16; engine 3/250/25, airscrew 13539/T28020. **SAD** allotted to BEF, re-allotted to 57 Sqn 6.10.16 and damaged in forced landing near Wakefield on delivery flight 17.10.16 (Lt Napier/Lt RA Grosvenor OK). **57 Sqn** dd ex 1 AD 25.1.17 and burnt out after hitting wires during forced-landing 5.3.17 (flying time 22hr 55min). **2 AD** ex 57 Sqn 10.3.17 and deleted 12.3.17.

A1934 Allotted to BEF 11.9.16. **RAF** 25.9.16; engine No.97, airscrew 13537/T28020. **1 AD** by 1.10.16. **20 Sqn** dd ex 1 AD 15.11.16 and damaged in forced-landing on patrol 17.3.17 (flying time 74hr 54min).

A1935 RAF 25.9.16; engine 1/250/11, airscrew 13572/T28020. Allotted to BEF 29.9.16. **1 AD** by 1.10.16. **20 Sqn** dd ex 1 AD 16.11.16 and damaged when propeller disintegrated 1.3.17 then victs 17.3.17 (Capt J Blackwood/Sgt S Smith sent an Albatros D.III OOC

Blaze away: FE2b A873 at Yatesbury, a frightening but unexplained spectacle.

near Becelaere at 12.15), 3.5.17 (2Lt FF Babbage/AM2 B Aldred sent an Albatros D.III OOC near Poelcapelle at 17.10), 5.5.17 (2Lt FF Babbage/AM2 B Aldred captured an Albatros C-type near Hollebeke at 17.45 – Uffz F Stegmann & Vzfw J Wenzl, Sch.2) and 7.5.17 (2Lt FF Babbage/AM2 B Aldred destroyed an Albatros D.III near Courtrai at 11.00) then damaged in combat on bombing sortie 12.5.17 (2Lt FF Babbage/Sgt B Aldred OK).

A1936 RAF 27.9.16; engine 1/250/71, airscrew 13551/T28020. **46 RS** dd ex Farnborough, via Grantham, 18-19.10.16 (2Lt TH Gladstone), allotted to Training Brigade but re-allotted to BEF 16.7.17. En-route Norwich – SAD, allotment to BEF cancelled 23.7.17 and on charge E1 Repair Section.

A1937 RAF 2.10.16; engine No.79, airscrew 13528/T28020. **46 RS** by 17.11.16 and wrecked in crash near Leeds 10.1.17 (Capt R Burdon/Lt HF Turner KIFA – due to bad flying).

A1938 RAF 5.10.16; engine 1/250/69, airscrew 13532/T28020. **46 RS** by 13.11.16 and crashed in forced landing after engine failure 14.2.17 (crew injured).

A1939 RAF 6.10.16; engine 3/250/3, airscrew 13535/T28020. **SAD** allotted to BEF 19.2.17. Lympne 6.3.17 with BEF allotment cancelled and on charge DAE2a Repair Section.

A1940 RAF 7.10.16; engine No.23, airscrew 13529/T28020. **57 Sqn** by 7.1.17 and damaged in forced-landing on test flight 24.2.17 (Lt RA Grosvenor/2Lt WW Glenn OK. Flying time 40hr 45min). **2 AD** wrecked ex 57 Sqn 28.2.17 and deleted 2.3.17.

A1941 RAF 9.10.16; engine No.69, airscrew 13555/T28020. **19 RS** crashed 1.1.17 (crew injured, one named Knox). **SAG** and wrecked in crash from stall after engine failure 2.1.17 (Lt AJ McWha/Sgt G Wilkes KIFA – casualty card gives unit as Southern Aircraft Depot Lympne – possibly crashed at Hythe on delivery flight?).

A1942 RAF 12.10.16; engine 3/250/65, airscrew 13561/T28020. At Northolt, allotted to BEF 10.1.17. **20 Sqn** dd ex 1 AD 11.2.17 and LIA on bombing sortie 5.5.17 (2Lt LG Bacon POW wdd/AM2 G Worthing KIA – probably shot down by OffSt W Göttsch, Jasta 8. Engine 1/275/27/WD13891).

A1943 RAF 16.10.16; engine 3/250/63, airscrew 13582/T28020. At Northolt, allotted to BEF 10.1.17. **20 Sqn** dd ex 1 AD 11.2.17.

A1944 RAF 18.10.16; engine 3/250/59, airscrew 13583/T28020. **57 Sqn** by 11.16 and LIA in combat with 6 EA near Lens on patrol 2.4.17 (Lt HP Sworder/2Lt AH Margolouth KIA – probably by Vzfw S Festner, Jasta 11. Flying time 98hr 22min, engine 3/250/59/WD10054).

A1945 RAF 3.11.16; engine 3/250/55, airscrew 13588/T28020. **46 RS** and wrecked in crash into woodland during snowstorm 13.1.17 (2Lt TH French KIFA).

A1946 RAF 22.10.16; engine 3/250/81, airscrew 13574/T28020. **SAD** allotted to BEF for 57 Sqn 12.12.16. Allotted to 57 Sqn 22.12.16. At Northolt, allotted to BEF 10.1.17. **SAD** under repair 27.1.17 with BEF allotment cancelled.

A1947 RAF 26.10.16; engine 3/250/85, airscrew 13536/T28020.

A1948 RAF 26.10.16; engine 3/250/89, airscrew 13584/T28020. **57 Sqn** by 15.11.16 and LIA in combat near Bapaume on OP 6.3.17 (2Lt FE Hills/2Lt AG Ryall POW – probably shot down by Ltn H Gontermann, Jasta 5. Engine RR3/250/89 WD10056).

A1949 RAF 8.11.16; engine 3/250/91, airscrew 13620/T28020. **57 Sqn** and wrecked in crash after engine failure 27.11.16 (Lt EH Hall KIFA).

A1950 Allotted to BEF 8.11.16. **RAF** 10.11.16;

engine 3/250/29, airscrew 13614/T28020. **1 AD** ex England 21.11.16. **57 Sqn** dd ex 1 AD 5.1.17 and LIA on OP 13.4.17 (2Lt GW Gillespie/Pte RE Sibley KIA – possibly shot down by Ltn K Schneider, J.5, or Ltn H Klein, J.4. Engine 3/250/29/WD8148).

A1951 Allotted to BEF 9.11.16. **RAF** 10.11.16; engine 4/250/3, airscrew 13536/T28020. **1 AD** ex England 21.11.16. **20 Sqn** dd ex 1 AD 4.1.17 and LIA in combat near Lille on recce 1.2.17 (2Lt WA Reeves POW wdd/2Lt FH Bronskill POW – probably shot down by OffSt W Göttsch, Jasta 28). Engine 1/250/3 WD10062, flying time 10hr 59min.

A1952 **RAF** 17.11.16; engine No.13, airscrew 13573/T28020. **57 Sqn** by 7.1.17 and wrecked in crash following combat with 6 EA near Cambrai on OP 6.4.17 (Capt AC Wright WIA/Pte RET Sibley OK. Flying time 49hr 24min, engine 4/250/71/WD10085).

A1953 **RAF** 19.11.16; engine 4/250/21, airscrew 13594/T28020. **57 Sqn** by 7.1.17 and LIA in combat near Bapaume 6.3.17 (Capt WSR Bloomfield/2Lt VO Lonsdale POW – probably shot down by Ltn A Schulte, Jasta 12. Flying time 38hr 25min).

A1954 Allotted to BEF for 57 Sqn 22.11.16. **RAF** 28.11.16; engine 4/250/25, airscrew 13546/T28020. **57 Sqn** dd ex 1 AD 5.1.17 and vict 24.3.17 (2Lt HR Harker/2Lt VD Fernauld sent an Albatros D.II OOC near Lens at 11.45) then damaged in forced-landing on practice flight with engine vibrating badly 27.4.17. **2 AD**, wrecked ex 57 Sqn, 29.4.17.

A1955 **RAF** 21.11.16; engine 3/250/99, airscrew 13562/T28020. **57 Sqn** as a/c **B** by 7.1.17 and severely damaged in combat near Arras 8.4.17 (Lt AD Pryor/AM2 C Goffe WIA). **2 AD** wrecked ex 57 Sqn 15.4.17 and for reconstruction 30.4.17.

A1956 **RAF** 21.11.16; engine 4/250/103, airscrew 13596/T28020. **SAD** allotted to BEF 18.12.16. **20 Sqn** and damaged by AA on bombing sortie 29.4.17 (2Lt GC Heseltine/2Lt FJ Kydd OK) then victs in combat 27.7.17 (Lt HGET Luchford/Lt MW Waddington sent 1 Albatros D.V down in flames and another OOC near Menin 19.45-20.40) and 28.7.17 (2Lt RM Makepeace/Pte SE Pilbrow sent an Albatros D.III OOC near Kezelbars at 09.20) then LIA in combat near Verbrandenmolen 14.45 on 31.7.17 (Lt CH Beldam POW/2Lt WH Watt POW wdd – probably shot down by Vzfw K Wusthoff, Jasta 4). Engine RR2/275/5 WD13954.

A1957 **RAF** 28.11.16; engine 1/250/81, airscrew 13615/T28020. **SAD** allotted to BEF for 57 Sqn 3.1.17. **57 Sqn** dd ex 1 AD 7.1.17, damaged in combat 8.4.17 (Lt RA Grosvenor OK/2Lt WW Glenn WIA) and vict 29.4.17 (Lt JH Ryan/2Lt B Soutten sent an Albatros D.III OOC near Noyelles at 10.30) then damaged in crash following combat near Chateau du Sart on bombing sortie 7.6.17 (2Lt GH Pollard POW fatally wdd/2Lt FS Ferriman KIA – possibly by Uffz Heiligers, J.30 near Kuelberg. Engine 3/250/99/WD10066).

A1958 **RAF** 29.11.16; engine No.83, airscrew 13624/T28020. **AID** allotted to BEF for 57 Sqn 4.12.16. **SAD** allotted to 57 Sqn 9.12.16. **57 Sqn** as a/c **B-2** by 7.1.17 and vict 29.4.17 (2Lt AW Erlebach and observer sent an Albatros D.III OOC near Noyelles at 10.20) then wrecked in crash near St Ouen following collision on formation practice 1.5.17 (2Lt W Woodward/Pte A Richards injured).

A1959 **RAF** 30.11.16; engine 4/250/71, airscrew 13627/T28020. **AID** allotted to BEF for 57 Sqn 7.12.16. **1 AD** ex England 30.12.16. **57 Sqn** dd ex 1 AD 5.1.17 and in successful combat near Arras 2.4.17 (2Lt EEE Pope/Lt AW Nasmyth destroyed 1 Albatros D.III in flames near Arras at 09.45 and sent another OOC) then LIA in combat with 6 EA near

FE2d A1959, one of four combat losses suffered by 57 Sqn on 6 April 1917 during a morning offensive patrol. Alongside Hptm Hünerbein, its victor Ltn H. Gontermann of Jasta 5 stands in the pilot's cockpit.

Cambrai on OP 6.4.17 (Lt TF Burrill POW/Pte F Smith POW wdd – probably shot down by Ltn H Gontermann, Jasta 5. Flying time 60hr 50min, engine 4/250/145/WD12117).

A1960 **RAF** 9.12.16; engine No.129, airscrew 13557/T28020. **AID** allotted to BEF for 57 Sqn 15.12.16. **20 Sqn** dd ex 1 AD 9.1.17 and vict 2.2.17 (Capt HE Hartney/2Lt HR Wilkinson destroyed a Halberstadt D.II near Lille at 14.15) then wrecked in crash after successful combat on photo sortie 14.2.17 (Capt HE Hartney/2Lt WT Jordan IIA had sent an Albatros D.III down in flames and destroyed another, both near Passchendaele at 17.00 – possibly shot down by Untoff Flemmig, Jasta 18, after sending 2 Albatros D.II OOC. Flying time 84hr 33min). **1 AD** and deleted 19.2.17.

A1961 **RAF** 9.12.16; engine 4/250/73, airscrew 13641/T28020. **AID** allotted to BEF for 57 Sqn 15.12.16. **1 AD** dd ex Farnborough 26.2.17. **20 Sqn** and victs 5.4.17 (Capt GJ Mahony-Jones/Capt RM Knowles sent an Albatros D.II OOC near Courtrai at 11.35 and another OOC near Houthulst at 11.40) then LIA in combat near Ploegsteert Wood on bombing sortie 18.15 on 7.4.17 (Capt GJ Mahony-Jones/2Lt WB Moyes KIA – a/c fell in flames, possibly shot down by Ltn W v Bülow, Jasta 18. Flying time 46hr 16min, engine 4/250/73/WD12084).

A1962 **RAF** 15.12.16; engine 4/250/99, airscrew 13564/T28020. **AID** allotted to BEF 23.12.16. **20 Sqn** dd ex 1 AD 7.1.17. **1 AD** and deleted 17.4.17 (NWR, flying time 67hr 40min).

A1963 **RAF** 21.12.16; engine No.77, airscrew 13622/T28020. Allotted to BEF for 57 Sqn 1.1.17. **57 Sqn** dd ex 1 AD 15.1.17 and wrecked in crash after combat near Arras on patrol 6.3.17 (Lt WFW Hills/2Lt W Sutton-Gardner KIA – probably by Obltn H Kummetz, Jasta 1. Engine 4/250/55/WD12114). Intended for deletion with 7hr 29min flying time but re-taken on charge for reconstruction. **2 AD** ex 57 Sqn 10.3.17, being rebuilt 30.4.17. **1 AD** ex 2 AD 2.7.17. **20 Sqn** and overturned in crash into shell-hole after combat near Zandvoorde 11.7.17 (2Lt RM Makepeace/2Lt WD Kennard OK).

A1964 **RAF** 30.12.16; engine 4/250/63, airscrew 13636/T28020. **AID** allotted to BEF 4.1.17. Folkestone 7.1.17 in forced landing on delivery flight Farnborough – St-Omer. **1 AD** ex Folkestone 15.1.17. **57 Sqn** and damaged in forced landing 3.4.17 after cartridge cases missed bag and hit propeller on practice flight (2Lt FAW Handley/2Lt E Percival). **2 AD** ex 57 Sqn 5.4.17 deleted 27.4.17 (NWR, flying time 31hr 10min). BUT **8 TDS** as FE2b and wrecked in crash from spinning nose dive following steep turn at 600ft 5.7.18 (Lt JG Moore KIFA).

FE2d A1942 of 20 Sqn, lost on a bombing raid on 5 May 1917 to the guns of OffSt W. Göttsch of Jasta 8.

A1965 **RAF** 28.12.16; engine 4/250/69, airscrew 13618/T28020. AID Farnborough allotted to BEF 4.1.17. **20 Sqn** dd ex 1 AD 8.2.17 and vict but damaged by AA on OP 8.6.17, controls shot up but landed on aerodrome (2Lt W Durrand/Sgt EH Sayers OK – destroyed an Albatros D.III in flames near Comines at 07.45).

A1966 **RAF** 1.1.17; engine 4/250/139, airscrew 13644/T28020. **SAD** allotted to BEF 5.1.17. **57 Sqn** dd ex 1 AD 20.1.17 and wrecked in forced landing after combat near Douai

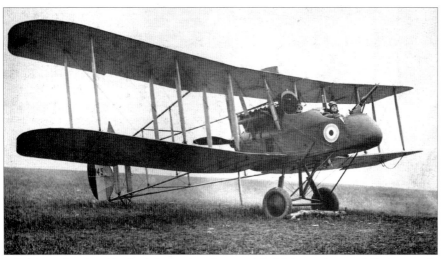

FE2d A5145 after a forced landing during ferrying to France, with Sgt E.E. Jones at the controls. The improvised wheel chocks are interesting.

FE2d A5149 of 20 Sqn was lost to Ltn W. von Bülow of Jasta 18 on 7 May 1917. Ltn P. Strähle of Jasta 57 subsequently used it extensively for filming from the air.

The staining on the tail assembly of A5150 suggests it may have been hit in the engine.

30.4.17 (Lt CS Morice/Lt F Leathey OK. Engine 2/275/47 WD13917).

A5143 – A5152: 10 RAF FE2d (250hp Rolls-Royce Mks.I, II or III or 275hp Rolls-Royce Eagle V) ordered under War Office authority, Extract 113 dated 20.10.16 and built by the Royal Aircraft Factory, Farnborough.

A5143 **RAF** 9.1.17; engine 4/250/35, airscrew 13640/T28020. Allotted to BEF 19.1.17. **20 Sqn** dd ex 1 AD 9.2.17. and vict 26.4.17 (Lt DY Hay/AM2 TE Allum sent an Albatros D.III

OOC near Moorslede at 19.00) then wrecked in forced landing at Eykhoek after hit by AA on bombing sortie 30.4.17; controls shot up, overturned and caught fire (Lt DY Hay/AM2 EH Sayers IIA. Flying time 42hr 45min).

A5144 **RAF** 22.1.17; engine 4/250/111, airscrew 13654/T28020. Allotted to BEF 30.1.17. **20 Sqn** dd ex 1 AD 15.2.17 and vict 7.4.17 (Lt NL Robertson/2Lt LG Fauvel destroyed an Albatros D.III near Tourcoing at 18.30) then LIA in combat near Ypres on escort 24.4.17 (Lt NL Robertson/Capt RM Knowles MC WIA – a/c fell in flames, probably shot down by Ltn W v Bülow, Jasta 18. Flying time 38hr 5min).

A5145 **RAF** 22.1.17; engine 4/250/95, airscrew 13081/T28020. **AID** allotted to BEF 14.2.17. **20 Sqn** and damaged landing from patrol 24.3.17. **1 AD** and deleted 17.4.17 (NWR, flying time 8hr 47min).

A5146 **RAF** 24.1.17; engine 12117/4/250/145, airscrew 13630/T28020. **SAD** allotted to BEF 5.2.17. **57 Sqn** and damaged in landing collision with A5148 after OP 24.3.17 (flying time 11hr 17min). **2 AD** ex 57 Sqn 23.3.17, for reconstruction, 30.4.17.

A5147 **RAF** 24.1.17; engine 4/250/147, airscrew 13643/T28020. Allotted to BEF 5.2.17. **20 Sqn** (engine RR3/250/97 WD8192) damaged in successful combat 5.5.17 (2Lt GC Heseltine/2Lt FJ Kydd OK – forced to land near Bailleul, possibly brought down by Ltn E Weissner, J.18, or Vzfw Flemmig, J.18, after sending an Albatros D.III OOC near Houthem at 17.30) then further victs 9.8.17 (Capt AN Solly/Lt CA Hoy sent an Albatros D.III OOC near Polygon Wood at 18.15) and 10.8.17 (Capt AN Solly/2Lt JJ Cawley sent an EA C-type down in flames at 08.45 near Becelaere and shared sending an Albatros D.V OOC near Wervicq with A6456 and B1890 at 09.00 then Capt AN Solly/Lt CA Hoy sent another OOC over Polygon Wood at 18.15).

A5148 **RAF** 26.1.17; engine 4/250/89, airscrew 13655/T28020. **SAD** allotted to BEF 5.2.17. **1 AD** dd ex Farnborough 26.2.17. **57 Sqn** and damaged in landing collision with A5146 after OP 24.3.17. **2 AD** ex 57 Sqn 23.3.17, for reconstruction 30.4.17, but deleted 5.7.17.

A5149 **RAF** 31.1.17; engine 4/250/105, airscrew 13652/T28020. **SAD** allotted to BEF 12.2.17. **20 Sqn** and vict 26.4.17 (2Lt HL Satchell/AM2 M Todd sent an Albatros D.III OOC near Roulers at 19.15) then LIA on bombing sortie 7.5.17 (Lt AW Martin/Pte WC Blake POW – possibly shot down by Ltn v Bulow Jasta 18; a/c landed on J.18 aerodrome, was repaired, re-marked and flown by Germans. Possible alternative claim by OffSt M Muller, J.28). Engine RR4/250/105 WD12095.

A5150 **RAF** 9.2.17; engine 1/250/0/39, airscrew 13546/T28020. RAF allotted to BEF 15.2.17. **1 AD** dd ex Farnborough 4.12.16. **2 AD** ex 1 AD 4.3.17. **57 Sqn** dd ex 2 AD 19.3.17 and LIA on OP 13.4.17 (Capt LS Platt/2Lt T Margerison KIA – probably shot down by Ltn H Gontermann, Jasta 5. Engine 4/250/89/ WD12113).

A5151 **RAF** 10.2.17; engine 13880/1/275/79, airscrew 13662/T28020. RAF allotted to BEF 15.2.17. **57 Sqn** by 6.3.17 and LIA in combat with 6 EA near Lens on patrol 2.4.17 (Capt H Tomlinson MC POW fatally wdd/Lt NC Denison POW wdd – probably shot down by Ltn Krefft, Jasta 11. Flying time 25hr 12min, engine 4/89/WD13/250880).

A5152 **RAF** 17.2.17; engine 1/250/35, airscrew 13599/T28020. **SAD** allotted to BEF 27.2.17. **57 Sqn** by 3.17. **25 Sqn** and vict near Drocourt 17.3.17 (2Lt JLB Weir shot down an EA scout) and on charge until @ 1.6.17. **20 Sqn** and LIA when wrecked in crash after hit by AA near Dickebusch on patrol

15.8.17 (2Lt CH Cameron OK/Pte SE Pilbrow KIA. Engine RR2/275/35 WD13926).

A5338 – A5437: Cancelled order for 100 RAF FE2b (120hp Beardmore).

A5438 – A5487: 50 RAF FE2b (120/160hp Beardmore) built by Boulton & Paul, Norwich under Contract 87/A/658.

A5438 Presentation a/c *Zanzibar No 9*. At Norwich allotted to BEF (160hp Beardmore) 20.10.16. **1 AD** ex England 6.11.16. **2 AD** ex 1 AD 9.11.16. **23 Sqn** dd ex 2 AD 9.11.16. **2 AD** ex 23 Sqn 11.3.17 with 160hp engine, SOC BEF charge 9.4.17 (NWR, flying time 73hr 37min) and to England in packing case 9.4.17.

A5439 Presentation a/c *Zanzibar No 10*. At Norwich allotted to BEF (160hp Beardmore) 20.10.16. **1 AD** ex England 10.11.16. **25 Sqn** dd ex 1 AD 12.11.16 and vict 4.3.17 (Lt AE Boultbee/Sgt JH Brown shared the destruction of an LVG C-type near Courrières 11.15 with 7025, 7693 and A780) then LIA in combat near Annoeulin on photo escort 17.3.17 (Lt AE Boultbee/AM2 F King KIA – shot down by Ltn M Fr v Richthofen, Jasta 11. 160hp engine 854/WD7464, Lewis guns A19633 & A19901, flying time 74hr 42min).

A5440 Presentation a/c *Zanzibar No 11*. At Norwich allotted to BEF (160hp Beardmore) 20.10.16. **SARD** under repair BEF allotment cancelled 19.12.16, repaired and allotted to BEF 22.1.17 and tested 6.2.17 (throttle jammed) and 9.2.17 (OK). **ES Orfordness**? **2 AD** ex 1 AD 18.2.17 and serviceable, 28.2.17. **23 Sqn** ex 2 AD 11.3.17. **18 Sqn** and wrecked in crash after losing speed on test flight 29.6.17. **2 AD** ex 18 Sqn 1.7.17 and deleted 2.7.17.

A5441 Presentation a/c *Zanzibar No 12*. At Norwich allotted to BEF (160hp Beardmore) 20.10.16. **1 AD** ex England 8.11.16. **2 AD** ex 1 AD 9.11.16. **22 Sqn** dd ex 2 AD 27.12.16 (2Lt TH Gladstone) destroyed in forced landing after combat on patrol 4.3.17 (2Lt LW Beal/AM2 AG Davin OK – possibly brought down by Ltn R Theiller, Jasta 5. Engine 160hp 829/WD7189, flying time 52hr 16min).

A5442 Presentation a/c *Malaya No 26*. At Norwich allotted to BEF (160hp Beardmore) 1.11.16. **1 AD** ex England 9.11.16. **2 AD** ex 1 AD 10.11.16. **11 Sqn** dd ex 2 AD 14.11.16 and vict 25.1.17 (Capt JB Quested/2Lt HJH Dicksee sent an EA scout OOC near Beaurains at 14.25) then wrecked in forced landing after vict on recce 24.3.17 (Capt CN Lowe IIA/2Lt G Masters OK – had sent an Albatros D.III OOC near Fontaine-les-Croisilles at 09.30. Possibly brought down by UntOff R Yorke, J.12, or Ltn A Schulte, J.12. Flying time 79hr 39min, engine 906/7516). **2 AD** and deleted 6.4.17.

A5443 Presentation a/c *Malaya No 27*. At Norwich allotted to BEF (160hp Beardmore) 1.11.16. **1 AD** ex England 13.11.16. **2 AD** ex 1 AD 16.11.16. **23 Sqn** dd ex 2 AD 19.11.16 and LIA in combat near Bapaume on photo escort 11.3.17 (2Lt A Holden/AM2 AG Walker POW – possibly by Ltn F Hengst & Ltn Criege, SS3). Deleted on unit 12.3.17 (flying time 87hr 30min, 160hp engine 697/WD7087).

A5444 Presentation a/c *Malaya No 28, The Singapore*. At Norwich allotted to BEF (160hp Beardmore) 1.11.16. **1 AD** ex England 15.11.16. **2 AD** ex 1 AD 16.11.16. **23 Sqn** dd ex 2 AD 20.11.16. **2 AD** ex 23 Sqn 26.12.16. **23 Sqn**. **2 AD** ex 23 Sqn 26.2.17 and serviceable and trued up, 28.2.17. **100 Sqn** dd ex 2 AD 31.3.17 (120hp Beardmore) and wrecked in storm 19/20.9.17. **2 AD** ex 100 Sqn and deleted 29.9.17. BUT flown to England 16.6.17 (120hp Beardmore).

A5445 Presentation a/c *Malaya No 20*. At Norwich

FE2d A5151 of 57 Sqn was lost on 2 April 1917. A German soldier helps the wounded observer, Lt N.C. Denison; the pilot, Capt H. Tomlinson MC, did not survive.

allotted to BEF (160hp Beardmore) 1.11.16. **1 AD** ex England 26.11.16. **18 Sqn** dd ex 1 AD 24.12.16 and vict 15.2.17 (2Lt VH Huston/2Lt PS Taylor destroyed an EA C type near Grevillers at 10.15) then damaged in crash taking off from forced landing 5.4.17 (160hp engine, flying time 60hr 45min). **2 AD** ex 18 Sqn 9.4.17 and to England in packing case 18.4.17.

A5446 Presentation a/c *Malaya No 11*. At Norwich allotted to BEF (160hp Beardmore) 1.11.16. **1 AD** ex England 17.11.16. **18 Sqn** dd ex 1 AD 27.11.16 and LIA near Le Transloy on OP 20.12.16 (2Lt LG D'Arcy/2Lt RC Whiteside KIA – probably by Ltn M Fr v Richthofen, Jasta 2. Engine 791/WD7151).

A5447 Presentation a/c *Australia No 6, New South Wales No 5, The White Belltrees* wef 15.11.16. At Norwich allotted to BEF (160hp Beardmore) 1.11.16. **SARD** dd ex Norwich, via Chingford, 11.11.16 (Capt JL Jones). **1 AD** ex England 13.11.16. **2 AD** ex 1 AD 15.11.16. **23 Sqn** ex 2 AD 16.11.16 and force landed after damaged by AA on photo sortie near Beaumont Hamel 7.12.16 (2Lt JC Griffiths WIA/Lt R Affleck OK, machine unsalvageable. 160hp Beardmore, flying time 29hr).

A5448 Presentation a/c *Australia No 7, New South Wales No 6* wef 15.11.16. At Norwich allotted to BEF (160hp Beardmore) 1.11.16. Folkestone ex Farnborough with engine trouble, 20.11.16. **1 AD** ex Folkestone 21.11.16. **18 Sqn** dd ex 1 AD 4.12.16 and crashed landing on aerodrome from OP with engine trouble 16.12.16 (2Lt GA Master/AM2 Watt OK). **2 AD** ex 18 Sqn 19.12.16 and deleted for spares 20.12.16.

A5449 Presentation a/c *Australia No 8, New South Wales No 7* wef 15.11.16. At Norwich allotted to BEF (160hp Beardmore) 1.11.16. **1 AD** ex

England 16.11.16. **2 AD** ex 1 AD 16.11.16. **23 Sqn** dd ex 2 AD 17.11.16, damaged by AA 7.12.16. **2 AD** ex 23 Sqn in exchange for SPAD S.VII 12.2.17. HQ Wing ex 2 AD 15.3.17. **100 Sqn** dd ex 2 AD 4.17 and crashed in forced landing on night bombing sortie after engine failure 27/28.5.17, catching fire when bomb exploded (2Lt WE Kemp/2Lt RJ Housden OK). Deleted 8.17.

A5450 Presentation a/c *Australia No 9, New South Wales No 8* wef 15.11.16. At Norwich allotted to BEF (160hp Beardmore) 1.11.16. **1 AD** ex England 21.11.16. **18 Sqn** dd ex 1 AD 28.11.16 and wrecked in forced landing on OP after British shell exploded near a/c 26.12.16 (2Lt GA Masters WIA/2Lt PS Taylor IIA). **2 AD** ex 18 Sqn 3.1.17 and deleted 4.1.17.

A5451 Presentation a/c *Punjab No 29* wef 18.11.16. At Norwich allotted to BEF (160hp Beardmore) 10.11.16. **1 AD** ex England 4.12.16. **25 Sqn** dd ex 1 AD 10.12.16 and crashed in spin after engine failed on night bombing sortie 28.12.16 (Lt A Maurice/Lt WG Meggitt IIFA). **1 AD** ex 25 Sqn 28.12.16 with 160hp engine. Deleted at 1 AD by 15.1.17 (NWR with 10hr 40min flying time) BUT **18 Sqn**, wrecked 8.5.17. Deleted 8.5.17.

A5452 Presentation to a/c *Baroda No 17*. At Norwich allotted to BEF (160hp Beardmore) 10.11.16. **1 AD** ex England 26.11.16. **18 Sqn** dd ex 1 AD 18.12.16 and LIA in combat near Gommecourt on OP 20.12.16 (Lt CH Windrum/Lt JA Hollis POW – possibly by Ltn Wortmann or Ltn H Immelmann, Jasta 2).

A5453 Presentation a/c *Montreal No 3* wef 18.11.16. At Norwich allotted to BEF (160hp Beardmore) 10.11.16. **1 AD** ex England 26.11.16. **18 Sqn** dd ex 1 AD 16.12.16 and crashed in shell-hole after combat on OP

FE2b A5449 of 100 Sqn, whose crew avoided a bomb explosion during a forced landing on 27/28 May 1917.

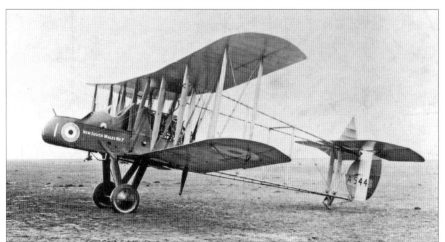

FE2b A5461 carried the 22 Sqn flight markings 'C1' under the lower wings. It was generally flown by Canadian ace Capt C.M. Clement. In the first half of 1917 he downed several enemy machines, including the unit's last FE2b claims with it on 5 June. As a rather tired machine it then passed to 101 Sqn to become a night bomber. The elaborately painted name on the front of the nacelle may begin 'Kery...'.

26.12.16 (Capt HLH Owen OK/Lt R Mayberry IIA – possibly brought down by Ltn R Theiller, J.5). **2 AD** ex 18 Sqn 3.1.17 and for deletion 4.1.17. **18 Sqn** and vict 23.4.17 (Capt CE Bryant/2Lt N Couve sent an Albatros D.III OOC near Baralle at 17.30). **100 Sqn** and crashed 3.8.17.

A5454 Presentation a/c *Junagadh No 2*. At Norwich allotted to BEF (160hp Beardmore) 10.11.16. **1 AD** ex England 4.12.16. **22 Sqn** dd ex 1 AD 16.12.16 damaged in combat on recce escort 11.3.17 (2Lt JFA Day and 2Lt LC Davies MC WIA – possibly by Vzfw F Kosmahl/Obltn Neuberger FlAb 261) and vict 8.4.17 (Lt LW Beal/2Lt GG Bell shared the destruction of an Albatros D.II near Regny 07.00 with 4883, 4891, 7681 and A796 A5461). **2 AD** ex 22 Sqn 3.7.17. **101 Sqn** dd ex 2 AD 12.7.17 and damaged in forced landing crash near Neuve Eglise on night bombing sortie 4.10.17 (2Lt HF Lind/Lt SG Barlow OK). **1 AD** ex 101 Sqn 6.10.17.

A5455 Presentation a/c *Gold Coast No 5*. At Norwich allotted to BEF (160hp Beardmore) 10.11.16. **1 AD** ex England 27.11.16. **18 Sqn** dd ex 1 AD 16.12.16 and vict 15.2.17 (2Lt VH Huston/2Lt PS Taylor destroyed an EA C-type near Grevillers) then damaged when propeller burst on patrol 2.3.17. **2 AD** ex 18 Sqn with 160hp engine, 15.3.17 and SOC BEF charge 7.4.17 (NWR, flying time 53hr 18min) and to England in packing case 7.4.17.

A5456 Presentation a/c *Punjab No 32 Montgomery*. At Norwich allotted to BEF (160hp Beardmore) 10.11.16. **1 AD** ex England 4.12.16. **22 Sqn** dd ex 1 AD 19.12.16 and damaged in forced-landing near Trones Wood 4.2.17 (2Lt TH Gladstone/2Lt GO McEntee OK after fuel tank holed in combat). **18 Sqn** and crashed in forced landing near Bernes after becoming lost 8.4.17 (Lt JW Shaw/2Lt PH West OK) and wrecked by wind 10.4.17. **2 AD** wrecked ex 22 Sqn 14.4.17 with 160hp engine, SOC BEF charge 20.4.17 (NWR, flying time 60hr 1min) and to England in packing case ex 2 AD 20.4.17.

A5457 Presentation a/c *Punjab No 3* wef 18.11.16. At Norwich allotted to BEF (160hp Beardmore) 10.11.16. **1 AD** ex England 4.12.16. **22 Sqn** dd ex 1 AD 16.12.16 and LIA in combat with 5 EA near Gouzeaucourt on patrol 19.5.17 (2Lt MS Goodban/2Lt PHB Ward KIA – shot down in flames, possibly by Ltn FO Bernert or Vzfw Holler, Jasta 6.) Engine 626/ WD6986.

A5458 Presentation a/c *River Plate* wef 21.11.16. At Norwich allotted to BEF (160hp Beardmore) 10.11.16. **1 AD** ex England 4.12.16. **18 Sqn** dd ex 1 AD 16.12.16 and vict 26.12.16 (2Lt WF Macdonald/2Lt JR Smith sent an Albatros D.II OOC near Velu at 09.50) then crashed landing due to wind on weather test 7.3.17 (Major RS Maxwell/Cpl L Alcock OK. 160hp engine, flying time 65hr 40min). **2 AD** ex 18 Sqn 9.3.17.

A5459 Presentation a/c *Baroda No 14*. At Norwich allotted to BEF (160hp Beardmore) 27.11.16. **1 AD** ex England 4.12.16. **22 Sqn** dd ex 1 AD 16.12.16 and damaged in combat near St Quentin on patrol 15.3.17 (2Lt EA Mearnes OK/AM2 CS Belton WIA). **2 AD** ex 22 Sqn 8.7.17 and deleted 17.7.17. BUT **1 AD** and deleted 11.10.17.

A5460 Presentation a/c *Manitoba*. At Norwich allotted to BEF (160hp Beardmore) 27.11.16. **SARD** dd ex Hendon 4.12.16 (Lt Clappen). **1 AD** ex England 20.12.16. **18 Sqn** dd ex 1 AD 27.12.16 and vict 4.2.17 (2Lt RW Farquhar/2Lt GN Blennerhasset sent an Albatros D.II OOC near Le Sars at 16.00) then wrecked in crash at Guillemont after combat on patrol 26.2.17 (2Lt G Vaughan-Jones KIA/ Lt JF Ferguson WIA. Flying time 45hr 15min). **2 AD** ex 18 Sqn 4.3.17 and deleted 5.3.17.

A5461 Presentation a/c *Montreal No 2*. At Norwich allotted to BEF (160hp Beardmore) 27.11.16. **1 AD** ex England 4.12.16. **22 Sqn** dd ex 1 AD 19.12.16 and victs 5.2.17, 8.4.17 (Capt CM Clement/2Lt LC Davies shared the destruction of an Albatros D.II near Regny at 07.00 with 4883, 4891, 7681, A796, A5454) (Capt CM Clement/2Lt MK Parlee shared the destruction of an Albatros D.II near Rocquigny with DH2 7930 of 24 Sqn), 9.5.17 (Capt CM Clement/2Lt MK Parlee sent an Albatros D.III OOC near Honnecourt at 15.45 and destroyed another near Lesdains at 15.50) and 5.6.17 (Capt CM Clement/2Lt LC Davies destroyed 1 Albatros D.III near Lesdains at 07.15 and sent another OOC at 07.30). **101 Sqn** by 7.17, crashed 10.9.17 (Capt SW Vickers/Lt SG Barlow OK) and reported as old and generally shot up. **1 ASD** by 4.18.

A5462 Presentation a/c *Punjab No 30*. At Norwich allotted to BEF (160hp Beardmore) 27.11.16. **1 AD** damaged on delivery flight from England 28.12.16 and recorded 15.1.17 with 160hp engine as unserviceable, 'for home in case' and to England in packing case 17.1.17 (5hr flying time). En-route to SAD for repair 26.1.17. **18 Sqn**. Flown to England and deleted 10.4.17.

A5463 Presentation a/c *Malaya No 22*. At Norwich allotted to BEF (160hp Beardmore) 27.11.16. **1 AD** ex England 4.12.16. **22 Sqn** dd ex 1 AD 19.12.16 and damaged in forced landing among shell holes 17.3.17. **2 AD** wrecked ex 22 Sqn 31.3.17, with 160hp engine, SOC BEF charge 7.4.17 (NWR, flying time 64hr 13min)

and to England in packing case 7.4.17.

A5464 Presentation a/c *Sind* wef 18.11.16. At Norwich allotted to BEF (160hp Beardmore) 27.11.16. **SAD** under repair 11.12.16 with BEF allotment cancelled. **2 AD** ex 1 AD 24.2.17 and serviceable, 28.2.17. **18 Sqn** ex 2 AD 12.3.17 and victs 5.4.17 (Capt RH Hood/2Lt JR Smith sent an Albatros D.II OOC near Inchy at 12.00) and 6.4.17 (Capt RH Hood /Lt JR Smith captured an Albatros D.III at Beaumetz at 10.00) then wrecked in crash landing near aerodrome on night bombing sortie 10.5.17 (2Lt CG Shaumer/2Lt N Couve OK).

A5465 Presentation a/c *Punjab No 26* wef 18.11.16. At Norwich allotted to BEF (160hp Beardmore) 27.11.16. **1 AD** ex England 11.12.16. **11 Sqn** dd ex 1 AD 24.12.16 and on charge until @ 2.17. **2 AD** ex 1 AD 14.7.17. **100 Sqn** dd ex 2 AD 26.7.17 and reported as old (135hr) 29.7.17. **2 AD** ex 100 Sqn 31.7.17 and deleted 8.8.17.

A5466 Presentation a/c *Baroda No 13*. At Norwich allotted to BEF (160hp Beardmore) 27.11.16. Folkestone ex Farnborough 11.12.16 with engine trouble and in fog. **1 AD** dd ex Folkestone 16.12.16. **18 Sqn** dd ex 1 AD 24.12.16 and damaged in combat with 4 EA near Marquion 29.4.17 (2Lt RW Reid OK/2Lt RC Doughty WIA). **2 AD** ex 18 Sqn 9.8.17 (226hr). **1 AD** ex 2 AD 10.8.17 and flown to England 14.8.17. **51 HDS** B Flt by 28.10.17 and wrecked catching fire in crash when spun in on 20.3.18 (Lt EA Worrall/2Lt ARC Hodges KIFA). Deleted 9.8.17 with 225 flying hours.

A5467 Presentation a/c *Newfoundland No 3* wef 18.11.16. At Norwich allotted to BEF (160hp Beardmore) 27.11.16. Crashed at Felstead on delivery and BEF allotment cancelled 11.12.16. **SARD** tested 25.3.17. Deleted 22.6.17. BUT **100 Sqn** by/until 22.6.17 and Reception Park to 1 AIS 31.1.18.

A5468 Presentation a/c *Malaya No 8* wef 18.11.16. At Norwich allotted to BEF (160hp Beardmore) 27.11.16. **1 AD** ex England 16.12.16. **18 Sqn** dd ex 1 AD 26.12.16 and victs 6.4.17 (2Lt RW Reid/2Lt GN Blennerhassett destroyed an Albatros D.III around Beugny-Beaumetz at 10.00) and 1.5.17 (2Lt MM Kaizer/Sgt F Russell sent an Albatros D.III OOC near Epinoy at 10.30). **2 AD** ex 18 Sqn 8.6.17 (no prefix letter noted). **22 Sqn** dd ex 2 AD 16.6.17 until @ 8.7.17. **1 AD** St-Omer tested 10.7.17. **2 AD** ex 1 AD 11.7.17. **101 Sqn** and damaged in crash on test flight 17.10.17 (reported as old with 168hr 32min flying time). BUT flown to England 23.9.17.

A5469 Presentation a/c *Ceylon*. At Norwich allotted to BEF (160hp Beardmore) 27.11.16. At Croydon 5.1.17 with BEF allotment cancelled. **SAD** allotted to BEF 10.2.17 and 12.2.17. **11 Sqn** and damaged in successful combat on recce 25.3.17 (2Lt H Calvey/AM F Hadlow OK after destroying an Albatros D.III over the Scarpe Valley at 09.30). **2 AD** wrecked ex 11 Sqn 30.3.17, SOC BEF charge 1.4.17 (160hp engine, NWR, flying time 10hr 53min) and to England in packing case 1.4.17.

A5470 Presentation a/c *Zanzibar No 3* wef 9.12.16. At Norwich allotted to BEF (160hp Beardmore) 27.11.16. **23 Sqn** dd ex 1 AD 7.1.17 and crashed. **2 AD** with 120hp engine ex 23 Sqn in exchange for SPAD S.VII 4.2.17, engine adjusted 28.2.17. HQ Wing ex 2 AD 1.3.17. **2 AD** ex HQ, wrecked, 5.3.17 and SOC BEF charge 7.4.17 (NWR, flying time 21hr 3min) and to England in packing case 7.4.17.

A5471 Presentation a/c *Shanghai Race Club No 2* wef 9.12.16. At Norwich allotted to BEF 11.12.16. **23 Sqn** dd ex 1 AD 12.1.17 and wrecked in crash near Bavincourt after combat on recce escort 6.3.17 (2Lt GH Harrison/2Lt OGS

158

Crawford WIA – 160hp engine, 54hr 44min flying time). **2 AD** ex 23 Sqn 11.3.17 and to England in packing case 7.4.17.

A5472 Presentation a/c *Gold Coast No 1* wef 9.12.16. At Norwich allotted to BEF 11.12.16. **RAF** dd ex Norwich via Cambridge 21-24.12.16. **1 AD** ex England 26.12.16 (160hp Beardmore). **2 AD** ex 1 AD 7.1.17. **11 Sqn** dd ex 2 AD 6.2.17 and wrecked overturning in forced landing crash on patrol 17.3.17 (Capt CN Lowe/2Lt G Masters OK.160hp engine, flying time 30hr 10min). **2 AD** ex 11 Sqn 24.3.17 and to England in packing case 30.3.17.

A5473 Presentation a/c *Bikanir No 5*. At Norwich allotted to BEF 11.12.16 (160hp Beardmore). **SAD** with BEF allotment cancelled 12.1.17 – under repair. **SAD** allotted to BEF 3.2.17. **11 Sqn** and damaged in landing crash after patrol 21.3.17. **2 AD** wrecked ex 11 Sqn 24.3.17 with 160hp engine and deleted 5.4.17 (NWR, flying time 12hr 15min).

A5474 Presentation a/c *Bikanir No 6*. At Norwich allotted to BEF 11.12.16. **1 AD** ex England 24.12.16. **18 Sqn** dd ex 1 AD 5.1.17 and LIA after successful combat near Queant on recce 27.5.17 (2Lt E West-White/Sgt JR Cumberland OK after brought down in flames possibly by Ltn K Schneider, J.5– had sent an Albatros D.V OOC at 07.15). Engine 1012/WD7622. **2 AD** and deleted for spares 3.6.17.

A5475 Presentation a/c *Bikanir No 7*. At Norwich allotted to BEF 11.12.16 (160hp Beardmore). **1 AD** ex England 24.12.16. **18 Sqn** dd ex 1 AD 5.1.17 and LIA near Bapaume on photo escort 11.3.17 (Sgt HP Burgess/2Lt HM Headley KIA – shot down in flames. Flying time 48hr 45min, engine 689/WD7058).

A5476 Presentation a/c *Bikanir No 8*. At Norwich allotted to BEF 22.12.16 (160hp Beardmore). **1 AD** ex England 24.12.16, still there 15.1.17, with 160hp engine, unserviceable and 'for home in case' and to England in packing case 17.1.17 (flying time 6hr 15min). En-route to SAD for repair 26.1.17. **100 Sqn**. Deleted 14.6.17.

A5477 Presentation a/c *Gold Coast No 9*. At Norwich allotted to BEF 22.12.16 (120hp Beardmore). **1 AD** 15.1.17, with 160hp engine, unserviceable and 'for home in case'. Flown to England 16.6.17. **100 Sqn** and wrecked when crashed in storm 19/20.9.17 and deleted.

A5478 Presentation a/c *Gold Coast No 10*. At Norwich allotted to BEF 22.12.16. **23 Sqn** dd ex 1 AD 12.1.17. **2 AD** ex 23 Sqn 12.2.17 in exchange for SPAD S.VII (160hp Beardmore). HQ Wing ex 2 AD 27.2.17 (120hp Beardmore). **100 Sqn** by 3.6.17 and crashed in forced landing near St Venant on night bombing sortie 11.8.17 (2Lt P Kent/ Sgt W Doyle OK). **2 AD** ex 100 Sqn 13.8.17 and deleted 18.8.17.

A5479 Presentation a/c *Gold Coast No 11*. At Norwich allotted to BEF 23.12.16. **2 AD** ex 1 AD 7.1.17. **23 Sqn** dd ex 2 AD 4.2.17 and wrecked in crash landing on 7 Sqn aerodrome after patrol 10.2.17 (Sgt JA Cunliffe/AM RE Upson OK). **2 AD** wrecked ex 23 Sqn with 160hp engine 13.2.17 and deleted 14.2.17 (NWR, flying time 12hr 14min).

A5480 Presentation a/c *Gold Coast No 12*. At Norwich allotted to BEF 23.12.16. **23 Sqn** dd ex 1 AD 7.1.17. **2 AD** ex 23 Sqn in exchange for SPAD S.VII 16.2.17 and 120hp engine fitted 28.2.17. HQ Wing ex 2 AD 11.3.17. **100 Sqn** and LIA night bombing 6.5.17 (2Lt TH Holmes/AM2 AW Ekins KIA. Engine 347/WD1411, flying time 66hr 45min).

A5481 Presentation a/c *Gold Coast No 13*. At Norwich allotted to BEF 1.1.17 (160hp Beardmore). **18 Sqn** dd ex 1 AD 23.1.17 and wrecked in forced landing with combat damage (tank hit) near Monchy-au-Bois on photo escort 30.4.17 (2Lt SH Bell/Lt DW McLeod OK. 160hp engine, flying time 105hr 20min). Deleted 1.5.17.

A5482 Presentation a/c *Gold Coast No 14*. At Norwich allotted to BEF 1.1.17 (160hp Beardmore). **2 AD** ex 1 AD 14.2.17 and serviceable, 28.2.17. **22 Sqn** ex 2 AD 13.3.17. **2 AD** ex 22 Sqn 27.7.17. Flown to England 5.8.17. **100 Sqn** and wrecked when crashed in storm 19/20.9.17.

A5483 Presentation a/c *Gold Coast No 15*. At Norwich allotted to BEF 1.1.17. **23 Sqn** by 2.17. **18 Sqn** and LIA in successful combat over lines on escort 29.4.17 (2Lt GH Dinsmore OK/2Lt GB Bate KIA after destroying an Albatros D.III – possibly shot down by Ltn K Wolff, Jasta 11. 160hp engine 904/WD7514, flying time 57hr 27min).

A5484 Presentation a/c *Gold Coast No 16*. At Norwich allotted to BEF 1.1.17 (160hp Beardmore). 18 Sqn? **25 Sqn** dd ex 1 AD 13.2.17 and victs 16.3.17 (Lt J Whittaker/AM2 F King sent an EA scout OOC near Neuvireuil at 15.10 in combat between 6 FEs and 16 EA) and 17.3.17 (Capt CHC Woollven/Sgt JH Booth sent an Albatros D.II OOC near Oppy at 11.30) then wrecked in forced landing 14.4.17 (160hp engine). **1 AD** ARS ex 25 Sqn 29.4.17.

A5485 Presentation a/c *Bombay No 1*. At Norwich allotted to BEF 1.1.17 (160hp Beardmore). **2 AD** ex 1 AD 14.2.17, serviceable, 28.2.17. **23 Sqn** ex 2 AD 13.3.17 and wrecked in forced landing near Achiet-le-Grand after combat on photo escort 24.3.17 (Sgt EP Critchley WIA/AM1 F Russell KIA – possibly by Ltn W Voss, Jasta 2). **2 AD** ex 23 Sqn 28.3.17 with 160hp engine 894/WD7504 packed for England 28.3.17, SOC BEF charge 29.3.17 (NWR, flying time 7hr 47min). To England 30.3.17.

A5486 Presentation a/c *City of Adelaide*. At Norwich allotted to BEF 1.1.17 (160hp Beardmore). **2 AD** ex 1 AD 16.3.17. **22 Sqn** dd ex 2 AD 31.3.17 and shelled to destruction after forced landing near Moslains following combat 3.4.17 (2Lt GM Hopkins/AM1 H Friend OK). **2 AD** wrecked ex 22 Sqn 7.4.17 and for England in packing case, 30.4.17 (160hp Beardmore).

A5487 Presentation a/c *British Subjects in Siam No 2*. At Norwich allotted to BEF 1.1.17 (160hp Beardmore). **SARD** under repair 26.1.17 and tested 8.4.17. Re-allotted to BEF 10.4.17 but **1 AD** 9.4.17. **25 Sqn** and damaged when overturned by wind in forced landing on patrol 10.4.17. **2 AD** ex 1 AD for 18 Sqn (160hp Beardmore) 30.4.17. **18 Sqn** and LIA on photo escort 7.5.17 (2Lt MM Kaizer/ Sgt F Russell POW – possibly shot down by Ltn Reisen, Jasta 5). Engine 1000/WD7610.

A5500 – A5649: 150 RAF FE2b (120/160hp Beardmore) built by G & J Weir Ltd, Cathcart under Contract 87/A/1233.

A5500 **AID** allotted to BEF 26.3.17. **11 Sqn** and damaged in forced landing following combat damage near Arras on recce 6.4.17 (2Lt DS Kennedy/AM2 JF Carr OK – possibly brought down by Ltn W Frankl, J.4). **2 AD**. **11 Sqn** ex 2 AD 12.4.17 and wrecked in landing crash following combat on photo sortie 22.4.17 (2Lt JJ Paine/2Lt J Rothwell IIA – 160hp engine 1044/7654, flying time 17hr 5 min). **2 AD**, wrecked ex 11 Sqn, 29.4.17.

A5501 **AID** allotted to BEF 4.4.17. **11 Sqn** dd ex 1 AD 19.4.17 and LIA on photo sortie 22.4.17 (Sgt JK Hollis POW wdd/Lt BJ Tolhurst KIA – probably shot down by Ltn K Wolff, Jasta 11. 160hp engine 939/WD7549, flying time 11hr 30min).

A5502 **RAF** 29.3.17. **AID** allotted to BEF 4.4.17. **25 Sqn** dd ex 1 AD 19.4.17 and on charge until @ 24.4.17. **18 Sqn** damaged 18.5.17 (engine 1048/WD7658) and LIA near Cambrai on photo sortie 23.5.17 (2Lt WF Macdonald/Lt FC Shackell KIA – possibly shot down by Ltn W Voss, Jasta 5).

A5503 En-route from Renfrew, allotted to BEF (160hp Beardmore) 25.4.17. **100 Sqn** by 6.17 and destroyed in shelling of aerodrome 22.7.17. **2 AD** ex 100 Sqn 26.7.17 and deleted 1.8.17.

A5504 At Renfrew allotted to HD Wing, re-allotted to BEF (160hp Beardmore) 14.4.17. Re-allotted to Training Brigade 5.6.17. **2 (Aux) SAG** as a/c *67* until @ 10.17. **199 DS** by 11.17 until @ 3.12.17.

A5505 **AID** allotted to BEF 4.4.17. **25 Sqn** dd ex 1 AD 19.4.17 and on charge until @ 1.5.17. **18 Sqn** and vict 25.5.17 (2Lt CF Horsley/Lt L Murphy sent an Albatros D.III OOC around Pronville/Baralle at 09.15) then listed as old machine 9.8.17 (182hr 34min). **1 AD** ex 2 AD 10.8.17 and flown to England 11.8.17. **8 AAP** by 12.8.17 (Lt PRT Chamberlayne AGP). **199 NTS** by 12.18.

A5506 **AID** allotted to BEF 4.4.17. **2 AD** ex 1 AD 21.4.17 (160hp Beardmore). **18 Sqn** ex 2 AD 21.4.17 and vict 1.5.17 (Lt CG Shaumer/ Lt FC Shackell sent an Albatros D.III OOC near Epinoy at 10.30) then damaged forced landing in old trenches on patrol 13.7.17. **2 AD** ex 18 Sqn 17.7.17 and deleted 17.7.17.

A5507 **AID** allotted to BEF 4.4.17. **1 AD** dd ex Farnborough 15.4.17. **11 Sqn** and vict 20.5.17 (2Lt AW Gardner/Lt DD McIntosh

FE2b A5508, involved in two training crashes. The presence of a DH1 in the background suggests that this was taken during its time at East Retford.

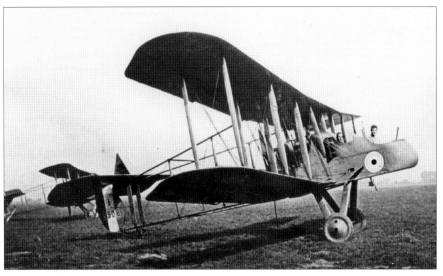

A5517 and A5523 after a collision on the ground at East Retford. The view from the reverse angle is shown on p25.

sent an Albatros D.III OOC near the Sensée Canal at 12.15). **2 AD** ex 11 Sqn 14.6.17. **101 Sqn** dd ex 2 AD 15.7.17 and burnt out following crash when hit tree taking off for new aerodrome 7.8.17 (2Lt C Kerpen IIFA/ AM2 HR Kitchingman fatally IIFA). Deleted on 101 Sqn 31.8.17.

A5508 At Renfrew allotted to HD Wing, re-allotted to BEF (160hp Beardmore) 14.4.17. Re-allotted to Training Brigade. **28 TS** damaged in crash after engine cut 26.6.17 (pilot OK/observer injured). **38 HDS** and wrecked in crash following stall on low turn 4.4.18 (2Lt L Roebuck KIFA).

A5509 **22 Sqn** by 5.17. **199 NTS** by 12.2.18 until @ 15.2.18. **1 AIS** dd ex 1 ASD 5.7.18.

A5510 **AID** allotted to BEF 12.4.17. **25 Sqn** dd ex 1 AD 29.4.17 (160hp Beardmore) and on charge until @ 1.5.17. **22 Sqn** and damaged in combat with 4 EA on patrol 19.5.17,

force landing on 9 Sqn aerodrome (2Lt GW Foreman/2Lt ND Robinson OK). **2 AD** in packing case for England 3.6.17 but deleted 16.7.17.

A5511 **AID** allotted to BEF (160hp Beardmore) 12.4.17. **11 Sqn** and vict 7.5.17 (2Lt CA Parker/AM2 SA Mee sent an Albatros D.III OOC near Douai at 14.50) then LIA by AA on photo sortie 20.5.17 (2Lt TJ Hudson/2Lt LH Horncastle MC KIA. Engine 1040/WD7650).

A5512 **AID** allotted to BEF (160hp Beardmore) 12.4.17. **25 Sqn** Lozinghem dd ex 1 AD St-Omer 27.4.17.

A5513 **AID** Farnborough allotted to BEF (160hp Beardmore) 12.4.17. **1 AD** ex 2 AD 28.4.17. **2 AD** ex 1 AD (160hp Beardmore) 30.4.17. **18 Sqn** ex 2 AD 30.4.17. **2 AD** ex 1 AD 25.8.17. Flown to England ex 1 AD 14.10.17 (160hp Beardmore 1010/WD7620).

A5514 **AID** allotted to BEF 12.4.17. **RAF** (160hp

Beardmore 1076/WD7686) 18.4.17. **2 AD** ex 1 AD 8.8.17. **100 Sqn** dd ex 2 AD 12.8.17 and wrecked in crash following engine failure on night bombing sortie 20.4.18. **2 ASD** ex 100 Sqn 20.4.18. On BEF charge 30.6.18.

A5515 **AID** allotted to BEF (160hp Beardmore) 19.4.17. **RAF** (160hp Beardmore 1073/ WD7683) 20.4.17. **SARD** tested 25.4.17. **1 AD** 26.4.17.

A5516 **AID** allotted to HD Wing, re-allotted to BEF 9.5.17.

A5517 **AID** allotted to BEF 9.5.17. **11 Sqn**, vict 20.5.17 (Capt ER Manning/2Lt AM West sent an Albatros D.III OOC near the Sensée Canal at 12.15) then LIA near Cherisy on recce 24.5.17 (2Lt WDG Turner KIA/2Lt L Holman POW wdd – possibly shot down by Ltn K Allmenröder, Jasta 11). Engine 1088/ WD7698.

A5518 **AID** allotted to BEF 9.5.17. Presentation a/c *Mauritius No 15*. **20 Sqn 1 AD** tested 12.6.17. **100 Sqn** and damaged overturned in gulley in forced landing on night bombing sortie 25.7.17 (Lt Clayton/AM2 S Harkins OK). **2 AD** ex 100 Sqn 27.7.17 and deleted 1.8.17.

A5519 **51 HDS** B Flt by 23.3.17 (Lt Parnell & AM Held 2 AZPs) until @ 5.18.

A5520 **51 HDS** C Flt Marham by 23.3.17 (2Lt HE Duncan/AM Bishop AZP). **51 HDS** C Flt Mattishall dd ex Marham 14.10.17 – photographed overturned in accident, date unknown.

A5521 **AID** allotted to HD Wing, re-allotted to BEF 9.5.17.

A5522 **RAF** 28.4.17 (160hp Beardmore 1089/ WD7699). **AID** allotted to BEF 1.5.17. **18 Sqn. 2 AD** ex 18 Sqn 4.7.17. **101 Sqn** dd ex 2 AD 6.7.17. **1 AD** ex 101 Sqn, old and poor climb, 14.12.17 (175hr). Flown to England ex 1 ASD 23.12.17 (flying time 178hr).

A5523 **200 DS**, damaged in ground collision with A5517 by Lt Morrice 12.10.17. **199 NTS** by 15.1.18 until @ 5.18. Photographed at Marham, possibly 191 NTS. **200 NTS** by 8.10.18 until @ 20.10.18.

A5524 **38 HDS**. **51 HDS** B Flt dd ex Farnborough 11.10.17 (Lt TH Gladstone) and burnt out in crash after hitting tree on gliding approach to landing 9.7.18 (2Lt JG Winks KIFA).

A5525 **51 HDS** C Flt by 3.9.17 and AZPs 24.9.17 (2Lt AW Simon and Lt Lynn). Allotted to HD Wing, re-allotted to BEF (160hp Beardmore) 10.10.17. **8 AAP** ex 51 HDS B Flt 10.10.17 (Lt TH Gladstone). **1 AD** dd ex England 10.10.17 (160hp Beardmore 1141/WD20050). **101 Sqn** dd ex 1 AD 15.10.17 (160hp Beardmore 1141/WD20050) and wrecked 15.10.17 in crash landing on night bombing sortie (Lt WG Ryan/2Lt HS Scott injured). **AD** ex 101

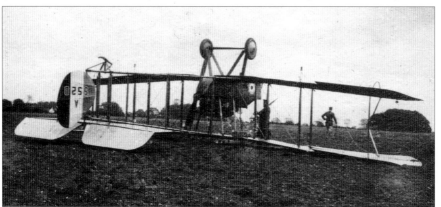

FE2b A5519 in a 51 HDS lineup, and FE2b A5520 of the same unit under guard after overturning.

Sqn 23.10.17.

A5526 **AID** allotted to BEF 1.6.17. **RAF** 7.6.17 (160hp Beardmore). **2 AD** ex 1 AD 12.6.17. **22 Sqn** dd ex 2 AD 15.7.17. **2 AD** ex 22 Sqn 27.7.17. **101 Sqn** dd ex 2 AD 8.8.17 and damaged by ground fire (tank hit) night bombing Rumbeke 27.9.17 (2Lt TJC Martyn/2Lt HW Steele OK) and wrecked 5.10.17. **1 AD** ex 101 Sqn 7.10.17 (160hp Beardmore 1060/ WD7670) and deleted 8.10.17.

A5527 **AID** allotted to BEF 5.6.17 (160hp Beardmore). **SARD** tested 8.6.17 (OK) and 10.6.17 (OK – but slight knock on engine). **100 Sqn** and damaged in landing crash on night bombing practice 27.7.17.

A5528 **AID** allotted to BEF 5.6.17 (160hp Beardmore). **100 Sqn** and damaged in forced landing at Le Foret, due to fog on night bombing sortie 25.9.17 (Lt JA Harman/Lt JA Stedman OK). **1 AD** and deleted 30.9.17.

A5529 **19 TS** Hounslow by 18.6.17 until @ 21.6.17.

A5530 **36 HDS** B Flt by 9.9.17. **192 NTS** by 12.4.18 until. Marham (51 HDS?), dd ex Newmarket 2.8.18.

A5531 **19 TS** Hounslow by 19.6.17 until @ 22.6.17.

A5532 **SARD** tested 20.6.17 (OK). **51 HDS** C Flt by 27.5.18 and on charge until @ 16.6.18.

A5533 **199 DS** by 18.8.17. **51 HDS** dd 5.11.17. **199 NTS** by 24.1.18 until @ 24.2.18. **187 NTS** by 7.18. **200 NTS** by 8.18 until @ 16.10.18.

A5534 **36 HDS** C Flt by 8.17 and wrecked in crash after sideslipping in off low turn during night bombing practice 5.2.18 (2Lt JM Black KIFA/2Lt E Nicholls fatally IIFA. 160hp Beardmore 1254/WD20163).

A5535 **33 HDS**. **36 HDS** B Flt by 18.10.17. **192 NTS** dd ex 36 HDS 12.11.17 (Lt JH Matthews) until @ 5.18.

A5536 **33 HDS** A Flt by 21.8.17 (Lt EG Roberts/2Lt AR Kingsford AZP) and further AZPs 24.9.17 (2Lt EG Roberts) and 19.10.17 (2Lt DR Brook/ Lt GE Lucas). **33 HDS** C Flt by 14.2.18.

A5537 Presentation a/c *Zanzibar No 1*. 25 Sqn? **76 HDS**. **38 HDS** by 5.9.17. **8 TDS** by summer 18.

A5538 **SARD** tested 1.7.17 (OK) and 4.7.17 (OK). **36 HDS**.

A5539 **SARD** tested 4.7.17 (engine rough, pressure dud), 6.7.17 (OK), 7.7.17 (pressure dud, 2nd magneto cutting out), force-landed at Cheddington, Bucks, 13.7.17 and tested at SARD 16.7.17 (OK). **36 HDS** B Flt by 10.9.17 until @ 4.10.17.

A5540 **SARD**, tested 6.2.17 and 9.2.17. **ES Martlesham Heath** (160hp Beardmore) by 8.17 for Trials Report M132. **ES Orfordness** by 8.17 for bombsight tests and on charge until @ 12.17.

A5541

A5542 **36 HDS** C Flt by 24.9.17 (2Lt RJ Paull/2Lt GH Box AZP) and in unsuccessful attack on submarine 2 miles SE of Seaham 26.4.18 (Lt MacDonald/Lt McMillan dropped 1 bomb) and another unsuccessful attack on submarine 15 miles E of Redcar 8.5.18 (Lt Ainscon dropped 1 bomb) and another 19.6.18 (Lt Toyne/AM Taplin on convoy patrol dropped 2 bombs on another submarine 1 mile south of Seaham and then force-landed at Littlethorpe, near Easington).

A5543 **RAF** 20.7.17 (160hp Bearmore 957/WD7567). **51 HDS** C Flt by 3.9.17, AZP 24.9.17 (Capt LC Angstrom) and further AZP 19.10.17 (2Lt AW Simon).

A5544 **192 NTS** and wrecked in crash when landing 2 miles from Thetford 2.3.18 (Capt Campbell OK/2Lt AR Aitken KIFA – seated too high).

A5545 **51 HDS** by 3.9.17 and wrecked in crash 6.10.17. **38 Sqn**.

A5546 **SARD** 20.10.17 allotted to BEF. **2 AD** by 11.17. **A Sqn RNAS** dd ex 2 AD 19.11.17. **16N Sqn** 8.1.18. **100 Sqn** ex 16N Sqn 5.3.18. **3 AD** ex 100 Sqn 2.9.18 and deleted.

A5547 **SARD** allotted to BEF 2.7.17 and tested 7.7.17 (OK). **1 AD** tested 12.7.17. **2 AD** dd ex 1 AD 13.7.17. **101 Sqn** and LIA night bombing 3.9.17 (2Lt F Scarborough/AM2 TH Taylor POW. Engine 1105/6875).

A5548 **64 Sqn**. **51 HDS** C Flt by 24.9.17 (Lt DH Montgomery AZP) and further AZP 5.8.18 (Capt TJC Martyn).

A5549 **SARD** tested 19.6.17 (OK). **51 HDS** B Flt Marham by 27.9.17 until @ 29.9.17. **51 HDS** C Flt Marham by 25.5.18 and on charge until @ 15.7.18. **51 HDS** B Flt Tydd-St-Mary 5.8.18 (Lt LA Bushe AZP).

A5550 **RAF** 29.7.17.

A5551 **RAF** 29.7.17. **51 HDS** B Flt by 24.9.17 (Lt OE Ridewood AZP) and further AZP 19.10.17 (Lt OE Ridewood) and still on charge 21.1.18.

A5552

A5553

A5554

A5555 **36 HDS** B Flt by 5.11.17 until @ 15.11.17. **36 HDS** A Flt by 5.4.18, fitted with dual control by 7.6.18 and on charge until @ 23.7.18 . **131 Sqn** . **191 NTS** by 9.18.

A5556 **SARD** tested 21.10.17 (OK) and allotted to BEF 22.10.17. **1 AIS** ex 1 AD RP 19.11.17. **101 Sqn** dd ex 1 ASD 6.12.17, force-landed by Capt ED Hall/2Lt KJ Hook 22.5.18 and force landed due to engine trouble on night recce 8.7.18 (crew shaken). **2 ASD** deleted 21.7.18, NWR (flying time 183hr 49min).

A5557 **83 Sqn** dd ex 1 AIS 25.3.18 and recorded as poor and unserviceable 16.4.18. **1 AD** ex 83 Sqn 17.4.18 for overhaul and repair. **1 ASD** ex Advanced Salvage and deleted 25.4.18 NWR (flying time 13hr 5min).

A5558 **AID** allotted to BEF 27.8.17. **102 Sqn** dd ex 2 AD Candas 13.9.17 and recorded as poor 17.4.18 (120). **2 ASD** ex 102 Sqn for overhaul 17.4.18 (flying time 120hr). **1 ASD** and flown to England 22.4.18 (flying time recorded as 119hr 27mins).

A5559 **2 AD** by 12.17. **101 Sqn** dd ex 1 AD 27.1.18 and damaged in crash near Bertangles after auxiliary tank hit by ground fire on night bombing 3.4.18 (Capt ED Hall/Lt WS Aulton OK, flying time 50hr). **2 ASD** ex 101 Sqn 3.4.18.

A5560 **33 HDS**. **1 AIS** ex 1 AD RP 19.11.17. **102 Sqn** and damaged hitting hole in forced landing due to mist and wind after becoming lost on night bombing sortie 24.4.18. **2 ASD** ex 102 Sqn 26.4.18 (flying time 21hr 24min). **101 Sqn** and damaged in forced landing after engine failure 23.11.18.

A5561 **SARD** tested 28.7.17 (engine revs down), 30.7.17 (engine rough) 31.7.17 (revs down but OK) and 3.8.17 (OK). **38 HDS** by 5.8.17. **76 HDS** 8.17. **36 HDS** B Flt by 11.9.17 then **36 HDS** A Flt by 22.4.18 until @ 25.4.18 then **36 HDS** C Flt and lost at sea after engine failed 5 miles north of R.Tyne 25.5.18 (crew rescued).

A5562 **8 AAP** allotted to BEF 14.8.17. **102 Sqn** and damaged in forced landing when engine failed on night bombing sortie 8 (10?).2.18 (2Lt H Fall/2Lt FN Phillips OK. Flying time 48hr). **AD** ex 102 Sqn 8.2.18. **102 Sqn** dd ex 1 AD 11.9.18.

A5563 **AID** allotted to BEF 27.8.17. **101 Sqn** and damaged in crash near aerodrome on engine test. **1 AD** ex 101 Sqn 18.10.17.

A5564 **AID** allotted to BEF 22.8.17. **RAF** .8.17 (160hp Beardmore 40/WD9488). **2 AD** ex 1 AD 22.8.17. **16N Sqn**. **100 Sqn** dd ex 16N Sqn 5.3.18 and wrecked in crash after hit rut on take-off for night bombing sortie 31.5.18. **2 ASD** 31.5.18 and deleted 27.6.18 (NWR, 1 flying time 17hr 7min).

A5565 **1 AD**, nacelle only, 31.8.17.

A5566 **SARD** tested 24.7.17 (OK). **33 HDS**. **38 HDS** B Flt by 24.9.17 (Lt GH Harrison/2Lt CC Abraham AZP) and force landed with fuel problems at Stamford on further AZP 19.10.17 (2Lt AE Iken/Lt Blyth). To BEF with **38 Sqn** and force landed safely 24.6.18. **102 Sqn** ex 38 Sqn 20.1.19.

A5567 **AID** allotted to BEF 27.8.17. Allocation cancelled 14.9.17, on charge E.1 Repair Section. **102 Sqn**.

A5568 **38 HDS** B Flt by 19.10.17 (Capt LP Watkins/ Sgt Edwards AZP).

A5569 **AID** allotted to BEF 20.8.17. **102 Sqn** dd ex 1 AD 5.9.17 and crashed into railway after becoming lost on night bombing sortie 30.10.17 (2Lt DP Wilson/Lt EV Collett OK). **1 AD** ex 102 Sqn..

FE2b A5548 at Spittlegate, probably a visitor, in 1918, with a close-up of the broad white nacelle marking above.

161

FE2b A5573 with modified nacelle profile. This photograph, taken at Spittlegate, probably dates from the machine's later service. East Retford was some 40 miles away, while Ashington was nearer 170.

A5570 **AID** allotted to BEF 27.8.17. **SARD** tested 31.8.17 (OK). **102 Sqn** dd ex 1 AD 3.9.17 force landed after engine failure on night bombing sortie 25.1.18 (2Lt BCW Windle/Lt Shaw OK). **1 RP** ex 102 Sqn 25.1.18. **1 ASD** deleted 31.1.18. (NWR, flying time 62hr).

A5571 **AID** allotted to BEF 21.8.17. **102 Sqn** dd ex 1 AD St-Omer 5.9.17, recorded as poor 17.4.18 (114hr). **2 ASD** ex 102 Sqn for overhaul 17.4.18 (114hr flying time). **1 ASD** and flown to England 8.5.18 (115hr flying time).

A5572 **2 AD** deleted 6.8.17. BUT **36 HDS** B Flt by 10.10.17.

A5573 **36 HDS** B Flt. **200 DS** dd ex 36 HDS 21.10.17, unit retitled **200 NTS** 21.12.17 and on charge until @ 3.18.

A5574 **36 HDS** B Flt by 4.11.17 (Lt JH Matthews force landed in mist at Cleadon NLG, OK). **199 NTS**. **200 NTS** by 22.7.18 until @ 24.7.18.

A5575 **36 HDS** B Flt by 11.9.17. **200 NTS** by 10.7.18 and wrecked in crash 26.7.18 (Flt Cdt EA White KIFA). **1 SNBD** by 8.18.

A5576 **102 Sqn** by 3.18.

A5577 **SARD** allotted to BEF 3.8.17. **102 Sqn** dd ex 1 AD 11.9.17 and LIA night bombing 7.11.17 (Capt EE Barnes/Lt EDS Caswell KIA).

A5578 **38 HDS** C Flt by 19.10.17 (Sgt CRL Faley/2Lt JO Holliday AZP) and further AZP 19.10.17 (2Lt SN Pike/AM1 GW Moorhouse) then crashed near Coventry aerodrome on AZP 12.4.18 (Lt WA Brown OK).

A5579 **8 AAP** allotted to BEF 8.8.17. **101 Sqn** and damaged by ground fire on night bombing 2.11.17 but landed on aerodrome (2Lt RS Larkin/2Lt S Ellis OK).

A5580 **8 AAP** allotted to BEF 9.8.17. **2 AD** ex 1 AD 22.8.17. **100 Sqn**, hit rut and wrecked in take-off for night bombing 30.5.18. **2 ASD** ex 100 Sqn 30.5.18 and deleted 27.6.18 (NWR, flying time 114hr 33min).

A5581 **8 AAP** allotted to BEF 28.8.17. **100 Sqn** and damaged in forced landing after engine cut on night bombing sortie 29.9.17 (2Lt JR Cudemore IIA/Lt RS Greenslade OK). **1 AD** ex 100 Sqn 29.9.17 and deleted 4.10.17 (160hp Beardmore 1076/WD7686).

A5582 **8 AAP** allotted to BEF 9.8.17. **1 AD** dd ex 2 AD 28.9.17. **101 Sqn** dd ex 1 AD 30.9.17 (160hp Beardmore 1266/WD20175) and force landed safely on night bombing sortie 24.4.18. **2 ASD** ex 101 Sqn for repair 25.4.18 (flying time 146hr 28min). **102 Sqn** Surcamps by 5.8.18 and wrecked hitting road in forced landing after engine trouble on night bombing sortie 21.8.18. **2 ASD** 24.8.18 (flying time 208hr 7min).

A5583 **8 AAP** allotted to BEF 9.8.17. **102 Sqn** dd ex 1 AD St-Omer 11.9.17 and damaged in forced landing near Nieppe after engine cut on night bombing sortie 29.10.17 (Lt AL Sinclair/2Lt R Bruce OK). **1 AD** ex 102 Sqn 29.10.17.

A5584 **76 HDS**. **38 HDS** A Flt by 9.17 until @ 19.10.17 (Capt MD Barber AZP). **192 NTS** by 12.3.18.

A5585 **192 NTS** by 25.2.18 until @ 26.6.18. **1 SNBD**.

A5586 **AID** allotted to BEF 25.9.17. **101 Sqn** and crashed after hit by AA night bombing Douai 30.11.17 (Capt T Grant WIA/2Lt Shand OK). **1 ASD** ex 101 Sqn 3.12.17.

A5587 **SARD** tested 21.10.17 (OK) and allotted to BEF 22.10.17. **8 AAP** dd ex SARD 22.10.17. **102 Sqn** by 5.11.17, involved in heavy landing 14.5.18 and damaged by ground fire night bombing 22.5.18 (Capt AL Chick/Lt WO Patey OK) and recorded as poor with 124hr 56min flying time. **2 AIS** ex 102 Sqn 25.5.18 (unserviceable for further war service) and deleted by 2 ASD 29.5.18 (NWR, flying time 124hr 56min).

A5588 **8 AAP** allotted to BEF 4.10.17. **1 AD** dd ex 8 AAP 14.10.17 (160hp Beardmore 115/WD9563). **101 Sqn** by 23.10.17 and damaged in crash at Westoutre on night bombing sortie 7.11.17 (2Lt DL Lynn/2Lt AW Janes OK). **1 AD** ex 101 Sqn 12.11.17 and deleted 15.11.17.

A5589 **SARD** tested 21.10.17 (OK) and allotted to BEF 22.10.17. **101 Sqn** by 23.10.17 and damaged in crash returning from forced landing 1.12.17 (2Lt Day). **1 AD** ex 101 Sqn 2.12.17.

A5590 **2 AIS** dd ex 1 ASD 28.7.18.

A5591 **SARD** allotted to BEF 20.10.17, tested 20.10.17 (OK) and 23.10.17 (pressure dud). **8 AAP** dd ex SARD 23.10.17. **102 Sqn** by 31.10.17 and crashed into fields after hitting pipe on take off for test flight 3.1.18. **1 AD** ex 102 Sqn 3.1.18. **2 ASD** deleted 12.2.18 (NWR, flying time 35hr). BUT **2 AI** dd ex Marquise 28.7.18.

A5592 **8 AAP** allotted to BEF 8.10.17. **1 AD** dd ex England 18.10.17 (160hp Beardmore 1314/WD20223). **100 Sqn** dd ex 2 AD Candas 1.11.17. and wrecked when hit tree taking off on night bombing sortie 5.1.18 (2Lt H Moreley injured). **2 AD** ex 100 Sqn 5.1.18. **2 ASD** and deleted 21.1.18 (NWR, flying time 14hr).

A5593 **8 AAP** allotted to BEF 6.10.17. **1 AD** dd ex England 14.10.17 (160hp Beardmore 1307/WD20216). **2 AD** dd ex 1 AD 21.10.17 (Sgt Mitchell). **100 Sqn** dd ex 2 AD 22.11.17 and damaged by EA while in hangar 22.11.17. **2 ASD** and deleted 17.12.17 (NWR).

A5594 **8 AAP** allotted to BEF 8.10.17. Presentation a/c *Johore No 4* wef 10.10.17. **1 AD** dd ex 8 AAP 23.10.17 (Lt CH Drew). **102 Sqn** by 5.11.17 and wrecked in forced landing near Bethune on night bombing sortie 27.11.17 (Lt H Hammond OK/2Lt H Howard injured). **1 AD** ex 102 Sqn 28.11.17.

A5595 **8 AAP** allotted to BEF 12.10.17. Re-allotted to HD Brigade 17.10.17. **33 HDS** C Flt by 27.2.18 until @ 4.18.

A5596 **8 AAP** allotted to BEF 6.10.17. **1 AD** dd ex England 15.10.17 (160hp Beardmore 131/WD9579). **101 Sqn** and force landed on night bombing sortie 20.4.18 (flying time 91hr 4min). **102 Sqn** dd ex 2 ASD 21.9.18 and crashed after hitting E7048 on take off for night bombing sortie 9.11.18.

A5597 **8 AAP** allotted to BEF 4.10.17. **1 AD** dd ex England in packing case 15.10.17 (160hp Beardmore 107/WD9553). **102 Sqn** by 23.10.17 and crashed in forced landing in fog near Le Havre after becoming lost on night bombing sortie 28.2.18 with crew burning machine, thinking they were in enemy territory (Lt P Sim/Lt W Zeigler OK, flying time 48hr).

A5598 **AID** allotted to BEF 12.9.17. **101 Sqn** dd ex 1 AD 8.10.17 (160hp Beardmore 83/WD9531) and damaged in forced landing near Berck-sur-Mer on night bombing sortie 19.12.17 (2Lt GT Wix/2Lt FJ Lain OK). **1 ASD** ex 101 Sqn 20.12.17. On BEF charge 30.6.18.

A5599 **AID** allotted to BEF 12.9.17. **8 AAP** dd ex SARD 23.9.17. **101 Sqn** and LIA night bombing Gontrode 29.9.17 (Lt GF Westcott/2Lt EAV Ellerbeck POW – shot down by ground fire – had taken off 20.15). BUT **199 DS**, crashed in gale at Kirton Lindsey 24.11.17 (Lt JH Matthew/Lt Davies OK).

A5600 **8 AAP** allotted to BEF 28.8.17. **101 Sqn** and crashed in mist near Brancourt on night bombing sortie 12.3.18 (Lt AHG Dunkerley/Lt WS Aulton OK. Flying time 102hr 8min). **2 ASD** for deletion 19.3.18, NWR (flying time 102 hours). BUT 5600 recorded wrecked in forced landing at Market Rasen on 33 HDS A Flt 17.3.18 (2Lt J Helingoe).

A5601 Presentation a/c *Gold Coast No 10*. **8 AAP** allotted to BEF 4.9.17. **100 Sqn** dd ex 1 AD 30.9.17 (160hp Beardmore 16/WD9544) and LIA night bombing 18.2.18 (Lt GG Jackson/AM2 JC Guyat POW. Flying time 48hr 57min).

A5602 **8 AAP** Lympne allotted to BEF 21.9.17. **101 Sqn** Clairmarais South by 9.10.17. **1 AD** ex 101 Sqn 9.10.17 (160hp Beardmore 86/WD9534, surplus to establishment). Flown to England ex **1 ASD** Marquise 21.4.18 (flying time 112hr 22min).

A5603 **8 AAP** allotted to 58 Sqn mobilising at Dover and re-allotted to BEF 8.1.18. **58 Sqn** dd ex 1 AIS 23.3.18 and damaged in forced landing after engine overheated on night bombing sortie 22.8.18 (Lt WR Greathead/2Lt LH Bell OK). **1 AD** ex 58 Sqn 24.8.18 (flying time 166hr 35min). **1 ASD** deleted 28.8.18 (NWR, flying time 167hr 5min).

A5604 **58 Sqn** dd 23.2.18. **58 Sqn** dd 27.9.18. **2 ASD** ex 58 Sqn 28.9.18. **83 Sqn** dd ex 2 ASD 28.9.18 and wrecked in crash in mist on night recce 7.10.18 (flying time 251hr 51min). Deleted on unit 7.10.18.

A5605 **83 Sqn** by 3.18 and wrecked in crash after engine hit by ground fire on night bombing sortie 20.4.18 (Lt GW Higgs/2Lt PA Bankes MC IIA. Flying time 32hr 59min). **1 ASD** ex Advanced Salvage and deleted 25.4.18.

A5606 **SARD** allotted to BEF 14.1.18. **100 Sqn** dd ex 2 ASD 5.3.18 and wrecked in crash after hitting ridge on take off for night bombing sortie 5.6.18. **2 ASD** ex 100 Sqn 5.6.18.

A5607 **1 ASD** 14.5.18. **58 Sqn** dd ex 1 AIS 18.5.18 ? and damaged in forced landing with engine vibrating badly on night bombing sortie 3/4.9.18 (Sgt EE Jones/2Lt FW

Roadhouse OK. Flying time 106hr 05min). **1 AD** ex 58 Sqn 5.9.18, deleted 5.11.18 and reconstructed as H7230 wef 5.11.18.

A5608 **83 Sqn**. **SD Flt** dd ex 83 Sqn 12.3.18 and wrecked landing on aerodrome after night bombing sortie to Bapaume 2.6.18 (Lt J Wingate/2Lt LA Taylor OK. Flying time 54hr 30min). **1 AD** ex SD Flt 7.6.18. **1 ASD** deleted 10.6.18, NWR (flying time 61hr 10min).

A5609 **SARD** tested 9.1.18 (OK) allotted to 58 Sqn mobilising at Dover and re-allotted to BEF 9.1.18. **1 AIS** dd ex 1 AD St-Omer 25.1.18. **58 Sqn** dd ex 1 AIS 20.2.18 and wrecked 3.5.18 when hit on test flight by F2B B1245 of 62 Sqn (2Lt HW Gardner/2Lt DR Goudie OK). **1 ARD** ex 58 Sqn 5.5.18 (flying time 67hr 35min). On BEF charge 30.6.18.

A5610 **51 HDS**. **58 Sqn** and wrecked hitting tree in forced landing near Pitgem after engine failed on night bombing sortie to Menin 15.3.18 (2Lt HW Gardner/2Lt a Brock OK). **1 ASD** to **2 ASD** 4.18. **102 Sqn** by 2.6.18 and LIA on night recce 16.9.18 (Lt CB Naylor/Lt H Mercer POW. Flying time 198hr 20min, 160hp Beardmore 154/WD9602).

A5611 **8 AAP** allotted to BEF 5.1.18. **1 ASD** damaged after stall on take-off for delivery to 83 Sqn 13.3.18, reconstructed and tested 16.4.18. **102 Sqn** and wrecked in crash following stall when zoomed over tree on night bombing sortie 16.5.18 (2Lt SC Mimmack/Lt AEG Bailey injured. Flying time 20hr 43min). **2 ASD** deleted 28.5.18.

A5612 **199 NTS** and wrecked in crash from stall 5.2.18 (AM2 TA Condron KIFA).

A5613

A5614

A5615 **199 DS** by 11.17 until @ 3.18.

A5616 **38 HDS** A Flt by 11.17. **199 NTS** by 26.1.18 and burnt out in crash after hitting tree on landing at 01.35 on 24.4.18 (2Lt HG Achurch KIFA).

A5617 **SARD** allotted to BEF 2.10.17 (160hp Beardmore) and tested 12.10.17 (OK) and 13.10.17 (pressure dud). **8 AAP** dd ex SARD 13.10.17. **1 AD** dd ex England 15.10.17 (160hp Beardmore 801/WD7161). **101 Sqn** by 23.10.17 and damaged in forced landing after engine failed on night bombing sortie 27.3.18 (Capt JA Middleton/2Lt CW Phillips OK).

A5618 **SARD** allotted to BEF 12.10.17 (160hp Beardmore). **8 AAP** dd ex SARD 15.10.17. **1 AD** dd ex England 15.10.17 (160hp Beardmore 928/WD7538). **101 Sqn** dd ex 1 AD 16.10.17 (160hp Beardmore 928/WD7538). and crashed landing in mist on night bombing sortie 12.3.18. **2 ASD** for deletion 19.3.18, NWR (flying time 76hr 33min).

A5619 **SARD** allotted to BEF but re-allotted to HD Brigade 2.11.17, tested 11.11.17 (engine very rough) and 14.11.17 (engine still rough) and 17.11.17 (OK). **51 HDS** B Flt by 11.1.18 until @ 13.1.18. **51 HDS** C Flt by 18.8.18.

A5620 **AID** allotted to BEF 9.1.17.

A5621 **200 NTS** and crashed in sideslip from downwind turn 25.3.18 (crew injured).

A5622 **36 HDS** C Flt by 4.4.18.

A5623 **38 Sqn** by 8.6.18 and force landed after engine failure on night bombing sortie 25.7.18. **4 ASD** ex 38 Sqn 31.7.18, beyond repair. **2 Salvage Section** ex 4 ASD 19.9.18.

A5624 **AID** allotted to BEF 9.11.17. **1 AIS** ex 1 AD 14.12.17. **101 Sqn** by 22.12.17 and damaged in enemy bombing of aerodrome 1.4.18 (flying time 72hr 40min). **2 ASD** ex 101 Sqn 1.4.18. **1 ASD** Reception Park 24.5.18. **2 ASD** 25.5.18. **102 Sqn** dd ex 2 ASD 27.5.18 and lost in forced landing on night bombing sortie 16.9.18 - unsalvageable. BUT **2 ASD** and deleted 9.10.18 (NWR flying time 24hr 50min).

A5625 **8 AAP** allotted to BEF 4.1.18 (160hp

FE2b A5635 being tested. The photograph was probably taken at Kirton Lindsey, a 33 Sqn aerodrome. This FE2b has toned-down markings, which were uncommon on such machines used in Home Defence.

Beardmore). **100 Sqn** dd ex 2 ASD 20.2.18 and damaged in forced landing in field en-route for Ochey 9.5.18 (crew shaken). **2 ASD** ex 100 Sqn via 6 AP, 9.5.18 and deleted 21.6.18 (NWR, flying time 26hr 50min).

A5626 **8 AAP** allotted to BEF 12.10.17 (160hp Beardmore) but re-allotted to HD Brigade 17.10.17. **33 HDS** HQ Flt and wrecked in crash, landing too steeply, 12.1.18 (2Lt FJH Livingstone KIFA).

A5627 **AID** allotted to BEF 9.11.17. Allocation cancelled 10.11.17. Re-allotted to BEF 4.1.18. **83 Sqn** and crashed in forced landing after engine failure on night recce 27.6.18. **2 AD** ex 83 Sqn 29.6.18. **2 ASD** deleted 6.7.18 (NWR, flying time 117hr 15min).

A5628 **AID** allotted to BEF 9.11.17. Allocation cancelled 10.11.17. Re-allotted to BEF 7.1.18. **100 Sqn** (engine 313/WD9761) dd ex 2 AD 21.2.18 to replace machine lost 18/19.2.18. **3 ASD** ex 100 Sqn 26.7.18.

A5629 Presentation a/c *Malaya No 11*. **8 AAP** allotted to BEF 16.10.17 (160hp Beardmore). **1 AD** ex England 16.11.17. **1 AD** ex Repair Park 23.11.17. **1 AIS** ex 1 AD 23.11.17. **102 Sqn** by 30.11.17 and force landed after engine failure on night bombing sortie 3.1.18 (Lt PH Cummings/Lt HA Parry OK). **1 ASD** deleted 4.2.18 (NWR, flying time 14hr). BUT **148 Sqn** flown Auchel–Sains-lès-Pernes 3.5.18 (2Lt J Helingoe/Cpl Carpenter). **1 ASD** 5.5.18. **2 ASD** 8.5.18 and on BEF charge 30.6.18.

A5630 Presentation a/c *Punjab No 5*. **8 AAP** allotted to BEF 16.10.17 (160hp Beardmore). **1 AD** ex England 18.11.17. **102 Sqn** and force landed near Acq after engine failed on night bombing sortie 13.3.18. **2 ASD** for deletion 21.3.18, NWR (flying time 133hr 15min).

A5631 **8 AAP** allotted to BEF 7.1.18 (160hp Beardmore). **2 ASD** and crashed near aerodrome on ferry flight to VIII Brigade after engine cut 20.2.18. **1 ASD** 5.5.18. **2 ASD** 8.5.18. **102 Sqn** by 5.8.18 and damaged in forced landing on night bombing sortie 24.8.18 (crew OK). **2 ASD** 24.8.18 and deleted 14.9.18 (NWR, flying time 133hr).

A5632 **8 AAP** allotted to BEF 5.1.18 (160hp Beardmore). **101 Sqn** and crashed landing near Longre after hit by French AA on night bombing sortie 13.4.18 (Lt GEP Elder IIA/2Lt SM Sproat OK). Flying time 37hr 3min). **2 ASD** ex 2 Salvage Dump and deleted 23.4.18.

A5633 **SARD** tested 4.6.18 (OK).

A5634 **33 HDS** 17. **36 HDS** B Flt and wrecked in crash during night-landing practice 15.1.18 (2Lt AF Quelch KIFA – 3 landings

then crashed from 700ft. 160hp Beardmore 1427/WD20336).

A5635 **33 HDS** B Flt by 19.10.17 (2Lt AS Harris AZP) BUT **51 HDS** dd ex AID 6.12.17.

A5636 **SARD** tested 5.1.18 (OK). **58 Sqn** by 31.5.18 and wrecked in crash near Bethune after engine failed on return from night recce 4.7.18 (2Lt HG Jeffrey KIA/2Lt H Booth IIA – initially reported missing). **1 AD** ex 58 Sqn 10.7.18. **1 ASD** deleted 13.7.18 (NWR – listed as A8636).

A5637 **33 HDS** C Flt by 1.3.18 until @ 13.3.18.

A5638

A5639 **33 HDS** and wrecked in crash due to bad flying on night flight 6.2.18 (Lt HS Marshall fatally IIFA/AM2 Bradshaw IIFA).

A5640 **192 NTS** by 1.18.

A5641 **101 Sqn** reported shot up night bombing and in need of overhaul 5.9.18 (flying time 212hr 20min).

A5642 **ES Orfordness** by 1 18 until @ 4.18. **ES Martlesham Heath** by 7.7.18 (night bomb sight tests, Lt JAW Armstrong/Sgt Kinneard).

A5643 Allotted to BEF 31.1.18. **101 Sqn** and damaged in enemy bombing of aerodrome 1.4.18 (flying time 5hr 55min). **2 ASD** ex 101 Sqn 3.4.18. **1 ASD** Repair Park 18.5.18. **1 AIS** ex 1 ASD 20.5.18. **58 Sqn** dd ex 1 AIS 5.7.18. **2 ASD** ex 58 Sqn 27.9.18. **83 Sqn** dd ex 2 ASD 28.9.18. **102 Sqn** dd ex 83 Sqn 20.1.19.

FE2b A5648 stands behind this machine which displays the 'lazy M' marking of 199 NTS.

FE2b A5660. The overpainted rudder stripes were a concession to its nocturnal role.

A5644 **58 Sqn** dd ex 1 AIS 3.4.18 and crashed into hole taking off too slowly on night bombing sortie 8.5.18 (Lt GL Castle/2Lt AH Harrison OK). **1 RP** ex 58 Sqn (flying time 27hr 50min).

A5645 **199 DS** by 11.17.

A5646 **199 NTS** by 4.18. **187 NTS** by 7.18.

A5647 **3 AAP** allotted to 58 Sqn mobilising and dd 27.10.17. Re-allotted to BEF 7.1.18. **58 Sqn** dd ex 1 RP 6.2.18 and wrecked in crash returning from night bombing 26.9.18 (Lt AH Thompson/2Lt LH Bell KIA. Flying time 189hr 35min).

A5648 Presentation a/c *Baroda No 14*. **199 NTS** by 15.1.18. **200 NTS** and wrecked in crash 16.10.18, hitting tree during forced landing (Flt Cdt EV French KIFA).

A5649 **SARD** tested 19.6.17 and 31.8.17 (OK). **8 AAP** allotted to BEF 31.1.18 (160hp Beardmore) . **102 Sqn** by 3.18 and propeller damaged by ground fire and force-landed near Ficheux on night bombing sortie 23.5.18 (Lt AB Whiteside/Lt EF Howard MC OK). **2 ASD** ex 102 Sqn 26.5.18 and deleted 7.6.18, NWR (flying time 92hr 24min).

A5650 – A5899: 250 RAF FE2b (120/160hp Beardmore) ordered from G & J Weir Ltd, Cathcart under Contract 87/A/1233. Last 100 cancelled.

A5650 **AID** allotted to BEF 18.7.17 (160hp Beardmore). **1 AD** tested 22.8.17. **2 AD** ex 1 AD 22.8.17. **100 Sqn** by 2.18. **3 AD** ex 100 Sqn 27.8.18 in exchange for HP 0/400. Sold to US government for USAS.

A5651 **SARD** allotted to BEF 2.7.17, tested 3.7.17 and 4.7.17. **100 Sqn** dd ex 2 AD 23.7.17 and damaged in enemy bombing of aerodrome

4.12.17 (repairable). **2 AD** ex 100 Sqn 4.12.17. **2 ASD** and deleted 12.1.18 (NWR, flying time 105hr).

A5652 **AID** allotted to BEF 18.7.17. **1 AD** tested 27.7.17. **100 Sqn** dd ex 2 AD 31.7.17 and LIA near Courtrai special night bombing 10.8.17 (2Lt EP Fulton/AM2 AW Hawkins POW – took-off at 02.05, became lost in bad weather, shot down by AA of Flakzeug 12).

A5653 **36 HDS** C Flt by 8.17.

A5654 **33 HDS** A Flt and burnt out in crash after side-slipping in from stall on night flying practice 26.7.17 (Lt TH Coupe KIFA, engine 160hp 775/WD7135).

A5655 **33 HDS** B Flt returned early from AZP with engine trouble 19.10.17 then took off again (2Lt JD Watson). **33 HDS** C Flt by 4.18. **33 HDS** B Flt by 21.8.18. **131 Sqn**. **199 NTS** by 12.18.

A5656 **33 HDS** HQ Flt by 21.8.17 (Major AAB Thomson/2Lt JR Smith 2 AZPs, landing at Scampton on the second). **33 HDS** B Flt by and crashed from 200ft after take-off in mist for AZP 19.10.17 (2Lt HP Solomon KIA/2Lt H Preston OK. Engine 160hp 20088).

A5657 **36 HDS** A Flt crashed on take-off 20.2.18 (Sgt AJ Joyce OK). **192 NTS** by 10.3.18. **33 HDS** B Flt by 3.9.18.

A5658 **1 AD** dd in case 25.8.17. **8 AAP** allotted to BEF 4.10.17. **1 AD** dd ex England 14.10.17 (160hp Beardmore 124/WD9572). **101 Sqn** by 22.10.17. **1 AD** tested 6.2.18. **2 AIS** 15.2.18. **1 ASD** 16.2.18. **2 ASD** 1.3.18. **101 Sqn** crashed landing on aerodrome after night bombing sortie to Bouchoir 1.4.18 (Lt R Affleck/Lt HJ Townson OK, flying time 87hr 28min). **2 ASD** ex 101 Sqn for repair. BUT **83 Sqn** dd 10.3.18 and damaged

in forced landing after engine seized on night bombing sortie 2.4.18. **1 ASD** for repair 3.4.18. **RP** 1 ASD 31.5.18 and deleted 25.6.18 when reconstructed as F5852. BUT **2 AI** 1.6.18. **101 Sqn** dd ex 2 ASD 12.6.18 and reported as old machine 21.10.18. **2 ASD** Repair Park ex 101 Sqn 23.10.18 for overhaul and reported there 26.10.18 with enquiries made 20.12.18 re this double identity.

A5659 **33 HDS** A Flt by 24.9.17 (2Lt DR Brook AZP landing at Kelstern NLG with engine failure) and further AZPs 19.10.17 (2Lt AR Kingsford/Lt CW Reid) and 12.3.18 (2Lt FA Benitz). **33 HDS** C Flt by 15.2.18 until @ 4.18. **33 HDS** B Flt by 12.8.18. **199 NTS** by 12.18 until @ 1.19.

A5660 **33 HDS** A Flt by 21.8.17 (Capt SW Price/2Lt DR Brook AZP). **33 HDS** C Flt by 12.2.18. **33 HDS** B Flt by 5.8.18 (2Lt JTG Murison AZP) until @ 21.8.18.

A5661 Presentation a/c *Montreal No 2*. **8 AAP** allotted to BEF 16.10.17 (160hp Beardmore). **102 Sqn** by 5.12.17, and recorded as unfit for service 2.8.18 (flying time 219hr). **2 ASD** ex 102 Sqn 5.8.18 ('unfit for further war service' flying time 219hr). **1 ASD** ex 2 Air Issues Section 9.8.18. **2 ASD** 13.8.18 (flying time 219hr 35min). Flown to England 13.8.18. BUT **149 Sqn** by 23.4.18 unitl @ 17.5.18.

A5662 **8 AAP** allotted to BEF 9.8.17 (160hp Beardmore). Allocation cancelled 14.8.17. **SARD** tested 31.8.17 (OK) and allotted to BEF. **8 AAP** dd ex SARD 2.9.17. **1 AD** dd ex Lympne 4.9.17. **102 Sqn** dd ex 1 AD 6.9.17 and wrecked in forced landing after radiator hit by ground fire on night bombing sortie 27.10.17 (Capt IAJ Duff WIA/Lt Davis OK). **1 AD** ex 102 Sqn.

A5663 **AID** allotted to BEF 24.10.17. **100 Sqn** and burnt out after bomb went off during loading for night bombing sortie 26.2.18 (24hr 23min flying time).

A5664 **SARD** tested 21.8.17. **8 AAP** dd ex SARD 21.8.17. **100 Sqn** dd ex 2 ASD 21.2.18. **16N Sqn** dd ex 100 Sqn 5.3.18, re-titled **216 Sqn** from 1.4.18. **100 Sqn** ex 216 Sqn 10.5.18.

A5665 **100 Sqn** damaged by fire 26.2.18. **83 Sqn** dd ex 1 AIS 24.3.18 and crashed after stall on take off for night bombing sortie 31.5.18. **2 ASD** 2.6.18 and deleted 13.6.18, NWR (flying time 41hr 20min).

A5666 **7 AAP** and wrecked in crash 3.3.19 – side-slipped in avoiding hangar after engine failed on take-off (both crew injured).

A5667 **AID** allotted to BEF 18.7.17. **2 AD** ex 1 AD 5.8.17. **18 Sqn** dd ex 2 AD 9.8.17 and wrecked overshooting landing, too fast, on travelling flight 10.8.17. **2 AD** ex 18 Sqn 13.8.17 and deleted 18.8.17.

A5668 On BEF charge 30.6.18.

A5669 **AID** allotted to BEF (160hp Beardmore). Allocation cancelled 10.12.17 – lost in Channel.

A5670 **1 AD** tested 16.11.17. **1 AIS** ex 1 AD RP 19.11.17. **102 Sqn** by 28.11.17 and recorded as tired 1.7.18. **2 ASD** deleted 17.7.18, NWR (flying time 191hr 8min).

A5671 **1 AIS** ex 1 AD RP 19.11.17. **100 Sqn** dd ex 2 ASD 20.2.18. **16N Sqn** dd ex 100 Sqn 5.3.18, re-titled **216 Sqn** from 1.4.18. **100 Sqn** ex 216 Sqn 10.5.18 and damaged hitting rut in forced landing on night bombing sortie 26.6.18. **2 ASD** ex 100 Sqn 26.6.18. Sold to US government. **USAS Aviation Centre** from 9.18.

A5672 **SARD** allotted to BEF 3.8.17 (160hp Beardmore). **101 Sqn** and LIA night bombing Roulers 21.9.17 (Capt AC Hatfield/2Lt RR Macgregor POW. Engine 65/WD9512).

A5673

A5674 **8 AAP** allotted to BEF 10.8.17 (160hp Beardmore). **2 AD** ex 1 AD 18.9.17. **100 Sqn** dd ex 2 AD 24.10.17 and in forced landing

A poor quality but interesting photo of A5650 'JESS' in American hands in France after service with 100 Sqn – still fitted with twin underwing tanks and brackets for Holt's flares.

after engine failed on take off for travelling flight 7.3.18. **2 ASD** ex 100 Sqn 7.3.18. On BEF charge 30.6.18.

A5675 **58 Sqn** dd ex 1 AIS 3.4.18 and wrecked when hit hole and overturned on take off for night bombing sortie 15.5.18 (2Lt JE Philpott injured/2Lt FW Roadhouse OK). **1 ASD** ex 58 Sqn 17.5.18 (23 flying hours) and deleted 20.5.18.

A5676 **SARD**, allotted to BEF 3.8.17 (160hp Beardmore), tested 12.8.17 (tail heavy) and 13.8.17 (OK). **2 AD** ex 1 AD 20.8.17. **102 Sqn** and LIA when wrecked in forced landing after engine hit on night bombing sortie 26.11.17 (Lt PH Cummings/Lt HA Parry OK). **1 AD** ex 102 Sqn 29.11.17.

A5677 **8 AAP** allotted to BEF 7.8.17 (160hp Beardmore). **102 Sqn** dd ex 1 AD 6.9.17 on charge until 17.4.18 when recorded as poor (flying time 118hr 41min). **2 ASD** ex 102 Sqn for overhaul 17.4.18 (118hr 41min flying time) and deleted 25.4.18, NWR (recorded as 116hr 41min flying time).

A5678 **SARD** allotted to HD Brigade but re-allotted to BEF 5.10.17, tested 6.10.17 (revs down, pressure dud) and 8.10.17 (OK) and 9.10.17 (OK). **8 AAP** dd ex SARD 10.10.17. **1 AD** dd ex England 10.10.17 (160hp Beardmore 93/WD9541). **102 Sqn** dd ex 1 AD 19.10.17 (160hp Beardmore 93/WD9541) and LIA night bombing 21.10.17 (Lt EH Kann/2Lt HD Barbour KIA).

A5679 **51 HDS** B Flt by 19.1.18 and wrecked in crash due to engine trouble, hitting tree, 12.2.18 (2Lt HG Donaldson fatally IIFA/2Lt AG Taylor IIFA). Sold to US government. **USAS Aviation Centre** by 30.9.18.

A5680 **SARD** allotted to BEF 3.9.17 (160hp Beardmore). **102 Sqn** dd ex 1 AD 6.9.17 and LIA night bombing 6.10.17 (2Lt RH Richardson/2Lt CE Carroll POW).

A5681 **SARD** allotted to BEF 3.8.17 and tested 13.8.17 (OK). **2 AD** ex 1 AD 16.8.17. **18 Sqn** ex 2 AD 21.8.17. **102 Sqn** dd ex 1 AD 9.10.17 (160hp Beardmore 1131/WD6954) and recorded as poor 11.5.18. Flown to England ex 1 ASD 14.5.18 (flying time 135hr).

A5682 **8 AAP** allotted to BEF 4.10.17 (160hp Beardmore). **1 AD** dd ex England 15.10.17 (160hp Beardmore 1066/WD7676). **2 AD** ex 1 AD 17.10.17 (160hp Beardmore 1066/WD7676). **2 ASD** by 19.2.18, allotted to 101 Sqn Auchel – aborted delivery flight that day. **101 Sqn** and force landed with overheated engine on night bombing sortie 16.5.18 (crew OK – a/c caught fire but extinguished). On BEF charge 30.6.18.

A5683 **36 HDS** C Flt by 12.1.18 and wrecked landing on aerodrome 00.01 after AZP 14.3.18 (Lt C MacLaughlin).

A5684 **36 HDS** B Flt Ashington as single-seat conversion by 14.10.17 (Lt JH Matthews) and in unsuccessful attack on submarine 13 miles SE of Seaham 8.5.18 (Lt Taylor dropped 1 bomb).

A5685 **8 AAP** allotted to BEF 4.8.17 (160hp Beardmore). **102 Sqn** dd ex 1 AD 5.9.17 and damaged in landing crash after night bombing sortie 16.3.18 (crew OK – had confused lights on aerodrome). **1 ASD** ex 2 ASD for deletion 15.4.18, NWR.

A5686 **8 AAP** Lympne allotted to BEF 4.8.17 (160hp Beardmore). **101 Sqn** Clairmarais South and damaged by ground fire night bombing 28.9.17 (Capt LGS Payne/Lt FP Worthington OK. Flying time 16hr 20min). **1 AD** dd wrecked ex 101 Sqn 5.10.17 (160hp Beardmore 753/WD7113) and deleted 8.10.17.

A5687 **8 AAP** allotted to BEF 10.8.17 (160hp Beardmore). **102 Sqn** dd ex 1 AD 13.9.17 and damaged in forced landing after engine cut on night bombing sortie 30.9.17 (Lt Taylor/Lt EV Collett OK). **2 AD** ex 102 Sqn

Night flying FE2b A5678 of 102 Sqn lost, along with its crew, on an early evening bombing raid on 21 October 1917. Its mainplanes, as was usual for night bombers, retained their standard cockades, but the rudder appears to have been overpainted with PC10 before a black serial number was applied.

30.9.17.

A5688 **8 AAP** allotted to BEF 9.8.17 (160hp Beardmore). **102 Sqn** and damaged in landing crash at Lealvillers, after night bombing sortie, when wheel came off 3.12.17 (2Lt Behm/2Lt EW Grant OK).

A5689 **38 Sqn** by 11.6.18 and LIA night bombing Thourout 24.6.18 (2Lt WC Tempest/2Lt W Turner POW).

A5690 **38 HDS** A Flt by 11.17.

A5691 **38 HDS** and wrecked 22.11.17. Deleted 28.11.17.

A5692 Presentation a/c *Punjab No 1, Bahawalpur* wef 10.10.17. **8 AAP** allotted to BEF 9.10.17 (160hp Beardmore). **2 ASD** ex 1 Ad 15.11.17. **100 Sqn** dd ex 2 ASD 18.2.18. **3 ASD** ex 100 Sqn 2.9.18. Sold to US government. **USAS Aviation Centre** by 16.9.18 until @ 30.9.18.

A5693 **38 Sqn**, damaged in landing crash 16.6.18 and crashed on beach near Dunkerque after engine failed on night bombing sortie 22.6.18. **2 Salvage Section** 19.9.18, beyond repair by 4 ASD.

A5694 **AID** allotted to BEF 25.9.17 (160hp Beardmore). **1 AD** dd ex England 30.9.17 (160hp Beardmore 871/WD7481). **101 Sqn** dd ex 1 AD 11.10.17 (160hp Beardmore 871/WD7481) and damaged by ground fire on night bombing sortie 28.6.17 and recorded with 180hr flying time 30.6.18.

A5695 **8 AAP** allotted to BEF 4.10.17 (160hp

Beardmore). **1 AD** dd ex England 14.10.17 (160hp Beardmore 125/WD9573). **100 Sqn** dd ex 2 AD 22.11.17 and LIA night bombing 21.1.18 (2Lt AH Peile/Lt CW Reid POW. Flying time 11hr 35min).

A5696 **8 AAP** allotted to BEF 6.10.17 (160hp Beardmore). **1 AD** dd ex England 14.10.17 (160hp Beardmore 1315/WD20224).

A5697 **200 NTS** by 3.18.

A5698 **38 HDS** A Flt and wrecked in crash after hit by AA on training flight 3.1.18 (Lt EF Wilson OK).

A5699 **200 NTS** by 8.18 until @ 26.10.18.

A5700 **AID** allotted to HD Brigade, re-allotted to BEF 5.10.17 (160hp Beardmore). **SARD** tested 6.10.17 (OK) and 8.10.17 (OK). **1 AD** dd ex England 9.10.17 (160hp Beardmore 3/WD9453). **102 Sqn** dd ex 1 AD 11.10.17 (160hp Beardmore 3/WD9453) and force landed after engine failed on night bombing sortie 25.1.18. **1 RP** ex 102 Sqn. **1 ASD** deleted 1.2.18 (NWR, flying time 54hr).

A5701 **AID** allotted to BEF 29.9.17 (160hp Beardmore). **SARD** tested 6.10.17 (OK) and 8.10.17 (OK). **1 AD** dd ex England 10.10.17 (160hp Beardmore 943/WD7553). **102 Sqn** by 18.10.17. **1 AD** ex 102 Sqn 18.10.17 (160hp Beardmore 943/WD7553). **101 Sqn** and wrecked in take off crash on night flying practice 18.12.17 (2Lt D Sinclair KIFA. Flying time 28hr).

FE2 A5689 (with index letter missing) of 38 Sqn, captured after force-landing on the beach at Blankenberghe on 24 June 1918. The rudder has been overpainted to reduce the white stripe, with the serial crudely and incompletely reapplied.

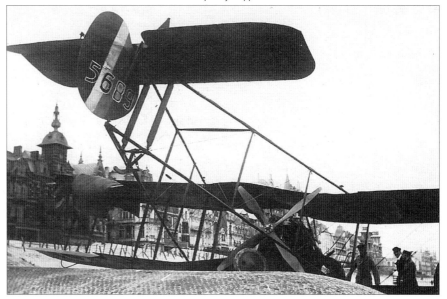

A dozen night bombing FE2bs of 83 Squadron ready to leave England in March 1918 while the crews hold a final discussion. A5712 and A5720 are in the centre.

A5702 **AID** allotted to BEF 25.9.17 (160hp Beardmore). **1 AD** ex England 5.10.17 (160hp Beardmore 109/WD9557). **2 AD** ex 1 AD 18.10.17 (160hp Beardmore 109/WD9557). **100 Sqn** dd ex 2 AD 21.10.17 and LIA night bombing railways between Falkenburg and Saarbrucken 24.10.17 (2Lt LM Archibald/Lt RS Greenslade POW. Flying time 10hr 45min).

A5703 **8 AAP** allotted to BEF 4.10.17 (160hp Beardmore). **1 AD** dd ex England in packing case 16.10.17 (160hp Beardmore 1308/WD20217). **102 Sqn** dd ex 2 ASD 12.1.18 and recorded as tired 2.7.18 with 157hr 15min flying time. **2 ASD** deleted 13.8.18, NWR.

A5704 **AID** allotted to BEF 12.9.17 (160hp Beardmore). **SARD** tested 26.9.17 (OK). **101 Sqn** dd ex 1 AD 1.10.17 (160hp Beardmore 77/WD9925) and damaged in crash on aerodrome on night bombing sortie. **1 AD** ex 101 Sqn 30.10.17 (flying time 18hr).

A5705 **8 AAP** allotted to BEF 28.8.17 (160hp Beardmore). **101 Sqn** dd ex 1 AD 3.11.17.

A5706 **8 AAP** allotted to BEF 6.9.17 (160hp Beardmore). **100 Sqn** dd ex 1 AD 5.10.17 (160hp Beardmore 1236/WD20195) and LIA night bombing railways 24.10.17 (2Lt WH Jones/Lt JS Godard POW – flying time 14hr 8min).

A5707 **38 HDS** B Flt and crashed near Coventry on AZP 12.4.18 (Lt CH Noble-Campbell WIA – possibly hit by AA).

A5708 **83 Sqn** by 2.8.18 and wrecked in forced landing after Michelin flare ignited on rack during night recce sortie 22.8.18 (flying time 133hr 15min).

A5709 Presentation a/c *Junagadh No 3*. Deleted 18. **83 Sqn** and damaged when hit by A5712 as it landed 15.5.18. On BEF charge 30.6.18.

A5710 **83 Sqn** by 16.2.18, to BEF with unit 6.3.18, via St-Omer and LIA on recce (15.00hr take-off) 16.3.18 (2Lt WH Taylor/2Lt CV Shakesby POW – brought down near Mericourt by AA).

A5711 **83 Sqn** by 17.2.18, and to BEF with the unit and force-landed after tank hit on night recce 21.9.18 (Major DA MacRae OK) then wrecked in crash avoiding tree in forced landing on travelling flight 27.9.18 (flying time 226hr 10min). **2 AD** 29.9.18 and deleted 30.9.18.

A5712 **83 Sqn** and wrecked landing from night bombing sortie when hit A5709 on aerodrome (crew injured). **2 Salvage Dump**, deleted by 2 ASD 29.5.18 (flying time 40hr 37min).

A5713 **8 AAP** by 7.3.18. **83 Sqn** and wrecked hitting firing butts in forced landing after engine failed on night recce 27.6.18. **2 ASD** deleted 5.7.18 (NWR, flying time 193hr 57min).

A5714 **ES Orfordness** (engine 160hp Beardmore) by 2.18 until @ 4.3.18. **8 AAP** by 7.3.18.

A5715 **199 DS** crashed into trees 10.10.17 by Lt Morris.

A5716

A5717 **199 DS**, damaged in ground collision with A5523 by Lt Morrice 12.10.17.

A5718

A5719 **36 HDS** B Flt by 15.10.17 (Lt JH Matthews) then **36 HDS** C Flt and LIA on patrol 6.11.17 (2Lt HD Crisp missing over North Sea on 17.00 night patrol).

A5720 **83 Sqn** by 15.2.18, to BEF with unit and wrecked in crash forced landing in hop field near Berthen after catching fire at 4000ft on night bombing sortie 23.3.18 (2Lt KW Payne/2Lt TH Singleton OK). **1 ASD** for deletion 8.4.18, NWR (flying time 17hr 15min).

A5721

A5722 **AID** allotted to BEF 25.9.17 (160hp Beardmore). **SARD** tested 30.9.17 (OK). **1 AD** dd ex England 2.10.17 (160hp Beardmore 102/WD9580). **102 Sqn** dd ex 1 AD 8.10.17 (160hp Beardmore 102/WD9550). **51 HDS** and damaged in forced landing after engine failure 15.2.18 (pilot OK, observer injured). **102 Sqn** by 3.18, crashed on take off for night bombing sortie 19.4.18. **2 ASD** ex 102 Sqn 23.4.18 (flying time 130hr 50min). **102 Sqn** by 5.8.18 and damaged in forced landing 17.8.18 after engine boiled on night bombing sortie. **2 ASD** 19.8.18 and deleted 10.9.18 (NWR, flying time 148hr 35min).

A5723 **AID** allotted to BEF 2.10.17 (160hp Beardmore), re-allotted to HD Brigade 9.10.17. **51 HDS** B Flt dd 10.10.17, on AZP 19.10.17 (Lt AR Nock), converted to single-

A5723 and A5724 in a lineup of 51 HDS machines; and A5723 (above) now with V undercarriage, flipped over after a landing accident that destroyed the front of the nacelle.

Force-landed at Skegness, FE2b A5732 of 51 HDS has the front cockpit faired over to adapt it to a single-seater for anti-zeppelin work.

seater and fitted with twin fixed Lewis guns and on charge until @ 2.18.

A5724 Re-allotted to HD Brigade 9.10.17 (160hp Beardmore). **51 HDS** B Flt dd 11.10.17, on AZP 19.10.17 (2Lt TH Gladstone), flight re-designated C Flt 2.18, converted to single-seater and fitted with twin fixed Lewis guns and further AZPs 12.4.18 (2Lt JR Smith) and 5.8.18 (Lt HW Steele).

A5725 **83 Sqn** and wrecked in forced landing after engine failed on gunnery practice 21.3.18. **1 AD** ex 83 Sqn 21.3.18. **102 Sqn** dd ex 2 ASD 25.5.18 and damaged in forced landing after engine failed on night bombing sortie 27.6.18 (pilot OK/observer injured). **2 ASD** deleted 4.7.18 (NWR, flying time 68hr 45min).

A5726 **AID** allotted to BEF 29.10.17 (160hp Beardmore).

A5727 **AID** Farnborough allotted to BEF with allotment cancelled 10.11.17 (160hp Beardmore). **SARD** Farnborough allotted to BEF with allotment cancelled 11.12.17, machine written off.

A5728 **AID** allotted to BEF with allotment cancelled 10.11.17 (160hp Beardmore). **1 AI** ex 1 AD 8.12.17. **101 Sqn** and wrecked on night bombing 12.4.18 (2Lt JP Holdsworth KIA/2Lt HJ Collins WIA – hit by French AA. Flying time 62hr 40min). **100 Sqn** dd ex 2 ASD 26.6.18 and wrecked 28.7.18. **3 AD** ex 100 Sqn under repair 28.7.18.

A5729 Presentation a/c *Gold Coast No 9* wef 10.10.17. **51 HDS** B Flt dd ex 8 AAP 12.10.17, flight re-designated C Flt 2.18, AZP 12.4.18 (Lt TH Gladstone) and on charge until @ 11.5.18.

A5730 **51 HDS** B Flt dd ex 8 AAP 12.10.17. and on charge until @ 24.2.18. **51 HDS** C Flt by 8.8.18.

A5731 Presentation a/c *Sultan of Kedah*. **51 HDS** C Flt dd 12.10.17 and wrecked 24.10.17. Deleted 3.11.17.

A5732 Presentation a/c *Malaya No 30* wef 10.10.17. **51 HDS** C Flt dd 10.10.17 transferred to 51 HDS A Flt by 12.4.18 (Lt Coombs AZP) and further AZP 5.8.18 (2Lt JL Drummond – force-landed at Skegness).

A5733 Presentation a/c *Waringford, Burma*. **51 HDS** C Flt dd 10.10.17 transferred to **51 HDS** B Flt dd 3.11.17, AZP 12.4.18 (2Lt CO Bird). **51 HDS** C Flt by 30.6.18 and crashed at Skegness 6.8.18 (Lt JL Drummond).

A5734 **83 Sqn**, overturned and wrecked in crash after hitting haystack near flares on night bombing sortie (2Lt JC Hopkins/2Lt MD Joseph injured). **2 ASD**, deleted 12.5.18. (NWR, flying time 46hr 19min).

A5735 Presentation a/c *Mauritius No 13*. **51 HDS** B

Another 51 HDS FE2b with a faired cockpit: A5733.

Flt by 30.11.17 until @ 15.2.18. **51 HDS** A Flt by 7.9.18 until @ 24.9.18. **1 (S) ARD** by 1.19.

A5736 **58 Sqn** (160hp Beardmore) by 22.3.18 and wrecked in forced landing after engine cut over Arras on night bombing sortie 1.4.18 (2Lt RN Iverach/Lt CE Jenkinson OK). **1 AD** ex 58 Sqn 1.4.18 (flying time 24hr 45min). On BEF charge 30.6.18.

A5737 **200 DS** by 8.17 (too early?). **199 DS** tested new 13.11.17 and photographed wrecked in crash.

A5738 **36 HDS** B Flt and in unsuccessful attack on submarine 5 miles E of Beadnell 31.5.18 (Lt Riley/Lt de Escolet dropped 2 bombs, one exploded on edge of conning tower). **36 HDS** A Flt by 29.9.18. **191 NTS** by 10.18.

A5739

A5740 Presentation a/c *Zanzibar No 3*. **36 HDS** A Flt and crashed below Pontop Pike on AZP at 22.45 14.3.18 (Sgt AJ Joyce KIA after side-slipping in. Engine 160hp Beardmore 201/ WD9649).

A5741 **36 HDS** B Flt Ashington by 14.3.18 (2Lt HE Ebrey AZP). **36 HDS** A Flt Hylton by 24.10.18.

A5742 **191 NTS**.

A5743 **38 Sqn** and LIA 12.8.18 when force-landed in water on night bombing sortie and sank in sea off Calais 11.8.18 (Lt HC McDonald/2Lt ER Bull OK). Shot up in water by EA). Deleted (general fatigue) 15.8.18.

A5744 FE2c converted at **SARD**. **AID** allotted to BEF 28.11.17. **2 AD** dd ex 1 ASD 6.12.17. Dispatched **2 ASD** to Montdidier 24.1.18 en-route 41 Wing. **100 Sqn** dd ex 2 ASD 26.1.18 and crashed after hitting wires on landing during enemy bombing of aerodrome 19.2.18 (2Lt HJ Crofts/2Lt JCE Price OK but shaken, flying time 12hr).

A5745 **8 AAP** allotted to BEF 1.2.18 (160hp Beardmore). **101 Sqn** dd ex 2 ASD 15.4.18 and damaged in force landing following AA hit on engine while on night recce 26.6.18 (Capt R Affleck/Major AB Mason OK). **2 ASD** deleted 6.7.18 (NWR, flying time 73hr 25min).

A5746 **8 AAP** allotted to BEF 25.1.18 (160hp Beardmore). **100 Sqn** dd ex 2 ASD 26.1.18 and destroyed by fire when starting up for practice flight 11.4.18 (flying time 25hr 20min).

A5747 **8 AAP** allotted to BEF 25.1.18 (160hp Beardmore). **101 Sqn** by 3.18. **102 Sqn** listed as 'poor' 26.7.18. **2 ASD** 29.7.18 for repair (flying time 155hr 35min). **1 ASD** dd ex 2 Air Issues Section 8.8.18. Flown to England 9.9.18 (flying time 156hr 50min). **8 TDS** by late summer 18.

A5748 **192 NTS** by 31.1.18 and damaged in crash from stall and spinning nose dive 17.7.18 (Flt Cdt JL Smith KIFA). BUT recorded on **100 Sqn** 24.7.18.

A5749 FE2d. **SARD** tested 12.2.17. Converted FE2b. **83 Sqn** dd ex 2 AIS 17.4.18 and damaged landing in mist from night bombing sortie 10.8.18 (crew OK). **2 ASD** ex 83 sqn 11.8.18 and deleted 16.8.18 (NWR, flying time 95hr 50min).

A5750 **58 Sqn** and crashed in forced landing near Hazebrouck after fuel pipe failure on night bombing sortie 21.4.18 (Capt D Gilley/2Lt JA Blythe OK. Flying time 73hr 35min). On BEF charge 30.6.18.

A5751

A5752 **1 SNBD** by 2.6.18.

A5753 **51 HDS** B Flt dd engine-less 9.11.17 and on charge until @ 12.4.18 (Lt F St C Sergeant AZP – fired on L62). **51 HDS** C Flt by 28.7.18 until @ 14.8.18.

A5754 **51 HDS** A Flt dd engine-less 9.11.17 with AZP 12.4.18 (Capt AR Nock) and further AZP 5.8.18 (Lt J Day) then wrecked in crash from nose dive 18.9.18 (both crew injured).

A5755 **192 DS** dd ex SARD 2.11.17, unit retitled **192 NTS** 21.12.17 and on charge until @ 16.5.18.

FE2b A5756 of 192 NTS being returned to the sheds after overturning. Sgt E.E. Jones instructed on this aircraft, which was fitted with dual controls.

8 AAP dd ex 1 ASD Marquise 17.9.18.

A5756 **192 DS** dd ex SARD 2.11.17, unit retitled **192 NTS** 21.12.17, instructional a/c of Sgt EE Jones and on charge until @ 11.6.18.

A5757 **192 NTS** by 21.12.17 until @ 15.5.18. **38 HDS** B Flt dd ex Newmarket 27.5.18. **38 Sqn** by 11.6.18. **102 Sqn** Serny ex 38 Sqn 19.1.19.

A5758 **192 NTS** by 5.2.18 and wrecked in crash after engine failure 5.4.18 (both crew injured).

A5759 **33 HDS** C Flt by 5.2.18. **192 NTS**. Crashed and overturned on landing in UK 31.7.18 (crew injured).

A5760 Presentation a/c *Johore No 4*. **1 SNBD** and wrecked in crash from stall and then caught fire 8.2.18 (2Lt FG Smith/FSL C Jewell KIFA).

A5761 Presentation a/c *Mauritius No 15*. **1 AD** tested 16.6.17. **33 HDS** C Flt by 23.3.18. **148 Sqn**. **149 Sqn** dd ex 148 Sqn 17.4.18. **97 Sqn** by 12.7.18. **115 Sqn**. **1 (S) ARD** by 18.1.19.

A5762 **3 AAP** allotted to 58 Sqn (moblising), re-allotted to BEF 7.1.18. **1 AIS** ex Reception Park 29.1.18. **58 Sqn** and LIA night bombing near Bray after engine failure 27.3.18 (2Lt JD Vaughan POW/Lt JC Thompson POW wdd – attached to 102 Sqn).

A5763 **51 HDS** C Flt by 4.18 and crashed in spin from 100ft after forced landing 2.8.18 (both crew injured) but returned to service by 15.5.18.

A5764 Presentation a/c *Sultan of Kedah No 2*. **51 HDS** by 2.18. **83 Sqn** by 3.18. 26 TS? **51 HDS** C Flt by 25.4.18 and crashed from slow turn 30.5.18 (both crew injured).

A5765

A5766 **101 Sqn** and deleted 4.4.18 after damage by bomb shrapnel (flying time 8hr).

A5767

A5768 **1 SNBD** by 12.4.18 until @ 13.4.18.

A5769 **1 SNBD** F Flt by 5.18 until 9.18. **8 TDS** by 27.9.18.

A5770 **102 Sqn**.

A5771 **2 ASD** dd ex **1 AD** 30.9.17.

A5772 **1 SNBD** E Flt by 25.4.18 until 9.18. **8 TDS** by 13.9.18.

A5773 **WEE** 1918.

A5774

A5775 **WEE** B Flt. **1 SNBD** by 4.18. **8 TDS** by 9.9.18.

A5776 **1 SNBD** by 24.3.18 until @ 4.18. **WEE** B Flt.

A5777 **4 AAP**, allotted to BEF (160hp Beardmore) 7.1.18. **192 NTS** by 19.3.18 and crashed in slow landing 7.7.18 (both crew injured).

A5778 **4 AAP**, allotted to BEF (160hp Beardmore) 7.1.18. **51 HDS** C Flt by 27.2.18, fitted with dual control by 25.4.18 and on charge until @ 15.7.18. **192 NTS** by 8.18. **191 NTS** by 11.18 and crashed after stalled on turn following engine failure on take-off 15.1.19.

A5779 **100 Sqn** dd ex 2 ASD 7.4.18 and force landed night bombing 23.5.18 (Lt LD Kirk/ Lt W Richards OK – initially reported MIA with 31hr 25min flying time).

A5780 **83 Sqn** and LIA night bombing Cambrai 16.6.18 (Sgt SC Bracey POW fatally WIA/2Lt P Kemp POW wdd. Flying time 81hr 35min).

A5781 **192 NTS**. **83 Sqn** and wrecked in crash when hit mast on take-off for engine test 11.4.18 (Capt JN MacRae/Flt Sgt A Westwood KIFA. Flying time 33hr 40min).

A5782 **83 Sqn** and wrecked in crash after tyre burst on take-off for night bombing sortie 23.3.18. **1 AD** ex 83 Sqn 24.3.18. **2 ASD** ex 1 ASD 8.5.18. **100 Sqn** dd ex 2 ASD 20.5.18 and wrecked 14.7.18.

A5783 **58 Sqn** dd ex **1 AIS** 21.3.18 and wrecked when swung and hit hangar on landing

from night bombing sortie 3.6.18 (Lt HG Jeffery/2Lt H Booth OK). **1 AD** ex 58 Sqn 5.6.18 (flying time 89hr 25min). On BEF charge 30.6.18. Deleted at 1 ASD 17.9.18 (flying time still 89hr 25min) and reconstructed as H7145 wef 17.9.18.

A5784 **8 AAP** allotted to BEF (160hp Beardmore) 28.1.18. **58 Sqn** dd 8.6.18. **100 Sqn** dd ex 2 ASD 13.8.18. **3 ASD** wrecked ex 100 Sqn 23.8.18 and deleted 9.18 (flying time 100hr).

A5785 **8 AAP** allotted to BEF (160hp Beardmore) 28.1.18. **1 SNBD** by 23.3.18 until @ 7.18. **102 Sqn** by 5.8.18 and recorded as old 2.9.18 (flying time 246hr 53min). **2 ASD** dd 5.9.18 ('unfit for war service'). **1 ASD** ex 2 ASD and flown to England (flying time 250hr 3min). **8 AAP** ex Marquise 17.9.18 (160hp Beardmore 1204/WD20113).

A5786 **101 Sqn** dd ex 2 ASD 31.3.18 and damaged in enemy bombing of aerodrome 1.4.18. **2 ASD** ex 101 Sqn 1.4.18. **1 ASD**. **2 ASD** ex 1 ASD 31.5.18. **58 Sqn** dd ex 2 AIS 9.6.18. **2 ASD** ex 58 Sqn 3.10.18.

A5787 **8 AAP** allotted to BEF (160hp Beardmore) 28.1.18. **100 Sqn** dd ex **2 ASD** 8.3.18 and wrecked in crash after hit rut on take-off for practice flight 14.6.18. **2 ASD** ex 100 Sqn 14.6.18 and deleted 27.6.18 (NWR, flying time 57hr 35min) BUT **102 Sqn** by 7.18.

A5788 **8 AAP** allotted to BEF (160hp Beardmore) 28.1.18. **101 Sqn** damaged in crash when controls broke on take-off for night bombing sortie 12.4.18 (crew OK, flying time 24hr). **2 ASD** for repair. **101 Sqn** dd ex 2 ASD 7.6.19 and crashed after hitting A6482 on landing from night bombing 17.7.18 (crew OK). **2 ASD** deleted 8.8.18, NWR.

A5789 **58 Sqn** dd ex **1 AIS** 1.4.18, damaged when propeller came off on night recce 28.5.18 (Capt GK Palmer/Lt JM Faquhar OK) and overturned and wrecked in forced landing when night bombing 6/7.6.18 (Lt CH Weir injured/Lt CE Jenkinson OK). **1 AD** ex 58 Sqn 9.6.18 (flying time 79hr 15min). On BEF charge 30.6.18. Deleted 5.11.18 and reconstructed as H7233 wef 5.11.18.

A5790 **192 DS** dd ex Glasgow 7.11.17. **1 SNBD** by 6.19.

A5791 **192 DS** dd ex Glasgow 7.11.17. **83 Sqn** and wrecked and burnt when shot down by ground fire near Avion on day recce 16.3.18 (Capt OE Ridewood WIA/Lt FF Hutchison OK).

A5792 **192 DS** dd 7.11.17. **1 SNBD** by 17.5.18 until 9.18. **8 TDS** by 15.9.18.

A5793 **192 DS** dd 7.11.17. **2 AD** by 19.11.17. **100 Sqn** dd ex 2 AD 19-22.11.17. **1 SNBD** by 12.4.18 and wrecked in crash after engine cut 25.4.18 (Lt EG Goy KIFA/Lt CE Black IIFA). Crashed in nose dive from low turn after engine cut at South Farnborough 8.7.18 (Lt GMV Bidie injured/AM1 Manning KIFA).

FE2b A5764 at 51 NTS. The observer's canvas windscreen is raised, showing the supporting framework.

FE2d A6355 of 57 Sqn, before and after capture. It was lost in a big dogfight on 29 April 1917 after going to the assistance of SE5 fighters, being shot down by Untoff F. Gille of Jasta 12.

A5794 **192 DS** dd ex Glasgow 7.11.17. **1 SNBD** by 23.3.18 until @ 1.8.18.

A5795 **199 DS** by 11.17. Hit by A6590 taking off 22.4.18 (Lt Roy OK) – 199 NTS?

A5796

A5797 On BEF charge 30.6.18. **83 Sqn** by 1.8.18. **102 Sqn** ex 83 Sqn 20.1.19.

A5798 **199 DS/NTS** by 19.12.17 until @ 5.18. **200 NTS** by 4.10.18 until @ 8.10.1918 (fitted with dual control).

A5799 **199 NTS** and crashed and burnt following stall and spinning nose dive 2.1.18 (crew injured).

A6351 – A6600: 250 RAF FE2d (250hp Rolls-Royce Mk.I/III/IV or 275hp Rolls-Royce Mk.I/II) to Contract 87/A/658 and erected by Boulton & Paul Ltd, Norwich, with nacelles built by Richard Garrett & Sons Ltd, Leiston. Many completed as/converted to FE2b (160hp Beardmore).

A6351 FE2d. Presentation a/c *Newfoundland No 2*. Allotted BEF. Flown to England 2.17. **46 RS/TS** by 27.3.17 until @ 5.17. **33 HDS** and crashed into house near New Holland NLG on night flying 14/15.8.17 (Lt AW Rowlands KIFA, engine 1/250/63/WD6196).

A6352 FE2d. Presentation a/c *Malaya No 29* wef 18.1.17. At Norwich 27.1.17 allotted to BEF. **2 AD** ex 1 AD 25.4.17. **57 Sqn** dd ex 2 AD 25.4.17 and LIA in combat near Douai on patrol 30.4.17 (2Lt ED Jennings/2Lt JR Lingard POW – possibly brought down by Ltn L v Richthofen, Jasta 11. Flying time 25hr 1min, engine 1/279/59/WD13885).

A6353 FE2d. Presentation a/c *Johore No 2* wef 18.11.16. **28 Sqn** by 26.5.17, allotted to 'K' Replacement squadron BEF 28.3.17. Re-allotted to Training Brigade 24.4.17. Allotted to BEF 4.7.17. Lympne 5.7.17. **20 Sqn** and crashed after hitting road on landing after OP 12.7.17 (2Lt CH Beldam OK/2Lt RM Madhill IIFA). **33 HDS** A Flt by 19.10.17 (2Lt TE Carley/Cpl Smith AZP).

A6354 FE2d. At Norwich 14.2.17 allotted to BEF. Allotment cancelled 3.3.17, on charge DAE2a Repair Section. **SARD** allotted to BEF 18.4.17. **20 Sqn** by 12.5.17 and victs 13.5.17 (Lt AN Solly/AM2 C Beminster destroyed an EA C-type near Menin at 11.00), 15.5.17 (Lt AN Solly/AM2 C Beminster sent an Albatros D.III OOC near Quesnoy at 07.00) and 12.6.17 (Lt AN Solly/2Lt FJ Kydd sent an Albatros D.III OOC near Zandvoorde) then damaged in force landing crash after wire broke on OP 2.7.17.

A6355 FE2d. Presentation a/c *Gold Coast No 6*. **2 AD**

ex 1 AD 15.3.17. **20 Sqn** ex 2 AD 18.3.17. **2 AD** ex 20 Sqn 23.3.17 (250hp RR). In France, allotted to ES Orfordness, re-allotted to BEF 27.3.17. **57 Sqn** as a/c B3 dd ex 2 AD 5.4.17 and LIA in combat near Barelle on patrol 29.4.17 (2Lt FAW Handley/2Lt E Percival POW after sending an Albatros D.III OOC near Noyelles at 10.30 – probably shot down by Untoff F Gille, Jasta 12. Flying time 64hr 57min, engine 4/250/131/WD12102).

A6356 FE2d. Presentation a/c *Ceylon No 4, Flying Fox* wef 18.1.17. **28 Sqn** by 14.5.17 until @ 24.5.17. **33 HDS** C Flt by 24.9.17 (Lt Carruthers AZP – aborted due to engine trouble). Converted to FE2b. **NARD** 12.18 allotted to BEF, allotment cancelled 9.1.19 and awaiting deletion18.1.19.

A6357 FE2d. Presentation a/c *Punjab No 27*. **28 Sqn** by 15.3.17. In France allotted to 'K' Replacement squadron BEF 28.3.17. **20 Sqn** by 25.5.17 and damaged hitting ditch in forced landing near aerodrome on patrol 4.6.17. BUT flown to England 8.3.17.

A6358 FE2d. Presentation a/c *Bombay No 2*. At Norwich 14.2.17 allotted to BEF. **20 Sqn** and LIA near Bellewaarde on bombing sortie 6.4.17 (2Lt R Smith/Lt R Hume KIA – probably shot down by OffSt W Göttsch, Jasta 8. –Flying time 13hr 1min, engine 4/250/135/WD12116).

A6359 FE2d. Presentation a/c *Overseas Club Empire Day 16 No 4*. Gosport by 22.3.17 (28 Sqn?). In France allotted to 'K' Replacement squadron BEF 28.3.17. **20 Sqn** and vict 29.4.17 (2Lt RE Conder/2Lt HG Neville sent an Albatros D.III OOC near Courtrai at 17.00) then damaged in forced landing after lost propeller on OP

1.5.17 then victs 15.8.17 (Lt HW Joslyn/2Lt JP Adams destroyed an Albatros D.V near Poelcapelle at 18.10) and 19.8.17 (2Lt JL Boles/L-Cpl W Harrop sent an Albatros D.V OOC near Menin at 17.00). Flown to England 12.9.17.

A6360 FE2d. Presentation a/c *Australia No 10, NSW No 9*, donated 19.10.16. At Norwich 14.2.17 allotted to BEF. **2 AD** ex 1 AD 25.3.17. **57 Sqn** dd ex 2 AD 25.3.17. **25 Sqn** by 1.6.17 and damaged in successful combat with 4 EA near Habourdin on bombing sortie 8.6.17 (Sgt R Mann WIA/AM2 J Harris OK – had sent an Albatros D.III OOC near Haubourdin at 07.35). Flown to England 9.9.17.

A6361 FE2d. Presentation a/c *Australia No 11, NSW 10, 'Duplicate Tweed No 9'* donated 20.10.16 and wef 18.1.17. **9 RS** by 2.17 until @ 3.17.

A6362

A6363

A6364 FE2d. Presentation a/c *Mauritius No 3* wef 18.1.17. Gosport by 23.3.17 (28 Sqn?). Yatesbury (59 RS/TS ?) by late 17.

A6365 FE2d. **AID** allotted to BEF 14.2.17. **RAF** 19.2.17, re-engined with 275/91/WD13889, airscrew 13889F. **25 Sqn** by 1.6.17 and vict 6.6.17 (Sgt JHR Green/Pte H Else shared sending an Albatros D.III OOC near Sallaumines at 12.05 with A6401 and A6500) then wrecked after engine failed on take-off for photo sortie/patrol 7.7.17 (Capt MGB Copeman KIFA). **2 AD** deleted 8.7.17.

A6366 FE2d. **SAD** allotted to BEF 3.3.17. **20 Sqn** by 7.5.17 and shelled to destruction following forced landing after combat on OP 25.5.17 (2Lt JH Baring-Gould WIA/Lt CA Hoy IIA – possibly shot down by Ltn A Hanko, Jasta

25 Sqn FE2d A6378 was lost on reconnaissance on 28 May 1917. The banded nacelle markings are typical of this unit, three bands signifying C Flight.

28). Engine RR1/250/41 WD6164.

A6367 FE2d. **AID** allotted to BEF 17.2.17. **RAF** 23.2.17, engine 4/250/149/WD12138. BEF allotment cancelled and on charge DAE2a Repair Section 7.3.17.

A6368 FE2d. At Lympne allotted to BEF 27.2.17. **20 Sqn** and vict 9.5.17 (Lt DY Hay/Sgt TE Wait sent an Albatros D.III OOC near Menin at 13.30) then damaged by AA near Weegscheede on OP 17.6.17 (Lt HW Joslyn/Lt SF Trotter OK). **1 AD** deleted 29.6.17 (NWR).

A6369 FE2d. At Lympne allotted to BEF 2.3.17. **25 Sqn** dd ex 1 AD 19.4.17 and on charge until @ 11.7.17.

A6370 FE2d. At Lympne allotted to BEF 2.3.17. **20 Sqn** and vict 6.4.17 (2Lt EO Perry/Pte TE Allum destroyed an Albatros D.III near Ledeghem at 10.10). **25 Sqn** by 1.6.17 brought down in forced landing at Monchy Fosse Farm after successful combat near La Bassée on patrol 11.7.17 (2Lt HS St C Sargant WIA/Lt JH Kirk OK – shot down by Obltn A Ritt v Tutschek, Jasta 12, after sending an Albatros D.V OOC near Oppy Wood at 17.30, engine 2/275/25/WD 13928).

A6371 FE2d. **RAF** 13.3.17, engine 2/275/3/WD13912. **AID** allotted to BEF 27.3.17. **25 Sqn** dd ex 1 AD 2.4.17 and LIA in combat near Lens on photo sortie 3.4.17 (Lt L Dodson POW wdd/2Lt HS Richards POW fatally wd – probably shot down by Ltn K Schaefer, Jasta 11. Flying time 3hr 45min).

A6372 FE2d. **RAF** 13.3.17, engine 2/275/7/WD13913. **AID** allotted to Training Brigade, re-allotted to BEF 27.3.17. **25 Sqn** dd ex 1 AD 4.4.17 and LIA on return from bombing Hénin-Liétard 13.4.17 (Capt LL Richardson/2Lt DC Wollen KIA – probably brought down by Obltn H Klein, Jasta 4).

A6373 FE2d. **AID** allotted to BEF 15.3.17. **RAF** 20.3.17, engine 2/275/9/WD13914. **25 Sqn** dd ex 1 AD 4.4.17 and victs 13.4.17 (2Lt RG Malcolm/2Lt JB Weir brought down an Albatros D.III near Hénin-Liétard at 19.30) and 21.4.17 (2Lt RG Malcolm/2Lt JB Weir captured an Albatros D-type neat Thelus – shared with Sopwith Triplane N5458 of 8N Sqn) then wrecked in crash when undercarriage lost on take off for test flight 11.5.17 (crew injured).

A6374 FE2d. 300hp Rolls-Royce (1st installation). **SARD** tested 13.5.17 and allotted to BEF 12.5.17. **20 Sqn** I and damaged in forced landing, hiting wires near Brandhoek after combat 24.5.17 (2Lt WP Scott/2Lt ES Cogswell IIA).

A6375 FE2d. **SARD** tested 6.6.17 (pressure dud – force-landed Laffans Plain), allotted to BEF 7.6.17 and re-tested 19.7.17 (OK). **8 AAP** dd ex **1 AD** 15.8.17. **33 HDS** B Flt by 19.10.17 (Lt JA Harman/AM1 Booth AZP and 2Lt NJ Whittingham/2Lt FC Dixon AZP) and further AZP 5.8.18 (Lt RE Butler).

A6376 FE2d. **SARD** allotted to BEF 7.6.17 and tested 19.6.17 (OK). **20 Sqn** (275hp RR) and victs 29.6.17 (2Lt OHD Vickers/AM2 JJ Cowell sent an Albatros D.V OOC near Becelaere at 16.10), 3.7.17 (2Lt OHD Vickers/2Lt SF Thompson sent an Albatros D.V OOC near Becelaere at 17.00), 12.7.17 (2Lt OHD Vickers/AM2 JJ Cowell destroyed an Albatros D.V at 17.00 and sent another OOC at 17.15, both near Ploegsteert Wood), 20.7.17 (2Lt OHD Vickers/AM2 JJ Cowell sent an Albatros D.V OOC near Wervicq at 09.55), 22.7.17 (2Lt OHD Vickers/AM2 JJ Cowell sent an Albatros D.V OOC near Menin at 16.50), 28.7.17 (2Lt OHD Vickers/AM2 JJ Cowell sent an Albatros D.V OOC near Messines at 18.45), 16.8.17 (2Lt OHD Vickers/Lt JA Hone sent an Albatros D.V OOC near Passchendaele at 08.55 and destroyed another near Zonnebeke at 09.17). Damaged in successful combat on OP 17.8.17 (2Lt OHD Vickers/Lt JA Hone sent 4 Albatros D.V OOC near Halluin 10.10-10.15 but force landed near Dickebusch – probably shot up by Vzfw F Altemeier, Jasta 24).

A6377 FE2d. En-route Lympne to BEF 22.5.17. **20 Sqn** by 25.5.17 and vict 26.5.17 (Lt N Boucher/Lt W Birkett sent an Albatros D.III OOC near Comines at 10.45) then damaged from stall on landing from OP 4.6.17.

A6378 FE2d. Lympne allotted to K Replacement Squadron BEF 28.3.17. **2 AD** ex 1 AD 30.3.17. **57 Sqn** dd ex 2 AD 3.4.17. **25 Sqn** and LIA on recce 28.5.17 (Capt A de Selincourt/Lt H Cotton POW wdd – possibly shot down by Ltn K Schneider, Jasta 5). Engine RR1/275/15 WD13895.

A6379

A6380 FE2d. En-route to Lympne allotted to K Replacement Squadron BEF 28.3.17. Shoeburyness, allotted to BEF 4.4.17. En-route to SARD from Rochford with allotment cancelled and on charge DAE2a Repair Section 5.4.17. **98 DS** allotted to BEF 25.4.17. **57 Sqn** and damaged in forced landing after combat on patrol 30.4.17 (Lt JH Ryan fatally WIA/2Lt B Soutten WIA). **20 Sqn** by 6.17.

A6381 FE2d. **28 Sqn** allotted to K Replacement Squadron BEF 28.3.17. **25 Sqn** in successful combat 21.5.17 (Lt A Roulstone/Lt H Cotton sent an Albatros D.III OOC near La Bassée at 16.30) and damaged in crash on aerodrome on photo sortie 3.6.17.

A6382 FE2d. Lympne allotted to K Replacement Squadron BEF 28.3.17. **25 Sqn** dd ex 1 AD 31.3.17 and LIA in combat near Lagnicourt on photo sortie 3.4.17 (2Lt DP MacDonald POW/2Lt JIM O'Beirne KIA – probably shot down by Ritt M Fr v Richthofen, Jasta 11. Engine 1/275/73 WD13896, flying time 8hr 48min).

A6383 FE2d. Lympne allotted to K Replacement Squadron BEF 28.3.17. **25 Sqn** dd ex 1 AD 31.3.17 and victs 13.4.17 (2Lt RG Malcolm/2Lt JB Weir shared the destruction of an Albatros D.III near Hénin-Liétard with 7003 at 19.30) and 21.4.17 (Capt JL Leith/Lt GMA Hobart-Hampden sent an Albatros D.III OOC near Oppy at 18.55 but a/c hit, force-landed and overturned). **20 Sqn** dd 7.6.17 and burnt out in forced landing after engine failed on take-off for OP 12.6.17 (Lt WR MacAskill/2Lt DW Stacey both fatally IIFA).

A6384 FE2d. Presentation a/c *Newfoundland No 2*. Lympne allotted to K Replacement Squadron BEF 28.3.17. Allotted to BEF 4.4.17. **25 Sqn**. **20 Sqn** and damaged in combat and forced to land in Ypres Salient 5.6.17 (Lt WW Sawden fatally WIA/Lt R McK Madill OK – probably by Ltn Schaefer, J.11. Unsalvageable engine 4/250/147/WD12118).

A6385 FE2d. Presentation a/c *Punjab No 27*. Norwich allotted to K Replacement Squadron BEF 28.3.17. **20 Sqn** and victs 5.4.17 (2Lt HG White/Pte TE Allum captured an Albatros D.III at Neuve Eglise at 11.45 – Ltn J Flintz, J.18, POW) and 13.4.17 (2Lt RG Malcolm/Cpl L Emsden destroyed an Albatros D.III near Hénin-Liétard) then LIA in combat near Becelaere on photo escort 24.4.17 (2Lt AR Johnston/Lt HR Nicholson KIA – probably in collision with Albatros D.III of MFJ 1 flown by Vzflgmstr J Wirth, who was also killed. Flying time 22hr 21min, engine 1/275/95/WD13900).

A6386 FE2d. Presentation a/c *Overseas Club Empire Day No 4*. To France allotted to K Replacement Squadron BEF 28.3.17. **25 Sqn** dd ex 1 AD 4.4.17 and wrecked in crash taking off for target practice 19.4.17. **1 AD** ARS ex 25 Sqn 22.4.17. **20 Sqn** and wrecked

Most likely seen in England before going to war are FE2ds A6353 and A6382.

in crash 3.6.17 (2Lt H Ross).

A6387 FE2d. Presentation a/c *Punjab No 44, Lahore No 4*. **28 Sqn** allotted to Training Brigade, re-allotted to BEF 4.7.17. **8 AAP** ex 28 Sqn 5.7.17. **20 Sqn** and crashed on aerodrome on landing after OP 14.7.17.

A6388 FE2d. Presentation a/c *Punjab No 45, Jhelum River*. At Norwich allotted to BEF 21.3.17. **2 AD** ex 1 AD 30.3.17. **57 Sqn** dd ex 2 AD 3.4.17 and LIA in combat with 6 EA near Marquion on OP 6.4.17 (2Lt HD Hamilton/Pte E Snelling POW – probably shot down by OffSt E Nathanael, Jasta 5. Flying time 7hr 13min, engine 1/275/23/WD13902).

A6389 FE2d. Presentation a/c *Punjab No 46, Chenab*. At Norwich allotted to BEF 21.3.17. BEF allotment cancelled and with DAE2a Repair Section 13.4.17. **SARD** allotted to BEF 7.6.17 and tested 14.6.17 (force-landed Laffans Plain after throttle detached) and 15.6.17 (weak pressure). **20 Sqn** and wrecked in forced landing near Hondeghem after engine failure on OP 27.6.17 (2Lt RM Makepeace/Lt MW Waddington).

A6390 FE2d. Presentation a/c *Punjab No 47, Ravi*. At Norwich allotted to BEF 21.3.17. **20 Sqn** and vict 1.5.17 (Capt FJH Thayre/Capt FR Cubbon destroyed an Albatros C-type in flames near Ploegsteert Wood at 11.20) then wrecked in forced landing at Vlamertinghe after combat on bombing sortie 3.5.17 (2Lt RG Dalziel/Lt LG Fauvel WIA. Engine RR1/275/39 WD13892).

A6391 FE2d. Presentation a/c *Punjab No 48, Bess*. At Norwich allotted to BEF 21.3.17. **20 Sqn** and LIA in combat with 20 EA near Courtrai on bombing sortie 29.4.17 (2Lt VLA Burns/2Lt DL Houghton POW – brought down by Ltn P Strähle, Jasta 18. Flying time 19hr 55min, engine 1/275/99/WD13901).

A6392 FE2d. Presentation a/c *Punjab No 49, Sutley*. At Norwich allotted to BEF 21.3.17. **20 Sqn** and victs 24.4.17 (Lt RE Johnson/Capt FR Cubbon destroyed an Albatros D.III around

Ledeghem-Roulers at 07.20 and sent another OOC) and 1.5.17 (2Lt RG Dalziel/L-Cpl R Bradley destroyed an Albatros C.III near Messines at 11.15) then damaged in combat on OP 5.6.17 (Lt HGET Luchford/Pte C Lloyd OK – landed on aerodrome).

A6393 FE2d. Presentation a/c *Punjab No 50, Manjha*. At Norwich allotted to K Replacement Squadron 28.3.17. Allotted to BEF 4.4.17. **20 Sqn** and shelled following forced landing near Le Biset after hit by AA near Comines on OP 8.6.17 (Lt HL Satchell/Lt AN Jenks OK).

A6394 FE2d. Presentation a/c *Punjab No 51, Malwa*. At Norwich allotted to K Replacement Squadron 28.3.17. Allotted to BEF 4.4.17. **57 Sqn** and wrecked in forced landing on patrol 22.4.17. **2 AD** wrecked ex 57 Sqn 26.4.17, for reconstruction 30.4.17 but deleted 14.5.17.

A6395 FE2d. Presentation a/c *Udaipur No 1*. At Norwich allotted to BEF 24.3.17. **2 AD** ex 1 AD 30.3.17. **57 Sqn** and wrecked on landing from gunnery practice 20.4.17. Intended for deletion 20.4.17, with 15hr 58min flying time, but re-taken on charge for reconstruction. **2 AD**, wrecked ex 57 Sqn 21.4.17, for reconstruction 30.4.17 but deleted 5.5.17.

A6396

A6397

A6398 FE2b. **58 Sqn** dd ex **1 AIS** 29.3.18 and wrecked in forced landing near Arras after hit by AA over Douai on night bombing sortie 1.4.18 (Lt GL Castle OK/Lt FC Dixon IIA – a/c shelled but salvaged. Flying time 3hr 20min, 160hp Beardmore). **1 ASD** deleted 14.4.18.

A6399 FE2b. **101 Sqn** dd ex 2 ASD 2.4.18 and recorded as poor 7.6.18. **2 ASD** for rebuild 14.6.18 and deleted 24.6.18 (NWR, flying time 60hr 32min).

A6400 FE2d. At Norwich allotted to K Replacement

Above: FE2d A6385 of 20 Sqn was lost on 24 April 1917, most likely the result of an air collision with Vzfw J. Wirtz of MFJa1, who was also killed.

Below: FE2d A6387 of 20 Sqn being dismantled after its crash on 14 July 1917.

FE2d A6393 of 20 Sqn took an AA hit on 8 June 1917, but the unhurt crew managed a safe forced landing. FE2d A6384 is in the background.

Squadron 27.3.17. Allotted to BEF 4.4.17. **20 Sqn** damaged in forced landing crash following combat near Ploegsteert Wood on bombing sortie 7.4.17 (2Lt J Lawson OK/2Lt HN Hampson fatally WIA) and vict 5.5.17 (2Lt RE Conder/AM JJ Cowell sent an Albatros D.III OOC near Poelcapelle at 17.10) then damaged in forced landing after Lewis drums hit propeller on instructional flight 11.5.17.

A6401 FE2d. Flown Joyce Green to Hainault Farm 25.2.17 (with forced landing at Polhill). At Norwich allotted to K Replacement Squadron 27.3.17. Allotted to BEF 4.4.17. **25 Sqn** by 1.6.17 and vict 6.6.17 (Capt C Dunlop/Lt F Cornish shared sending an Albatros D.III OOC near Sallaumines at 12.05 with A6365 and A6500) until @ 6.8.17. **20 Sqn** and wrecked in forced landing on road near Bailleul aerodrome on photo recce 11.8.17 (Lt WD Chambers OK/Flt Sgt FA Potter fatally injured).

A6402 FE2d. At Norwich allotted to K Replacement Squadron 27.3.17. **2 AD** ex 1 AD 5.4.17. **57 Sqn** dd ex 2 AD 7.4.17 and LIA in combat near Douai on patrol 30.4.17 (Lt PT Bowers/2Lt ST Wills POW – probably brought down by Obltn A Ritt v Tutschek, Jasta 12. Flying time 41hr 17min, engine 1/275/87/WD13887).

A6403 FE2d. At Norwich allotted to K Replacement Squadron 27.3.17. Allotted to BEF 4.4.17. **20 Sqn** by 19.4.17, damaged in successful combat and force-landed near Ypres on recce escort 24.4.17 (2Lt EO Perry/AM2 EH Sayers OK after sending an Albatros D.III down in flames near Becelaere at 07.55 – probably brought down by Vzfw J Wirtz, MFJa 1). **25 Sqn** dd ex 1 AD St-Omer 29.5.17. **20 Sqn** ex 25 Sqn 6.6.17 and LIA on OP 17.6.17 (2Lt BS Marshall KIA/Pte C Lloyd POW – probably hit by AA, engine 1/250/57/

WD6808).

A6404 FE2d. At Norwich allotted to K Replacement Squadron 27.3.17. Allotted to BEF 4.4.17. **2 AD** ex 1 AD 8.4.17. **57 Sqn** dd ex 2 AD 9.4.17 and tested new 10.4.17 until @ 3.5.17. **25 Sqn** by 1.6.17 until @ 16.7.17.

A6405 FE2b. **192 NTS** by 8.18.

A6406 FE2b. **148 Sqn** by 15.3.18, to BEF and crashed in fog during forced landing without flares on night bombing sortie 27.5.18 (flying time 19hr 10min). **1 AD** ex 148 Sqn 27.5.18. On BEF charge 30.6.18.

A6407 FE2b. **25 Sqn** flown by Capt A Roulstone/Lt D Taylor-Fox. **SARD** tested 3.11.17 (pitot tube dud). **2 ASD** dd ex 1 ASD 5.5.18. **102 Sqn** by 6.18 and listed as old 25.9.18 (193hr 20min and to be returned to 2 ASD for overhaul). **1 ASD** and flown to England 5.10.18.

A6408 FE2b. **101 Sqn** dd ex 2 ASD 6.4.18 and wrecked in crash near Dommartin on night bombing sortie 18.4.18 (Capt JA Middleton IIA/Lt RE Smith KIFA – a/c shelled to destruction). For deletion at 101 Sqn 23.4.18 (flying time 11hr 20min).

A6409 FE2b. **148 Sqn** dd ex 8 AAP 29.3.18 and LIA night bombing Estaires 17.6.18 (Lt HB Evans/Lt HS Collet POW. Flying time 35hr 10min).

A6410 FE2d. **SARD** allotted to BEF 18.4.17. **25 Sqn** and LIA on recce 28.5.17 (Lt TN Southorn POW/Lt V Smith POW wdd – possibly shot down by Vzfw O Koennecke, Jasta 5). Engine RR2/275/69 WD13968

A6411 FE2b. **148 Sqn** by 2.4.18, to BEF with unit dd 8.5.18 via **2 AIS** and wrecked after engine failure on bombing sortie 5.7.18 (crew injured. Flying time 29hr 30min).

A6412 FE2d. **SARD** allotted to BEF 18.4.17. **20 Sqn** and victs 29.4.17 (2Lt EJ Smart/2Lt TAMS Lewis destroyed an Albatros D.III around

Courtrai-Ypres at 17.25), 13.5.17 (2Lt MP Scott/AM2 JJ Cowell destroyed an EA C-type near Reckem aerodrome at 10.40), 20.5.17 (2Lt RE Conder/AM JJ Cowell sent an Albatros D.III OOC near Menin at 09.20), 23.5.17 (2Lt HG White/2Lt TAMS Lewis sent an Albatros D.III OOC near Zandvoorde at 10.45) and 26.5.17 (2Lt HG White/2Lt TAMS Lewis sent an Albatros D.III OOC near Quesnoy at 10.45), damaged in landing crash after patrol 6.6.17 and still on charge 27.7.17.

A6413 FE2d. **SARD** allotted to BEF 18.4.17. **20 Sqn** by 7.5.17 and victs 20.5.17 (Lt RE Johnson/Lt LG Fauvel sent an Albatros D.III OOC near Houthem at 09.35) and 31.5.17 (2Lt FJ Taylor/2Lt W Lingard sent an Albatros D.III OOC near Comines at 19.20) then damaged by ground fire near Locre on OP 3.6.17 (2Lt ER Robins WIA/Pte C Lloyd OK, engine 2/275/65/WD13965).

A6414 FE2d. In France allotted to CTD, re-allotted to BEF 2.6.17. **20 Sqn** (275hp engine) and vict 5.6.17 (Lt DC Cunnell/Sgt AH Sayers destroyed an Albatros D.V in flames near Coucou at 08.00) then damaged in forced landing after propeller burst on OP 9.6.17.

A6415 FE2d. At Norwich allotted to BEF 10.4.17. **2 AD** ex 1 AD 21.4.17. **57 Sqn** as a/c A-6 dd ex 2 AD 21 4.17. **20 Sqn** by 12.5.17 and victs 20.5.17 (Lt N Boucher/Lt W Birkett sent an Albatros D.III OOC near Ypres at 09.30), 25.5.17 (2Lt RE Conder/AM2 JJ Cowell sent an Albatros D.III OOC near Wervicq at 08.50), 26.6.17 (2Lt RE Conder/AM2 JJ Cowell sent an Albatros D.III OOC near Comines at 10.30 and destroyed another in flames near Ypres at 20.10), 29.6.17 (Lt HW Joslyn/Pte FA Potter destroyed an Albatros D.V in flames near Houthem at 13.15), 2.7.17 (Lt HW Joslyn/Pte FA Potter sent an Albatros D,V OOC near Houthem at 12.45), 7.7.17 (Lt HW Joslyn/Pte FA Potter sent an Albatros D.V OOC near Wervicq at 19.00) then crashed landing after successful combat followed by AA damage to undercarriage on OP 27.7.17 (Lt HW Joslyn/AM2 FA Potter OK – had sent an Albatros D.V OOC near Menin 19.45-20.40).

A6416 FE2d. At Norwich allotted to BEF 10.4.17. **25 Sqn** by 1.6.17 until @ 11.7.17. **20 Sqn** by 19.5.17 and vict 26.5.17 (2Lt RE Conder/AM2 JJ Cowell destroyed an Albatros D.III in flames near Ypres at 20.10) then listed as old 17.8.17 (flying time 172hr). Flown to England ex 1 AD 19.8.17. **33 HDS** and crashed from low turn at Gainsborough 30.11.17 (2Lt C Pinnock KIFA).

A6417 FE2d. At Norwich allotted to BEF 10.4.17. **25 Sqn** and victs 21.5.17 (2Lt JHR Green/Pte H Else sent an Albatros D.III OOC near La Bassée) and 6.17 (Lt CT Lally/2Lt LF Williams sent 2 Albatros D-type OOC near Lille at 07.00) then wrecked hitting trees on take off for patrol 13.6.17. **1 AD** ARS ex 25 Sqn 16.6.17.

A6418 At Norwich allotted to BEF 10.4.17. Flown to England ex 1 AD 25.9.17.

A6419 FE2d. At Norwich allotted to BEF 10.4.17. **25 Sqn** dd ex **1 AD** St-Omer 24.4.17 and victs 21.5.17 (Sgt JHR Green/Pte H Else sent an Albatros D.III OOC near La Bassée at 16.30) and 24.6.17 (Sgt AN Stretton/AM1 W Trezise sent an Albatros D-type OOC near Lille at 16.45 but own engine hit and force-landed at Chocques). **20 Sqn** and crashed in forced landing following combat on OP 6.7.17 (2Lt W Durrand OK/Lt SF Trotter fatally WIA. Engine 4/250/63).

A6420 FE2d. **9 RS** by 24.4.17 until @ 28.4.17. Converted to FE2b. **2 ASD** ex 1 ASD 29.5.18. **100 Sqn** dd ex 2 ASD 2.6.18 and wrecked 11.7.18.

A6421 FE2b. **36 HDS** A Flt by 20.5.18 until @ 22.5.18.

The crew of FE2d A6410 of 25 Sqn became prisoners on 28 May 1917 after a forced landing.

A6422 FE2d. **38 HDS** A Flt by 11.17. **36 HDS** C Flt by 25.1.18 until @ 14.3.18 (2Lt EC Morris/2Lt RD Linford on 20.49 AZP – unsuccessfully chased Zeppelin L42 and landed at Hylton 23.15 due to mist at base).

A6423 FE2b. **149 Sqn** by 26.4.18. **192 NTS** dd ex 149 Sqn 7.6.18.

A6424 FE2b. **101 Sqn** dd ex 2 ASD 15.4.18 and LIA on night recce near Peronne 16.6.18 (Capt RO Purry/2Lt WHA Rickett POW. Flying time 6hr 40min).

A6425 FE2b. **58 Sqn** dd ex **1 AD** 1.4.18. **1 AD** ex 58 Sqn 30.8.18.

A6426 FE2d. **9 RS** by 27.4.17 until @ 29.4.17.

A6427 FE2d. Presentation a/c *Udaipur No 2*. At Norwich allotted to Training Brigade, re-allotted to BEF 20.4.17. **25 Sqn** dd ex **1 AD** 25.4.17. **20 Sqn** dd ex 25 Sqn 6.6.17 and vict 9.6.17 (2Lt B Strange/2Lt J Tennant sent an Albatros D.III OOC near Wervicq at 19.00) then wrecked in landing crash when undercarriage collapsed on instructional flight.11.6.17 (Lt HGET Luchford/2Lt OHD Vickers OK). Deleted 16.6.17.

A6428 FE2d. Presentation a/c *Jodhpur*. At Norwich allotted to Training Brigade, re-allotted to BEF 20.4.17. Allotted to Training Brigade 23.4.17. **28 Sqn** by 8.5.17 until @ 6.6.17. **17 Wing ARS** re-allotted to BEF 20.7.17. Allotted to Training Brigade 28.7.17.

A6429 FE2d. Presentation a/c *Bundi No 1*. At Norwich allotted to Training Brigade, re-allotted to BEF 20.4.17. **20 Sqn** and damaged by AA near Vlamertinghe on bombing sortie 9.5.17 (2Lt EJ Smart OK/2Lt HG Neville fatally WIA) then victs 22.7.17 (2Lt NV Harrison/Lt RND O Earwaker sent an Albatros D.V OOC near Menin at 16.50) 28.7.17 (Lt HW Joslyn/Pte FA Potter sent an Albatros D.V OOC near Kezelbars at 09.15). Flown to England 9.9.17. **36 HDS** A Flt by 24.2.18 with AZP 10.3.18 (Sgt R Mann/Cpl Douglas) and crashed at Hylton by Lt Downing 12.3.18 and deleted 26.4.18.

A6430 FE2d. Presentation a/c *Ajmer*. At Norwich allotted to Training Brigade, re-allotted to BEF 20.4.17. **20 Sqn** and victs 29.4.17 (Capt FJH Thayre/Capt FR Cubbon destroyed 2 Albatros D.III in flames, one near Menin at 17.05 and the other near Zillebeke at 17.10), 3.5.17 (Capt FJH Thayre/Capt FR Cubbon destroyed an Albatros D.III near Moorslede at 17.20 and another near Westroosebeke at 17.25 and claimed an Albatros C.III OOC near Rumbeke), 5.5.17 (Capt FJH Thayre/Capt FR Cubbon destroyed an Albatros D.III in flames near Poelcapelle at 17.00 and two more near Houthem at 17.20 and 17.30, 1 in flames), 12.5.17 (Capt FJH Thayre/Capt FR Cubbon sent an Albatros D.III OOC near Tournai at 08.10), 13.5.17 (Capt FJH Thayre/Capt FR Cubbon destroyed an Albatros D.III in flames near Gheluvelt at c.10.45, and another near Rumbeke at c.10.45), 23.5.17 (Capt FJH Thayre/Capt FR Cubbon destroyed an Albatros D.III near Zandvoorde at 15.10 and sent another OOC near Ploegsteert at 15.15), 25.5.17 (Capt FJH Thayre/Capt FR Cubbon destroyed an Albatros D.III near Reckem at 07.30 and another, in flames, near Wervicq at 09.00), 27.5.17 (Capt FJH Thayre/Capt FR Cubbon destroyed an Albatros C-type at 07.30 and an Albatros D.III at 07.35, both near Ypres), 31.5.17 (Capt DC Cunnell/Lt WC Cambray destroyed an Albatros D.III near Comines at 19.20), 5.6.17 (Capt FJH Thayre/Capt FR Cubbon destroyed an Albatros D.III, and possibly a second, near Coucou aerodrome at 08.10), 7.6.17 (Capt FJH Thayre/Capt FR Cubbon destroyed an Albatros D.III near Houthem) and 8.6.17 (Capt FJH Thayre/Capt FR Cubbon sent an EA C type OOC near Houthem at 21.00) then LIA near Comines in

FE2d A6435 Mauritius No 2, with the observer demonstrating a hand-held camera.

combat on bombing sortie 9.6.17 (Capt FJH Thayre MC/Capt FR Cubbon MC KIA. Engine 2/275/85/WD13952).

A6431 FE2d. Presentation a/c *Kotah No.1*. At Norwich allotted to BEF 21.4.17. **20 Sqn** and victs 2.5.17 (Capt DC Cunnell/AM2 AH Sayers destroyed an Albatros D.III in flames near Comines at 11.15), 26.5.17 (Capt DC Cunnell/Lt WT Gilson destroyed an Albatros D.III near Quesnoy at 10.35), 9.6.17 (2Lt RM Trevethan/2Lt M Dudbridge destroyed an Albatros D.III in flames near Ploegsteert at 06.00), 17.6.17 (2Lt 2Lt CR Richards/2Lt AE Wear destroyed an Aviatik C type in flames near Zonnebeke at 07.20), 29.6.17 (Lt HL Satchell/Lt AN Jenks destroyed an Albatros D.V near Becelaere at 16.10) and 2.7.17 (Lt HL Satchell/Lt AN Jenks destroyed an Albatros D.V in flames near Houthem at 12.45) then wrecked hitting road in landing crash after patrol 4.7.17 (Lt J Pattersen/Lt M Waddington).

A6432 FE2d. Presentation a/c *Kotah No 2*. At Norwich allotted to BEF 21.4.17. **2 AD** ex 1 AD 27.4.17. **57 Sqn** dd ex 2 AD 28.4.17. **25 Sqn** (250hp engine) by 1.6.17 and damaged in forced landing after engine failed on patrol 24.6.17. **2 AD** ex 25 Sqn 26.6.17 and deleted 26.6.17.

A6433 FE2d. Presentation a/c *Rajputana No 1*. **28 Sqn** by 5.17, on charge until @ 12.6.17. Allotted to BEF, but re-allotted to Training Brigade 5.7.17. Allotted to HD Wing, re-allotted to Training Brigade 28.7.17. Deleted 13.8.17.

A6434 FE2d. Presentation a/c *Waringford, Burma*. **28 Sqn** by 25.5.17 until @ 11.6.17. **33 HDS** HQ Flt by 21.8.17 (2Lt FH Barton AZP).

A6435 FE2d. Presentation a/c *People of Mauritius No 2*. **59 TS** by 7.17. **NARD** 12.18, allotted to BEF with allotment cancelled 9.1.19 and awaiting deletion.

A6436 FE2d. **20 Sqn**. Converted to FE2b. **148 Sqn** by 2.4.18. **102 Sqn** dd ex 2 ASD 23.4.18 and recorded as old 21.9.18. (flying time 211hr 55min and to be returned to 2 ASD for overhaul). **1 ASD** and flown to England 10.8.18.

A6437 FE2d. **20 Sqn** and vict 2.7.17 (Lt GTW Burkett/Pte H Grenner sent an Albatros D.V OOC near Houthem at 12.45). Converted to FE2b. **58 Sqn** dd ex **1 AIS** 5.5.18 and crashed on take-off 17.5.18 (flying time 11hr 30min). **1 AD** ex 58 Sqn 19.5.18. On BEF charge 30.6.18.

A6438 FE2b. **51 HDS** by 18. **149 Sqn** by 30.4.18, to BEF and Alquines with the unit until @ 3.8.18.

A6439 FE2d. Imperial Gift to Canada. **4 SMA** Toronto 1917.

A6440 FE2b. **1 ASD** by 4.18. **101 Sqn** dd ex 2 ASD 17.4.18 and force-landed after engine failure on night recce/bombing sortie 5.7.18. **2 ASD** deleted 17.7.18, NWR (flying time 89hr 5min).

A6441 FE2b. **101 Sqn** dd ex 2 ASD 15.4.18 and damaged landing in cornfield during night bombing sortie 5.8.18 (Lt CB Mellor/2Lt RD Hughes OK). **2 ASD** deleted 11.9.18, (NWR, flying time 114hr 10min).

A6442 FE2d. Presentation a/c *Toungoo District of Burma*. **46 RS** by 4.17 until @ 5.17. **36 HDS** B Flt by 2.4.18 with 275hp engine and wrecked in crash 9.8.18 (Major McRae).

A6443 FE2d. Presentation a/c *Punjab No 29, Rawlpindi*. At Norwich allotted to BEF 30.4.17

Pictured half the world away: FE2d A6439 at 4 School of Military Aeronautics, Toronto.

FE2d A6446 of 20 Sqn was lost on 15 May 1917, the likely victim of Ltn J. von Bertrab of Jasta 30.

(275hp engine). **20 Sqn** and damaged in forced landing crash at Everdinghe after combat on bombing sortie 13.5.17 (Lt AC Lee/Pte C Lloyd OK).

A6444 FE2d. Presentation a/c *Johore No 7*. At Norwich allotted to BEF 30.4.17 (275hp engine). **20 Sqn** and victs 3.5.17 (Lt FD Stevens/Lt HR Wilkinson sent an Albatros D.III OOC near Westroosebeke at 17.15), 5.5.17 (Lt AN Solly/AM2 C Beminster sent two Albatros D.III OOC near Poelcapelle at 17.15 and 17.20) and 7.5.17 (Lt AW Martin/ AM2 C Beminster sent an Albatros D.III OOC near Poelcapelle at 17.20) then overturned in forced landing at St Sylvestre Capelle after combat on OP 20.5.17 (Lt HB Howe IIA/ LCpl R Bradley KIA – radiator had been hit).

A6445 FE2d. Presentation a/c *Sultan of Kedah*. At Norwich allotted to BEF 30.4.17 (275hp engine). **20 Sqn** by 11.5.17 and and vict 9.5.17 (2Lt HB Howe/2Lt FJ Kydd destroyed an Albatros D.III near Menin at 13.25) then damaged in crash near Brandhoek after combat on bombing sortie 13.5.17 (2Lt GC Heseltine WIA/2Lt LG Fauvel OK – possibly shot down by Ltn P Strähle, Jasta 18).

A6446 FE2d. Presentation a/c *Malaya No 17, The Alma Baker No 3*. At Norwich allotted to BEF 30.4.17 (275hp engine). **20 Sqn** and LIA near Lille after successful combat on patrol 15.5.17 (2Lt EJ Grout/AM2 A Tyrrell POW after destroying an Albatros D.III near Fort Carnot at 07.00 – possibly shot down by Ltn J v Bertrab, Jasta 30 – claimed a FE at 07.20).

FE2d A6448 took part in a couple of 20 Sqn victories, including those on 6 July 1917 when 20 Sqn wounded and shot down Manfred von Richthofen. AA then forced it down to crash here on 16 August 1917.

Engine 2/275/55 WD13955.

A6447 FE2d. Presentation a/c *Mauritius No 1*. At Norwich allotted to Training Brigade, re-allotted to BEF 5.5.17. **25 Sqn** and LIA in combat with 4 EA Near Vermelles on patrol 21.5.17 (2Lt JH Blackall/2Lt BC Moody POW wdd – possibly shot down by Ltn E Mohnicke, Jasta 11). Engine 1/250/97 WD5455.

A6448 FE2d. Presentation a/c *Mauritius No 2*. **28 Sqn** allotted to Training Brigade. Re-allotted to BEF 5.3.17. Lympne ex 28 Sqn 5.3.17. **20 Sqn** and victs 6.7.17 (Lt CR Richards/2Lt AE Wear sent an EA Scout OOC near Wervicq at 10.30), 17.7.17 (Lt CR Richards/2Lt AE Wear shared sending an Albatros D.V OOC near Menin at 10.30 and shared the destruction of another at 10.40, both near Menin and shared with SPADs) and 16.8.17 (2Lt HGET Luchford/2Lt J Tennant sent an Albatros C-type OOC near Menin at 11.45 then damaged by AA 16.8.17 and force landed, crew OK).

A6449

A6450 FE2b. **148 Sqn** dd ex 2 AIS 9.5.18 and damaged in forced landing after engine failed on test/instructional flight 23.5.18. **1 AD** ex 148 Sqn 24.5.18 and deleted 20.6.18 (NWR, flying time 18hr 10min).

A6451 FE2d. **36 HDS** C Flt by 12.3.18 (Lt AH Hinton/2Lt RD Linford 22.00 AZP) and further AZP 20.15 on 13.3.18 (Lt AH Hinton/2Lt H Hutchinson).

A6452 FE2b. **148 Sqn** by 26.3.18, to BEF with unit 3.5.18 and damaged in forced landing on bombing sortie 17.6.18 (flares failed to ignite). **1 ASD** ex 148 Sqn for repair 21.6.18 but deleted 8.10.18 and reconstructed as H7177 8.10.18.

A6453 FE2b. **51 HDS** B Flt by 12.4.18 (2Lt LA Bushe AZP) and further AZP 5.8.18 (2Lt AE Rowell).

A6454 FE2b. **192 NTS** and wrecked when hit tree while landing in fog near Sudbury 25.3.18 (crew injured).

A6455 FE2d. Presentation a/c *Mauritius No 3* wef 18.1.17. Deleted 28.5.17.

A6456 FE2d. Presentation a/c *Mauritius No 4*. **59 TS**, allotted to HD Wing, re-allotted to BEF 4.7.17. **8 AAP** and AZP 7.7.17 (Lt RA Grosvenor/air mechanic, 10.10 – 11.30). **1 AD** dd ex Lympne 7.7.17 (Lt RA Grosvenor). **20 Sqn** and victs 10.8.17 (Lt DY Hay/2Lt M Todd shared sending an Albatros D.V OOC near Wervicq with A5147 & B1890 at 09.00), 16.8.17 (2Lt AGV Taylor/2Lt M Todd sent an Albatros D.III OOC near Zonnebeke at 09.30) and 17.8.17 (2Lt W Durrand/2Lt JP Flynn shared destruction of an Albatros D.V near Polygon Wood with B1897 at 20.00) then) then wrecked in crash hitting ditch on landing from practice flight 7.9.17 (2Lt AGV Taylor/Lt M Todd).

A6457 FE2d. Presentation a/c *Australia No 9, NSW No 8, The FJ White Sumarez & Baldblair*. At Norwich allotted to BEF 10.5.17. **20 Sqn** and LIA near Menin on OP 20.5.17 (Lt AC Lee/AM2 C Beminster POW – possibly shot down by Ltn K Schaefer, Jasta 28). Engine RR1/250/23 WD6168

A6458 FE2d. **20 Sqn** and 11.9.17 (2Lt AGV Taylor/ Lt GA Brooke sent an Albatros D.V OOC near Wervicq).

A6459 Converted to FE2b. **101 Sqn** Famechon and wrecked in forced landing crash near Treport after becoming lost in mist on recce 9/10.8.18 (Lt Alcock/2Lt KJ Hook IIFA). **2 ASD**, wreckage to salvage dump and deleted 18.8.18 (NWR, flying time 121hr).

A6460 FE2b. **100 Sqn** dd ex **2 ASD** 12.4.18. Sold to US government for USAS 9.18.

A6461 FE2d. **36 HDS** C Flt and missing over

North Sea on 01.50 AZP 25.9.17 (2Lt HJ Thornton/2Lt CA Moore KIA – assumed ran out of fuel. Engine 4/250/111/WD12106).

A6462 FE2b. **36 HDS** A Flt by 14.3.18 (2Lt NS Jones/2Lt JM le Mee 20.10 AZP - reported as A6642 – engine cut but landed back at base – possibly FE2d A6442). **58 Sqn** dd ex **1 AIS** 24.4.18 and crashed on aerodrome after engine cut at 500ft on test flight 30.6.18 (2Lt RK Fletcher/Capt CC Cole OK). **1 AD** ex 58 Sqn 1.7.18. **1 ASD** deleted 5.7.18 (NWR, flying time 73hr 30min).

A6463 FE2b. **148 Sqn** by 2.4.18, to BEF with unit dd via 1 AIS and 2 ASD 25.5.18 and wrecked after engine failed on night bombing sortie 17.9.18 (crew shaken, flying time 100hr 50min). **1 ASD** deleted 23.9.18.

A6464 FE2b. **148 Sqn** by 2.4.18, to BEF with unit dd ex 2 AIS 8.5.18 and, forced landed at Hesdin on night bombing 18.5.18 (Lt JH Matthews/ Lt A Outhwaite OK) and crashed in forced landing due to weather on night bombing sortie 25.5.18 (Lt JH Matthews/Lt Outhwaite OK). **1 ASD** ex 148 Sqn 1.6.18 (flying time 21hr 5min). On BEF charge 30.6.18. **1 ASD** and deleted 14.9.18 (flying time 26hr 5min).

A6465 FE2b. **51 HDS** C Flt by 12.4.18 (2Lt SW Smith AZP).

A6466 FE2d. At Norwich allotted to BEF 11.5.17. **20 Sqn** and damaged in combat and forced landed near Vlamertinghe on OP 23.5.17 (2Lt W Howarth WIA/Sgt F Bird KIA – engine RR3/250/103 WD10072). Converted to FE2b. **100 Sqn**. **3 ASD** ex 100 Sqn 2.9.18.

A6467 FE2d. At Norwich allotted to BEF 11.5.17. **20 Sqn** and LIA in combat on OP 23.5.17 (2Lt RG Masson KIA/2Lt FW Evans fatally WIA – possibly shot down by Ltn K Schaefer, Jasta 28). engine RR2/275/115 WD13975.

A6468 FE2d. At Norwich allotted to BEF 11.5.17. **20 Sqn** and damaged in combat and force-landed on OP 24.5.17 (Lt RAP Johns POW wdd/Sgt B Aldred KIA – possibly shot down by OffSt M Muller, Jasta 28). Engine RR2/275/117 WD13976.

A6469 FE2d. At Norwich allotted to BEF 19.5.17. **20 Sqn** and victs 26.5.17 (2Lt HL Satchell/ Lt AN Jenks destroyed an Albatros D.III near Comines at 10.30 and sent another OOC in Comines-Menin area at 10.40) and 5.6.17 (Lt HL Satchell/2Lt TAMS Lewis destroyed an Albatros D-type near Becelaere at 14.35 – pilot was Ltn K Schaefer, Jasta 28) then LIA in combat near St Eloi 21.20 on 17.6.17 (Lt N Boucher WIA/Lt W Birkett IIA. Shot down in flames, possibly by Obltn E von Dostler, J.6, engine 2/275/83/WD13972).

A6470 FE2d. At Norwich allotted to BEF 19.5.17. **20 Sqn** wrecked in landing crash following stall on delivery flight 24.5.18.

A6471 FE2d. En-route Norwich – BEF 19.5.17. **1 AD** dd ex Farnborough 10.5.17. **20 Sqn** and damaged in forced landing after combat near Poegsteert on OP 25.5.17 (Lt RE Johnston/2Lt LG Fauvel IIA – engine RR2/275/23 WD13971).

A6472 FE2d. Allotted to BEF 4.7.17. Flown to England ex 1 AD 24.9.17. **33 HDS** C Flt by 4.18. Converted to FE2b. **NARD** 12.18 (160hp Beardmore) allotted to BEF, allotment cancelled 9.1.19 and deleted.

A6473 FE2b. At Boulogne 3.17. **148 Sqn** by 2.4.18. **102 Sqn** dd ex 2 ASD 21.4.18 and recorded as old 20.8.18 (199hr 25min flying time). **2 ASD** 31.8.18 ('unfit for further war service'). **1 ASD** and flown to England 12.9.18 (flying time 200hr 35min).

A6474 FE2b. At Boulogne 3.3.17. **1 AD** dd 5.3.17. **36 HDS** A Flt by 5.2.18 with AZP 13.3.18 (Lt ET Carpenter/2Lt TV Preedy on 20.20) and on charge until 18.8.18. **36 HDS** B Flt dd ex A Flt 18.8.18.

A6475 At Boulogne 2.3.17. **1 AD** dd 8.3.17.

Photographed at Narborough with 83 Sqn, A6460 was an FE2b night bomber with 100 Sqn in 1918.

A6476 FE2b. At Boulogne 3.3.17. **1 AD** dd 6.3.17. **33 HDS** B Flt by 7.8.18. **199 NTS** by 1.19.

A6477 FE2b (160hp). **187 NTS** by 7.18. **33 HDS** B Flt by 8.8.18 until @ 12.8.18.

A6478 FE2b. **101 Sqn** dd ex 2 ASD 2.4.18 and damaged when hit by A6494 on aerodrome 5/6.6.18. **2 ASD** salvage dump 8.6.18 and deleted 21.6.18 (NWR, 45hr 45min flying time).

A6479 FE2b. **58 Sqn** dd ex **1 AIS** 31.3.18 and damaged in landing crash from stall over hangar on test flight 25.4.18 (Lt KY Gliddon OK). **1 AD** ex 58 Sqn 25.4.18 (flying time 12hr 20min). **1 ASD** for deletion 29.4.18, NWR but on BEF charge 30.6.18.

A6480 FE2d. Presentation a/c *Mauritius No 5*. At Norwich allotted to BEF 21.5.17. **20 Sqn** by 26.5.17 and vict 2.6.17 (2Lt RM Trevethan/ AM2 JJ Cowell destroyed an Albatros D.III near Gheluvelt at 09.45) then wrecked in forced landing crash near Abeele after hit by British AA on patrol 6.6.17 (2Lt RE Conder WIA/Sgt JJ Cowell OK).

A6481

A6482 FE2b. **148 Sqn** by 2.4.18. **101 Sqn** dd ex 2 ASD 20.4.18 and damaged on aerodrome when hit by A5788 17.7.18 and damaged in forced landing near Estrées, due to wind, on night bombing sortie 29.9.18. **2 ASD** and deleted 5.10.18 (NWR).

A6483 FE2b. **148 Sqn** by 2.4.18. **58 Sqn** dd ex 1 AIS 9.5.18 and LIA on night recce to Lille 1.7.18 (Lt GL Castle/Lt AH Harrison POW – had transmitted message 'engine konked'. Flying time 69hr 55min).

A6484 FE2b. **149 Sqn** by 27.4.18. **192 NTS** dd ex Ford Junction 7.6.18 until @ 8.18.

A6485 FE2d. Presentation a/c *Mauritius No 6*. At Norwich allotted to BEF 21.5.17. **20 Sqn**. Deleted 3.7.17.

A6486 FE2b. **148 Sqn** by 11.4.18. 102 Sqn. On BEF charge 30.6.18.

A6487 FE2b. On BEF charge 30.6.18. **101 Sqn** by 1.7.18 and damaged in forced landing after radiator hit on return from bombing sortie 15.7.18 (Lt EH Lyon-Hall/Lt E Clark OK).

A6488
A6489
A6490
A6491

A6492 FE2b. On BEF charge 30.6.18. **102 Sqn** by 7.18 and wrecked avoiding trenches in forced landing crash on night bombing sortie 17.8.18 (crew injured). **2 ASD** 19.8.18 and deleted 21.8.18 (NWR, flying time 68hr 30min).

A6493 FE2b. **38 Sqn**, force landing safely on night bombing sorties 12.6.18 and 17.6.18. **102 Sqn** ex 38 Sqn 19.1.19.

A6494 FE2d. **20 Sqn**. Converted to FE2b. **101 Sqn**

dd ex 2 ASD 2.4.18 and hit A6478 when landing from night bombing sortie 5/6.6.18. **2 ASD** 8.6.18 and deleted 15.6.18, NWR (flying time 68hr 50min, time also recorded as 72hr).

A6495 FE2b. **58 Sqn** dd ex 1 AIS 23.4.18 and wrecked in crashed landing on test flight 24.6.18 (Major JH TyssenOK/AM2 PA Young injured). **1 AD** ex 58 Sqn 25.6.18 (flying time 60hr 20min). **1 ASD** deleted 14.8.18, NWR (flying time 60hr 45min).

A6496 FE2b. **149 Sqn** by 26.4.18 until @ 3.818.

A6497 FE2b. **149 Sqn** by 30.4.18 and crashed in forced landing on night bombing sortie 25.6.18 (crew injured). **1 ASD** ex 149 Sqn 26.6.18 and deleted 30.6.18 (NWR, flying time 36hr 40min).

A6498 FE2d. Presentation a/c *Mauritius No.7*. At Norwich allotted to BEF 29.5.17. **25 Sqn**. **20 Sqn** ex 25 Sqn and victs 14.6.17 (2Lt CR Richards/Lt AE Wear sent an Albatros D.V OOC near Becelaere), 29.6.17 (2Lt RM Makepeace/Lt MW Waddington sent an Albatros D.III OOC near Houthem at 13.30), 6.7.17 (2Lt M McCall/Lt MW Waddington destroyed an Albatros D.V in flames near Comines at 18.30) and 7.7.17 (2Lt Lt CR Richards/2Lt AE Wear sent an Albatros D.V OOC near Becelaere at 15.00) then LIA on OP 7.7.17 (Lt J Crafter POW wdd/Sgt WDA Backhouse KIA c.19.45 – possibly by Ltn W v Bulow or Ltn H Bongartz, Jasta 36. Engine 2/275/159/WD16074).

A6499 FE2d. Presentation a/c *Mauritius No 8*. At Norwich allotted to BEF 29.5.17. **20 Sqn** by 5.6.17 and vict 17.6.17 (Lt CR Alston/2Lt WH Chester destroyed an Albatros D.III near Houthem at 20.30) then burnt out after hitting wires in forced landing due to storm on OP 19.6.17 (Lt CR Alston/Lt WH Chester OK).

A6500 FE2d. Presentation a/c *Mauritius No 9*. At Norwich allotted to BEF 29.5.17. **25 Sqn** dd ex **1 AD** 3.6.17 and vict 6.6.17 (Lt D Maclaren/Lt EC Middleton shared sending an Albatros D.III OOC near Sallaumines with A6365 and A6401 at 12.05). **20 Sqn** and damaged in forced landing after combat near Ypres 15.8.17 (2Lt JM McLean WIA/ Gnr A Owen fatally WIA – possibly brought down by Ltn H Kroll, J.24). Deleted 19.8.17.

A6501 FE2d. Allotted to Ransomes, Sims & Jefferies, Ipswich. Converted to FE2h (230hp Siddeley Puma) and nacelle modified to accommodate 6lb Davis gun. Re-serialled E3151.

A6502 FE2d. Allotted to Ransomes, Sims & Jefferies, Ipswich. Converted to FE2h (230hp Siddeley Puma) and nacelle modified to accommodate 6lb Davis gun. Re-serialled

No details of A6509's history have come to light, but the absence of foliage on the trees in this photograph suggests that its demise was during a winter month, probably of 1917-18.

E3152.

A6503 FE2d. Allotted to Ransomes, Sims & Jefferies, Ipswich. Converted to FE2h (230hp Siddeley Puma) and nacelle modified to accommodate 6lb Davis gun. Re-serialled E3153.

A6504 FE2b. **148 Sqn** by 11.4.18 and wrecked in forced landing through low cloud on bombing sortie 31.5.18. **1 ASD** ex 148 Sqn 4.6.18 (flying time 24hr 14min). On BEF charge 30.6.18. Deleted 5.11.18 and reconstructed as H7228 wef 5.11.18. BUT recorded on 192 NTS 25.4.18 – mistaken for A6540?

A6505

A6506 FE2b. On BEF charge 30.6.18. **101 Sqn** dd ex 2 ASD 19.6.18 and crashed in crops taking off from forced landing on practice night recce 6.7.18. **2 ASD** deleted 21.7.18, NWR (flying time 10hr 35min).

A6507 FE2b. **148 Sqn** by 5.4.18. **149 Sqn** dd ex 148 Sqn by 22.4.18 and wrecked when hit tree on take-off from forced landing 26.4.18 (pilot OK/observer injured). Deleted 30.4.18.

A6508 **3 AAP** Norwich ex 6 SD for use as spares in building night-flying FE2bs.

A6509

A6510 FE2b. Presentation a/c *Baroda No.13*. **2 AIS** dd ex **1 ASD** 28.7.18. **2 ASD** and wrecked in

crash at Le Bourget on delivery flight to 3 AD. **2 ASD** deleted 22.8.18 (NWR, flying time 1hr 55min).

A6511 FE2d. Presentation a/c *Mauritius No 10*. At Norwich allotted to BEF 5.6.17. **20 Sqn** and wrecked in crash after hit by AA on OP 25.6.17 (2Lt M McCall/Rfm WJ Benger IIA – engine RR1/250/77 WD5453).

A6512 FE2d. Presentation a/c *Mauritius No.11*. At Norwich allotted to BEF 5.6.17. **20 Sqn** by 12.6.17 and victs 6.7.17 (Capt DC Cunnell/2Lt AE Woodbridge sent 4 Albatros D-types OOC near Wervicq at c.10.30 – including Albatros D.V of Ritt M Fr v Richthofen – and 2Lt HE Luchford/2Lt J Tennant sent 2 Albatros D.III OOC near Comines at 18.30), 11.7.17 (Capt DC Cunnell/Lt AG Bill destroyed an Albatros D.V in flames near Wervicq at 14.00), 17.7.17 (Lt DY Hay/2Lt M Tod sent an Albatros D.V near Houthem at 09.50 and 2Lt RM Trevethan/Lt CA Hoy destroyed an Albatros D.V near Polygon Wood at 19.55), 22.7.17 (Lt HL Satchell/Lt AN Jenks sent an Albatros D.V OOC near Menin at 19.00), 27.7.17 (2Lt GTW Burkett/Lt TAMS Lewis destroyed 2 Albatros D.V near Menin 19.45-20.40) and 11.7.17 (Capt DC Cunnell/Lt AG Bill destroyed an Albatros D.V in flames near Wervicq) then wrecked in crash 15.8.17 (Lt Hay & Lt Tod).

A6513 FE2d. Presentation a/c *Mauritius No 12*. **ES**

FE2d A6516 with its usual crew, Capt F.D. Stevens (left) and Lt W.C. Cambray MC.

Orfordness by 4.7.17 (Capt LJ Wackett/Lt FW Musson AGP). **ES Martlesham Heath** by 20.4.18. Deleted 2.5.18.

A6514 FE2b. **3 AAP** tested 15.5.18 (OK). **58 Sqn** dd ex 1 AIS 23.8.18. **1 AD** ex 58 Sqn 30.8.18. **102 Sqn** Surcamps dd ex **1 ASD** 10.9.18 and force landed safely after engine overheated on night bombing sortie 21.9.18. **2 ASD** 22.9.18 and deleted 1.10.18 (NWR, flying time 23hr 45min).

A6515 FE2d. **20 Sqn**. Converted to FE2b. On BEF charge 30.6.18. **102 Sqn** dd ex 2 ASD 13.8.18 and crashed after hitting wires landing at new aerodrome at Hurtebise Farm after travelling flight 27.10.18 (2Lt CA Grant injured/Sgt R Daniels OK).

A6516 FE2d. Presentation a/c *Mauritius No 13*. At Norwich allotted to BEF 8.6.17. **20 Sqn** and victs 13.6.17 (2Lt HCE Luchford/2Lt J Tennant sent an Albatros D.III OOC near Houthem at 08.45), 18.6.17 (Lt AN Solly/Lt WC Cambray sent an Albatros D.III OOC near Quesnoy at 13.15), 29.6.17 (2Lt HE Luchford/2Lt WD Kennard destroyed an Albatros D.III in flames near Zonnebeke at 13.20) 3.7.17 (Capt FD Stevens/Lt FJ Kydd sent an Albatros D.III OOC near Becelaere at 16.00), 6.7.17 (Lt FD Stevens/Lt AN Jenks sent an Albatros D.III OOC near Comines at 18.30), 17.7.17 (Lt FD Stevens/Lt WC Cambray sent an Albatros D.III OOC near Polygon Wood at 19.55) and 16.8.17 (Lt FD Stevens/Lt WC Cambray sent an Albatros D.III OOC near Polygon Wood at 11.00) then damaged in combat on patrol 20.9.17 (Capt FD Stevens/2Lt WC Cambray OK). **1 AD** ex 20 Sqn and deleted 26.9.17.

A6517 FE2b. **148 Sqn** by 19.3.18. **102 Sqn** dd ex 148 Sqn 19.1.19.

A6518 FE2d. **20 Sqn**, possibly the machine on which Lt B Strange was injured 25.6.17. Converted to FE2b. **2 AIS** dd ex 1 ASD 8.8.18. **101 Sqn** dd ex 2 ASD 15.8.18 and burnt out after overturned when taxiing for test flight 31.10.18 (Capt F Woodcock KIFA/ AM1 J Murray IIFA).

A6519 FE2b. **2 ASD** ex 1 ASD 27.5.18. **100 Sqn** dd ex **2 AIS** 31.5.18. **3 AD** ex 100 Sqn 29.8.18 and deleted 9.18 (flying time 63hr).

A6520 **3 AAP** dd ex **6 SD** 10.18 and deleted for spares for building night-flying FE2b.

A6521 FE2b. **200 NTS** by 2.18. **2 AIS** dd ex **1 ASD** Marquise 8.8.18. **102 Sqn** dd ex 2 ASD 11.8.18 and LIA on night bombing sortie 25.9.18 (Capt PM McSwiney/Lt ER Canning OK. Hit by AA, force-landed in lines and shelled to destruction, flying time 72hr 40min).

A6522 FE2d. Presentation a/c *Mauritius No 14*. At Norwich allotted to BEF 9.6.17. **20 Sqn** and wrecked in forced landing after take-off for OP 25.6.17 (2Lt JR Patterson/2Lt WD Kennard OK). **1 AD** ex 20 Sqn 28.6.17. Converted to FE2b. **102 Sqn** and crashed in orchard near Candas on return from night bombing sortie 8.9.18 (Lt GA Brown/Lt ME Brown injured).

A6523 FE2d. **20 Sqn** and vict 2.7.17 (2Lt RM Trevethan & Lt CA Hoy sent an Albatros D.III OOC near Houthem at 12.45). Converted to FE2b. **101 Sqn** dd ex 2 ASD 20.8.18 and damaged in landing crash after night bombing sortie 27.10.18 (2Lt AE Sharp OK).

A6524 FE2b. **1 ASD** Marquise 4.18. **102 Sqn** dd ex 2 ASD 20.4.18 and recorded as old 29.8.18. **2 ASD** 31.8.18 ('unfit for further war service' flying time 187hr 50min). **1 ASD** Marquise and flown to England 3.9.18 (flying time 186hr 10min).

A6525 FE2d. **1 ASD** 4.18. **3 AAP** dd ex 6 SD 10.18 and deleted for spares for building night-flying FE2b.

A6526 FE2b. **148 Sqn** by 2.4.18. **58 Sqn** dd ex 1 AIS 14.5.18. **2 ASD** ex 58 Sqn 27.9.18. **102**

FE2d A6527 saw operational service with 20 Sqn but the sheen on the nacelle nose, undercarriage struts and gravity tank, as well as the unblemished fabric and cockade on the lower mainplane, suggest that this was taken before delivery, probably at Norwich. A detail view of the cockpit appears on p 103.

Sqn dd ex 2 ASD 28.9.18 and damaged hitting shell hole in forced landing on night bombing sortie 8.10.18. **2 ASD** and deleted 16.10.18 (NWR).

A6527 FE2d. Presentation a/c *Mauritius No 15*. **20 Sqn** and victs 8.8.17 (2Lt RM Trevethan/ Lt CA Hoy sent 2 Albatros D.V OOC near Messines) and 9.8.17 (2Lt RM Trevethan/ Lt CA Hoy sent an Albatros D.V OOC near Becelaere).

A6528 FE2d. Presentation a/c *Australia No 12, NSW No 11, The Macintyre Kayuga Eatate* wef 4.6.17. At Norwich 13.6.17, allotted to BEF. **20 Sqn** and victs 7.7.17 (2Lt RM Trevethan/ Lt CA Hoy destroyed an Albatros D.V in flames near Wervicq at 19.00), 12.7.17 (2Lt RM Trevethan/Pte Arkley destroyed an Albatros D.V in flames near Ploegsteert Wood at 17.25) and 27.7.17 (2Lt RM Trevethan/Lt CA Hoy sent an Albatros D.V OOC near Menin at 16.50), 22.7.17 (2Lt RM Trevethan/Lt CA Hoy destroyed an Albatros D.V in flames near Menin), 27.7.17 (2Lt RM Trevethan/Lt CA Hoy sent an Albatros D.V OOC near Menin 19.45-20.40), 28.7.17 (2Lt RM Trevethan/Lt CA Hoy sent 2 Albatros D.V OOC near Kezelbars at 09.15 and 09.20) and 8.8.17 (Lt RM Trevethan/Lt CA Hoy sent an Albatros D.V OOC at 10.30 and destroyed another at 10.40, both near Messines) then damaged in forced landing 10.8.17 (2Lt Cameron/AM2 Potter OK). Converted to FE2b. **100 Sqn** and wrecked in crash 26.7.18 (2Lt JL Gower OK).

A6529 FE2b. **148 Sqn** by 15.3.18 and wrecked 10.9.18. (flying time 86hr 10min). **1 ASD** 10.9.18.

A6530 FE2b. **192 NTS** by 8.4.18 until @ 21.5.18. **38 Sqn** by 9.6.18. **102 Sqn** dd ex 38 Sqn 19.1.19.

A6531 FE2d. **ES Martlesham Heath** by 8.17 (250hp Rolls-Royce Mk.IV) for Trials Report M132. Converted FE2b. **1 ASD** Repair Park 1.5.18. **51 HDS** C Flt by 6.5.18, fitted with dual control by 27.5.18 and on charge until @ 31.7.18. **192 NTS** and wrecked hitting Avro 504 during take-off 15.1.19 (2Lt FA Goodman injured/Lt HE Duncan OK).

A6532

A6533

A6534 **3 AAP** dd ex 6 SD Ascot 10.18 and deleted for spares for building night-flying FE2b.

A6535 FE2b. **36 HDS** C Flt by 3.18 and in successful attack on submarine 5 miles E of Seaham 31.5.18 (Lt Beal dropped 2 x 100-lb bombs, attack followed-up by HMS *Locust* to destroy

UC49) and still on charge 17.6.18.

A6536 FE2b. **EC&AD** by 25.5.18, tested with flotation gear 30.5.18, fitted with hydrovane and successfully ditched again 29.6.18. Crashed 7.18 during ferry flight to 36 Sqn. Repaired at Grain.

A6537 FE2b. **8 TDS** by 20.6.18 until @ 17.7.18 and wrecked in crash after engine failed on take-off 9.9.18 (2Lt JF Clarke fatally IIFA).

A6538 FE2b. **8 TDS** E Flt by 5.7.18 until @ 9.8.18.

A6539 FE2d. **20 Sqn** and vict 29.3.17 (2Lt RE Conder/2Lt HG Neville sent an Albatros D.III OOC near Courtrai).

A6540 FE2b. **192 NTS** by 7.4.18. **38 Sqn** by 24.6.18 and recorded as unserviceable 30.6.18. **4 ASD** ex 38 Sqn 17.7.18. **2 Salvage Section** 19.9.18, beyond repair by 4 ASD.

A6541 FE2b. **1 ASD** dd ex **8 AAP** 20.3.18. **101 Sqn** dd ex 2 ASD 3.4.18 and crashed taking off from forced landing on dummy aerodrome 12.4.18 (flying time 7hr 35min). On BEF charge 30.6.18.

A6542 FE2b. **102 Sqn** by 29.7.18.

A6543 FE2b. **1 SNBD** E Flt by 6.18 until @ 9.18.

A6544 FE2b. **58 Sqn** until 8.5.18. **8 TDS** by 7.18.

A6545 FE2d. Allotted to Ransomes, Sims & Jefferies, Ipswich, 21.11.17. Converted to FE2h (200hp BHP 5512/WD23186). **ES Martlesham** Heath for erection 27.2.18, tested with oleo and V-strut undercarriages. **ES Orfordness** dd ex Martlesham 17.5.18 and used for tests with bomb sights etc until @ 25.2.19.

A6546 FE2d. **20 Sqn**. Converted to FE2b. **8 TDS** E Flt by 7.7.18 until @ 20.8.18.

A6547 FE2d. Presentation a/c *Australia No 13, NSW No 12, The Macintyre Kayuga Estate*. At Norwich allotted to BEF 22.6.17. **20 Sqn** and victs 29.6.17 (Lt JR Patterson/Lt CA Hoy

destroyed an Albatros D.V near Becelaere at 16.10), 3.7.17 (Lt HE Luchford/2Lt J Tennant destroyed an Albatros D.III near Becelaere at 15.00) and 6.7.17 (2Lt RM Makepeace/2Lt WD Kennard sent an Albatros D.V OOC near Comines at 18.30) then damaged in forced landing in cornfield on OP 16.7.17.

A6548 FE2d. Presentation a/c *Malaya No 30, The Ashworth Hope*. At Norwich allotted to BEF 23.6.17. **20 Sqn** and victs 17.7.17 (Lt W Durrand/2Lt SF Thompson sent an Albatros D.V OOC near Polygon Wood at 08.45 and 2Lt HE Luchford/Lt MW Waddington sent an Albatros D.III OOC near Polygon Wood at 19.55), 21.7.17 (2Lt HE Luchford/Lt MW Waddington sent an Albatros D.III OOC near Menin at 18.50), 22.7.17 (Lt HW Joslyn/ Pte FA Potter destroyed an Albatros D.V in flames near Menin at 16.45), 27.7.17 (2Lt RM Makepeace/Pte SE Pilbrow destroyed 3 Albatros D.V, one in flames, near Polygon Wood 19.45-20.40), 12.8.17 (2Lt JL Boles/2Lt J Cawley sent an Albatros D.V OOC near Becelaere at 08.15) then crashed and wrecked in forced landing during storm on recce 13.9.17 (2Lt JW Seward/AM A Townsend injured).

A6549 FE2b. **149 Sqn** by 3.4.18. To France for Independent Force 10.8.18. **3 AD** dd 16.8.18. To BEF 28.8.18. **102 Sqn** dd ex 2 ASD 4.9.18.

A6550 FE2b. **199 NTS** by 6.18.

A6551 FE2b. **1 SNBD** by 18.8.18 until @ 24.8.18. BUT **101 Sqn**. **2 ASD** ex 101 Sqn 12.8.18. **102 Sqn** dd 4.9.18 until @ 1.19.

A6552

A6553 FE2d (275hp). At Ascot 30.8.17 allotted to BEF. **8 AAP**, re-allotted for HD 13.9.17.

A6554 FE2d. **20 Sqn** and vict 12.6.17 (Lt AN Solly/

A6544 photographed at a UK aerodrome that had the 1915 pattern flight sheds, again making Norwich a likely candidate.

FE2b A6589, seen here in the markings of 1 SNBD, also served with 36 HDS in 1918.

Lt FJ Kydd sent an Albatros D.III OOC near Zandvoorde at 12.15).

A6555 FE2d. Presentation a/c *Malaya No 31, The Kuala Kangsar*. At Norwich 25.6.17 allotted to BEF. **20 Sqn** and crashed on aerodrome with engine failure and hit ditch after becoming lost on OP 7.7.17 (Lt JM McLean/ Lt MW Waddington).

A6556

A6557 FE2b. **3 AAP** tested 3.7.18. **83 Sqn** dd ex 2 AIS 20.7.18 and wrecked in forced landing near Grevillers after radiator hit by ground fire during night bombing raid 21.9.18 (Lt LGW Howles/2Lt JR Crowe OK, flying time 29hr 50min). **2 AD** 22.9.18 and deleted 25.9.18.

A6558 FE2b. **101 Sqn** dd ex 2 ASD 18.6.18 and wrecked in crash landing from side slip and nose dive on test flight 2.8.18 (Lt JB Small/2Lt TA Nutcombe KIFA). **2 ASD** deleted 3.8.18, NWR (flying time 51hr).

A6559

A6560

A6561 FE2b. **8 TDS** by 6.18 until @ 15.7.18. **12 TDS** by 13.9.18.

A6562 FE2b. **2 ASD** dd ex 1 ASD 25.5.18. **102 Sqn** dd ex 2 ASD 25.5.18 (and crashed in forced landing on return from night bombing sortie 8.9.18 (2Lt GA Brown/2Lt ME Brown injured? – flying time 162hr 50min – or A65222?). **2 ASD** 8.9.18 and deleted 11.9.18.

A6563 FE2b. On BEF charge 30.6.18. **101 Sqn** dd ex 2 ASD 21.6.18 and damaged in crash landing from night bombing sortie 26/27.10.18 (2Lt

GE Stevens/Lt WAS Blucke OK).

A6564 FE2b. **1 SNBD** and wrecked in crash from spinning nose-dive 6.10.18 (2Lt WH Russell KIFA).

A6565 FE2b. On BEF charge 30.6.18. Deleted 11.10.18 and reconstructed as H7176 wef 11.10.18.

A6566

A6567 FE2b. **191 NTS** by 12.18.

A6568

A6569 FE2b. **8 AAP** Lympne dd ex Norwich 10.5.18 (Lt King/2Lt JW Partridge). **1 AIS** ex 1 ASD 15.5.18. **148 Sqn** dd ex 1 AIS 20.5.18 and wrecked in crash after engine failed on take off for night bombing sortie 16.7.18 (Lt GEN Bullock KIFA/2Lt WG Perry IIFA. Flying time 44hr 35min).

A6570 FE2b. On BEF charge 30.6.18. **101 Sqn** and destroyed by fire when force landed near Ailly-sur-Noye following hit by AA on night recce 15.8.18 (2Lt PJ Williams/2Lt RL Williams OK – flying time 45hr 40min).

A6571 FE2b. At Norwich allotted to BEF 7.5.17. **2 AD** ex 1 AD 10.8.17. **102 Sqn** and wrecked in forced landing crash after pressure failed on night bombing sortie 31.10.18 (Lt H Hammond/2Lt H Howard OK).

A6572 FE2d. **3 AAP** allotted to BEF 27.5.17. **20 Sqn** and damaged in successful combat near Ypres 16.6.17 (2Lt PJ Gardiner WIA/Pte J MacLeod OK after destroying an Albatros D-type). Converted to FE2b. **2 AD** ex 1 AD 5.8.17. **100 Sqn** dd ex 2 AD 10.8.17 and wrecked hitting tree in forced landing on

night bombing sortie 20.8.17. **2 AD** ex 100 Sqn 23.8.17 and deleted 25.8.17.

A6573 FE2b. **8 AAP** allotted to BEF 29.1.18 (160hp Beardmore). **2 AD** 2.18. **16N Sqn** dd ex 2 AD 26.2.18 (engine 1560/WD20594). **100 Sqn** ex 16N Sqn 5.3.18 and damaged in forced landing after engine failed on practice flight 10.3.18 (recorded as 5hr 35min flying time – with 100 Sqn?). **2 ASD** ex 100 Sqn 10.3.18 and for deletion 26.3.18, NWR.

A6574 FE2b. **102 Sqn**. **83 Sqn** dd 18.3.18 and wrecked hitting wires on take off from forced landing on travelling flight 11.10.18 (flying time 20hr 2min).

A6575 FE2b. **101 Sqn** recorded as always poor 31.5.18 (flying time 43hr 10min). **2 ASD** for rebuild 1.6.18 and deleted 15.6.18, NWR (flying time 43hr 10min).

A6576 FE2b. **102 Sqn** dd ex 1 AIS 27.2.18, shot down KB behind Albert 27.3.18 then crashed in hop garden at Droglandt after becoming lost on night bombing sortie 21.4.18 (reported wrong signal from No12 lighthouse). **2 ASD** ex 102 Sqn 26.4.18 (flying time 51hr 54min). **101 Sqn** dd ex 2 ASD 27.9.18 and wrecked in forced landing after engine failure 13.11.18.

A6577 FE2b. **83 Sqn** dd 22.3.18 and damaged in landing crash on test flight 6.5.18. On BEF charge 30.6.18.

A6578 FE2b. **8 AAP** allotted to BEF 1.2.18 (160hp Beardmore). **101 Sqn** and burnt out/ unsalvageable in forced landing crash near trenches after camshaft failed on night bombing sortie 25.5.18 (flying time 45hr 30min). On BEF charge 30.6.18.

A6579 FE2b. **58 Sqn** crashed after hitting ridge on landing 1.3.18 (2Lt RA Vosper OK/Lt HC Hyde injured. Flying time 17hr 15min). **1 AD** ex 58 Sqn 1.3.18. **58 Sqn** dd 1.4.18. **1 ASD** ex 58 Sqn 4.4.18. **148 Sqn** dd ex 1 AD 5.6.18. **102 Sqn** dd ex 148 Sqn 19.1.19.

A6580 FE2b. **8 AAP** allotted to BEF 31.1.18 (160hp Beardmore). **58 Sqn** dd 3.4.18 ex 1 AIS and damaged in forced landing after propeller shaft failed in night recce 28.5.18 (Capt GK Palmer/Lt JM Farquhar OK). **1 AD** ex 58 Sqn 31.5.18 (flying time 58hr 55min). **1 ASD** ex 58 Sqn and deleted 14.9.18 (flying time 58hr 55min).

A6581 FE2b. Presentation a/c *Malaya No 6*. **83 Sqn** I dd ex 1 AIS 25.3.18 and wrecked landing after travelling flight 27.9.18 (pilot OK/2Lt WC Benton injured. Flying time 196hr 12min). **2 ASD** and deleted 3.10.18.

A6582 FE2b. **36 HDS** B Flt and crashed on night flight into sea from 150ft near Widdrington 26.4.18 (Lt NS? Jones/Lt Lance injured).

A6583 FE2b.

A6584 FE2b. **36 HDS** C Flt by 10.6.18 until @ 17.6.18.

A6585 FE2b. **36 HDS** C Flt by 17.6.17 until @ 3.8.18. **36 HDS** A Flt Hylton. **1 SNBD** by 16.5.18 until @ 6.18. **8 TDS** by 19.9.18.

A6586 FE2b. **36 HDS** C Flt and in unsuccessful attack on submarine 4 miles E of Seaham 8.5.18 (Lt EJ Penny/Lt Bell dropped 1 bomb, attack followed-up by a drifter) and on charge until @ 1.7.18. **191 NTS** by 12.18 until @ 1.19.

A6587 FE2b. **33 HDS** C Flt 17 until 4.18. **33 HDS** A Flt by 12.4.10 (2Lt J Heyes/2Lt EH Canning force-landed on AZP). **33 HDS** B Flt by 23.8.18. **199 NTS** by 10.18.

A6588 FE2b.

A6589 FE2b. **1 SNBD** by 16.5.18 until @ 16.5.18. **36 HDS** B Flt and sank under tow after forced landing in sea 7.6.18 (Capt Stanley/Lt Lock OK).

A6590 FE2b. In UK accident, hitting A5795 on take-off 22.4.18 both crew injured, one Lt Nicholl – 199 NTS?). **33 HDS** B Flt by 25.9.18 until @ 30.9.18.

A6591 FE2b. **148 Sqn**. **149 Sqn** allotted ex 148 Sqn

FE2b A8950, a presentation aircraft built from spares at Leeds in April 1917.

20.3.18 and used by 4.4.18 until allocation cancelled 14.5.18. Ternhill (13 TDS?) and South West Group 15.5.18. **8 TDS** by summer 1918.

A6592 FE2b. **148 Sqn**. **149 Sqn** allotted ex 148 Sqn 20.3.18 but cancelled 14.5.18. Ternhill (13 TDS?) and South West Group 15.5.18. Deleted 5.6.18.

A6593 FE2b. 33 HDS 17. **148 Sqn**. **149 Sqn** allotted ex 148 Sqn 20.3.18 but cancelled 14.5.18. Ternhill (13 TDS?) and South West Group 15.5.18. Deleted 17.5.18.

A6594 FE2d. **1 AD** dd ex England 10.7.17. Converted to FE2b. **148 Sqn**. **149 Sqn** allotted ex 148 Sqn 20.3.18 but cancelled 14.5.18. Netheravon (8 TDS?) 15.4.18. Deleted 14.5.18.

A6595 FE2b. **1 SNBD** by 19.5.18 and crashed from stall at 30ft 14.6.18 (crew injured).

A6596 FE2b. **1 SNBD** by 6.18 and wrecked in crash after stall 25.7.18 (2Lt GB McSweeney KIFA/ Flt Cdt CC Haskew KIFA).

A6597 FE2b. **1 SNBD** by 6.18. **102 Sqn**.

A6598 FE2b. Flown Eastbourne to Stonehenge 24.5.18. **1 SNBD** by 12.6.18 until @ 8.18.

A6599 FE2b. **33 HDS** C Flt by 16.3.18 until @ 1.4.18. **148 Sqn** by 3.6.18 and wrecked in forced landing crash on return from night bombing sortie 1.7.18 (Capt LP Watkins MC KIFA/2Lt CW Ridgway IIFA). **1 ASD** ex 148 Sqn 3.7.18.

A6600 FE2b. **148 Sqn** by 16.3.18, to BEF with unit and crashed in forced landing after engine cut on night bombing sortie 3.6.18 (crew OK – flying time 40hr 40min). **1 ASD** for repair 9.6.18 but deleted 7.7.18 (NWR, flying time recorded as 65hr 50min) and reconstructed as H7178 wef 8.10.18.

A8895: 1 RAF FE2b (120hp Beardmore) rebuilt by the Southern Aircraft Repair Depot, Farnborough under War Office Reference 87/A/528.

A8895 SARD No 006. **SARD** tested 15.3.17, 17.3.17 and 23.3.17.

A8950: 1 RAF FE2b (160hp Beardmore) built from spares by the Blackburn Aeroplane & Motor Co Ltd, Leeds and completed 23.4.17.

A8950 Presentation a/c *Leeds*. **AID** allotted to BEF 23.4.17. **RAF** 28.4.17. **25 Sqn** dd ex 1 AD 29.4.17 and on charge until @ 1.5.17. **22 Sqn** dd 4.6.17. **2 AD** ex 1 AD 20.7.17. **100 Sqn** dd ex 2 ASD 7.3.18 fitted with pom-pom and wrecked landing too slowly on practice flight 29.5.18. **2 ASD** ex 100 Sqn 30.5.18 and deleted 1.7.18 (NWR, flying time 178hr 1min).

B401 – B500: 100 RAF FE2b (120/160hp Beardmore) built by Ransomes, Sims & Jefferies, Ipswich under Contract 87/A/1033 dated 9.2.17 and fitted with V-strut undercarriage.

B401 Passed by AID 4.17 (130hp [*sic*] Beardmore). **10 RS** by 16.6.17. **ES Orfordness** by 5.17 and vict 17.6.17 (Lt FD Holder/Sgt S Ashby shared destruction of Zeppelin L48 at Theberton with DH2 A5058 and BE12 6610) and used in a variety of tests with bomb sights, compasses, bombs and silencers then fitted with 'bowsprit' as balloon fender (Capt R Hill) and on charge until 6.7.18. **ES Martlesham Heath** 7.7.1917. **51 HDS**.

B402 At Lympne allotted by BEF 11.6.17 (160hp Beardmore). **2 AD** ex 1 AD 20.7.17. **101 Sqn** dd ex 2 AD 28.7.17 and damaged by ground fire night bombing Roulers 22.9.17 (2Lt WH Jones/AM2 Muff OK). **1 AD** and deleted 3.10.17 (160hp Beardmore 73/WD9521).

B403 **192 NTS** by 3.18 until @ 29.6.18.

B404 **33 HDS** 17. **192 NTS** by 18.3.18 until 8.5.18.

B405 At Lympne allotted by BEF 11.6.17 (160hp

FE2b B401 had a meritorious career, sharing in the destruction of a Zeppelin on 17 June 1917 before being used extensively in some notable experiments (see p75).

Beardmore). **1 AD** dd ex 8 AAP 16.7.17. **101 Sqn** Clairmarais and wrecked taking off on night bombing sortie 15.10.17 (Lt CC Gadsden fatally IIFA). **1 AD** and deleted 19.10.17.

B406 At Lympne allotted by BEF 11.6.17 (160hp Beardmore). **2 AD** ex 1 AD 17.7.17. **101 Sqn** dd ex 2 AD 27.7.17 and burnt out after landing crash on practice flight 18.8.17 after controls had detached (Lt EL Roberts/AM2 A Hughesdon OK). **2 AD** ex 101 Sqn 22.8.17 and deleted 22.8.17.

B407 **SARD** tested 2.7.17 (OK – right wing slightly low). **33 HDS** damaged in landing crash when engine cut on low turn 22/23.10.17 (2Lt AS Harris injured) with C Flt by 25.2.18 and wrecked in crash when flew into ground 26.4.18 (2Lt Van Staden KIFA/2Lt WR Bilson IIFA, 160hp engine 7112/WD752).

B408 **36 HDS** B Flt dd ex SARD with Lt HT Leslie injured swinging propeller at Knaresborough 20.7.17 after back-fire (160hp engine 953/ WD7563).

B409 **33 HDS** B Flt by 19.10.17 (2Lt GEP Elder/AM1 Bayley on aborted AZP).

B410

B411 At Lympne allotted by BEF 11.6.17 (160hp Beardmore). **1 AD** dd ex Lympne 22.7.17 with forced landing at Samer en-route (Lt RA Grosvenor). **2 AD** ex 1 AD 22.7.17. **100 Sqn** dd ex 2 AD 4.8.17 and damaged in landing when over-ran flares and hit hedge on return from night bombing 22.8.17 (2Lt JF Bushe/2Lt LA Colbert injured). **2 AD** ex 100 Sqn 23.8.17 and deleted 25.8.17.

B412 **AID** allotted to BEF 2.8.17. RAF Farnborough 4.8.17 (160hp Beardmore 1231/WD20140). **102 Sqn** dd ex 1 AD 3.9.17 and wrecked on travelling flight, hitting wire when landing in mist. 101 Sqn dd ex Serny 17.1.19 (2Lt J Helingoe). **1 RP** ex 102 Sqn 30.1.18. **1 ASD** deleted 7.2.18 (NWR, flying time 76hr). BUT '412' dd 101 Sqn ex Serny 17.1.19 (2Lt J Helingoe).

B413 **AID** allotted to BEF 26.10.17 (160hp Beardmore). **1 AIS** ex 1 AD RP 19.11.17. **102 Sqn** by 5.12.17 and damaged in forced landing near Merville when engine failed on night bombing sortie 24.12.17. **2 AD** ex 102 Sqn 24.12.17. **1 ASD** deleted 4.2.18 (NWR, flying time 14hr).

B414 **AID** allotted to BEF 29.10.17 (160hp Beardmore). **101 Sqn** by 4.11.17 and damaged in forced landing in trenches on Bethune-Cambrai road after engine failed on night bombing sortie 3.12.17 (2Lt JA Paull/Lt WS McKenzie OK). 1 AD ex 101 Sqn 6.12.17.

B415 **102 Sqn** by 5.11.17 and damaged in forced landing near Busens after engine failed on night bombing sortie 3.12.17 (2Lt Day/2Lt H Smith OK). **2 AD** ex 102 Sqn 5.12.17.

B416 **33 HDS** HQ Flt and wrecked in crash on night flight 17.11.17 (Lt JA Harman KIFA).

B417 **51 HDS** C Flt by 17.9.17, AZP 24.9.17 (2Lt Simon) and further AZPs 19.10.17 (Lt HC Burdett landed at Tibenham NLG due to weather) and 12.4.18 (2Lt Munro force landed).

B418 **AID** allotted to BEF 29.10.17 (160hp Beardmore). **102 Sqn** by 9.11.17 and damaged when hit trench landing at St Eloi on night bombing sortie 3.12.17. **2 AD** ex 102 Sqn 7.12.17.

B419 **76 HDS** by 8.17. **38 HDS** A Flt force-landed on AZP 19.10.17 (Lt HC Calvey/Lt RA Varley OK). **38 HDS** C Flt by 19/20.10.17 converted to single seat configuration (2Lt E Vredenburg AZP and force landed near Great Gonerby), to BEF with **38 Sqn** by 13.6.18 (restored to two seat configuration?) and damaged in crash landing after controls failed on night bombing sortie 9.10.18. **4 ASD** ex 38 Sqn 10.10.18 and still on unit charge 25.10.18.

B420 **33 HDS** C Flt by 3.3.18 until @ 14.3.18. **33 HDS** B Flt by 10.8.18.

B421 **36 HDS** B Flt by 4.18.

B422 **38 HDS** C Flt damaged in combat 19.10.17 (Lt GH Harrison attacked Zeppelin L45 over Leicester, a/c sustained hits from return fire), to BEF with **38 Sqn** by 12.6.18, damaged landing 16.6.18 and wrecked when hit beacon on take-off for night bombing sortie 30.7.18. **4 ASD** ex 38 Sqn 31.7.18. Deleted 31.8.18.

B423 At Lympne allotted to BEF 7.8.17 (160hp Beardmore). **101 Sqn**. **100 Sqn** dd ex 101 Sqn 3.10.17 and damaged on aerodrome by bomb off A5663 26.2.18. **2 ASD** Reception Park by 30.6.18. **100 Sqn** by 15.7.18. **3 ASD** ex 100 Sqn 13.8.18. **100 Sqn** ex 3 ASD by 18.8.18. **3 ASD** ex 100 Sqn 21.8.18. **102 Sqn** by 1.19.

B424 At Lympne allotted to BEF 7.8.17 (160hp Beardmore). **2 AD** dd ex 1 AD 5.9.17. **1 AD** 28.9.17. **101 Sqn** dd ex 1 AD 30.9.17 (160hp Beardmore 69/WD9517) and damaged hitting pole in forced landing near Coudekerque after becoming lost on night bombing sortie 18.12.17 (Lt JP Owen-Holdsworth OK/2Lt GW Hockey injured). **1 AD** ex 101 Sqn 18.12.17. **1 ASD** and deleted 23.12.17 (NWR, flying time 41hr).

B425 **100 Sqn**. **2 ASD** ex 100 Sqn 26.2.18. Flown Eastbourne–Dover 30.5.18. **38 Sqn** by 8.6.18, damaged landing 16.6.18 and LIA night bombing Zeebrugge 29.6.18 (2Lt G Balance/2Lt EG Turner POW). Deleted 15.7.18.

B426

B427 **76 HDS** by 8.17. **38 HDS** by 2.9.17.

B428 **38 HDS** C Flt and wrecked in crash on night flying instruction 11.3.18 (Lt GRG Smeddle KIFA, 160hp engine WD20179).

FE2b B453 served with 101 Sqn until it crashed on a night take-off on 21 April 1918, killing its observer 2Lt H.J. Townson.

B429   **76 HDS** C Flt by 7.17. **38 HDS** by 23.9.17, to BEF with **38 Sqn** and crashed on beach during raid on Ostende 7.8.18 (Lt B de Salaberry IIA). **4 ASD** ex 38 Sqn 12.8.18 and deleted 15.8.18.

B430   **33 HDS** C Flt by 24.2.18. **33 HDS** B Flt by 10.3.18 (Capt WE Kemp aborted AZP).

B431   **38 Sqn** by 4.6.18 and LIA night bombing Ostende 18.7.18 (Lt LWDT Tratman/2Lt H Bosher POW). Deleted 31.7.18.

B432

B433   **199 NTS** 5.18. **187 NTS** by 7.18. **200 NTS** by 10.18. **199 NTS** by 1.19.

B434   Converted to FE2c at **SARD**. **AID** allotted to BEF 28.11.17 (engine 1247/WD20156). **100 Sqn** dd ex 2 AD 22.1.18 and damaged in enemy bombing of aerodrome 19.2.18. **2 ASD** ex 100 Sqn 19.2.18. **100 Sqn** ex 2 ASD 25.2.18. **2 ASD** 8.5.18, NWR (flying time 15hr 35min).

B435

B436

B437   **38 HDS** C Flt and wrecked landing from night flight 9.3.18 (Capt RG Somervell injured, 120hp Beardmore WD2352).

B438   **8 AAP** allotted to BEF 11.10.17 (160hp Beardmore). **101 Sqn** by 27.10.17 and wrecked crash after engine failed on take-off for night bombing/recce sortie from Famechon 18.6.18 (crew OK – flying time 164hr 35min). **2 ASD** deleted 24.6.18 (NWR, flying time recorded as 166hr 5min).

B439   Presentation a/c *Malaya No 17*. **8 AAP** allotted to BEF 10.10.17 (160hp Beardmore). **100 Sqn** dd ex 2 AD 13.11.17 and LIA night

bombing Courcelles 9.2.18 (2Lt OB Swart/2Lt A Fielding-Clarke POW, 20hr flying time).

B440   Presentation a/c *Gold Coast No 14*. **8 AAP** allotted to BEF 10.10.17 (160hp Beardmore). **1 AD** ex England 16.11.17. **1 AD** ex Repair Park 23.11.17. **1 AIS** ex 1 AD 19.11.17. **101 Sqn** by 3.12.17, force landed 5.12.17 and damaged in forced landing after engine choked on take-off for night bombing sortie 21.3.18. Deleted 25.8.18.

B441   Presentation a/c *Mauritius No 4* wef 10.10.17. **8 AAP** allotted to BEF 10.10.17 (160hp Beardmore), re-allotted to HD Brigade 17.10.17. **38 Sqn** by 12.6.18 and wrecked in crash landing after night bombing sortie 25.6.18 (2Lt RE Conder/Sgt JJ Cowell).

B442   Presentation a/c *Malaya No 28* wef 10.10.17. **8 AAP** allotted to BEF 10.10.17 (160hp Beardmore), re-allotted to HD Brigade 17.10.17. **38 Sqn** by 16.6.18 and damaged by AA and force landed near La Panne 22.8.18 (Lt E Everett/2Lt W Morginson OK). **4 ASD** ex 38 Sqn 31.8.18 and beyond repair. **2 Salvage Section** ex 4 ASD 19.9.18.

B443   Presentation a/c *Johore No 7*. **38 HDS** by 10.17 (160hp Beardmore).

B444   **AID** allotted to BEF 28.11.17 (160hp Beardmore). Allotment cancelled 8.12.17 and deleted.

B445   Converted to FE2c at **SARD**. **AID** allotted to BEF 28.11.17 (160hp Beardmore). **2 AIS** dd ex Reception Park 27.1.18 (Lt RA Grosvenor, recorded as FE2c 544). **100 Sqn** dd ex 2 AD 29.1.18 and shot up on aerodrome by EA when ready for bombing sortie 19.2.18,

flying time 99hr 45min). **2 AD** ex 100 Sqn 19.2.18. **2 ASD** 8.5.18, NWR (flying time 11hr 15min).

B446   **AID** allotted to BEF 28.11.17 (160hp Beardmore). **1 AI** dd ex 1 AD 22.12.17. **101 Sqn** dd ex 1 AI 22.12.17 and crashed after hitting bomb crater when landing from travelling flight 26.3.18 (crew OK). **58 Sqn** dd ex 1 AIS 1.7.18. **1 AD** ex 58 Sqn 30.8.18. **1 ASD** and flown to England 26.10.18. **192 NTS**.

B447   Converted to FE2c at **SARD**. **AID** allotted to BEF 28.11.17 (160hp Beardmore). **100 Sqn** dd ex 2 AD 26.1.18 and wrecked and burnt in enemy bombing of aerodrome 19.2.18 (flying time 13hr).

B448   **AID** allotted to BEF 28.11.17 (160hp Beardmore). **1 AIS** ex 1 AD 27.12.17. **100 Sqn** dd 14.1.18 ex 2 AD Candas (had left 9.1.18 but damaged skid at Fismes) and LIA night bombing Metz 28.5.18 (2Lt VR Brown/Pte AJ Johnson POW. Flying time 76hr 20min).

B449   Converted to FE2c at **SARD**. **AID** allotted to BEF 28.11.17 (160hp Beardmore). **100 Sqn** dd ex 2 AD Candas 12.12.17. **2 ASD** wrecked ex 100 Sqn 17.2.18. On BEF charge 30.6.18.

B450   Converted to FE2c at **SARD**. **AID** allotted to BEF 28.11.17 (160hp Beardmore). **2 AD** dd ex Marquise 24.1.18. Allotted 41 Wing and dispatched 25.1.18. **100 Sqn** dd 27.1.18 and wrecked in crash after hitting flare on take-off for night bombing sortie 19/20.4.18 (flying time 32hr 35min, 160hp engine 1295/WD20204).

B451   **AID** allotted to BEF 30.11.17 (160hp Beardmore). **102 Sqn** dd ex 1 RP 28.1.18 and LIA night bombing 21.2.18 (2Lt BCW Windle/2Lt SG Williams MC POW, flying time 16hr).

B452   **58 Sqn** and damaged in forced landing in field near aerodrome after engine failed on take-off for engine test 30.1.18 (2Lt GN McBlain/2Lt JS Rough OK). **1 RP** ex 58 Sqn. **1 ASD** deleted 2.2.18 (NWR, flying time 4hr). BUT **Armament ES** for camouflage experiments and dispatched to BEF for low-flying tests c.3.18.

B453   Presentation a/c *Junagadh No 2*. **8 AAP** allotted to BEF 15.11.17. AAFS? **101 Sqn** and wrecked in crash after hitting light on take-off for night bombing sortie 21.4.18 (2Lt AC Hine IIFA/2Lt HJ Townson KIFA– machine had 76hr flying time).

B454   Presentation a/c *Shanghai Exhibition*. **8 AAP** allotted to BEF 16.11.17 (160hp Beardmore). **102 Sqn** by 25.12.17 and crashed near Armentières after engine failed on take-off for night bombing sortie 30.1.18 (Capt M Richardson/2Lt C Marshall IIFA). **1 RP** ex 102 Sqn 30.1.18. **1 ASD** deleted 2.2.18 (NWR, flying time 14hr). BUT **2 ASD** ex 102 Sqn for overhaul 17.4.18 (flying time 75hr).

FE2b B456 was a night bomber with 58 and 102 Squadrons in 1918.

Another night bombing FE2b of 102 Sqn, B457, is manoeuvred by its handlers. It has darkened rudder and fin surfaces.

B455 Presentation a/c *Rajpipla*. **8 AAP** allotted to BEF 16.11.17 (160hp Beardmore). **102 Sqn** dd ex 1 AIS 29.1.18 and damaged after hitting wires in forced landing after becoming lost on night bombing sortie 26.3.18 (2Lt AS Kelly/2Lt C Batty OK). **148 Sqn** dd ex 2 AIS 8.4.18 and wrecked in forced landing crash into ploughed field during night flying practice 17.5.18 ((Lt W Perry/Lt GEN Bullock OK). **1 AD** ex 148 Sqn 18.5.18 (flying time 2hr 25min??). **1 ASD** and deleted 14.9.18 (flying time 48hr 59min).

B456 Presentation a/c *Malaya No 8*. **8 AAP** allotted to BEF 20.11.17 (160hp Beardmore). **58 Sqn** dd ex 1 AIS 31.1.18 and recorded as poor 19.3.18. 1 AD ex 58 Sqn 21.3.18. **1 ASD** tested 4.18. **102 Sqn** dd ex 2 ASD 21.4.18 and damaged in crashed landing due to mist after night bombing sortie 19.8.18 (crew OK). **2 ASD** deleted 11.9.18 (NWR).

B457 Presentation a/c *Zanzibar No 5*. **8 AAP** allotted to BEF 16.11.17 (160hp Beardmore). **102 Sqn** dd ex 1 AD 4.1.18, recorded as poor 17.4.18 (with 75 flying hours). BUT **102 Sqn** dd ex 2 ASD 22.4.18 and crashed into hedge after becoming lost in mist on night bombing sortie 3.5.18 (crew OK). Deleted 25.6.18.

B458 **8 AAP** allotted to BEF 16.11.17 (160hp Beardmore). **102 Sqn** dd ex 1 AIS 16.2.18 and wrecked in forced landing crash after engine failed on night bombing sortie 26.5.18 (Lt FW Butt KIFA/2Lt HN Phillips IIFA. Flying time 95hr 15min). **2 ASD** ex 102 Sqn 28.5.18.

B459 **8 AAP** allotted to BEF 29.11.17 (160hp Beardmore). **101 Sqn** and wrecked in forced landing crash after engine failed on test flight 17.5.18 (crew OK).

B460 **1 ASD** Reception Park to 1 AI 26.1.18 (160hp Beardmore). **58 Sqn** dd ex 1 RP 6.2.18 and wrecked after hitting ridge on landing after night bombing sortie 3/4.9.18 (2Lt JM Brown/2Lt TMR Riggs OK). **1 AD** ex 58 Sqn 5.9.18 (flying time 169hr). Deleted 5.11.18 and reconstructed as H7231 wef 5.11.18.

B461 **199 NTS** by 12.1.18 until @ 30.1.19.

B462 **199 NTS** by 14.1.18 until @ 30.1.19.

B463 **1 AD** by 10.3.18. **83 Sqn** dd ex 1 ASD 13.4.18 and wrecked in forced landing after engine cut on night bombing sortie 1.7.18 (crew shaken). **2 AD** ex 83 Sqn 2.7.18. **2 ASD** deleted 17.7.18, NWR (flying time 87hr 25min).

B464 **SARD** allotted to 58 Sqn mobilising at Dover 9.1.18 and tested 11.1.18 (160hp engine cutting). **58 Sqn** dd ex 1 RP 6.2.18 and wrecked in forced landing near La Clytte after engine failed on night bombing sortie 21.3.18 (2Lt HW Gardner/Lt CE Jenkinson OK). **1 AD** ex 58 Sqn 22.3.18 (flying time 35hr 40min). On BEF charge 30.6.18.

B465 **58 Sqn** and wrecked hitting tree in forced landing near Savy after engine failed on night bombing sortie to Bapaume 27.3.18 (2Lt TE Carley IIA/Lt FC Dixon OK. Flying time 54hr 55min). **1 AD** ex 58 Sqn.

B466 **83 Sqn** by 27.1.18. **102 Sqn** dd ex 83 Sqn 20.1.19.

B467 **58 Sqn** and damaged when hit new hangar when landing in mist after night bombing sortie to Lille 12.3.18 (2Lt JD Vaughan/Lt JC Thompson OK). **101 Sqn** dd ex 2 ASD 22.4.18 and recorded as poor 8.8.18. **2 ASD** as salvage 12.8.18 and deleted 18.8.18 (NWR, flying time 162hr).

B468

B469 **148 Sqn** by 6.3.18. **149 Sqn** dd ex 148 Sqn 17.4.18 and wrecked in crash after hitting hedge on take off 9.5.18 (crew injured). Deleted 12.5.18.

B470

B471 **8 AAP** tested 24.10.17 and still on charge 12.17. **58 Sqn** and wrecked in forced landing in fog at Droglandt on night bombing sortie 3.2.18 (2Lt RK Fletcher OK/2Lt H Kearley KIA – had misjudged flare height and overshot). **1 RP** ex 58 Sqn 3.2.18. 1 ASD deleted 9.2.18 (NWR, flying time 13hr).

B472 **8 AAP** allotted to BEF 3.12.17, re-allotted to 58 Sqn mobilising at Dover 19.12.17 (160hp Beardmore). **58 Sqn** and wrecked hitting tree in forced landing near Coquelles after engine failed on night bombing sortie 16.2.18 (2Lt MC Healy OK/Lt CC Abraham injured). **1 RP** ex 58 Sqn 16.2.18 (flying time14hr 40min). **1 ASD** deleted 28.2.18 (NWR).

B473 **8 AAP** allotted to BEF 3.12.17, re-allotted to Training Division 8.1.18 (160hp Beardmore). **148 Sqn** Ford Junction. **ARS** Ford Junction ex 148 Sqn 20.3.18.

B474 **8 AAP** allotted to BEF 3.12.17, re-allotted to 58 Sqn mobilising at Dover 19.12.17 (160hp Beardmore). **58 Sqn** by 12.17 and LIA night bombing 4.2.18 (2Lt A Holmes/2Lt PAB Lytton KIA, 8hr flying time).

B475 **8 AAP** allotted to BEF 7.1.18, (160hp Beardmore). **100 Sqn** dd ex 2 AD. **3 ASD** ex 100 Sqn 12.8.18.

B476 **AID** allotted to BEF 26.10.17 (160hp Beardmore). **101 Sqn** by 8.11.17 and wrecked hitting pole in forced landing near Ribemont after becoming lost on night bombing sortie 16.2.18 (2Lt R Locke/2Lt GW Hockey injured – had taken off from Vivaise aerodrome, reported wrecked for deletion 18.2.18, 46hr flying time).

B477 **AID** allotted to BEF 9.11.17 (160hp Beardmore). **8 AAP** dd ex SARD 21.11.17. **1 AI** ex 1 AD 8.12.17. **58 Sqn** dd ex 1 AIS 2.2.18 and damaged when tyre burst while taxiing out for night bombing sortie 12.5.18 (2Lt HN Hampton/2Lt LA Taylor OK). **1 AD** ex 58 Sqn for repair 14.5.18 (68hr 15min flying time). On BEF charge 30.6.18.

B478 **AID** allotted to BEF 9.11.17 (160hp Beardmore). **101 Sqn** by 16.12.17 and wrecked in crash landing at Auchel after pilot fainted on travelling flight 7.2.18 (2Lt AE Iken/2Lt FJ Lain OK). **1 RP** collected from Courcelles 7.2.18. **1 ASD** deleted 9.2.18 (NWR, flying time 19hr).

B479 **AID** allotted to BEF 26.10.17 (160hp Beardmore). **101 Sqn** by 2.11.17 and damaged in forced landing after engine failed on practice flight 15.12.17 (2Lt Macdonnell/2Lt EE Lockwood OK). **1 AD** ex 101 Sqn 15.12.17. **1 ASD** and deleted 21.12.17 (NWR).

B480 **AID** allotted to BEF 29.10.17 (160hp Beardmore). **1 AD**. **1 AIS** ex 1 AD RP 19.11.17. **2 AD** dd ex 1 AD 3.12.17. **101 Sqn** by 3.12.17. **1 AD** ex 101 Sqn. **101 Sqn** ex 1 AD 26.1.18 and wrecked in crash landing in mist at Le Nieppe on night bombing sortie 26.1.18 (2Lt RC Lovell/Lt WS McKenzie KIFA

The observer's cockpit of FE2b B469 is worked on from a stepladder.

FE2b B485, with a bold but indecipherable inscription on the starboard side of the nacelle, in pristine condition, probably at Lympne, before delivery to France.

– hit trees). **1 ASD** deleted 29.1.18 (NWR, flying time 24hr).

B481 **AID** allotted to BEF 29.10.17 (160hp Beardmore). **2 ASD** dd ex 1 AD 3.12.17 (engine 974/WD7584). **100 Sqn** dd ex 2 ASD 11.1.18 (had force landed at Ormes on delivery flight 9.1.18) and damaged in forced landing at Ochey on night bombing sortie 19.2.18. **2 ASD** ex 100 Sqn. BUT 100 Sqn crashed on night bombing sortie 24.2.18 (Lt WA Barnes/2Lt JCE Price injured). **1 ASD** deleted 29.6.18 (NWR, flying time 29hr 27min).

B482 **AID** allotted to BEF 9.11.17 (160hp Beardmore). **1 AD** ex England 18.11.17. **102 Sqn** by 5.12.17 and damaged in forced landing near Neuve Berquin after engine seized (no water in radiator) on night bombing sortie 17.12.17 (2Lt AD Whiteside/2Lt WJ Harvey OK). **1 ASD** and deleted 27.12.17 (NWR, flying time 8hr).

B483 Presentation a/c *Mauritius No 15*. **8 AAP** allotted to BEF 9.10.17, re-allotted to HD Brigade 17.10.17 (160hp Beardmore). **199 NTS** by 10.17 until @ 12.17. Deleted 21.12.17.

B484 **58 Sqn** and wrecked in forced landing near Roeux after sustaining hits on night recce sortie 10.3.18 (Capt CH Brewer MC/2Lt DS Broadhurst WIA. Flying time 22hr 45min).

B485 Presentation a/c *Punjab No 29* wef 10.10.17. **8 AAP** Lympne allotted to BEF 11.10.17 (160hp Beardmore). **100 Sqn** Ochey by dd ex 2 AD Candas 26.11.17 and damaged by EA raiding aerodrome 19.2.18 (Lt HL Miles/Lt HA Sampson OK). **2 AD** ex 100 Sqn 19.2.18. **58 Sqn** ex 58 Sqn and deleted 14.4.18, NWR (flying time 32hr 57min).

B486 **8 AAP** allotted to BEF 19.10.17 (160hp Beardmore). **1 AIS** ex 1 AD 24.1.18. **102 Sqn**

by dd ex 1 AIS 30.1.18 and wrecked hitting corn stack in forced landing after engine boiled on night bombing sortie 3.9.18 (crew OK). **2 ASD** 3.9.18 and deleted 14.9.18, NWR (flying time 264hr 4min).

B487 **AID** allotted to BEF 31.10.17 (160hp Beardmore), allotment cancelled 24.11.17 and on charge E1 Repair Section.

B488 **AID** allotted to BEF 19.11.17 (160hp Beardmore). **102 Sqn** dd ex 1 RP 29.1.18 and crashed with engine problems in overshot landing from night bombing sortie 26.2.18 (2Lt RW Loudon/Lt GL Zeigler OK). **1 RP** ex 102 Sqn 26.2.18. **83 Sqn** dd ex 1 AIS 20.4.18 and reported as poor and in need of repair 25.5.18. **2 ASD** ex 83 Sqn 30.5.18 for repair and deleted 13.6.18, NWR (flying time 34hr 26min).

B489 **8 AAP** allotted to BEF 19.11.17 (160hp Beardmore), re-allotted to 58 Sqn mobilising at Dover 19.12.17. **58 Sqn** I (engine 327/ WD9775) by 21.2.18, named *Black Eyed Queen*, temporarily armed with Vickers 1.59in breech-loading gun by 13.3.18 (raid on Menin) and wrecked in crash landing on aerodrome after night bombing sortie 1.4.18 (Capt HJ Whittingham/Lt RA Varley OK). **1 AD** ex 58 Sqn 1.4.18 (flying time 56hr 40min. **1 ASD** for deletion 14.4.18 (flying time 57hr 25min).

B490 At Dover allotted to 58 Sqn, mobilising, re-allotted to BEF 14.1.18 (160hp Beardmore). **58 Sqn** dd 17.3.18 and damaged in forced landing into ploughed field after engine vibrations on night bombing sortie 14.5.18 (2Lt RG Clough/2Lt AP Ledger OK. Flying time 47hr 40min). **1 AD** ex 58 Sqn 17.5.18.

B491 **58 Sqn** dd ex 1 RP 4.2.18 and crashed in forced landing in fog near 7 Sqn aerodrome after fuel problems on night bombing sortie

4.2.18 (2Lt JFB Ewan injured/2Lt JD Watson OK). 1 RP ex 58 Sqn 4.2.18. 1 ASD deleted 13.2.18 (NWR, flying time 12hr).

B492 At Dover allotted to 58 Sqn, re-allotted to BEF 14.1.18 (160hp Beardmore). **100 Sqn** dd ex 2 ASD 26.2.18 and LIA night bombing Thionville 17.5.18 (2Lt JC Williamson/Lt NF Penruddocke POW. Flying time 48hr 10min).

B493 **58 Sqn** and wrecked in forced landing in mist near Retonval on practice night recce 25.1.18 (2Lt WA Leslie/2Lt F Wilkinson UK). 1 RP ex 58 Sqn 29.1.18. 1 ASD deleted 1.2.18 (NWR, flying time 11hr).

B494 **58 Sqn** by 1.1.18 and 1.7.18 recorded as poor with no climb: 10min to 1000ft, ceiling 3200ft (flying time 157hr 45min). **1 AD** ex 58 Sqn 4.7.18.

B495 At Dover allotted to 58 Sqn, re-allotted to BEF 14.1.18 (160hp Beardmore). **83 Sqn** and crashed in forced landing after fuel pipe hit by ground fire on night bombing sortie 22.5.18 (Lt NS Jones/2Lt TH Singleton OK – fuel ran out). **2 ASD** ex 83 Sqn 24.5.18 and deleted 7.6.18, NWR (flying time 39hr 1min).

B496 **58 Sqn** and crashed in forced landing after engine stopped on test flight 18.2.18 (2Lt EG Roberts injured/Lt KR Anderson OK). 1 RP ex 58 Sqn 18.2.18 (flying time 18hr 15min). 1 ASD deleted 24.2.18 (NWR, flying time 18hr).

B497 **58 Sqn** and LIA night bombing 12.5.18 (Lt J Handley/2Lt JB Birkhead POW wdd) and deleted on unit 14.5.18 (flying time 79hr 20min).

B498 At London Colney allotted to 58 Sqn (mobilising), re-allotted to BEF 8.1.18. **100 Sqn** dd ex 2 AD 20.2.18. 100 Sqn collected from Villesneux and missing on delivery flight to Ochey 15.5.18 (2Lt DS Anderson/AM2 H O'Connor POW). Deleted on unit 16.5.18 (flying time 29hr 15min).

B499 **58 Sqn** by 1.18, force landed safely 27.3.18 (2Lt RN Smith/Lt WLH Davies OK) and wrecked in forced landing after engine failed on take off on collection from Repair Depot 1.4.18 (Lt CH Smith OK). **1 AD** ex 58 Sqn 1.4.18 (flying time 60hr 35min). **2 ASD** for repair 18.5.18 (flying time 80hr). On BEF charge 30.6.18.

B500 **8 AAP** allotted to BEF 7.1.18. **102 Sqn** by 23.2.18 and damaged on night bombing sortie 21.7.18 (Lt JA Hoogterp/Lt EC Harris OK – initially reported MIA. Flying time 201hr 40min).

B704 & B767: 2 RAF FE2b (160hp Beardmore) rebuilt by the Southern Aircraft Repair Depot, Farnborough.

B704 Fitted with Trafford Jones undercarriage. **199 DS/NTS** by 10.17 until @ 25.2.18 and

FE2b B487 in the Ransomes, Sims & Jefferies factory at Leiston, Suffolk.

fitted with dual control.

B767   **SARD** tested 22.11.17 (water boiling away).

B1851 – B1900: 50 RAF FE2d (250hp Rolls-Royce Mks.I or II or 275hp Rolls-Royce Eagle III) built by Boulton & Paul Ltd, Norwich under continuing Contract 87/A/658 dated 24.3.17. Many converted to FE2b (120 &160hp Beardmore).

B1851

B1852

B1853   FE2b. **200 NTS** by 10.18.

B1854   FE2b. **199 NTS** by 7.6.18 until @ 17.6.18

B1855   FE2b. **3 AAP**, tested 4.7.18 (OK). **149 Sqn** ?.18.

B1856   FE2b. **1 SNBD** and force landed Harlestone, Northants 26.9.18 (Lt WJ Kelly killed by propeller attempting to put out fire/Lt AC Taylor OK).

B1857

B1858   FE2b. **200 NTS** by 10.18.

B1859   FE2b. **3 AAP**, tested 11.8.18 (OK).

B1860   FE2b. **ES Martlesham Heath. RAE** dd ex AES 16.6.19.

B1861   FE2b. **8 TDS** by summer 1918.

B1862   FE2b. **102 Sqn**. Yatesbury 1917 (reported as 66 TS but more likely 59 TS). **12 TDS** by 4.8.18.

B1863   Presentation a/c *Malaya No 32*. FE2d. **3 AAP** allotted to BEF 9.7.17 (275hp RR). **20 Sqn** and and vict 12.7.17 (Capt DC Cunnell/Lt AG Bill sent an Albatros D.V OOC near Menin at 17.10) wrecked in crash after hit by AA near Menin 12.7.17 (Capt DC Cunnell KIA/Lt AG Bill IIA – observer landed the a/c).

B1864

B1865   Presentation a/c *Falkland*. FE2d. **3 AAP** allotted to BEF 9.7.17 (250hp RR). **20 Sqn** and vict 17.7.17 (Lt CH Beldam/2Lt WH Watt sent an Albatros D.V OOC near Polygon Wood at 20.00) LIA 23.7.17 (damaged when shot down in combat with EA on OP near Menin – 2Lt M McCall WIA/Lt R McK Madill KIA. Engine RR3/250/5 WD5170).

B1866   FE2b. **3 AAP** tested 8.7.18 (OK). **8 TDS** by 13.7.18. **Armament School** by 10.18.

B1867   FE2b. **3 AAP** tested 3.7.18 (OK) and 5.7.18. **8 TDS** by 7.7.18 until @ 14.7.18.

B1868   FE2b. **3 AAP** tested 6.7.18 (tail high) and 8.7.17 (OK). **1 SNBD** by 9.18. **Armament School** by 10.18.

B1869

B1870   FE2b. **101 Sqn** dd ex 2 ASD 3.9.18 and damaged in crash landing after night bombing sortie 27.10.18 (Lt J Harkin/Lt RE Carles OK).

B1871   FE2b. **3 AAP** tested 29.7.18 (OK). **102 Sqn** until @ 1.19.

B1872   FE2b. **Reception Park** allotted to Independent Force 26.7.18 but replaced by

FE2b B704 was built from spares by SARD and served with 199 DS/NTS.

B18xx 5.8.18. **2 AIS** by 31.7.18. **102 Sqn** dd ex 2 ASD 31.8.18 and damaged in forced landing in trenches following engine failure on night recce 8.10.18 and deleted 16.10.18 (NWR).

B1873   Presentation a/c *Punjab No 5, Nabha*. FE2b. **100 Sqn. 3 ASD** ex 100 Sqn 21.8.18. Transferred to USAS 9.18.

B1874   Presentation a/c *Junagadh No 2*. FE2b. **58 Sqn. I Flt** dd ex 58 Sqn via 1 AIS 22.8.18. **148 Sqn** dd ex I Flt 17.1.19. **102 Sqn** dd ex 102 Sqn 19.1.19.

B1875   **6 SD** 10.18 intended for preservation.

B1876   FE2b. **Reception Park**, 1 ASD e, dd ex 8 AAP 30.7.18. **83 Sqn** dd ex 2 AIS 18.8.18, crashed on aerodrome 25.9.18 and repaired by 13.10.18. **102 Sqn** dd ex 83 Sqn 20.1.19.

B1877   FE2b. Presentation a/c *St Andrews No 1*. **2 AIS** dd ex 1 ASD 30.7.18. At Paris en-route to Independent Force 31.7.18. **100 Sqn**

dd 31.7.18. **83 Sqn. 102 Sqn** dd ex 83 Sqn 20.1.19. Transferred to USAS 9.18.

B1878   **3 AAP**, tested 24.7.18. **Central Dispatch Pool** crashed 29.7.18 (Lt WWM Dulin). **1 ASD** ex Reception Park 4.8.18 and deleted that day, NWR (flying time 30min).

B1879   FE2b. **148 Sqn** dd ex 1 ASD 29.8.18 and wrecked in forced landing near Souchez, night bombing, after propeller hit by ground fire 2.9.18 (Lt E Alder OK/Lt AV Collins WIA. Flying time 8hr 55min). **1 ASD** deleted 8.9.18.

B1880   Presentation a/c *Punjab No 29*. FE2b. **100 Sqn** by 6.8.18. **3 ASD** ex 100 Sqn 27.8.18. **102 Sqn** dd ex 2 ASD 4.9.18 and damaged in forced landing after engine failure on night bombing sortie 23.9.18. **2 ASD** 23.9.18 and deleted 29.9.18 (NWR, flying time 45hr).

B1881   FE2d. **3 AAP** allotted to BEF 16.8.17 (275hp RR). **8 AAP** by 22.8.17 (Lt H Slingsby AGP).

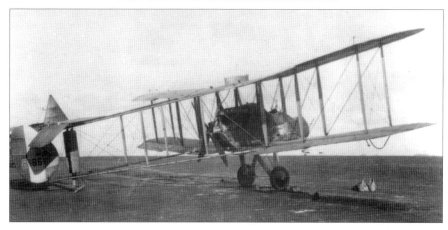

FE2b B1868 saw service as a school machine in late 1918.

A crisp photo of FE2b B1877 with its night bombing V-strut undercarriage. In addition to the bomb/flare release levers visible in the view on p50, this angle shows yet another double lever on the port side of the pilot's cockpit and also offers a very clear view of the tail light.

A celebration(?) while swinging the compass of this 33HDS FE2b, B4005.

B1882 FE2d. **33 HDS** B Flt by 21.8.17 (Capt DH Dabbs AZP). **39 HDS**. **78 HDS** by 24.9.17 (2Lt FH Barton/AM1 E Cooper AGP) and further AGPs 25.9.17 (2Lt FH Barton/AM1 HL Daws), 29.9.17 (2Lt FH Barton/AM1 WT Merchant), 30.9.17 (2Lt FH Barton/Lt HI Fordred) and 1.10.17 (2Lt FH Barton/AM1 WT Merchant) then wrecked in crash after hitting wires on night flying practice 4.10.17 (Capt DH Dabbs/2Lt TH Barton injured, engine 2/275/23/WD13971).

B1883 FE2d. **33 HDS** A Flt by 21.8.17 (2Lt NL Garstin/2Lt JD Watson AZP). **39 HDS**. **78 HDS** by 24.9.17 (2Lt NL Garstin/Lt HI Fordred AGP) and further AGP 28.9.17 (2Lt NL Garstin/Lt HI Fordred). **36 HDS** B Flt by 26.1.18 with AZP 10.3.18 (2Lt NS Jones/2Lt H Cock 20.24) and further AZP 21.10 14.3.18 (Capt JA Boret/2Lt LJ Ingram). **36 HDS** A Flt by 26.5.18 until @ 15.6.18.

B1884 FE2d. **33 HDS** A Flt by 24.9.17 (Capt SW Price AZP) and further AZPs from 19.10.17 (2Lt EG Roberts/Lt Tatham and Lt JA Harman/Lt Stevenson).

B1885 FE2d. **33 HDS** HQ Flt by 24.9.17 (Major AAB Thomson AZP) and further AZPs 19.10.17 (Major AAB Thomson 3 sorties). Converted to FE2b. **33 HDS** C Flt by 18.2.18. **2 (N) ARD** 12.18, allotted to BEF but allotment cancelled 9.1.19 and to be deleted.

B1886 FE2b. With HD Group re-allotted to BEF 29.8.17 (275hp RR). **199 NTS**, crashed due to dazzle when landing 19.2.18 (crew injured – recorded as '1336').

B1887 FE2b. **83 Sqn** dd ex 2 ASD 10.8.18. **102 Sqn** dd ex 83 Sqn 20.1.19. **2 ASD** 20.1.19.

B1888 Presentation a/c *British Residents in the Netherlands East Indies No 1*. **1 ASD** and damaged in crashed from stall while landing on ferry flight 7.8.18.

B1889 Presentation a/c *Bundi No 1*. FE2b. **3 AAP** tested 18.7.18 (knocking) and 29.7.18 (OK). **2 AI** dd ex 1 ASD 9.8.18. **101 Sqn** dd ex 2 ASD 16.8.18, overturned and damaged hitting searchlight on landing from night bombing sortie 30.9.18 (crew OK). **2 ASD** and deleted 13.10.18 (NWR).

B1890 FE2d. **3 AAP** allotted to BEF 1.8.17 (275hp RR). **20 Sqn** and victs 9.8.17 (Lt CR Richards/ Lt AE Wear sent an Albatros D.V OOC near Becelaere at 09.50), 10.8.17 (Lt CR Richards/ Lt AE Wear sent 1 EA C-type OOC near Polygon Wood at 08.40 and shared sending an Albatros D.V OOC near Wervicq at 09.00 with A5147 and A6456), 16.8.17 (Lt CR Richards/Lt AE Wear sent an Albatros D.V OOC near Passchendaele on 09.15) and 17.8.17 (2Lt AGV Taylor/2Lt M Tod destroyed an Albatros D.III near Polygon Wood at 20.00) then LIA near Wervicq on photo

sortie 18.00 on 20.8.17 (2Lt CR Richards MC/2Lt SF Thompson POW wdd – possibly shot down by Ltn E Hess, Jasta 28). Engine RR/275/39 WD13963.

B1891 FE2d. **3 AAP** allotted to BEF 1.8.17 (275hp RR). **20 Sqn** and vict 14.8.17 (2Lt GS Lee/2Lt A Urquart destroyed a DFW C type in flames near Armentieres at 09.40) then LIA near Zonnebecke on OP 17.8.17 (Lt HW Joslyn & 2Lt A Urquart KIA – probably shot down by Vzfw F Kosmahl, Jasta 26). Engine RR2/275/105 WD13973.

B1892 FE2d. **3 AAP** allotted to BEF 3.8.17 (275hp RR). **20 Sqn** and vict 21.9.17 (2Lt W Durrand/ Lt AN Jenks sent an Albatros D.V OOC near Becelaere). **1 ASD** deleted 22.1.18 (NWR).

B1893 **3 AAP** allotted to BEF 7.8.17 (275hp RR). **1 ASD** deleted 24.1.18 (NWR).

B1894 **3 AAP** allotted to BEF 7.8.17 (250hp RR). **8 AAP** by 12.8.17 (Lt M Campbell AGP) and further AGP 22.8.17 (Lt PRT Chamberlayne).

B1895 FE2d. **3 AAP** allotted to BEF 7.8.17 (275hp RR). **20 Sqn** and LIA near Boesinghe on OP 6.9.17 (Lt JO Pilkington/AM2 HF Matthews KIA – shot down in flames by Ltn W Voss, Jasta 10). Engine RR1/275/39 WD13892.

B1896 Presentation a/c *Orissa States No 1*. **3 AAP** allotted to BEF 30.7.17 (250hp RR). Flown from France to England 16.8.17. **8 AAP** by 22.8.17 (2Lt AN Dupont AGP). **33 HDS** C Flt by 24.9.17 (Lt EEH Hamilton-Jackson AZP – landed at Beverley) and further AZP 19.10.17 (Lt R Affleck/2Lt D Fraser).

B1897 Presentation a/c *Australia No 14, NSW No 13*. FE2d. **3 AAP** allotted to BEF 30.7.17 (250hp RR). **20 Sqn** and victs 17.8.17 (2Lt HE Luchford/2Lt J Tennant destroyed an Albatros D.V near Houthem at 14.45 and Lt RM Makepeace/Gnr J McMechan shared destruction of an Albatros D.V near Polygon Wood with A6456 at 20.00) then damaged when hit ditch on landing from OP 4.9.17.

B1898 **3 AAP** allotted to BEF 11.8.17 (250hp RR). **8 AAP** by 22.8.17 (2Lt O Matson AGP). **1 AD** dd ex Lympne 29.8.17 (Lt RA Grosvenor) and tested 31.8.17. Flown to England 24.9.17. **33 HDS** B Flt by 5.8.18 (Lt GN Smith/Capt ST Goodman AZP). **2 (N) ARD** 12.18, allotted to BEF but allotment cancelled 9.1.19 and to be deleted.

B1899

B1900 Presentation a/c *British Residents in the Netherlands East Indies No 1*. **33 HDS** and wrecked in crash from low turn 26.3.18 (2Lt JL Browne fatally IIFA/Lt GW Ross KIFA).

B4005 & B4050: 2 RAF FE2b (160hp Beardmore) rebuilt by 2 (Northern) Aircraft Repair Depot, Coal Aston under Reserve Aeroplane Scheme.

B4005 Issued for training w/e 28.1.18. **33 HDS** A Flt and damaged landing after AZP 13.4.18 (Lt L Murphy/AM2 W Taylor OK). **33 HDS** B Flt by 13.8.18.

B4050 **148 Sqn**. **149 Sqn** dd ex 148 Sqn 17.4.18.

37 RAF FE2b (120/160hp Beardmore) rebuilt by the Southern Aircraft Repair Depot, Farnborough under the Reserve Aeroplane Scheme.

B7779 **148 Sqn** dd 8.4.18. Issued for Expeditionary Force w/e 22.4.18. **2 AIS**. **148 Sqn** dd ex 2 AIS 8.5.18. **102 Sqn** dd ex 148 Sqn 19.1.19.

B7782 Issued for Expeditionary Force w/e 22.4.18 (160hp Beardmore). **1 ASD** tested 22.4.18. **102 Sqn** dd ex 2 ASD 25.4.18 and damaged by AA night bombing and force-landed near Douchy-les-Ayette 17.5.18 (Lt AS Kelly/Lt WJ Harvey OK. Flying time 20hr 27min).

B7788 **SARD** tested 9.4.18 (OK). Issued for Expeditionary Force w/e 22.4.18. **148 Sqn** 4.18. **2 ASD** dd ex 1 ASD 9.5.18. Allotted to 100 Sqn but forced landed on delivery flight and returned to 2 ASD. **101 Sqn** dd ex 2 ASD 25.5.18 until @ 23.10.18.

B7794 **SARD** tested 13.3.18 (pressure dud) and 3.6.18 (OK). Issued for **148 Sqn** w/e 11.3.18 until @ 2.4.18. Issued for Expeditionary Force w/e 10.6.18. **83 Sqn** by 2.8.18. **102 Sqn** dd ex 83 Sqn 20.1.19.

B7795 Issued for **148 Sqn** w/e 11.3.18. to BEF with the unit by 3.6.18 and, although picketed, wrecked by wind 5.11.18. **1 ASD** 17.11.18.

B7799 **148 Sqn** by 3.6.18. **1 ASD** ex 148 Sqn 9.6.18.

B7800 **SARD** tested 4.1.18 (OK – recorded as A7800) and allotted to BEF 5.1.18 (160hp Beardmore). **100 Sqn** dd ex 2 ASD 13.3.18 and wrecked in forced landing near Fargniers 27.4.18. **2 ASD** wrecked ex 100 Sqn 30.6.18.

B7808 Issued for **148 Sqn** w/e 4.3.18, to BEF with the unit by 3.6.18 and LIA night bombing 16.6.18 (Lt CE Wharton/Lt JW Pryor POW. Flying time 57hr 8min).

B7809 **SARD** tested 5.4.18 (OK). Issued for Expeditionary Force w/e 8.4.18. **148 Sqn** by 4.18. **102 Sqn** dd ex 2 ASD 20.4.18 and wrecked in forced landing after engine failed on night bombing sortie 16.5.18. On BEF charge 30.6.18.

B7812 **148 Sqn** dd 27.5.18.

B7813 Issued for Expeditionary Force w/e 20.5.18. **2 ASD** by 29.5.18. **148 Sqn**. **101 Sqn** dd ex 2 ASD 1.6.18 and LIA night bombing 7.8.18 (2Lt JD Anderson/2Lt CEA Lovell POW – flying time 66hr 35min).

B7814 Issued for Expeditionary Force w/e 13.5.18 (160hp Beardmore). **1 ASD** dd ex 1 ASD 18.5.18. **58 Sqn** dd ex 1 AIS 5.7.18 and wrecked in overturned landing on aerodrome after engine overheated on night bombing sortie 22.8.18 (2Lt JC Belford/2Lt AG Thistle OK). **1 ASD** deleted 26.8.18 (NWR, flying time 37hr 25min).

B7815 **SARD** tested 5.5.18 (nose heavy), 6.5.18 (rigging OK, engine overheating), 8.5.18 (test again) and 9.5.18 (OK). Issued for Expeditionary Force w/e 13.5.18 (160hp Beardmore). **1 AIS** dd ex 1 ASD 18.5.18. **148 Sqn** dd ex 1 AIS 29.5.18 **102 Sqn** dd ex 148 Sqn 19.1.19.

B7816 **SARD** tested 10.4.18 (pressure pipe broken) and 12.4.18 (OK). **148 Sqn** by 4.18. Issued for Expeditionary Force w/e 22.4.18. **2 AIS**. **148 Sqn** dd ex 2 AIS 8.5.18 and listed as 'old' 28.9.18. **2 ASD** by 2.10.18 (unfit for service). **1 ASD** and flown to England 4.10.18.

B7817 **SARD** tested 30.7.18 (pressure dud) and 2.8.18 (OK). **51 HDS** A Flt by 9.9.18.

B7818 **SARD** tested 8.5.18 (OK).

B7836 **SARD** tested 5.4.18 (OK). Issued for **148 Sqn** w/e 1.4.18. **2 AIS**. **148 Sqn** dd ex 2 AIS 2.5.18 and damaged overshooting landing from

night recce 8.7.18 (crew OK). **1 ASD** 9.7.18 and deleted 7.7.18 (NWR, flying time 49hr 50min). BUT **148 Sqn** by 9.18.

B7837 **SARD** tested 27.3.18 (revs down) and 5.4.18 (OK). Issued for **148 Sqn** w/e 25.3.18. **101 Sqn** dd ex 2 ASD 22.4.18 and overturned in crash in cornfield taking off on night recce 19.6.18 (2Lt CR Dove injured/Lt RB Lane injured – flying time 64hr 43min). **2 ASD** deleted 27.7.18, NWR.

B7838 **SARD** tested 15.4.18 (NBG), 22.5.18 (NBG – test again) and 26.5.18 (OK). Issued for **148 Sqn** w/e 25.3.18 and w/e 3.6.18. **1 ASD**. **148 Sqn** dd ex 1 ASD 17.6.18 and wrecked hitting tree in overshoot on landing from night bombing sortie 23.8.18. **1 ASD** ex 148 Sqn 24.8.18 and deleted 27.8.18 (NWR, flying time 51hr 15min).

B7839 Issued for **148 Sqn** w/e 1.4.18. **1 AIS**. **58 Sqn** dd ex 1 AIS 14.5.18 and damaged in forced landing in trenches after engine failed on night recce to Lille/Tournai 21/22.7.18 (2Lt RG Clough/2Lt GR Thornley OK). **1 ASD** deleted 27.7.18, NWR (flying time 62hr 25min). BUT **2 ASD** deleted 27.6.18 (NWR, flying time 57hr 35min).

B7840 Issued for **148 Sqn** w/e 25.3.18 (160hp Beardmore), to BEF with unit and force landed near aerodrome when engine failed on night bombing sortie 22.5.18 (flying time 21hr). **1 ASD** deleted 14.8.18, NWR (flying time 28hr??).

B7841 **SARD** tested 8.5.18 (temperature gauge changed then OK). Issued for Expeditionary Force w/e 13.5.18 (160hp Beardmore). **1 ASD** and wrecked hitting trees when engine failed taking off on ferry flight to 2 ASD 18.5.18. **148 Sqn** and damaged in crash after engine failed 29.8.18 (2Lt RN Gosling injured).

B7843 Issued for Expeditionary Force w/e 13.5.18 (160hp Beardmore). **1 ASD** dd ex England 14.5.18. **2 ASD** ex 1 ASD 17.5.18. **1 AIS**. **148 Sqn** dd ex 2 AIS 25.5.18 and wrecked in crash spinning in from 500ft on test flight 13.8.18 (Lt RWF Angus/AM1 GW King KIFA). **1 ASD** 13.8.18 and deleted 16.8.18 (NWR – flying time 13hr 55min).

B7844 **SARD** tested 14.6.18 (OK but tail heavy). Issued for SW Area w/e 17.6.18.

B7845 **SARD** tested 17.7.17 (test stopped by storm) and 18.7.18 (OK). **2 AAP** dd ex SARD 20.7.18. **51 HDS** C Flt by 30.7.18.

B7846 **SARD** tested 22.8.18 (OK).

B7847 **SARD** tested 9.5.18 (thermometer dud). **2 ASD** dd ex 1 ASD 21.5.18. **148 Sqn** dd ex 1

ASD by 6.7.18 and wrecked in forced landing after engine failed on night bombing sortie 29.8.18 (pilot injured/observer OK. Flying time 29hr 5min). **1 ASD** 31.8.18 and deleted 2.9.18.

B7848 **SARD** tested 2.5.18 (pressure dud, engine rough) and 3.5.18 (engine still rough, airlock in tank). Issued for Expeditionary Force w/e 13.5.18. **1 AIS** dd ex 1 ASD 21.5.18. **83 Sqn** dd ex 2 ASD 27.5.18 and burnt after forced landing when engine failed on night bombing sortie 10.11.18. **2 ASD** ex 83 Sqn 14.11.18

B7856 **SARD** tested 19.8.18 (OK).

B7872 **SARD** tested 22.4.18 (OK – rather tail heavy). **1 AIS** dd ex 1 ASD 9.5.18. **148 Sqn** dd ex 1 AIS 29.5.18. **102 Sqn** dd ex 148 Sqn 19.1.19.

B7874 **SARD** tested 25.6.18 (petrol leaking), 26.6.18 (twice – weak wind pump then wind pump seized) and 27.6.18 (OK at last).

B7877 **SARD** tested 6.6.18 (OK). Issued for training w/e 10.6.18.

B7922 **SARD** tested 27.8.18 (OK).

B7923 Sold to US government for USAS.

B7926 **SARD** tested 1.9.18 (OK).

B7932 **SARD** tested 30.8.18 (pump seized), visited Worthy Down 30.8.18 (ferrying pilot) and re-tested 31.8.18 (OK).

B7936 **12 TDS** by 24.8.18 until @ 26.8.18 (no prefix given to serial).

B7952 **SARD** tested 30.8.18 (pressure dud).

C9786 – C9835: 50 RAF FE2b (160hp Beardmore) built by Ransomes, Sims & Jefferies, Ipswich under Contract A.S.29675 dated 25.10.17.

C9786 Presentation a/c *Malaya No 11*. **2 AIS** dd ex 1 ASD 3.5.18. **83 Sqn** and crashed on take-off for night bombing practice 21.7.18 (2Lt V Rogers injured/2Lt D Fraser OK). On RAF charge 1.19.

C9787 **101 Sqn** dd ex 2 ASD 25.4.18 and LIA night recce 6.5.18 (Lt SA Hustwitt/Lt NA Smith POW. Flying time 14hr).

C9788 **1 AIS** ex 1 ASD 11.5.18. **1 ASD** 28.5.18. **58 Sqn** dd ex 1 AIS 30.5.18 and wrecked in forced landing at ammunition dump after pump failed on night recce 26.9.18 (2Lt EE Jones/2Lt J Warren OK. Flying time 112hr 15min). **1 AD** ex 58 Sqn 28.9.18

C9789 Presentation a/c *Malaya No 17*. **2 ASD** ex 1 ASD 3.5.18. **83 Sqn** by 2.8.18 and wrecked in forced landing crash after engine cut on night bombing sortie 17.8.18 (2Lt E Hooper/2Lt JWR McPhail OK). Deleted on unit with 106hr 24min flying time.

C9790 Presentation a/c *Gold Coast No 10*. **2 ASD** ex 1 ASD 3.5.18. **101 Sqn** and LIA night bombing 1.9.18 (Lt ME Challis/2Lt RD Hughes POW. Flying time 116hr).

C9791 Presentation a/c *Shanghai Exhibition* wef 1.18. Deleted 29.4.18.

C9792 **148 Sqn** by 5.4.18. **149 Sqn** dd ex 148 Sqn 29.4.18 and wrecked in landing crash after side slip developed into nose dive 19.5.18 (Capt G Robinson KIFA/2Lt CHP Hughes IIFA).

C9793 **36 HDS** A Flt by 9.6.18 until 15.6.18. **36 HDS** B Flt and wrecked in crash when spun in near aerodrome night flying 23.00 on 11.8.18 (Lt A Wald KIFA).

C9794 **2 ASD** ex 1 ASD 19.5.18. **148 Sqn** dd ex 2 AIS 25.5.18. **102 Sqn** dd ex 148 Sqn 19.1.19.

C9795 **38 Sqn** by 11.6.18. **102 Sqn** ex 38 Sqn 19.1.19.

C9796 **2 ASD** ex 1 ASD 18.5.18. **83 Sqn** dd ex 2 ASD 23.5.18 and damaged in crash after night bombing sortie 9.11.18 (2Lt JM Brown/2Lt CR Cook IIFA). **2 ASD** ex 83 Sqn 14.11.18.

C9797 **1 AIS** dd ex 1 ASD 14.5.18. **1 ASD** by 21.5.18. **I Flt** dd ex 1 AIS 7.6.18 and damaged by ground fire on Special Mission 21.8.18 crashing near aerodrome (Lt J Wingate/Capt

Two views of FE2b C9795 which served first with 38 and then 102 Squadron. The white rudder stripe is narrower than usual.

FE2b D3832 with excited passengers aboard after the war (see also p21).

CC Cole OK). **1 AD** ex I Flt 24.8.18 (flying time 54hr 40min). **1 ASD** deleted 27.8.18 (NWR, flying time 54hr 40min).

C9798 On BEF charge 30.6.18. **83 Sqn** dd ex 2 ASD 17.6.18 and wrecked in forced landing after engine cut on night bombing sortie 17.8.18. **2 ASD** deleted 22.8.18 – flying time 66hr 45min.

C9799 **149 Sqn** by 30.4.18, to BEF with unit unit, wrecked 17.8.18 and deleted on unit 18.9.18 with 66hr 45min flying time. BUT **1 ASD** deleted 22.9.18 (flying time 71hr 20min).

C9800 **3 AAP** tested 12.7.18. **1 SNBD** by 8.18. **2 SNBD** Andover.

C9801 **149 Sqn** by 3.5.18 until @ 14.6.18. On BEF charge 30.6.18.

C9802 **100 Sqn** dd ex 2 ASD 16.6.18. **3 ASD** ex 100 Sqn 2.9.18. Sold to US government for USAS 9.18.

C9803 **38 Sqn** dd ex 4 ASD 29.6.18 and LIA when force landed in sea off Calais by EA and sank 11.8.18 (Lt H McAndrew/Sgt Harris OK). **4 ASD** ex 38 Sqn 14.8.18 (salved?). Deleted 30.9.18 (completely wrecked).

C9804

C9805 On BEF charge 30.6.18. **101 Sqn** and crashed landing from test flight 23.7.18 (crew OK). **2 ASD** deleted 11.8.18, NWR – flying time 32hr 10min.

C9806 **38 HDS** Depot by 5.8.18 (2Lt AJ Marsden AZP from Leadenham). **199 NTS** by 12.18.

C9807 **100 Sqn** dd ex 2 ASD 29.6.18 and wrecked (burnt) 16.8.18. **3 AD** and deleted 9.18 (flying time 49hr).

C9808 **149 Sqn** by 30.4.18, to BEF and with unit and wrecked in forced landing after engine cut on night bombing sortie 18.8.18. **1 ASD** ex 149 Sqn 18.8.18 and deleted 22.8.18 (NWR, flying time 67hr 35min).

C9809 **38 HDS** Depot by 5.8.18 (Capt PW Rutherford aborted AZP from Buckmister).

C9810 **8 TDS** by 8.18.

C9811 On BEF charge 30.6.18. **58 Sqn** dd ex 2 AIS 1.7.18 and overturned into field near aerodrome on take off for night recce to Lille 24.7.18 (2Lt SGE Inman-Knox/2Lt FW Roadhouse OK. Flying time 12hr 15min). **1 ASD** ex 58 Sqn 26.7.18 and deleted 28.7.18 (NWR, 1 flying time 2hr 15min).

C9812 **83 Sqn** dd ex 2 AD 29.6.18 and crashed hitting wires in forced landing on night recce 7.9.18 (crew shaken). Deleted on unit (flying time 79hr 15min – given as D9812) but to 2 ASD and deleted 16.9.18.

C9813 On BEF charge 30.6.18. **101 Sqn** and wrecked in crash after take off for night bombing sortie 21.9.18 (2Lt GN Troth injured, flying time 89hr 30min). Deleted in the field.

C9814 **58 Sqn** dd ex 1 AIS 25.6.18. **2 ASD** ex 58 Sqn 3.10.18. **102 Sqn** dd 1.19.

C9815 **149 Sqn** by 16.6.18 and crashed on take off for night bombing sortie 15.8.18. **1 ASD** ex 149 Sqn (wrecked) 16.8.18 and deleted 22.8.18 (NWR, flying time 46hr 10min).

C9816 **3 AAP** tested 7.7.18. **149 Sqn** dd ex 1 ASD 19.7.18 and damaged in forced landing after engine seized on night bombing sortie 29.9.18 (crew OK). Deleted 1.10.18.

C9817 On BEF charge 30.6.18. **83 Sqn** dd ex 2 AIS 1.7.18 and wrecked in forced landing in trenches near Brie on night recce 7.9.18 (Lt WC Pierce/2Lt A Macinnes shaken). Deleted on unit (flying time 72hr 15min).

C9818 **1 SNBD** by 8.18. **2 SNBD.**

C9819 **61 Wing**, Dover. **102 Sqn** by 5.8.18 and wrecked when crashed through wall after engine failed at 15ft on take off for night bombing sortie 13.8.18 (crew OK. Flying time 37hr 25min). **2 ASD** ex 102 Sqn 15.8.18.

C9820 **8 TDS** by 8.18. **12 TDS** by 15.8.18.

C9821 **38 Sqn** by 24.6.18. Sold to US Government. **1 Aviation Centre** USAS by 3.10.18.

C9822 **149 Sqn** dd ex 1 ASD 10.7.18

C9823 **101 Sqn** and listed as old 4.11.18.

C9824 **148 Sqn** dd ex 1 ASD 9.7.18 and damaged in forced landing after engine failed on take off for night bombing sortie 4.9.18 (Capt LHL Lindsay-Young injured). **1 ASD** ex 148 Sqn 10.9.18. Flying time 18hr 5min.

C9825 On BEF charge 30.6.18. **101 Sqn** by 8.18 and crashed in forced landing after engine failed on night recce 3.9.18 (2Lt EH Lyon-Hall injured). **2 ASD** ex 101 Sqn 4.9.18 and deleted 8.9.18 (NWR, flying time 65hr).

C9826 **148 Sqn** dd ex 1 ASD 14.8.18. **102 Sqn** ex 148 Sqn 19.1.19.

C9827 **1 AIS** dd ex 1 ASD 30.7.18. **149 Sqn** dd ex 1 ASD 14.8.18.

C9828 Presentation a/c *Presented by the Colony of Mauritius No 4* wef 18.8.18. **1 ASD** dd ex 8 AAP 17.8.18. **102 Sqn** dd ex 2 ASD 25.8.18 and wrecked in forced landing crash after engine failed on night bombing sortie 24.9.18 (2Lt W Jaggs/2Lt R Gibson IIFA). **2 ASD** 24.9.18 and deleted 29.9.18 (NWR, flying time 43hr 45min).

C9829 Presentation a/c *Malaya No 19* wef 18.8.18. **83 Sqn** collected ex 1 AIS 7.9.18 and wrecked when crashed into shell holes after becoming lost in dark on delivery flight (flying time 97hr 30min). Deleted 7.9.18 but re-taken on charge 19.9.18. Deleted 10.10.18 and reconstructed as H6888 1.11.18.

C9830 **148 Sqn** dd ex 1 ASD 24.8.18. **102 Sqn** ex 148 Sqn 19.1.19.

C9831 **58 Sqn** dd ex 1 AIS 23.8.18 and wrecked in forced landing crash in field near Moulle on night bombing sortie to Ramegnies 24.9.18 (Lt CM McLean/2Lt TA Evans OK – a/c salvaged. Flying time 27hr 35min).

C9832 **102 Sqn** dd ex 2 ASD 21.8.18 and in safe forced landing after propeller burst on night bombing sortie 23.8.18 (crew OK). **2 ASD** 23.8.18 and deleted 14.9.18, (NWR – flying time 12hr 45min).

C9833 Presentation a/c *Punjab No 27* wef 18.8.18.

C9834 Presentation a/c *Shanghai Exhibition* wef 18.8.18. **101 Sqn** dd ex 2 ASD 4.9.18 and LIA night bombing after hit by AA 18.9.18 (Capt HW Stockdale/2Lt Shergold OK, evaded capture – a/c abandoned in enemy territory. Engine 471/WD9919, flying time 10hr 35min).

C9835 Arrived in France for Independent Force 11.8.18. **2 AIS** dd ex 1 ASD 17.8.18. **2 ASD** tested 30.10.18 (Lt RA Grosvenor, pressure dud, mechanical pump not working and then thermostat dud). **83 Sqn** Serny. **102 Sqn** dd ex 83 Sqn 20.1.19.

D3776 – D3835: 60 РАГ ГЕ2b (160hp Beardmore) built by Richard Garrett & Sons, Leiston under Contract A.S.34281 dated 14.11.17 – some conversions to FE2c.

D3776 **3 AAP** tested 15.6.18 (engine knocking). On BEF charge 30.6.18. **58 Sqn** dd ex 1 AIS 3.7.18. **2 ASD** ex 58 Sqn 3.10.18. **102 Sqn** by 1.19.

D3777

D3778

D3779 **149 Sqn** dd ex 1 ASD 25.6.18 and LIA night bombing 18.7.18 (Lt RA Vosper/Lt A Smith POW. Flying time 5hr 10min).

A night bomber FE2b D9091, assembled by Alexander Stephen & Sons, Linthouse, Glasgow, awaits its engine.

D3780 **3 AAP** tested 9.7.18. **38 Sqn** dd ex 4 ASD 8.8.18. **102 Sqn** ex 38 Sqn 19.1.19.

D3781 **3 AAP** tested 9.7.18 and 10.7.18. **38 Sqn** by 10.18. Sold to US government for USAS. **1 Aviation Centre** USAS ex 38 Sqn 14.10.18.

D3782 **3 AAP** tested 17.7.18. **38 Sqn** dd ex 4 ASD 1.8.18. Sold to US government for USAS. **1 Aviation Centre** USAS ex 38 Sqn 3.10.18. **48th Aero Sqn** USAS.

D3783 **3 AAP** tested 3.7.18 (pump seized). Dispatched to 5 Group, 7.7.18. **101 Sqn** by 6.8.18 and LIA night bombing 15.9.18 (Lt EJ Stockman/2Lt P Payne POW. Flying time 56hr).

D3784 **38 Sqn** crashed in sea on night bombing sortie 4.11.18, in water for 4 days and unserviceable. Deleted in the field 11.11.18.

D3785 FE2c. **3 AAP** tested 13.7.18. **38 Sqn**. Sold to US government for USAS. **1 Aviation Centre** USAS dd ex 38 Sqn 18.10.18.

D3786

D3787 Dispatched to 5 Group but not arrived by 2.10.18.

D3788 **12 TDS** and wrecked in crash and burnt following steep landing after becoming lost on night flight 23.10.18 (2Lt HB Ward fatally IIFA).

D3789

D3790

D3791 **1 SNBD** by 9.18. 38 Sqn.

D3792

D3793

D3794

D3795 **191 NTS** and overturned in crash after struck wheel when landing 6.9.18.

D3796

D3797 **8 TDS** by summer 1918 and overturned in landing crash on aerodrome. **Armament School** by 10.18.

D3798

D3799 **101 Sqn** dd ex 2 ASD 23.8.18 and damaged taxiing on soft ground when throttle broke 23.9.18. **2 ASD** ex 101 Sqn 24.9.18. **2 ASD** 24.9.18 and deleted 29.9.18 (NWR, flying time 29hr 05min).

D3800

D3801

D3802

D3803

D3804

D3805

D3806

D3807

D3808 **191 NTS** by 10.18.

D3809 **83 Sqn** dd ex 2 ASD 1.11.18. **102 Sqn** Serny ex 83 Sqn 20.1.19.

D3810 **191 NTS** by 10.18.

D3811 **101 Sqn** and wrecked hitting trees on take-off for night bombing sortie 5.11.18 (Lt WJ Cooper/2Lt HC Bowler KIA).

D3812

D3813 **38 Cqn** dd ex 4 ASD 23.8.18. **102 Sqn** ex 38 Sqn 19.1.19.

D3814 **83 Sqn** dd ex 1 AIS 7.9.18 and wrecked in collision near Beauchamp after night-bombing Charleroi railway station 29.10.18 (2Lt VH Lawrence/2Lt R Chapman IIFA) BUT wrecked in forced landing with engine valve trouble on night bombing sortie 31.10.18 (crew shaken).

D3815

D3816 **58 Sqn** dd ex 1 AIS 4.9.18 and crashed taking off on poor ground for night bombing sortie 25.9.18 (2Lt R Adams/2Lt W Kew OK). **1 ASD** ex 58 Sqn (flying time 12hr 30min).

D3817 Arrived in France for Independent Force 19.8.18 but not required and re-allotted to BEF. **102 Sqn** dd ex 2 ASD 22.8.18 and damaged in heavy landing on night practice flight 22.8.18 (crew OK). **2 ASD** 22.8.18 and deleted 14.9.18, (NWR, – flying time 5hr 55min).

D3818 **83 Sqn** dd ex 2 AIS 22.8.18 and crashed into

FE2b D9105 in night bombing livery, but at an unknown English location.

orchard in forced landing on night bombing sortie 30.10.18 (Lt C Mitchell/2Lt W Grayson IIFA).

D3819 **2 AIS** dd ex 1 ASD 5.7.18. **102 Sqn** dd ex 2 ASD 23.8.18 and damaged hitting low road in forced landing after engine lost revs on night bombing sortie 7.9.18 (crew OK). **2 ASD** 7.9.18 and deleted 10.9.18 (NWR, flying time 29hr 25min).

D3820 **102 Sqn** dd ex 2 ASD 13.9.18 and damaged hitting shell hole in forced landing on night bombing sortie 28.9.18 (crew OK). **2 ASD** and deleted 5.10.18 (NWR).

D3821 **3 AAP** tested 21.8.18. **38 Sqn** dd ex 4 ASD 31.8.18. Sold to US government for USAS. **1 Aviation Centre** USAS dd ex 38 Sqn 14.10.18.

D3822 **102 Sqn** dd ex 2 ASD 5.9.18 and damaged in forced landing after engine failed on night bombing sortie 8.9.18. 2 ASD 7.9.18 and deleted 12.9.18, NWR (flying time 5hr 35min).

D3823 **3 AAP** tested 18.10.18.

D3824 Presentation a/c *Punjab No 16* wef 10.18. **83 Sqn** dd ex 1 ASD 26.9.18 and crashed from sideslip to avoid wires after engine cut on night practice flight 29.10.18 (2Lt A Hart OK).

D3825 **149 Sqn** dd ex 1 ASD 18.9.18.

D3826 **83 Sqn** dd ex RP 23.9.18. **102 Sqn** ex 83 Sqn 20.1.19.

D3827

D3828 **3 AAP** tested 16.10.18. **83 Sqn** by 16.11.18. **102 Sqn** ex 83 Sqn 19.1.19.

D3829 Presentation a/c *Kaffraria* wef 10.18. **8 AAP** by 1.1.19 allotted to BEF, allotment cancelled 23.1.19 and to be deleted.

D3830 Presentation a/c *Punjab No 36* wef 10.18. **101 Sqn** tested new 7.10.18 (2Lt J Helingoe) and crashed after engine failed on take off for night bombing sortie 26.10.18 (2Lt A Allen injured/2Lt G Williams OK).

D3831

D3832 **RAE** by 10.18. To Civil Register as G-EAHC.

D3833

D3834

D3835

D9081 – D9230: 150 RAF FE2b (160hp Beardmore) D9081-D9180: assembled by Alexander Stephen & Sons, Linthouse, Glasgow from material supplied by G & J Weir under Contract A.S.40817. D9181-D9250 erected by Barclay, Curle & Co Ltd, Whiteinch, Glasgow under Contract 35a/1076/C908.

D9081 **1 SNBD** F Flt by 5.18 and crashed landing 6.8.18 (pilot OK/observer injured), repaired and on charge until 9.18. **8 TDS** by 1.10.18.

D9082 **2 AIS** dd ex 1 ASD 3.5.18. On BEF charge

30.6.18. **83 Sqn** by 1.8.18. **102 Sqn** dd ex 83 Sqn 22.1.19.

D9083 **2 ASD** ex 1 ASD 8.5.18. **101 Sqn** dd ex 2 ASD 18.5.18 and crashed in forced landing after engine failed on night recce 3.9.18. **2 ASD** ex 101 Sqn 4.9.18 and deleted 8.9.18 (NWR, flying time130hr).

D9084 **3 AAP** tested 1.5.18. **2 ASD** ex 1 ASD 8.5.18. **102 Sqn** by 7.6.18 and wrecked in crash after engine failed on take-off for night bombing sortie 27.6.18 (Lt GE Reynolds KIFA/Lt ET Clarke injured). **2 ASD** deleted 4.7.18 (NWR, flying time 60hr 50min).

D9085 **1 AIS** dd 15.5.18. **2 ASD** ex 1 AIS 17.5.18. **100 Sqn** dd ex 2 ASD 18.5.18. **3 ASD** ex 100 Sqn 29.7.18.

D9086

D9087 **200 NTS** by 10.18.

D9088 **200 NTS** and wrecked in crash from sideslip 26.6.18 (Lt RdeN Coape-Arnold KIFA).

D9089 **149 Sqn** by 30.4.18, to BEF with the unit 2.6.18 and on still charge at Namur 12.18. Flown Cologne – Serny 8/9.3.19.

D9090 On BEF charge 30.6.18. **101 Sqn** and wrecked in crash on take off for night bombing sortie 7.8.18 (Lt AJ Hunter/Lt WW Sproson KIFA). **2 ASD** ex 101 Sqn 7.8.18 for salvage and deleted 8.8.18 (NWR, flying time 3hr 35min).

D9091 **149 Sqn** by 3.5.18 until @ 3.8.18.

D9092

D9093 To BEF 31.5.18. **83 Sqn** dd ex 2 ASD 1.6.18 and crashed returning after engine failed on night recce 1.7.18 (crew OK). **2 AD** ex 83 Sqn 2.7.18. **2 ASD** deleted 21.7.18, NWR (flying time 20hr 30min).

D9094 To BEF 31.5.18. **2 ASD** ex 1 ASD 31.5.18. **100 Sqn** dd ex 2 ASD 9.6.18 until struck off 18.8.18.

D9095

D9096

D9097 **13 TDS** and wrecked in crash and burnt after steep glide developed into nose-dive 2.7.18 (2Lt EG Nicholls-Pratt KIFA). BUT at Bickendorf 7.3.19.

D9098 **36 HDS** B Flt, and photographed visiting Cramlington early summer 18.

D9099 On BEF charge 30.6.18. **83 Sqn** by 2.8.18 and wrecked in forced landing after hit by ground fire (or EA?) on night bombing sortie 9.8.18 (Capt AO Lewis-Roberts DFC/2Lt EN Lohmeyer DFC OK. Flying time 66hr 3min). **2 ASD** deleted 13.8.18.

D9100 On BEF charge 30.6.18. **102 Sqn** by 5.8.18 and wrecked in crash when overshot landing in heavy mist after night bombing sortie 10.8.18 (crew OK. Flying time 76hr 50min). **2 ASD** ex 102 Sqn 12.8.18.

D9101 **1 SNBD** by 2.6.18 and in ground accident

FE2b D9108 with large 'light-shades' on its wing-tip flares. It was extensively used for testing well into the early 1920s [see also p68].

7.9.18 (Pte H Richardson killed by propeller).

D9102

D9103 **1 SNBD** F Flt by 9.18. **8 TDS** by 30.9.18.

D9104 #

D9105

D9106 On BEF charge 30.6.18. **149 Sqn** dd ex 1 ASD 5.7.18 and burnt out in crash after engine stalled on take off for night bombing sortie 15.9.18 (Lt AJG King/2Lt JW Hogan KIFA. Flying time 29hr 05min). Deleted on unit 18.9.18 but to 1 ASD and deleted 20.9.18.

D9107 **8 TDS** by summer 18.

D9108 **ES Martlesham Heath** by 11.8.18 until @ 23.3.19 (compass, sextant and gyro tests). **Instrument Design Establishment**, by 13.9.19 and scheduled to appear at 1921 Hendon Pageant but petrol pump failed and returned to Biggin Hill. **RAE** dd ex IDE 15.5.1922 until @ 11.1924.

D9109 **102 Sqn** by 1.19.

D9110 **102 Sqn** dd ex 2 ASD 19.8.18 until @ 1.19.

D9111 **102 Sqn** dd ex 2 ASD 11.8.18 until @ 17.9.18.

D9112

D9113

D9114

D9115 Sold to US government for USAS 9.18.

D9116 **WEE**.

D9117 **148 Sqn** dd ex 1 ASD 18.6.18 and rear end collapsed on roll out 19.11.18. **1 ASD** 5.12.18 (prefix uncertain).

D9118 **15 TDS** by 10.18.

D9119

D9120 Arrived in France for Independent Force 8.8.18. **3 AD** dd dismantled.

D9121 **51 HDS** C Flt by 29.6.18 until @ 17.7.18, as two seat machine. **51 HDS** B Flt, converted to single-seater configuration.

D9122

D9123 **192 NTS** by 7.9.18, forced landed near Kettering 17.11.18 and on charge until @ 2.19.

D9124 **51 HDS** B Flt, converted to single-seater configuration.

D9125 **191 NTS** and force-landed due to water leakage at Wilburton, near Ely, 3.1.19 (PFO WF Clark).

D9126

D9127 **12 TDS** by 11.8.18 until @ 18.8.18.

D9128 **12 TDS** by 19.8.18.

D9129

D9130 **12 TDS** Netheravon and wrecked in crash from spin after engine failed on low turn 11.8.18 (2Lt IW Hathaway KIFA).

D9131

D9132 **13 TDS** and crashed in undershot landing 21.10.18 (crew injured).

D9133 **15 TDS** by 10.18.

D9134 **51 HDS** B Flt, as single seat conversion.

D9135

D9136

D9137

D9138

D9139 **199 NTS** and wrecked in crash 24.1.19 after engine failed on take-off.

D9140 On BEF charge 30.6.18.

D9141 On BEF charge 30.6.18. **8 TDS** crashed from stall 20.10.18 (crew injured).

D9142 On BEF charge 30.6.18.

D9143 On BEF charge 30.6.18.

D9144 On BEF charge 30.6.18. **199 NTS** by 1.19.

D9145 On BEF charge 30.6.18.

D9146 On BEF charge 30.6.18. **58 Sqn** by 9.7.18. In UK based training accident 29.10.18 when forced to land downwind after engine failure (crew injured).

D9147

FE2b D9142 interestingly reveals its serial under its lower wings, which probably indicates one of the home-based training units.

FE2b D9154 after it crashed at 1 School of Navigation and Bomb Dropping in June 1918.

D9148 On BEF charge 30.6.18. **200 NTS** by 9.18.

D9149

D9150 On BEF charge 30.6.18.

D9151

D9152 **58 TDS** and wrecked in crash from spin after stalled 28.10.18 (2Lt MF Thwaite KIFA).

D9153 **8 TDS** by summer 18 and crashed in side-slip from turn 23.12.18 (both crew injured). BUT **Armament School** by 10.18.

D9154 **1 SNBD** and crashed night flying 6.18.

D9155

D9156

D9157 On BEF charge 30.6.18. **58 Sqn** until @ 3.7.18. **8 TDS** and crashed due to bad flying 22.10.18 (crew injured).

D9158

D9159 On BEF charge 30.6.18. **58 Sqn** until @ 9.7.18.

D9160

D9161 On BEF charge 30.6.18.

D9162 On BEF charge 30.6.18.

D9163 **58 Sqn** dd 3.6.18 and damaged in crash 20.6.18. **13 TDS** by summer 1918.

D9164 On BEF charge 30.6.18.

D9165

D9166

D9167

D9168

D9169

D9170

D1971

D9172

D9173 **4 AAP** in store and dismantled, allotted to BEF but allotment cancelled 9.12.18 and to be deleted.

D9174 **4 AAP** in store and dismantled, allotted to BEF but allotment cancelled 9.12.18 and to

be deleted.

D9175 **4 AAP** in store and dismantled, allotted to BEF but allotment cancelled 9.12.18 and to be deleted.

D9176 On BEF charge 30.6.18. **4 AAP** in store and dismantled, allotted to BEF but allotment cancelled 9.12.18 and to be deleted.

D9177

D9178 On BEF charge 30.6.18.

D9179 On BEF charge 30.6.18.

D9180

D9181 On BEF charge 30.6.18.

D9182

D9183 **58 Sqn** dd 18.6.18. On BEF charge 30.6.18.

D9184

D9185

D9186 On BEF charge 30.6.18. **83 Sqn** by 20.7.18 and crashed when bomb detached on take off for night bombing sortie 4.11.18 (Lt AF Corker/2Lt V Nutter injured).

D9187 **148 Sqn** dd ex 1 ASD 7.10.18. **102 Sqn** ex 148 Sqn 21.1.19.

D9188 **58 Sqn** dd 30.5.18.

D9189

D9190

D9191

D9192 RAE 1.1.19 used for Sperry gyro tests.

D9193

D9194

D9195

D9196

D9197

D9198

D9199

D9200

D9201

D9202

D9203

D9204

D9205

D9206

D9207

D9208

D9209

D9210

D9211

D9212

D9213

D9214

D9215

D9216

D9217

D9218 Delivered mid 11.18.

D9219

D9220

D9221

D9222

D9223

D9224

D9225

D9226

D9227

D9228

D9229

D9230 Delivered 14.12.18.

D9740 – D9789: 50 RAF FE2b (120/160hp Beardmore) erected from spares at 3 (Western) ARD, Yate under the Reserve Aeroplane Scheme.

D9740 **149 Sqn** by 26.4.18, to BEF with unit, wrecked in crash from nose dive on practice flight 7.7.18 (pilot injured) and deleted in the field 8.7.18 (flying time 29hr 25min).

D9741 **149 Sqn** by 26.4.18, to BEF with unit and wrecked when overshot flarepath and ran through sleeper fence on landing from night bombing sortie 13.8.18. **1 ASD** 15.8.18, to Repair Park for repair but deleted 18.8.18 (NWR, flying time 54hr 35min).

D9742 **149 Sqn** by 26.4.18, to BEF with unit, wrecked in forced landing on 58 Sqn dummy aerodrome after throttle cable snapped on night bombing sortie 4.7.18 and deleted in

FE2b D9750 was a night bomber with 149 Sqn, but no further details are known.

the field 6.7.18 (flying time 20hr 20min).

D9743 **149 Sqn** by 26.4.18, to BEF with unit and damaged in crash taking off from soft ground 9.12.18. **215 Sqn** Alquines by 12.18.

D9744 **149 Sqn** by 26.4.18, to BEF with unit and damaged when stone hit propeller on test flight 19.8.18. **1 ASD** wrecked ex 149 Sqn 20.8.18 and deleted 23.8.18 (NWR, flying time 55hr 40min).

D9745 **149 Sqn** by 25.4.18, to BEF with unit and force landed with engine trouble on night recce 10.7.18. **1 ASD** wrecked ex 149 Sqn 10.7.18 and deleted 14.7.18 (NWR, flying time 22hr).

D9746 **58 Sqn** dd ex 1 AIS 9.7.18. **1 AD** ex 58 Sqn 30.8.18. **149 Sqn** dd ex 1 ASD 16.9.18.

D9747 **3 AAP** tested 28.6.18 (water leak).

D9748 **1 AIS** dd ex 1 ASD 29.5.18. **101 Sqn** dd ex 2 ASD 7.6.18 and damaged in forced landing on night bombing sortie 23.8.18 (crew OK). **2 ASD** as salvage ex 101 Sqn 23.8.18 and deleted 14.9.18, (NWR, flying time 98hr, also recorded as 31hr 40min).

D9749 **148 Sqn** dd ex 1 ASD 17.7.18. **102 Sqn** ex 148 Sqn 19.1.19.

D9750 **149 Sqn** by 26.4.18, to BEF with unit until @12.18.

D9751 **149 Sqn** by 16.6.18.

D9752 **149 Sqn** by 2.5.18. **192 NTS** dd ex Ford Junction 7.6.18 until @ 14.6.18.

D9753 **3 AAP** tested 20.6.18 (pump seized) **191 NTS** and wrecked in crash from stall then spinning nose-dive 7.9.18 (2Lt AE Parks/2Lt AH Thompson KIFA).

D9754 **1 SNBD** by 8.18. **2 SNBD**.

D9755

D9756 **2 ASD** dd ex 1 ASD 26.5.18. **100 Sqn** dd ex 2 ASD 30.5.18. **3 ASD** ex 100 Sqn for repair 29.7.18.

D9757 **1 ASD** Repair Park 11.5.18. **1 AIS** ex 1 ASD 14.5.18. **58 Sqn** dd ex 1 AIS 16.5.18 and reported with poor climb on test flight 29.6.18 (Capt HJ Whittingham/Lt RA Varley.

Flying time 40hr 50min). **1 AD** ex 58 Sqn 3.7.18. Deleted 5.11.18 and reconstructed as H7229 wef 5.11.18.

D9758 **100 Sqn** dd ex 2 ASD 18.5.18, also 31.5.18, damaged in forced landing near Toul 1.6.18 (to be dismantled and under rebuild on unit 8.6.18) and LIA bombing enemy aerodromes 17.8.18 (1Lt JJ van Schaack USAS/Capt JA King USAS POW).

D9759 **1 AIS** dd ex 1 ASD 6.5.18. **58 Sqn** dd ex 1 AIS 16.5.18 and crashed when propeller hit pole on take off for night bombing sortie 7.7.18 (Lt AH Padley/Capt CC Cole OK). **1 AD** ex 58 Sqn 9.7.18 (flying time 57hr 10min). Deleted 8.10.18 and reconstructed as H7179 wef 8.10.18.

D9760

D9761 **1 AIS** dd ex 1 ASD 15.5.18. **149 Sqn** dd ex 1 ASD 2.7.18 until @ 3.8.18.

D9762 **2 ASD** 8.5.18. **83 Sqn** and LIA on night recce 12.6.18 (Capt J Weaver/2Lt JL Brown POW – WT transmission had been jammed – flying time 43hr 15min).

D9763 **1 AIS** dd ex 1 ASD 14.5.18. **58 Sqn** dd ex 1 AIS 3.6.18, damaged in forced landing after hit by AA on night raid 7.6.18 (Lt WA Leslie/Lt F Wilkinson OK, only engine salvaged by 10 AP) and deleted 20.6.18 with 22hr flying time.

D9764 **1 AIS** dd ex 1 ASD 2.5.18. **148 Sqn** dd ex 1 ASD 5.6.18 (delivered in error). **1 ASD** ex 148 Sqn 6.6.18. **148 Sqn** ex 1 ASD 17.6.18. **102 Sqn** ex 148 Sqn 19.1.19.

D9765 **2 ASD** ex 1 ASD 27.5.18. **100 Sqn** dd ex 2 ASD 2.6.18. **3 ASD** ex 100 Sqn 21.8.18. **100 Sqn** ex 3 ASD 25.8.18. **3 ASD** ex 100 Sqn 2.9.18. Sold to US government for USAS 9.18.

D9766 **2 ASD** ex 1 ASD 29.5.18. **100 Sqn** dd ex 2 ASD 3.6.18 and damaged hitting rut in forced landing after engine failed on night bombing sortie 23.6.18 (crew OK). **2 ASD** ex 100 Sqn 23.6.18.

D9767 **36 HDS** stalled doing low spiral during

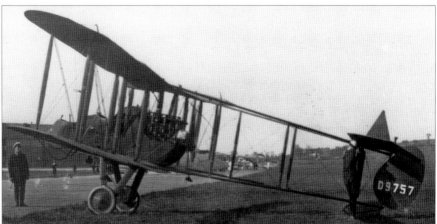

FE2b D9757 at Cranwell, before delivery to France where it served with 58 Squadron.

FE2b D9911 was on the strength of 100 Sqn for barely a week. Here it is seen flipped over after landing. Its transfer to 3 ASD on 27 July 1918 was probably the result of this accident.

D9768 **1 SNBD** by 1.6.18.

D9769 **8 TDS** A Flt by 18.6.18. **Armament School** by 10.18.

D9770 **192 NTS** crashed in flames after take-off 13.25 on 17.6.18 (pilot OK/observer injured).

D9771 **51 HDS** crashed force-landing when engine cut 29.7.18 (pilot injured/observer OK).

D9772

D9773 **36 HDS** C Flt as a/c *D* by 3.6.18 until @ 8.18. **36 HDS** A Flt by 30.8.18. Bury/Upwood (190 NTS?) dd ex Hylton, via Doncaster, 30/31.8.18.

D9774 **3 AAP** tested 2.6.18 (OK). **90 HDS** A Flt by 20.8.18 until @ 22.8.18.

D9775 **149 Sqn** by 2.5.18. SW Area ex Ford Junction 8.6.18.

D9776 **148 Sqn** and crashed after hitting trees when overshot landing from engine test 4.7.18 (crew OK). Deleted 8.10.18 and reconstructed as H7180 wef 8.10.18.

D9777 **149 Sqn** by 30.4.18 and LIA night bombing Armentières 23.6.18 (Lt JW Thompson/2Lt IJW Ingram POW. Flying time 23hr 25min).

D9778 **149 Sqn** by 2.5.18 and damaged when stones hit propeller on take off for weather test 1.7.18. **1 ASD** wrecked ex 149 Sqn 1.7.18 and deleted 7.7.18 (NWR, flying time 34hr 50min).

D9779 **149 Sqn** by 30.4.18, to BEF and Alquines with unit and crashed in forced landing on bad ground after engine cut 17.9.18. Deleted on unit 19.9.18 (flying time 75hr 30min) but then to 1 ASD and deleted 22.9.18.

D9780 **1 SNBD** and wrecked in crash from stall after engine cut with fuel problem 30.6.18 (Lt JR Taylor OK/Sgt BJ Allen fatally IIFA).

D9781 **148 Sqn** dd ex 1 ASD 5.7.18. **102 Sqn** ex 148 Sqn 19.1.19.

D9782 **1 SNBD** E Flt by 8.18 until 9.18. **8 TDS** by 7.9.18 (dual control). **2 SNBD**.

D9783 **58 Sqn** dd ex 1 AIS 18.6.18. **2 ASD** ex 58 Sqn 3.10.18. 13.6.18. **102 Sqn** dd 1.19.

D9784 **3 AAP** tested 24-26.6.18. **38 Sqn**. **4 ASD** ex 38 Sqn 2.10.18. **191 NTS**.

D9785 **38 Sqn** by 25.6.18 and crashed in forced landing after losing water on night bombing sortie 2.10.18. **4 ASD** ex 38 Sqn 2.10.18 and still on unit charge 28.10.18.

D9786 **3 AAP** tested 14.6.18 (OK). **83 Sqn** dd ex 2 AIS 2.7.18 and crashed after engine failed on night recce 18.7.18. **2 ASD** ex 83 Sqn 24.7.18 and deleted 8.8.18 (NWR). BUT. **38 Sqn**. **4 ASD** ex 38 Sqn 10.18.

D9787 **3 AAP** tested 19.6.18 (OK). **1 SNBD** F Flt by 9.18. **8 TDS** by 9.9.18 (dual control).

D9788 **3 AAP** tested 24.6.18 (OK).

D9789 **3 AAP** tested 15.6.18 (pressure dud).

D9794: 1 RAF FE2b rebuilt by 3 (Western) ARD Yate under the Reserve Aeroplane Scheme.

D9794 **148 Sqn** dd ex 2 AIS 25.5.18 (2Lt J Helingoe) until 5.8.18.

D9900 – D9999: 100 RAF FE2b (160hp Beardmore) built by Ransomes, Sims & Jefferies Ltd, Ispwich under Contract A.S.2974.

D9900 **38 Sqn** by 5.18, retained for night testing 4.9.18. **102 Sqn** ex 38 Sqn 19.9.19.

D9901 **149 Sqn** dd ex 1 ASD 18.8.18 and retained for night testing 4.9.18.

D9902 **3 AAP** tested 2.7.18 (valve clatter) and 6.7.18 (float sticking). **58 Sqn** dd ex 1 AIS 22.7.18. **1 AD** ex 58 Sqn 30.8.18.

D9903 **3 AAP** tested 3.7.18 (OK). **149 Sqn** dd 8.7.18 until @ 11.18.

D9904 **3 AAP** tested 16.7.18 (overheating). **102 Sqn** dd ex 2 ASD 5.8.18 and damaged on aerodrome for night bombing sortie when hit by another machine which overshot on landing 4.9.18. **2 ASD** 4.9.18 and deleted 8.9.18 (NWR, flying time 59hr 55min).

D9905 **3 AAP** tested 6.7.18 (rough). **58 Sqn** dd ex 1 AIS 25.7.18 and damaged in forced landing crash following engine vibration on night bombing sortie 15.8.18 (Lt SGE Inman-Knox/2Lt HJ Tinker OK). **1 AD** ex 58 Sqn 17.8.18 (flying time 19hr). **1 ASD** deleted 21.8.18 (NWR, flying time 19hr 40min).

D9906 **3 AAP** tested 2.7.18 (OK).

D9907 **8 TDS** and wrecked in crash following stall on landing overshoot 21.7.18 (Lt EM Scovil/Flt Cdt GWA Beet KIFA).

D9908 **100 Sqn** by 29.7.18. **3 ASD** ex 100 Sqn 21.8.18 in exchange for HP 0/400. **100 Sqn** ex 3 ASD 24.8.18. **3 ASD** ex 100 Sqn 27.8.18. Sold to US government for USAS 9.18.

D9909 **149 Sqn** dd ex 1 ASD 21.8.18 and force landed with engine trouble on night bombing sortie 3.9.18. **1 ASD** wrecked ex 149 Sqn 4.9.18, to Repair Park 5.9.18 (flying time 8hr 50min).

D9910 **100 Sqn** by 29.7.18. **3 ASD** ex 100 Sqn 27.8.18. Sold to US government for USAS 9.18.

D9911 **100 Sqn** by 18.7.18. **3 ASD** ex 100 Sqn 29.7.18.

D9912 **100 Sqn** by 10.8.18. **3 ASD** ex 100 Sqn 2.9.18. Sold to US government for USAS 9.18.

D9913 **3 AAP** tested 13.7.18 (rudder sticking, valve clatter) and 15.7.18 (windscreen broken). **83 Sqn** dd ex 2 ASD 7.8.18 and wrecked in crash landing on aerodrome after night bombing sortie 6.9.18 (2Lt CF Kirby KIFA/2Lt JWR McPhail IIFA). Deleted on unit 7.9.18 (flying time 41hr 34min).

D9914 Allotted to Independent Force and wrecked at Le Bourget on delivery flight to 2 ASD 30.7.18 (Lt AB Taylor injured). **2 ASD** on BEF charge and deleted 16.8.18 (NWR, flying time 3hr 25min). Subject of query re its whereabouts 24.9.18 – still thought to be on Independent Force charge.

D9915 **38 Sqn** dd ex 4 ASD 31.7.18 until @ 30.8.18. Sold to US government for USAS. **1 Aviation Centre** USAS dd 18.10.18.

D9916 **3 AAP** tested 15.7.18 (magneto dud). **100 Sqn** by 10.8.18. **3 ASD** ex 100 Sqn 2.9.18. Sold to US government for USAS 9.18.

D9917 Presentation a/c *Montreal*. **83 Sqn** dd ex 2 ASD 11.8.18. **1 ASD** ex 83 Sqn 11.1.19 (2Lt J Helingoe). **102 Sqn** Serny dd 20.1.19.

D9918 Allotted for Independent Force and dispatched from England 29.7.18. Arrived in France 31.7.18. Replaced in/for Independent Force by D99xx 5.8.18. **101 Sqn** dd ex 2 ASD 8.8.18 and damaged in forced landing after engine boiled on night bombing sortie 4.10.18. **2 ASD** and deleted 26.10.18 (NWR).

D9919 **101 Sqn** dd ex 2 ASD 9.8.18 and wrecked

D9954, shown minus propeller and engine cowling, served with 191 NTS at Bury (Upwood). DH6 machines of that unit are visible in the background and the temporary Bessonneau hangars at that station were used until its permanent GS sheds were completed.

in forced landing near Aubercourt after hit by ground fire on night recce 13.8.18 (2Lt LH Phillips/2Lt RG Miller OK – a/c initially unsalvageable but being dismantled 15.8.18). **2 ASD** 17.8.18 and deleted 11.9.18, (NWR, flying time 7hr 5min).

D9920 **102 Sqn** dd ex 2 ASD 29.7.18 and wrecked crashing into houses on night bombing sortie 5.10.18 (Lt LJ Forrest/Lt EH Canning DFC KIFA). Deleted as unsalvable 5.10.18.

D9921 **2 AIS** dd ex 1 ASD 6.8.18. **101 Sqn** dd ex 2 ASD 7.8.18. **102 Sqn** dd ex 2 ASD 23.8.18. **101 Sqn** Lahoussoye and damaged in crash 19.9.18 (Lt FA Browning fatally IIFA/2Lt BML Bunting OK) then LIA night bombing 24.9.18 (Lt BH Kewley/2Lt JW Brown POW. Flying time 82hr 10min).

D9922 **102 Sqn** dd ex 2 ASD 23.8.18 and damaged in forced landing at Sailleaumont on night bombing sortie 25.9.18, after engine hit by ground fire (2Lt W Lloyd-Williams/Lt O Reilly-Patey DFC OK). **2 ASD** 26.9.18 and deleted 9.10.18 (NWR, flying time 54hr 55min).

D9923 **3 AAP** 8.8.18. **1 ASD** and damaged in forced landing after engine failed at 500ft on ferry flight 18.8.18.

D9924 **101 Sqn** dd ex 2 ASD 9.8.18 and damaged hitting corn on landing from night bombing sortie 19.8.18. **2 ASD** ex 101 Sqn 20.8.18 and deleted 10.9.18 (NWR, flying time 28hr).

D9925 **149 Sqn** dd ex 1 ASD 16.8.18 and damaged landing on bad ground after night bombing sortie 2.11.18.

D9926 **83 Sqn** dd ex 2 AIS 18.8.18 and wrecked in forced landing, due to weather, on travelling flight 27.9.18 (flying time 33hr 45min). **2 ASD** 29.9.18 and deleted 30.9.18.

D9927 **3 AAP** tested 7.8.18 (pressure dud). Arrived in France for Independent Force 9.8.18. 3 AD dd 16.8.18. **1 AIS** ex 3 AD 30.8.18 for transfer to USAS.

D9928 **3 AAP** tested 29.7.18 (aneroid dud, accumulator loose). **101 Sqn** dd ex 2 ASD 16.8.18 (Lt RA Grosvenor) and wrecked hitting tree in forced landing near No 22 lighthouse on night bombing sortie 16.8.18 (2Lt PT Somerville KIFA/2Lt F Hartford IIFA). **2 ASD** ex 101 Sqn 18.8.18 and deleted 20.8.18 (NWR, flying time 4hr 20min).

D9929 **2 AIS** dd ex 1 ASD 7.8.18. **101 Sqn** dd ex 2 ASD 14.8.18 and LIA night bombing 9.11.18 (2Lt HT Eyres KIA/2Lt GE Williams WIA).

D9930 **13 TDS** and wrecked in crash from stall on low turn 30.8.18 (2Lt HK Stevens KIFA).

D9931

D9932 13 TDS.

D9933

D9934

D9935

D9936 **148 Sqn** dd ex 1 ASD 3.9.18. **102 Sqn** dd 19.1.19.

D9937 **148 Sqn** dd ex 1 ASD 9.9.18. **102 Sqn** dd 19.1.19.

D9938 **83 Sqn** dd ex 1 AIS 5.10.18, used in camouflage trials (NIVO?) and crashed hitting gun pit on take off for night bombing sortie 29.10.18 (Lt G Carroll/2Lt E Hardwidge injured).

D9939 **3 AAP** tested 26.8.18 (OK). **149 Sqn** dd ex 1 AIS 4.9.18.

D9940 **3 AAP** tested 23.8.18 (OK). **148 Sqn** dd ex 1 ASD 4.9.18. **102 Sqn** dd 19.1.19.

D9941 **3 AAP** tested 9.11.18 (OK). **83 Sqn**.

D9942 **101 Sqn** by 8.18. Sold to US government for USAS and transferred 2.10.18.

D9943 **1 AIS** dd ex 1 ASD 1.9.18. **58 Sqn** dd ex 1 AIS 5.9.18. **2 ASD** ex 58 Sqn 27.9.18. **83 Sqn** dd ex 2 ASD 28.9.18. **102 Sqn** dd 20.1.19.

D9944 **4 ASD** and crashed on test flight 1.10.18 (pilot injured) and still on unit charge 25.10.18.

D9945 **102 Sqn** dd ex 1 ASD Repair Park 13.9.18 until @ 1.19.

D9946 **3 AAP** tested 6-11.9.18. **102 Sqn** by 1.19.

D9947 **102 Sqn** dd ex 1 ASD Repair Park 10.9.18 until @ 1.19.

D9948 **3 AAP** tested 13.9.18 (tail heavy, swings to right).

D9949 **3 AAP** tested 8.9.18 (OK). **102 Sqn** dd ex 2 ASD 17.9.18 until @ 1.19.

D9950 **101 Sqn** 'new' on 19.7.18 and destroyed by hangar fire 16.8.18. **2 ASD** deleted 29.8.18 with 30hr 8min flying time.

D9951

D9952 **102 Sqn** dd ex 2 ASD 29.9.18, used for night camouflage trials (NIVO?) and damaged in landing crash on aerodrome after engine failed on night bombing sortie 3.10.18 (Lt G Shepherd/2Lt A Bairstow IIFA). **2 ASD** and deleted 7.10.18 (NWR).

D9953 **1 SNBD** F Flt by 9.18. **8 TDS** by 2.10.18.

D9954 **191 NTS** by 10.18.

D9955 **102 Sqn** dd ex 1 ASD 18.9.18 and damaged in forced landing after engine failed on night bombing sortie 25.9.18. **2 ASD** 28.9.18 and deleted 1.10.18 (NWR, flying time 12hr 30min, also recorded as 16hr 25min).

D9956 **3 AAP** tested 6.10.18 (magneto dud) and 7.10.18 (vibrating, missing). **38 Sqn**. **102 Sqn** ex 38 Sqn 20.1.19.

D9957

D9958 **2 ASD** dd ex 1 ASD 8.5.18.

D9959 Sold to US government for USAS.

D9960 **101 Sqn** dd ex 2 ASD 17.9.18.

D9961

D9962 **101 Sqn** dd ex 1 ASD 7.8.18. **1 ASD** 26.9.18. **83 Sqn** by 9.18.

D9963 **148 Sqn** dd ex 1 ASD 8.10.18. **102 Sqn** dd 19.1.19.

D9964 Presentation a/c *Gold Coast Aborigines*. On RAF charge 1.19. **101 Sqn** and damaged in forced landing onto soft ground in fog 24.12.18.

D9965 **3 AAP** tested 17.9.18 (OK).

D9966

D9967 **3 AAP** tested 12.9.18 (magneto dud, small leak). **101 Sqn** dd ex 2 ASD 19.9.18 and wrecked when side-slipped into hangar 18.2.19 (2Lt KL Graham/2Lt JH Pringle injured).

D9968 **4 AAP**, in store and dismantled, allotted to BEF but allotment cancelled 9.12.1918 and to be deleted.

D9969 Sold to US government for USAS 10.9.18. **4 AAP** dismantled for USAS (160hp Beardmore), re-allotted to storage 9.12.18.

D9970 Sold to US government for USAS 10.9.18. **4 AAP** dismantled for USAS (160hp Beardmore), re-allotted to storage 9.12.18.

D9971 **4 AAP**, in store and dismantled, allotted to BEF but allotment cancelled 9.12.18 and to be deleted.

D9972 **4 AAP**, in store and dismantled, allotted to BEF but allotment cancelled 9.12.18 and to be deleted. BUT 9972 tested for 101 Sqn by 2Lt J Helingoe (83 Sqn) 30.11.18.

D9973 **4 AAP**, in store and dismantled, allotted to BEF but allotment cancelled 9.12.18 and to be deleted.

D9974 **4 AAP**, in store and dismantled, allotted to BEF but allotment cancelled 9.12.18 and to be deleted.

D9975 **4 AAP**, in store and dismantled, allotted to BEF but allotment cancelled 9.12.18 and to be deleted.

D9976 **4 AAP**, in store and dismantled, allotted to BEF but allotment cancelled 9.12.18 and to be deleted.

D9977 **4 AAP**, in store and dismantled, allotted to BEF but allotment cancelled 9.12.18 and to be deleted.

D9778 **4 AAP**, in store and dismantled, allotted to BEF but allotment cancelled 9.12.18 and to be deleted.

D9979 **4 AAP**, in store and dismantled, allotted to BEF but allotment cancelled 9.12.18 and to be deleted.

D9980

D9881

D9982

D9983

D9984

D9985

D9986

D9987

D9988

D9989

D9990

D9991 Presentation a/c *API* wef 10.18. **I Flt** dd 4.10.18 and damaged when overturned in forced landing after engine failure 11.12.18 (Lt J Wingate OK). **1 ASD** ex I Flt 12.18.

D9992 **3 AAP** tested 23.9.18. **102 Sqn** dd ex 1 ASD 29.9.18 and damaged in forced landing after engine failed on test flight 22.10.18 (Lt FR Witham/Cpl Scanlon OK).

D9993 Presentation a/c *Australia No 6* wef 5.10.18. **148 Sqn** dd ex 1 ASD 27.8.18. **102 Sqn** ex 148 Sqn 19.1.19.

D9994 **102 Sqn** by 1.19.

D9995 **38 Sqn** dd ex 1 ASD 4.11.18. **102 Sqn** ex 38 Sqn 20.1.19.

D9996 **3 AAP** tested 3-5.10.18.

D9997

E5151, one of three FE2ds converted to FE2h configuration by Ransomes, Sims and Jefferies. Shown fitted with its 6lb Davis gun, the extra bay added to the nacelle (probably to counter the weight of the weapon) is apparent.

FE2b E7067 at an unknown location.

D9998 Presentation a/c *Australia No 1, South Australia No 1*. **102 Sqn** dd ex 2 ASD 28.9.18 and damaged when hit road on landing on aerodrome after night bombing sortie 9.11.18.

D9999 Presentation a/c *Australia No 16*. **102 Sqn** and crashed taking off from forced landing after engine failure on night bombing sortie 8.10.18. **2 ASD** and deleted 13.10.18 (NWR).

E3151 – E3153: 3 RAF FE2h (230hp Siddeley Puma) converted from existing airframes by Ransomes, Sims & Jefferies Ltd, Ipswich to Contract AS3981/18A dated 13.3.18.

E3151 Ex A6501. Fitted with 6lb Davis gun in modified nacelle. **EAD Grain** by 25.5.18, awaiting wings and tail.

E3152 Ex A6502. Fitted with 6-lb Davis gun in modified nacelle. **EAD Grain.**

E3153 Ex A6503. Fitted with 6lb Davis gun in modified nacelle. **EAD Grain.**

E6687 – E6736: 50 RAF FE2b (160hp Beardmore) ordered from Richard Garrett & Sons, Leiston under Contract 35a/285/C255 dated 3.4.18. Order apparently cancelled.

E6687

E6688

E6689 **3 AAP** Norwich allotted to BEF but allocation cancelled and to be deleted 23.1.19.

E7037 – E7136: 100 RAF FE2b (160hp Beardmore) built by Ransomes, Sims & Jefferies, Ipswich under Contract 35a/348/C225 dated 3.4.18.

E7037 Presentation a/c *Hawkes Bay, New Zealand.*

On RAF charge 18.1.19.

E7038 **3 AAP** tested 11.10.18. **38 Sqn** by 11.18.

E7039 **3 AAP** tested 23.9.18. **38 Sqn**. **102 Sqn** ex 38 Sqn 19.1.19.

E7040 **3 AAP** tested 12.10.18.

E7041 **38 Sqn**. **102 Sqn** ex 38 Sqn 19.1.19.

E7042 Presentation a/c *Baroda No 6* wef 5.10.18. **3 AAP** tested 26-27.9.18. On RAF charge 18.1.19.

E7043 Presentation a/c *Johannesburg No 2* wef 10.18. **83 Sqn** dd ex 1 AIS 9.10.18 and crashed after engine failure 13.12.18. **1 ASD** Salvage Section ex 83 Sqn 27.12.18. On RAF charge 1.19.

E7044 Presentation a/c *British Residents in Netherlands East Indies*. **1 ASD** Repair Park ex Tourignies 22.1.19.

E7045

E7046 Presentation a/c *Malaya No 4* wef 10.18. On RAF charge 1.19.

E7047 **3 AAP** tested 10.10.18.

E7048 **102 Sqn** by 14.10.18 and destroyed by fire after hit by A5596 prior to take-off for night bombing sortie 9.11.18.

E7049 **83 Sqn** by 27.11.18. **102 Sqn** ex 83 Sqn 20.1.19.

E7050 **2 ASD** dd ex 1 ASD 17.10.18. **101 Sqn** overturned and wrecked in landing crash when wheel broke on practice flight 10.11.18 (2Lt FE Dafoe OK).

E7051 **3 AAP** Norwich tested 18.10.18.

E7052 Presentation a/c *Argentine Central Railway* wef 10.18. **8 AAP** allotted to BEF but allocation cancelled and to be deleted 23.1.19.

E7053 **102 Sqn** and damaged after landing on sloping ground and running onto road on test flight 11.10.18. **2 ASD** and deleted 16.10.18 (NWR).

E7054 **38 Sqn** wrecked when hit breakwater landing in mist after night bombing sortie 30.10.18 (2Lt AC Scott/2Lt ER Bull OK). Deleted in the field 6.11.18.

E7055 **3 AAP** tested 13.10.18.

E7056 Presentation a/c *Malaya No 16 'The Menang'*. **101 Sqn** Hancourt and LIA night bombing 29.10.18 (Lt J Malley-Martin/2Lt TLW Leonard KIA).

E7057 **3 AAP** tested 7.10.18. **148 Sqn** dd ex 1 ASD Marquise 8.11.18. **102 Sqn** ex 148 Sqn 19.1.19.

E7058

E7059 **38 Sqn** by 26.10.18. **102 Sqn** dd ex 38 Sqn 19.1.19.

E7060 **38 Sqn** wrecked when hit tree and crashed on night bombing sortie 5.11.18.

E7061 **3 AAP** tested 14.10.18.

E7062

E7063 **3 AAP** tested 1.10.18. **102 Sqn** Serny by 1.19.

E7064 Presentation a/c *South Africa* wef 26.10.18. **3 AAP** tested 22.10.18. On RAF charge 1.19.

E7065 **3 AAP** tested 10.10.18.

E7066

E7067

E7068 Presentation a/c *Baroda No 13* wef 26.10.18. Transferred to USAS.

E7069 **3 AAP** tested 14.10.18. **38 Sqn** dd ex 1 ASD Marquise 4.11.18. **102 Sqn** ex 38 Sqn 19.1.19.

E7070 **3 AAP** tested 20.10.18. **83 Sqn**. **102 Sqn** dd ex 83 Sqn 20.1.19.

E7071 **3 AAP** tested 17.10.18. At Rochford allotted to BEF, allotment cancelled 23.1.19 and to be deleted.

E7072 **3 AAP** tested 20.10.18. Sold to US government for USAS.

E7073 **83 Sqn** by 11.18. **102 Sqn** dd ex 83 Sqn 20.1.19.

E7074 Presentation a/c *Madras No 1* wef 26.10.18. On RAF charge 18.1.19.

E7075 Sold to US government for USAS.

E7076 Sold to US government for USAS.

E7077 **38 Sqn** by 12.11.18. **102 Sqn** dd ex 38 Sqn 19.1.19.

E7078 Presentation a/c *Mauritius No 1*. **101 Sqn** and wrecked in forced landing on night bombing sortie 9.11.18 (2Lt J Cave/2Lt BML Bunting thought MIA but OK).

E7079

E7080 Presentation a/c *Punjab No 6, Nabha* wef 26.10.18. On RAF charge 1.19.

E7081 Presentation a/c *Faridhot No 3* wef 26.10.18. **83 Sqn** Serny by 1.19. **102 Sqn** dd ex 83 Sqn 20.1.19.

E7082 Presentation a/c *Leeds* wef 26.10.18. **83 Sqn** by 26.10.18 until @ 27.11.18. On RAF charge 1.19.

E7083 **3 AAP** allotted to BEF but allocation cancelled and to be deleted 23.1.19.

E7084 **I Flt** dd ex 1 AI 18.12.18. **2 ASD** ex I Flt 7.1.19.

E7085 **3 AAP** tested 23.10.18. Presentation a/c *Toongoo District of Burma* wef 26.10.18. On RAF charge 18.1.19.

E7086 Presentation a/c *Punjab No 5, Nabha* wef 26.10.18. **101 Sqn** recorded as exposed (to weather) 30.1.19.

E7087 Presentation a/c *Malaya No 24* wef 26.10.18. **3 AAP** tested 6.10.18 and still there (in store) allotted to BEF but allocation cancelled and to be deleted 23.1.19.

E7088 Presentation a/c *Malaya No 17* wef 26.10.18. **3 AAP** tested 26-28.10.18. **102 Sqn** and wrecked hitting bank during forced landing in mist when lost 14.11.18.

FE2b E7075, one of a number which were transferred for service with the USAS in France.

FE2b E7090, also transferred to the USAS, exhibits an unusual jet-shaped hinged fitment beneath its nacelle, which is perhaps a signal light.

E7089 Presentation a/c *Zanzibar No 10* wef 12.10.18. **38 Sqn** dd ex 1 ASD 12.11.18. **102 Sqn** ex 38 Sqn 20.1.19.

E7090 Presentation a/c *Punjab No 11* wef 26.10.18. Sold to US government for USAS. **48th Aero Sqn** USAS.

E7091 **8 AAP** allotted to BEF but allocation cancelled and to be deleted 23.1.19.

E7092 Presentation a/c *Britons Overseas No 11*. **83 Sqn**. **102 Sqn** dd ex 83 Sqn 20.1.19.

E7093 Presentation a/c Presentation a/c *Musapha No 1* wef 26.10.18. **148 Sqn** dd ex 1 ASD 1.12.18. **102 Sqn** ex 148 Sqn 19.1.19.

E7094 Presentation a/c *Makhabane* wef 26.10.18. **3 AAP** tested 10.11.18. On RAF charge 1.19.

E7095 Presentation a/c *Non Mihi Sed Patriae* wef 26.10.18. Sold to US government for USAS. **48th Aero Sqn**.

E7096 Presentation a/c *Junagadh No 3* wef 26.10.18. On RAF charge 1.19.

E7097 Presentation a/c *Britons Overseas No 10* wef 26.10.18. **83 Sqn**. **102 Sqn** by 1.19.

E7098 **3 AAP** allotted to BEF but allocation cancelled and to be deleted 23.1.19.

E7099 **NARD** allotted to USAS but cancelled 11.12.18 (crashed).

E7100 Presentation a/c *Huddersfield* wef 26.10.18. Sold to US government for USAS. **48th Aero Sqn**.

E7101 Presentation a/c *North China Aeroplane*. **101 Sqn** Morville recorded as exposed (to weather) 28.1.19.

E7102 Presentation a/c *Rio de Janiero Britons No 3* wef 26.10.18. Sold to US government for USAS. **48th Aero Sqn**.

E7103 Presentation a/c *Britons in Nicaragua*. **3 AAP** Norwich tested 29.10.18. **8 AAP** Lympne allotted to BEF but allocation cancelled and to be deleted 23.1.19.

E7104 Presentation a/c *Presented By The Citizens Town & District of Thana*. **3 AAP** allotted to BEF but allocation cancelled and to be deleted 23.1.19.

E7105 Presentation a/c *Lepoqo*. **192 NTS** by 1.19. **8 AAP** Lympne allotted to BEF but allocation cancelled and to be deleted 23.1.19.

E7106 Presentation a/c *Australia No 21, New South Wales No 19*. Sold to US government for USAS. **48th Aero Sqn**.

E7107 Presentation a/c *Imperial Order of Daughters of the British Empire (USA)* wef 26.10.18. On RAF charge 1.19.

E7108 Sold to US government for USAS.

E7109 Allotted to BEF, re-allotted to SW Area for Controller of Technical Department, 4.1.19.

E7110 **3 AAP** tested 2.11.18. Sold to US government for USAS.

E7111 **3 AAP** allotted to BEF but allocation cancelled and to be deleted 23.1.19.

E7112 Completed as FE2c 13.7.18. Allocated to BEF but crashed on arrival 20.7.18. **1 ASD**, deleted 25.7.18 (NWR, flying time 5hr 45min).

E7113 Completed as FE2c 25.8.18.

E7114

E7115 Delivered to storage by 11.1.19.

E7116 Delivered to storage by 11.1.19

E7117 Delivered to storage by 11.1.19

E7118 Delivered to storage by 11.1.19

E7119 Delivered to storage by 11.1.19

E7120 Delivered to storage by 11.1.19

E7121 Delivered to storage by 11.1.19

E7122 Delivered to storage by 11.1.19

E7123 Delivered to storage by 11.1.19

E7124 Delivered to storage by 11.1.19

E7125 Delivered to storage by 11.1.19

E7126 Delivered to storage by 11.1.19

E7127 Delivered to storage by 11.1.19

E7128 Delivered to storage by 11.1.19

E7129 Delivered to storage by 11.1.19

E7130 Delivered to storage by 11.1.19

E7131 Delivered to storage by 11.1.19

E7132 Delivered to storage by 11.1.19

E7133 Delivered to storage by 11.1.19

E7134 Delivered to storage by 11.1.19

E7135 Delivered to storage by 11.1.19

E7136 Delivered to storage by 11.1.19

F2945 – F2994: 50 RAF FE2b (160hp Beardmore) ordered from Barclay, Curle & Co Ltd, Whiteinch, Glasgow under Contract 35a/1076/C908 dated 22.5.18. Contract for 100 erected machines and material for the remainder transferred from A. Stephens & Son ex Contract AS40817. No evidence of delivery.

F3498 – F3547: 50 RAF FE2b (160hp Beardmore) built by Barclay, Curle & Co Ltd, Whiteinch, Glasgow.

F3498

F3499 **8 TDS** by summer 18.

F3500 **8 TDS** by 12.8.18.

F3501 **8 TDS** by summer 18.

F3502

F3503
F3504
F3505
F3506
F3507
F3508
F3509
F3510
F3511
F3512
F3513
F3514
F3515
F3516
F3517
F3518
F3519
F3520
F3521
F3522
F3523
F3524
F3525
F3526
F3527
F3528
F3529
F3530
F3531
F3532
F3533
F3534
F3535
F3536
F3537
F3538
F3539
F3540
F3541
F3542
F3543
F3544
F3545
F3546
F3547

F3768 – F3917: 150 RAF FE2b (160hp Beardmore) ordered from Ransomes, Sims & Jefferies Ltd, Ipswich. Order cancelled.

F4071 – F4170: 100 RAF FE2b (160hp Beardmore) ordered from Alexander Stephen

One of the last FE2bs to be built: H9939 constructed in Ipswich.

& Sons Ltd, Linthouse, Glasgow under Contract 35a/1126/C977 dated 27.5.18 (against Weir's material contract 35a/1125/C976). Serial numbers allocated 27.8.18. Order cancelled.

17 RAF FE2b airframes reconstructed at Aircraft Depots in France.

F5851 **148 Sqn** dd ex 1 ASD 20.9.18 and damaged in force landing crash after engine failed on night bombing sortie 26.9.18 (crew OK, flying time 3hr 55min).

F5852 Reconstructed from A5658 25.6.18. **102 Sqn** dd ex 2 ASD 17.8.18 and wrecked in forced landing crash after engine failed on night bombing sortie 7.9.18 (crew OK). **2 ASD** 7.9.18 and deleted 10.9.18 (NWR, flying time 33hr 5min).

F5853 **58 Sqn** dd ex 1 AIS 16.8.18. **1 AD** ex 58 Sqn 30.8.18. **83 Sqn** dd ex 1 AIS 10.9.18 and wrecked in landing after hit by AA near Cambrai on night bombing raid 20.9.18 (Lt DDA Greig/2Lt WA Armstrong shaken, flying time 18hr 20min).

F5854 **101 Sqn** dd ex 2 ASD 17.8.18 and shelled after forced landing crash following engine failure on night bombing sortie 8.10.18 (Lt J Malley-Martin/2Lt G Williams OK).

F5856 **38 Sqn** dd ex 1 AI 13.11.18. **102 Sqn** ex 38 Sqn 19.1.19.

F5857 Photographed equipped for night flying, probably winter 1918-19.

F5858 **1 AIS** and wrecked on delivery flight 7.11.18.

F5859 **101 Sqn** and damaged in forced landing after throttle broke 30.1.19.

F5861 **102 Sqn** by 1.19.

F5862 **149 Sqn** burnt out in forced landing on delivery flight from 1 ASD 16.1.19 (crew OK)

F5863 **101 Sqn** dd ex 2 ASD 5.9.18 and damaged night bombing 17.9.18 (Lt AW Allen/Lt EH Clarke OK after hit by AA and force-landing in trench lines – a/c salvaged but deleted, flying time 100hr 50min).

F6071 **2 ASD** Reception Park dd 4.7.18. **83 Sqn** dd ex 2 AIS 26.7.18 and crashed taking off on bad ground for night bombing sortie 7.8.18 (crew injured). 2 ASD deleted 9.8.18, (flying time 10hr 50min).

F6079 **2 ASD** tested 21.10.18 (Lt RA Grosvenor, cut out on main tank/pressure dud).

F6080 **102 Sqn** by 1.19.

F6081 **2 ASD** by 9.18. **83 Sqn** dd ex 1 AIS 15.9.18 and crashed in forced landing after fuel failed on recce 31.10.18 (Capt G Allen/2Lt W Armstrong IIFA).

F6109 **101 Sqn** and wrecked in forced landing crash in trenches after engine failed on night bombing sortie 4.10.18 (2Lt RT Watkins/Lt S Thomas OK).

F6128 **102 Sqn** by 1.19.

F6173 **102 Sqn** dd ex 2 ASD 7.9.18 (Lt RA Grosvenor) and damaged in forced landing after engine failed on night bombing sortie 8.9.18. **2 ASD** 8.9.18 (flying time 3hr 45min) and deleted 11.9.18.

F6174 **2 ASD** by 9.18.

F9296 – F9395: 100 RAF FE2h (230hp Puma) ordered from Richard Garrett & Sons Ltd, Leiston. Order cancelled.

F9550: 1 RAF FE2b (160hp Beardmore) reconstructed from spares/salvage by 4 Wing ARS Netheravon under the Reserve Aeroplane Scheme.

F9550

F9566: 1 RAF FE2b (160hp Beardmore) reconstructed from spares/salvage by 4 Wing ARS Netheravon under the Reserve Aeroplane Scheme.

F9566

F9585: 1 RAF FE2b reconstructed from spares/salvage under the Reserve Aeroplane Scheme.

F9585 **1 SNBD** by 9.18.

12 RAF FE2b airframes reconstructed at Aircraft Depots in France.

H6888 Reconstructed from C9829 1.10.18.
H7145 Reconstructed from A5783 17.9.18.
H7176 Reconstructed from A6565 5.11.18.
H7177 Reconstructed from A6452 8.10.18.
H7178 Reconstructed from A6600 8.10.18.
H7179 Reconstructed from D9759 8.10.18.
H7180 Reconstructed from D9776 8.10.18.
H7228 Reconstructed from A6504 5.11.18.
H7229 Reconstructed from D9757 5.11.18.
H7230 Reconstructed from A5607 5.11.18. 83 Sqn.
H7231 Reconstructed from B460 5.11.18.
H7232 Reconstructed ex B7817 20.10.18.
H7233 Reconstructed from A5789 5.11.18.

H9913 – H9962: 50 RAF FE2b/c (160hp Beardmore or 230hp Siddeley Puma) ordered from Ransomes, Sims & Jefferies Ltd, Ipswich under Contract 35A/2958/C3391 dated 26.9.18. First 20 ordered as FE2c.

H9913 FE2c.
H9914 FE2c.
H9915 FE2c.
H9916 FE2c.
H9917 FE2c.
H9918 FE2c.
H9919 FE2c.
H9920 FE2c.
H9921 FE2c.
H9922 FE2c.
H9923 FE2c.
H9924 FE2c.
H9925 FE2c.
H9926 FE2c.
H9927 FE2c.
H9928 FE2c.
H9929 FE2c.
H9930 FE2c.
H9931 FE2c.
H9932 FE2c.
H9933 FE2c.
H9934 FE2c.
H9935 FE2c.
H9936 FE2c.
H9937 FE2b. **3 AAP** allotted to the BEF 12.18, but cancelled 23.1.19 and to be deleted.
H9938 FE2b. Visited Harling Road 6.11.18. **3 AAP** allotted to the BEF 12.18, but cancelled 23.1.19 and to be deleted.
H9939 FE2b. **3 AAP** allotted to the BEF 12.18, **8 AAP** with BEF allotment cancelled 23.1.19 and to be deleted.
H9940 FE2b. **3 AAP** allotted to the BEF 12.18, but cancelled 23.1.19 and to be deleted.
H9941 FE2b. **3 AAP** allotted to the BEF 12.18, re-allotted to SE Area 18.12.18 and to be delivered to Brooklands for erection.
H9942 FE2b. **3 AAP** allotted to the BEF 12.18, but cancelled 23.1.19 and to be deleted.
H9943 FE2b. **3 AAP** allotted to the BEF 12.18, re-allotted to Experiment & Design (Photography), Kenley Common 19.12.18.
H9944 FE2b. **3 AAP** allotted to the BEF 12.18, but cancelled 23.1.19 and to be deleted.
H9945 FE2b. **3 AAP** allotted to the BEF 12.18, but cancelled 23.1.19 and to be deleted.
H9946 FE2b. **3 AAP** allotted to the BEF 12.18, but cancelled 23.1.19 and to be deleted.
H9947 FE2b. **3 AAP** allotted to the BEF 12.18, but cancelled 23.1.19 and to be deleted.
H9948 FE2b. **3 AAP** allotted to the BEF 12.18, but cancelled 23.1.19 and to be deleted.
H9949 FE2b. **3 AAP** allotted to the BEF 12.18, but cancelled 23.1.19 and to be deleted.
H9950 FE2b. **3 AAP** allotted to the BEF 12.18, but cancelled 23.1.19 and to be deleted.
H9951 FE2b. **3 AAP** allotted to the BEF 12.18, but cancelled 23.1.19 and to be deleted.
H9952 FE2b. **3 AAP** allotted to the BEF 12.18, but cancelled 23.1.19 and to be deleted.
H9953 FE2b. **3 AAP** allotted to the BEF 12.18, but cancelled 23.1.19 and to be deleted.
H9954 FE2b. **3 AAP** allotted to the BEF 12.18, but cancelled 23.1.19 and to be deleted.
H9955 FE2b.
H9956 FE2b.
H9957 FE2b.
H9958 FE2b.
H9959 FE2b.
H9960 FE2b.
H9961 FE2b.
H9962 FE2b.

J601 – J650: 50 RAF FE2b (160hp Beardmore) ordered from Barclay, Curle & Co Ltd, Whiteinch, Glasgow under Contract 35a/3047/C3518 dated 21.9.18. Order cancelled.

F13 & F17: 1 FE2b and 1 FE2d in the special series for ground instructional airframes (preceding the M-series)

F13 FE2d. Issued to **SMA** Watford w/e 4.2.18.
F17 FE2b. Intended for issue w/e 4.2.18 but cancelled.

Unidentified Incidents

'6925' FE2b. **46 TS** crashed from low stall 12.6.17 (Lt L Stephens KIFA).

'7212' FE2b. **35 TS** crashed 26.11.17 (crew injured). Mistaken entry for Bristol F2B A7212?

'4128' FE2b. 2 (Aux) SAG recorded 20.4.17 (2Lt RS Davies).

'707' FE2b recorded on 33 HDS C Flt 24.2.17 by 2Lt CW Wridgway. Very early date for a FE2b on 33 HDS and BE2c B707 wasn't reconstructed until April/May.

'600' '2D' recorded as dd 148 Sqn ex Dover 16.1.19 (2Lt J Helingoe/Lt Marshall).

'576' recorded as dd Dover ex Izel 15.1.19 (2Lt J Helingoe/Lt Marshall)

Name Index

Airmen mentioned in the FE2a/b/c/d Serials Database

A
Abraham, 2Lt, Lt CC **B472, A5566**
Achurch, 2Lt HG **A5616**
Adams, FltSgt (23 Sqn) **6369**
Adams, 2Lt JP **A6359**
Adams, 2Lt R **D3816**
Adams, Capt RN **4918, 6354**
Adamson, Capt WC **4227**
Adcock, AM2 LB **A779**
Affleck, Capt R **A5745**
Affleck, Lt R **A5447, A5658, B1896**
Ainscon, Lt (36 Sqn) **A5542**
Aitken, 2Lt AR **A5544**
Aked, Lt HLC **5202, 5206**
Albu, Capt WG **A865, A867**
Alcock, Lt (101 Sqn) **A6459**
Alcock, Cpl L **A5458**
Alder, Lt E **B1879**
Alder, 2Lt S **A24, A34**
Aldred, AM2, Sgt B **A1935, A6468**
Alexander, AM1 H **A24**
Allen, 2Lt A **D3830**
Allen, Lt AW **F5863**
Allen, Sgt BJ **D9780**
Allen, 2Lt EF **5235**
Allen, Capt G **F6081**
Allen, 2Lt GM **7008**
Allen, Lt J **7700**
Allen, Sgt J **6947**
Allum, AM2, Pte TE **A29, A5143, A6370, A6385**
Alston, Lt CR **A6499**
Ambler, Lt E **4267**
Anderson, Lt A **7026**
Anderson, 2Lt DS **B498**
Anderson, 2Lt GN **7008**
Anderson, 2Lt JB **6944**
Anderson, 2Lt JD **B7813**
Anderson, Lt KR **B496**
Anderson, Lt RH **6328**
Anderson, Lt W **A27**
Anglin, Lt JV **A801**
Angstrom, 2Lt, Lt, Capt LC **6334, 7679, 7682, A5543**
Angus, Lt RWF **B7843**
Annersley, Capt JFStJ **7668**
Appleton, Sgt SC **4930, A817**
Archer, Lt RR **A1**
Archibald, 2Lt LM **A5702**
Arkle, 2Lt GW **5240, 5243**
Arkley, Pte (20 Sqn) **A6528**
Armstrong, 2Lt JLP **5209, 6938**
Armstrong, 2Lt W **F6081**
Armstrong, 2Lt WA **F5853**

Sgt SC Appleton

B
Ashby, Sgt S **B401**
Aspinall, 2Lt JV **4983, 7012, 7681, 7711, A796**
Attwater, Sgt S **A19**
Atwell, AM2 GF **5210**
Aulton, Lt WS **A5559, A5600**

Babbage, 2Lt FF **A1935**
Backhouse, Sgt WDA **A6498**
Bacon, 2Lt RG **A1942**
Bailey, Lt AEG **A5611**
Baillie, Lt W **7023**
Baines, Lt MT **7002**
Bairstow, 2Lt A **D9952**
Baker, Capt FC **4842, 4917**
Balance, 2Lt G **B425**
Baldwin, Sgt CG **7010**
Bankes, 2Lt PA **A5605**
Barber, Capt MD **A5584**
Barbour, 2Lt HD **A5678**
Barclay, 2Lt IC **A779**
Baring-Gould, 2Lt JH **A6366**
Barlow, Lt SG **A5454, A5461**
Barltrop, Lt EA **6929**
Barnard, 2Lt FL **4929**
Barnes, Capt (51 Sqn) **7676**
Barnes, Capt EE **A5577**
Barnes, AM2 EW **7714**
Barnes, Lt WA **B481**
Barnes, Sgt WA **4997, A780**
Barraclough, 2Lt JC **4909, 6343, 6366**
Barton, 2Lt FH **A6434, B1882**
Bastable, Sgt (51 Sqn) **4890**
Bate, 2Lt GB **A823, A5483**
Bates, 2Lt AH **4997**
Batten, AM2 WJ **A831**
Batty, 2Lt C **B455**
Bayes, AM1 (23 Sqn) **6976**
Bayley, AM1 (33 Sqn) **B409**
Beal, Lt (36 Sqn) **A6535**
Beal, 2Lt Lt LW **7685, A5441, A5454**
Bean, 2Lt CO **4890**
Beauchamp, Cpl C **7672, 7686, 7687**
Beaumont, 2Lt CL **7668**
Beebee, Cpl A **4898, 6987**
Beet,FltCdt.GWA **D9907**
Behm, 2Lt, (102 Sqn) **A5688**
Beldam, Lt CH **A1956, A6353, B1865**
Belford, 2Lt JC **B7814**
Bell, Lt (36 Sqn) **A6586**
Bell, 2Lt EVA **7686, A813**
Bell, 2Lt GG **A855, A5454**
Bell, 2Lt LH **A5603, A5647**
Bell, 2Lt SH **A5481**
Bell-Irving, 2Lt M **5221, 5222, 5228**
Belton, AM2 CS **A5459**
Beminster, AM2 C **A6354, A6444, A6457**
Benitz, 2Lt FA **A5659**
Bennett-Boggs, 2Lt JLN **4847**
Bentham, 2Lt GA **7010**
Benton, 2Lt WC **A6581**
Bidie, Lt GMV **A5793**
Biette, 2Lt FC **4863, 5220**
Bill, Lt AG **A6512, B1863**
Billinge, 2Lt, Lt F **6336, 6339, 6366**
Billon, Pte J **A4**
Bilson, 2Lt WR **B407**
Birch, 2Lt DC **A21**
Birch, 2Lt E, **A10**
Birch, Cpl, Sgt S **A4, A6, A8, A33**

Birch, 2Lt W **A863**
Bird, 2Lt CO **A5733**
Bird, Lt EH **5212**
Bird, Sgt F **A6466**
Birdmead, Lt CH **4841**
Birkett, Lt W **A6377, A6415, A6469**
Birkhead, 2Lt JB **B497**
Bishop, AM (51 Sqn) **A5520**
Black, Lt CE **A5793**
Black, 2Lt JM **A5534**
Black, 2Lt W **4867, 7678**
Blackall, 2Lt JH **A6447**
Blackwood, 2Lt, Capt J **A32, A1935**
Blake, 2Lt CL **5249, 6969, 6970**
Blake, Pte WC **A5149**
Blatherwick, Capt R **A16**
Blenkiron, 2Lt, Lt AV **4925, A782, A784**
Blennerhasset, 2Lt GN **4969, 7003, A5460, A5468**
Bloomfield, Capt WSR **A1953**
Blucke, Lt WAS **A6563**
Blyth, Lt (38 Sqn) **A5566**
Blythe, 2Lt JA **A5750**
Boddy, 2Lt JAV **7677, 7694, 7708**
Boles, 2Lt JL **A6359**
Booth, AM1 (33 Sqn) **A6375**
Booth, 2Lt H **A5636, A5783**
Booth, AM2 JH **6997**
Booth, Sgt JH **7024, A5484**
Booth,, AM1 JM **4272**
Booth, Sgt L **4970**
Boret, Capt JA **B1883**
Borton, 2Lt CVJ **5235**
Bosher, 2Lt H **B431**
Boucher, Lt N **A6377, A6415, A6469**
Boultbee, Lt AE **A5439**
Bousfield, Lt JK **A21**
Boustead, Lt HAR **4967, 4984**
Bowen, 2Lt, Lt EGA **4267, 4921**
Bower, Cpl AG **4877, 6990, 7672**
Bowerman, Lt AJ **6366, 6368**
Bowers, Sgt CWH **6975**
Bowers, Lt PT **A6402**
Bowler, Lt HC **D3811**
Bowman, Lt WP **6985, 7670**
Box, 2Lt GH **A5542**
Bracey, Sgt SC **A5780**
Bradley, LCpl R **A6392, A6444**
Bradshaw, AM2 (33 Sqn) **A5639**
Bradyll, Lt ECRG **2864, 4227, 4253**
Brain, AM1 NL **7684**
Brandon, Lt ETC **A808**
Brewer, Capt CH **B484**
Brock, 2Lt A **A5610**
Bronskill, 2Lt FH **A32, A1951**
Brook, 2Lt DR **A5536, A5659, A5660**
Brooke, Lt GA **A6458**
Brooker, AM (51 Sqn) **4876**
Brothers, AM2 H **4918**
Brotherton, AM1 ER **4840**
Brown, 2Lt C **7025**
Brown, AM2 G **4957**
Brown, 2Lt, Lt GA **A6522, A6562**
Brown, Cpl H **7003**
Brown, Sgt JH **7003, 7024, A5439**
Brown, 2Lt JL **D9762**
Brown, 2Lt JM **B460, C9796**
Brown, 2Lt JW **D9921**
Brown, 2Lt, Lt ME **A6522, A6562**
Brown, 2Lt VR **B448**

Brown, Lt WA **A5578**
Browne, 2Lt JL **B1900**
Browning, Lt FA **D9921**
Bruce, 2Lt R **A5583**
Bryant, Capt CE **7699, A5443**
Bryom, Lt JF **A779**
Buchanan, Sgt CWB **4847**
Buckenridge, Lt GD **7676**
Bull, 2Lt ER **A5743, E7054**
Bullock, Lt GEN **A6569, B455**
Buntine, 2Lt WHC **6988, A817**
Bunting, 2Lt BML **D9921, E7078**
Burdett, Lt HC **B417**
Burdon, Capt R **A1937**
Burgess, Sgt HP **A5475**
Burgess, Lt R **6365**
Burkenshaw, Sgt WJ **7003**
Burkett, 2Lt GTW **A6437, A6512**
Burns, 2Lt VLA **A6391**
Burrill, Lt TF **A1959**
Burtenshaw, Sgt J **7007**
Burton, 2Lt E **4290**
Bushe, 2Lt JF **A822, B411**
Bushe, 2Lt Lt LA **A802, A5549, A6453**
Butler, 2Lt AS **4840**
Butler, Sgt C **7683**
Butler, 2Lt CJ **7025**
Butler, Lt L **7669**
Butler, Lt RE **A6375**
Butt, Lt FW **B458**
Butt, 2Lt LAK **5202**
Butterworth, 2Lt HW **5233**

C
Cairne-Duff, 2Lt A **6345**
Cairns, 2Lt JA **4850**
Callaghan, 2Lt JC **5232**
Callender, 2Lt GG **A6**
Calvey, 2Lt HC **4954, A5469, B419**
Cambray, 2Lt, Lt WC **A6430, A6516, A6516**
Cameron, 2Lt CH **A5152, A6528**
Campbell, Capt (192 NTS) **A5544**
Campbell, Lt (199 DS) **4892**
Campbell, Lt C **4963**
Campbell, 2Lt, Lt JK (22Sqn) **4891, 7703**
Campbell, Cpl JK (22Sqn) **4288**
Campbell, Lt M **B1894**
Canning, 2Lt, Lt EH **A6587, D9920**
Canning, Lt ER **A6521**
Capper, Cpl (22 Sqn) **6966**
Carbert, Capt CM **A28, A36**
Carles, Lt RE **B1870**
Carley, 2Lt TE **A6353, B465**

Capt WSR Bloomfield, New Zealand

2Lt JW Brown

Carpenter, Lt ET **A6474**
Carr, AM2 JF **5000, A5500**
Carroll, 2Lt CE **A5680**
Carroll, Lt G **D9938**
Carruthers, Lt (33 Sqn) **A6356**
Carter, 2Lt RN **4934**
Castle, Lt GL **A5644, A6398, A6483**
Caswell, Lt EDS **A5577**
Cathie, 2Lt AJ (11Sqn) **6992**
Cathie, Cpl .AJ, (23Sqn)**5235**
Catton, AM1 S **6332**
Cave, Lt EHP **5642, 5643**
Cave, 2Lt J **E7078**
Cawley, 2Lt JJ **A5147**
Chadwick, 2Lt EL **4915, 7693**
Chadwick, AM2 H **6334**
Chadwick, 2Lt, Lt HL **6374, 6978, 7025**
Chadwick, Capt R **7022**
Challis, Lt ME **C9790**
Chamberlayne, Lt PRT **A5505, B1894**
Chambers, 2Lt HC **A866**
Chambers, 2Lt PW **4855**
Chambers, Lt WD **A6401**
Champion, 2Lt HF **6338**
Chancellor, 2Lt C **6332**
Chancellor, Lt GE **A20**
Chaplin, 2Lt (100 Sqn) **5228**
Chapman, AM1, Sgt DAR **6354**
Chapman, Sgt LC **6938**
Chapman, 2Lt R **D3814**
Chaworth-Musters, 2Lt RM **6375, 6972**
Chester, Lt WH **A3, A6499**
Chester-Walsh, 2Lt JH **6930**
Chick, Capt AL **A5587**
Chidlaw-Roberts, 2Lt R **5243**
Clappen, Lt (SARD) **A5460**
Clark, Lt E **A6487**
Clark, PFO WF **D9125**

2Lt JFA Day, Ireland

Clarke, Lt EH **F5863**
Clarke, 2Lt JF **A6537**
Clarke, 2Lt, Lt SH **4289, 6372**
Clarkson, Sgt A **6973, 6983**
Clarkson, FltSgt LC **4278**
Clayton, Lt, (100 Sqn) **A5518**
Clayton, 2Lt G **7670**
Clement, 2Lt, Capt CM **4286, 4288, 7703, A5461**
Clifton, Lt N **4227**
Clifton, 2Lt WGT **7691, 7709**
Cloete, 2Lt, Lt DC **4892, 6351, 6354**
Clough, 2Lt RG **B490, B7839**
Coape-Arnold, Lt RdeN **D9088**
Cobbold, Lt FRC **A37**
Cock, 2Lt H **B1883**
Cogswell, 2Lt ES **A6374**
Colbert, 2Lt LA **A822, B411**
Cole, Capt CC **A6462, C9797, D9759**
Collet, Lt HS **A6409**
Collett, Lt EV **A5569, A5687**
Collins, Lt (11 Sqn) **7014**
Collins, Lt AV **B1879**
Collins, 2Lt HJ **A5728**
Collins, 2Lt LE **A844**
Collinson, 2Lt(25 Sqn) **6335**
Collinson, AM2 F **6974**
Collis, 2Lt R **6364**
Collison, Pte J **A789**
Collison, Lt, Capt WE **5210, 7004**
Conder, 2Lt RE **A6359, A6400, A6412, A6415, A6416, A6480, A6539, B441**
Condron, Sgt TA **A5612**
Cook, 2Lt CR **C9796**
Cook, 2Lt LCL **5250**
Coombs, Lt (51 Sqn) **A5732**
Cooper, 2Lt CA **4926**
Cooper, AM1 E **B1882**
Cooper, Lt WJ **D3811**
Cooper-King, 2Lt MK **2864**
Cooper-Wilson, 2Lt J **4866**
Coops, 2Lt FC **7713**
Copeland, Lt AHM **4292**
Copeman, Capt MGB **A6365**
Corker, Lt AF **D9186**
Cornish, Lt F **A6401**
Cotton, Lt H **A6378, A6381**
Cotton, AM1 S **6332**
Coupal, Sgt, 2Lt AP **6951, 7023**
Coupe, Lt TH **A5654**
Court, AM2, AM1 LS **4283, 4922, 6932**
Court, Cpl, Sgt LS **4839, 6993, 7693, 7695**
Couve, 2Lt N **A5453, A5464**
Cowell, Sgt J, (38Sqn) **B441**
Cowell, AM2, Sgt JJ, (20Sqn) **A6376, A6400, A6412, A6415, A6416, A6468, A6480**
Cowie, 2Lt JD **7701**
Cox, Sgt CJ **A35**
Cox, Capt CR **4855**
Cox, Pte FD **6950**
Cox, 2Lt RC **4979**
Crafter, Lt J **A6498**
Creasey, 2Lt AA **A861**
Crichton, Lt CJW **4918**
Crickmore, AM2 CB **4882**
Crisp, 2Lt AR **6346**
Crisp, 2Lt F **7677**
Crisp, 2Lt HD **A5719**
Critchley, 2Lt A **7004**
Critchley, 2Lt GA **6987, A851**
Critchley, Sgt EP **4957, A5485**
Crofts, 2Lt HJ **A5744**
Cropper, 2Lt A **4924, 6963**
Cross, 2Lt RW **7695**
Crowe, 2Lt JR **A6557**
Cruselle, Cpl (51 Sqn) **4885**
Cubbon, Capt FR **A6390, A6392, A6430**

Cudemore, 2Lt JR **A5581**
Cumberland, Sgt JR **A5474**
Cummings, Lt PH **A5629, A5676**
Cunliffe, Sgt JA **4897, 4970, A831, A5479**
Cunnell, 2Lt, Capt DC **A36, A6414, A6430, A6431, A6512, B1863**
Curling, Lt ET **7694, A819**

D

D'Arcy, 2Lt LG **A5446**
da Costa, 2Lt WRC **6963**
Dabbs, 2Lt, Lt, Capt DH **A8, A13, A30, B1882**
Dafoe, 2Lt FE **E7050**
Dalziel, 2Lt RG **A3, A6390, A6392**
Daniels, Sgt R **A6515**
Darnell, 2Lt CV **A837**
Davey, 2Lt, Lt, Capt HB **4907, 5201, 5209, 5238, 6938, 7694**
Davies, 2Lt DS **A11**
Davies, 2Lt JE **A19**
Davies, 2Lt LC **A5454, A5461**
Davies, 2Lt RS **Unidentified a'c:4128**
Davies, 2Lt WE **4877**
Davies, Lt WLH **B499**
Davin, AM2 AG **7685, A5441**
Davis, Lt (102 Sqn) **A5662**
Davis, 2Lt, Lt ER **5212, 5238**
Davis, Lt HE **6990**
Daws, AM1 HL **B1882**
Day, 2Lt (101 Sqn) **A5589**
Day, 2Lt (102 Sqn) **B415**
Day, Lt J **A5754**
Day, 2Lt, Lt JFA **4935, 7681, A796, A5454**
de Pomeroy, 2Lt NR **4867**
de Salaberry, Lt B **B429**
de Selincourt, Capt A **A6378**
Deakin, 2Lt D **A838**
Dearing,, AM1 F **A8**
Dempsey, Sgt J **A784, A813**
Denison, Lt NC **A5151**
Dennistoun, Lt JR **6348**
des Brisay, Spr EM **4272**
Deuchar, Capt AG **A13**
Dewar, 2Lt A **A30**
Dickinson, 2Lt AH **5643**
Dicksee, 2Lt HJH **7666, A5442**
Dingley, 2Lt RL **5239**
Dinsmore, 2Lt GH **A5483**
Dixon, Capt CH **6990, 6997**
Dixon, 2Lt, Lt FC **A6375, A6398, B465**
Dixon, 2Lt H **5212**
Dixon, 2Lt RS **A29**
Dixon-Spain, Capt G **A11, A19**
Dodson, Lt L **A6371**
Don, Capt FP **A857**
Donaldson, 2Lt HG **A5679**
Doughty, 2Lt G **4848**
Doughty, 2Lt RC **4895, A5466**
Douglas, Cpl (36 Sqn) **A6429**
Doune, 2Lt, Lt Lord **5209, 6938**
Dove, 2Lt CR **B7837**
Dowling, 2Lt, Capt BL **6981, A3**
Doyle, Sgt W **A5478**
Drummond, 2Lt, Lt JL **A5732, A5733**
Dudbridge, 2Lt M **A6431**
Duff, Capt IAJ **6970, A5662**
Duffus, 2Lt CS **4855, 4883, 6931, 7697**
Dulin, Lt WWM **B1878**
Duncan, 2Lt, Lt HE **A5520, A6531**
Dunkerley, Lt AHG **A5600**
Dunlop, Lt, Capt C **4839, 4847, 7024, A6401**
Dunn, Lt (1AD) **5202**
Dupont, 2Lt AN **B1896**
Durrand, 2Lt, Lt W **A1965, A6419, A6456, A6548, B1892**
Dye, Cpl (51 Sqn) **7689**

Dyer, Pte HH **7691**

E

Earwaker, Lt RND'O **A6429**
Eastwood, Lt, Capt GH **5201, 5202**
Ebrey, 2Lt HE **A5741**
Eccles, 2Lt HEK **4989**
Edwards, AM1 (22 Sqn) **4849**
Edwards, Sgt (38 Sqn) **A5568**
Ekins, AM2 AW **A5480**
Elder, 2Lt, Lt GEP **A5632, B409**
Ellerbeck, 2Lt EAV **A5599**
Elliot, 2Lt HS **4960, 7699**
Ellis, 2Lt S **A5579**
Else, Pte H **A6365, A6417, A6419**
Elsley, Lt L **A805**
Emery, FltSgt AC **6364**
Emsden, Cpl L **4839, 4847, 7672, 7683, 7693, A797, A6385**
Erlebach, 2Lt AW **A1958**
Escolet, Lt de **A5738**
Evans, 2Lt (18 Sqn) **6933**
Evans, Sgt FH **A811**
Evans, 2Lt FW **A6467**
Evans, Lt HB **A6409**
Evans, 2Lt TA **C9831**
Everett, Lt E **B442**
Ewan, 2Lt JFB **B491**
Exley, 2Lt GA **6340, 6361**
Exley, 2Lt WR, **A795**
Eyres, 2Lt HT **D9929**

F

Faley, Sgt CRL **A5578**
Fall, 2Lt H **A5562**
Faquhar, Lt JM **A5789, A6580**
Farquhar, 2Lt RW **A5460**
Fauvel, 2Lt, Lt LG **A35, A5144, A6390, A6413, A6445, A6471**
Fearnside-Speed, 2Lt KA **4898, 6987**
Ferguson, Lt JF **A5460**
Fernauld, 2Lt VD **A1954**
Ferriman, 2Lt FS **A1957**
Field, Capt ACW **6945**
Fielding-Clarke, 2Lt A **B439**
Fincham, 2Lt GEH **5645**
Findlay, 2Lt WF **A19**
Finer, 2Lt HJ **4938**
Finevan, Sgt G **4930**
Firbank, 2Lt GJ **4851, 6369**
Firstbrook, Lt JH **6365**
Fiske, 2Lt H **4884**
Fitzgerald, 2Lt WW **7003**
Fleming, 2Lt JAM **A801**
Fletcher, 2Lt RK **A6462, B471**
Fletcher, Lt WF **4960, 7020**
Floyd, 2Lt J **6952**
Flynn, 2Lt JP **A6456**
Foord, Lt EA **4990, 4998, A779**
Foote, 2Lt EL **7016**
Forbes, Capt EW **6328, 6359**
Ford, 2Lt N **A844**
Fordred, Lt HI **B1882, B1883**
Foreman, 2Lt GW **A861, A5510**
Forrest, Lt LJ **D9920**
Francis, 2Lt JW **A37**
Franklin, Lt W **7020**
Fraser, 2Lt D **B1896, C9786**
Freeman, Lt HP **4279**
Freeman-Smith, 2Lt HE **5247, 7683**
French,FltCdt,EV **A5648**
French, Lt GS **A815**
French, 2Lt TH **A1945**
Friend, AM1 H **A5486**
Frudge, FltSgt **6989**
Fuller, 2Lt, Lt LA **7686, 7687**
Fulton, 2Lt EP **A5652**
Furlonger, 2Lt CAM **4883, 4983, 4991**

G

Gadsden, Lt CC **B405**
Galley, 2Lt EDG **4971, 4986**
Gardiner, 2Lt PJ **A6572**
Gardner, 2Lt AW **7702, A5507**

2Lt F Hall

Capt JR Howett

Sgt F Johnson

Kent, 2Lt EAW	**4876**
Kent, 2Lt P	**A5478**
Kerpen, 2Lt C	**A5507**
Kew, 2Lt W	**D3816**
Kewley, Lt BH	**D9921**
King, Lt AJG	**D9106**
King, 2Lt, Lt B	**4847, 7683, A782,**
	A815, A842
King, AM2 F	**A5439, A5484**
King, AM1 GW	**B7843**
King, Capt JA, USAS	**D9758**
Kingsford, 2Lt AR	**A5536, A5659**
Kinnear, Lt, Capt JL	**2864, 4227,**
	5643, 5644
Kirby, 2Lt CF	**D9913**
Kirby, 2Lt H	**A23**
Kirk, Lt JH	**A6370**
Kirk, Lt LD	**A5779**
Kirton, 2Lt, Lt JT	**6336**
Kitchingman, AM2 HR	**A5507**
Knight, 2Lt NL	**7715**
Knowlden, 2Lt WE	**6374**
Knowles, Capt RM	**A1961, A5144**
Kolligs, 2Lt FFHE	**7697**
Kydd, 2Lt, Lt FJ	**A1956, A5147,**
	A6354, A6445, A6516, A6554
L	
Lain, 2Lt FJ	**A5598, B478**
Lally, Lt CT	**A6417**
Lambourne, Lt H	**A789**
Lance, Lt (36 Sqn)	**A6582**
Lane, Sgt (25 Sqn)	**6330**
Lane, 2Lt CW	**4883, 4983, 4991**
Lane, Lt RB	**B7837**
Langwill, 2Lt (11Sqn)	**7709**
Lansdale, Lt EC	**6973**
Larkin, 2Lt RS	**A5579**
Law, 2Lt HMB	**4276, 4903, 6941**
Law, Cpl LO	**6993**
Law, 2Lt R	**4970**
Lawrence, Tptr JG	**A842**
Lawrence, 2Lt VH	**D3814**
Lawson, 2Lt J	**A6400**
Le Fevre, Lt FE	**A852**
le Mee, 2Lt JM	**A6462**
Learmount, Maj LW	**7703**

Capt CT Maclean, New Zealand

Leathey, Lt F	**A1966**
Ledger, 2Lt AP	**B490**
Lee, Lt AC	**A6443, A6457**
Lee, 2Lt GS	**B1891**
Lees, Lt WF	**7704**
Leggatt, 2Lt EW	**2864**
Leishman, 2Lt D	**A4**
Leith, 2Lt, Capt JL	**4946, 7683,**
	7693, 7695, A782, A6383
Leonard, 2Lt TLW	**E7056**
Le Royer, Capt JA	**A795**
Leslie, 2Lt, Lt WA	**B493, D9763**
Lewes, Lt MV	**6337**
Lewis, 2Lt JE	**A785**
Lewis, 2Lt M	**A22**
Lewis, 2Lt TAMS	**A6412, A6469,**
	A6512
Lewis-Roberts, Capt AO	**D9099**
Libby, Lt F	**6994, 7027, 7678**
Lind, 2Lt HF	**A5454**
Lindsay, Cpl R	**A865**
Lindsay-Young, Capt LHL	**C9824**
Linford, 2Lt RD	**A6422, A6451**
Lingard, 2Lt JR	**A6352**
Lingard, 2Lt W	**A6413**
Littlewood, 2Lt SCT	**A5**
Livingstone, 2Lt (trav)	**4920**
Livingstone, 2Lt AF	**A8**
Livingstone, 2Lt FJH	**A5626**
Lloyd, Pte C	**A6392, A6403,**
	A6413xxx
Lloyd, Pte C	**A6443**
Lloyd-Williams, 2Lt W	**D9922**
Lock, Lt, (36 Sqn)	**A6589**
Locke, 2Lt R	**B476**
Lockhart, Lt WE	**A853**
Lockwood, 2Lt EE	**B479**
Lodge, Lt CF	**6981, 7695**
Logan, 2Lt D	**A863**
Lohmeyer, 2Lt EN	**D9099**
Lonsdale, 2Lt VO	**A1953**
Loudon, 2Lt RW	**B488**
Loveland, Lt H	**6953, 7707**
Lovell, 2Lt CEA	**B7813**
Lovell, 2Lt RC	**B480**
Lowe, Capt CN	**7027, A5442,**
	A5472
Lowson, 2Lt CPF	**4286, 4288**
Loyd, 2Lt AT	**4855, 6993**
Lucas, Capt Lord AT	**7026**
Lucas, Lt GE	**A5536**
Lucas, Lt TCH	**A31, A32**
Luchford, 2Lt, Lt HGET	**A1956,**
	A6392, A6427, A6448, A6512,
	A6516, A6547, A6548, B1897
Lutyens, Lt FD	**7016, 7669**
Lyall-Grant, Lt D	**A5**
Lynn, Lt (51 Sqn)	**A5525**
Lynn, 2Lt DL	**A5588**
Lyon-Hall, 2Lt, Lt EH	**A6487,**
	C9825
Lytton, 2Lt PAB	**B474**
M	
Macaskie, 2Lt DSC	**6351**
MacAskill, Lt WR	**A6383**
MacDonald, Lt (36 Sqn)	**A5542**
MacDonald, 2Lt DP	**A6382**
Macdonald, 2Lt, Lt GK	**6373, 6933,**
	6942
Macdonald, 2Lt WF	**A5458, A5502**
Macdonnell, 2Lt, (101 Sqn)	**B479**
Macfie, 2Lt JDA	**5235**
Macgregor, 2Lt RR	**A5672**
Macinnes, 2Lt A	**C9817**
Macintyre, 2Lt DH	**6952**
Mackay, 2Lt WA	**4863**
Mackie, Sgt GJ	**4841, 7024**
Mackie, AM2 J	**4897, 4898**
Mackintosh, 2Lt G	**4967**
Mackrell, Capt G	**A869**
Maclaren, Lt D	**A6500**
MacLaughlin, Lt C	**A5683**
Maclean, Capt CT	**6343, 6366**
Maclean, 2Lt EV	**4917**

MacLennan, Lt JE	**6997**
MacLeod, Pte J	**A6572**
MacRae, MajDA	**A5711**
MacRae, Capt JN	**A5781**
Madhill, 2Lt RM	**A6353**
Madill, Lt RMcK	**A6384, B1865**
Mahony-Jones, Capt GJ	**A1961**
Makepeace, 2Lt, Lt RM	**A3, A1956,**
	A1963, A6389, A6458, A6498,
	A6547, A6548, B1897
Malcolm, MajCJ	**A20**
Malcolm, 2Lt RG	**4839, 7672, 7693,**
	A782, A6373, A6383, A6385
Malley-Martin, Lt J	**E7056, F5854**
Malloy, 2Lt (11 Sqn)	**6986**
Mann, 2Lt, Lt JA	**4269, 5209, 5245,**
	6330, 6996
Mann, Sgt R	**A797, A6360, A6429**
Manning, AM1 (1 SNBD)	**A5793**
Manning, 2Lt, Capt ER	**5235, A810,**
	A5517
Mannock, 2Lt E	**4972**
Mansell, 2Lt WS	**4267, 5250**
Mansfield, Lt WHC	**4253**
Marchant, 2Lt CH	**7024**
Margerison, 2Lt T	**A5150**
Margolouth, 2Lt AH	**A1944**
Marsden, 2Lt AJ	**C9806**
Marshall, 2Lt BS	**A6403**
Marshall, 2Lt C	**B454**
Marshall, 2Lt DE	**4998, 7003**
Marshall, Capt E	**A856**
Marshall, Lt HS	**A5639**
Marshall, 2Lt HWH	**4871**
Marshall, Lt	**unidentified a'c**
	(148 Sqn)
Martin, Lt AW	**A5149, A6444**
Martin, AM2 JH	**6362**
Martyn, Maj RB	**4935**
Martyn, 2Lt, Capt TJC	**A5526,**
	A5548
Mason, Maj AB	**A5745**
Masson, 2Lt RG	**A6467**
Master, 2Lt GA	**A5448**
Masters, 2Lt G	**A808, A5442,**
	A5472
Masters, 2Lt GA	**A5450**
Matheson, Sgt, 2Lt WD	**7007,**
	A780
Mathewson, Lt K	**4272**
Matson, 2Lt O	**B1898**
Matthews, AM2 HF	**B1895**
Matthews, Lt JH	**A874, A5574,**
	A5684, A5719, A6464
Maule, Lt EB	**A38**
Maurice, Lt A	**A5451**
Maxsted, Lt OD	**4984**
Maxwell, Cpl G	**6345**
Maxwell, 2Lt, Capt, Maj RS	**6341,**
	A1, A13, A23, A29, A5458
May, Cpl, Sgt T	**6339, 6359**
Mayberry, Lt R	**A785, A5453**
McAndrew, Lt H	**C9803**
McBlain, Lt GN	**B452**
McCall, 2Lt M	**A6498, B1865**
McCallum, 2Lt AHK	**A813**
McClean, Capt CT	**4909, 6343**
McCubbin, 2Lt, Lt GR	**4272, 6346**
McCudden, Sgt, Capt JTB	**4955,**
	A7, A15
McDonald, Lt HC	**A5743**
McDonald, Lt WN	**4971**
McEntee, 2Lt GO	**4883, 4991,**
	7697, A5456
McEwan, Capt JHF	**5233**
McIntosh, Lt DD	**A5507**
McIntosh, 2Lt FG	**5235**
McKenzie, Lt WS	**B414, B480**
McLean, Lt CM	**C9831**
McLean, 2Lt, Lt JM	**A6500, A6555**
McLeod, Lt DW	**A5481**
McMaster, Cpl D	**6341**
McMechan, Gnr J	**B1897**
McMillan, Lt (36 Sqn)	**A5542**

McMurray, 2Lt A	**4998**
McNaughton, 2Lt, Lt NG	**6332,**
McPhail, 2Lt JWR	**C9789, D9913**
McRae, Maj (36 Sqn)	**A6442**
McRobert, AM1 J	**7703**
McSweeney, 2Lt GB	**A6596**
McSwiney, Capt PM	**A6521**
McWha, Lt AJ	**A1941**
Mearnes, 2Lt EA	**7707, A5459**
Mee, AM2 SA	**A5511**
Meggitt, 2Lt, Lt WG	**4877, 7007,**
	7022, 7686, A5451
Mellor, Lt CB	**A6441**
Menzies, Lt JA	**A12**
Mercer, Lt H	**A5610**
Merchant, AM1 WT	**B1882**
Mews, Lt B	**4925**
Middleton, Lt EC	**A6500**
Middleton, Capt JA	**A5617, A6408**
Middleton, Lt JR	**A803**
Miles, Lt HL	**B485**
Miller, 2Lt GB	**4968, 4969**
Miller, 2Lt JMR	**7681, 7711**
Miller, 2Lt RG	**D9919**
Millington, 2Lt CB	**4992**
Milne, Capt W	**5212, 5238**
Mimmack, 2Lt SC	**A5611**
Mitchell, Sgt (trav)	**A5593**
Mitchell, Lt C	**D3818**
Mitchell, 2Lt HBO	**4933**
Mitchell, 2Lt J	**5232**
Moller, 2Lt FS	**6331, 7683**
Molloy, 2Lt TPL	**4844, 6947**
Monk, Cpl G	**6965**
Montgomery, Lt DH	**A5548**
Montgomery, 2Lt DM	**A823**
Moody, 2Lt BC	**A6447**
Moore, 2Lt CA	**A6461**
Moore, Lt JG	**A1964**
Moore, Cpl W	**A11**
Moorhouse, AM1 GW	**A5578**
Moreley, 2Lt H	**A5592**
Morgan, Lt RC?	**2864**
Morginson, 2Lt W	**B442**
Morice, Lt CS	**A1966**
Morley, Capt HC	**5238**
Morris, 2Lt EC	**A6422**
Morris, 2Lt LBF	**6983, 7018, 7019**
Morrison, 2Lt (11 Sqn)	**A799**
Morrison, Lt NW	**4877**
Morrison, TFSL RB	**A826**
Morrison, 2Lt WS	**4912**
Morton, Sgt GJ	**4844, 6988**
Morton, 2Lt JR	**6359**
Mottershead, Sgt T	**4848, 4859,**
	4946, 6998, A39
Moyes, 2Lt WB	**A1961**
Muff, AM2 (101 Sqn)	**B402**
Munk, Cpl G	**6985**
Munro, Lt (51 Sqn)	**B417**
Munro, 2Lt RNL	**7025, 7693**
Murchie, 2Lt CP	**4258**
Murison, 2Lt JTG	**A5660**
Murphy, Lt L	**A5505**
Murray, AM1 J	**A6518**
Musson, Lt FW	**A6513**
Myers, 2Lt FM	**A15**
N	
Nasmyth, Lt AW	**A1959**
Naylor, Lt CB	**A5610**
Nelson, Lt C	**6991**
Nesbitt, Lt A	**4863**
Nevile-Smith, 2Lt L	**7694**
Neville, 2Lt HG	**A6359, A6429,**
	A6539
Newbold, 2Lt LA	**6338**
Nicholl, Lt (199NTS?)	**A6590**
Nicholls, 2Lt E	**A5534**
Nicholls-Pratt, 2Lt EG	**D9097**
Nicholson, Capt GCN	**6362**
Nicholson, Lt HR	**A6385**
Nixon, Lt O	**5643**
Noble-Campbell, Lt CH	**A5707**
Nock, Capt AR	**A5754**

Nock, Lt AR A5723
Norman, Capt GH 4258, 5241
Norris, Lt (25 Sqn) 6342
Nunn, Sgt CHN 7693, A813
Nutcombe, 2Lt TA A6558
Nutter, 2Lt V D9186

O

O'Beirne, 2Lt JIM A6382
O'Beirne, 2Lt TM 5228
O'Connor, AM2 H B498
Ogg, Lt GJ 4918
Ordish, 2Lt BWA 6374
Orr-Ewing, 2Lt AI A856
Osmaston, 2Lt RS 4857, 6964
O'Sullivan, 2Lt F 4855
Outhwaite, Lt A A6464
Owen,Gnr.A A6500
Owen, Capt HLH A5453
Owen-Holdsworth, Lt JP B424

P

Padley, Lt AH D9759
Paine, 2Lt JJ A5500
Palmer, Capt GK A788, A5789, A6580
Parke, Sgt (11 Sqn) 6951
Parker, Lt CA 4227, 4228, A820, A5511
Parker, 2Lt JK 4866
Parkinson, 2Lt, Lt C 4896, 6968, A801
Parks, 2Lt AE D9753
Parlee, 2Lt MK 4983, 7681, A796, A5461
Parnell, Lt (51 Sqn) A5519
Parnell, Lt IW 7025
Parry, Lt HA A5629, A5676
Parsons, 2Lt LWB 4288, 5214
Partington, 2Lt OJ A851
Patey, Lt WO A5587
Pattersen, Lt J A6431
Patterson, 2Lt, Lt JR A6522, A6547
Paull, 2Lt JA B414
Paull, 2Lt RJ A5542
Paull, Cpl W 5238
Pawley, AM2 G A837
Payn, 2Lt, Lt HJ 2864, 5644
Payne, 2Lt KW A5720
Payne, Capt LGS A5686
Payne, 2Lt P D3783
Payze, Lt A? 4227
Pearce, Lt AD 5248, A19
Pearson, 2Lt HA 5220
Pebder, 2Lt WG A3
Peile, 2Lt AH A5695
Pemberton, Capt (28 Sqn) 4904
Pemberton, Capt AJM 5250
Penny, Lt EJ A6586
Penruddocke, Lt NF B492
Percival, 2Lt E A1964, A6355
Perry, AM1 EG 4850
Perry, 2Lt EO A29, A6370, A6403
Perry, Lt W B455
Perry, 2Lt WG A6569
Peters, 2Lt GC A838
Phillips, 2Lt AW 6976
Phillips, 2Lt CW A5617
Phillips, 2Lt FN A5562
Phillips, 2Lt HN B458
Phillips, 2Lt LH D9919
Philpott, 2Lt JE A5675
Pierce, Lt WC C9817
Pike, 2Lt SN A29, A5578
Pilbrow, Pte SE A1956, A5152, A6548
Pilkington, Lt JO B1895
Pinder, 2Lt FG 6352
Pinkerton, 2Lt AL 6999
Pinnock, 2Lt C A12, A6416
Pither, 2Lt CE 6354
Pitman, Lt RC A796
Pitman,ProbLt RC 4936
Pixton, Capt (trav) 7007
Platt, Capt LS A5150
Pollard, 2Lt GH A1957

Pope, 2Lt EEE A1959
Pope, AM2 R A39
Potter, AM2, Pte, Sgt FA A6401, A6415, A6429, A6528, A6548
Powell, Lt DG 4969
Powell, 2Lt, Lt LC 5235, 6364
Preedy, Lt TV A6474
Preston, 2Lt H A5656
Price, 2Lt G 5645
Price, 2Lt JCE A5744, B481
Price, Lt JW 7016
Price, Capt SW 6994, 7027, A5660, B1884
Pringle, 2Lt JH D9967
Pruen, 2Lt ET 5241
Pryor, Lt AD A1955
Pryor, Lt JW B7808
Pulleyn, 2Lt JL 6965
Purry, Capt RO A6424

Q

Quelch, 2Lt AF A5634
Quested, 2Lt, Capt JB 6965, 7016, 7666, A5442

R

Randall, Lt BD 5234
Randall, Lt BF 4937
Rankin, Lt FS 4929, 6373, 6968
Rawnsley, 2Lt L A838
Raymond-Barker, 2Lt, (6 Sqn) 5643
Read, Lt (25 Sqn) 4269
Read, Lt NH 4850, 7694
Rees, Lt L 6983
Rees, Lt T 7018, 7019
Reeves, 2Lt WA A1951
Reid, Lt CW A5659, A5695
Reid, 2Lt GPS A11, A19
Reid, 2Lt, Capt GRM 6330, A19, A22, A39
Reid, Lt JL 6980
Reid, 2Lt RW A5466, A5468
Reilly-Patey, Lt O D9922
Richards, Pte A A1958
Richards, 2Lt ARM 7714
Richards, 2Lt, Lt CR A6448, A6431, A6498, B1890
Richards, 2Lt HS A6371
Richards, Lt W A5779, A6388
Richardson, 2Lt CR A845
Richardson, 2Lt GT 6330
Richardson, Pte H D9101
Richardson, 2Lt, Capt LL 4283, 4839, 6337, 6932, 7686, A6372
Richardson, Capt M B454
Richardson, 2Lt RH A5680
Richman, AM2 W 4900
Rickett, 2Lt WHA A6424
Ridewood, Lt, Capt OE 7689, A5551, A5791
Ridgway, Lt CW A6599
Riggs, 2Lt TMR B460
Rilett, 2Lt WH 4922
Riley, Lt, (36 Sqn) A5738
Riley, 2Lt CG 6963
Riley, Lt RCB 5212
Ringer, 2Lt ECS A801
Roadhouse, 2Lt FW A5607, A5675, C9811
Robarts, Lt GW 4860
Robb, AM2 R 7669
Roberts, 2Lt CL 6965, 7014
Roberts, 2Lt, Lt EG A5536, A5536, B496, B1884
Roberts, Lt EL B406
Robertson, 2Lt JL 5238
Robertson, Lt NL A5144
Robins, 2Lt ER A6413
Robinson, AM2 (25 Sqn) 4909, 5201
Robinson, Capt G C9792
Robinson, 2Lt ND A5510
Robinson, 2Lt P 7698
Roebuck, 2Lt L A5508
Rogers, 2Lt CE 6940

Rogers, 2Lt V C9786
Rooke, 2Lt CE 4279
Ross, Lt JW B1900
Rossi, 2Lt JA 7681
Rothwell, 2Lt J A5500, A819
Rough, Capt (11 Sqn) 6945
Rough, 2Lt JS B452
Roulstone, 2Lt, Lt, Capt A 5247, 7686, A6381, A6407
Rowell, 2Lt AE A6453
Rowlands, Lt AW A6351
Royffe, 2Lt HS 4854
Rushby, Capt RH 6963
Russell, Lt (35 Sqn) 4264
Russell, AM1 F, (23 Sqn) A5485
Russell, Sgt F (18 & 25 Sqn) 6987, A5468, A5487
Russell, Lt HB 6348
Russell, 2Lt PA 6953
Russell, 2Lt WH A6564
Rutherford, Capt PW C9809
Ryall, 2Lt AG A1948
Ryan, Lt JH A1957, A6380
Ryan, Lt WG A5525

S

Salter, Capt WE 4986
Sampson, Lt HA B485
Sampson, 2Lt RD 6332
Sams, 2Lt FDH 6934
Sanders, Lt JW 6999
Sandys-Thomas, 2Lt CI 6351
Sargant, 2Lt HSStC 4850
Satchell, 2Lt, Lt HL A3, A6393, A6431, A6469, A6469, A6512
Savage, 2Lt, Lt JRB 4909, 5201, 6347
Savery, 2Lt, Capt RC 7004, A799
Sawden, Lt WW A6384
Sayers, AM2, Sgt AH A29, A1965, A5143, A6403, A6414, A6431
Scandrett, 2Lt H 7024
Scanlon, Cpl (102 Sqn) D9992
Scarborough, 2Lt F A5547
Schaumer, Lt CG A5506
Schreiber, Lt RTB A22
Schweitzer, Lt, Capt VE 4857, 4885
Scott, 2Lt AC E7054
Scott, Lt DH 4926
Scott, 2Lt HS A5525
Scott, Lt LH A19, A22, A39
Scott, 2Lt MP A6412
Scott, 2Lt PG 6331, 6340
Scott, 2Lt WP A6374
Scovil, Lt EM D9907
Seagrave, Capt H 6342
Sellers, 2Lt H 7003
Sergeant, Lt FStC A5753
Severs, 2Lt AG 4946, 7715
Seward, 2Lt JW A6548
Shackell, Lt FC A5502, A5506
Shakesby, 2Lt CV A5710
Shand, 2Lt, (101 Sqn) A5586
Sharp, 2Lt AE A6523
Sharpe, 2Lt SA 6341
Shaumer, 2Lt, Lt CG 4856, 4895, 4969, 5234, 6968, A5464
Shaw, Lt, (102 Sqn) A5570
Shaw, Lt JW A5456
Shellington, 2Lt PG 4871
Shepherd, 2Lt ALM 7684
Shepherd, Lt G D9952
Shergold, 2Lt, (101 Sqn) C9834
Sherwell, 2Lt, Lt AV 4842, 4952
Sherwell, 2Lt R 6334, 6339
Shirtcliffe, 2Lt AW A782, A784
Shum, 2Lt CAR 7713
Sibley, Pte RE A1950, A1952
Sievwright, 2Lt RH 6980
Sim, Lt P A5597
Simon, 2Lt AW A5525, A5543, B417
Simpson, 2Lt CB A6456
Sinclair, Lt AL A5583

Capt ER Manning, Australia

Sinclair, 2Lt D A5701
Sinclair, 2Lt HS A792
Singleton, 2Lt TH A5720, B495
Slingsby, 2Lt, Lt H 7704, B1881
Small, Lt JB A6558
Smart, 2Lt EJ A3, A6412, A6429
Smeddle, Lt GRG B428
Smith, Cpl , (33 Sqn) A6353
Smith, Lt A D3779
Smith, 2Lt C 4285
Smith, Lt CH B499
Smith, Pte F A1959
Smith, 2Lt FG A5760
Smith, Lt GN B1898
Smith, 2Lt H B415
Smith,FltCdt.JL A5748
Smith, 2Lt JR,(18 Sqn) 4984, A5458, A5464, A5656, A5724
Smith,Spr.JR, (25 Sqn) 6991
Smith, 2Lt LN 4850
Smith, Lt NA C9787
Smith, Lt P 7007
Smith, 2Lt R 4884, A6358
Smith, Lt RN A6408
Smith, 2Lt RN B499
Smith, 2Lt SW A6465
Smith, Lt V A32, A6410
Smyth, 2Lt PJ 5220, 6971
Snelling, Pte E A6388
Solly, Lt, Capt AN 5213, 5215, 6345, A5147, A6354, A6444, A6516, A6554
Solomon, 2Lt HP A5656
Somervell, Capt RG B437
Somerville, 2Lt PT D9928
Soulby, 2Lt HW A6
Southorn, Lt TN 7683, A6410
Soutten, 2Lt B A1957, A6380
Sowery, Capt J 4882
Spearpoint, Lt HG 4891
Spence, 2Lt WG 6957
Spencer, Lt HTL 6949
Spicer, 2Lt ED A8, A28
Sproat, 2Lt SM A5632

Capt H Tomlinson

Sproson, Lt WW **D9090**
Stacey, 2Lt DW **A6383**
Stachell, 2Lt HL **A5149**
Staden, 2Lt Van **B407**
Stalker, 2Lt RM **4921**
Stanley, Capt (36 Sqn) **A6589**
Stanley, AM2 A **A3, A16**
Stead, Sgt G **4898**
Stead, 2Lt, Capt JK **A26, A30, A31**
Stedman, Lt JA **A5528**
Steele, 2Lt, Lt HW **A5526, A5724**
Stephens, Lt L **unidentified**
Stevens, 2Lt EH **A32**
Stevens, Lt, Capt FD, **A6444, A6516**
Stevens, 2Lt GE **A6563**
Stevens, 2Lt HK **D9930**
Stevenson, Lt (33 Sqn) **B1884**
Stevenson, 2Lt J **6975**
Stewart, AM1 DA **A1, A13, A23**
Stewart, 2Lt DJ **A823**
Stewart, 2Lt JCM **6339, 6932**
Stewart, 2Lt JO **7697**
Stockdale, Capt HW **C9834**
Stockman, Lt EJ **D3783**
Strange, 2Lt B **A6427, A6518**
Strange, Capt LA **2864, 4228**
Strange, Lt LAT **7691**
Strathy-Mackay, 2Lt, Lt H **6368, 6928, 6366**
Street, 2Lt C **6998**
Stretton, Sgt AN **A6419**
Stringer, Cpl JW **A18**
Stronach, FltSgt J **5207**
Stubbs, Lt EW **5642**
Sturruck, LCpl C **A32**
Sullivan, 2Lt FO **6929**
Summers, Cpl W **6934**
Summers, Capt WA **4278, 6375, 6972**
Sutton-Gardner, 2Lt W **A1963**
Swart, Capt JG **5250**
Swart, 2Lt OB **B439**
Sworder, Lt HP **A1944**

T
Talbot, AM1, (20 Sqn) **6332**
Taplin, AM (36 Sqn) **A5542**
Tatham, Lt (33 Sqn) **B1884**
Taylor, Lt (102 Sqn) **A5687**
Taylor, Lt (36 Sqn) **A5684**
Taylor, 2Lt (11 Sqn) **7708**
Taylor, Cpl AA **A840**
Taylor, Lt AB **D9914**
Taylor, Lt AC **B1856**
Taylor, 2Lt AG **A5679**
Taylor, 2Lt AGV **A6456, A6458, B1890**
Taylor, 2Lt FJ **A15, A6413**
Taylor, Sgt H **6940**
Taylor, AM2, Cpl, Sgt HG **6990, 7025, 7683, A782**
Taylor, Lt JR **D9780**
Taylor, 2Lt LA **A5608, B477**
Taylor, Lt LG **A852**
Taylor, 2Lt PS **4896, A5450, A5445, A5455**
Taylor, AM2 TH **A5547**
Taylor, 2Lt WH **A5710**
Taylor, 2Lt, Lt WM **7012, 7681, A796**
Taylor-Fox, Lt D **A6407**
Taylor-Loban, Capt G **6340**
Teale, Capt GN **A18**
Tedder, Capt AW **4915**
Tempest, 2Lt WC **A5689**
Tennant, 2Lt J **A6427, A6448, A6512, A6516, A6547, B1897**
Thayre, Capt FJH **A6390, A6430**
Thiery, 2Lt FG **4852**
Thistle, 2Lt AG **B7814**
Thomas, Lt AM **5207**
Thomas, Lt MW **2864**
Thomas, Lt S **F6109**
Thompson, Sgt (11 Sqn) **6983, 6989**
Thompson, 2Lt AH (191NTS) **D9753**
Thompson, Lt AH (58Sqn) **A5647**
Thompson, 2Lt H **6994**
Thompson, Lt JC **A5762, B467**
Thompson, Lt JW **D9777**
Thompson, 2Lt SF **A6376, A6548, B1890**
Thomson, Maj AAB **A5656, B1885**
Thornley, 2Lt GR **B7839**
Thornton, 2Lt HJ **A6461**
Thwaite, 2Lt MF **D9152**
Tibbetts, 2Lt JL **4853**
Tilley, AM2 H **7698**
Tillie, 2Lt AR **5201**
Tinker, 2Lt HJ **D9905**
Todd, Lt A **4984**
Todd, AM2, 2Lt, Lt M **A5149, A6456, A6512, B1890**
Tolhurst, Lt BJ **A5501**
Tolhurst, 2Lt NH **7706**
Tollerfield, AM2, Cpl RE **7027, A799, A810**
Tomlinson, Capt H **A5151**
Tooley,AM., (11 Sqn) **A799**
Toone, 2Lt JW **6357**
Topliffe, Sgt G **5209**
Towlson, AM2 II **4926**
Townend, Lt, (36 Sqn) **4976**
Townsend,AM.A **A6548**
Townson, 2Lt HJ **B453**
Townson, Lt HJ **A5658**
Toyne, Lt, (36 Sqn) **A5542**
Trafford-Jones, Lt E **6359**
Tratman, Lt LWDT **B431**
Trayles, 2Lt HA **6987**
Trevethan, 2Lt RM **A6431, A6480, A6498, A6512, A6523, A6527, A6528**
Trezise,, AM1 W **A6419**
Troth, 2Lt GN **C9813**
Trotter, Lt SF **A6368, A6419**
Truesdale, Pte WH **6374**
Tudor-Hart, Lt WO **6928**
Turk, 2Lt, Lt HH **4926, 7666, 7677, 7700**
Turner, 2Lt EG **B425**
Turner, Lt HF **A1937**
Turner, 2Lt W **A5689**
Turner, 2Lt WDG **A5517**
Tylee, Lt AK **5228, 5229**
Tyrrell, AM2 A **A6446**
Tyssen, Capt, Maj JH **4289, 6372, A6495**

U
Upson, AM RE **A5479**
Urquart, 2Lt A **B1891**

V
van Schaack, 1Lt JJ, USAS **D9758**
van Schaik, Cpl L **5201**
Varley, Lt RA **B419, B489, D9757**
Vaughan, 2Lt JD **A5762, B467**
Vaughan-Jones, 2Lt G **A5460**
Vaughan-Lewes, Lt M **4283**

Lt RA Varley

Veitch, Lt (16 Sqn) **5202**
Vernon, 2Lt LGH **4851**
Vickers, 2Lt FWA **6964**
Vickers, 2Lt OHD **A6376, A6427**
Vickers, Capt SW **A5461**
Villers, 2Lt HL **7023**
Vosper, 2Lt, Lt RA **A6579, D3779**
Vredenburg, 2Lt E **B419**

W
Wackett, Capt LJ **A6513**
Waddington, Lt MW **A3, A1956, A6389, A6431, A6498, A6548, A6555**
Wainwright, 2Lt RB **A28, A29, A33**
Wait, Sgt TE **A23, A6368**
Waite, Cpl A **A783**
Wald, Lt A **C9793**
Walder, AM2 (25 Sqn) **6347**
Walker, Cpl, Sgt (11Sqn) **6985, 6986**
Walker, AM2 AG **4970, A5443**
Walker, 2Lt HF **7024**
Walker, AM2 J **4896, 4898**
Walker, AM2 JC **4995**
Walker, Lt RD **4285, 6966**
Walker, 2Lt RE **6938**
Walker, 2Lt RU **5209**
Waller, Cpl J **4272**
Waller, Cpl JH **6344, 6346**
Walsh, 2Lt C **6928**
Walter, 2Lt DP **7025**
Walter, Lt SRP **4907**
Walton, Lt OT **4995**
Ward, Cpl CGS **7701**
Ward, 2Lt EAH **A855**
Ward, 2Lt PHB **A5457**
Wardale, AM3 (19 Res Sqn) **6363**
Wardill, Lt A **A843**
Warn, Lt WG **4853**
Warren, 2Lt J **C9788**
Watkins, Capt LP **A5568, A6599**
Watkins, 2Lt RT **F6109**
Watson, 2Lt, Capt AT **5249, 6969, 6970**
Watson, 2Lt JD **A5655, B491, B1883**
Watt, AM2 (18 Sqn) **A5448**
Watt, 2Lt WH **A1956, B1865**
Watts, AM1 O **4915**
Wear, 2Lt, Lt AE **A6431, A6448, B1890**
Weaver, Capt J **D9762**
Webb, Capt GW **6928**
Webb, 2Lt NWW **4839, 4841, 5245, 6993, 7003**
Wedgwood, 2Lt WA **6949**
Weir, Lt (25 Sqn) **A5152**
Weir, Lt CH **A5789**
Weir, 2Lt JB **4839, 4847, A6373, A6383**
Welford, Pte (22 Sqn) **5242**
Welford, 2Lt LC **4855**
Wells, 2Lt, Lt FW **4936, A796**
Wells, 2Lt HMW **6947**
Welsford, 2Lt GK **7016, 7674**
West, 2Lt AM **A5517**
West, 2Lt PH **7681, A5456**
Westcott, Lt GF **A5599**
West-White, 2Lt E **A5474**
Westwood, FltSgt A **A5781**
Wharton, Lt CE **B7808**
Wheldon, 2Lt EG **6976**
White, Capt CHC **7003, A5484**
White,FltCdt.EA **A5575**
White, 2Lt HG **A39, A6385, A6412**
White, Lt RW **A24, A34**
Whitehead, Lt WHN **5239**
Whitehouse, AM2 AG **A800**
Whiteman, Sgt T **6987, 6998**
Whiteside, Lt AB **A5649**
Whiteside, 2Lt AD **B482**
Whiteside, 2Lt RC **A5446**
Whitney, 2Lt RT **7705**
Whittaker, Lt J **A5484**

Whittingham, Capt HJ **B489, D9757**
Whittingham, 2Lt NJ, (HJ?) **A6375**
Wigglesworth, Sgt (51 Sqn) **A787**
Wilkes, Sgt G **A1941**
Wilkinson, 2Lt, Lt F **B493, D9763**
Wilkinson, Lt HR **A33, A1960, A6444**
Williams, 2Lt G **D3830, F5854**
Williams, 2Lt GE **D9929**
Williams, 2Lt JS **4860**
Williams, 2Lt LF **A6417**
Williams, 2Lt PJ **A6570**
Williams, 2Lt RL **A6570**
Williams, 2Lt SG **B451**
Williamson, 2Lt JC **B492**
Wills, 2Lt ST **A6402**
Wilson, Cpl A **4954**
Wilson, Lt CW **A782**
Wilson, 2Lt DP **A5569**
Wilson, Lt EF **A5698**
Windle, 2Lt BCW **A5570, B451**
Windrum, Lt CH **4952, A5452**
Wingate, Lt J **A5608, C9797, D9991**
Winks, 2Lt JG **A5524**
Winsor, Lt HTO **7016**
Winterbottom, Cpl A **4938, 6931**
Witham, Lt FR **D9992**
Wix, 2Lt GT **A5598**
Wollen, 2Lt DC **4839, 7693, A6372**
Wood, AM2 E **A811**
Woodbridge, 2Lt AE **A6512**
Woodcock, Capt F **A6518**
Woodman, Lt AC **4979, 6981**
Woods, 2Lt JM **7703**
Woods, 2Lt ME **A38**
Woodward, 2Lt W **A1958**
Woolley, Lt DB **A27**
Woollven, 2Lt CHC **6991, 7024**
Workman, 2Lt, Lt CS **4839, 4841, 6993**
Worrall, Lt EA **A5466, A841**
Worthing, AM2 G **A1942**
Worthington, Lt FP **A5686**
Wren, 2Lt LR **7020**
Wridgway, 2Lt CW **unidentified a'c: 707**
Wright, Capt AC **A1952**
Wyatt, 2Lt WJ **6965**
Wyllie, Capt H **5213, 5215**
Wynn, AM2 JH **6998**

Y
Young, LCpl (11 Sqn) **7020**
Young, 2Lt (6 Sqn) **5643**
Young, AM2 PA **A6495**

Z
Zeigler, Lt GL **B488**
Zeigler, Lt W **A5597**
Zink, 2Lt EL **4896, 4898, A823**

Capt SW Vickers